CHANGE
FOR
AMERICA

CHANGE
FOR
AMERICA

A Progressive Blueprint
for the 44th President

MARK GREEN
MICHELE JOLIN

EDITORS

with Ed Paisley and
Lauren Strayer

BASIC
BOOKS

A Member of the Perseus Books Group
New York

Published by Basic Books,
A Member of the Perseus Books Group

Books published by Basic Books are available at special discounts for bulk purchases
in the United States by corporations, institutions, and other organizations.
For more information, please contact the Special Markets Department at the
Perseus Books Group, 2300 Chestnut Street, Suite 200, Philadelphia, PA 19103,
or call (800) 810-4145, ext. 5000, or e-mail special.markets@perseusbooks.com.

DESIGN BY JANE RAESE
Text set in 11-point Dante

Library of Congress Cataloging-in-Publication Data is available for this book.
ISBN 978-0-465-01387-6

2 4 6 8 10 9 7 5 3 1

Contents

ECONOMIC POLICY

DOMESTIC POLICY

NATIONAL SECURITY POLICY

Preface

JOHN D. PODESTA

On January 20, 2009, the new president of the United States will take the oath of office on the steps of the U.S. Capitol. Behind the speeches, parades and celebrations that will accompany this ritual transfer of democratic power lies a difficult and complex transition period that will determine whether the symbolic changing of the guard is matched by an equally precise and effective handover of executive authority.

In order to facilitate this presidential transition, the Center for American Progress Action Fund and the New Democracy Project are pleased to present this volume, *Change for America: A Progressive Blueprint for the 44th President*, a collection of essays by 67 of the nation's leading authorities on government and policy detailing their thoughts on how best to structure the priorities, policy needs, management decisions, and personnel requirements of the next administration. Although the ideas expressed here reflect a progressive viewpoint, I had hoped that the recommendations would be useful and instructive regardless of who was elected to be the 44th president.

All of the contributors to this book have either direct cabinet-level or White House experience in past presidential administrations or long-standing legislative and executive policymaking experience at the federal level. At the same time, the essays in this volume are non-technical and intended to be of interest to those outside of government in academia and the media, or to lay readers interested in how the government works.

Since the Presidential Transition Act of 1963, the process of turning over the executive branch has become increasingly specialized and fine-tuned. For the 2008–2009 transition, President George W. Bush requested $8.5 million for transition-related activities for the president-elect and issued an executive order assigning 15 of his highest-ranking advisers to work with the president-elect in making sure that all relevant information and activities are coordinated between the outgoing and incoming administrations. The president-elect and his transition team will be responsible for naming the heads and top positions of 15 statutory cabinet offices, more than 10 White House divisions, and countless agencies, boards, and commissions that help to advise and run the government. The new president will inherit a vast federal bureaucracy of civil employees that his administration must manage along with several layers of personnel that must be selected, hundreds of whom must go through Senate confirmation.

The 11-week period between the November election and Inauguration Day also requires a rapid succession of political and governing decisions that will ultimately determine how successful the new president will be in implementing his policies and building public support for his agenda. What is the basic organizational structure of the White House and executive branch? What are the major priorities of the new administration? Who must be brought on board to help develop and communicate the president's policy agenda? How will the executive and legislative branches coordinate action on the president's priorities? How will the new president and administration work to handle immediate crises while also maintaining a focus on their larger goals for the country?

Every successful presidential transition requires vision and talent. But the transfer of power in 2009 will demand extraordinarily clear and focused strategic thinking from the president-elect and his team given the economic and foreign policy challenges facing the country. When the new president takes over in January 2009, he will confront a range of challenges that have emerged since the last presidential transition in 2001.

More than 150,000 American troops are fighting in Iraq and 33,000 in Afghanistan, Osama bin Laden remains at large, and Al Qaeda and the Taliban are resurgent in Afghanistan and western Pakistan. The U.S. military is under enormous stress from repeated conflicts, hardware use, and troop rotations. And new global challenges ranging from climate change and disease to poverty and nuclear proliferation threaten international stability.

At home, Wall Street and Main Street are undergoing a financial crisis of proportions not seen since the Great Depression. The American middle class is imperiled as unemployment continues to rise, wages stagnate, benefits decline, and household costs increase. Economic inequality is higher than it has been since the late 1920s. The national debt has doubled to more than $10 trillion and annual budget deficits are approaching $500 billion per year. Over the past eight years, four million more Americans have fallen into poverty, and seven million more have joined the ranks of the uninsured.

Whether he likes it or not, the new president faces a monumental task in first righting the ship of state and then charting a new course to smooth water for the country. This book aims to make this navigation a bit easier and more coherent. The first section focuses on the structure of the White House Office and Executive Office of the President. It provides detailed recommendations for the organization and agenda of all existing offices including the National Security Council, the National Economic Council, White House Counsel, the Office of the Vice President, and others as well as suggestions for three new executive offices to carry out the nation's need for energy transformation, innovation, and research: the National Energy Council, the Office of Social Entrepreneurship, and Chief Technology Officer.

The second section provides a specific outline of what the new president's economic policy should look like, and it offers detailed recommendations for carrying out this policy within the six most relevant departments and agencies, including the Departments of Treasury, Labor, and Commerce; the Office of Management and Budget; the Office of the U.S. Trade Representative; and the Securities and Exchange Commission. The primary goal of the new administration should be to build a strong platform for economic growth that is both fair and effective. The new president must deal immediately with the global financial and mortgage crisis and focus long term on enhanced global trade, economic mobility for workers, and innovation and technological advancement.

The third section provides a broad overview of the domestic landscape, focusing on everything from changing demographics and immigration to energy and climate change to health care and government transparency. The final section presents a new national security strategy for the incoming president focused on terrorist threats and the war in Iraq; homeland security; emerging transnational challenges on weapons proliferation and economic development; and renewed focus on human and civil rights and public diplomacy in the new security environment.

By way of example, let me finish by offering my direct thoughts on presidential transitions. I have been involved at both ends of the transition process—on the incoming side as staff secretary to President William J. Clinton in 1993, and later, on the outgoing side as the president's chief of staff in 2001. Based on my experience on both sides of the equation, I have learned that the office of the presidency requires both flexibility and endurance. Despite the president's best-laid plans, unforeseen circumstances or events can quickly consume the new administration.

At the same time, if the president and his administration do not take the time upfront to develop a clear and coherent blueprint for action—and find ways to move this agenda regardless of the environment—then they will quickly find the windows of opportunity shutting before their eyes and will face increased public frustration and disappointment.

In a spirit of cooperation, respect, and support for our new president, I hope the recommendations within this volume offer some measure of guidance for a smooth transition and a successful term in office that serves the country well.

October 2008

Progressive Patriotism

How the 44th President Can Change Washington and America

MARK GREEN

From Politics to Governance

It was a "change" election all right, but will it actually change Washington and America?

November 2008 wasn't so much a culmination as it was the beginning of a new chapter in our national story. For America is as much a notion as a nation, the notion being that a government "of, by and for the people" (still the best definition of democracy) is a continuously self-correcting mechanism where the pursuit of progress is our secular religion. "America," wrote Walt Whitman, "is always becoming."

But that idealized process presumes a continuing conversation between leaders and citizens so that government reflects popular opinion and therefore produces good results. This is the opposite of President George W. Bush's almost authoritarian assertion after his reelection that the country had had its "accountability moment" and, as the "decider," he'd lead where he chose. November 5, then, shouldn't end, but rather ignite, a public conversation about what's next. As politics now elides into policies, the story of 2009 is only starting to be written.

Hence *Change for America*.

The Center for American Progress Action Fund and the New Democracy Project began working on this non-partisan volume in mid-2007 based on the belief that the "charisma of ideas"[1] could help whoever was elected the 44th president.[2] Presidential candidates rationally concentrate far more on money, media and primaries than on how to actually run the government post-election. That's why we thought that the winner would benefit from the best thinking of 67 progressive scholars, authors, advocates, and officials pooling their collective years of experience and thinking into one volume of solutions. *Change for America* consequently contains both detailed agency-by-agency proposals as well as thematic overview essays about how to best renew and reform the next America.

The model was President John F. Kennedy, who said he "threw his hat over the wall of space" when he predicted in 1962 that America would land a man on the moon by decade's end. So let's imagine America in 2016: how do we want our government and country to look then, by the end of the 44th president's possible two terms in office? Unless the new administration has a clear destination, it will never get there.

This book offers several hundred ways both to fix our broken government and to provide benchmarks against which the new administration can be measured. It focuses far more on prescription than description, on ideas for the future rather than the failures of the past. Change, however, is hard. Machiavelli rightly noted that "there is nothing more difficult and dangerous, or more doubtful of success, than an attempt to introduce a new order of things in any state. For the innovator has for enemies all those who derived advantages from the old order of things whilst those who expect to be benefited by the new in situations will be lukewarm defenders." Indeed, the American democratic system—with its bicameral legislature, Senate filibuster rules, and executive veto—bends more toward stasis than reform. Still, dramatic change can occasionally happen all at once—as it did in 1933 and 1965—when public pressure forces tectonic plates to shift and when there's presidential leadership to direct the released energy.

Teddy Roosevelt, for example, realized that only government could protect the environment and police big corporations—and he acted on that realization. Of course, Franklin Delano Roosevelt was elected to respond boldly to the Great Depression. Harry Truman understood that Europe's recovery after World War II would enhance America's recovery—hence the Marshall Plan. Monumental civil rights laws emerged from the combination of Kennedy's assassination and Lyndon Johnson's legislative acumen.

As the co-founder of this transition project, I believe that 2009 will commence not only a transition between presidencies but potentially also between eras. Based on two significant books from this past year—Rick Perlstein's *Nixonland* and Sean Wilentz's *Era of Reagan*—that both analyze the two leading conservative presidents of the late 20th century, it is safe to conclude that 1968 was the start of a 40-year conservative reign, interrupted by the anomaly of Watergate and Bill Clinton's unusual talents. Clinton, though, understood well the era he governed in, once confiding to an aide that he was "a progressive president in a conservative era."

Barack Obama, on the other hand, now has the historic opportunity to be a progressive president in a progressive era and therefore take America to a different place, where elected leaders focus on issues beyond *only* taxes and terrorism.

Preconditions for a New Era

The late Arthur Schlesinger, Jr., articulated the theory that, in a two-party country, there are political cycles of 30 years or so that swing like a pendulum from right to left and back. While he did not think there was such a thing as historical inevitability, it is true that, looking back, there has been something of a pendulum effect from McKinley/TR to FDR/Truman/JFK to the Reagan/Bushes.

The assumption that we may soon see a progressive president in a progressive era requires several preconditions to come true. If he's the match, here's the kindling:

Bush and Conservatism Failed. Every presidency makes mistakes, blunders, and shades the truth: conversations about presidential administrations usually permit a healthy debate on whether the gains exceed the failures.

George W. Bush is actually, provably different. He and his allies were the dog that caught the car when in 2001 they controlled the executive branch, the legislative branch, a majority of the judiciary, and the corporate community as well—and then proceeded to blow it.

His eight years in office were a complete, abysmal failure. How else can one describe ruining our global reputation; condoning torture; invading a country that never attacked us, based on false information; borrowing trillions from the future and Chinese in order to enrich our wealthiest citizens; generating only one third of the jobs produced in the prior administration; ignoring global warming; failing to react adequately to Hurricane Katrina yet overreacting to Terry Schiavo; watching 50 top appointees resign after scandals alongside two White House aides who were convicted of crimes, the first such staff in 150 years; and—for an encore—presiding over the near collapse of our financial system and ushering in an economic recession? All this while waving both the flag and the bloody shirt of 9/11.

Bush's dwindling supporters are now left with predicting a Truman-like vindication in 50 years; the last refuge for those losing a debate on the facts is to hypothesize future redemption, since it cannot be logically disproved today. Already only two of 109 historians have concluded that Bush's presidency is a success—98 percent is a big negative vote whether in elections or among historians.[3]

Nor can conservatives argue that President Bush and Vice President Cheney betrayed conservatism. That administration was plenty conservative on the core tests of national security, taxes, choice and culture. But when confronted with 21st-century problems of slow job growth, accelerating gas prices, and stunning income and wealth inequality, conservatism had no ready answers. A domestic policy based on laissez-faire had nothing to say to families with shrinking incomes who were losing their homes to shady mortgage brokers.

America Is More Progressive. In large measure because of this failure, America is changing into a more progressive place. Karl Rove's grandiose plan for a 50-year conservative realignment is obviously in ruins.

Rhetorically, it's still a fairly conservative country, with more citizens self-identifying with the word "conservative" than the word "liberal" and with denunciations of "tax-and-spend liberals" and "activist judges" continuing to find an audience. But *operationally,* the country is becoming more liberal—all polls indicate significant majorities who are pro-environment, pro-choice, pro-civil rights, pro-Social Security, as well as anti-Iraq war, anti-big business and anti-tax breaks for the top one percent. When asked in a Pew poll whether a person favored "bigger government, more services" over "smaller government, fewer services," Americans favored the smaller government option by 15 percentage points in 2001 and the bigger government option by a point in 2008.[4] And on the issue of race: while mixed marriages were illegal in 22 states in 1961, a man born that year of just such a relationship will be sworn in as president of the United States in 2009.

At the same time, the country's minorities, professional families and single-person households are all on the rise as a percentage of the entire population. And all on average are more supportive of progressive positions. Indeed, it's hard to come up with *any* issues where the country is growing less progressive.

Grass-roots Fervor Is Rising. Because in a democracy intensity can count every bit as much as a majority, leaders often follow movements rather than vice-versa. Labor organizers pushed FDR to propose many of his New Deal reforms. The civil rights laws of the 1960s were preceded by protests comprised largely of blacks and students. Environmentalists organizing Earth Day, not

President Richard Nixon's walks on the beach in his dress shoes, crystallized into the Environmental Protection Agency.

In the late 1970s, due to stagflation, the Iranian hostage crisis and a very spirited conservative movement, the public began demanding less government and taxes. That led in 1978 both to enactment of Prop 13 in California, which slashed property taxes, and the defeat of the federal Consumer Protection Agency bill, and then of course to the election of Ronald Reagan in 1980. Anti-tax libertarians and pin-striped populists were on the march.

Today the new energy appears to be far more economically populist, anti-war and pro-environment. There was an explosion of new voters in primaries and the general election as compared to the previous cycle. The explosive growth of the Internet and the net-roots community heavily tilts to Blue America. Six years ago, the Center for American Progress, the HuffingtonPost, Media Matters and Air America Media didn't exist, and Move On had only a fraction of its current reach. This new democratization of news and views means that millions now get their information directly, quickly and inexpensively from independent advocates, not just through intermediaries such as the major corporate news media.

Indeed, while presidents must calculate how to speak to America through the major networks, the 44th president is *himself* a network with 10 million email names he can text or talk to at will. He and future 21st-century presidents will not have to wait for fireside chats or weekly radio addresses to have a one-way conversation with a public increasingly expecting to have two-way conversations with an internet-savvy chief executive.

Historian Doris Kearns Goodwin framed it well.

History suggests that unless a progressive president is able to mobilize widespread support for significant change in the country at large, it's not enough to have a congressional majority. For example, Bill Clinton had a Democratic majority when he failed to get health reform. When you look at the periods of social change, in each instance the president used leadership not only to get the public involved in understanding what the problems were but to create a fervent desire to address those problems in a meaningful way.[5]

Smart Government Is Back. For years government has been a four-letter word indistinguishable from bureaucracy. Governors Carter and Reagan rode anti-government sentiment into the White House, as the belief that government can help people fell by half from the 1970s to the 1990s. Even Bill Clinton famously said that "the era of big government is over" (although the blame-government-first crowd blithely chose to ignore his next qualifier, "but we cannot go back to the time when our citizens were left to fend for themselves").

Ironically, it was government failures such as the Vietnam War and Watergate—epochal events having nothing to do with the progressive community or values—which shrank the credibility of government, which is often the instrument of progressive reform. But Reagan's inaugural observation that "Government is not the solution, government is the problem" has now fallen flat after events ranging from Hurricane Katrina to E-coli outbreaks, from dangerous Chinese toys to collapsed mines in West Virginia and Utah, from millions losing their homes in foreclosures to inadequate care in veterans facilities. No, the "problem" wasn't government regulation but weakened levees; uninsured and unemployed Americans; mortgage crooks; Enron executives; dangerous food, drugs and workplaces; and tax cuts to billionaires while fighting two wars. Explained author Jacob Hacker in *The Great Risk Shift*: "People are more worried about Big Insecurity than Big Government."

Surely, market fundamentalism as a reigning economic philosophy reached its nadir with former Fed chair Alan Greenspan's testimony before Chairman Henry Waxman's Government Affairs Subcommittee in late October 2008. When asked whether the near collapse of capital markets of late 2008 didn't expose the failure of his exuberant view that markets were perfectly self-correcting, this oracle of free markets and Ayn Rand replied, "absolutely ... I was shocked ... I made a mistake." In other words, laissez *wasn't* always fair.

Clinton's and Bush's presidential terms, then, for very different reasons, have helped to restore public faith in the power of positive government. For his part, Clinton's agenda of crime reduction, welfare reform and budget balancing not only worked programmatically but also helped take the historic monkey of "big, bloated government" off the backs of federal regulators. And Bush's failures made the public yearn for real solutions rather than merely invoking the "greed is good" ethic of Gordon Gekko in *Wall Street*.

At the same time, a progressive community used their time out-of-power after 2000 to rethink and re-plan at least as well their conservative counterparts did after the 1964 Goldwater shellacking. So by 2008, a body of work had developed over time—in think tanks, universities, congressional offices—that together constituted a progressive plan to renew Washington and America. *Change for America*, therefore, is not based simply on more-big-government—"cap-and-trade" is not just old-fashioned command-and-control regulation—

but on more transparent, accountable and common-sense government that looks to the market when it can as well as to regulation when it must.

Four Values for America

The 44th president can find early success if he were simply able to appoint competent people, obey the law and tell the truth, unlike recent history. Assuming, however, that the new president wants to do more than go back to the future, there's the need for a *plan*. We call it "Progressive Patriotism" because there's nothing more American than always seeking to do things better.

Franklin Delano Roosevelt and Ronald Reagan especially understood that broad themes and big ideas move America more than any particular program or policy. Historian Sean Wilentz reports that Reagan once told his barber that as president he had tried to lower taxes, raise morale, increase defense spending, face down the Soviet Union and shrink government. Contending that he had done all but the last, Reagan concluded, "four out of five ain't bad."

Only a new president can ultimately decide how his majority converts into his mandate. What changes *must* be on his early list; what *should be*? Will he be largely reactive, putting out fires, or visionary, creating fire prevention policies? Does he start with another economic stimulus and energy conservation ... or children's health and the policy on torture? What's an early win that can snowball into a landslide of legislation?

Does he listen to Cassandra's urging centrist caution or move boldly for more transformational change during a window of opportunity, especially in 2009–2010?

These are hard decisions for a new White House. To help that process, I propose a plan for Progressive Patriotism that is built on four cornerstones: democracy, diplomacy, economic opportunity, and a greener world. This Introduction and book will describe what's wrong and then what's next, based on these four core values with the expectation that 2009 may begin a transition not only between presidencies but also between governing paradigms.

Value 1: A Stronger Democracy

Whereas issues involving war and economy invariably trump other voter issues, and 2008 was no exception, the process of democracy should be a bedrock American concern because process *is* policy. "If we want to solve our problems," writes contributor Michael Waldman in his book, *A Return to Common Sense*, then "we have to fix our systems." When the mechanism of democracy is broken—when there's such secrecy, disenfranchisement, lawlessness, dishonesty, and special interest domination that people can't have access to decision-makers —the government won't act in the public interest. If you care about reforming, say, Pentagon contracting rules, environmental regulation, tax policy or foreign aide, Congress needs to reform democracy itself.

So just as Ronald Reagan kept referring back to *Freedom* as a primary value, Barack Obama can hold up *Democracy* as his primary value. It's a good time to not only wave the flag but also to pursue policies that honor what it represents, for the world's oldest democracy has become less democratic.

Over two centuries America has been lurching toward a "more perfect union." Slavery was abolished, women and then blacks won the right to vote, workers pioneered workplace democracy by winning the right to collectively bargain, and limits were put on what big interests could contribute to campaigns. Over the past eight years, however, a group of new authoritarians in the Executive Branch, the Congress and the courts have posed a clear and present danger to our democratic and constitutional traditions.

Consider voting rights, executive abuse and the rule of law.

Although our democracy ranks in the bottom fifth in turnout of all democracies, the Bush administration's Justice Department focused not on expanding voter turnout but on so-called voter fraud. As discussed in the chapters on civil rights and the Department of Justice, the Civil Rights Division did not bring one case against the suppression of minority voters, but instead pressured U.S. Attorneys to concentrate on cases against people presumably voting illegally. This happens, however, about as often as someone getting hit by lightning, according to a study by the Brennan Center for Justice at New York University, since it's extremely unlikely that a person will risk prosecution and jail to join a conspiracy that adds his/her one extra vote to an election total.

Then citing the "war on terror" after 9/11, the Bush-Cheney Administration came up with a theory of the "unitary executive," which basically assumed that the president could ignore any law during wartime as commander-in-chief. This was both unprecedented and radical since the war on terror would never be over and the president, per the Constitution, is commander-in-chief of the military, not the country. (The theory should not have been surprising, however, for it was Representative Richard Cheney whose dissent to the 1987 congressional Iran-Contra Report concluded that a president, in emergencies, should resort to "monarchical" remedies.)[6]

This was too much for even a U.S. Supreme Court with a majority of Republican appointees. Four times it ruled that the Bush administration was denying due process of law to Guantanamo detainees. "A state of war," wrote then justice Sandra Day O'Connor, "is not a blank check for the president." It was a combination of Kafka and Orwell for an American government to argue that it could imprison people forever without a hearing or a charge—in the name of protecting Western values.

The Bush White House again and again ignored precedent—by using 1,100 so-called Signing Statements; neglecting 4th Amendment requirements for probable cause under the Foreign Intelligence Surveillance Act; employing politicized hiring practices at the Justice Department; failing to enforce the Clean Air and Clean Water Acts; and ignoring domestic law and international treaties against torture. Apparently when George W. Bush took his oath of office "to faithfully execute the laws," he took it literally.

As this era of extremism posing as patriotism is ending, the 44th president can pursue a Democracy Agenda—expanding the franchise, transparency, accountability and the rule of law. He could

- create universal voter enrollment, which could add up to 50 million voters to the rolls;
- make it a crime for any person or official to actively suppress the vote by any form of intimidation;
- enact a public finance law to help provide a funding floor under congressional candidates to help level the financial playing field;
- establish federal standards for electronic voting, with paper-verifiable ballots, same-day registration, voting by mail and felony enfranchisement laws, so all states come into the 21st century in technology and process;
- encourage instant runoff elections assuming that primary winners would have majority support in one round of voting;
- create an independent, bi-partisan commission, with subpoena power, to investigate all the allegedly illegal conduct by administration officials, as proposed by the author and lawyer Frederick A.O. Schwarz of the Brennan Center for Justice;
- instruct the Federal Communications Commission to make sure every home has affordable access to a broadband network of at least 100 megabits per second by the year 2012; and
- create a White House Office of Democracy ("Democracy Czar") to push for all of these and other pro-democracy reforms throughout the government, since the only way such important but non-headline reforms can be enacted by the congressional and executive branch bureaucracies, in my view, is if there's a known emissary advocating on behalf of a committed president.

Value 2: Economic Opportunity

America has never begrudged people becoming rich, so long as everyone has a shot at it. As Abraham Lincoln said, all should have "an open field and a fair chance [for their] industry, enterprise, and intelligence."

By that standard, the American economy in 2008 is failing. As the wide-ranging chapters on the economy detail, most Americans feel as if they are always running faster after an accelerating bus called prosperity.

Economic metrics reflect this split-level economy, with a new aristocracy of wealth and a floundering middle class. Between 1979 and 2005, the top 1 percent of income earners have enjoyed a 176 percent income rise, while the bottom 20 percent experienced only a 9 percent rise. Based on data going back to 1913, income is now more concentrated among the top 1 percent of households than any year except one—1928. While economic insecurity is up, economic mobility is down. About two-fifths of Americans born into a family in the bottom fifth stay in that rut as adults, while nearly the same percentage born into the top quintile stay there as adults—the only industrialized country with less upward mobility is Great Britain.[7]

Half of all workers report total savings and investments of under $50,000, while a quarter of all workers and retirees report no savings of any kind. In this past decade alone, the number of people without health insurance rose to over 46 million in 2006 from 38.4 million in 2000. And in 2005, the head of Exxon-Mobil, Lee Raymond, earned more (counting stock options) *per hour* than his average blue-collar worker did *per year*. Yet the minimum wage has fallen a third in real terms over the past two decades.

Hence the "hollowing out" of the middle class, as tax cuts engorge the super-rich while the flight of manufacturing jobs, higher unemployment, and growth of low wage/low-benefits service sector jobs shrink median incomes. This is partly due to the "invisible hand" of global economic trends, where $3-an-hour Mexican laborers and 67¢-an-hour Chinese can produce cheaper cars than their $24-an-hour American counterparts. But it is also due to the very visible hand of public policy. Just as Franklin Roosevelt's labor and regulatory policies and Truman's GI bill helped create the American middle class, Reagan's and the Bush's labor, tax and deregulatory policies are shrinking it.

The best way to lift people up from poverty and help the middle class is for the 44th president to concentrate on the value of economic opportunity for all, on linking GDP growth with real income growth for those with median incomes.

While any economic reforms will have to adapt to the ongoing financial and credit crisis, an Economic Opportunity Agenda would aim to:

- create a true progressive tax system by reducing rates on those earning under $200,000 and raising top rates on the fortunate few back at least to 38 percent, as in the 1990s when the economy was steaming ahead—and extend the estate tax, with exemptions on the first $3.5 million;
- expand the federally funded State Children's Health Insurance Program so all children have health care irrespective of their parents' employment—and then push for some version of universal health insurance, ideally with a "Medicare for All" program that the public would understand;
- cut poverty by half by 2016, as Peter Edelman and Angela Glover Blackwell argue, by focusing on programs that help children from birth to 5 years of age, starting with a program for "Universal Pre-K" for 4-year-olds to make sure that they're ready to learn when they enter kindergarten, and requiring a "Children's Impact Statement" for every federal law that might have an impact on children;
- shift $150 billion annually spent on nation building in Iraq to nation building in America by creating a National Infrastructure Bank that would invest in economic growth over the next decade;
- strengthen unions—one of the few mechanisms able to improve real income for workers—by enacting the Employee Free Choice Act, appointing NLRB commissioners who don't ignore the labor laws, hiring enough inspectors to effectively enforce labor health/safety laws at the Occupational Safety and Health Administration, and implementing ergonomics standards;
- establish a wage-loss insurance program to help workers, for a specific period of time, who lose their jobs and are forced to take a new job at a lower wage;
- create a single toll-free number as well as one-stop centers that handle all reemployment issues, from job search to training, health, mortgage and unemployment insurance; and
- enact a program to give four-year scholarships annually to 10,000 college students who will become primary-school teachers of science, math, engineering and technology.

Is all this just "class warfare," according to the rhetoric of conservatism? Answers Warren Buffett, now the wealthiest American: "It's class warfare only because my class started it and is winning."[8] What's required is nothing less than a new social compact between managers/owners, workers, and government.

Value 3: Diplomacy for Security

Winston Churchill and FDR understood the value of collective security and diplomacy. Both were witness to the fierce nationalism and pride that helped ignite World War I and both were determined toward the end of the next World War to make sure that allies with common interests had common institutions. Therefore, they began to put in place international organizations like the United Nations, the International Monetary Fund, and the World Bank—as one scholar put it, "the architecture of internationalism that Woodrow Wilson dreamed of."[9] To these men, talking to your enemies was not a form of appeasement, which Churchill knew plenty about since he succeeded Neville Chamberlain, but a rational means to avoid conflict. In Churchill's famous aphorism, "to jaw jaw is always better than to war war."

George W. Bush graduated from a very different school of thought. In the eyes of the world and many Americans, our leading exports seem to be war and financial calamity. Given our participation both in preemptive war and in a policy of torture and since so many international problems cannot be solved by nations acting alone, it's time for the 44th president to return to FDR's and Churchill's vision by issuing in effect a Declaration of Interdependence. Pollution, extreme weather, AIDs and other pandemics, terrorism, refugee flows, and nuclear proliferation don't respect sovereign borders. The only way to defeat these threats is for nation states to engage in collective security rather than hide behind Maginot lines or oceans. As the author of the State Department chapter, Gregory B. Craig, puts it, "There are other, more effective ways of exercising influence in this world than military force, such as an America more active and engaged diplomatically on every front." Recall also the presidential nominee in 2008 who said, "We must be willing to listen to our democratic allies. Being a great power does not mean that we can do whatever we want whenever we want …"[10] That nominee was John McCain.

Diplomacy simply means using a mix of carrots and sticks to advance our interests, which so often now are also the interests of others. When we are seen as doing good by talking rather than bullying—as Truman did with the Marshall Plan, as Bush 43 has done on HIV / AIDS in much of Africa—we recruit others to join us in common problem-solving. The goal is to convince powerful and emerging states to become stakeholders in the global economy and in joint responses to terrorism. Our foreign policy authors explain how a new president should:

- withdraw responsibly from Iraq and repudiate the strategy of preemptive regime change by military means—and engage in diplomatic efforts with the parties in Iraq and then with its neighbors Iran, Syria, Turkey, Jordan, Saudi Arabia, and the Gulf States;

- shut down Guantanamo, provide due process rights to remaining detainees, as the Supreme Court has insisted, and end the practice of torture by again complying with the Geneva Conventions, the Convention Against Torture and the International Covenant on Civil and Political Rights;

- give a speech in a major European capital calling for a new alliance to combat and prevent terrorism throughout the world by coordinating the work of police and military, conducting special operations, sharing information more quickly, and creating an international legal framework that's more effective in capturing, trying and convicting terrorists;

- support the creation of an International Peace Corps modeled on our domestic version, first proposed by Crown Prince Hamzah of Jordan five years ago;

- promote more trade with provisions for labor and environmental standards so we don't have a "race to the bottom" like industrial America did in the 1890s;

- seriously participate in the Copenhagen round to reduce global warming, not just issue late rhetorical appeals for reductions decades hence; and

- aspire to the abolition of nuclear weapons worldwide by, first, establishing the primary strategic objective of preventing any new actors—state or non-state—from seeking or acquiring nuclear weapons and, second, reducing towards zero the risk that actors who already have nuclear arms will use them.

Value 4: A Greener World

Not that long ago conservatives regularly mocked liberals as "tree huggers" and George H. W. Bush referred to Al Gore as "the ozone man." But that was before human-made climate change produced six of the hottest eight years of the past century, four of the most severe hurricanes, and the melting of Arctic and Antarctic ice—and before the concept of "peak oil" boosted price by the barrel and at the pump, and nearly all scientists agreed that unmitigated climate change would lead to massive casualties as oceans surged and desperate neighboring nations went to war.

Despite this amount of evidence, the past eight years have been lost time when it comes to the problems of environmental pollution and global warming. At the final G8 Summit of his presidency, Bush agreed to the unanimous goal "of moving to a carbon-free society" by hoping to reduce heat-trapping greenhouse gases 50 percent by the year 2050—and then actually joked as he walked off the stage, "goodbye from the world's biggest polluter."

Given all these sins of emission and omission, the 44th president will have public support to launch an Apollo-like project to produce a green, low-carbon economy that delivers more prosperity by making our nation more energy efficient and internationally competitive. The only way to serve as a model to China and India is to build a green consciousness into every economic decision, every transportation decision, every tax decision, every regulatory decision. It will no longer do to treat energy and environment as "an" issue in its own silo—like, say, education or fiscal policy or antitrust enforcement. For climate change is "the" only issue simultaneously affecting our economic health, physical health, and national security.

Since America has been responsible for some 30 percent of worldwide carbon emissions over the past century, we must acknowledge our responsibility and lead the world in declaring that this country cannot "drill and burn" our way out of our addiction to fossil fuels but instead must "invest, invent and conserve" our way forward. As Bracken Hendricks and Van Jones write in their overview on the climate crisis, "The 'clean tech' revolution and the transformation of our aging energy infrastructure is poised to become the next great engine for American innovation, productivity and job growth, as well as social equity gains. Building a clean energy economy can generate hundreds of billions of dollars of productive new investments on the scale of the greatest periods of past American economic expansion." A "clean tech revolution" requires:

- the creation of a new White House "National Energy Council" that is the equivalent of the National Security Council for climate change—coordinating all other energy-related departments to advance the president's message and program for a greener world—and it should oversee producing biennial reports for the White House and Congress on the ongoing effects of extreme weather on human health and the environment, like a Census on the climate;
- the implementation of a carbon "cap and trade" system that sells corporations permits to emit greenhouse gases and that can push us from a high carbon to a renewable energy economy, generate hundreds of billions in revenues annually to promote alternative energy sources like wind, solar and biomass and provide rebates to struggling Americans hit with higher energy prices;
- the application of a National Energy Efficiency Resource Standard to require utilities to cut energy use by 10 percent by 2020, including retrofits

of non-weatherized housing;

- the implementation of the Renewable Energy Policy Project's plan of a $62 billion investment to expand wind capacity by 125,000 megawatts over 10 years to help stabilize U.S. carbon emissions and create nearly 400,000 domestic manufacturing jobs;
- stronger appliance efficiency standards that are mandatory and reflect the best available technology;
- a program to develop a new line of ultra-efficient vehicles, such as plug-in hybrids that can get 100 miles per gallon as well as new battery systems— and also to insist on far stricter auto fuel efficiency standards since auto fuel efficiency was flat for two decades and today Europe has achieved averages of 40 mpg as contrasted with our 27 mpg;
- mandatory policies to increase electricity generated from renewables, something dropped from the 2007 Energy Bill;
- a joint U.S.-China R&D project to develop new carbon capture-and-storage technology for coal-fired plants; and
- a program requiring that the federal government, which controls billions of square feet of building space and hundreds of billions of dollars in procurement contracts, reduce its carbon footprint by altering purchasing decisions, improving vehicle fleet management, retrofitting buildings and providing bonus points for bidders who meet green standards.

Conclusion: Teacher-In-Chief in the New Mainstream

Not since 1933 has there been a presidential handoff involving a bigger gap in philosophy at a more difficult time. The economy is suffering from a crisis of confidence and credit, as jobs disappear and real incomes shrink over a decade. With the backdrop of an intractable war in Iraq in the most fractious region on earth, America is reviled by many nations around the world for appearing to emphasize the power of our arms rather than the power of our values. Terrorism is on the rise around the globe—and at home, plutocracy seems to be growing just as democracy is eroding. Human-made climate change threatens our country and planet while hyper-partisanship and special interest money seem to be in the saddle in Washington.

While exceptional, America may not be immune. Will she fade like Rome, Russia, Japan and Great Britain did in earlier epochs? Or is there a real chance for a renewal?

Walt Kelly's cartoon character Pogo once referred to a dire situation as presenting "insurmountable opportunities"—and as author Tom Friedman keeps reminding us, "a crisis is a terrible thing to waste." Now, in the midst of these multiple crises, the 2008 election has put in place the first progressive president and progressive congressional majority in nearly 50 years. For Obama to rise to this occasion and become a 21st-century FDR or LBJ requires that he seize two approaches during his transition and early months.

Stylistically, while of course the commander-in-chief during wartime, the president is also the teacher-in-chief, what Teddy Roosevelt famously called the Bully Pulpit. Here we should give George W. Bush credit: while he won office by one vote, in the Supreme Court, he acted like a huge Electoral College winner in unapologetically describing and pursuing his conservative agenda, especially after the unifying tragedy of 9/11. In a similar display of leadership, the 44th chief executive should send to the rhetorical dustbin all talk of "death taxes," "mushroom clouds," and "the culture of life" and instead constantly remind citizens of the urgency of equal justice in America, global warming, a low carbon economy, universal health care, and wage-insurance. Think of the way FDR spoke not of a "bank moratorium" in his first week in office but a "bank holiday." And remember how fast America went from golf to Ian Fleming when we went from Ike to JFK? With a smart teacher-in-chief in the White House knowing George Lakoff's and Drew Westin's phone numbers, the frames of policy must now surely change.

Substantively, four huge policy problems are being left on the new president's doorstep. Yet each has answers that are practicable, plausible and linked to the four core values articulated earlier:

- Withdraw from Iraq safely, end torture and restore our global standing by means of collective security to solve other transnational challenges;
- Stabilize the economy and advance economic opportunity so that average income finally starts rising after a stagnant eight years and all families have access to quality, affordable health care;
- Shift to a green economy so we enhance our national, family and economic security;
- Fix our democracy so we don't again have public opinion going in one direction but public policy in another.

The obstacles to these transformational changes are not facts but stale thinking.

Anachronistic analysts will argue that this is still a "center-right" country and the 44th president shouldn't move too far left, as *Newsweek* cautioned in anticipation of Obama's Inaugural.[11] But the suggestion that Obama should "move" to the center ignores that recently the center has moved to the left. "For Much of the Country, a Sizeable Shift," was a banner post-election headline in the *New York Times*.[12] Voters appeared to render a negative verdict on preventive wars, trickle-down economics, financial deregulation, executive abuses, and theocracy over science. Precisely because conservative values crashed into a reef called reality, it has created a new mainstream, a new mandate for change. This collapse and the '08 elections alone did not create a new progressive era—Rove's earlier hubris should caution us to that—but the *opportunity* for a new progressive era.

It's now up to the new president during his transition and "first hundred days" to tactically deploy executive orders, major addresses, well-chosen visits and proposed legislation to convey his substance, his strategy, his plan, his *narrative*. He got elected by focusing on "change," presumably from Bush—now he has to explain change for what? As this book describes in detail, Barack Obama can ideally reframe the American conversation around democracy, diplomacy, opportunity and a greener world.

What's at stake is a better America by 2016.

CHANGE
FOR
AMERICA

THE WHITE HOUSE

Managing the White House for a Successful Presidency

JOHN D. PODESTA AND
SARAH ROSEN WARTELL

The White House chief of staff is the senior manager of the administration, a key advisor to the president, and a decision maker in his or her own right, making choices in service of the president's goals and strategics. As the top administration manager, the chief of staff must marshal organizational resources in support of the president.

Managing the administration entails oversight of almost 2,000 White House employees and approximately 3,000 cabinet officials and other political appointees. The chief of staff also manages how the administration engages with the media, Congress, and state and local policymakers, as well as business, labor, and a myriad of interests. In establishing the procedures by which decisions are brought to the president, made, and executed, the chief of staff must ensure the team remains focused on big-picture objectives and strategy, while responding nimbly to the inevitable day-to-day crises. And he or she must ensure the highest possible standards of ethical government to protect the president.

The job also entails managing the president himself—working with him to allocate his scarce time and attention to achieve the most important objectives and sustain his mental acuity and physical strength. At its heart, the chief of staff's job is to manage the process by which decisions are brought to the president or made at lower levels. As the administration's ultimate "honest broker," the chief of staff should first oversee an inclusive process in which ideas are tested and improved by discourse; but he or she may also add his or her own view as an important presidential advisor as well. Almost every other senior advisor, other than the vice president, has a portfolio—national security, the economy, Congress, communications, etc.—but very few are in a position to see the full picture.

The precise balance of manager and advisor will depend on the temperament and management style of the new president and his chief of staff and the understanding reached between them. But in any model it is in the president's best interest for his chief of staff to be a powerful decision maker on both process and substance on issues of significance, within parameters established by, and in service of the goals and strategies of the president.

Without impairing the chief of staff's effectiveness as an honest broker, the president can encourage him or her to exercise authority on his behalf. The chief of staff's authority, however, will stem principally from the perception of the White House's success. Rather than seeking to become the "second most powerful person in Washington" in his or her own right, the chief of staff should accrue and sustain power by skillfully enhancing the president's own success. A chief of staff consequently must not selectively limit the information flow to the president to advantage his own view, but instead should insist on a fair, internally transparent decision making process that uses the president's time efficiently.

The new president, however, has a corresponding obligation. He should agree to not consider requests for decisions when the policy process enforced by the chief of staff is circumvented. By so empowering the chief of staff, the president gets someone who can say no, even to the president's closest friends and strongest supporters, without requiring the president to own every hard call.

Recommendations

While picking the cabinet is the most visible focus of the presidential transition, staffing the White House quickly is of greatest importance. There will inevitably be delays in obtaining senate confirmation of agency officials, but a full complement of White House staff will allow the president to get his agenda going on day one.

During the transition, the chief-of-staff designee should be responsible for working with the new president to fill top administrative jobs, particularly the key White House staff positions. The selection should produce a well-rounded staff that both meets the needs of the 44th president and fills the gaps in his policy knowledge. Two essential hires for the chief of staff are two deputies— one engaged with policy and the other with White House management— though the portfolios may change depending on the skill set of the individuals in question.

Staffing the White House requires skills different than required by the campaign, but the new president should have some advisors who were with him on the stump. The chief of staff must help find the right mix of talents and experience from among the most senior advisors including: policy expertise, communication skills, knowledge of the White House, knowledge of Congress, knowledge of the president and his campaign, and intellectual independence.

Other criteria might also be added to the mix. For instance, the team should include those with experience dealing with important constituencies for reform, including both key business sectors—such as health, finance, and energy—as well as labor and consumer interests. It also would be valuable to have some individuals with experience gained from working in government agencies, to balance the instinctive desire of White House staff to develop all policy internally. The team will be stronger if it also represents a broad array of racial, ethnic, faith, geographic, socioeconomic, and sexual orientation backgrounds. In light of the unique role played by the Internet in enhancing civic participation of people previously uninvolved, any president would want advisors who can take advantage of its democratizing power to engage more Americans.

The new president should put special emphasis on having a staff with strong Capitol Hill relationships. The coming legislative agenda will be daunting. Winning support from Congress for the new administration's program will be hard even if there is shared party affiliation. If there is a divided government, the likelihood of stalemate is very high. The most essential factor in winning congressional approval for any initiative is earning the support of the American people, but disrespect of Congress' prerogatives can give rise to enormous obstacles to the president's goals, even if public support is mobilized.

Short- and Long-Term Objectives

The number of issues that could command the president and White House staff's attention is enormous. The chief of staff must lead a process to determine a limited number of short- and long-term objectives which should command the lion's share of White House time and attention.

Presidential priorities, of course, must compete with emerging challenges. The greatest tests of a presidency, such as 9/11 or the recent financial market meltdown, are rarely things specifically anticipated before Inauguration Day. The challenge for a chief of staff is to get the balance right between advancing established priorities, reacting to the unanticipated, and stepping back to reassess periodically how well the administration is making progress against its larger goals and in the eyes of the American people.

To ensure that events do not completely overtake the presidential agenda, the president should decide on goals and measures against which he wants his administration and the White House work to be evaluated. He should strive to leave these goals largely constant, despite changing circumstances. His administration should not blindly push its policy agenda without considering the shifting landscape. Rather, decisions on emerging challenges should be made with reference to long-term objectives. The chief of staff must ensure at least some consideration of these larger objectives in the heat of the moment.

Beyond day-to-day crises, much of the White House focus is driven by an annual cycle of predictable events, such as the State of the Union address, submission of the president's budget, negotiations with Congress on appropriations, major legislative reauthorizations, international summits, international trips, and visits by heads of state. Presidential priorities and emerging challenges are often addressed within these cycles. Each should be seen as a key opportunity to advance some of the small set of large objectives by which the presidency will be judged.

Sustaining political capital and momentum for the agenda requires early victories on the key issues on which the president campaigned. To achieve early victories, the president needs to take advantage of the power of the executive branch to make change happen on its own. Executive orders, regulatory waivers, reallocation of appropriated program resources, and changes in program policies are routes available in many circumstances to show that change can happen quickly. The submission of the president's first budget is another key way to demonstrate the new direction—even if it takes at least nine months for the budget to become law.

Beginning new rulemakings under existing laws, while not immediately effective, can also show the country concretely the direction the new president intends to take. These battles will also take energy and political capital, so the fights picked should be strategic, ideally ones that are emblematic of the policy direction the administration will advance in time through larger battles. Small victories on well-fought fights will demonstrate to reluctant lawmakers the political benefits of following the president's course, winning converts for the heavier lift to come.

With a change of party, some administrations have spent great energy in reversing the regulations and agency policies of the prior administration. Some reversals will be important to show the change in direction the president wants to achieve, but the demands from interest groups to focus on policy restoration should be resisted. The reason: It lets the president's predecessor and his political party continue to pick the issues around which the debate is held. Administrations are notoriously slow to get their own regulatory agenda into gear. Doing so is one of the best ways to shape the debate quickly, while legislative agendas are developed.

Driving Policy Through Inclusion

The White House policy council structure presents the chief of staff with a good way to ensure that a limited set of key objectives receive ongoing heightened attention. The major challenges facing the new administration will all involve more than one council. Making clear assignments for presidential priorities (and making clear the imperative for coordination and inclusion) means that a senior member of the team will "own" responsibility for driving policy to reach an overriding objective of the presidency.

The best assignment of issues to policy councils will depend upon the talents and perspective of the individuals selected as the president's policy advisors. In fact, in picking advisors the president and his chief of staff should consider not only expertise, excellence, and temperament, but also how closely the advisor's approach to the challenge aligns with the president's own ideas. The advisor's capacity to coordinate easily with his or her fellow policy advisors should also be a major consideration, given that these issues greatly overlap policy categories.

The National Security Council. Ending two wars, rebuilding our strained military capacities, redeploying our resources to address ongoing and emerging security risks, and re-establishing America's leadership in international affairs are the enormous coordination responsibilities of the NSC. In a global economy, the security of the United States is increasingly tied to our economic vitality and global competitiveness, suggesting the need for close collaboration with the National Economic Council on international economic issues. The security implications of climate change and energy dependence mandate intense NSC involvement in energy security deliberations as part of a larger national energy strategy run by the new National Energy Council.

The National Economic Council. Coordinating a strategy for economic recovery, rebuilding an effective social safety net, improving global competitiveness, emphasizing infrastructure, and spurring widely shared long-term growth should all be the policy responsibility of the NEC. But key components of such an economic strategy logically fall into other policy council baskets, especially universal health care and the transformation to a low-carbon economy. The overlap suggests the need for collaboration and joint management of policy development and processes. The NEC can knit the pieces together and focus on bringing sound economic analysis, a long-term fiscal strategy, and the perspective of the American worker and consumer to the table. Stabilizing our financial markets will be the preoccupation of the new Treasury secretary, although the reform strategy there also needs to be developed and vetted through NEC processes.

The Domestic Policy Council. DPC should have the lead responsibility for driving the enormous reform of our health delivery and insurance system. The Health and Human Services secretary or a White House official could be appointed as the reform effort leader and spokesperson. But it needs to be run through the deliberative policy process of the DPC. Budget, entitlement, and fiscal implications of health care reform require the NEC's economic expertise, suggesting collaboration and negotiation of a clear allocation of responsibilities on various components of health reform. Similarly, education reform for pre-K through 12th grade should be led by the DPC. New strategies for higher education and workforce development belong with the NEC, but the two pieces must come together in an education and human capital strategy developed jointly to ensure coherence. Other domestic issues that require coordination with NSC and NEC include immigration reform and food safety, for example. Finally, the DPC needs to drive an effort to restore the rule of law, ethics, and confidence in government.

The National Energy Council. As described in a subsequent chapter in this section, the 44th president should create a new National Energy Council to drive the transformation to a low-carbon economy. While this goal is best seen as an economic transformation, not merely an energy policy, assigning this responsibility to the National Economic Council would not produce the essential focus or deliver the energy policy expertise required given so many simultaneous economic challenges. But some components of the strategy around job creation and trade require shared responsibility. Similarly, the security aspects of the transformation will require close collaboration with the NSC.

Beyond making clear the assignments of the policy councils, the president and his chief of staff must establish the norms in which the cabinet agencies and policy councils advance policy proposals and craft strategy. "No drama" is perhaps most important, sending a clear signal that there will be no reward for subverting process or stepping on others' prerogatives. As an honest broker, the chief of staff should insist that all key advisors have a chance to be heard on any relevant issue. The staff secretary should be empowered by the chief of staff to refuse to give the president anything when norms of inclusion and transparency are not respected. Operating under these norms, the president's cabinet and senior advisors will come to see the chief of staff as their ally, ensuring their voice is heard on relevant issues and their access to the president is never blocked, although often structured.

Develop Trust with the National Security Advisor

The chief of staff must recognize that the national security advisor has some unique statutory and operational responsibilities that differentiate the role from that of other policy advisors. The NSC has a unique ability to get the commander in chief's time and attention, starting with a regular morning security briefing. Its staff, including many career government employees detailed from other agencies, is many times larger than that of other policy councils, sometimes replicating other White House functions internally.

If not well managed, the parallel NSC operation can result in the president moving between two separate worlds—with little coordination between the two. The chief of staff cannot ensure a fair and transparent deliberative process on policy issues of overlapping domestic and international import if matters are brought to the president through NSC channels without inviting the addition of any domestic or economic considerations. Similarly, if some of the president's speeches are written inside the NSC and not by centralized speechwriters, they will be less likely to present a coherent and integrated view of America's place in the world and its central challenges. What's more, domestic considerations could end up too far subordinated to international and security concerns.

By virtue of the dangers anticipated each and every day, a national security advisor will always think the incursion of Russia into Georgia is a greater threat to American safety than is the loss of wealth and income stemming from the housing crisis. Beside matters of war and peace, almost any consideration seems petty and political. Without the chief of staff's involvement in security matters to ensure a balanced presentation of interests, the new president could find himself with the same criticism leveled against George H.W. Bush's administration: inadequate attention paid to the lives of the American people.

An alternative model where security considerations and the national security advisor are subordinate would serve the public interest no better. Condoleezza Rice, for example, served as the president's NSC advisor, but in fact ended up subordinate to Vice President Cheney on national security affairs, giving her little credibility and authority with the other national security-related agencies. Decision making was skewed as a result of these power imbalances, allowing one perspective to dominate despite contrary evidence.

A third and more effective approach gives the national security advisor an independent line of communication to the president, but in exchange the advisor agrees to operate within the larger White House management system, play by its rules, and share—at least with the chief of staff—all information flows. To implement this approach in the second term of the Clinton administration, the chief of staff served on the NSC and the national security advisor was in the chief of staff's office with the other policy and political advisors early each morning where the issues of the day were discussed and coordinated. All information flowing to the president from the NSC also went to the chief of staff, and the national security advisor was included in a far wider array of domestic and economic policy matters. In this way, the NSC advisor was given an opportunity to weigh in on those issues' international and security implications.

This partnership between the chief of staff and the national security advisor works, however, only if the president picks people for these jobs who can respect one another's roles and understand how their own objectives could be advanced best through cooperation. It is therefore imperative that the new president, chief of staff, and national security advisor reach an agreement about the objectives and form of this integration.

The Vice President and First Lady

There is a wide array of models for integration of the offices of the vice president and first lady into the White House operation. Once the president and these individuals reach their own agreement about roles and particular areas of emphasis and leadership, the key to making these inherently complex relationships work is the signal that the chief of staff sends to the rest of the White House staff about the respect and integration that is expected.

Like the chief of staff, the vice president can be a valuable presidential advisor, with a broad perspective on balancing competing concerns. But that wisdom can only be shared if the vice president is in the information flows to begin with. That's why the vice president and his or her staff should be fully integrated into executive branch decision making. The VP should be a principal on all policy councils with his staff invited to all relevant meetings to represent his interests and share his perspective early in policy analysis and development.

By mutual agreement, the vice president should be given the opportunity to lead key initiatives in his or her area of interest and expertise. The relevant policy councils should understand it to be their obligation to support and enhance the VP's capacity to lead these efforts. But as we have learned from the Bush administration, the vice president's policy initiatives should be subject to the same broad vetting and deliberation as are other initiatives.

The first lady's areas of leadership are historically more targeted, and were even when Sen. Hillary Clinton was first lady. The president and first lady must decide early on the issues for which they want the first lady's views and input to be solicited. Better decision making and internal buy-in to decisions will result when the first lady's input comes through the regular order of advice and decision making in the White House, rather than directly to the president at the beginning or end of a process. Internal transparency goes a long way to avoid suspicions that sometime arise around spousal influence. As with the vice president, initiatives assigned to the first lady by the president should also go through the regular order of business and should receive the same level of support from relevant White House staff as would a presidential initiative. Additionally, the ability of the first lady to generate political capital to augment the president's is an asset that can only be developed thorough inclusion of her staff, particularly her chief of staff and communications team.

National Security Council

SAMUEL BERGER AND
TOM DONILON

The National Security Act of 1947 created the National Security Council, the nation's first institutionalized structure for the coordination of foreign and defense policy. The NSC remains today the core mechanism for the development of national security policy (as well as crisis management). In the 60 years since its creation, the authority and effectiveness of the NSC have ebbed and flowed. Its structures and processes have varied depending principally on the outlook and the decision-making style of the president, the personalities and skills of the president's national security advisors, and the challenges facing the country.

It is generally acknowledged that against any reasonable criteria, the NSC process during the Bush administration functioned poorly. Indeed, the past eight years marked the worst management of modern national security decision machinery since the council's establishment in 1947. The process has been described by former Bush administration officials and a range of analysts as "dysfunctional," resulting in national security failings with roots in a variety of sources, among them: the multiple and, in some cases, unprecedented challenges that confronted the administration; a number of process breakdowns and behaviors specific to the administration; and the general deficiencies that have affected the NSC process through several administrations.

Correcting these deficiencies—both those specific to the Bush administration as well as long-standing fundamental weaknesses—is of critical importance to the new administration. The new president will face the most daunting set of international challenges of any president since World War II, including two active wars, jihadist terrorism, instability in Pakistan, nuclear programs in Iran and North Korea, a fraying global nonproliferation regime, turmoil throughout the Middle East, a rising China, and global warming. Such a challenging agenda demands an effective, efficient policymaking process—one whose organization and operation match the current environment's demands.

Creating a strong and effective interagency process by which policy is made and carried out, however, should not detract from the essential roles and responsibilities of the key cabinet officials. The secretary of state should be the face of the new administration's foreign policy, the chief spokesperson for that policy, and the chief negotiator with foreign governments. The secretary of defense should be responsible for carrying out the use of military power, the chief architect of our military capabilities, and the custodian for maintaining and modernizing our overwhelming military apparatus, as well as the key interlocutor with his or her counterparts abroad.

Other cabinet secretaries also have important roles to play in national security policy, from the secretary of the treasury to the director of the Office of Management and Budget. But there must be a strong and energetic process at the center which assures that policy is made with due regard for all points of view, differences are identified and sharpened, the president is presented with all of the viable options, and his decisions are executed in an effective manner consistent with the president's intent.

The deficiencies specific to the Bush administration have been widely reported and provide a number of lessons for future administrations. The NSC

failed to reach policy decisions at critical times, resulting in the failure to resolve differences and policy paralysis for long periods of time. Vice President
Dick Cheney's office, with its parallel staff and expansive portfolio, pulled influence away from and fomented conflict within the NSC. Key players (specifically the secretary of defense) opted out of and circumvented the NSC process.
And the national security advisor (particularly in the first term) served as a sur-
rogate for President Bush rather than as an honest broker seeking to sharpen
differences and present them clearly to the president. This meant President
Bush often was not presented with competing viewpoints.

But there are also deficiencies in the NSC process that go beyond the Bush
administration, fundamental issues that have persisted under both Democratic
and Republican administrations for several decades that should be addressed.
Lack of long-term planning is one key deficiency. In national security as well as
other policymaking, the "urgent" usually drives out the "important." Developments and trends brewing beneath the surface or over the horizon often are
not addressed in a systemic fashion.

Inadequate mechanisms for implementing policy decisions are another troubling long-term problem. Reaching the "right" answer is just the beginning. Often there has been a failure to obtain congruence between policy as developed
and policy as implemented. And lack of accountability has led in the past to bureaucratic rivalries in carrying out policy that often defeat effective implementation. The new president and his national security advisor would be well
advised to consider these recent and more enduring deficiencies in the NSC
policymaking structure.

Recommendations

An effective interagency process requires a strong National Security Council
led by a national security advisor who sees his or her role as honest broker in
the policymaking process and chief watchdog in the implementation process
to assure that the president makes the most informed judgments possible and
that his or her decisions are, in fact, executed as intended. That's why the national security advisor needs only four deputies, not the current six or seven
deputies.

The national security advisor's principal deputy should chair the deputies
committee and handle crisis management. There should be a deputy national
security advisor for counterterrorism and homeland security, and a deputy responsible for coordination between the NSC and the National Economic

Council on national security-related, international economic issues. And there should be a deputy national security advisor for strategic planning who would chair a new strategic planning board and be responsible for national security policy development as it relates to long-term strategic issues.

The basic NSC structure, however, remains sound and should be preserved. The current NSC is supported by two working committees: a principals committee and a deputies committee. This model was designed and first implemented by President George H.W. Bush and his national security advisor Brent Scowcroft and has been carried forward through the subsequent two administrations. The Bush/Scowcroft system significantly streamlined and simplified the NSC system and provided a mechanism that was designed to bring decisions to the president in an efficient and informed manner. The success of the system is, however, dependent on the dedication of the principals (as well as the president and vice president) to the system as the central means by which decisions are made and agreement among the principals to participate in the process in good faith.

The principals committee is chaired by the national security advisor and consists of the key national security cabinet members with the addition of the chairman of the Joint Chiefs and the director of national intelligence serving as statutory advisors. The new president should re-include the ambassador to the United Nations as a formal and permanent member of the committee. The principal functions of the committee are to resolve issues where there is consensus and do not rise to the presidential level, and in other cases, in the words of General Scowcroft, to "clarify issues and positions among the principals before the issues are taken to the president."

The deputies committee is chaired by the principal deputy national security advisor and consists of the second- or third-ranking official of the key national security agencies. This body resolves mid-level issues, handles crisis management, and fully considers options of issues for consideration by the principals committee. Interagency working groups at the assistant-secretary level would deal with policy recommendations in the first instance and report to the deputies committee.

The Homeland Security Council should be integrated into the established NSC system, as recommended by the 9/11 Commission, to improve coordination. Homeland security directorates would have dual reporting to the Domestic Policy Council as well. Combating terrorism is a domestic and global challenge. Many of the critical tools required to protect the homeland involve formal agreements with and cooperation from international partners. Broader definitions of national and homeland security require the elimination of policy "silos" that previously categorized challenges as "foreign" and "domestic."

The new president should create four new significant structures to supplement the current system. The first is an NSC strategic planning board. A chronic problem with national security policymaking is the failure to anticipate or to see the broader and deeper issues that may confront the president over the six-month to three-year time horizon. What are the implications of China's rise over the next decade? What happens if the leadership of a key ally, Egypt or Saudi Arabia, collapses? What are the implications of large changes in capital flows for the U.S. population? What are the implications of global population and demographic changes? What are the national security implications of climate driven changes, such as water shortages in the Middle East?

The U.S. government currently lacks the capacity to do serious, comprehensive, multifaceted, and long-term strategic planning. There are planning offices and assets throughout the government, but nowhere is planning brought together comprehensively and strategically. Nor is it done at a level to inform and affect presidential decision making. The charter of such a new body would resemble that of George Marshall's 1947 vision for the State Department's policy planning staff and the Eisenhower administration's blueprint for its NSC planning board. This new body would reside in the Executive Office of the President and would be composed of deputy or assistant secretaries from the key agencies. It would report to the principals committee through a new deputy national security advisor who will be dedicated to this responsibility.

The strategic planning board's discussions would be informed by analyses of the CIA's National Intelligence Council as well as by outside experts from universities, think tanks, and business. In addition, the board could commission studies from experts outside the government or possibly create a think tank dedicated to the national security policy process serving a function much like RAND has done historically for the Defense Department. In short, the strategic planning board would serve as the president's dedicated strategic planning arm, situated at the heart of the national security process, to assess the most important emerging international issues facing the nation.

The second structure the new president will need from day one is a new National Energy Council, which is detailed later in the White House section. The new council's director would also be a member of the NSC principals committee.

The third new structure would be a National Security Law Committee. The Bush administration has seen profound process and planning breakdowns in the area of national security law. Many of the decisions made were done so without careful review by the responsible officials and the results have been exceedingly damaging. Indeed a number of crucial law-related decisions were made without the meaningful participation of the appropriate officials—including in some cases the attorney general. A National Security Law Committee, chaired by the attorney general and supported by the Office of Legal Counsel, would advise the president and the principals on national security law policy issues, including war-making authority, surveillance policy, detention and interrogation practices, rules of engagement, and others.

This committee would be a formal interagency process where all relevant agencies would participate in the development of administration positions and advice to the president through the nation's chief legal officer, the attorney general. The committee's first task should be a thorough review of existing national security-related orders, policies, practices, and positions with the goal of a report to the president within 90 days of his taking office.

Finally, the new president will require a number of executive committees for policy implementation. Where policies cut across more than one agency, such as post-conflict reconstruction in Iraq, the formulation of policy and the supervision of implementation would be vested in an executive committee, chaired by a senior official of the agency with the greatest responsibility, such as the departments of State or Defense, and composed of senior officials of the affected agencies. These executive committees would not be responsible for the day-to-day conduct of policy but rather for the process by which policy is made and accountability is established.

President Dwight D. Eisenhower once said, "Good organization does not guarantee success but bad organization guarantees failure." The NSC process suffered badly in the past eight years under mismanagement, but also from several key structural inadequacies. The proposals outlined here address a number of those needs. They would be the most significant changes to the White House structure in many years and would substantially enhance the ability of the next president to meet the unprecedented array of national security challenges he will face in January 2009.

National Economic Council

SARAH ROSEN WARTELL

The National Economic Council, directed by the president's national economic advisor, is the White House unit that should coordinate the development of the president's domestic and international economic program. The NEC should embody a commitment to a fair process of inquiry and debate among the president's top advisors, in which ideas are tested and improved by discourse. Many perspectives, from inside and outside of government, must be given voice, ensuring that the president has informed advice in a timely and efficient way. Cabinet secretaries and other senior White House staff all should have an opportunity to be heard on important decisions in private and can then speak in public in unison—knowing they had a fair shot at shaping the decision. The result: a good policymaking process that provides more time for all the key policymakers to advance the needs of the country and less time wasted in bureaucratic jockeying.

Most modern presidents had some structure for economic policy coordination,[1] though the specific form of the NEC first appeared under President Bill Clinton. The model used by his predecessor, President George H. W. Bush, included a small White House staff supporting an Economic Policy Committee overseen by the Treasury secretary, but Bush relied on it little. For domestic matters, Bush relied heavily upon the Office of Management and Budget Director Dick Darman, although he would also turn to individual agency heads for different projects.[2]

On the campaign trail, presidential candidate Bill Clinton first proposed the creation of a National Economic Security Council, arguing that (unlike President Bush) his focus in world affairs would be on the economic interests of Americans. But from campaign to transition, the brief for what was ultimately termed the National Economic Council expanded. After running a campaign whose lodestar was "it's the economy, stupid," Clinton needed to fulfill a domestic job creation pledge and tackle deficit reduction. The creation of a White House-led policy council to drive a broad international and domestic economic agenda helped his administration to "focus like a laser beam on the economy."[3] Adding the NEC to the White House staff also meant Clinton had top posts available for two key team members: Sen. Lloyd Bentsen of Texas and the Goldman Sachs Group, Inc.'s Robert Rubin, each of whom was believed essential to reassuring important audiences.

President Clinton called the NEC the single most significant organizational innovation that his administration made in the White House.[4] The reason was clear: it pulled international and economic policy together in a single White House-based coordinating council commited to a deliberative process with the NEC serving, first and foremost, as the honest broker. While far smaller and operating more informally than the National Security Council on which it was modeled, the Clinton NEC developed strong procedural norms that were held largely constant through the terms of its three directors, Robert Rubin, Laura Tyson, and Gene Sperling.

The NEC had the support of the president and each of his chiefs of staff, who typically insisted that economic policy recommendations come through the NEC process. After Rubin, for example, left the White House and became a hugely influential Treasury secretary, he had the ability to reach the president directly. But his commitment to the process was such that he brought policy proposals forward through NEC mechanisms. Some cabinet officials even used the NEC strategically to win broader administration support for their initiatives. As a result, most of the major economic policy initiatives of President Clinton were developed around a table convened by the NEC. Those that were not, most notably the health care plan of 1994, did not fare as well, for many reasons perhaps, but also because ideas are tested and improved by the deliberative process.

President George W. Bush retained the NEC structure, although the entire policy council apparatus appears to have been less influential, with more policy direction flowing from Vice President Dick Cheney's office and political advisors.[5] The outcome of the Bush administration's politically driven economic policy—flat to declining real wage gains, less competitive industries, housing and financial markets in continual crisis, and a sea of federal red ink—is what the new president inherits on day one. He will sorely need a proactive, pragmatic, well-respected NEC to sort through the many immediate economic policy priorities to shape a coherent plan to rebuild our economy for long-term, widely shared growth.

Recommendations

The NEC executive order issued by President Clinton remains in place and the NEC under his successor remained largely the same in structure if not function. The 44th president should use the same mechanism—an NEC composed of his top economic advisors, managed by an assistant to the president and director of the NEC.[6] In naming its membership, the president should make clear to all his commitment to an inclusive and transparent deliberative policy process and unwillingness to entertain those who subvert that process.

The new president should appoint a director of the NEC who has the temperament to serve as an honest broker. A trusted relationship with the president can and should be earned, not simply by providing good advice but also by ensuring that the best advice from the president's entire team informs his economic policy. It is less important that the director have specific expertise in economics, financial markets, business, labor, or the intersection of economic policy and politics, although the cabinet should include a mix of such experiences. It is more important that he or she be someone committed to rigorous analysis of all kinds, who can work collegially and earn respect from all quarters, melding them into an economic team.

The NEC director should be supported by two deputies with the responsibilities divided between domestic and international economic issues. One notable difference between the Bush and Clinton administrations was the relationship between the NEC and NSC on international economic policy. Early in his administration, President Bush made a conscious effort to get the National Security Council more involved "in the economic changes that have caused upheaval around the world," hiring more economic experts for the NSC. "It's a way to make sure the economic people don't run off with foreign policy and vice versa," Bush said.[7]

He made the NEC deputy assistant to the president for international economic affairs explicitly "dual-hatted," so he or she served also as the deputy national security advisor. In practice, the deputy operated largely within the NSC's orbit, with offices for the international economic team at the NSC. To ensure a more optimal balance of national security and diplomatic concerns and concern for American companies, workers, and consumers, the new president should name a deputy economic advisor for international economics who operates through the NEC, with good coordination with his or her NSC counterparts.

Careful thought should be given to building the rest of the NEC staff team. The NEC benefits from having staff from many disciplines: business, finance, labor, and social entrepreneurship, along with those with executive agency, White House, and Capitol Hill experience. The range of issues that will arise is as broad as American society itself, so employing those with a wide range of racial, ethnic, faith, geographic, and socioeconomic backgrounds will strengthen the capacity of the NEC team as well. Important qualities to consider are entrepreneurialism, judgment, humility, and endurance.

The NEC Process

The NEC must serve as an honest broker among agencies and viewpoints. Working groups should be established in the key areas of administration policy focus—for example, the housing market or retirement savings. Working groups should also convene to develop a new presidential initiative or a response to a new situation or major legislation. An NEC decision memo should lay out the background, detail a set of options, and argue the advantages and disadvantages of each in an unbiased way. A recommendation section allows each advisor or agency to specify their own recommendation regarding the options described and reasoning in brief.

The NEC's recommendation follows the others. Cabinet officials can ask to have a dissenting memorandum laying out their own views accompany the NEC decision memorandum. Encouraging the president's staff secretary to grant that courtesy, while allowing other principals to see the dissenting communication, is the best way to ensure that the opportunity is taken rarely and officials do not seek end runs around the process. The president will receive the best possible advice if the president and his chief of staff are supportive of the NEC process and that of all of the policy councils. If major policy decisions are made that preempt this process, then the credibility of the NEC will be diminished, as will be its ability to demand adherence to its process norms in the future. Ultimately, the quality of the president's decisions would lack well-rounded input and proper vetting. And the president's time will not be used most efficiently.

As the new occupants of the White House settle in, the NEC director should request a regular weekly briefing with the president and vice president. The NEC director should set the agenda, bringing along and showcasing evidence and analyses from the Council of Economic Advisors, Treasury, the Office of Management and Budget, and others depending upon the topic. The president receives a national security briefing daily, but economic conditions do not change as quickly nor require the same level of everyday engagement. Still, our country faces uniquely challenging economic conditions as the new president assumes office. Regular briefings on economic conditions will help to place these concerns at the front of his mind as the president goes about his schedule and sets his priorities.

The economic issues that are most effectively handled through the NEC process generally share certain characteristics. Typically, more than one agency has a stake in the decision, requiring interagency input and coordination. The NEC, however, also might coordinate presidential decision making on an issue affecting only a single agency, especially if the issue received significant public or congressional attention and the press or members of Congress would look to the president directly. The NEC also helps to coordinate the development of new initiatives that represent the president's priorities. Although the NEC is not an implementation agency, it should periodically check in on implementation of key initiatives to ensure the president's objectives are being met.

Some coordination functions should remain with relevant agencies. In the response to international financial market crises in the late 1990s, for example, Treasury coordinated closely with the NEC and NSC, but it had the lead. It could conduct essential coordination with the Federal Reserve and with finance ministers around the world on critical market issues without the appearance of political interference. Similarly, a framework strategy for trade agreements was developed through White House coordination, but the U.S. Trade Representative's office still managed the interagency process around the details. Buy-in at the front helped to ensure that the process of winning congressional approval for these agreements was a White House-wide effort.

The rhythms of the NEC are determined in significant part by regular and predictable events that drive policy development. In the fall, the NEC should convene a meeting with the president, his chief of staff, and other key presidential aides, where the OMB director and the Treasury secretary should present budget and tax options, and the framework for the budget should be established. Meanwhile, agencies submit their budget requests to OMB. The NEC should be consulted on these proposals and initiatives.

The NEC also should lead a simultaneous effort to develop new economic ideas for the president's State of the Union address in January, so that the budget can be built to accommodate the new initiatives picked by the president. Recent presidents used the month of January leading up to the speech to roll out a number of major proposals in advance and sustain focus on his agenda. The president is required to submit his budget to Congress by the first week in February. CEA's Economic Report of the President, which should reflect NEC and agency input, is submitted to Congress within 10 days of the president's budget. Other key dates that can drive the NEC's work include major international meetings like the Group of Eight industrialized nations.

While these predictable events establish a natural cycle for the NEC, unforeseeable events in the economy or international financial markets also will drive the agenda. These core and ad hoc responsibilities can be consuming, yet it is important to find time amid these pressures for strategic planning over a long-term horizon. In particular, keeping one eye on history, the NEC must reflect on the progress achieved against the president's fundamental economic objectives. This process of reflection and strategic planning benefits from broad consultation. No good policy is developed from inside the bubble alone. The NEC should draw upon the ideas and analyses of a deep bench of experts from non-governmental organizations, universities, other governments, former government officials, and think tanks—all eager to be of service and press their ideas. Consistent with the guidance of the White House counsel, the NEC also must work with allies of the president's policies to forge common advocacy strategies and messages.

Most importantly, the credibility of the president's policy requires that the NEC have strong ties to both American business and American labor. Business must be given an opportunity to gain confidence in a new progressive president. Organized labor, too long unwelcome in any agency other than the Department of Labor, has important insights and can be mobilized on behalf of the president's agenda to restore economic opportunity and mobility. Other key allies include mayors and governors around the country, each of whom shares the new chief executive's interest in fixing many of these same challenges in their own communities.

Critical Relationships

The NEC's core value is transparency, essential to assuring the NEC principal that the council is serving as an honest broker, which at times makes dealing with its most important co-council, the National Security Council, difficult to navigate. The national security community operates with a norm of secrecy, with information shared only on a need-to-know basis. While some national security advisors have been honest brokers, others saw themselves as advocates first. These different traditions can exacerbate the natural tension that flows from the different worldviews of those with different experiences and expertise at the NEC and NSC.

Managing these inherent tensions constructively is necessary to best serve the new president. The NEC director should be a member of the NSC and vice versa. When matters involve international economic policy, the NEC should chair the relevant meetings and drive the process with heavy NSC consultation. Planning for trips overseas, international meetings, and visits by foreign dignitaries, however, should be led by the NSC, except when economic issues are paramount, as for meetings of the G8, the Asia-Pacific Economic Cooperation, and the Summit of the Americas. NEC inclusion in planning and briefing for international meetings, even when NSC-led, is an important way to ensure that economic implications are given due weight in foreign affairs.

The president's chief of staff plays a key role in managing this tension by insisting on mutual respect and comity. When presented with important issues with both security and economic dimensions, the NSC and NEC advisors can be asked to run a joint process—with co-chaired meetings and co-signed memoranda—ensuring both perspectives are appropriately reflected from the start. If the president's staff secretary always insists on giving one advisor an opportunity to comment on a relevant memoranda from another advisor before the memo reaches the president, then both advisors will learn to bring each other into discussions earlier. Finally, interactions between the two councils work best when the relationship between the relevant NEC and NSC deputies is strong and collegial.

The responsibility for international economic issues must rest with the NEC, working closely (even sharing responsibility at times) with the NSC. A new mechanism, the National Energy Council, should have the responsibility to oversee single-mindedly the transformation to a low-carbon economy, partnering with the NEC on processes that determine how the transformation fits into the 44th president's overall economic strategy. Similarly, responsibility for creation of a plan to achieve universal health care should be shared between the Domestic Policy Council and NEC, with consideration of the fiscal and budget implications driven by the NEC and issues regarding our health care system led by the DPC. Finally, the new president also should make clear assignments for education, with policies related to primary and secondary schools going to the DPC and higher education policy to the NEC. Where issues overlap these borders, it may ease tension to ask two assistants to the president to co-chair the process in which the key decisions get made.

President Clinton's creation of the NEC threatened the traditional role of the Council of Economic Advisors more than any other agency. Over time, however, the bifurcation of economic responsibilities worked. The CEA should have responsibility for forecasting and core economic analysis; the NEC should ensure that the CEA has a seat at the table whenever a decision affecting the economy is made. The CEA also has the ability to give the president unfettered economic advice, even where the NEC believes other considerations should dictate a different outcome. The CEA in turn helps to ensure that policy debate is grounded in sound economics and that unfounded economic arguments for the president's policy are not advanced, weakening his credibility. Rubin described the CEA to Tyson as "the hand of economic analysis within the NEC glove."[8]

The Role of Politics and Messaging

The new president is assuming leadership of a country that faces profound economic challenges. The success of his presidency hinges on addressing these challenges and winning public and congressional support for his economic policies. Even the best substantive policy made in a vacuum without consideration of communication and politics is unlikely to survive. The NEC process is where these political realities and public communication challenges intersect with the development of policy. Legislative and messaging strategy should be developed along with the policy positions themselves.

However, if political considerations simply drive the policy process, as appears to have happened during the Bush administration, then the NEC and other policy councils serve little serious purpose. A commitment to the deliberative process of the NEC and its sister policy councils is a commitment to serving the best interests of the country and its citizens. Of course, political considerations must be brought to bear in weighing the range of options available and the best strategy for achieving the public interest, but strengthening a party's hold on power should not ever become the object of governance. The culture and traditions of the NEC, if supported by the new president and his chief of staff, offer a mechanism to get this balance right in economic policy.

National Energy Council

TODD STERN AND DAVID HAYES

Both nationally and globally, we are on a trajectory for energy use and greenhouse gas emissions that is incompatible with the preservation of a safe and livable world. World primary energy use and carbon dioxide emissions are expected to grow 55 percent to 57 percent between 2005 and 2030, including around 75 percent in developing countries. American CO_2 emissions, on a business-as-usual path, are expected to increase 25 percent between 2006 and 2030.[1] At the same time, leading scientists estimate that to avoid the worst risks of climate change, the world will have to *reduce* emissions by at least 50 percent as compared to now, with some estimating the needed reduction to be more than 80 percent.

The scope of this challenge is immense. Many leading climate scientists say we need to limit the increase in global average temperature to 2° Celsius above pre-industrial times, or about 1.2°C (2.2°F) above current temperature. In a February 2007 statement to U.N. Secretary General Ban Ki-moon and the U.N. Commission on Sustainable Development, Harvard's John Holdren, a pre-eminent climate scientist, said that "if the build-up of greenhouse gases pushes the global average surface temperature past 2–2.5°C above the pre-industrial level, the danger of intolerable and unmanageable impacts of climate change on human well-being becomes very high."[2] And James Hansen, the noted physicist at the NASA Goddard Institute, whose June 1988 Senate testimony helped put global warming on the map, testified in June 2008 that allowing temperature to increase even to 2°C above pre-industrial levels would be "a recipe for global disaster."[3]

The scale of needed change is formidable. In a noted article, Stephen Pacala and Robert Socolow of Princeton University describe a variety of major energy initiatives or "wedges," any seven of which, in combination, could hold global emissions to today's level in 50 years.[4] This is a level of reduction most scientists would regard as quite inadequate, but even this would require a massive effort. The wedges include, for example, increasing the fuel efficiency of 2 billion cars from 30 miles per gallon to 60 mpg; improving the efficiency of buildings and appliances enough to cut their CO_2 emissions by 25 percent; introducing carbon capture-and-storage capabilities at the equivalent of 1,600 large (500 megawatt) power plants; and a huge increase in the use of renewable fuels like wind, solar, and biomass to produce electricity.

The Intergovernmental Panel on Climate Change, the U.N. body of over 2,000 scientists that shared the 2007 Nobel Peace Prize, estimates in its fourth assessment report that holding emissions in 2050 to a level between 30 percent below and 5 percent above 2000 levels would correspond to an increase in global average temperature of 2.8–3.2° C above pre-industrial levels—well above what scientists regard as plausibly safe. To hold temperatures to 2.4–2.8° C above pre-industrial levels, the IPCC estimates that emissions in 2050 would need to be reduced between 30 and 60 percent below 2000 levels; a temperature range of 2.0–2.4° C would require a reduction between 50 and 85 percent below 2000 levels.

Solving the energy and climate challenge will require interrelated policy efforts at home and abroad. Our capacity to enact a robust, mandatory domestic program will depend in part on the energy and climate programs that other major emitters of greenhouse gases are implementing, while our capacity to achieve meaningful agreements for global reductions will depend in part on the scope and ambition of our domestic program. And there will be tricky issues of tactics and sequencing as a new president works to make break-through progress on both fronts.

Recommendations

The president-elect should nominate the new energy team early, shortly after the national security team and the economic team, signaling the importance of this issue. This new team would form the core of a new White House National Energy Council, which would include the secretaries of most cabinet agencies and the heads of the Council on Environmental Quality, the National Economic Council, and National Security Council, and would be led by a national energy advisor with stature comparable to the national security advisor and the national economic advisor.

Transforming the energy base of the economy will demand top-level participation across the executive branch. It will require the concerted engagement of the president, and the kind of single-minded attention that only a fully empowered national energy advisor and council can bring. The National Energy Council would serve as the new president's agent in driving both policy and strategic options with respect to energy and climate change. At the first cabinet meeting, the president should make clear the centrality of this issue and the authority of his new national energy advisor.

The National Energy Council should have a lean staff. We would propose a deputy; two policy experts to cover the range of domestic policy issues; a technology research, development, and deployment expert; a financial and business expert focused on public-private partnerships, designing the right incentives for the private sector, etc.; a scientist; an economist; an international expert focused on climate diplomacy; a congressional liaison; and an advisor on press and communications. Most of this staff could be dual-hatted with other White House offices such as NSC, NEC, CEQ, OSTP.

To guide our federal investment decisions, which are now uncoordinated, the new president should establish an interagency Energy Innovation Council to develop an integrated, multiyear national energy research, development, and deployment strategy. We cannot transition to a low-carbon economy without enormous technological innovation. Technologies on the shelf can get us started, but we will need a host of new discoveries and refinements to get us where we need to go. Against this reality, the federal government's investment in energy R&D—around $2 billion last year—is woefully inadequate, only a third of what it spent 25 years ago. By contrast, the government spends $28 billion on medical research and $75 billion on military research.

The new president should also create a quasi-public entity—an Energy Technology Corporation—dedicated to managing large-scale energy demonstration projects in low- or no-carbon technologies. Historically, the government's efforts to support the late-stage demonstration projects essential to commercialization have foundered because they have not been done in a manner seen as financially credible to investors and the private sector.

The new president will also need to mobilize the public and the political establishment to support the low-carbon transformation of our economy. He will need to use the bully pulpit, his schedule, and the full reach of his administration to do this. Working with the national energy advisor, the new president should convey a set of core messages to the public, beginning with the fact that the science is clear: global warming poses an enormous, growing threat to the health and safety of our world and that of our children. The fight against climate change and the fight against our dependence on foreign oil is the same fight—we must take on these twin threats together.

The new president should also make clear that failing to take strong action will do great damage to our economy, national security, environment, and well-being, conveying the message that this is a national imperative, beyond political parties. Finally, he should explain that the transformation to a low-carbon economy represents a huge opportunity to create millions of jobs and lead in the development of new clean technologies, and that this is a global problem so we must ensure our competitors do their fair share.

In his inaugural address, the president should highlight the urgency and opportunity of these challenges, underscoring his belief that the low-carbon transformation is essential to building a successful economy in the 21st century. To this end, he should announce a 100-day pledge to introduce energy and climate legislation. In his State of the Union address, he should again underscore the essential nature of this priority. And in the early weeks of the new administration, he should make a major address devoted to this issue.

The president should also convene a series of meetings with key players in the first weeks of his administration. These should include a National Energy Conference with business and financial leaders, labor leaders, farmers, scientists, public health experts, national security experts, environmentalists, leaders from the faith community, and others. He should also establish an ongoing advisory council of such leaders. The president should also meet with governors and mayors who have been the leaders on climate change during the past seven years, as well as with congressional leaders, underscoring this energy transformation must be a genuine collaboration to succeed.

The new national energy advisor should also begin working with a core group of leading scientists with the credibility and skill to deliver a message about the dire threat we face and the scientific urgency of action. This group should promote our economic and technological capacity to meet this challenge if we have the political courage to act. Business and other leaders should be deployed as well.

The president should also request the National Academy of Sciences to report back promptly with its view of a tolerable range of warming and greenhouse gas concentration limits. The IPCC has done related work, but the National Academy of Sciences speaks with an authoritative voice to an American audience that will only support aggressive action if it appreciates the dangers. The academy should review its conclusions every few years in light of new facts on the ground and new science.

The president should also take several key executive actions (all discussed in more detail in the Environmental Protection Agency and Department of Energy chapters of this book) promptly after assuming office. First and foremost, he should direct EPA to consider the so-called California waiver so that the state can set its own tailpipe emissions standards. He then should ask the agency to: establish a low-carbon fuel standard; issue performance standards for power plants; establish the regulatory framework for carbon capture-and-storage systems (in league with DOE); and announce strong federal measures to sharply boost both energy efficiency in the government's operations and the use of renewable energy.

Finally, the president will have to take swift action to reengage internationally. With 80 percent of emissions released outside the United States, climate change cannot be solved without global action. Moreover, approximately 40 percent of energy-related CO_2 emissions come from developing countries now, and 55 percent will come from such countries by 2030.

The international community is now focusing on negotiating a new climate change agreement that will bring both the United States and key developing countries into the fold. The stated intention is to conclude such an agreement in Copenhagen in December 2009. This calendar leaves little time for a new president to confirm his team and develop substantive and tactical ideas. At the same time, there are high hopes for a committed new approach by the United States, and it will be important not to undercut those hopes. There will thus be tricky issues to handle, both of substance and of diplomacy.

While it isn't possible at this early stage to spell out the elements of a new global agreement, certain core principles should guide a new president. He will need to negotiate with a clear sense of what science tells us must be done to reduce emissions, and what the implications of that are both for developed and major developing countries. He must understand that real progress internationally won't be possible without a strong, mandatory U.S. program at home. He must be flexible with regard to the kinds of commitments that countries make, as long as the scale of the commitments is significant enough. And he must bear in mind that a new global agreement must be the beginning, not the end, of international collaboration.

Following any agreement, there will be an urgent need for active partnerships to develop, transfer, finance, and commercialize low-carbon technologies in ways that are beneficial to developing and developed countries alike. Early on, the new president should deliver a major climate change speech with a global audience in mind, making clear his understanding of the scale of the problem, his plan to implement a far-reaching program at home, and his commitment to working cooperatively with other countries. The new president needs to convey a sense of responsibility, humility, and determination.

Within its first weeks, a new administration should conduct targeted bilateral diplomacy with key nations such as Great Britain, France, Germany, Japan, China, India, and Brazil. It will be imperative to convey the message that it is a new day in the United States and that we are once again ready to engage vigorously on this issue. The United States should anchor its climate diplomacy in a core group of major emitting nations, both developed and developing. A small group process can be conducive to honest, forthright, substantive discussion. The group should be understood as a jointly owned process, akin to the Group of Eight industrialized democracies, rather than as a U.S. undertaking.

The new president will also need to devote special attention to China, without whom significant global progress on climate change is impossible, both for substantive and political reasons. China has now surpassed us as the largest emitting nation. We need to work with China on a new energy and climate change partnership, involving other allies such as the European Union and Japan where appropriate. Understandings reached bilaterally or in a core group will need to be brought back into the U.N. process itself, which will ultimately need to accept and adopt a new global accord.

Domestic Policy Council

TOM FREEDMAN

The new president must create a strong, well-organized White House Domestic Policy Council (DPC) to ensure that he has substantive control over domestic policy formulation, access to the best information on domestic policy issues, and a forum for strategic coordination of domestic issues. The DPC was developed in response to a challenge for presidents: the expansion of federal government in the latter half of the 20th century meant key agenda items and strategic planning were increasingly being shaped outside their direct knowledge and control in the domestic agencies. Presidents from Lyndon Johnson to Richard Nixon to Bill Clinton all have sought to redress that balance by using the DPC to formulate and coordinate domestic policy. The DPC can play a critical role in spearheading and implementing the 44th president's domestic policy agenda and priorities, particularly for those issues that cut across the jurisdiction of a number of agencies and departments in the executive branch.

Recommendations

An effective Domestic Policy Council should be led by an assistant to the president for domestic policy who has a variety of skills. The head of the DPC must have the intellectual ability to evaluate and direct myriad policy proposals. He or she must also have the ability to manage a diverse staff, a temperament that can push sometimes-unpopular positions through agencies and unhappy civil servants, and yet be collegial enough to work cooperatively with the National Economic Council, cabinet secretaries, and others without alienating them.

In addition, the new president should consider choosing someone as head of the DPC with a strong policy background in one or more of the president's top policy priorities. The new head of the DPC should be someone who can immediately lead on the hardest domestic policy issues that will face the administration—whether those are health care, climate change, or education reform—while still having the skills to help supervise developments in other policy areas.

Many of the most successful domestic policy advisors—including Joseph Califano, Daniel Patrick Moynihan, and Bruce Reed—had distinct, often idiosyncratic policy views, and were effective in part because they were heterodox and not hemmed in by the traditional interest-group politics that stymied agencies. For that reason, the new president should err on the side of picking a strong-minded thinker rather than someone who will simply be an "honest broker" among agencies and White House offices. In practice, the leader of the DPC should focus on a few major domestic policy agenda items and then delegate significant background work on other issues to a strong deputy and a number of strong special assistants to the president.

The first function the DPC must undertake is as lead strategist and coordinator on domestic policy issues, helping to create a coherent message that reflects the president's direction. It should also work seamlessly with the other White House offices that deal with domestic policy issues, including the NEC, the new National Energy Council, the Office of Management and Budget, and the White House Offices of Legislative Affairs, Political Affairs, Public Liaison, and Communications.

Particularly important relationships for the DPC are with Congress and the White House Office of Legislative Affairs. How well the DPC supports the president's agenda on Capitol Hill and responds to congressional proposals has a major impact on the ultimate success of the president's overall domestic program. The role of coordinator and strategist may take up the bulk of the DPC's time, especially during the run up to the State of the Union addresses, periods in which most presidents roll out a number of policy announcements.

A second role of the DPC is to support the development of domestic policies in key issue areas. The DPC should work with agency experts to make sure the new president has the specific policy proposals he needs to tackle tough problems. It must be able to provide thinking not only about key issues, but also the big, interconnected problems the country faces. In addition, the DPC needs to be able to provide prompt updates and options on emerging issues and crises. When a specific crisis emerges—for instance, an outbreak of school violence or a food safety issue—the DPC must focus the agency response and coordinate the president's policy response.

Finally, the DPC must be a "go-to" source of information for the new president. It should provide easy one-stop shopping for information on any domestic policy, from what is going on in particular arenas to who is handling a certain issue and what policy options exist. The alternative for the White House is no alternative at all—guessing which cabinet agency has the issue, making inquiries, and getting ad hoc, inconsistent, uncoordinated responses back.

Inevitably, there will be tensions between the DPC and the cabinet secretaries and their senior staff at the agencies. If the council provides a common strategy and is a source of clear communication, then the president will get the most out of the vast set of agency know-how and resources. In turn, the agencies will get the chance for input and direction that helps them execute the president's agenda. Moreover, the DPC can be a powerful advocate for the agencies' perspectives from within the White House.

A Policy Agenda

The council works best when it helps develop new policy ideas that reinforce and demonstrate the president's overall positive vision for the role of government. The DPC must both implement the policy ideas the president outlined in his campaign and balance the need to make progress on a couple of the biggest priorities with the multiplicity of other issues that inevitably arise.

The first of these larger issues is building a strong social safety net. In a global, technological, modern economy, with sharp demographic changes, the question of how to reduce economic and social insecurity while still promoting widely shared economic growth will be paramount.

The DPC should help with the development and passage through Congress of extraordinarily important policies in this arena, including: health care reform, better child care and senior care, and policies that touch on work-life balance issues such as paid sick leave and child and parental care leave. Social safety net issues also will require working closely with the NEC on policies to reduce economic insecurity. This will include rethinking unemployment insurance and trade adjustment assistance programs, and supporting secure retirements for Americans by strengthening Social Security and considering additional retirement tools such as universal 401(k) accounts.

The White House's domestic policy agenda should make it a priority to address the challenges faced by nearly 40 million Americans living in poverty. There are numerous ways to increase opportunity for these Americans, including expanding the Earned Income Tax Credit, extending and reforming programs to fight hunger, using innovative means to provide affordable housing, and implementing a program to help former prisoners reintegrate successfully into society. All of these policies to build a stronger social safety net share some common features: the problems they confront have been overlooked for almost a decade; they often defy common ideological stereotypes; and there is public will for bold action.

A second important area of work for the DPC is to reduce economic insecurity by helping expand opportunity in the new economy. Education policy is a key way to generate more opportunity. The council should explore ideas for re-forms and investments, including improving teacher pay and accountability, re-ducing drop-out rates, promoting early childhood education, expanding after-school programs, and making college more affordable. Working with the Department of Education and the Office of Science and Technology Policy, the DPC should also help coordinate the development of more robust educational programs in science, technology, engineering, and mathematics—the so-called STEM disciplines—to boost our nation's future global competitiveness.

A third area of work involves helping the new president break Washington stalemates that have been caused by polarization and special-interest gridlock. Among the big issues where significant steps can be taken are governmental and lobbying reform, immigration, protecting civil rights, fighting crime, and expanding consumer protection. In each of these areas, critical developments have been stymied for the last eight years, but progressive change has public backing. Compromise in some of these fields may be necessary, but in all of them a majority in Congress can likely be built.

Finally, the DPC should work cooperatively with the NEC and other policy shops in the White House on issues in which the DPC is not necessarily the lead entity. These include energy, the environment, rural and urban develop-ment strategies, and promoting and regulating technology. It will be useful for the new president early on to make clear how policy responsibilities are di-vided. One option will be for the president-elect to task his chief of staff to oversee the preparation of a plan for his approval that shows clear lines of pol-icy authority. The plan should show which issues will be under the purview of the DPC, the NEC, other entities, or new councils and task forces.

Sequencing the Policy Agenda
The new president must pay special attention to the sequencing and timetable used to unveil and seek passage of his domestic policy program. The first 100 days of a new administration and the several months after each State of the Union Address serve notice of priorities and are the best opportunity to lead.

The reality is that finding the right sequence for policy proposals should fol-low Supreme Court Justice Potter Stewart's approach: "You know it when you see it." History suggests that having early accomplishments can build momen-tum and support. Biting off too much, however, or refusing to compromise can sink a president's popularity and damage his reputational capital, making sub-sequent new policy announcements less likely to pass.

Staggering day one, first week, and first month signings of executive orders and bills on medium-sized issues while undertaking a major set of policy initiatives that might pass in the early part of the administration is the right balance to strike.

The trick is to lead with something big enough to inspire, but not so impossible to achieve that it will get bogged down and diminish the sense of presidential potential.

Events will dictate some policy developments, but having an internal game plan and schedule will maximize the chance of fulfilling the new president's domestic agenda. The DPC can play an important role in making sure the president has the information, specific proposals, and agency coordinating tools he needs to achieve his long-term domestic goals for the country.

White House Counsel

ELENA KAGAN

The new president must appoint a strong, knowledgeable, experienced White House counsel who can restore the professionalism and credibility of the office, help infuse the entire Executive Office of the President with an appreciation for the rule of law and its application to political activities, respect the responsibilities of other branches of government while protecting presidential prerogatives, and coordinate with other parts of the administration to provide the president with excellent legal advice.

The counsel's office is involved in some of the most important and sensitive issues in the White House. These attorneys will often find themselves in positions of some tension with others in the White House, administrative agencies, or Congress. The most effective counsel's offices in the past were those that were sensitive to political and policy interests and eager to help advance the president's goals, but aware above all that they need to comply with the highest legal standards and preserve our underlying constitutional system.

Responsibilities

The White House Counsel's four most important responsibilities are enforcing ethical standards and general rules of behavior in the executive branch, handling congressional and other investigations, advising the president on legal questions in coordination with the Justice Department, and handling judicial nominations.

The office polices all ethical standards and policies applicable to Executive Office of the President personnel, including financial disclosures and conflicts of interest. It enforces rules relating to campaign or other political activities to ensure that government funds are not inappropriately spent for partisan ends. And the office polices rules concerning appropriate contacts between EOP personnel and administrative agencies, including—perhaps most sensitively—the Department of Justice.

The bulk of the office's work in some administrations has been spent handling investigations, while in other administrations that work has constituted only a small amount. Much depends on whether Congress is in the hands of the other political party. Included in this set of activities are negotiating the proper scope of any investigation; responding to document and testimony requests arising from such an investigation; and evaluating, asserting, and negotiating privilege claims arising from these requests.

In any administration, legal questions will arise in which the president has a great interest. Some of these are more accurately described as policy questions relating to the legal system such as whether to narrow or widen the scope of federal class actions. Others will concern the United States' litigating positions on significant statutory and constitutional questions; the legality of certain executive or administrative actions, relating to both foreign and domestic policy and including questions of national security; or the outcome of a legal process such as a rulemaking occurring elsewhere in the government. The office must coordinate, depending on the nature of these questions, with the Justice Department and/or lawyers in other agencies to determine the appropriate scope and nature of presidential and other EOP involvement. Assuming involvement is appropriate, the office must provide the president and other EOP personnel with the soundest possible legal advice.

The counsel's office also takes the lead role within the White House in vetting possible judicial nominees and presenting recommendations to the president. These include nominees to all levels of the federal judiciary—senatorial involvement in selection is usually most significant for district court judges—as well as certain nominees to the D.C. courts. The counsel's office will also usually work with the Legislative Affairs Office to ensure congressional confirmation of these nominees.

Priorities

The White House counsel's single most important job, transcending all the specific activities listed above, is to ensure a respect for law throughout the EOP. This means, at a minimum, ensuring that all personnel comply with legal requirements relating to their job performance. But more broadly, it means infusing the EOP with an understanding of the importance of legal processes and norms throughout the government, including an appreciation for the constitutional significance of separation of powers.

To perform this core function, the counsel will have to restore the protocols that govern requests for and communication of legal advice. The counsel must establish clear lines of communication and authority with other lawyers in the EOP, particularly in the Vice President's Office and the National Security Council. And the office must put in place and enforce appropriate rules for dealing with the Department of Justice and lawyers in other administrative agencies to ensure that the appropriate people in the EOP are dealing with the appropriate people in DOJ or other agencies. Time and again in the last eight years, important legal issues have been discussed and resolved in ways that bypassed actors possessing clear authority and knowledge or that evaded long-standing consultative processes. The first task of a new White House counsel will be to ensure that everyone in the EOP knows and understands who may initiate requests for legal advice, to whom those requests should be directed, and how to engage in discussion and debate concerning the issues involved.

The counsel's office should also play a key role in fostering productive relationships with members of Congress. The office often will be on the frontline of conflict as Congress goes about performing its investigatory or oversight duties. The counsel's office must be able to assert appropriate presidential prerogatives while showing respect for Congress' constitutional responsibilities. Once again, recent experiences are instructive: too often in recent years the counsel's office has acted as though Congress had no proper role in reviewing administrative decision making. The counsel's office in the next administration needs to be able to protect presidential power while respecting congressional authority—and communicate this same understanding of the virtues of our separated governmental system to other members of the EOP.

Leadership and Organization

The counsel's position is one of the most difficult jobs in the White House. The counsel needs to be a great lawyer—the kind of lawyer who knows when to say "no," but also how to facilitate a client's objectives. The counsel needs, at the same time, to be a knowledgeable and skilled political actor who has experience with and a feel for the institutional environment of Washington, particularly Congress and the agencies.

The work of the counsel's office is varied, and a sensible organization of the office will almost surely involve a number of different "practice groups." The office's ethics work—policing financial disclosures, preventing conflicts of interest, distinguishing governmental from political expenditures—is highly technical and specialized; the best people for these positions will have substantial experience in the field already and little or no desire to involve themselves in the political or policy dimensions of the White House's activities. The group of lawyers involved in congressional investigations and judicial selections should have serious knowledge of Capitol Hill.

A third group should have substantial national security expertise; these might report both to the counsel and to the director of the National Security Counsel. A final set of attorneys might be tasked with interacting with the Department of Justice and other administrative agencies on constitutional and other significant legal issues outside the realm of national security; these attorneys should have the same kind of elite legal credentials that attorneys typically have in DOJ's Office of the Solicitor General or Office of Legal Counsel to ensure they have real credibility in these discussions.

White House Communications and Press Operations ₍

MICHAEL WALDMAN

Communications is an essential tool for governing. Richard Neustadt memorably explained in *Presidential Power* that the power of the president is primarily "the power to persuade." Building an effective communications operation requires balancing the impulses of the president and the demands of the presidency.

The White House communications operation reflects the president himself: his personality, his quirks, his goals, even his work habits. At the same time, the structure and function of the communications operation must be guided, in part, by the dictates of the office, recognizing the distinct and unique voice of the White House in our governmental system.

A frenetic "permanent campaign" atmosphere risks diminishing the aura of the office. Rather, the new president should use the tools of communications to convey big themes and speak honestly and in detail to the public about policy, all while managing—but not being consumed by—the day-to-day minutiae of the White House press corps.

A new president has one distinct advantage: coming fresh from the campaign trail, he will likely have an especially sensitive awareness of the current media environment. This skill—especially in the use of new technology—will be remarkably useful to build a strong and effective voice for the president and his administration.

Recommendations

One initial and significant organizational decision will be whether to include the communications and press functions in one department or to structure them separately. Some presidents have chosen to have two separate departments and a co-equal director of communications and press secretary, both at the level of assistant to the president. Others have chosen to put the press office under the auspices of the communications department. This combined arrangement can work, but only if the press secretary has direct access to the president and the chief of staff. If the press secretary does not have this access, he or she will not have credibility with the press corps.

The press office usually includes three deputy press secretaries—two who serve as deputy spokespeople and one who oversees the logistical needs of the press corps and serves as chief of staff of the press office. Other key elements of a successful press office include a regional press team, radio and television bookers, and press advance staff.

Recent presidents have also enlisted a close, trusted "senior advisor" or "counselor to the president," such as George Stephanopoulos for President Bill Clinton or Karl Rove for President George W. Bush, to set tone and message strategy, and possibly supervise various aspects of the communications shop.

Press Office
Former White House Press Secretary Michael McCurry has aptly described the

location of the press secretary's office—halfway between the Oval Office and the press briefing room—as a perfect metaphor for the role of the White House press secretary. Inside the Briefing Room, the press secretary is an advocate for the president. Inside the White House, the press secretary is an advocate for the press and the public's right to know.

Press secretaries must have access to decision making—and be seen by the press as having that access—to succeed. The press secretary will fail if she or he is viewed as merely a hack, robotically repeating administration talking points. The relationship between the White House and the press corps is inherently adversarial, but the most successful press secretaries drain much of the tension from this relationship by gaining the trust of the press. The press corps must have faith that the press secretary is knowledgeable and speaking with authority, but also looking after the press corps's interests within the White House.

Incoming presidents often seek to use symbolic changes at the White House as a means of signaling change and a new way of doing business. That can be an effective communications strategy, but it is ill advised to make symbolic changes in the White House staff's relationship with the White House press corps.

The press hate change and love covering stories about themselves. So there would be a great temptation for the press to focus on process stories at the beginning of a term, rather than the new president's policy agenda. Precipitous changes in how the White House interacts with, or grants access to, the press will result in endless speculation on what is behind this new move and would unnecessarily antagonize the press.

The press also, rightly or wrongly, judge a new White House's competency in part by how well it manages the press. A well-run press office operation will not ensure positive coverage, but you can be portrayed as a White House unprepared for prime time if briefings start late and press travel is chaotic.

In addition to the daily White House press briefing, recent administrations have held an "off-camera" morning briefing called the "gaggle." Different administrations have chosen to televise different parts of the briefing; a good middle ground is the first 10 minutes, which allows television networks to get the video footage they need, while giving print reporters the chance to ask questions off camera without preening.

Speechwriting

In the country's first century, the president spoke infrequently. It was considered improper for a president to stump for his policies; in fact, one of the impeachment counts against Andrew Jackson berated him for speaking in public in a "loud voice." Modern presidents changed that. Theodore Roosevelt began to use the "bully pulpit," and Woodrow Wilson addressed Congress for the first time in a century. The presidency and the president's voice changed first with radio, then broadcast TV, then 24-hour cable news, then the Internet. In a typical year, Harry Truman spoke in public 88 times; Ronald Reagan, 320 times; Clinton, 550 times.

The most effective presidential communicators are intimately involved in crafting speeches, often writing major addresses themselves or closely with others. The key to the success of speechwriting, as scholars have noted, is access to the president, and to the White House policy councils as well. Presidents typically have about six speechwriters in an office of speechwriting, a number that has remained unchanged for decades. As with the press secretary, the director of speechwriting has been an assistant to the president for most of the past two decades.

Presidents have long had help with their addresses. Some, such as Franklin D. Roosevelt, Harry S. Truman, and John F. Kennedy, vested the role in a special counsel (Samuel Rosenman, Clark Clifford, and Ted Sorensen, respectively), who was a key policy aide. Nixon began to wall off speech writing, giving it its own department and a fleet of writers who just crafted prose. When Peggy Noonan crafted the famous D-Day commemoration for Ronald Reagan, she had never met the man.

Clinton began to push the pendulum back. Historian Carol Gelderman wrote, "By bringing policy experts and other senior advisers into the speech-writing process, Clinton began to reverse the long-held practice of keeping the wordsmiths separated from the inner circle. As a result, his speeches revitalized his presidency and enabled him to win a second term, an achievement realized by only two other Democrats—FDR and Woodrow Wilson—in the 20th Century."[1] Key speechwriters were drawn from policy backgrounds, and top policy aides at both the National Security Council and Domestic Policy Council began their careers as speechwriters.

The Clinton administration instituted one innovation that should *not* be repeated. The speechwriting department produced speeches on domestic policy and the international economy, but not foreign policy. Those talks were written by staff members of the National Security Council. No other president has done it this way, for good reason. The president must speak with one clear, consistent voice regardless of the topic, domestic or foreign.

New Media
The communications department must be structured to give appropriate atten-

tion to new media. When Bill Clinton took office in 1993, there were 50 sites on the World Wide Web. The 44th president will enter government amid a media ecosystem that would have seemed like nonsense syllables just a few years ago. (Blogs? Facebook? Twitter?) Successful presidents master new technology. Theodore Roosevelt relished the new nautical maps and newspapers able to print rotogravure photos. FDR used radio. (He did not *overuse* it: he gave only two or three Fireside Chats per year.) JFK used TV to broadcast his witty press conferences. Reagan applied his thespian's craft to elaborate, prime-time State of the Union addresses.

The new president will be the first to truly use the Internet—at least as much, if not more than, a newspaper. How? The campaign offers intriguing hints. For example, many more citizens watched many candidate speeches in full on YouTube than ever saw news summaries of the talk. The White House will have to structure its communications operation to make full use of the Internet and cater to the highly attentive public now following politics closely through blogs and political websites. The White House website still resembles a slightly enhanced electronic version of the printed record. The 44th president should find a way to vastly upgrade the site so that it is far more content-rich and provides much greater interactivity with the public.

Office of the Vice President

LISA BROWN

The vice president's constitutional role is famously limited to succeeding the president and serving as president of the Senate. Yet the president and the country are best served when the vice president is a strong partner and when the relationship between the president and his number two is based on mutual trust and respect. Everything flows from this relationship, which means the president and vice president must have a clear understanding at the very beginning of the transition process for how they and their staffs will work together and implement this cooperative, supportive relationship.

Recent examples of vice presidents with little authority such as Vice President Dan Quayle, or with undue and unchecked power such as Vice President

Dick Cheney, have one thing in common: staffs that operate independently from the president's. In the case of Vice President Quayle, his staff was not even on the same email network as the president's. In Vice President Cheney's case, the staff created a rogue government, abrogating to themselves decisions, actions, and orders that should have belonged to the president and his staff.

The new vice president's policy roles and responsibilities must be clear, and the vice president's staff must be integrated into the work and operations of the rest of the White House, in order for the vice president and his or her staff to operate effectively and advance the president's agenda. This can include taking leadership on specific projects. During Vice President Gore's time in office, for example, he led several efforts and programs clearly delegated to him by President Clinton, such as the "Reinventing Government" effort, which he undertook through a staff integrated fully into the president's operations. This is the ideal.

Recommendations

The White House should be organized from day one to seamlessly and fully integrate the vice president and his or her staff fully, with the vice president offered full access and capacity for input at all levels of decision making. This will enable the vice president to give the president honest, informed advice and best advance the president's agenda. To accomplish this, the vice president's staff must have parallel access and opportunity for input. It is vital not only that the president and vice president be committed to this level of communication, but also that their staffs honor and respect the relationship and create a culture of cooperation and teamwork—something that they will take their cues on from their bosses.

This integration can be best achieved if a clear agreement is reached during the transition on issues related to access and process. The vice president should, for example, have a regular, weekly, unstaffed meeting with the president, with a recognition that those meetings operate within a well-ordered White House decision-making process. The vice president or the vice president's chief of staff should be welcome to attend any Oval Office meeting or other White House or cabinet meeting, and the vice president should receive all paper that goes to the president.

The vice president's staff should have parallel access to paper and meetings; any paper that goes to a member of the president's staff should also go to the corresponding member of the vice president's staff, and meetings including the president's staff should include the corresponding staff in the vice president's office. At least one member of the vice president's staff, for example, should attend the president's chief of staff and scheduling meetings, as well as meetings on domestic, economic, and national security policy, judicial nominations, and other matters.

The vice president's senior staff should have a role equivalent to that of their White House and cabinet counterparts on policy councils such as the Domestic Policy Council, the National Economic Council, and the National Security Council, as well as on ancillary bodies such as the President's Council of Advisors on Science and Technology. The staffs of the policy councils should be clearly instructed on their responsibility to support and report to the vice president as well as the president.

Because of the unique relationship between the vice president and the president, it is particularly important that the vice president choose a chief of staff and other senior staff who understand the unique role of the vice president and are committed to building strong relationships with their counterparts on the president's staff and in the cabinet. These personal relationships are vital to the success of the office and will create a positive environment for addressing the inevitable issues that will arise.

The vice president's chief of staff and other appropriate senior staff should have titles that reflect their joint role as advisors to the vice president and president (e.g., assistant to the president and chief of staff to the vice president) to facilitate their integration into the White House team. The vice president's chief of staff will be most successful if it is clear that he or she is close to the vice president and can speak for the vice president. The chief of staff is a diplomat, mediator, and manager who should keep firmly focused on how the office can best further the vice president's interests. While the chief of staff needs strong political, policy, and press skills, he or she does not necessarily need to be an expert in any particular area.

The vice president is well suited to take the lead on particular White House initiatives. Particular areas of responsibility will inevitably flow from the vice president's particular interests and expertise, as well as from the relationship between the president and vice president and circumstances that arise during the administration. The issues could be domestic and international—such as, for example, former Vice President Gore's focus on the environment, telecommunications, Russia, and South Africa. Even when the vice president takes the lead on issues, he and his staff must be sensitive to the fact that the vice president does not displace the president. The vice president should also pick specific spots to have a visible role and a personal impact, keeping in mind that choosing an area where he or she is likely to be successful is more important than picking an area because it is large.

The structure of the Office of Vice President will flow from his or her particular role and focus. Key staff members should include the chief of staff, deputy chief of staff, counsel, domestic policy advisor, national security advisor, national economic advisor, communications director, and scheduler. Beyond that, the exact offices and the number of staff in each will depend upon the vice president's focus. The office may, for example, have more staff dedicated to national security or legislative affairs if those are particular focal points for the vice president.

Staffing will require some tradeoffs due to the small size of the Office of the Vice President's budget. The vice president's chief of staff needs to carefully orchestrate the office's budget, which comes from the Senate and the White House office, and make the most of legitimate mechanisms for building a sufficiently large staff. As part of this, there needs to be a routine and transparent process for assigning White House fellows, detailees, agency representatives, and others to the Office of the Vice President. His staff can also enlist a cross-cabinet group of key policy experts to support and advise their work, as, for example, Vice President Gore did on telecommunications.

The vice president's transition staff should also take advantage of all opportunities to obtain information from the outgoing administration as part of the transition so he or she learns as much as possible about the context in which he or she will be working.

A New Office of Social Entrepreneurship

MICHELE JOLIN

The new president will take office with ambitious goals to solve our nation's most urgent social problems, but he will be operating in a climate with limited tolerance for new government spending or government-only solutions. The new president has a historic opportunity to turn to leading social entrepreneurs and the non-profit sector to help develop and implement effective solutions.

By creating a new White House Office of Social Entrepreneurship, the 44th president can support these new actors and ideas through policy tools, spurring greater innovation, creativity, and success in the non-profit sector. The non-profit sector in the United States has become an increasingly important and vital third sector of the economy, with over 1.5 million nonprofits accounting for more than $1 trillion in revenues annually.[1] Non-profit organizations employed roughly 9.4 million people in 2004, or approximately 7.2 percent of the U.S. economy—more than the number of people employed by the financial services sector.[2]

Non-profit organizations have stepped in to fill gaps where the government and private sector have been unable to provide adequate services and support, particularly in areas such as education, economic development, and access to health care. Non-profit organizations are the leading source of innovation in some areas, such as school reform, and many of their efforts are more effective and more innovative than what is being done by either government or the private sector.

Within this vital and growing non-profit sector, "social entrepreneurs"[3]— individuals who have developed system-changing solutions to solve serious social problems—are playing a unique role. Leading social entrepreneurs such as Geoffrey Canada of Harlem Children's Zone, which provides comprehensive support to low-income children in New York's toughest neighborhoods, and Nobel Prize–winning Muhammad Yunus of the Grameen Bank, which is the world's most famous microlender, have developed innovative models that are reorienting the way philanthropists, the private sector, and—increasingly— policymakers address intractable problems.

Fostering Non-Profit Growth and Innovation

Despite the non-profit sector's growth and the success of these social entrepreneurs, the next president can do more to support this work. At the most basic level, social entrepreneurs offer the new president and his administration examples of successful approaches that government should be using to tackle problems. Government support for and investment in models developed by nonprofits is not new: the non-profit sector has been a laboratory to test what works for governments at all levels since the 1960s.

Services provided by the non-profit sector are not a substitute for adequately funded health care, social services, education, and other vital government programs. But the non-profit sector can be a source of innovation and experimentation, and serve as a testing ground for these new ideas. The federal government has adapted a number of successful non-profit approaches into full-scale programs. City Year's national service successes led to AmeriCorps, for example, and a federal appropriation expanded YouthBuild into a national government program in 1993.

To fundamentally address these problems on the scale and scope required, the new administration will need to focus both on replicating successful individual programs and reorienting the government's relationship toward the non-profit sector to create a better climate for innovation. The federal government should play a defined and limited role in developing this policy effort without creating a new bureaucracy that runs counter to the culture of social innovation and entrepreneurship. It should remain flexible in its approach, using both policy tools that can adapt to changing circumstances and new evidence about what works. The federal government should not pick specific "winners" in the non-profit sector; it should invest in a range of solutions designed to meet national goals. Government investments should not replace current funding streams; they should fill important gaps and catalyze funding by foundations, the private sector, and individuals.

In short, the new president needs to focus on creating a policy environment that over the long term fosters new entrepreneurship, improves nonprofits' access to growth capital, and removes outdated tax and regulatory barriers to innovation.

Access to capital is a key factor limiting the ability of most successful nonprofits to spread and grow. The total number of non-profit organizations has doubled in the last 25 years, but only a small number have actually grown to the size or scale needed to have a significant effect on a national or international scale. A recent analysis by the Bridgespan Group found that of the more than 200,000 nonprofits created in the United States since 1970, only 144 have reached over $50 million in annual revenue.[4]

Unlike for-profit capital markets, there is not a natural and reliable source of capital for high-performing nonprofits or social entrepreneurs who are ready to expand their reach. Traditional foundations and other philanthropists often have restrictions on the number of years or the types of organizations they can fund over time. Not all nonprofits should grow significantly, but the federal government can act as a source of capital in instances where a social entrepreneurial model has shown concrete results and has the infrastructure and plan to support expansion. Federal funding can be used to catalyze investments by the private and philanthropic sectors.

Funding constraints also mean that many nonprofits cannot devote enough time or resources to evaluate the success of their particular approach or conduct research to better understand underlying problems. The problems are often complicated, and too many nonprofits lack adequate tools to evaluate their impact. Nonprofits must have access to high-quality data to inform appropriate investments and support good management decisions. The federal government can fund independent research and evaluation and provide a multidisciplinary team of analysts to better understand effective solutions.

Outdated legal, regulatory, or tax regimes also can constrain innovation and results in the non-profit sector, especially in instances where the line between the non-profit and for-profit sectors has blurred. Business entrepreneurs are increasingly using for-profit investments to produce greater social good, especially in the areas of micro enterprise, health care, and the environment. Pierre Omidyar, founder of online auction house eBay, created a private equity fund to expand the use of microloans and encourage the development of a commercial equity market to serve global microfinance institutions. The federal government needs to identify, catalogue, and remove outdated tax and other rules that likely constrain innovation and limit other kinds of hybrid for-profit investments with a social purpose.

The Office of Social Entrepreneurship

The new president should create a White House Office of Social Entrepreneurship to coordinate the reorganization of the federal government and its resources. This office will use the president's platform to highlight the importance of relying on social entrepreneurs and nonprofits to solve social problems, in many cases in partnership with the government or the private sector. The OSE will also give social entrepreneurs and other non-profit leaders a greater voice in the public policy debates of the day by being part of the White House domestic and economic policymaking processes. It should work closely with the Office of Faith-Based and Community Initiatives to ensure that faith-based organizations have access to resources to support the growth and spread of their work.

The OSE should develop tools to ensure that all relevant federal agencies will direct government resources toward scaling proven solutions in the social sector. It should also lead the creation of a series of "Grow What Works Funds" in key agencies, such as the Department of Education, which would invest in social entrepreneurial models that have demonstrated concrete results.

The office could also work to establish an "Impact Fund," housed at the Corporation for National Service, that would provide federal dollars for nonprofits to collect data on and better evaluate their success.

The OSE also should catalyze larger-scale, multi-sector problem solving by creating an annual multimillion-dollar "prize" for developing the most creative, sustainable, and high-impact solution to a defined social challenge. This prize, which could be run out of an agency such as the Department of Treasury, would encourage cross-sector partnerships and create enormous publicity and energy around solving a social problem while limiting direct government involvement or bureaucracy.

The OSE also would explore ways to eliminate barriers to innovation in the tax code by identifying appropriate changes to the current corporate structure and tax treatment of 501(c)(3) organizations' provisions. The office would explore possible revisions to the tax code to reward partnerships between nonprofits and businesses, and increase charitable giving that would help successful nonprofits grow. The office should identify and advocate for the elimination of regulatory barriers to success in various sectors, especially education, health care, and housing.

The White House Office of Social Entrepreneurship, in addition to these large-scale changes, should undertake smaller, daily efforts to boost innovative nonprofits. It could, for example, raise the profile of successful problem-solvers through a weekly "Changemakers" announcement or award, issued by the president to highlight the work of inspiring, effective social entrepreneurs, faith-based organizations, and leaders in the non-profit or philanthropic world. It could host an annual White House Social Entrepreneurship and Social Innovation Conference, and several targeted workshops around the country, designed to highlight successful programs and best practices.

The OSE also should coordinate with the Corporation for National and Community Service's Commission on Cross-Sector Solutions to America's Problems, which would be made up of non-profit, philanthropic, and corporate social responsibility leaders, as well as representatives from key agencies. The commission will advise the president on policy issues directly affecting the non-profit sector's competitiveness. The OSE also should coordinate with the Corporation for National and Community Service on finding ways that national service can leverage the work of social entrepreneurs and build the capacity of social entrepreneurs and others in the non-profit sector.

On the global level, the OSE should work with the U.S. Agency for International Development to create an Innovation Investment Fund to support new social-sector actors and ideas in the global development field such as the Acumen Fund, which provides growth funding for successful economic development projects, or the Grameen Bank. It also could help large, successful U.S. nonprofits replicate ideas in countries around the world, helping connect innovators and ideas. One of the most powerful American exports over the next decade could be successful ideas for social change demonstrated by leaders in the U.S. non-profit sector. Last year, for instance, Teach for America responded to the growing demand for international replication of its model by creating Teach for All, which will provide advice and support for local adaptations of TFA.

Office of Faith-Based and Community Initiatives

SHAUN CASEY

President George W. Bush established the White House Office of Faith-Based and Community Initiatives with an executive order in January 2001. Despite its lofty rhetoric and noble goals, the office has been widely considered a failure by supporters and critics on both ends of the ideological spectrum.

The Faith-Based Office's activities and events have been in large part symbolic and political, designed to win political support from conservative clergy. The domestic poverty-fighting mission of the office was largely ignored; the Bush administration claims it has distributed over $2 billion to faith-based organizations, but this number simply counts the funds that were already being distributed to these groups. There was no new federal government money devoted to faith-based organizations.

Many faith-based organizations, moreover, lacked the technical capacity to apply for and manage federal grant funding, and there was no systematic analysis of faith-based grantees' effectiveness. The Bush administration also made no effort to protect the important separation between church and state that draws a bright line between direct service, poverty-fighting program funds going to faith-based groups, and programs that proselytize and permit discrimination in hiring.

There are powerful practical and policy reasons for the new president to reform and reconstitute this faith-based office with adequate constitutional and statutory protections. The federal government in the past successfully partnered with faith-based organizations for large-scale social service provisions using safeguards to protect the integrity of the ministry and ensure that government funds are not used to subsidize religious activity or impermissible discrimination. There also is ample research showing that people under duress are likely to first turn to houses of worship, faith-based groups, and community organizations for assistance.

These faith-based social service providers need to have access to the same resources and support from the federal government as other community groups in order to serve community needs. The faith community's voice and wisdom also can inform the policy debate on some of the most pressing problems facing our nation and the world, including domestic and global poverty alleviation and the global spread of HIV/AIDS.

Recommendations

The 44th president should indicate his intention to reform the Bush initiative by issuing a new executive order within his first 100 days in office to reauthorize and rename the Faith-Based Office. He would ideally connect the work and priorities of this office with the White House Office of Social Entrepreneurship described in this book.

The White House should make clear that the central mission of the office is to support an agenda to fight domestic and global poverty. The organizing purpose of this office will be to mobilize the ideas and energies of organizations run by people of faith in tackling the immoral and intolerable levels of poverty in this country and around the world. This office should be the designated portal for faith-based groups to submit policy advice to the White House national security, economic, and domestic policy councils, and work with the White House Office of Social Entrepreneurship to identify organizations that have demonstrated success and are ready to grow to scale. These organizations will play an important role in leading innovation and alleviating poverty in communities throughout the United States and the world. The new president also should announce that he intends to increase overall funding for federal poverty-reduction programs and for grants for which faith-based and other groups can apply.

The White House also should reinforce that the Faith-Based Office will operate within the framework of the Constitution. The Constitution does not allow the government to directly finance "inherently religious" activities such as religious worship, instruction, or proselytizing; this is at the heart of the separation of church and state. More importantly, most religious leaders would not want this government funding for their religious activities, in the interest of protecting the integrity of their ministry. The government should take steps to ensure that the recipients of any federal funds meaningfully segregate any programs involving faith-intensive activities from programs that are directly funded by the government.

The Faith-Based Office also must ensure that its funds do not subsidize any form of discrimination in a manner prohibited by the Constitution or by federal, state, or local statutes. This means that recipients of federal funds may not discriminate against beneficiaries on the basis of race, sex, national origin, religion, or disability. It also means that recipients of federal funds may not discriminate against employees in a federally funded program on the basis of race, sex, or national origin. Faith-based programs that receive federal funding also should operate within federal statutes prohibiting discrimination on the basis of religion, although faith-based recipients of federal funding retain any right they may have under Title VII of the 1964 Civil Rights Act to favor coreligionist employees outside federally subsidized programs. The Justice Department's Office of Legal Counsel should help promulgate clear guidance on the law in this complex area of hiring practices by recipients of federal funds.

Over the longer term, the president and his Faith-Based Office will need to communicate the importance of faith-based and secular non-profit community organizations in fighting poverty to Congress, where members across the political spectrum are skeptical of such initiatives. The president must make the case that the office is committed to focusing on accountability and results, and will ensure that the office will not be used for political purposes or for discrimination for or against any religion. Bipartisan consensus on the importance of this effort will allow the White House to secure authorizing legislation for the office and its work, along with adequate funds, congressional oversight, and a place for the office that lasts beyond the current administration.

The Faith-Based Office also should work with the Office of Social Entrepreneurship to develop tools to evaluate the effectiveness of all non-profit groups receiving federal funds. As with all other federal grants, it is important that limited dollars be directed toward groups that demonstrate results in their efforts to alleviate poverty. Public funding should go only to organizations that deliver verifiable results. All recipients of federal funds should maintain clear performance and results data and be required to share the data with research entities that evaluate their programs.

Finally, the Faith-Based Office also should work with the appropriate federal agencies to create local and state databases of available services. These so-called "benefits banks" would empower local organizations fighting domestic poverty to provide accurate information to impoverished people about how to seek help for health insurance, food stamps, and a host of other social services. There are over 315,000 houses of worship in America, but the average membership is somewhere around 100 members. These small religious communities are often on the front lines when families or individuals seek help with basic necessities. Establishing these kinds of "benefits banks" would help clergy and volunteers in faith-based groups, as well as employees and volunteers in other community organizations, identify the appropriate local, state, and federal services that could support people in their neighborhoods and communities.

Office of Science and Technology Policy

NEAL LANE

U.S. science and technology—our nation's capability to discover new knowledge, invent new technologies, and then apply them to create new products and markets—are at the core of innovation. U.S. science and technology are the engines of our economic growth, our national security, our health and quality of life, and the eventual basis of our nation's energy self-sufficiency and global environmental stewardship. The United States has been the world's leader in scientific discovery and technological innovation for at least the past six decades, yet we risk falling rapidly behind many other parts of the world on both the discovery side of scientific exploration and the applied technology side of creativity and inventiveness.

The recent report from the National Academy of Sciences, "Rising Above the Gathering Storm," makes clear the myriad challenges we face to preserve our nation's preeminent place in science and technology. A few cases in point:

Addressing the implications of climate change for energy, the environment, economy, and human health; enhancing our global leadership in science, technology, and innovation; improving the nation's health care; confronting terrorism and pandemics; and training the best generation of scientists and engineers in the world. Worse yet, the outgoing administration compounded the problems by taking decidedly anti-science stances on climate change, stem cell research, and even fundamental health issues such as the effects of emissions from coal-fired power plants on the quality of the air we breathe.

Current U.S. federal science and technology programs—structure and policies—are the result of six decades of experience and incremental adaptation to forces of evolving change since the end of World War II. Today, however, change in science and technology is coming more quickly than ever. The U.S. system must be able to respond. Many laws, regulations, institutions, and programs need updating. A progressive agenda must take on some of the most challenging needs for substantial policy and structural reform, especially as the next president takes on the greatest challenge of his administration—simultaneously reducing carbon emissions, dealing with climate change, and attaining energy security. This is why the role of the Office of Science and Technology Policy in the White House will be more important to our 44th president than at any time in history.

The new president's science advisor, formally known as the assistant to the president for science and technology, also serves as director of OSTP. He advises the president on all aspects of science and technology policy and provides him with the scientific and technical analysis needed to make sound policy decisions on these issues. Most areas of public policy today depend on science and technology, and many of the next administration's policymakers in these arenas will be counting on innovative new ideas, technical information, interagency coordination, and policy analysis to help them achieve the goals of the new president. Staffing OSTP with the right mix of professionals and ensuring they are empowered by the president to set a tight policymaking agenda while working with a variety of other White House offices and federal agencies could well define the success of the new administration.

Recommendations

The challenge for the new president and his OSTP director will be to keep their science and technology policy focus tight enough to achieve success, yet broad enough to influence the many overlapping policies that include science and technology components. The first step is to spell out the overall responsibilities of the office. Second is to get the policymaking infrastructure right. Third is to reaffirm the importance of integrity (openness, honesty, trust) in the new administration's handling of science and technology matters. And the fourth step is planning and launching the president's overall science and technology agenda, priorities, and budget initiatives.

Within the White House, OSTP should have the principal responsibility for policy development and interagency coordination in all areas that relate to the funding, regulation, and management of research and development—particularly basic and applied science, engineering, and medical research—and assessments and dissemination of information on the current status of scientific and technical understanding in all areas of national importance. This is indeed a tall order, since most federal agencies are involved in R&D, but only OSTP will have the staff and expertise to deal with the broad array of science and technology matters. OSTP's responsibilities should also include the U.S. nonmilitary space program—science and technology as well as human exploration.

The director of OSTP should be the president's top advisor on all such matters, and should be a member of the National Security Council, the National Economic Council, and the new National Energy Council proposed in another chapter in the White House section of this book. The new president's science advisor should attend White House meetings where science and technology matters are discussed and be consulted on any policies that relate to science and technology, including issues of national and homeland security. He or she should attend all cabinet meetings.

The 44th president will need to move quickly to put in place the personnel and policymaking infrastructure necessary to ensure that he receives the best analysis and advice about science and technology issues and that the new president's science and technology agenda is coordinated among the appropriate agencies and White House offices. On some policy matters, such as stem cells and climate change, the new president will want advice right away.

As a first step, the new president should choose his science advisor before assuming office, quickly nominate him or her to be director of OSTP, and then seek early confirmation by the Senate. This was the practice during the administrations of presidents Bill Clinton and George H.W. Bush. On both occasions, OSTP was able to staff up quickly, establish an effective interagency coordination mechanism (through the National Science and Technology Council in the Clinton administration), and issue science and technology policy position documents early in the president's first term.

The OSTP director should have scientific credentials and a number of special attributes. He or she must be well respected in the academic and the high-technology industrial communities, be an effective spokesperson for science and technology issues, and be a determined and skilled advocate for the president's priorities and initiatives. The director should not appear to be a "representative" of the science and technology community, but should know how the federal government works and how policy is made, and should have good standing with both parties in Congress or be capable of establishing that standing quickly.

Once the director is in place, he or she should ensure that the president nominates or appoints the key government science and technology positions, as outlined in the National Academies list of critical science and technology appointments in its "Science and Technology for America's Progress: Ensuring the Best Presidential Appointments in the New Administration" report. Particularly important early appointments include: the directors of the National Science Foundation, National Institutes of Health, and National Institute for Standards and Technology; the administrators of NASA and the National Oceanic and Atmospheric Administration; the head of the United States Geological Survey; the Department of Commerce Undersecretary for Technology; the Department of Energy Undersecretary for Science; and the associate directors of OSTP, all of which require Senate confirmation.

All four authorized associate director positions should be filled (only two were filled during the Bush administration), and the OSTP director and associate directors and OSTP staff should be returned to the Eisenhower Old Executive Office Building so they can interact in real time with other senior White House policy officials and integrate informed, science-based decision making into White House policy. There is a special argument to be made for OSTP staff being located within the White House security fence, since OSTP, more than any other office, is likely to be called upon in connection with the broad sweep of policy matters the White House considers each day.

In selecting his or her team, the OSTP director should consider the need for expertise in areas that will be increasingly critical to our economy, sustainability, and national security. These areas include alternative energy, energy efficiency, cybersecurity, nanotechnology, climate change, ecology, and, in the life sciences, genomics, proteomics, regenerative medicine and non-reproductive somatic cell nuclear transfer (often known as non-reproductive human cloning), neuroscience, and synthetic biology.

The director also should develop a plan and framework to work with federal officials and alongside state and local leaders and the heads of universities to find ways to integrate federal efforts to support science and innovation in regional economies across the country. Similarly, he or she will need to coordinate on climate change policies with states and regions that are already reducing their carbon footprints and adapting to the potential consequences of global warming, or are planning to do so because of the lack of any progress on the national level by the Bush administration in dealing with carbon emissions and climate change.

Finally, the director should recommend that the new president re-issue the executive order that is still in place from the Clinton administration to re-establish the National Science and Technology Council, chaired by the president, as the principal mechanism for coordinating all interagency efforts that involve science and technology in any significant way. The National Science and Technology Council should be a cabinet-level council with no members or substitutions below deputy secretary and should include as well the heads (or deputies) of the National Science Foundation, the National Institutes of Health, NASA, the National Institute of Standards and Technology, the National Oceanic and Atmospheric Administration, and the U.S. Geological Survey. The council should be operated by OSTP and be responsive to the new president's agenda, particularly as it requires multi-agency cooperation.

Rely on the Best Scientific Evidence
After eight years of political interference by the Bush White House whenever science-based policy proposals did not match the demands of economic or cultural conservatives, the new president must reinforce that the policymaking process and decisions in the new administration will be informed by the best scientific evidence and analysis. In addition, the new administration must have in place explicit guidelines to ensure government officials respect and support the process of open scientific inquiry and dissemination of research results.

To reinforce this, he should issue within the first week after the Inauguration an executive order on the "Integrity of Science in the Federal Government." The order should state that: all federal policy and information provided to the public by the federal government will be based on the best scientific evidence; membership on federal scientific advisory committees will be based on scientific qualifications; and scientists within the federal government or funded by federal agencies will be free to publish and speak openly about their results, unless restricted due to national security concerns.

Within the first week after the Inauguration, the 44th president should also issue an executive order to permit federal funding for embryonic stem cell research on all ethically derived stem cell lines as defined by the National Academies' guidelines or International Society for Stem Cell Research guidelines. This executive order should also allow for the creation of new lines from embryos remaining in fertility clinics that are donated by their progenitors after they are not needed for reproduction in accordance with NAS or ISSCR guidelines, and by means of somatic cell nuclear transfer (non-reproductive human cloning), as well as other research involving SCNT, such as studies of disease at the cellular level.

At the same time, the new president should be clear in the executive order that any effort to clone a human being is altogether banned. The president should also call for Congress to pass legislation that makes this policy a matter of law and that avoids unnecessary measures that could slow ethically conducted science. The OSTP director should also advocate for the repeal of the misnamed Data Quality Act (also known as Information Quality Act), which is an obscure rider on a 2001 appropriations bill that has become an ideal vehicle for industry attacks on the science underlying health and environmental regulation decision making.

New Agenda and Budget Initiatives
OSTP should immediately develop and advance, through the cabinet-level National Science and Technology Council, a strong science and technology agenda and corresponding R&D program in coordination with the Office of Management and Budget and the White House National Economic Council, Domestic Policy Council, National Security Council, and the new National Energy Council and Chief Technology Officer, as well as the relevant federal agencies. The new president's science and technology agenda should include new budget initiatives focused on strengthening the U.S. science base, and enhancing American innovation, the economic competitiveness of U.S. industry, and the capability of the U.S. workforce. For more detail on a progressive science and technology agenda, see the Science, Technology, and Innovation Overview chapter by Tom Kalil.

The office should work with the Office of Management and Budget and the agencies to ensure that the agencies' programs and budget requests reflect the president's priorities. When necessary, the coordinating body, the National Science and Technology Council, can be used to ensure compliance. This agenda should articulate the vital role that each federal agency will play in accomplishing the goals set out by the new administration. A failing of many policymakers in the past has been their inability to understand how the various parts of government can best support an important common national agenda while carrying out their respective missions. The whole needs to be greater than the parts; the new president's science and technology agenda should make that clear, and the point should be clearly articulated during the budget process.

One set of budget initiatives should focus on increasing investments in R&D, especially research. These budget initiatives should include proposals for multiyear increases in research funding at 10 percent annual real growth, after accounting for inflation, for key agencies and programs. These key federal allocations should go to: the National Science Foundation; the National Institutes of Health; the Department of Energy's Office of Science; the National Institute of Standards and Technology; the Department of Defense's basic and applied research programs and Defense Advanced Research Projects Agency; and the NASA, NOAA, and USGS science programs.

The new president's budget initiatives should place a particularly high priority on support for early career researchers and potentially transformational (high-risk, high-reward) research. High priority should be given to long-term basic research in the physical and biological sciences that relates, broadly, to a national goal of making revolutionary advances in information technology, nanotechnology, modern materials, and synthetic biology. By focusing on long-term basic research, the federal government will avoid "picking winners and losers."

Given how rapidly many developing nations are expanding their research infrastructure and science and technology workforce, increased emphasis should also be placed on international collaborations that are proposed by U.S. researchers in their funding requests. And the president's budget initiatives should also include a broad set of multidisciplinary "Grand Challenges" in areas where significant R&D is required to respond to vital societal needs in such areas as health and safety, energy, climate change and the environment, food and water, and domestic and national security in cyberspace, as detailed in the Science, Technology, and Innovation Overview chapter.

A second critical budget initiative should address the many failings of the U.S. primary school public education system in teaching science, technology, engineering, and mathematics. OSTP should develop a STEM education, training, and workforce development program through its coordinating body, the National Science and Technology Council, alongside the Department of Education and National Science Foundation, but also include other agencies involved in education and the technical workforce, with clear goals and budget proposals for relevant programs within the agencies. OSTP should take an active role not only in the development of the initiative but in seeing it implemented, since its success will require an unprecedented partnership between the NSF and the Department of Education, which in turn will require strong White House involvement.

The principal goal of this initiative should be to ensure that all secondary school American boys and girls receive a quality education in the STEM skill sets to build a diverse next generation of well-educated women and men, including the skilled scientists, engineers, and technical professionals who will be needed to meet the challenges of the 21st century. This initiative should include federal funding for STEM teachers and future teachers. The bipartisan "America Competes Act" provides an excellent starting point for authorizing legislation for this initiative and could be revised to reflect the new administration's priorities.

Specifically, the new administration should provide four-year scholarships each year to 10,000 or more promising college students who will become primary school science, math, engineering, and technology teachers, thus educating 10 million minds. The initiative would also include summer institutes for 100,000 or more STEM teachers across the nation by providing federal matches to state funds, and fund new master's degree programs (full or part time) focused on science, math, or technology education, offered to current K–12th grade teachers (with or without undergraduate science, math, or technology degrees).

New White House Offices

OSTP and its coordinating body, the National Science and Technology Council, should work closely with the newly created National Energy Council to provide the scientific evidence and analysis to support the next president's efforts to protect U.S. energy security needs, as well as develop mitigation and adaptation to alleviate the effects of climate change. The head of the new council should be a member of the National Science and Technology Council, and the director of OSTP should be a member of the new council.

OSTP should have the principal responsibility in all matters that relate to the funding, regulation, and management of R&D, and it should support the new council on broader policy matters. In particular, OSTP should focus on increasing the funding for R&D related to climate change and carbon-free energy. At the present time, progress is seriously hampered by the lack of strong interagency cooperation and collaboration in monitoring the effects of climate change from satellites. OSTP should develop recommendations to create a strong coordination mechanism involving NOAA, USGS, and NASA.

OSTP should also coordinate with and support the work of the new White House chief technology officer, whose role will be to ensure that the vast federal government is using the best information technologies to ensure that government is more effective, more open, and our nation more secure. (See the CTO chapter in the White House section of this book.) The CTO should be a member of the National Science and Technology Council. OSTP should work with the CTO as he or she coordinates the work of federal agencies responsible for regulating and supporting information technology, including broadband access to the Internet. OSTP should have the principal responsibility for White House policies related to the funding, regulation, and management of R&D, but the CTO should be consulted on all matters that might affect the government's capabilities in information technology.

White House Chief Technology Officer

MITCHELL KAPOR

Technology, especially information technology, is increasingly vital to the life of the nation, economically and culturally. The Internet has become integral to the nation's economy and is transforming our media landscape. Like the telephone more than a century ago, the Internet is weaving itself into the daily lives of Americans in direct and personal ways: it is taking the place of the library, the mall, and the neighborhood hangout.

Yet the continued health of the information and communications technology ecosystem today is precarious. For instance, the United States lags badly in broadband deployment and the speed of broadband access. Our country recently slipped to 15th place among developed nations in broadband subscribers—a full 12 percentage points behind Denmark, which ranked first. Telecommunications oligopolies still control the so-called "last mile" between customers and the Internet, and continually threaten to choke innovation or impose enormous opportunity costs on it.

Similarly, overly broad intellectual property rights reward rent-seeking behavior and, contrary to popular views, act as a disincentive to entrepreneurial innovation. Finding a new, balanced regime for intellectual property is one of the major challenges of the digital era. There also will be opportunities to promote new approaches such as reuse of spectrum in an open and collaborative way as it is being freed in the conversion from analog to digital.

Various executive agencies have well-established responsibilities that bear upon technology, such as the Office of Science and Technology Policy, the Patent and Trademark Office, and Copyright Office for intellectual property, but there are broad concerns that require higher levels of attention related to the new information and communications technologies. Moreover, when the benefits of a policy are highly concentrated but costs widely distributed, federal departments and agencies are subject to capture by their immediate constituency and are unable to serve a broader mission. By appointing a White House Chief Technology Officer, the 44th president would signal an understanding of the importance of technology and innovation to the nation's future.

Rather than being thought of as alien territory or an implementation detail, the next president can use information and communications technology, or ICT, to proactively drive both the vision and the strategy for a progressive agenda that emphasizes democratic renewal, opportunity creation, and a broader vision of security. The United States led in ICT innovation in no small part because of far-sighted policies, such as the deregulation of telecommunications infrastructure, which promoted the competition that in turn led to successful commercialization of the Internet.

A 21st-century, technologically sophisticated White House CTO could help shape policies that would allow such breakthroughs in the future. The CTO in particular could advise on investments in learning technologies to develop more domestic science, technology, engineering, and mathematics talent, especially among underrepresented minorities, in order to remain globally competitive.

Specifically, the CTO would have three key roles. The first: advising the president on the federal government's efforts to expand the use of technology in government operations to create a more open and efficient government. The second: working with OSTP to advise the president and the policymaking processes on all issues that have a critical ICT component, from the economy and national security to health care and education, providing a sophisticated understanding of technology's influence and its promise for innovation, as well as its perils. One key example of this second role would be the digitalization of health records as national health insurance policy gets overhauled.

The third task would be playing a new and important coordination role in ensuring that the information and communications technology platforms deployed across the United States are robust in their capabilities, broadly available and affordable to all sectors, and organized in a way that embodies openness and interoperability. This coordinating role will straddle the public and private sectors to permit the greatest innovation by the private sector for the benefit of the public.

Recommendations

The 44th president should immediately appoint a White House CTO who deeply understands information and communications technology policy issues, has concrete experience implementing and managing actual technology systems, and is a skilled and collegial advocate for technology issues. The new appointee must be able to advise the new president immediately on the delivery of real e-government and e-democracy reforms, in which government services are delivered with increasing effectiveness, and citizens participate actively in self-government.

The CTO should be a champion of principles of open government, in which government data (from weather and climate measurements and statistics to the state of legislation in progress) are made available in ways that are complete, timely, reviewable, accessible, and nonproprietary. In this capacity, the CTO should also identify and develop important new policy ideas and innovative strategies that involve interagency and government-public collaboration for consideration by the next president.

For instance, as the new president seeks to reverse the civil liberties incursions of the past eight years and invests instead in genuine improvements in security, the strategy and implementation needs to be done with impeccable technical sophistication, as all forms of communications today are digitally mediated. The CTO would work with the White House's National Economic Council, OSTP, and other policy councils to drive these new ideas and strategies through the policy process.

More broadly, the CTO must serve as a public champion of the president's information and communications technology priorities with Congress, the media, the private sector, and civil society. The CTO could also serve as ombudsman to industry, academia, and non-profit groups, providing a place to hear out important concerns that are falling on deaf ears elsewhere.

Within government, too, the CTO could act as a unifying force to overcome departmental silos. He or she could help recruit and support a network of experts with similar roles at the agency level, such as those working on health in-formation technology implementation at the Department of Health and Human Services, on intelligent transportation systems at the Department of Transportation, on learning technology in the Department of Education and the Department of Labor, and on security technology at the Department of Homeland Security.

ECONOMIC POLICY

Overview
A Pro-Growth, Progressive Economic Agenda

GENE SPERLING

Our new president's largest challenge: ensure we grow together as a nation so that we do not grow apart as a people. A pro-growth, progressive economic agenda must focus on policies that both raise the economic tide and lift all boats—boosting productivity and our gross national product while fostering the shared prosperity that defines our nation's values. These progressive values require growth that makes room for those seeking to prosper in America without forcing others to share a smaller slice of the pie. These values support a new social compact that ensures a basic level of dignity in economic life for those who work and take responsibility for their lives. And they offer every worker real opportunity for upward mobility while ensuring that the accident of birth does not severely stack the deck against any child. To this end, the new administration and Congress should enact tax reforms and investments focused on new jobs, especially in alternative energy on our shores, a new Universal 401(k) pension plan to promote savings for working families, a new strategy to promote early intervention in middle school to promote college enrollment and completion for disadvantaged students, a universal health care program, and a broad range of policies designed to both boost our national competitiveness and economic security.

The new president will most likely be forced to deal with the fallout of the financial meltdown and the need to jumpstart what could be an economy in recession in his first days in office. Yet over the full course of the next eight years the larger issue is more likely to be how we are growing rather than whether we are growing. Will we have an economy that both raises the tide and lifts all boats? Will we grow together with shared prosperity, or grow apart because of rising inequality and economic insecurity?

Thirty-five years ago, the fundamental economic challenge was the decline in productivity growth, which outside of the farm sector fell to a disappointing

1.4 percent from 1974 to 1995 after growing by 2.8 percent from 1948 to 1973.[1] Starting in 1996, however, strong productivity growth resurfaced, bolstered by the spread of information technology, more productive workers, strong public policies, and the efficiencies of a more integrated global economy. While many economic commentators like to look at inequality or wage growth as a 30-year trend, there is much the 44th president can learn from looking at this most recent period from 1995 to 2007—which I have called the "new productivity decade."

Far from being part of an unbroken 30-year trend, the history of the new productivity decade is in many ways a tale of two cities.[2] In the first half, productivity grew 13 percent overall from 1995 to 2000, and the benefits were broadly spread among working families. Median working household income kept up, growing 11 percent during this period. From 1993 to 2000, every income group experienced real family income growth of at least 16 percent, with the bottom 20 percent doing the best at nearly 24 percent growth.[3] Overall, working household income increased by $7,748 from 1993 to 2000.

In contrast, in the second half of the new productivity decade there was a complete reversal of fortune. While productivity growth kept rising, the majority of the middle class experienced stagnant or falling real income growth. From 2000 to 2007, productivity expanded at an average rate of 2.5 percent per year, yet the typical working-age household saw its income fall by $2,010. Even average incomes for college-educated men, which rose $12,224 from 1993 to 2000, declined by $3,687 between 2001 and 2007.

Most troubling for many workers was the sense that rising productivity and historic corporate profits—averaging 13 percent as a share of gross national income in recent years—seemed predicated on disappointing wages. According to Goldman Sachs Group, Inc., more than 40 percent of record corporate profit growth over the past five years was due to the historically low share of national income going to labor.[4] The widespread deployment of information technology may have helped increase U.S. wages in the 1990s, but in this decade the interaction between IT and globalization seemed to put downward pressure on many service job categories, allowing companies to lower labor costs by searching out the cheapest option in a global labor force, or threatening to do so to keep labor costs down at home.

The two halves of the new productivity decade demonstrate that the forces of technology and globalization can lead to either wage stress or shared prosperity for typical American families—depending on both economic trends and our public policies. This presents a fundamental challenge for a new president seeking a pro-growth and progressive economic policy. Some policies that promote economic efficiency and productivity may put downward pressure on middle-class wages, yet efforts to simply halt dynamic competition and techno-logical change in the interest of stability, security, and protecting existing jobs can inhibit long-term growth and innovation. That is why the 44th president must work with both sides of the political spectrum to design policies that boost shared prosperity by strengthening and growing the middle class, not policies that focus just on growth or on equity alone.

Conservatives often speak of gross domestic product growth as if it were the whole ball game, with the question of whether most people benefit from it defined as a quaint "distributional" issue. Yet this misses the degree to which the American aspiration for strong growth always included a focus on the de-gree to which that growth was widely shared. Benjamin Franklin's critique of England 250 years ago was not of its economic growth record but of a society in which economic outcomes were overly determined by accident of birth. In modern day terms, he asked colonial Americans whether they wanted to create a new nation that would replace a dumbbell society—an upper class and a lower class and a thin middle class—with a bell curve economy that featured a majority middle class and only a few in poverty or wealthy, in which anyone could rise with inspiration and perspiration.

Explaining the difference between Europe and America, Franklin wrote: "[P]ersons of moderate Fortunes and Capitals, who, having a Number of Chil-dren to provide for, are desirous of bringing them up to Industry, and to secure Estates for their Posterity, have Opportunities of doing it in America, which Europe does not afford."[5] Progressives today must likewise shape globalization and technological change to ensure shared prosperity rather than downplay the intense global and innovative pressures America faces—pressures we must re-spond to in order to remain on the economic cutting edge. Strong and dynamic growth—even with its dislocation—is critical to ensuring the United States al-ways makes room for anyone from anywhere who is willing to work hard and play by the rules without having to force existing groups to settle for less. In short, it is easier to have a melting pot if you have a growing pot.

Recommendations

The progressive growth agenda of the new president must from day one pro-mote four core progressive values—shared prosperity, economic dignity, real opportunity for upward mobility, and the chance to succeed regardless of the accident of birth.[6] These values must be translated into pragmatic policies.

First and foremost, the 44th president must address whether the forces that promote productivity growth translate into good jobs, strong wages, and new opportunities for working families in the United States. Simply put, we cannot assume that what promotes corporate efficiency for U.S. multinationals necessarily results in shared economic growth for working families, or that what is good for Intel is good for U.S. workers. Part of the reason for updating this famous quip by former General Motors Corp. chief executive Charlie Wilson is that it was Intel Corp. founder Andy Grove who explicitly articulated the tension between what was best for his company and what was best for his country. "Those of us in business have two obligations in my opinion," he said in 2003. "The one that's un-debatable is we have a fiduciary responsibility to run our business for the shareholders who put us in our place, gave us the decision making power." But Grove also said that he "feels a responsibility for doing the right thing for the country," and that "these two are pulling us in different directions."[7]

Indeed, the second half of the new productivity decade under President George W. Bush confirms at a macroeconomic level Grove's instinct concerning Intel. Despite previous economic studies indicating that economic expansion overseas generally creates growth and jobs at home, it is not necessarily so. For the new president this means he must carefully analyze where the intersection is between what is best for U.S. multinationals and U.S. workers' standards of living. While incentives for alternative energy innovation in the United States and incentives for moving jobs overseas may both help the corporate bottom line, the former clearly intersects with job creation in the United States while the latter may have the opposite effect. When developing shared-prosperity policies we must first ask "who is us?" as former Secretary of Labor Robert Reich did in his prescient book, *The Work of Nations*.

In performing this analysis, policymakers must be willing to take a broad look at our economic policies, including trade, regulatory issues, and job creation strategies—not just cost-sharing and job-adjustment policies, however important. Indeed, much of the hostility among labor unions toward ideas such as wage insurance may be because of the suspicion these policies reflect an uncritical attitude toward the structural challenges facing the U.S. economy. While stronger adjustment policies are needed for those losing jobs in the United States, policymakers cannot limit a progressive policy approach only to re-employment strategies for what is too often described in patronizing terms as compensating losers.

Yet, a willingness to look broadly at how larger structural, technological, and global issues impact job and wage opportunities in the United States is not an excuse to resort to inappropriate "picking winners" policies or other public measures that would dampen the competitive and innovative pressures that are essential to the United States staying on the cutting edge of the global economy. The new president must be creative, finding ways to make changing market conditions work for more Americans while ensuring our economy faces competitive pressures to innovate. Fortunately, the 44th president will be armed with a number of shared-prosperity policies to implement upon taking office.

Job-Creating Tax Reform

In an open global economy, U.S. employers are essentially free to locate jobs, production, and services where they see fit. But that does not mean the federal government should be neutral about where they want jobs to be located. Currently, our tax laws allow a U.S. company located in tax havens or low-tax jurisdictions abroad to defer paying U.S. taxes indefinitely on their active overseas income. This practice gives U.S. companies that expand by building a new factory abroad to make products for sale overseas a competitive advantage over a rival company who chooses to expand a similar factory to make export products in the United States. The rationale for this tax advantage is that if U.S. companies have to pay higher U.S. income taxes when they are locating in tax havens, they will be less competitive with foreign rivals, which only have to pay the lower rate in the tax haven.

At times this rationale should be applied. If a U.S. hotel chain wants to locate in Hong Kong, for example, it makes little sense to force them to immediately pay higher U.S. tax rates where there is obviously no way to service those hotel needs from the United States. But when a U.S. company wishes to move a U.S. factory to China and eliminate U.S. jobs to make products to export to other nations, why should we give them lower taxes than other U.S. competitors by letting them defer their foreign income from U.S. taxation?

There is also no reason to make it so easy for hedge funds and U.S. citizens to park their wealth in tax havens at the expense of ordinary working families who pay their full taxes. Legislation proposed by Sens. Carl Levin (D-MI), Barack Obama (D-IL), and Norm Coleman (R-MN) in February 2007 smartly allows the IRS to shift the burden to those U.S. taxpayers who have set up accounts or companies that formed in well-known tax havens like the Cayman Islands to show that they are not engaging in tax evasion. The bill would require the companies and U.S. citizens to prove they have legitimate business abroad through opening their offshore books to auditors, or else the government would assume that they are fronts for income shifting or other tax avoidance schemes.

Such measures could be part of a revenue-neutral, pro-job tax reform by using the increased revenues from these reforms to increase the amount of positive tax incentives for job creation in the United States. This could be done by expanding the research-and-development tax credit and basic research tax credit, providing incentives for new small business job creation in the United States, especially green jobs, and by expanding incentives for locating jobs in harder-hit rural and urban areas in the United States.

We will never keep all U.S. jobs from being outsourced abroad or offshored, or stop all U.S. companies from establishing offshore production platforms in lower-wage nations. But that does not mean we should not even seek to enable our most underserved rural and urban areas with up to 40 percent lower labor costs than in larger cities from competing for jobs currently being outsourced to foreign nations. High-tech and call-center jobs could be well suited for rural sourcing and could be a significant source of growth for regional economies. The new president should build on policies like the New Markets Tax Credit that provide tax cuts for those investing in financial institutions serving underserved and low-income areas, and the wage and new job credits utilized in Empowerment Zones to encourage location of jobs in the untapped markets in our own nation.

Green Jobs

Rather than seeking to outguess the market about which technologies will provide the best results, the new president should adopt technology-neutral policies that require utilities to generate a respectable percentage of their power from renewable sources while providing incentives for major public and private investment in basic alternative energy technologies and research and development. Such policies will have enormous positive implications for our environment and national security while also spurring economic growth. There will be hundreds of billions of dollars worth of alternative energy investments made around the world over the next two decades, creating millions of new jobs. There is no reason the United States should not take all steps possible to ensure that a substantial number of those jobs are created here in this country, just as other nations are doing, and that our investment in research and technology development results in new industries and new opportunities for U.S. workers.

A policy framework that supports new green businesses means the new administration could help spur jobs in largely new professions that help work-ers in construction and advanced manufacturing as well as new innovators, re-searchers, and entrepreneurs. A variety of new jobs would be created, from solar panel installers and electricians who would perform energy efficiency retrofits or swap out old and inefficient lighting, to advanced manufacturing workers who will do the metal fabrication to build wind turbines and towers or produce advanced batteries for a new generation of cars.

A strong R&D and venture capital component will also work to direct the initiative and energies of our brightest research minds and budding entrepre-neurs aspiring to be the next Sergey Brin and Larry Page toward alternative en-ergy. The investments required to forge a low-carbon economy will improve the productivity of the workforce, spur new innovation and industry, and re-store the infrastructure that is the backbone of our economy.

Research and Innovation Jobs

At a time when new competition from China and India should be leading to a major national effort to compete for research jobs and create more university-centered innovation clusters to keep jobs and investment in the United States, the Bush administration sat on its hands. Funding for the National Institutes of Health, for example, was frozen for five years, creating an enormous and disil-lusioning deterrent to scores of young researchers.[8] Thomas Kalil's overview chapter on science and innovation details investment policies the new president and his administration could pursue.

The Bush administration also failed to invest in the so-called STEM educa-tional disciplines—science, technology, engineering, and math—at the primary, secondary, and postsecondary levels, leaving our nation with a human-resource policy that does not fill our high-level science, math, and research needs. The new administration needs to expand the education and opportunities of our own people, especially for minorities and young women who are currently un-derrepresented in these areas. Shirley Ann Jackson, president of the Rensselaer Polytechnic Institute, rightly calls this the "quiet crisis."[9] Cynthia Brown's edu-cation overview provides a vision of a comprehensive educational reform pro-gram required to teach all of our children and young adults well.

A Social Compact for Economic Dignity

Our nation's social compact has never been spelled out in a constitutional amendment or even a commercial contract. Yet this implicit contract is built around a few core principles: A career of hard work should command respect at the workplace, provide health care for your family and a secure retirement, and give you a chance to send your children to college so that they might lead a better life. Today, however, playing by what Americans thought were the rules too often means that a 30-year-old computer programmer is suddenly uncompetitive in the global economy, or a couple just entering retirement after working hard for four decades has to move into their child's cramped basement due to rising health costs.

The 44th president must take a number of steps to restore the American social compact, beginning with policies that de-link health care security, retirement savings opportunities, and higher education affordability from job retention and job loss. The new administration cannot guarantee that any particular industry, company, or job will be stable, but it could enact policies that provide American workers with incentives to save for retirement, with affordable and portable health care, with the ability to send their children to college, and with the capacity to survive job losses and the career changes characteristic of today's economy. These steps would help reduce poverty, too.

These sets of policies should not seek to de-link pension savings plans and health care from employment. Indeed, we know that people are more likely to save if they can elect to make automatic deductions from their paychecks, and that Americans are attached to receiving health care assistance through their jobs. But a policy that guarantees each American access to affordable health care would ensure that tens of millions of Americans are not one job loss or one illness away from financial devastation.

Similarly, a Universal 401(k) pension savings plan would provide major federal incentives for savings, even when a worker is voluntarily or involuntarily separated from the job market or simply working for himself or herself. And a more robust policy for both refundable tax credits for higher education and lifelong learning can enable workers to use higher education to improve their economic situations and allow them to give more opportunities to their children. A minimum wage that keeps up with inflation, combined with an Earned Income Tax Credit that is expanded for single workers and those with three or more children, will also help to continue to reward work and provide basic economic dignity for America's most hard-pressed working families.

In this way, the new administration can ensure a basic floor of economic dignity for those who have worked hard throughout their lives. Through affordable health care, retirement savings incentives and tax policies that reward students and workers who choose to upgrade their skills to compete in the global economy, the 44th president can rebuild several key components of our nation's historic social compact, even in a dynamic global economy.

Job Training and Adjustment Assistance

The new president must develop a full jobs and economic dignity agenda to make clear to workers that his agenda is more than just a "band aid" or "burial insurance" when they suffer job losses due to globalization. He must do more to create worker adjustment policies that provide both options for workers to get job training and other assistance and for localities to seek economic diversification before predictable mass layoffs occur. Bringing a community's stakeholders together could head off economic problems several years down the road before workers feel the sting of a pink slip.

These new job creation and pre-emptive policies for workers and hard-hit communities would make clear that a strong adjustment and re-employment agenda reflects not a focus on "burial insurance," but a means to ensure economic dignity for workers who, despite all reasonable efforts, find themselves between jobs. As we do reform worker adjustment assistance, we must make such help universal regardless of how a worker lost their job through no fault of their own.

The full focus of our policies should be on helping workers find new jobs, not on finding out how they lost their last job. There is no reason why the government should care more about a person who lost their job due to trade than one who lost it due to outsourcing or technological change. Sorting out the causal differences will only become harder over time.

If we are serious about adjustment assistance then it has to be simple, have universal eligibility, and be user friendly. If Costco can provide one-stop shopping for life's day-by-day necessities, then the government should be able to have a single toll-free number and one-stop centers that handle all re-employment issues, from job search, to training, to health, mortgage, and unemployment insurance. Such a one-stop shop could move us toward the consumer-oriented government that former Vice President Al Gore has championed.

Dignity and Rights of Workers

Working families have also lost their ability to stand up for their labor rights thanks to a prolonged weak labor market and the more-than-decade-long attack on the right of workers to organize. The growing hostility toward organized labor between 1994 and 2006 severely undercut the right of workers to organize. Labor journalist Steven Greenhouse notes in his new book, *The Big Squeeze*, the meteoric rise in the number of union-busting consultants in the last half-century. And Cornell University professor Kate Bronfenbrenner found that 75 percent of companies facing organizing drives hired anti-union consultants, some of whom have admitted to using shady tactics such as planting contraband in the lockers of pro-union workers with drug records or other personal attacks.[10] According to top union leader Richard Trumka, over 20,000 workers are illegally fired every year for exercising their most fundamental rights—freedom of opinion, expression, and association.

Furthermore, regulations promulgated by the Bush administration reduced those eligible for overtime and workplace protections. In 2003, the Department of Labor started a rulemaking process that, according to the Economic Policy Institute, will cause 8 million workers to lose access to overtime pay, giving employers free reign to require the exempt employees to work virtually any schedule for any number of hours, without providing additional compensation. The 500-page rule created new exemptions barring overtime for huge swaths of workers from pre-school teachers to sous chefs and funeral directors, while classifying others, such as fast-food assistant managers (who spend 90 percent of their time cooking) as full-time supervisors, making them ineligible for overtime.[11]

The Bush administration went even further, using its administrative powers to systematically attack organized labor and cut enforcement of safety standards and safety enforcement over the last eight years. Scott Lilly at the Center for American Progress noted that Occupational Safety and Health Office enforcement spending is down 8 percent from 2001 levels in real terms, and wage and child labor enforcement has dropped by 13 percent over that same period.[12] The tragic mine disasters of this decade came at a time when the Bush administration's Department of Labor was cutting enforcement. From 2002 to 2006 the Mine Safety Hazard Administration cut 100 safety officers (18 percent of the total), even though mining went up 9 percent during that period. Since then, congressional pressure brought over 250 more inspectors on board.[13]

Similarly, the number of wage-and-hour investigators at DOL dropped to 732 in 2007 from 945 in 2001, according to the Government Accountability Office.[14] This decline came during a time that labor journalist Greenhouse found shocking cases of immigrant workers being paid less than $3.35 an hour at a discount store in Brooklyn, others being barred from sitting down or even taking calls from a sick child, and grocery delivery men being classified as contractors, allowing their employers to pay effective wages of $2.43 an hour.

A new emphasis on worker safety, family leave and family-friendly policies, and working with labor when retrenchment is necessary to save jobs are the starting points. A first essential step would be the president's signature on the Employee Free Choice Act, which would level the playing field between unions and companies when workers decide to organize. Other proposed reforms related to the status of workers and their families are detailed in the economic mobility overview chapter by Angela Glover Blackwell and Peter Edelman, the Department of Labor chapter by Ed Montgomery.

Likewise, labor rights abroad have languished in the absence of leadership in the United States. The new president should prioritize the "decent work" agenda proposed by the International Labor Organization and supported by the Center for American Progress. Such core labor standards are crucial to ensure that U.S. workers and their counterparts abroad are not facing a race to the bottom in which unfair and shameful labor practices—including slave and coercive labor practices, abusive child labor, and violence against labor leaders—are used to achieve lower and more competitive prices. As Thea Lee, policy director and chief international economist at the AFL-CIO, noted, investigations into labor abuses in countries such as China are not aimed at stopping these nations' "right to compete in the global economy on the basis of low wages," but rather at the "incremental cost advantage that comes from the brutal and undemocratic repression of workers' human rights."[15]

Likewise, as seen in the U.S.-Cambodia textile agreement, labor standards should be part of a positive incentive structure that trades carrots such as U.S. market access for enforceable labor standards. There may be few places where the new president could so quickly unify progressives and gain quick legislative success on promoting, as President Bill Clinton used to say, "globalization with a human face" than a strong agenda to invest more resources in fighting abusive sweat shops and child labor and helping emerging economies build better safety nets and processes for enforcing labor rights. This can be done through increased funding for the international work of the Department of Labor and more resources, enforcement teeth, and monitoring capacity for the ILO. This commitment to focus on a decent work agenda should be adopted within the National Economic Council and National Security Council and in the policy considerations of the World Bank and International Monetary Fund. For a further description of policies in this area, see the chapter on the Office of the U.S. Trade Representative by Ira Shapiro and Richard Samans.

Strengthening Opportunities for Upward Mobility

It is not sufficient for progressives to promote merely greater economic security for working Americans. We should never underestimate the strength of Americans' desire for a fair chance to get ahead through their own efforts.[16] The new administration should refocus on policies that create opportunities for Americans to gain more access to and succeed at higher education, and to save so they can create their own wealth and nest egg for retirement or to pass on to their children.

Rising income inequality in our economy today is complemented by rising wealth inequality. Economist Edward Wolff has found that, excluding homes, 92.5 percent of our nation's wealth is held by the top 20 percent of individuals, while only 1.1 percent is held by the bottom 40 percent. The problem is worst for minorities—more than half of African Americans (54 percent) and Hispanics (55 percent) have less than $10,000 in savings and investments, according to the Employee Benefits Research Institute.

U.S. tax policy actually encourages this disparity. Out of the more than $200 billion in tax incentives offered each year for savings, only about 5 percent goes to the bottom 50 percent of Americans. The wealthiest Americans are triple winners, benefiting from pre-tax contributions to 401(k)-type pension savings plans with generous matching incentives, a menu of additional tax-preferred savings vehicles, and (because they are in the top 35 percent bracket) a 35-cent tax incentive on every dollar saved. Lower-income Americans most often have no pension, and if they do save a dollar, they get a mere 10 percent deduction.

This upside-down system is a disgrace from both equity and growth perspectives. Unlike savings incentives for working families, incentives for upper-income families cause a shift of existing savings, not an actual increase in new private savings. To spread wealth creation and savings, we must start by righting our "upside down" system of tax-preferred savings.

Other than the Universal Savings Accounts or USA Accounts program, which President Clinton proposed in 1999 but was never enacted, there have been few major progressive savings initiatives. The recent movement toward automatic savings deductions, in which workers opt out as opposed to opting in to employee-based savings plans, is a crucial reform, but it does not address the upside-down nature of our tax system. A Universal 401(k) savings plan would offer all Americans the opportunity to contribute to a new tax-deferred retirement account. This savings plan would provide middle-class and lower-income workers with matching contributions on initial retirement savings of up to $2,000 per year, deducted from their paychecks, in the form of refundable tax credits deposited directly into their Universal 401(k)s.

This plan would also provide for a refundable "flat savings tax credit" of 30 percent for all savings done by those in the lower- and moderate-income brackets. Other new progressive savings proposals in the policy arena include those by Rep. Rahm Emanuel (D-IL) and Professor Teresa Ghilarducci of Notre Dame. Rep. Emanuel's plan would establish voluntary personal savings accounts and strengthen the tax credit for families to save. Ghilarducci proposes a Guaranteed

Retirement Account system that would eliminate the current income tax and 401(k) tax preferences in favor of a government-subsidized annuity system that would guarantee employees at least a 3 percent real rate of return.

Proposals like the Universal 401(k) promote several critical progressive economic goals, including increasing our national savings rate, reducing wealth inequality, and spreading opportunities for wealth creation and a national culture for savings, while ensuring that on top of a strong guaranteed benefit for Social Security, tens of millions of Americans have a pension that will help ensure a more dignified and secure retirement.

Investing in and Completing a Higher Education
While there is understandable angst at the fact that a higher education no longer provides foolproof protection against downward wage pressures and job displacement from global labor competition, we cannot forget that a higher education is still the best ticket to sustained upward mobility. A higher education has never been less of a sure thing and yet never been more important. And with declining labor growth in the future, the U.S. economy cannot rely as it did in the past on a growing labor force to supply a growing pool of college-educated workers.

We have no choice but to increase the pool of Americans who not only enter college but also complete it. Low completion rates are systemic but are even more prevalent among minority and low-income students. According to the Pew Hispanic Center, white youth beginning at community colleges are nearly twice as likely as comparable Hispanic youth to finish a bachelor's degree, and among the best-prepared white and Latino college students at nonselective colleges and universities, 81 percent of whites complete a bachelor's degree and 57 percent of Latinos do so.[17]

The new administration needs to significantly increase college education financing for the broad middle class, but also to ensure that young African Americans, Hispanics, and Native Americans not only enter college but also complete it. The new president should seek to increase the college tax credit in three ways: by increasing its $1,650 maximum value, by extending it for four years, and by making it refundable. This recommendation has been made in recent presidential campaigns and is also supported by Louis Soares and Chris Mazzeo in the recent CAP report, "College-Ready Students, Student-Ready Colleges."

The new administration should also reform the lifelong learning tax credit by establishing a "Flexible Education Account," which would provide a pool of tax credits for each person per decade so that Americans in the workforce would have an opportunity to get considerable help for concentrated periods of retraining or retooling their skills as opposed to a small tax credit each and every year. While the current lifelong learning tax credit—20 percent of the first $10,000 of annual tuition—never allows anyone to get more than $2,000 of assistance in a given year, a $15,000 per decade Flexible Education Account would allow a worker to use up to $7,500 in each of the two years where he or she needed major training or educational assistance to make a critical job or career transition.

Finally, the new administration should create a College Completion Bonus Fund. This bonus fund should provide assistance to schools that are successful in increasing the *number* of young people that enroll and complete colleges as opposed to the *percentage* of those completing school. This design feature is crucial: if awards are based on the percentage of those completing, it might create an incentive for schools to take less risks on admitting more students from disadvantaged backgrounds. The goal of such a program should be to reward those who are willing to reach out to such young people and fund innovative pre-college and during-college programs to help such young people stay in college and succeed.

Spread Entrepreneurship
Part of our global competitive advantage is our ethic of entrepreneurship and risk taking. Prosperity-spreading opportunities for entrepreneurship are vital to create more jobs in the United States, to create new green technologies, and to ensure more entrepreneurial opportunities among minorities and women. The Center for Women's Business Research found that in 2006 only 29.7 percent of businesses (7.7 million) were majority-owned by women, even as women made up a full 46 percent of the labor force. And the Kauffman Foundation reports that despite making up approximately 13 percent each of the total population, African Americans and Hispanics respectively own only 4 percent and 6 percent of U.S. businesses.

One policy the new administration should consider restoring and expanding is the New Markets Venture Capital program started under President Clinton to ensure greater equity opportunities for entrepreneurs investing in our urban and rural communities. This initiative was designed to help create venture capital for those willing to invest in companies in at-risk communities, helping those companies to raise equity capital and to get the technical and start-up help they need in hiring the right people and creating a viable business plan. Though six NMVC companies were approved in 2003, President Bush subsequently eliminated the program, despite the fact that the existing NMVC companies have made significant investments in their at-risk communities.

Equal Opportunity, Not the Accident of Birth

One uniting principle of our founders was the notion that United States would be a nation without a perpetual elite or underclass. John Adams wrote that "no expense would be thought extravagant" when it came to educating poor children, and Thomas Jefferson supported a constitutional amendment guaranteeing free public education and calling for inheritance laws to "prevent the accumulation and perpetuation of wealth, in select families." We as a nation still cling to the ideal of America as a land where everyone can rise to the best of their abilities, but we are increasingly becoming a country where the accident of birth for the poorest children stacks the odds overwhelmingly against them while the perpetuation of wealth was strengthened by the Bush administration's insistence on gutting the estate tax even for the wealthiest estates.

A progressive administration must address the persistence of youth poverty, which stands at 34 percent for African-American children. A concern for economic mobility should compel a more expansive preschool effort, from birth to 5 years old, in universal pre-K programs. Research compiled by Arthur Rolnick and Rob Grunewald for the Federal Reserve Bank of Minneapolis and Rob Dugger for the Committee on Economic Development shows that the cognitive skills needed to succeed in the global economy are significantly developed during the first years of life, and that the cost of investing in Head Start for a child is returned 14 times over that child's lifetime.[18]

That is why the new administration needs to expand programs like Head Start and Early Head Start and ensure we develop a truly comprehensive education and child care initiative that offers all children from birth to age 5 from modest and low-income families access to quality infant, toddler, and preschool programs. Launching such an effort might cost $20 billion annually, but that is only 50 percent of what it would cost to repeal the estate tax for the wealthiest estates, further making the accident of birth more determinative in American life on both the poor and privileged side.

Reaching for College Early

Education reform cannot be just about small twists in testing metrics and standards based on those tests. Instead, the new president needs to push his new secretary of education to support the kind of in-school reform and afterschool opportunities that instill in students high expectations and a sense of belonging beyond performance on standardized tests. How often have we seen that it is the exceptionally motivational principal or teacher or afterschool theater or chess club that turns a young person's life around? Detailed proposals to bring public and private funding together at the federal, state, and local levels to expand these types of proven educational programs can be found in Michele Jolin's Office of Social Entrepreneurship chapter and Cynthia Brown's education overview chapter.

While high school reform efforts are important, an effective effort to ensure that more disadvantaged youth, including youths from African-American, Hispanic, and Native-American backgrounds, go to college requires early intervention through mentoring, enrichment, and college preparation classes beginning in elementary school and continuing through to college. As one education expert aptly put it, children "begin to drop out of college in grade school."[19]

Early intervention programs such as GEAR UP are the place to start. GEAR UP is an innovative program started in the late 1990s that reaches out to disadvantaged children at young ages and stays engaged with them through high school. Research by Steven Zwerling of the Ford Foundation validates the success of programs such as GEAR UP at increasing the pool of college-ready young people from disadvantaged backgrounds.

The federal government could lead universities and the private sector in greatly expanding GEAR UP and similar programs such as College Summit, Project GRAD, and the Harlem Children's Zone, and begin to create a national ethic of our nation's finest universities helping to increase the pool of well-qualified young people from disadvantaged communities in their own backyards.

Universal Education

No child's life should be determined by the accident of birth. Many Americans believe this bedrock applies to children born anywhere. Seventy-two million young children are out of primary school and another 226 million are out of secondary school worldwide. The leaders of the world are denying these children—particularly the girls who are out of school in higher numbers—a chance to grow, learn, and create healthier families, stronger economies, and more democratic nations.

These progressive growth values are furthered by universal quality education, especially for girls, in poor nations. Passage of the bipartisan Education for All Act of 2007 would go a long way toward positioning the United States as a leader in making that vision a reality by 2016. The act would empower the United States to build off the existing education fast track initiative to help lead a major global education fund, raising annual funding to $3 billion by 2012 to empower poor nations with strong plans to offer universal quality education and ensure special interventions for girls, children with disabilities, those impacted by abusive child labor, or those impacted by HIV/AIDS as well as the tens of millions losing their futures due to conflict or humanitarian emergencies.

Overview

A Progressive Agenda for Competitiveness and Trade

LAURA D'ANDREA TYSON

*Over the past 50 years, trade and economic integration with the rest of the world gener-
ated substantial economic and foreign policy benefits for the United States, yet not all
Americans shared in the economic benefits. Now, with the rise of emerging market competitors and the outsourcing or offshoring of production, rising imports are causing job
losses and wage declines, resulting in increasing insecurity for American workers at all
but the highest skill levels. The structural and technological forces making the world
economy more competitive and interdependent cannot be reversed, but the federal government can and must do much more to help U.S. workers compete and prosper in the global
economy. The new president must work with Congress to enact progressive policies that
include sustained investments in education, innovation, infrastructure, energy efficiency, and new energy technologies to strengthen the attractiveness of the United States
as a production location and to create and retain good jobs for American workers.*

*The new president must cooperate with Congress to enact a progressive competitive-
ness agenda with three key components. First, the new administration needs to invest in
education, research and development, infrastructure, and energy efficiency and new energy technologies to strengthen the attractiveness of the United States as a production location and to create and retain good jobs for American workers. Second, we need policies
to ensure a more equitable sharing of the costs and benefits of globalization through a
new social contract that includes increases in the minimum wage linked to increases in
inflation, an expansion of unemployment insurance, and healthcare reforms that break
the link between employment and access to health care. Third, the new administration's
trade policies must be part of an international economic strategy to promote the broad-
based expansion of living standards at home and abroad through enforceable labor and
environmental standards in the United States and among our trading partners—standards that foster a global agreement on climate change.*

During the past 30 years, American workers have become considerably
more productive, yet wages and family incomes have not risen at a commensurate rate. On average, the growth of real compensation per worker kept
pace with the growth of worker productivity, slowing when productivity
slowed between the early 1970s and the mid-1990s, and accelerating when productivity growth improved between 1996 and 2006. But as a result of increas-

ing inequality in the distribution of wages and family incomes, those averages are deceiving. The real hourly wages of blue-collar and non-supervisory workers—more than 80 percent of the American workforce—remained virtually unchanged despite significant gains in output per hour. Real hourly wages for male workers are actually lower now than they were three decades ago. Most of the productivity gains accrued to the top 10 percent of wage earners, with the fastest growth concentrated in the top 1 percent.

Family income trends show similar uneven results. Median family income grew 11 percent between 1995 and 2000, tracking productivity growth of 13 percent. During this period, every income group enjoyed strong income growth, with the most rapid gains enjoyed by the bottom 20 percent of families. But this period of "growing together" under progressive presidential leadership was short-lived. Between 2001 and 2006, real median family income actually declined despite strong productivity gains.

Now after decades of disappointing growth in wages and family incomes, a growing number of American workers find themselves competing for jobs with cheaper foreign workers and bearing the costs in the form of job losses, stagnating or falling real wages, and mounting financial insecurity. Reacting to these trends, a majority of Americans now believe that globalization is not working for them—despite the importance of global trade and investment to the U.S. economy.

The share of trade in the U.S. economy has tripled over the past 40 years, reaching 28.5 percent of U.S. gross domestic product by 2007. The United States is the largest importer and the third-largest exporter of goods and services. About 20 percent of all U.S. manufacturing jobs depend on exports, and jobs that depend on trade generally pay 13 percent to 18 percent more than the national average. The United States is the largest recipient of cross-border capital flows. Foreign lending reduced U.S. interest rates by as much as a percentage point between 2002 and 2007. The United States is also the largest source and recipient of foreign direct investment—outbound FDI amounts to 18 percent of GDP while inbound FDI amounts to 13 percent. U.S. multinational companies employ about 30 million people, about 70 percent of whom work in U.S. locations, while foreign multinational companies employ about 5 million workers in the United States.

Both economic logic and numerous empirical studies confirm the United States benefits from its strong economic ties with the rest of the world. The well-known economic benefits from trade include: lower prices and greater product variety; greater efficiency and lower costs of production; the dissemination of technological know-how; and higher productivity growth triggered by greater competition.[1] Growing interdependence also generates benefits for foreign and national security policy. The economic interdependence of nations in a rules-based international trading system is a powerful foundation for stability. No large economic and trading partners have gone to war with one another for more than half a century. Increased openness to trade also remains an essential ingredient in all cases of successful economic development.

Yet there are winners and losers in the United States from rising globalization and trade. Exports create high-wage jobs and enrich communities for some Americans, but imports destroy jobs and impoverish communities for others. Workers who lose their jobs to imports often suffer prolonged periods of joblessness, lose access to health care, and earn substantially lower wages when they find new jobs. That the benefits and costs of trade are not evenly distributed is well recognized in economic theory. But theory also predicts that the aggregate gains from trade outweigh the so-called dislocation costs of lost jobs and wages. Evidence confirms this prediction—at least so far.[2] Given large net gains from trade, the United States could easily afford to compensate workers and communities for their trade-related job and wage losses. But the U.S. safety net is full of holes, and compensation to offset such losses is marginal.

Today, there are reasons to fear these losses are getting larger and affecting a larger share of American workers. Often with the help of investment by U.S. companies, emerging market economies are developing export capabilities in goods and services that traditionally created high-wage jobs for American workers. In addition, many high-wage, information technology-enabled services jobs are more easily outsourced or offshored.

As a result of technological advances, any service that requires little face-to-face interaction and is IT-intensive with IT-transmittable output can be sent to lower-wage locations. Recent studies by economists Alan Blinder and Lori Kletzer suggest that as many as 40 million U.S. service jobs may be at risk. Most of these jobs pay substantially more than jobs in non-tradeable services such as retail, restaurant, and educational services.[3]

As a result, a large number of U.S. workers, irrespective of their experience, skill, or educational levels, are anxious about the security of their jobs and the level of their wages. Over the past 50 years, American workers enjoyed a productivity advantage over workers in low-wage countries. Now, the knowledge, skills, and technology that drive superior productivity are rapidly spreading around the world, helped by U.S. companies seeking to combine their capital and expertise with cheaper labor. As China and other emerging-market economies have opened their markets, the supply of foreign labor available to U.S. companies has soared. According to the International Monetary Fund, the available global labor supply has risen fourfold since 1980.[4] Most of the new workers are unskilled, with secondary-school educations or lower, but even the global supply of college graduates has increased by 50 percent.

The results are easy to predict: downward pressure on the wages of workers in the United States and other advanced industrial countries, and an increase in the returns to capital and to individuals with specialized skills that are in limited global supply. U.S. companies and their shareholders may earn higher returns by buying inputs from low-wage foreign sources or simply moving their production there, but many U.S. workers are now competing for jobs with cheaper foreign workers and facing lower wages, lost jobs, and greater job insecurity.

Evidence suggests their anxiety is warranted. Harvard University economist Robert Lawrence finds both that imports are now competing with domestic production in industries paying higher-than-average wages, and that jobs lost to trade have similar skill levels to jobs in the rest of the economy.[5] This means trade is now causing displacement and dislocation for workers at all but the highest skill levels. Lawrence's research, however, indicates that trade explains at most about 20 percent of wage inequality—even though he also concludes that trade may be exerting downward pressure on the wages of most American workers. Those most threatened today are middle-income workers.

Until the late 1980s, wage inequality was concentrated between the bottom and the middle of the wage distribution, but beginning in the mid-1990s, rising wage inequality became increasingly evident between middle-income workers and top earners.[6] The evidence suggests that rising imports of goods and services and offshoring by U.S. companies, are contributing to the polarization of employment into high- and low-wage jobs at the expense of middle-wage jobs.[7]

Recommendations: A Progressive Competitiveness Agenda

The United States continues to rank as one of the most attractive places in the world to do business. But there is stiff competition from other countries vying to attract high-value-added production and high-wage jobs. The new president and his administration must respond with policies to strengthen U.S. competitiveness by increasing investment in four areas: the education and skills of the workforce; research and development; physical infrastructure; and energy efficiency and clean-energy technologies.

Human Capital

In a world of footloose capital and technology, nations compete for high-wage jobs through the education and skills of their workers. The United States is falling behind in fostering the necessary talent. After being the world's leading nation in terms of education attainment for most of the 20th century, the

United States now ranks in the middle of the Organization for Economic Co-operation and Development countries, and now sits at the top of the list for dropout rates among high school students.[8]

The economic returns of completing high school and occupational training remain substantial, and the economic benefits to college and post-college schooling are at historically high levels. Sadly, millions of Americans are not getting the education they need to take advantage of new high-wage opportunities enabled by new technologies. The education chapters by Cindy Brown and Judith Winston offer specific recommendations to address these weaknesses in the U.S. educational system. Tom Kalil's chapter on science and innovation identifies complementary policy initiatives to bolster education in math, science, and engineering.

Immigration policy also affects the nation's talent supply and its attractiveness as a production site. An aging America faces shortages of workers across all occupation levels. Unfortunately, immigration policy in the United States is increasingly restrictive compared with the country's talent requirements. Immigration surged over the past decade, boosting the growth of the labor force by about half a percentage point a year, but highly skilled workers made up only about one-third of all immigrants.[9] The annual quota on the H1B visa program used by companies to hire highly educated foreigners to work in the United States is set so low that it is rapidly exhausted each year. Unable to get the talent they need, American companies have relocated some of their production to countries such as Canada, which have eased immigration policies to attract educated foreigners.

The new president must work with Congress to expand the number of permanent visas available for employment-based immigration; create a new temporary-worker visa program with adequate worker and labor-market protections; remove restrictions on the movement of foreign workers from one firm to another; and give the Department of Labor adequate administrative resources to enforce the new requirements. The immigration overview chapter of this book by Cecilia Munoz describes these policies in greater detail and underscores that these changes must take place in the context of broader immigration reform.

Innovation

Innovation drives global economic competitiveness—a fact not lost among policymakers in emerging market economies such as China and India, where governments are adopting policies to pursue innovation-based models of development.[10] On many dimensions the United States still holds the lead as the most attractive location for innovation-based businesses. Our nation is home to many of the world's best universities and research facilities, which will continue to attract talent provided immigration policies do not stand in the way. The strong links between U.S. universities and businesses encourage the rapid translation of scientific knowledge into commercial technologies. And access to university laboratories and graduate students is a big attraction for the venture capital industry.

But the United States now ranks only seventh among the OECD countries in the share of GDP devoted to research and development. Since the late 1960s, federal government spending on research and development has declined as a share of both total R&D spending and GDP. And a large fraction of government R&D spending—nearly 58 percent in 2007—goes to the Department of Defense.[11] Federal spending to support basic research has declined in real terms since 2000, and now accounts for only about 21 percent of its total R&D support. The federal government provides about 60 percent of the funding for such research, while the private sector devotes only about 5 percent of its R&D spending to this purpose.

Government funding for basic research created the knowledge behind America's leadership in many industries, including the Internet, biotechnology, and nanotechnology. Sustained increases in federal funding for basic research on broad national challenges, such as improving the quality of health care and developing clean-energy technologies, should be central components of a progressive competitiveness agenda. Strong tax incentives to encourage R&D spending by the private sector should also be part of the package. Tom Kalil's science and innovation overview chapter details the steps the new administration must take to ensure continued U.S. science and technology pre-eminence.[12]

America's physical infrastructure is outdated, worn, and in some cases failing. Its weaknesses were exposed by the collapse of New Orleans' levees during Hurricane Katrina in 2005 and the Minneapolis bridge disaster in 2007.[13] In a recent assessment, the American Society of Civil Engineers gave the United States a failing grade on its transportation infrastructure.[14] Government spending on physical infrastructure as a share of GDP declined markedly between the late 1950s and the mid-1980s, and since then has remained relatively constant at slightly more than 1 percent—compared to about 9 percent in China.[15] Current investment levels are woefully inadequate to address the infrastructure needs of the economy. A May 2008 study by the Congressional Budget Office identifies about $185 billion a year of real government spending (measured in 2004 prices) on transportation infrastructure justifiable on economic grounds. This is nearly 75 percent higher than current spending levels.[16]

A challenge for the new president and his administration is how to finance increased spending on infrastructure given other priorities, such as health care reform and bleak long-term federal budget projections. The good news is that both the Senate and the House of Representatives already have before them legislation to create a new independent federal entity to evaluate and help finance infrastructure projects of national significance. Both the Senate and House bills are designed to evaluate projects on their economic merits and to avoid the earmarking process.

The new president should forge a congressional agreement on this new infrastructure agency. This agency could take advantage of an estimated $400 billion in global funds available for equity investment in infrastructure projects, and several trillions of dollars in long-term investment funds available for debt investment in such projects. Europe is already using the European Investment Bank and unique forms of pooled securities to draw on global capital to finance infrastructure projects through private-public partnerships. The United States could quickly win a significant share of these resources.[17]

Clean Energy and Green-Collar Jobs

The United States must become less dependent on carbon-based fuels for economic, national security, and environmental reasons. Significant increases in the price of oil played a major role in 9 out of 10 recessions since World War II. Today, dependence on oil imports undermines our national security and compromises our foreign policy.

At present, we are forced to rely on several unstable and hostile states to satisfy our oil needs. Our spending on oil helps prop up unfriendly or authoritarian governments and provides a funding stream for terrorist activities. Finally, U.S. consumption of oil and other carbon-based fuels is a major contributor to global warming. The United States is the number one per capita contributor to global greenhouse gas emissions. It is responsible for 25 percent of annual global emissions and about 30 percent of cumulative emissions from 1850 through 2000.[18]

To reduce the nation's dependence on oil imports, the new president should work with Congress to implement a multi-part strategy to enhance energy efficiency and to promote the development and diffusion of clean-energy technologies. A price on carbon emissions must be established, which in turn will provide a powerful broad-based incentive for consumers, businesses, and investors to change their behavior, and will provide the fiscal resources to help our transition to a low-carbon economy.

According to the McKinsey Global Institute, profitable investments to increase energy efficiency could reduce projected energy demand by at least half between now and 2020.[19] Such investments include a wide variety of programs, such as retrofitting existing buildings for better insulation, applying higher energy-efficiency standards for appliances, and building more wind power systems. The government must foster energy efficiency and innovation at every stage, from basic research to demonstration and rapid deployment of new technologies.[20] Policies to accelerate the development of clean energy alternatives will help create green-collar jobs and build U.S. competitiveness in what promises to be one of the fastest-growing areas of the world economy over the next half-century.

But the new president and his administration will have to act fast. Many other countries, from Germany to China, are supporting the development of their own clean energy companies, often using U.S. technology to do so. Detailed recommendations to ensure the United States leads the green energy technology revolution are presented in the overview on creating a low-carbon economy.

Sharing Costs and Benefits of Globalization

A new social contract in the United States must be an essential component of a progressive competitiveness agenda. U.S. workers who lose their jobs, regardless of cause, face long spells of unemployment with lost income, significant reductions in wages, and the loss of health insurance and other benefits. Manufacturing workers who lose their jobs suffer an average of 14 weeks of unemployment and a 20 percent loss in wages in their new jobs, while service workers suffer an average of about 11 weeks of unemployment and a 13 percent reduction in wages.

Although the United States has the highest rate of job churn among the OECD countries, it spends only 0.5 percent of GDP on policies to assist dislocated workers—the lowest share among the OECD countries. The federal unemployment insurance program contains so many restrictions that only about 37 percent of jobless workers qualify for benefits. Workers seeking part-time employment, workers who experience long-term unemployment, and workers re-entering the labor force are not eligible. The Department of Labor's trade adjustment assistance program—designed specifically to help workers dislocated by trade—is so restrictive that it denies more than 40 percent of requests and serves fewer than 75,000 workers per year.

American workers deserve a much stronger safety net to bolster their economic security. The policies that make up this safety net should be universal, covering all displaced workers regardless of the industry in which they are employed and regardless of the cause of their job loss. New safety net policies should reflect the multifaceted needs of displaced workers for income support, health care, and retraining assistance.

The new administration should also undertake a thorough assessment of wage-loss insurance, a new program introduced on a very small scale in the 2002 trade bill. The idea behind wage-loss insurance is simple. If a worker loses a job and is forced to take a new job at a lower wage, he or she is eligible for insurance payments that cover a significant part of the shortfall between the new wage and the old one for a specific period of time. Concerns that wage-loss insurance may depress the wages of those who are already employed, and may favor middle-income workers over low-income wage earners, will need to be addressed.

Gene Sperling's chapter on progressive growth describes the key features of the social contract America needs, including: a higher minimum wage linked to inflation; an expansion of the earned income tax credit; tax policies that reduce the burden on middle-class families and that support education, training, and savings; universal health care; policies to bolster union membership and influence; and policies that protect workers from the costs of job and wage loss while providing incentives for them to find new employment opportunities.

Trade and International Economic Policies
The new president will have to make the case for trade and international economic engagement at a time when the congressional appetite for trade liberalization measures is limited, when protectionist pressures are strong, and when any action viewed as a significant retreat from America's commitment to trade will further undermine America's standing in the world.

Chapters in this book on trade policy by Ira Shapiro and Richard Samans, Gene Sperling's progressive growth overview, and Gayle Smith's foreign aid overview describe an ambitious agenda for an effective trade policy under these multiple constraints. This section highlights some of their recommendations and adds a few others that should be part of a progressive competitiveness agenda.

The trade policies pursued by the new president should support an international economic strategy designed to foster economic development and institution-building to create good jobs, provide social safety nets, and protect workers' rights in developed, emerging, and developing economies. The basic goals should be to increase the gains from globalization and to translate them into the broadest possible improvements in living standards for the United States and its trading partners.[21]

Consistent with this approach, future trade agreements, whether bilateral, regional, or multilateral, should include enforceable labor and environmental standards. As a result of progressive congressional leadership, both the United States-Peru Free Trade Agreement (ratified at the end of 2007) and the United States-Jordan Free Trade agreement (2001) have strong labor and environmental provisions and enforcement mechanisms. Both the Peru and Jordan agreements demonstrate that it is possible to embody reasonable safeguards for labor and the environment in trade agreements, policies which are supported by majorities in nations around the world.

The 44th president must also devote more attention and resources to enforcing existing trade agreements. Billions of dollars of export revenues, along with well-paying jobs for American workers, are lost each year as a result of inadequate enforcement of our trading partners' obligations. A strong presidential commitment to enforcement is essential to warn other nations that failure to implement commitments will not be tolerated.

To this end, the new president should issue an early executive order directing all government agencies to pursue all claims of trade-agreement violations by a specific time so that prompt responses can be pursued either through negotiation or through the World Trade Organization's dispute resolution process. The new president should also direct USTR to assess the effects of existing trade agreements before contemplating new ones. During this review period, he should call a temporary moratorium on the negotiation of new bilateral trade agreements, which were an ill-advised component of the Bush trade strategy.

In lieu of new bilateral initiatives, the 44th president should reiterate America's longstanding preference for multilateral or regional trade agreements, and then focus on those that promise sizeable economic benefits. At the same time, the president and Congress should explore ways to address the outstanding economic and labor rights issues in the bilateral trade agreements already negotiated by the Bush administration. Ratification of these agreements, which have been negotiated with countries friendly to the United States in important regions, would serve U.S. foreign policy interests and would send a strong signal of America's continuing commitment to trade liberalization for economic development.

The new president should also work to bring the Doha Round of WTO negotiations to completion. If the United States turns its back on Doha, it will be portrayed around the world as a historic retreat from U.S. leadership, and will discourage dialogue and cooperation with other nations on a wide range of global economic issues including climate change and development assistance. At the same time, the president must recognize that concluding an agreement with major breakthroughs on agriculture, manufactured goods, and other highly sensitive issues will remain a major challenge.

Finally, the new president should initiate discussions with both Mexico and Canada to review how NAFTA could be adjusted to work better for all three nations. The world economy has changed dramatically since NAFTA was negotiated. The inclusion of labor and environmental issues in side-agreements was state-of-the-art at that time, but this is no longer the case. The U.S.-Jordan Free Trade Agreement and U.S.-Peru Free Trade Agreement go much further and provide models for modernization of NAFTA's labor and environmental provisions.

Trade and Currency Issues with China

The economic relationship with China will require early attention by the next president. U.S.-China economic relations are broad, deep, and growing rapidly. In 2007, China became America's second-largest goods trading partner (after Canada), the largest source of goods imports, and the third-largest source of goods exports.[22] China is now America's fastest growing export market. But the United States runs a large bilateral trade deficit with China that accounted for 33 percent of the total U.S. trade deficit in 2007. In addition to concerns about the trade deficit, U.S. policymakers and citizens share many other concerns about trade with China, including labor and human rights, the environment, health and safety standards, intellectual property protection, and currency manipulation.

There are numerous areas that should be the focus of trade dialogue with China. To stem the theft of intellectual property, China must increase its penalties, while the United States must commit more resources to customs controls. If intellectual property theft continues, U.S. anti-dumping laws should be expanded to cover imports that enjoy an unfair cost advantage from embedded stolen IP. Many Chinese industrial policies, such as forced technology transfer as a condition for doing business in China, are illegal under China's WTO commitments, and should be topics of bilateral trade negotiations and possible WTO actions. China must also do more to ensure the safety of its exports while the United States strengthens its own enforcement mechanisms to ensure that imports from China and elsewhere are meeting U.S. standards.

The new president will also have to cooperate with Congress on how best to respond to China's intervention in currency markets. Some influential members of Congress have voiced their support for tariffs on Chinese imports to offset price advantages resulting from the undervaluation of the yuan. But the imposition of such penalties could trigger trade retaliation and a potentially disruptive large sale of U.S. financial assets by the Chinese government. China's intervention to control the yuan's value provides an implicit subsidy to Chinese exports, but it also contributes to lower U.S. import prices and lower U.S. interest rates. A significant yuan appreciation would reduce these twin benefits without having much effect on the U.S. trade deficit if production moves from China to other low-cost foreign locations such as Vietnam, Indonesia, and Mexico.

Finally, experts disagree about the extent to which the Chinese currency is undervalued relative to the dollar. Estimates range from parity to 50 percent. Since 2005, the yuan has appreciated 17.5 percent against the dollar, and the rate of appreciation has accelerated to 6.5 percent in 2007 from 3.3 percent in 2006. During the first half of 2008, the yuan appreciated 6.0 percent against the dollar.[23]

The new president should urge Congress to rely on multilateral channels to encourage China to make the yuan a fully convertible currency. Under IMF rules, China has the right to peg its currency but it does not have the right to intervene on a massive scale to maintain an undervalued currency to boost its international competitive position. With U.S. support, the IMF has agreed to take on a larger role to reduce global economic imbalances and to discourage China and other countries from undervaluing their exchange rates and accumulating large foreign exchange reserves. The new administration should seek to enhance the IMF's capacity to achieve these objectives. Multilateral pressure, particularly from the IMF in relation to its surveillance function, will reinforce support for those within the Chinese leadership who favor more rapid yuan appreciation to offset inflationary pressures.

At the broadest level, the goal of U.S. economic policy toward China should be to encourage China to assume greater responsibility for the global economic system, consistent with its growing share of global economic activity. Effective systemic responses to global economic challenges, including poverty reduction, energy security, and climate change, require China's active participation and cooperation with the United States and Europe. China will have to be a participant in the creation of new international norms and institutional arrangements to address these challenges. This will require adjustments in the governance of multilateral institutions to reflect China's economic power.

Global Engagement on Climate Change
Climate change is the most complex and important collective action problem in human history, requiring concerted action among unequal participants. Soon after the new president is elected, the United States is scheduled to participate in the next global summit on climate change. The goal is agreement on a long-term global cap on greenhouse gas emissions, with a trajectory for achieving it over time and a burden-sharing arrangement that defines national responsibilities. The United States will have to accept a cap on its own greenhouse gas emissions and will have to adopt policies to realize this cap.

An effective solution to global climate change will also require the participation of developing countries, which will be responsible for 60 percent to 70 percent of carbon emissions by 2030. The United States along with the other developed countries should help defray the costs of emissions reductions in these countries through financial, technological, and capacity-building assistance, and through broadening the United Nations' Clean Development Mechanism, which allows polluting companies to purchase offsetting emission-reduction credits from qualified participants in the program.

As part of these efforts, the United States should explore the possibility of a joint R&D project with China to develop new carbon capture-and-storage technologies for coal-fired power plants. Breakthroughs in these areas would be a win-win outcome for both countries, which have the largest coal reserves in the world.

The next president should also champion new global rules based on the principles of nondiscrimination and national treatment to head off trade disputes emanating from differences in national policies on carbon emissions. If developed countries adopt binding caps before developing and emerging countries do, there is a danger that carbon-intensive production and jobs will migrate from countries with caps to those without. National efforts to encourage domestic production of clean energy alternatives through trade-distorting policies such as the local-content conditions recently enacted in China are also potential sources of trade conflicts. New multilateral trading rules are required to support rather than undermine the implementation of an effective, efficient, and equitable global agreement on climate change. Ultimately, a new Global Environmental Organization may be required to realize this objective.

Overview
Science, Technology, and Innovation Challenges

THOMAS KALIL

The outgoing Bush administration's hostility toward science has cost our nation dearly. Federal investment in research and development underpins our economy, our national defense, our safety and health, and our future workforce. To ensure that the United States remains an "innovation superpower" in the 21st century, the 44th president must increase funding for research and development, improve the math and science skills of America's workforce, reform our nation's immigration laws to attract the "best and brightest," strengthen incentives for private sector investment in research and development, and expand the role that science, technology, and innovation can play in meeting some of our most important national and global challenges. These goals can be achieved, but only if the new president makes them a top administration priority. The new administration must restore America's preeminence in science, technology, and innovation.

Science, technology, and innovation have long provided the foundation for America's prosperity. Naturally inquisitive and inventive, the American people have developed new products and technologies that have fueled our economy and improved our quality of life. Consider how different our lives would be without electricity, air travel, antibiotics, computers, and the Internet. That's why science, technology, and innovation policy must be a central component of U.S. national economic strategy

Innovation—the development of new products, services, and processes—drives economic growth, job creation, and productivity. Innovation is important not only for high-tech sectors such as advanced manufacturing, aerospace, clean energy, the life sciences, semiconductors, and the Internet. It is also essential for companies that are using technology to develop products more rapidly, harness the "collective IQ" of their customers and employees, and orchestrate sophisticated global supply chains.

Even small differences in productivity have a huge impact on America's long-term standard of living. Our average standard of living will double every 23 years if our productivity growth rate is 3 percent, and every 70 years if it is 1 percent. High productivity growth rates will make it much easier to honor our commitments to older Americans, expand access to health care for the uninsured, and increase our investments in infrastructure, education, and worker training.

Innovation is currently a source of competitive advantage for the United States in the global economy. We have world-class research universities, an entrepreneurial culture, flexible labor markets, and deep capital markets. Americans are twice as likely as adults in Europe and Japan to be "high expectation" entrepreneurs—that is, to start a business with the intention of growing it rapidly.

Innovation also plays an important role in meeting many of the most important goals we have as a nation. Innovation can help provide all Americans with longer and healthier lives, fight global warming, maintain a strong defense at home and abroad, expand access to high-quality education and training, and make government more open and efficient. And innovation is important in the civic sector as well as the private sector. A new generation of "social entrepreneurs" is changing the way we educate our children, lift people out of poverty, prevent crime, and build vibrant communities.

Finally, increasing our understanding of ourselves and the world around us are worthy goals themselves. We want to understand the ultimate fate of the

universe, the nature of matter, the origin of life, and how human consciousness emerges from 100 billion neurons and 100 trillion synapses. We want to
know why civilizations rise and fall, and how to foster thriving, multicultural
societies. So it's vital to support unfettered inquiry to address these and many
other questions.

Challenges for Innovation Policy

Although the responsibility for developing new products, processes, and services rests with the private sector, the federal government has a catalytic role in
promoting and encouraging innovation. Government support for R&D has led
to technologies and industries such as computers, the Internet, and biotechnology. As our economy becomes dominated by new ideas, this role becomes
more urgent.

Unfortunately, while science, technology, innovation, and a highly skilled
workforce are becoming more important to our future prosperity, U.S. federal
investment in R&D, particularly in key disciplines such as the physical sciences
and engineering, has actually been declining as a fraction of gross domestic
product. Agencies such as the Defense Advanced Research Projects Agency, or
DARPA, which have traditionally backed breakthrough technologies such as
the Internet, have shifted to funding projects with more immediate payoffs.

America continues to do a mediocre job of preparing our children for careers in science, technology, engineering, and mathematics, the so-called
STEM disciplines. Ideologically driven policies such as the Bush administration's restrictions on stem cell research have slowed our scientists from developing potential cures for diseases such as spinal cord injuries, multiple sclerosis,
or Alzheimer's. And U.S. immigration policies make it difficult for the "best and
brightest" from other countries who receive advanced degrees from our colleges and universities to stay here and contribute to our economy.

The challenges we face today are momentous. As the Hart/Rudman Commission on National Security concluded, "Second only to a weapon of mass destruction detonating in a U.S. city, we can think of nothing more dangerous
than a failure to manage properly science, technology, and education for the
common good over the next quarter of a century."[1]

Essential Principles
What are the principles that should underpin a science, technology, and innovation agenda? First of all, the United States will only be an innovation superpower if all Americans are both participants in and beneficiaries of the
innovation economy. We must not think of innovation as the province only of

the highly educated. Innovation-driven business models require large numbers of technically proficient, scientifically literate, knowledge workers at every level of the organization who can solve rapidly changing problems.

Similarly, the principle of innovation must be applied to the very challenge of improving economic opportunity for all our citizens. Online learning, for example, can help working adults gain the skills they need to compete for higher wage jobs. Universal design principles can make information and communications technologies accessible for people with disabilities, increasing their independence, employability, and standard of living.

The role of the government is to make investments in areas that the private sector will underinvest in relative to their social return, such as fundamental research and a skilled workforce, and to create a policy environment that will foster competition, innovation, and entrepreneurship. The private sector takes the lead on the commercialization and adoption of new technologies.

There are significant "market failures" associated with the innovation process, such as the positive externalities associated with research and development, and the negative externalities associated with the emission of greenhouse gases. However, government intervention can lead to "government failures," such as pork-barrel politics, rent-seeking by interest groups, and regulatory capture by the industries that agencies are supposed to police. Decision making, too, can be made on the basis of faulty or incomplete information, policies crafted where costs exceed benefits, and guidelines enacted that lack flexibility to adapt to changed circumstances and new evidence.[2]

When the government does intervene, careful thought needs to be given to the design of the intervention so that the "cure" is not worse than the "disease." Whenever possible, governments should seek to take advantage of market forces as opposed to relying on government programs or top-down regulation.

No one can predict the future evolution of technology—not even the participants in the marketplace. In the early 1990s, most of the major players in the media and telecommunications industry were convinced that "video on demand" would drive the development of the "information superhighway." Few predicted the importance of the Internet. For this reason, the government should set broad goals and invest in a portfolio of approaches to achieve them.

Case in point: the government should support research that has the greatest potential to reduce greenhouse gas emissions, as opposed to the Bush administration's decision to pick the "hydrogen car" as the solution to the energy and climate crisis. Decisions about which research directions are most promising should be made in close consultation with the scientific and technical community, and a competitive, merit-based process should be used to allocate funding for individual research projects.

There are a large number of public policies that affect America's general ability to innovate, such as those with respect to research funding, education and training, immigration, intellectual property, regulation, antitrust enforcement, taxes, regional economic development, and international trade. The ability of particular research-intensive sectors to compete is affected by spectrum policy (wireless industry), the Food and Drug Administration approval process (biotech, medical devices, pharmaceuticals), and export controls (computers, satellites). So it's imperative that the new administration embrace innovation as a central organizing principle for its economic strategy. Policymakers in many different agencies need to understand the impact that their decisions have on America's long-term competitiveness.

America's innovation policy needs to recognize that even the way we change is changing. The executive director of the University of California–Berkeley's Center for Open Innovation, Professor Henry Chesbrough, observes that many leading companies are pursuing "open innovation" strategies. Increasingly, they are working with external partners to commercialize their internal innovations and to identify external innovations that they can commercialize.[3] More than 40 percent of Procter and Gamble's products have a major component that has been sourced externally. And online innovation marketplaces such as InnoCentive allow customers to post complex problems, where more than 125,000 engineers, scientists, inventors, business people, and research organizations from 175 countries can compete to solve them.

Professor Eric Von Hippel, the head of the Innovation and Entrepreneurship Group at the MIT Sloan School of Management, concludes that innovation is becoming democratized as more users of products and services are able to innovate for themselves. Savvy companies are encouraging this development by creating "toolkits" that empower their customers and allow them to quickly and easily customize products and services.[4]

A related concept is what scholars such as Harvard Law School professor Yochai Benkler have called "commons-based peer production," which is the creative energies of large numbers of people who are using the Internet to create information, knowledge, and culture, often without financial incentives or traditional hierarchical organizations. Many observers have called attention to the important role that design, aesthetics, user experience, and opportunities for self-expression are playing in the marketplace as companies seek to differentiate their products and services and avoid "commodity hell."

What's more, the capacity to innovate is becoming increasingly globalized, with entrepreneurs creating teams of Bangalore software engineers, Russian mathematicians, and Taiwanese product designers. U.S. policy needs to take into account these and other changes in the nature of innovation.

Finally, the role of the federal government should be to serve as a catalyst. A good example of the "ripple effect" that federal policy can have on national priorities is the National Nanotechnology Initiative, unveiled by President Bill Clinton in January 2000. After the NNI was announced, major research universities, venture capitalists, entrepreneurs, states, and Fortune 500 companies all launched new efforts in nanotechnology research, education, and commercialization. Such initiatives should be designed to spark additional investments by industry, academia, states, foundations, and other stakeholders.

An Innovation Agenda

The innovation agenda described below would increase funding for research and development, improve the math and science skills of America's workforce, reform our nation's immigration laws to attract the "best and brightest," strengthen incentives for private sector investment in R&D, and expand the role that science, technology, and innovation can play in meeting some of our most important national and global challenges.

There is a compelling case for sustained increases in federal research funding, particularly for university-based research. Federal investment in many key disciplines has actually declined as a fraction of GDP. Currently, agencies can fund only a fraction of the high-quality proposals that they receive. Even if a research grant is awarded, it is often too small or too short for a researcher to make meaningful progress. Young scientists are discouraged from pursuing a career in research because they must wait until they are, on average, 41.7 years of age before they receive their first grant from the National Institutes of Health as an independent investigator.[5]

Over the next 10 years, the federal government should provide 7 percent to 10 percent annual increases in the budgets of the key science agencies, such as the National Science Foundation, the National Institutes of Health, the Department of Defense, the Department of Energy, and the National Institute of Standards and Technology. Although increases in the physical sciences and engineering were proposed in the Bush administration's American Competitiveness Initiative, and authorized in the America COMPETES legislation, almost none of these proposed increases are likely to be appropriated before the end of the 2008 congressional term.

Most of the proposed increases in research funding should augment the core disciplinary programs of science agencies that support investigator-initiated projects in biology, the physical sciences, engineering, the behavioral sciences, and the social sciences. Some of the increase in funding should be targeted to multidisciplinary initiatives that respond to national priorities and emerging opportunities. Again, the new president and Congress should set broad goals, and rely on the scientific and technical community (and other stakeholders) to identify the most promising research directions. Existing initiatives that should be supported include the multiagency efforts in information technology and nanotechnology R&D.

New efforts should be launched in areas such as clean energy technologies, which will accelerate the transition to a low-carbon economy, including nanotechnology-based solar cells as cheap as paint, or intelligent grids that support distributed energy resources. Similar efforts should target advances in learning technologies, such as games for middle school math and science that are as compelling as those from the video game industry, and technologies that address major challenges faced by developing countries, such as infectious diseases and a lack of safe drinking water.

New discoveries should also be explored in synthetic biology. Although still in its infancy, synthetic biology can be used to lower the cost of making the most effective antimalaria drug by a factor of 10, discover and destroy tumors, turn sugar into gasoline, and clean up toxic waste sites. Due to the shortcomings of today's science policies, the new administration should expand support for high-risk, high-return research, particularly at agencies such as DARPA, and fill the void left by the demise of research labs such as Bell Labs with new university-industry partnerships, such as the Nanoelectronics Research Initiative. These new research efforts should encourage multidisciplinary research and education.

The 44th president also needs to increase the capacity of the federal government to foster innovation in support of a broader set of national goals. The Environmental Protection Agency, for example, currently has a limited ability to encourage innovations that minimize pollution, instead focusing much of its energy on "end of pipe" regulations. Finally, agencies should make greater use of "inducement prizes" such as the X Prize for stimulating technological innovation.

Workforce with World-Class Skills

America is not on track to create the workforce that we need to remain globally competitive in the 21st century, particularly in science, technology, engineering, and mathematics, the so-called STEM disciplines. Improved math and science literacy is becoming increasingly important in a wide range of jobs—not just for chip designers and computer programmers.

This problem exists along the entire education "pipeline." Sixty-eight percent of U.S. 8th graders receive instruction from a mathematics teacher who does not hold a degree or certification in mathematics. American 15-year-olds rank 24th out of 40 participating countries in an international test that meas-

ures the ability of students to apply mathematical concepts to real-world problems. In the United States, 15 percent of all undergraduates receive a degree in
the natural sciences and engineering, compared to 50 percent in China and 67
percent in Singapore.[6]

While there is no one single initiative that will address this challenge, the
new administration should improve the quantity and quality of K–12 math and
science teachers. The National Academy has recommended providing 10,000
four-year, merit-based scholarships to students who are receiving a K–12
teacher certification and a bachelor's degree in a STEM field. The new administration should also make it easier for science and technology professionals to
gain certification to teach in our classrooms.

Another top priority: increase funding for partnerships between industry
and community colleges to develop customized job training and associate's degrees for technicians. Supporting programs aimed at increasing the diversity of
the STEM workforce and getting more young men and women excited about
science and engineering is a critical step, as is providing grants to colleges and
universities that expand the number of undergraduates who receive a bachelor's degree in science and engineering.[7]

In higher education, we need to triple the number of the National Science
Foundation's Graduate Research Fellowships from 1,000 to 3,000.[8] The number
of NSF graduate fellowships has remained unchanged since the early 1960s, despite a large increase in the size of the undergraduate population. Funding fellowships also gives graduate students more autonomy in choosing their
research projects.

Finally, the new president needs to bring our immigration laws in line with
21st-century economic needs. The number of "green cards" in employment-
based categories must be doubled to clear up the backlog of skilled immigrants
waiting to become permanent residents, but not at the expense of family-based
immigration. A "fast track" system should be adopted that allows foreign students who receive advanced technical degrees from U.S. universities to receive an
employment-based visa without having to return to their home country; and the
H1-B visa program should be expanded and reformed to address current economic needs while ensuring that U.S. workers are protected. These steps need to
be taken as part of a comprehensive immigration reform initiative to require the
12 million undocumented immigrants living and working in the United States to
become legal, taxpaying, and contributing members of our society.

Expand Incentives for R&D
Private sector companies do not capture all of the benefits from their investment
in R&D. Economic analysis shows that the benefits to the economy as a whole

from private investment in R&D are significantly larger than the returns that flow to individual companies. Because companies will underinvest in R&D, federal law should again provide a tax credit for companies that invest in research and development. The United States has done so since 1981; unfortunately, this credit has been renewed 11 times and expired twice, most recently in 2007. This inconsistency seriously undermines its effectiveness since companies are not able to rely on the existence of the credit when making investment decisions.

Moreover, the United States in the 1980s once provided the most generous tax incentives for R&D among the industrialized member nations of the Organisation for Economic Cooperation and Development, but by 2004 we had fallen to 17th place. At a minimum, the United States should make its R&D tax credit permanent. The new administration should also consider proposals to expand and increase the effectiveness of the credit, such as increasing the credit's rate from 20 percent to 40 percent, or creating a flat credit for research that is conducted in partnership with industry consortia, universities, or national labs.

Benefits of an Information Society

The new administration should identify appropriate steps that the federal government can take to promote the economic and societal benefits of the information revolution. Among the steps it could take would be to eliminate or reform legal and regulatory barriers to the further expansion of global electronic commerce; ensure that IT is designed to be accessible to people with disabilities, thereby increasing their ability to work and improving their quality of life; and develop multimedia digital libraries that place our shared cultural and historic heritage at the fingertips of every American.

To improve our nation's human capital, the new administration should empower adults who are struggling to meet the competing demands of work and family to acquire new skills through online learning, which will allow them to gain new skills at a time, place, and pace that is convenient for them. Another important step is to promote applications that are specifically designed to address the needs of underserved and low-income communities, such as high-quality, compelling software for English as a Second Language and Adult Basic Education.

To improve government, the 44th president must make government more open, transparent, efficient, and user-friendly by taking a page from former Center for American Progress fellow Carl Malamud, who put the Securities and Exchange Commission's EDGAR database of corporate filings online, and successfully urged C-SPAN to expand citizen access to its online video of congressional hearings, agency briefings, and White House events. The new administration should require government to make it easy for citizens, community-based organizations, and the private sector to add value to data, especially given the power of "mash ups" and other Web 2.0 tools and techniques.

The United States should also make it a priority to restore our leadership in broadband technology. The United States, the birthplace of the Internet, ranks only 15th out of 30 OECD countries in broadband deployment.[9] A study commissioned by the Communication Workers of America concluded that average broadband speeds in the United States were less than 2 megabits per second, compared to 61 mbps in Japan and 45 mbps in South Korea.[10]

Some of the applications described above will help stimulate demand for broadband. Other actions that the government should take include creating tax incentives for companies that invest in next-generation broadband networks and provide access to underserved urban and rural communities.[11] The new administration should also push Congress to permanently extend the moratorium on Internet taxes.

Allocating additional broadband spectrum on a licensed and unlicensed basis, with the goal of making wireless a viable competitor to cable and phone companies in the residential broadband market, should be another key policy goal. The result would be lower prices, faster deployment of advanced networks, and a lower risk of anticompetitive behavior that stifles the openness of the Internet.[12] More federal investment in R&D would also allow us to make better use of the existing spectrum of technologies such as "cognitive radio," which allows wireless devices to automatically adjust transmission frequencies to maintain efficient and uninterrupted communications. Finally, the new administration should help the states boost broadband deployment.

Overview

Economic Opportunity for All or a New Gilded Age?

PETER EDELMAN AND
ANGELA GLOVER BLACKWELL

Economic mobility must be a vital priority for the new administration. Fulfilling the promise of equal economic opportunity for all depends on our success in growing the economy justly for all—a task neglected over the past eight years. Stimulating economic

growth that benefits everyone and closes ever-widening economic gaps requires a multi-
plicity of action. Economic mobility policies must invest more successfully in children,
youth, and young adults to prepare them for the challenges posed by globalization, in
part by preparing them for new careers in a low-carbon economy so essential to the sur-
vival of the planet. Children need to be ready to learn when they start school. Schools
need to teach 21st-century skills. Postsecondary education must reach far more people.
And options for further learning must be available throughout our lives. Responsibility
for action depends not just on public policymakers, but also on the full participation of
business, labor, faith-based groups, and other civic actors to ensure each of us assumes
individual and personal responsibility for ourselves, our families, and our communities.

New economic research and current economic conditions provide fresh insights on the issue of economic mobility.[1] The American Dream—that we can all move up the economic ladder—is far from reality for many people today. The U.S. economy grew for most of the current decade—before the housing crisis that began in 2007 threatened recession in 2008—but the benefits have not been widely shared. Income inequality and the wealth gap are widening, with disproportionate effects on racial and ethnic minorities. The current housing crisis is causing further downward mobility for many low-income families, endangering the effectiveness of homeownership as a vehicle for economic mobility and asset building.

These threats pose fundamental challenges to achieving full economic opportunity in America. But they are not new challenges. Over the past three decades, real wage growth (after adjusting for inflation) was slower for low- and middle-income workers and their families even though overall economic growth was quite robust. Slower income growth resulted in slower wealth accumulation outside of homeownership, which is why the current housing crisis is so truly alarming. In short, the promise of opportunity for all because of economic mobility has given way to a new Gilded Age, in which the wealthy thrive while most Americans struggle.

Economic mobility refers to economic success over time—both within the span of a lifetime and across generations. It includes two dimensions: "absolute mobility," the proverbial rising tide (or lack thereof) said to lift all boats; and "relative mobility," which results in changing places with others in the economic hierarchy.

Absolute mobility doesn't necessarily occur across the board. It refers to growth without people gaining or losing ground in the pecking order. The rich can get richer while others make small income gains. Or the least well off and the middle class could do better than the wealthy, shrinking the gap between the top and the bottom.

In contrast, relative mobility has winners and losers as people climb over one another on the economic ladder. The negative effects on those passed over can be ameliorated by absolute mobility if overall economic growth is robust enough, and is fairly distributed enough, to keep people's income on the rise even though their relative place in the economy goes down.

Focusing on both absolute and relative economic mobility compels policymakers to ask both how to end poverty and reduce gaps in income and wealth across income levels and racial groups, and how to increase the number of people who move from lower income levels to higher levels. These are complex policymaking tasks that involve an array of policy tools. The first is an agenda for the progressive distribution of the proceeds of economic growth to give low- and lower-middle-income workers and their families the opportunity to climb the economic ladder. The second is increased educational opportunities for children, youth, and young adults to boost intergenerational economic mobility. And the third is building healthy communities of opportunity across metropolitan regions to further absolute and relative economic mobility.[2]

Our recommendations emphasize relative mobility. But they should be seen as corollaries to an absolute mobility strategy centered on growing a productive, competitive, low-carbon economy that provides living-wage jobs for low-wage workers alongside economic opportunity to anyone willing to work hard seeking the American Dream.

Growing Economic Disparities

Economic mobility in the United States worsened considerably over the past three decades. Since 1973, wage growth was slower for most workers—particularly for low- and lower-middle-income wage earners—than it was in the initial decades after World War II. Because overall economic growth over this period was quite robust, wage stagnation among low- and middle-income families means that economic inequality increased while poverty remained about the same. Absolute economic mobility for those in the bottom half proved elusive.

What's more, intergenerational income growth and relative mobility were weak to nonexistent for many, and were particularly dire for many African Americans left behind in inner cities and rural communities as other African Americans clawed their way into the middle class—only to face trouble ahead due to the housing and credit crises. The upshot: thirty-five years of American prosperity left many people behind.

Economic restructuring and the shift to a knowledge-based economy reduced unionized, blue-collar manufacturing jobs, which were replaced by low-wage service and retail jobs. The supply of jobs grew enough to absorb an influx of new entrants to the labor market—mainly women and immigrants—but not at the same income levels as unionized workers. The 20th century closed with a low rate of overall unemployment that was the envy of other nations, yet the shift to a service economy hollowed out the manufacturing labor market, reducing the share of well-paying middle-class jobs, and limiting opportunities for upward mobility for a majority of Americans. The fruits of growth mainly accrued to the upper middle class and the wealthy.

The numbers, by now familiar to many, are dramatic. Between 1979 and 2005, the after-tax income of the top 1 percent of earners increased 176 percent, while the income of the poorest fifth only increased 9 percent.[3] The widening of the wealth gap is even more spectacular. The wealthiest 1 percent of Americans had 1,500 times more wealth than the bottom 40 percent in 1983, and this widened to a multiple of 4,400 by 2001.[4]

The median income of men aged 30 through 39 actually decreased by 12.5 percent from 1974 to 2004. In 1974 their median income was about $40,000 (in inflation-adjusted dollars); their counterparts 30 years later had a median income of about $35,000.[5] Family income increased over the same period, but only because millions of women went to work (some by choice and some by necessity), introducing a second wage earner into the family.

Forty-two percent of those children living in families in the bottom fifth of income in 1968 remained there as adults, and 39 percent of children whose families were in the top fifth of income in that same year stayed there as adults—what researchers call "stickiness" at both ends of the income spectrum.[6] The only industrialized country with less upward mobility over this period is Great Britain.[7]

Available data indicate major racial disparities in mobility. Thirty-one percent of African-American children in families in the middle tier of income in 1968 made more as adults than their parents, compared to 68 percent of whites.[8] The relative mobility figures for African Americans are especially troubling (although based on a relatively small sample). About 45 percent of African-American children in middle-income families in 1968 ended up in the bottom fifth of income earners as adults, compared to only 16 percent of white children who started in those circumstances.[9]

These trends are the result of a number of changes in our economy over the past several decades. The loss of manufacturing jobs means that the children of blue-collar parents lack the same job opportunities that were available to their parents. The increase in female-headed households—a population-wide trend that is more pronounced among African Americans—means that fewer families have two wage earners. And racial discrimination in the job market continues even today.

Homeownership has long been an important vehicle for economic mobility and wealth building, but people of color are less likely to own their homes than whites, largely due to historic, racially discriminatory public and private policies that prevent them from obtaining financing to purchase homes. A large share of the accumulated wealth of whites stems from the increase in value of homes purchased decades ago, an opportunity many African Americans were denied.

Indeed, home values are often stagnant, or even decreasing, in the neighborhoods where many people of color can afford to live. And the subprime mortgage and foreclosure crisis has disproportionately affected people of color: a 2008 study estimates that the total loss of wealth for people of color will be between $164 billion and $213 billion.[10]

Residential segregation by race and income plays a role as well. Many low-income people of color live in neighborhoods that lack the necessary ingredients for economic success: living-wage jobs, transportation access, good schools, safe and walkable streets, parks, housing choices, grocery stores, and services. They are often plagued by environmental problems, high crime rates, and racially disparate law enforcement.

It is hard to generalize about immigrants as a group. They arrive with different levels of education and skills and, depending upon their place of origin and skin color, they may face very different experiences in the United States. Unfortunately, mobility data are not broken down by national origin. Therefore, though research tends to show that immigrants have largely been successful in moving up economically, much more refined research will be needed before any nuanced conclusions can be reached about the economic mobility of immigrant groups.

What we do know is that the annual number of legal immigrants to the United States today now totals about 1 million a year, a trend evident since 1990, and up sharply from about 600,000 a year in the 1980s, and about 500,000 a year in the 1970s.[11] Over most of the past three decades, first-generation immigrants did better than comparable native-born groups, and second-generation immigrants did even better. In recent years, however, the educational attainment of immigrants declined on average, and the initial economic performance of immigrants declined. The trend of upward mobility continues, but at a slower pace.

The experiences of immigrants compared to native-born Americans leads to controversial conclusions about the possible negative effects of immigrants on the wages and employment levels of lower-income native-born workers. Respected researchers come to opposite conclusions. Our inclination is to side with those who conclude that legal immigrants add positive value to the economy. That conclusion, however, only further highlights why the new administration needs to meet the challenge of absorbing lower-skilled immigrant workers into the economy while also raising the incomes of all low-wage workers.

Developing databases to enable the analysis of economic mobility for different ethnic and racial groups is important for future research on economic scenarios and policy choices. Demographic trends—among them immigration rates, higher birth rates among racial and ethnic minorities, and the aging of the white population—will translate into a much more diverse American society in the coming decades. Our future national success will hinge on doing a much better job integrating everyone into the economy. Understanding these economic mobility trends in detail through better data will help government policymakers tremendously.

A New Agenda

The new president and his administration must pursue an agenda of economic growth that will lift all Americans to higher levels of income and asset accumulation. Upward absolute and relative economic mobility need to be conscious goals of national policy. The limited upward economic mobility for most people and the significant downward mobility for many others over the last 35 years must be acknowledged, addressed, and corrected.

That effort begins by achieving broad-based economic growth in a globalized economy—a major challenge. The weakness in wage growth (after factoring the effects of inflation) for low- and middle-income Americans since 1973 is due in large part to the increasing pace of globalization, and heralds a new era in which American workers will experience greater economic insecurity and downward wage pressure in many sectors of the economy. Yet the consequences of climate change and rising energy costs brought on by our fossil fuel–driven economic growth offer the new administration the opportunity to develop new economic arenas to spur robust economic growth, as the authors in other chapters of this book make clear.

Achieving widely shared absolute economic mobility through broad-based economic growth will require paying attention to a host of matters that are highly interdependent yet significant in themselves to create the most educated and adaptable workforce possible. These matters include fiscal and monetary issues, taxes, trade, energy and the environment, health policy, technology policy, foreign assistance, and lifelong learning programs. The growth policies of today and tomorrow must be premised on the creation of a low-carbon economy. To succeed, business, labor, and civic leaders, encouraged by leadership from the new president, must think broadly about the nation's economic interests and the human needs of the workforce.

Progressive Distribution of Economic Growth
Sustained and robust economic growth is one requisite, but it is not sufficient. Policies must also be in place to build a sustainable, inclusive economy that benefits all. The first step is to restore a progressive U.S. tax system in the wake of the Bush administration's tax cuts, which poured hundreds of billions of dollars into the hands of the wealthiest Americans and corporations. Everyone must pay a fair share of the cost of taking long-overdue action on matters of pressing national need, which in turn will help deliver the jobs, savings, and other assets needed to boost absolute economic mobility across American society.

The next policy aim to restore absolute mobility is to ensure that all Americans have both living-wage incomes that allow them to pay for needed expenses and savings to fall back on. A living wage for all wage earners and true equal opportunity for racial and ethnic minorities to climb into the middle class are not debatable in the most prosperous country in the world.

But we want overall relative mobility as well. We need to create more pathways of opportunity for many more low-income people to join the middle class, and more opportunities for middle-class families to join the ranks of the well-to-do. Indeed, policies need to be in place so that children from low-income families have the opportunity to succeed in reaching the very top. To achieve such positive economic mobility, more workers need opportunities to upgrade their skills and change directions throughout their working lives, through lifelong learning, trade adjustment assistance, and job retraining.

Improving economic mobility is inextricably linked to strategies to end poverty as well as strategies that create opportunities for the working poor to move up in the workforce. Economic mobility research shows that parental success tends in general to enhance children's success, signaling the need to focus on increasing the incomes of low-wage workers. Critical policies to achieve these ends include: raising and indexing the minimum wage; improving government support programs such as the Earned Income Tax Credit, Child Tax Credit, and food stamps; removing the barriers to union organizing to allow parents to earn more; and making health care available to all.

Because mobility outcomes vary by race, it is imperative that the policies adopted to pursue increased relative mobility and a living income for all adequately address the factors that perpetuate racial inequities. Critical barriers to relative mobility must be removed by improving education for lower-income minority children, offering housing vouchers to help alleviate concentrated poverty, and tackling the disproportionate incarceration of minorities. Equally important are policies that break the "disconnect" of many minority youth, and tackle continued discrimination in the job market and elsewhere in society—factors that severely handicap low-income ethnic and racial minorities from fully participating in the U.S. economy.

But national policy is only a part of the picture. It is an instrument to stimulate and empower people to act in their own communities for change. We view the needed actions as a tripod that will collapse unless all three of its legs are sturdy and strong—with the three legs being public policy at all levels of government, private and civic action, and individual and community responsibility. Educational policy reform exemplifies our tripod approach.

Increase Educational Opportunities

Nothing is more important for children to attain economic success than an excellent education. And nothing, it seems, is more difficult than providing an excellent education to low-income children given the welter of challenges involved and the multiplicity of federal, state, and local policies that must fire in sync to achieve sustained educational success. This task is especially challenging in schools where nearly every child is poor, which is too often the case for children of color.

To reduce the economic disparities that plague the educational opportunities of our nation's low-income children the new administration needs to make a national commitment to pre-kindergarten for all as part of an overall system of developmental care for children during the preschool years. The 44th president also needs to renew the government's commitment to quality elementary and secondary education for every child, embrace new strategies to boost college enrollment and retention across America, and make more widely available lifelong learning opportunities for those entering a rapidly changing workplace. Taking these steps—as outlined in detail in other chapters of this book— will create multiple upward pathways of opportunity and pave the way to successful entry into the job market.

The new president's economic mobility agenda must kick into gear for all Americans before birth, with policies to discourage teen pregnancy, ensure prenatal and neonatal care, and offer child care and child development programs. Every child should come to school at age 5 healthy and fully ready to start kindergarten. Parents and state and local community leaders must be equally engaged to get children ready to enter school. This is where presidential leadership from the bully pulpit, alongside federal funds, can stimulate local initiatives for programs that encourage reading to children and reduce violence at home and in communities.

The 44th president should set a national goal to ensure that our public education system is no longer limited to K–12. We need a national commitment to every child progressing successfully through a public education system that begins with pre-kindergarten and extends, for those who choose it, to community college, state colleges, and universities (with Pell Grants and other postsecondary financial aid as needed).

Attracting and retaining able and committed teachers and principals in low-income schools is certainly critical to a successful public education system, as are pay raises for effective teacher and principal performance. Other chapters detail the policies we need to enact these reforms, but there are three specific suggestions related to boosting economic mobility that are not necessarily front and center on other lists of needed reform.

The first is to increase social and economic integration in schools. We must find more ways for low-income children to go to school with children from different socioeconomic backgrounds. This includes choice within school systems, magnet schools, career academies, themed schools, charter and contract schools, and other innovative approaches. Federal funding could provide two creative policy initiatives: incentives for programs that cross school district boundaries to achieve greater integration; and efforts to promote economic mixing, affording access for low-income students to higher-income schools.[12]

Second, we must strengthen after-school and out-of-school programs. The new president must re-engineer federal funding for after-school programs to encourage local programs that follow children continuously through to successful integration into adult society. Much attention has been paid to after-school hours over the past decade, and some cities do have extensive citywide initiatives, but much more is needed. One effective model is the Harlem Children's Zone, which unlike too many after-school programs stays with children through childhood and adolescence until they are successfully into college or the job market.

Third, we need to invest in programs that reach at-risk and disconnected youth, particularly men and boys of color. The government must invest particularly in those young people who are most at risk of becoming disconnected from mainstream society, and in creating second chances for those who are already disconnected. The situation of young men and boys of color is truly dire. Between 1989 and 1999, the share of 18- to-24-year-old African Americans without a high school degree who had a job fell to only 52 percent from an already dismal 59 percent, and this does not include young men who were in prison. If anything, the situation has deteriorated further during the current decade.

The list of possible strategies to reach these young men of color includes supporting high schools that work with local employers to implement proven job training and placement programs, as well as encouraging community colleges to recruit and accept out-of-school youth or out-of-work youth in order to help them obtain a high school diploma and then an associate's degree. Other steps include expanding promising job-training programs such as YouthBuild and the Service and Conservation Corps, and pursuing new programs that train disconnected youth for jobs in the green sectors of the economy.

Above all, though, ensuring that our tripod of policies at the federal, state, and local levels are in place, and will help disconnected youth in particular, will require a range of incentives to spark partnerships among employers, schools and community colleges, and non-profit community organizations to create clear pathways to the job market. These same policies need to be in place to help ex-offenders surmount the huge barriers they confront on coming out of prison, including review of legal barriers that preclude employability.

Build Healthy Communities of Opportunity

Relative mobility is closely connected to issues of residential segregation, concentrated poverty, and geographic isolation. Where people live—and their level of access to locations throughout metropolitan regions—has a profound effect on their economic opportunities and life chances. Ensuring that all neighborhoods throughout metropolitan regions are "communities of opportunity," providing the supports necessary for economic success, is essential for helping low-income people help themselves climb up from the lower rungs of the economic ladder.

Racial and ethnic residential segregation and accompanying economic isolation are a lethal combination. Improving relative mobility requires understanding how geography and regional development patterns shape the economic and social opportunities of residents, and contribute to racial inequities. The work of coauthor Angela Glover Blackwell's organization, PolicyLink, in concert with local partners across the country, illustrates promising approaches.

Among these approaches are to increase the supply and financial accessibility of housing for lower-income people throughout regions, and implement targeted strategies to link inner-city residents to good jobs in the regional economy, including sectoral workforce development efforts, skills training, and transportation-to-work connections. We also need to build mixed-income neighborhoods by increasing the incomes of low-income residents and attracting middle-income people back to lower-income neighborhoods (in part by ensuring public safety and improving public schools) in a way that does not displace current residents.

On the economic front, the government should support initiatives and efforts of people to organize themselves on the ground to press for needed changes in public policy and corporate behavior, and promote entrepreneurship and small business development, particularly in communities of color, to build strong local economies. Reducing the high cost of being poor in inner-city neighborhoods can be done by attracting stores that sell goods at nationally competitive prices and regulating predatory and payday lenders and check-cashing proprietors.[13]

Creating housing choices throughout metropolitan regions is a particularly critical item for the new administration. The Federal Housing Trust Fund legislation that was pending in Congress for a number of years, was enacted during the summer of 2008. The new president should press for adequate funding of such legislation as part of a concerted federal effort to increase the supply of affordable housing. At the same time, the federal housing voucher program needs overhaul and expansion. Federal housing assistance currently reaches only one out of every four people who qualify for it.

Finally, transportation access to jobs is also an important federal policy priority. The federal transportation bill will be up for reauthorization in 2009. Facilitating economic mobility should be a key goal of the new legislation. Federal policy should support regional efforts by community organizations, government agencies, and business leaders to craft career training, placement, and transportation strategies to enable inner-city residents to access jobs located in different parts of the region. If more people can go out each day to work and bring back, collectively, more money to be spent in their own neighborhoods, then economic and social isolation will be reduced and a healthier community will result.

Overview

Meeting the Challenge of the Housing and Credit Crises

MICHAEL S. BARR

The U.S. economy is caught in a vicious downward spiral of declining home prices, escalating foreclosures, rising losses on mortgage-backed securities, and disappearing liquid-

ity. The crisis spread rapidly from the mortgage market in 2007 to engulf other forms of consumer credit, commercial real estate, and municipal debt, and reached far beyond American soil in the last year of the Bush presidency. Major financial institutions failed. The risk of sustained global economic crisis remains high. The new administration must act aggressively to contain the crisis, reform our home mortgage system, and develop new approaches to broad-scale housing and financial-sector reform—beginning with a clear understanding of the problem itself. Lax regulation, supervisory neglect, lack of transparency, and conflicts of interest all undermined the foundations of our financial system. Financial innovations in securitization and other factors brought increased liquidity but also broadened the wedge between the incentives facing brokers, lenders, borrowers, rating agencies, securitizers, loan servicers, and investors. The lack of transparency and oversight, coupled with rising home prices, hid the problems for some time. When home prices and other assets imploded, credit woes cascaded through the financial system, and the lack of trust in the system meant that even sound financial institutions faced contagion from the crisis. That is why we need fundamental change.

Understanding the Current Crisis

Alarmed by the specter of a prolonged economic slowdown, both the Federal Reserve and the U.S. Congress in 2008 acted aggressively to stimulate demand through monetary and fiscal levers. For too long, the U.S. Department of the Treasury simply pressed mortgage holders to restructure mortgages and suspend foreclosures on a voluntary basis. But continuing turmoil in financial markets confirmed that these actions were not enough. Restoring confidence and liquidity in credit markets requires bold action to restructure the overhang of distressed assets and contain the losses in the markets.

Rather than a measured market correction warranted solely by the underlying quality of assets, we have seen a freefall in mortgage-related financial assets and in U.S. home prices, with the crisis in credit quality extending across the financial sector. The total inventory of homes in foreclosure reached 2.75 percent by June 2008, and delinquencies reached 6.41 percent of all mortgages. More than 2 million foreclosures are anticipated within the next two years. As of September 2008, home prices had already fallen by approximately 20 percent from their peak two years ago, and the median home price has fallen for the first time since the Great Depression. Sharply falling home prices put a growing number of homeowners underwater, with nearly 10 million households already facing home mortgage debt levels that exceed the value of their homes. Negative equity is a strong predictor of default and foreclosures.

As the crisis spread, it helped to slow the U.S. and global economies and bring down major U.S. financial institutions. The investment banking firm, Bear Stearns Cos., with significant exposure to the subprime mortgage sector, failed, and was acquired by JP Morgan Chase & Co. with the support of Treasury and the financial backing of the Federal Reserve. IndyMac Bank, a federally insured depository and major subprime lender, faced an old-fashioned bank run and was taken over by the Federal Deposit Insurance Corporation. The vaunted home mortgage giants Fannie Mae and Freddie Mac, with $5 trillion in debt and mortgage-backed securities outstanding, succumbed to the crisis and were put into conservatorship by Treasury, with promises from the department to provide up to $100 billion in capital to each institution. Soon after, Wall Street investment bank Lehman Brothers Holdings Inc. went bankrupt, and rival Merrill Lynch & Co. sold itself to Bank of America to avoid the same fate.

The global insurance firm American International Group Inc. succumbed the next day, and the Federal Reserve agreed to loan the company up to $85 billion on an emergency basis as it sought to sell off its assets. After a run on historically "safe" money market mutual funds, which operate outside the FDIC-insured banking system, Treasury announced that it would extend the safety net by offering insurance to this entire industry as of September 19. The Fed then issued rules that temporarily weakened the firewalls between banks and other firms to provide additional liquidity from banks. By the end of that week, the last two remaining independent investment banks, Morgan Stanley and Goldman, Sachs Group Inc., converted to bank holding companies subject to the prudential supervision of the Federal Reserve. Washington Mutual Bank went into FDIC receivership and was sold to JP Morgan, and Wachovia Bank merged as well. Finally, Treasury declared that the time had come for Congressional authorization of a $700 billion program to have Treasury buy tranches of "toxic" mortgage-backed securities and collateralized debt obligations on the books of financial institutions.

This cascading collapse on Wall Street was preceded by legislation enacted in July 2008 aimed at restructuring troubled mortgages to prevent avoidable foreclosures and the resulting harm to neighboring homes and communities. Under the Housing and Economic Recovery Act of 2008, an estimated 400,000 at-risk mortgages could be restructured on affordable terms with credit enhancement from the Federal Housing Administration. Only loans on owner-occupied homes would be eligible for restructuring and speculators would be excluded.

Refinanced loans would take the form of new fixed-rate 30-year mortgages underwritten up to 90 percent of current home value. Borrowers would pay insurance premiums to the FHA and would share any equity appreciation in their home values. Lenders, participating on a voluntary basis, would negotiate to extinguish any second liens on the homes, agree to write down sufficient principal to meet loan-to-value and affordability guidelines, and pay a one-time insurance premium to the FHA. This "Hope for Homeowners" program was slated to begin insuring loans in the fall of 2008 as this book went to press. It remains to be seen whether a sufficient number of loans will be restructured to mitigate the crisis in foreclosures, and at the same time whether the federal government will be left with an adversely selected portfolio of the riskiest loans, with unknown exposure to the FHA and, potentially, taxpayers.

The legislation also included $3.9 billion for a Neighborhood Stabilization program based on a concept first published by Center for American Progress Senior Fellow David Abromowitz. These funds are available to help hard-hit states and localities purchase abandoned and foreclosed properties and put them to reuse as affordable housing. The legislation also includes funds for homeowner counseling and new flexibility for the Federal Housing Administration's core programs. Implementation of the program will undoubtedly take the time and attention of any new administration.

Significantly, the legislation put in place a new regulator—the Federal Housing Finance Agency—for the government-sponsored enterprises, Fannie Mae, Freddie Mac, and the Federal Home Loan Bank system, along with special authority for the government to backstop these agencies in the event of their inability to raise adequate capital to maintain mortgage market liquidity. But the new GSE authorities did little to stem the GSEs' problems raising capital, and their debt and mortgage-backed securities issuance became increasingly expensive relative to historical rates.

In September 2008, Treasury and the Federal Housing Finance Agency placed Fannie Mae and Freddie Mac into conservatorship. The FHFA is now responsible for running the GSEs. Treasury committed to cash infusions of up to $100 billion for each entity in the event that their liabilities exceed their assets, and Treasury is to receive stock senior in priority to all other equity, stock warrants representing 80 percent of the two companies' common stock, regular dividends, and commitment fees in exchange for Treasury's financial backing. Treasury also agreed on a temporary basis to purchase GSE mortgage-backed securities on the open market in the interest of market stability.

As this book went to press, Congress had just enacted the Bush administration's proposal for authority to buy up to $700 billion in mortgage-backed securities and collateralized debt obligations from financial institutions. The administration's proposal failed to include provisions required to help homeowners restructure their troubled mortgages, and left intact the conflicts of interest and legal barriers in the secondary markets blocking restructuring. The legislation failed to stem the bleeding. Just days later, with stock markets in steep declines and global financial markets still reeling, the Fed and Treasury announced a program to backstop commercial paper issued by any U.S. firm—extending the safety net across the U.S. economy.

During the transition, a new administration must quickly assess the current state of the mortgage market, the new tools enacted in 2008, and the challenges facing the broader economy. It must then implement a short- and long-term plan to restore financial stability and develop a sound housing and financial policy for the nation. Complicating matters, the new administration is likely going to need to develop these long-range plans while still in the midst of the current crisis.

Recommendations

The new president will need to put in place a crisis management team with strong experience. The team should be guided by a set of principles for crisis management, but they will need principles that can be maintained consistently throughout the crisis—not principles that will need to be abandoned as soon as reality strikes. The country cannot afford continued, haphazard crisis management, lurching from one financial bailout to the next. Nor can it afford another eight years of regulatory and supervisory neglect. We need attention focused on the financial crisis from day one, and we need fundamentally to reform our broken housing finance system.

The new administration will need to evaluate its predecessor's new securities buy-out program as well as the FHA voluntary restructuring tool, both as to take-up (how many mortgage lenders and investors avail themselves of the new program) and adverse selection (whether the mortgages they place into this program are their riskiest). With capital markets rife with divided ownership and conflicts of interest, both the voluntary plan pushed valiantly by FDIC Chair Sheila Bair, Treasury, and the new legislation may be met with foot-dragging by the market. If so, the time for loan-by-loan restructuring of threatened mortgages will have passed.

Under a loan plan called Saving America's Family Equity developed in January 2007 by this author along with colleagues at the Center for American Progress, the government would create a process for the rapid and transparent repricing and restructuring of existing home mortgages themselves—rather than the securities that were the focus of the Bush plan. The Federal Reserve would run auctions, in which Treasury and the private sector would purchase mortgages from current lenders and investors at discounts determined by the auction process. These mortgage holders would take a hit, trading a reduction in asset value and yield in exchange for liquidity and certainty.

Proposed changes to the tax code governing trusts holding mortgage-backed securities would give servicers and investors strong incentives and sound legal grounding to remove existing barriers to widespread loan restructuring through the auction process. By holding transparent auctions for pools of loans, the program could avoid many adverse selection problems associated with individual loan-by-loan applications for FHA insurance. Treasury would then work with responsible originators to restructure the loans they acquire on affordable terms.

As the new administration comes into office, it will also need to focus on maintaining stability and liquidity during this crisis so that homeowners maintain access to home mortgage credit across all regions of the country. The White House will need to ensure that the GSE conservatorship does not needlessly bail out the GSE investors, holds senior management accountable, and protects taxpayers by relying on the equity cushion represented by stock and preferred stock and by reducing the risk exposures of Fannie and Freddie. The new administration will need to ensure that the takeovers do not diminish the safety and soundness of other financial institutions.

The new administration should help lead the industry by example, as the FDIC is doing with its takeover of IndyMac by engaging in systematic restructuring rather than foreclosing on the failed bank's mortgages. The FHFA should turn carefully to restructuring troubled loans in the portfolios of the GSEs in a systematic manner, seeking to avoid further defaults and foreclosures by refinancing loans on a sound basis across its portfolio, rather than through piecemeal modifications. Similar restructurings must occur as part of the government's mortgage securities buy-out program.

The housing crisis we face today stems from serious systemic problems in the subprime and alternative lending markets that show our system of home mortgage regulation is seriously deficient and must be reformed. We need to fill what the late Federal Reserve Board Governor Ned Gramlich aptly termed "the giant hole in the supervisory safety net."[1] Banks and thrifts are subject to comprehensive federal regulation and supervision, but their affiliates far less so, and independent mortgage companies not at all. Moreover, many market-based systems designed to ensure sound practices in this sector—broker reputational risk, lender oversight of brokers, investor oversight of lenders, rating agency oversight of securitizations, and so on—simply did not work. Conflicts of interest, inadequate capital adequacy rules, lax regulation, and the "boom times" covered up the abuses—at least for a while. But no more.

The new administration, Congress, and the bank regulators could do much to restore integrity to mortgage markets and reduce the likelihood of such a crisis in the future. Federal regulation is necessary to combat abusive practices and restore integrity to our credit markets. We need to ensure that all participants in the mortgage process have the right incentives to engage in sound lending practices and are subject to regulatory oversight.

The House of Representatives in 2008 passed important legislation to clean up the mortgage process and regulate mortgage brokerage to drive out abuses, but the Senate has not followed suit.[2] While there are certainly improvements that could be made in the legislation, it forms a sound basis for the new administration and Congress to enact mortgage reform early in the next congressional session. Legislation should include provisions for judicially supervised modifications of home mortgages in certain narrow circumstances. In addition, the Federal Reserve's rulemakings to bar unfair and deceptive mortgage practices and to improve disclosures should be implemented immediately while the Fed works to strengthen them further. And to increase transparency, all borrowers need to be able to get firm price quotes on loans and settlement services in order to comparison shop.

The new administration also should develop an ex-post standard for truth in lending so that mortgage brokers and lenders do not have incentives to get around disclosure rules. Under this approach, an agency could determine whether a creditor's disclosure was objectively unreasonable, in that the disclosure would fail to communicate effectively the key terms and risks of the mortgage to the typical borrower. It should require brokers and lenders to disclose all information favorable to the borrower so that borrowers are no longer easily steered into loans that cost more than the loans for which they would qualify. The new law also needs to increase public disclosure of broker and lender conduct and regulatory monitoring of credit standards. To repair the broken trust and realign good incentives in our system, brokers should not be permitted to earn so-called yield spread premiums for steering borrowers into higher-cost loans.

Instead, we need a system under which brokers are accountable to borrowers. Over the long run, we could shift to a system under which borrowers paid for mortgage-broker services and brokers owed a fiduciary duty to borrowers, in a similar way that financial advisers owe such duties to their investment advisory clients. In the meanwhile, enhanced disclosures and barring yield spread premiums could help to reduce abuses.

Moreover, we need to ensure that our capital market regulations—across all financial sectors—provide for transparency, appropriate capital adequacy standards, and rules regarding conflicts of interest. Congress and the new administration need to reform our secondary market regulations as well as our tax and accounting rules so that securitizations enhance liquidity and transparency even in crises, rather than serving as obstacles to crisis resolution.

There is a long history of sound lending to low- and moderate-income borrowers. Banks and thrifts expanded their prime mortgage lending, consistent with safe and sound banking practices, under the Community Reinvestment Act. The results were impressive.[3] We should not blame the poor and learn the wrong lesson from the current crisis. Rather, we need to ensure that our mortgage finance system works for all creditworthy households.

In addition to reforming the mortgage market by taking on bad practices, we should take this opportunity fundamentally to rethink our approaches to regulation based on insights from behavioral economics. Harvard economist Sendhil Mullainathan, Princeton psychologist Eldar Shafir, and this author have argued for a new, opt-out mortgage plan.[4] While the causes of the mortgage crisis are myriad, a central problem is that brokers and lenders offered loans that looked much less expensive than they really are because of low initial monthly payments and hidden costly features. As Ned Gramlich asked, "Why are the most risky loan products sold to the least sophisticated borrowers?"[5] Many borrowers took out loans that they did not understand and could not afford, with predictable results.

In retirement policy, behavioral research led Congress to promote "opt out" plans under which employers sign workers up for retirement benefits unless the worker chooses not to participate. This policy has significantly improved people's retirement savings. Under an opt-out home mortgage plan, borrowers would be offered a standard set of mortgages, with sound underwriting and straightforward terms. And that's the mortgage they'd get unless they opted out after clear disclosures. Lenders and brokers would face increased scrutiny and the potential for liability if they provided alternative loans without reasonable disclosure. An opt-out system would mean borrowers would be more likely to get appropriate loans, without blocking beneficial financial innovation.

Long-Term Recommendations

The new administration should begin right away the sure-to-be time-consuming process of developing a home mortgage finance system for the 21st century, including evaluating the role of the GSEs and other participants in the system. Any such review would need to take account of the historically important role the GSEs play in developing and sustaining a home mortgage system that, prior to the current crisis, had been the envy of the world. In particular, we need to ensure that our system continues to sustain the market for 30-year, fixed rate, self-amortizing mortgages; provides liquidity throughout all regions of the country, including during economic crises; and promotes standardization of mortgage products that are in the interests of home mortgage borrowers.

These proposals should also include appropriate incentives for screening, monitoring, and enforcement for consumers, investors, and other stakeholders in the system. They should improve the alignment of the mortgage finance system with the public interest, and reduce systemic financial risk and the potential risk to taxpayers if the system fails. Developing principles based on what we need our financial system to do will help guide the process of figuring out how to get from our current crisis posture to that point.

More broadly, the new administration will also face important decisions regarding broad-scale financial reforms. The current U.S. home and global credit crises reveal significant weaknesses and glaring inconsistencies in our system of financial supervision. The government's response to the crisis raised new questions regarding moral hazard created by repeated government bailouts of a wide array of financial institutions, from deposit-taking commercial banks subject to comprehensive supervision and examination, to government-sponsored enterprises with historically weak oversight, to investment banks not generally subject to prudential supervision.

Treasury and the Federal Reserve in 2008 served as a lender of last resort to a broad array of institutions that, prior to the interventions, had no explicit authority to borrow and no comprehensive prudential supervision or serious capital requirements to contain the consequences of failure, or to protect the financial system and taxpayers. Ad hoc intervention, even if necessary, is no substitute for a system of financial regulation. Now that the Fed and Treasury have acted, there is no way to put the genie back in the bottle. The new administration should take a fresh look at proposals for regulatory rationalization, prudential supervision, and capital requirements across the financial sector, without either becoming bogged down in decades-old turf wars or succumbing to siren calls of special interest groups.

The new administration and Congress should undertake a series of initiatives to restore integrity and stability to our financial markets. Innovation is a hallmark of America's financial system, and with needed changes in governmental policies and regulatory supervision, we can expect our financial system once again to be vibrant and strong.

Department of the Treasury
Credibility and Flexibility for Economic Growth

JOSHUA L. STEINER

The effectiveness of the Department of the Treasury will ultimately depend on the quality of its team, its responsiveness to crises, and its ability to work effectively with other branches of government. Nothing illustrates the importance of these three qualities more acutely than the financial crisis of 2008, during which the Treasury had to demonstrate expertise, flexibility, and political agility. Success in each of these depends on acting quickly in recruiting good people and avoiding the kinds of early mistakes that can permanently damage a secretary's efficacy. It is equally important, however, that the new treasury secretary, working with the new president, lay out a clear set of economic goals and priorities and then stick to them. The policy agenda will need adjustment to reflect day-to-day crises and changing circumstances, but a clearly articulated set of overarching goals will help ensure that long-term objectives do not fall victim to the inevitable brush fires of domestic and international economics. Simply put, no treasury secretary will see his or her priorities implemented without building the right team, avoiding mistakes that have hobbled his or her predecessors and, perhaps most importantly, building the right relationships.

The core functions of the Department of the Treasury—tax policy, international economic coordination and regulatory coordination for financial institutions, and financial crimes enforcement—put the Treasury at the center of any administration's economic policy. The best treasury secretaries served as the president's key internal advisors and external leaders on matters relating to domestic and international economic policy. Treasury is statutorily at the center of all major economic debates, but the secretary's ultimate success in leading the economic agenda will depend largely on his or her ability to forge key working relationships, avoid mistakes, and set clear priorities.

Effective treasury secretaries balance long-term objectives such as crucial investments in human and physical capital with their responsibility as the ultimate guardian of fiscal prudence. While not removed from the political fray, the secretary has responsibility for protecting the country's long-term economic stability as well as responding to short-term objectives. That mix of long-term fiscal probity and short-term pragmatism is evident in the Treasury's statutory oversight of the Social Security and Medicare Trust Funds—the ultimate long-dated financial obligations of the U.S. government—and its immediate influence over tax policy.

Yet Treasury's central economic responsibilities only lend themselves partially to the kind of long-term planning envisioned by this book. Given that this chapter was written before the worst of the 2008 financial crisis, it does not try to address it in specificity. Indeed, much of what makes Treasury a vital part of any administration's agenda runs completely contrary to goals of advanced policy coordination. The very nature of the economic cycle suggests that the new administration and its treasury secretary should set forth clear objectives and then leave themselves the flexibility to enact the specific measures they would take when they have a clear picture of the country's economic health.

Consider our most recent treasury secretary, Henry Paulson, who came into office riding seemingly robust capital markets and wanted to highlight China and the environment as two major priorities. His legacy, however, will be determined by his handling of the housing and financial services crises. From a pure policy perspective, the Treasury Department under President George W. Bush shifted its attention from how to reform the charters of the government-sponsored housing finance giants—Fannie Mae and Freddie Mac—to how the government could provide the explicit guarantees needed to protect their viability to how they could effectuate a government takeover of both institutions. Those three pursuits—reform, guarantee, and ultimately conservatorship—all took place within a year.

This need for flexibility is only heightened by the fact that the new president will have a true transition. Without a sitting vice president running for office, the new president will almost certainly gain access to information during the transition that will alter his view of the correct economic imperatives. President Bill Clinton, for example, won the 1992 election with perhaps the most detailed economic plan of any candidate in history. By the time of the transition, planning largely focused on what stimulus efforts his first budget should include. By the time he actually presented a new budget based on the information that only became available when his team took office, the agenda had shifted to deficit reduction, which included certain tax increases.

All this does not and should not suggest that any planning is therefore ill-advised or a likely waste of time. While the new treasury secretary will by necessity focus intensely on the financial sector initiatives begun under the current administration, he or she, as the head of the economic team, must lay out a clear set of long-term objectives that transcend the current economic climate. At the outset, it is worth highlighting four areas of universal importance.

First and foremost, any new treasury secretary will confront the seemingly conflicting demands for deficit reduction and investment. The desire to make significant and badly needed investments in physical infrastructure, education, and health care—to name but three domestic priorities—would appear to run contrary to a similarly pressing need to reduce the deficit. Yet the judicious use of revenue increases and spending prioritization do not necessarily make these goals incompatible. Put differently, a focus on growth will drive clearer decision making and make seemingly intractable conflicts look less mutually exclusive.

Second, while the Department of the Treasury traditionally plays a more re-active role internationally, new global issues mean that the new secretary must develop a proactive global agenda early in the administration. Case in point: the current financial crisis will require sustained coordinated global responses. In addition, a wide variety of "new" issues, such as food scarcity, relations in China, and the strategic imperative of global economic development, suggest an enhanced role for Treasury in international affairs.

Third, the worldwide economy has undergone rapid change that requires a new urgency on some seemingly "old" issues. The rise of the service economy, the increasing reliance on technology in the workplace, and increased international competition with the United States all highlight the importance of helping U.S. workers transition to new jobs. Similarly, climbing income inequality in the United States and around the world has heightened tensions and threatens to undermine key elements of the domestic social fabric.

Finally, as the Center for American Progress points out in its papers on progressive growth, certain seemingly non-economic issues are of such pressing importance that they will go to the heart of the economic agenda. Most notably, climate change and the need to transform America's carbon usage should be part of any Treasury policy priority list.[1]

All of these challenges come against the backdrop of dramatic shifts in economic development and wealth creation around the world. Treasury will need to help develop an active strategy for how to position the United States for success in a world of rapid growth in India and China, massive wealth creation in the Middle East, and growing competition for scarce resources.

Personnel and Confirmations

Perhaps the single most important thing a treasury secretary can do is recruit individuals of exceptional competence and managerial skill. Treasury is such a vast operation, and the press of events on the treasury secretary and his or her senior staff so great, that even the most brilliant secretary cannot be successful without a talented team in place that operates with a clear set of objectives. This involves selecting a staff member to serve as the personnel liaison to screen resumes, talk to the relevant constituent groups, and, most importantly, make sure that personnel decisions get the attention they deserve. Accordingly, there are a few principles to consider.

The importance of the National Economic Council and the Council of Economic Advisors at the White House means that Treasury needs at least a few people who have deep personal relationships with senior members of the White House team. Given the current financial crisis, corporate experience alone will not suffice; Treasury truly needs people who have actual financial markets experience. Last, tax policy encompasses such a broad range of policy, economic, and political issues that building a well-rounded tax team is essential to Treasury's success. This will include expert tax lawyers, economists, and individuals with Washington experience.

Like any well-run organization, Treasury also needs clear lines of authority. For example, the deputy treasury secretary holds a position of tremendous seniority, yet he or she does not have a clear area of responsibility. It is therefore important for the secretary and his or her deputy to quickly define the deputy's purview. And like most modern organizations, the secretary will need legal advice on almost any matter of importance. Finding a general counsel in whom the secretary and deputy have the utmost confidence will greatly enhance the department's efficacy.

Since it is impossible to predict the issues that will arise, the department's credibility will depend as well on having senior members who truly represent a cross-section of Americans. The Treasury bureaus have immensely broad and important responsibilities. Once a bureau head is appointed, it is very difficult to remove him or her, which is why these personnel decisions should be given particular attention. Failure to use a deliberate, focused process that considers all of these principles at the outset will increase the risk that as the pool of remaining jobs narrows, the department will face pressure to fill the open slots with people who do not meet certain important criteria for the job.

The best selection process, however, is obviously for naught if the confirmation process fails. The Senate Finance Committee handles most nominations, with a portion going to the Senate Banking Committee and one residing at the Senate Select Committee on Intelligence. It is virtually impossible to overstate the importance of securing confirmations as quickly as possible. Without confirmation, appointees are limited in the actions that they can take, the way that they can interact with the press and public, and potentially their willingness to remain on the job.

Historical Lessons

History suggests that nothing limits a secretary's efficacy or credibility more severely than an early crisis. While each episode has its own nuances, one simple example to help set the stage: few secretaries enter office expecting to fight over increases in the debt ceiling. It would seem axiomatic that by authorizing increased borrowing, Congress would feel comfortable with the resulting increase in total outstanding government obligations. Yet in almost every administration, debt ceilings increases have created crises of varying severity.

The new secretary also must immediately determine a clear, easily repeated position on currency matters. When President Richard Nixon's treasury secretary, John Connally, announced to a group of European Finance ministers that "the dollar is our currency but your problem," he could not have known how problematic the dollar would become for his successors as secretary. Most recently, Bush administration Treasury Secretary John Snow caused dollar fluctuations throughout much of his first six months in charge, at one point causing the dollar to dip to its lowest level in four years when he explained that a weak dollar could boost exports. He was subsequently corrected the next day by White House Press Secretary Ari Fleischer, who said, "I haven't seen everything he said. [But] there's no change in dollar policy. The position of the government continues to support a strong dollar."[2]

The complexity of dollar commentary is not limited to the first few months in office. On October 21, 1994, the U.S. dollar hit an all-time low against the yen shortly after Secretary Lloyd Bentsen was quoted saying, "We have no plans to intervene" in the market to support the dollar.[3] The steep slide led him to revise his comments the next day, when he stated that "we are concerned about recent movements in the dollar. We would prefer a stronger dollar." His comments stabilized the markets.[4]

While Treasury can and should be a forceful and independent voice on economic policy within the administration, the perception of public disagreement or inconsistency with White House positions seriously undermines Treasury's ability to contribute to policy formation and the secretary's effectiveness as a steward of the economy. Former Bush administration Treasury Secretary Paul O'Neill, for example, resigned from his post as treasury secretary after consistently finding himself at odds with the political and economic agenda of the Bush White House. In the fall of 2002, during a period of continued uncertainty about the economic recovery, O'Neill was focused on a broad-based tax reform to simplify the code and questioned the need for more tax cuts in the name of economic stimulus. He was overruled by others in the administration, and amid dissatisfaction from the left and the right ultimately announced his resignation on December 6, 2002.[5]

Treasury also has responsibility for a variety of entities over which it has policy control but not specific administrative or enforcement control. The most obvious examples include the Internal Revenue Service and the Office of the Comptroller of the Currency. Both play crucial roles in enacting administration policies while also maintaining very important elements of independence. History is replete with well-intentioned political appointees who attempted to reform or improve regulatory agencies only to find themselves accused of political interference. The new treasury secretary and his or her team must be exceedingly careful to avoid similar missteps.

In light of the current economic environment, the new secretary is also almost certain to face a sovereign financial crisis of one sort or another. Since 1994, a series of economic crises in fast-growing developing economies has repeatedly tested the abilities of the United States and the International Monetary Fund to maintain market stability and encourage economic liberalization. From the $50 billion package created with the United States, IMF, World Bank, and Bank for International Settlements during the peso crisis in 1995, to the default on Argentine loans prompted by an IMF withdrawal in 2001, the nature of each sovereign failure and the efficacy of each remedy varied considerably. The immediate aftermath of each currency devaluation was sharply contractionary—Mexico's gross domestic product shrank by 6.2 percent in 1995, while Argentina's income per capita fell from $8,500 to $2,800.[6]

The policy lessons of these sovereign failures are still hotly debated, but the takeaways for crisis management at the U.S. Treasury are easier to draw. The simplest lesson is to recognize the pattern of instability in developing economies as they begin to realize the benefits of economic liberalization. Within the past 14 years, we have weathered major crises in Mexico, Thailand, Indonesia, South Korea, Russia, Argentina, Uruguay, Brazil, and Malaysia.

Within the new administration, Treasury will need to ensure that any crisis is on the agenda at both the National Economic Council and the National Security Council, and that the president is available to guide any aid and loan package. Externally, the treasury secretary—working with his or her Group of Eight counterparts from Japan, Germany, Great Britain, France, Italy, Canada, and Russia—will play a lead role in negotiating any package with the IMF, the World Bank, relevant regional institutions, and the leadership of the countries themselves.

As our capital markets are truly globalized, events in relatively small sectors of small economies can unravel economic calculations throughout the world. The primary source of economic imbalance in Thailand in 1997, for example, was speculation in real estate, but the subsequent currency collapse caused the Thai currency to lose 20 percent of its value in a single day, and caused the economy to contract by 10 percent in 1998.[7] As the crisis spread to Indonesia, the S&P 500 stock market index fell by 5 percent in August 1997.[8] The U.S. response to any future crisis will need to be both rapid and flexible to contain the risks of financial contagion and to mitigate the real economic impact of financial panics on poverty, living standards, and global growth.

Events in the United States, too, can cause sudden international financial disequilibrium. The U.S. subprime mortgage market crisis beginning in mid-2007, followed by the collapse of Wall Street investment bank Bear Stearns Cos. in March 2008, followed by the takeovers of Fannie Mae and Freddie Mac this past summer, followed by the global financial crisis in September that led to the collapse of investment bank Lehman Brothers Holdings Inc. and the government rescue of U.S. insurance giant American International Group Inc., are examples of the long string of financial crises that can confront Treasury. They usefully highlight, however, the department's power and its limitations.

Through its oversight of Fannie Mae and Freddie Mac and tax policy, Treasury played a key role in considering responses to rapid house-price declines and the resulting seizing up of credit markets. Treasury, however, had a more modest set of tools with which it could take immediate action after the crisis on Wall Street began to unfold. Indeed, aside from some quite obscure statutory authority relating to the Federal Reserve, nothing that it controlled unilaterally could have made much of an immediate difference relating to the systemic risk posed by Bear Stearn's weakening position. Instead, Secretary Paulson made himself a central actor in that drama by virtue of his insights and Treasury's ability to formulate longer-term reform. As the crisis evolved, it became clear that Treasury needed a broader set of statutory authorities.

This example goes directly to the importance of Treasury's credibility. Without Secretary Paulson's knowledge and relationships on Wall Street, Treasury would likely have played a lesser role in the Bear Stearns intervention. Equally important, unless Treasury had established real credibility with Congress, it would not have succeeded in pushing through the more fundamental changes at Fannie Mae and Freddie Mac, and securing passage of the Emergency Economic Stabilization Act of 2008.

Without its statutory authority over a variety of regulatory bodies, Treasury's influence would be diminished—an important point in the context of the current debate over financial services regulatory reform. A more proactive Treasury Department over the past eight years might have prevented the crises that now occupy much of the Bush administration's energy, and have cost the American economy so severely. The new treasury secretary will need to ensure his or her department does not make the same mistakes.

Key Relationships
The most successful Treasury secretaries have succeeded in maintaining key relationships with the White House, Congress, the Federal Reserve, other U.S. financial regulatory agencies, Wall Street, and Treasury's global counterparts around the world.

First and foremost is the importance of a close relationship with the new president and senior members of the White House staff. There are certain formal prerogatives that the secretary should seek and guard jealously, including participation in certain meetings with foreign heads of state, membership in the National Security Council, control over certain policy areas, and the ability to speak definitively about matters relating to the economy. For instance, after leaving the Clinton administration's National Economic Council to join Treasury in 1995, Treasury Secretary Robert Rubin continued to participate in the 8 a.m. White House senior staff meetings. This reflected his legacy ties to the White House staff as well as the central role of economic policy in that administration's priorities. Not all White House chiefs of staff would welcome a similar role for Treasury, but such participation might make sense given today's economic challenges.

While these formal protections matter, any treasury secretary ignores the importance of roaming the White House halls at his or her peril. Informal relationships with NEC and Office of Management and Budget directors as well as the head of the Council of Economic Advisers are essential, as are good working relationships with the chiefs of staff of the president and vice president and other senior members of the White House team. The secretary will want to pay particular attention to the role of the NEC, which at its best serves as an honest broker between varying cabinet views and formulates additional sets of policy recommendations. And as Treasury will work most closely with the Departments of State and Commerce and the Office of the U.S. Trade Representative, the secretary's relationship with each of these cabinet officers merits personal attention.

Then there are the critical relationships with Congress, which can begin with the confirmation process. The chairmen and ranking members of the Senate Banking Committee and House Financial Services Committee, the Senate Finance and House Ways and Means Committees, and more generally the leadership of both bodies will become essential allies or potential adversaries in most matters of importance to Treasury. Any treasury secretary who does not understand Congress will face a significant learning curve that will curtail his or her immediate efficacy during the first 100 days and the first year of the new administration.

Most treasury secretaries choose to meet privately on a weekly basis with the chairman of the Federal Reserve. This private, personal communication helps keep both institutions informed of the other's perspectives; helps coordinate policies in areas of overlapping jurisdiction, such as banking regulation; provides a forum for airing of perceived grievances; and fundamentally helps ensure that fiscal and monetary policy do not dramatically diverge. Yet the relationship will only succeed if complemented by two important elements.

First, a clear recognition by the new administration of the Fed's independence is essential. This does not suggest a willingness to capitulate on areas of overlapping responsibility, but rather an appreciation of the dangers of commenting on areas of Fed control, most notably interest rates. Second, the new treasury secretary must appreciate the Fed's bureaucratic strength and persistence. Treasury must remain firm on its views even if these involve disagreement with the Fed.

The financial crises of the past year have only increased the Fed's regulatory importance. The new administration will also want to ensure that decisions made in the heat of a very difficult environment will stand up well over the course of time. That's just one reason why the new secretary needs to develop good working relationships with the heads of the other federal financial regulatory agencies, including the Securities and Exchange Commission, the Federal Deposit Insurance Corporation, the Commodities and Futures Trading Commission, the Comptroller of the Currency, and the new regulator of Fannie Mae and Freddie Mac. At the same time, certain institutional bodies can serve to coordinate policy and bring important outside perspectives to the policy debate. The president's Financial Markets Working Group, for example, can serve to convene the right authorities on matters of cross-department concern.

Numerous trade associations representing Wall Street, industry, labor, and community groups will seek to present views on issues before the department. A formal relationship with these organizations serves both sides of this equation: the groups provide valuable insights while Treasury avoids the impression or reality of boasting ties that are too close with any one of them. Yet these groups should not substitute for direct interaction between the new secretary and the chief executives of major financial and industrial companies, and labor and community leaders.

Similarly, allocation of the secretary's scarce time should include direct ties to leading outside economists, labor unions, community and advocacy groups, and others representing a variety of perspectives in the economy. Building and maintaining a broad network will help inform decisions, provide a useful source of market intelligence, and prevent policy initiatives from arriving out of the blue. Previous Departments of the Treasury have found themselves well served by an office of Community Development that institutionalized the important role Treasury can play in community development and the importance of maintaining an active dialogue with community leaders.

Three other sets of relationships bear mentioning in the international sphere: the G7 finance ministers, the president of the World Bank, and the executive director of the IMF. In the past, these relationships seemed of particular importance in times of crisis. Today, enhanced economic interdependence, the rise of new global issues, and the growing importance of non-G7 economies all suggest that the new administration would do well to develop a more proactive approach to international economic relations. Certainly much of the new secretary's foreign travel will be dictated by the need to participate in G7 finance minister meetings and heads-of-state summits.

At times these meetings will seem at best pro forma. Yet these relationships will become a key form of communication in the current crisis or any future events that require international coordination, and could easily become the forum for important discussion about issues such as the economic consequences of climate change. This is not to suggest that new initiatives should replace a firm focus on central issues, such as funding for foreign military interventions or coordination on exchange rates. Rather, it reflects the fact that the new secretary will have an opportunity to expand the definition of issues that appropriately fall under Treasury's purview, and do so in a way that is less reactive than has traditionally been the case.

Focus on the G7 should not, however, preclude giving attention to emerging economies such as India and China, as well as important sources of global liquidity such as those in the Persian Gulf. Similarly, close allies and trading partners such as South Korea, Australia, Mexico, Canada, and Brazil should find their way on to the secretary's policy agenda.

In most administrations, neither the IMF nor the World Bank have occupied large amounts of the secretary's time, except during a crisis. During such crises, however, Treasury's close relationships with both the IMF and World Bank leadership are crucial to a sound response. Though the United States may sometimes wish otherwise, it does not control either the Fund or the Bank—making an understanding of their internal politics and leadership objectives essential to an effective working relationship. In addition, appointments of strong executive directors (the U.S. representatives to each group) will greatly enhance the influence the United States can exert in both institutions. Having the right representatives would enhance the potential to enact the serious reform that is badly needed, but unlikely—if not impossible—without active U.S. engagement.

Policy Initiatives

The macroeconomic agenda of the 44th president will determine how some of the most important pending policy issues will be resolved. The financial crisis will be the most pressing concern, but longer term issues will need immediate attention. Tax policy falls most squarely into this category. There is bipartisan support, for example, to reform the Alternative Minimum Tax but strong disagreements about how to pay for such reform. Similarly, all of President Bush's tax cuts will expire by January 1, 2011. Decisions relating to both issues will depend substantially on the overall economic plan embodied in the new president's first budget. Yet other areas, while not uncontroversial, allow for greater long-term planning and will likely require attention regardless of the president's macroeconomic agenda. The first challenge will be administering the massive government effort to remove illiquid assets from the balance sheets of financial institutions.

The housing crisis of 2008 highlighted the complexity of the government's relationship with Fannie Mae and Freddie Mac and the need for a comprehensive reevaluation of that relationship. Legislation passed in July 2008 was an important step forward in giving Treasury the authority it needed, and the decision to place them into conservatorship averted a serious crisis, but the major issues relating to their future remain unresolved.

The new administration will face the difficult decisions concerning their mission, ownership, size, and governance. Often wrapped into the Fannie and Freddie regulatory debate is the Federal Home Loan Bank system. The FHLB has grown rapidly and has been of considerable value in providing liquidity for banks and thrifts during the housing crisis. Some critics have noted, however, that governance of some banks, and regulation of the system more generally, has not kept pace with this growth, thus exacerbating the risk that one of the banks will face financial difficulty.

Financial regulatory modernization will also be at the top of the new secretary's list of policy priorities. The current financial crisis exposed the truth that our alphabet soup of regulatory agencies is out of date. Our antiquated methods of financial services regulation, which regulate banks heavily but other parts of the financial services sector hardly at all, are serious contributors to the current financial turmoil. Reform proposals vary dramatically, but some consensus exists around the following principles.

First, to the extent that investment banks wish to tap the Federal Reserve for funds previously limited to deposit-taking institutions, they must face closer regulatory scrutiny. Second, investors need greater transparency to understand the risks embedded in many balance sheets of financial institutions of all stripes. Third, executive compensation systems should reflect the long-term interests of shareholders. And fourth, overlapping regulatory jurisdictions and "venue shopping" undermine the entire regulatory regime.

The SEC and the Fed have begun to work more closely, so some action is likely even in the absence of dramatic new legislation. The new treasury secretary needs to continue those discussions immediately, while legislative proposals for more far-reaching financial markets regulation reform could be a major preoccupation of the new administration.

As outlined in other chapters of this book, the federal budget deficit, while very large, is not an insurmountable challenge, though it has become even more complicated given the obligations associated with addressing the financial crisis. The twin deficits in the federal budget and the current account deserve immediate attention. In the past seven years, both have ballooned.

The federal budget reached a record deficit of $413 billion in 2004, and is projected to come close to $500 billion in 2009, causing the total debt outstanding to increase from $5.7 trillion in January 2001 to $9.4 trillion in April 2008.[9] Meanwhile the trade gap reached a record of $763 billion in 2006, more than double the $361 billion in 2001.[10]

Any budget deficit is a deferred taxation, with interest. In 2007, 9 percent of federal spending—more than $200 billion—was used to pay interest on the federal debt.[11] The current account deficit is financed by a mirrored value in capital inflow, either because foreigners purchase U.S. debt (whether governmental, corporate, or personal) or because the ownership of assets is transferred to foreign parties (through foreign direct investment). Both are natural parts of a free and open economy, but are also unsustainable at these levels in the long term.

Demographic trends and policy realities will make it even harder to balance our twin deficits. As baby boomers age into the Medicare and Social Security systems, and as the cost of health care continues to rise, the financial strain on those programs will unavoidably constrain our fiscal policy. Even a basic analysis of the financial health of Social Security has been politicized in the aftermath of President Bush's 2005 efforts to change the structure of the system. So while proposals abound to fix the looming deficit, a political consensus has not emerged over the best way to fix it.

Medicare is equally contentious and at least as pressing. The largest portion of Medicare, Part A, which pays for inpatient hospital expenses, is funded, like Social Security, through a portion of federal payroll taxes; through 2007 these dedicated taxes collected more in revenue than was spent on Part A. The remainder is collected in a trust fund invested in U.S. Treasury Bonds. In 2007, Part A collected $223 billion in revenue and had program expenditures of $203 billion, leaving the trust fund an accumulated $326 billion in assets.

Starting in 2008, however, expenditures in Part A will exceed revenues. The program will draw down on the trust fund, which is currently projected to exhaust itself in 2019. In the absence of the depleted trust fund, general revenue or cuts in program spending will be required to make it whole.[12] The reason: surplus payroll taxes earmarked for Medicare in prior years were used by the government as a source of funding for general programs, and those debts will now begin to be redeemed.

The new secretary will also have to engage in government investment to grow the U.S. economy. It is clear that the economic policy focus of Treasury will need to expand beyond the Bush administration's view on the correlation between investment and growth. While economists can analyze the extent to which recent growth has come from consumption rather than investment, there is little doubt that the new administration will need to invest more heavily in our human and physical infrastructure, as Gene Sperling examines in his chapter on progressive growth in this book. It is important to note here, however, that the purview of Treasury should expand beyond the need to expand valuable programs such as the Earned Income Tax Credit that reward work, to supporting an economic infrastructure that spurs innovation and entrepreneurship.[13]

In the international arena, overseas financial services coordination and liberalization should become a key focus of the new secretary. Financial services are critical to both U.S. trade interests and to the economic growth in developing nations. From the U.S. perspective, financial services employ more than 6 million Americans, and contribute more than 8 percent of total U.S. GDP[14] (the 2008 financial crisis will diminish these numbers, but not change the industry's fundamental importance). Liberalization furthermore drives critical innovation in telecommunications and information technology.[15] Just as importantly, liberalization in financial services helps developing countries by providing competition in critical aspects of economic growth, allocating resources more efficiently and increasing access to capital.[16]

Economists Wendy Dobson and Pierre Jacquet estimate that financial services liberalization could have added $1.3 trillion to the global economy in the period from 2000 to 2010.[17] "Liberalizing services has a force-multiplier effect, reverberating across an entire economy," adds former U.S. Trade Representative and current World Bank President Robert Zoellick. "Every product, idea, or consumer benefits from a more effective and efficient service sector."[18]

This is not to suggest, however, that a blanket approach to liberalization either makes good policy or practical sense. From a policy perspective, emerging economies need the opportunity to develop indigenous financial markets and financial institutions. A robust domestic lending base can help minimize the risks associated with rapid transfers of foreign direct investment. The new treasury secretary, working with USTR, will need to develop policy that balances these concerns as the new administration considers how to pursue a general agreement on trade in services. Ira Shapiro and Richard Samans examine this topic in their chapter in this book on USTR, especially involving China. It will be incumbent on Treasury, however, to make sure that financial services remains a central element of trade liberalization efforts.

Similarly, the new treasury secretary will need to engage China directly over its exchange rate policies, but must do so within the context of a larger range of bilateral issues. As Shapiro and Samans argue elsewhere in this book, the Sino-U.S. Strategic Economic Dialogue started by Bush Treasury Secretary Paulson is the place to discuss not just exchange rates and other one-sided issues, but rather opportunities for the United States and China to work cooperatively. China has already made steps to strengthen worker rights, environmental protection, and product safety; strong engagement by the United States will allow China's economy to continue to grow without placing undue external risks on the rest of the world.[19] The Strategic Economic Dialogue provides a useful forum for these types of issues.[20] It is important to remember that Treasury will have a statutory obligation to opine on China's approach to currency shortly after the new administration takes office.

The new secretary's policy agenda will also include IMF and World Bank reform. The rise of middle-income countries such as China, India, and Brazil as economic powers has fundamentally altered the economic power dynamics within the IMF and the World Bank. Meanwhile, the integration of global capital flows and the buildup of foreign currency reserves have allowed middle-income countries to opt out of many IMF and World Bank lending programs.[21] These developments are unquestioned successes, but they now require the IMF and World Bank to engage in fundamental reform.

First, both institutions will need to redefine their role in the global economy, particularly in relation to middle-income countries. Secondly, both institutions are under pressure to reform their governance. While the IMF continues as the premier organization for global economic cooperation and the lender of last resort, its day-to-day lending operations have declined. In response to this change, the IMF will need to answer two key questions about its role. Should the fund retrench to focus on the core mission of exchange rate surveillance and global financial stability or invest in new tools and activities, such as expanded technical assistance programs? And can the fund engage all of its members, including rich nations, on economic reform and stability or will it increasingly focus on the development mission in low-income countries?

Underlying both these concerns is a question of how the IMF and the World Bank can collaborate while delineating clear areas of distinct responsibility.[22] Georgetown professor Dan Tarullo, a Senior Fellow at the Center for American Progress, argues that the mutual dependence of each organization's mission and the need for significant reform in both suggest that the reform agenda should support renewed focus on their unique missions—particularly for the fund. The IMF's core mission of monitoring exchange rate regimes and ensuring financial stability is as critical now as it was 60 years ago.[23]

Reform of the World Bank stems less from structural changes in the global economy than from questions about the bank's effectiveness in its mission. Over nearly 60 years, the World Bank's largest projects have often been linked with corruption in developing countries and the enrichment of political leaders there. Under former World Bank presidents James Wolfensohn and Paul Wolfowitz, anticorruption reforms were begun. These were neither popular nor entirely effective, but nevertheless deserve sustained attention. The new secretary must work with World Bank President Zoellick to ensure these efforts continue.

Though less insidious, doubts about the efficacy of World Bank programs are critical to its relevance. Allan Metzler, an economist and author of a 2000 report on World Bank reform, recently testified that the World Bank "spends or lends about $20 billion a year but neither we nor they know which programs are effective and warrant expansion or retention, and which are ineffective and inefficient and should be abandoned."[24] A third critical question facing the bank is whether to move from loans to grants in its development programs.

The Bush administration proposed that 50 percent of funds be dispersed in grants, while European nations and Japan have balked at such a large shift, instead proposing 10–20 percent levels. And a large opportunity also exists for the new treasury secretary to work his or her global relationships to press the bank to increase its role in the promotion of institutional capacity building outside of direct lending. These efforts could include helping emerging economies develop sound regulatory policies, environmental and labor protections, and incentives for environmentally sound infrastructure enhancements.[25]

Governance reform in the IMF and the World Bank will need to move hand in hand with these policy reforms. The new treasury secretary should focus on three basic goals. First, developed countries such as the United States, Japan, and most member nations of the European Union must maintain significant roles in the decision making of both organizations. Second, middle-income countries need to have a voice in these multilateral institutions commensurate with their rising economies. And third, low-income countries, despite being prime beneficiaries of both organizations, also need to play a meaningful role.[26] This will be a hard set of goals to square, but if other reforms are to proceed at both institutions then the new secretary will need take an active role in developing specific policy proposals in this arena.

Lastly, Treasury will continue to play a key policy role in the struggle with global terrorist networks. The Treasury Office of Terrorism and Financial Intelligence is primarily focused on freezing and seizing funds suspected of use for terrorist activities, enforcing economic sanctions against "rogue" nations, protecting the integrity of the financial system, fighting financial crime, and assisting in the hunt for Iraqi assets. Within the TFI is the Office of Foreign Assets Control, or OFAC, which has the power to designate a person or organization as a sponsor of terrorism and then freeze or seize the target's assets indefinitely while requesting that the United Nations take similar action on a worldwide basis. Also within TFI is the Financial Crimes Enforcement Network, or FinCEN, which has the power to designate a person or organization as a sponsor of terrorism.

Issues for the new treasury secretary will include coordinating on terrorism financing. Sixteen agencies or departments, including the Department of the Treasury, the Department of Justice, the FBI, the State Department, the Defense Department and the Defense Intelligence Agency, the CIA, and the Department of Homeland Security, are all involved in the effort to combat terrorism financing. The new secretary will also have to staff Treasury enforcement areas in order to pursue compliance with the Patriot Act, anti-money laundering statutes, and intelligence coordination, with priority setting especially around terrorism financing and hidden foreign assets. And the new secretary will also have to detail the role of the IRS in tracking whether non-profit organizations are linked to terrorists, and the use of IRS agents for investigating terrorism financing.

Office of Management and Budget
Ensuring Fiscal Responsibility and Government Accountability

SALLY KATZEN AND JACK LEW

The Office of Management and Budget is a tremendous resource to a new president, providing deep professional expertise and analytical capacity to help the administration build and execute its new policy agenda. After the election, the work at OMB starts at a run. Even before the Inauguration, the transition team working with OMB should begin preparing the 2010 Budget for transmittal to Congress by the end of February—a task requiring quick decisions on everything from Medicare and budget enforcement rules to the withdrawal of troops from Iraq. The new administration will face a difficult balancing job: to reestablish the importance of fiscal responsibility while simultaneously advancing a core policy agenda for economic growth and opportunity. The presidential transition team and the career OMB staff will also need to prepare to take control over the government regulatory process—a critical undertaking—immediately upon taking office. The 2010 Budget and especially the 2011 Budget will require significant time and attention, but OMB also has the opportunity for direct policy impact through focused attention on fixing government performance in targeted areas, through reform of government outsourcing policies, and through an in-depth review of all presidential Executive Orders issued over the past 8 years.

The new president will face the challenge of quickly taking control of the federal budget and federal bureaucracy. OMB is the single institution that will offer a ready, willing, and able team to provide the new administration with visibility across the entire government, and the ability to take immediate policy action. In the slightly longer run, OMB is also the institution that will work with the rest of the economic and national security team to allow the 44th president to lay out a detailed program for executive branch and congressional action.

When other policy councils in the White House are settling into new offices, without files or history, OMB offers institutional memory, context, and practical advice. That's why it's critical for the new president and his team to embrace OMB immediately, taking advantage of its fully operational analytic staff with a deep tradition that it serves both the president and the presidency—rather than make the mistake of previous administrations by taking the better part of a year to accept the idea that the OMB career staff are non-partisan.

Historically, OMB's staff, filled with experts on every federal department, program, regulation, and benefit, has exemplified the best of the federal civil service. As a small agency—490 employees today, down by approximately 30 from the end of the Clinton Administration—OMB has the capacity to be nimble, and is the one office that can consider issues and help the new president make policy on a sector- or government-wide basis selectively in the short-term and comprehensively over the course of his administration.

OMB, however, has lost some if its institutional clout during the Bush administration years. Budget enforcement laws in effect in the 1990s expired in 2002, eroding some of OMB's institutional influence that came from its score-keeping and forecasting functions. The new president should work with the Congress to reinstate those rules, which will help to restore OMB's role in the budget enforcement process. During the Bush administration, OMB's emphasis also shifted from program-by-program budget review to "performance" measurement exercises of questionable utility.

OMB's work will be fast and furious. Roughly 30 days after the Inauguration, the new president's first budget is due to Congress. Meanwhile, OMB will need on day one to gain control over pending regulations developed by the Bush administration during its waning months in office.

Indeed, taking control of the regulatory process will be the first major challenge at OMB for the new administration because many parts of the government are still moving forward regardless of the wishes of the electorate on the first Tuesday in November. But the first budget, for fiscal year 2010, which begins in October 2009, will almost immediately require attention as well.

By the end of the first summer, OMB will begin the process of developing the president's first bottom-up Budget for fiscal year 2011 for delivery to Congress the following February, a mid-session review of the 2009 budget is due, substantial progress should be made on reviewing Bush-era Executive Orders, and reviews of competitive outsourcing practices and government performance reforms should be well advanced. This is a clearly a fast-paced agenda that requires first and foremost the key top officials in place to make it happen quickly and efficiently.

Top Priorities: Filling Key Positions

Work on the new president's FY 2010 Budget should begin immediately after the election. The president-elect is likely to announce his nominee for OMB director in the initial round of cabinet selections, but the transition team will be the new administration's first point of contact with OMB staff. That team should include the president-elect's top budget advisors and those with budget experience, as well as lawyers with regulatory expertise who can advise the White House on critical near-term regulatory steps to forestall the late Bush administration efforts to implement policy after the election, and to initiate important initiatives of the incoming administration.

Hopefully, the incoming transition team will enjoy the access granted to the Bush transition team in late 2000, when the outgoing Clinton administration granted access to OMB staff immediately, so that the new transition team can gather the data and analysis essential to craft the first budget. This is important, as the president's initial budget is due to Congress just a month after the Inauguration.

The first appointees at OMB should include, in addition to the director, two top positions that also require Senate confirmation—deputy director and deputy director for management—as well as the associate director for communications who can serve as the lead budget writer, the program associate directors for health and defense/international, and a chief economist, none of whom require confirmation.

The new president should also rush to the Senate his nominee for administrator of the Office of Information and Regulatory Affairs, the most important government agency no one has ever heard of. Since there is often a delay in confirming officials below the cabinet and deputy level, the transition team is likely to play a particularly critical role in ensuring that day one steps are taken to stop publication of last-minute regulations by the outgoing Administration.

The First 30 Days

The new president will need to assume immediate control over a sprawling regulatory apparatus, operating in scores of executive branch agencies running full steam to promulgate hundreds of rules developed by the Bush administration over the previous eight years. It is common practice for an exiting administration to push out as many rules as possible before a new president takes control. The Bush administration's "midnight regulations" will probably include controversial actions intended to, among other things, roll back existing public health, safety, and environmental regulations, and set standards at levels well below those desired by state and local governments in an effort to preempt more protective measures.

Regulations are the most frequently used, and are often the most effective tool available to achieve a new administration's social, economic, environmental, and public health and safety policies. Much of the regulatory activity of executive branch agencies goes unnoticed by the media, but these actions often have the most profound impact on our nation's citizens, businesses, and communities.

It is a basic tenet of administrative law that once a regulation goes into effect, the only way to overturn it is through the same notice-and-comment process mandated by the Administrative Procedure Act. Thus, as soon as possible after taking the oath of office at noon on January 20, 2009, the incoming president should issue a government-wide "stop order" to immediately freeze all pending regulatory actions. By maintaining the status quo, the new administration will have breathing room to review rules under development, letting those that are consistent with the incoming president's agenda and policies move forward and modifying or withdrawing those that are not.

This is precisely what both President Clinton and President G.W. Bush did on their first day in office. They sent a memorandum, signed by the OMB director and the White House chief of staff, respectively, to the heads of all executive branch departments and agencies directing that, with certain very limited exceptions, no proposed or final regulations were to be sent to the Federal Register for publication (a key step under the APA in issuing a regulation in proposed or final form) until a department or agency head appointed by the new president had reviewed and approved the regulation. Both incoming administrations also required that any proposed or final regulations already sent to the Federal Register, but not yet published, should be withdrawn immediately for such review and approval.

The Bush memo went one step further, however, requiring agencies to delay the effective date of any final regulation that had been published in the Federal Register but not yet taken effect—a debatable legal step that was never ruled on by the courts. Rather than risk court challenge, the new president should instead work with Congress, using the Congressional Review Act to deal with any problematic regulations that have already been published in the Federal Register (whether or not they have taken effect). The CRA provides a limited window to disapprove a regulation, making it null and void.[1]

Both the Clinton and Bush "stop orders" contemplated that OMB would co-ordinate the review of pending agency actions, reaffirming the importance of the centralized regulatory review process carried out by OIRA, which has served as the principal and most effective means by which the president oversees and manages the regulatory activities of the federal bureaucracy.[2] OIRA's centralized review process enables a president to co-ordinate a government-wide regulatory policy and receive a relatively dispassionate and analytical "second opinion" on the output of Executive Branch agencies operating in his name.[3]

A centralized OMB review process, however, is not universally acclaimed. Various pro-regulatory groups are skeptical of or even hostile to the notion, arguing that because Congress has delegated the authority to regulate to the agencies that are expert and publicly accountable, OMB review is not an appropriate substitute for agency discretion. But those who have studied the issue from the perspective of the president, including liberal and conservative Democrats, have uniformly concluded that the president must have a centralized mechanism to review regulations as an important tool to implement policy.

Still, it may take some time for the new administration to develop its own policies for regulatory review. In the interim, then, the administration should revert to Clinton's E.O. 12866, which established a centralized review process that struck a balance between the need for centralized review and the role of agency discretion that was generally accepted by virtually all affected entities— agencies, state and local governments, public interest groups, and industry.[4]

By contrast, President Bush's amendments to E.O. 12866 have been criticized as inappropriately politicizing OIRA's review process by, among other things, expanding review to cover agency non-binding guidance documents, installing at each agency a presidentially appointed "regulatory policy officer" invested with the authority to review and disapprove rulemakings at the agency, and elevating "market failure" above other justifications for regulations.

The new president should therefore rescind—by Executive Order—Bush's E.O. 13422 as quickly as possible, preferably in conjunction with the "stop order" issued on January 20, 2009. This action will leave in place the Clinton regulatory review process, which is far more likely to be consistent with the new administration's policies.[5]

In addition, the president should invite discussion of how E.O. 12866 should be modified in light of the experience of the last 25 years under various Executive Orders. It is important that the new president reaffirm the legitimacy and importance of centralized review *and* clearly state that regulations are important in protecting public health and safety, our shared resources, and economic opportunities. He should announce the creation of a Task Force chaired by OIRA and the White House counsel's office to coordinate a transparent and inclusive process to develop a new centralized review E.O., which should be issued by the summer of 2009. This process should include a broad discussion of other Bush-era regulatory circulars and bulletins that, taken together, have imposed significant burdens and constraints on resource-limited regulatory agencies.[6]

A cautionary note is warranted here. Executive Orders tend to be overused at the start of an administration because they can be issued with few restrictions and no formal process. But many early attempts to implement policy through Executive Orders end in failure. Indeed, of the E.O.s issued during the first year of President Clinton's first term, 25 percent were later rescinded by the Clinton administration. There is a limited capacity to develop and implement policies during transition, and doing a few things right should be the guiding principle.

Preparing the First Budget

Since 1981, when the new Reagan administration used the budget reconciliation process to implement a broad program of budget and policy initiatives in an omnibus manner, an incoming president's first budget has been an opportunity to make dramatic policy statements and drive a new agenda, claiming an electoral mandate to accomplish large goals. In 1981, the first Reagan budget called for massive domestic spending and tax cuts, as well as massive defense spending increases. In 1993, the first Clinton budget charted a course for deficit reduction and fiscal responsibility, along with targeted investments in a progressive agenda. And in 2001, the first Bush budget proposed tax cuts that, once enacted, consumed virtually all of the surplus generated by Clinton-era policies.

In 2009, a new administration will face a difficult balancing job. It will need to reestablish the importance of fiscal responsibility while simultaneously advancing a core policy agenda for economic growth and opportunity. This agenda will likely include, at a minimum, investments in health care, education, the environment and alternative energy, and long-neglected infrastructure repairs and improvements, priorities discussed at greater length in other chapters of this book. But many other bills coming due threaten to crowd out these investments, among them financing issues in both Social Security and Medicare, expiring tax cuts, the Alternative Minimum Tax, spending on the wars in Iraq and Afghanistan, and ongoing defense requirements.

The Bush administration "kicked the can down the road" by allowing budget enforcement rules to lapse, cutting taxes for the wealthy while debt financing a war, and generally increasing government spending. And the Bush budgets did nothing to address the coming financial pressures presented by rising health costs across the economy. To chart a more responsible course, the new administration will need to make threshold decisions on whether the economy needs additional fiscal stimulus, how much of the 2001 tax cuts the administration wants to extend, the scope of action required to deal with the AMT, the pace and spending implications of withdrawal from Iraq, and spending growth in Medicare and Medicaid.

The answers to these questions, set against the cost of maintaining existing programs at their current levels—known as the current services baseline in budget parlance—will indicate whether it might be possible to aim for a balanced budget, and how much deficit reduction can be achieved in the near term. Both the scale and complexity of these spending and tax policy issues, combined with the desired investment agenda of the new administration, means that the new president should move cautiously before announcing a target year to reach surplus. And he should do so after extensive consultation with Congress as part of a broad deficit reduction and investment strategy.

The Deficit Context

While the past eight years represent a significant missed opportunity to address some of the most pressing fiscal issues, nonetheless the new president will inherit a fiscal context that is not as immediately dire as the one President Clinton found in 1993. At that time, the federal deficit was 4.7 percent of GDP, national debt was 48 percent of GDP, and both were growing rapidly. Fiscal discipline and a strong economy under President Clinton produced the large surplus and smaller debt President Bush inherited in 2001, which was deliberately consumed by tax cuts that reduced taxes from 19.8 percent of GDP in 2001 to 17.9 percent today. Despite massive fiscal deterioration under the Bush administration, including a national debt that today stands at $5.4 trillion, up from $3.3 trillion in 2001, the new president is likely to find a federal budget deficit of about 2.8 percent of GDP, and total debt of 38 percent of GDP.

This complicated picture is certainly not rosy. The nominal annual deficit will be $400 billion, the baby boomer generation is beginning to retire, and health costs across the economy are growing unsustainably. Prior to the financial crisis, there was not the imminent sense of urgency that existed in the early 1990s. The challenge will be to balance competing needs to reassert progressive priorities in the context of a serious deficit reduction effort.

There is an added level of complexity, however, because experts disagree on the current budget outlook. Whether the budget is heading towards deficit or surplus depends on both future policy choices and baseline conventions. The Congressional Budget Office baseline, for example, projects a budget surplus in 2012 because it mechanically extends current tax law—assuming that the Bush tax cuts expire at the end of 2010. In contrast, many independent experts use baselines that assume that some tax cuts were intended to be permanent, and therefore project a deficit hovering around 2 percent to 3 percent of GDP instead of surplus in 2012.

All these forecasts focus on the unified budget deficit, which includes the surplus in the Social Security Trust Fund and thus reduces the apparent size of the deficit in the rest of the budget. Excluding Social Security funds from federal budget projections, even the more optimistic CBO baseline projects a deficit continuing for the entire period from now through 2018.

At a minimum, it will be important to set a credible and achievable goal of stabilizing both the deficit and the federal debt as a share of GDP while accommodating targeted investments. Ideally, fiscal policy under the new administration would be on a trajectory to reduce the unified deficit as a percentage of GDP and reduce the need to draw on the Social Security surplus to fund the non-Social Security portions of the budget. It will be important to consult with Congress in setting immediate deficit reduction goals.

The short deadline to develop the 2010 Budget is an added challenge. Stretching the statutory deadlines, recent administrations have sent their initial budgets forward 20 days to 40 days after Inauguration, followed by more detailed documents a few months later. The president's budget is due by law to Congress on the first Monday in February.[7]

Budget Enforcement Rules

In addition to signaling the president's budget and policy priorities, the 2010 budget should communicate the level of his administration's commitment to fiscal discipline and honesty in budgeting. Reinstating effective and meaningful budget enforcement rules is central to any effort to restore fiscal discipline. President Bush and the Republican-led Congress allowed the rules from the Budget Enforcement Act of 1990 to lapse in 2002. Those rules had several key elements: statutory limits on discretionary spending; requirements that any new entitlement spending or tax cut would need a corresponding offset from cuts in mandatory spending or additional revenues; and regular scorekeeping by OMB to monitor the impact of policy changes and trigger any enforcement actions.

Since then, Congress has reinstated some of these mechanisms in annual budget resolutions, such as the "pay-go" commitment of the current Democratic-led Congress, but they are strictly a matter of congressional protocol and are not statutory. As a result, these mechanisms can be waived by Congress and do not involve OMB scoring. With strong leadership, the budget rules of the 1990s were effective, in part because they were established in statute and gave OMB the key role of scorekeeper. The new administration should pursue enactment of similar rules.

Because it will take some time to enact this proposed legislative package, new budget enforcement rules will not be in place in the president's first year in office, but his commitment to the principle will drive the dynamics of the budget process immediately and in subsequent years. During the transition, OMB should explore the possibility of reaching an agreement with Congress to build a realistic budget baseline and effective enforcement rules. One particularly important challenge will be how to address the status of expiring Bush tax cuts to recognize offsets from the repeal of provisions that benefit the very wealthy. CBO's opinion is viewed by many in Congress and outside observers as critical to validating the legitimacy of the administration's projections.

The key to developing a budget and enforcement rules is the baseline that determines whether new policies would result in savings or added costs compared to a continuation of current policies. The problem is, in many cases it is not clear what constitutes "current policy."

On the spending side, CBO is guided by statute and precedent in making choices. If Congress, for example, passed no additional legislation, then the food stamp program, the Temporary Assistance for Needy Families program, and the State Children's Health Insurance Program would all expire at no budgetary cost. But CBO's baseline assumes that these programs continue—for a total of $870 billion over the next decade.

In contrast, CBO assumes that the tax cuts enacted since 2001 expire because they were passed with sunset provisions, even though those end dates were designed to reduce the fiscal impact of the tax cuts, not because all the cuts were viewed as temporary. If the baseline assumes that a provision will sunset, extending that provision will require offsets if there is a pay-go rule similar to the rule in effect in the 1990s. Yet if a provision is assumed to be permanent, then there will be savings from repealing that provision—savings that can be used to either reduce the deficit or finance a new initiative.

The baseline issue is highly consequential because the expiration or reduction of the Bush tax cuts is frequently described as the source of offsets to finance a progressive agenda. Baseline adjustments should reflect only the continuation of provisions that were designed as permanent policy. But this should not apply to all tax provisions that require attention. One case in point is the Alternative Minimum Tax, which requires legislative action because there is no permanent policy in place to address the problem fully. Similarly, one-time fiscal stimulus tax cuts were not meant to be permanent.

Building a Budget

In a non-transition year, the bottom-up process to build the president's budget takes over seven months. OMB provides budget guidance to the agencies in April and May, which is followed by three months of line-by-line agency reviews through the fall, and then an end-of-year appeal process to the writing of the documents the President sends to Congress in early February. Compiling a new president's first budget in four weeks is no simple task.

The transition team can make best use of the time available by taking a few key steps. First, it needs to get started on the baseline right after the election. Developing the new president's budget will be much easier if the outgoing OMB team leaves behind a detailed current services baseline for the new team to use as a starting point, as the Clinton team did in 2001. The transition team may need to make revisions, but it should not be necessary or desirable to re-open every aspect of the baseline.

The transition team should also ask the exiting OMB director to make available OMB staff to work with the incoming team immediately after the election, both to prepare a baseline and begin estimating the economic impact of new initiatives. In December 2000, for example, the Clinton administration provided the incoming Bush team with full access to OMB resources literally the day the Supreme Court resolved the contested election.

Since Congress and the Bush administration are unlikely to agree on full year appropriations for the fiscal year beginning October 1, 2008, most of the government will be funded under a temporary or full-year stop gap appropriation that simply extends prior year funding levels. This will not address changing needs and priorities, or natural expansions and contractions of programs that reflect current economic conditions. Moreover, further emergency action may be needed to address the financial crisis and the economic downturn. The new administration, in consultation with Congress, should undertake a review to determine where emergency action, supplemental appropriations, and rescissions are necessary or whether full-year appropriations should be enacted in some cases.

Second, the OMB transition team should start narrowing the short list of initiatives to be highlighted in the budget, and then determine their rough magnitude. Given the short timeframe, the initial budget will not be more than an outline of priorities. But it should leave room for the president's key initiatives, even if only as a placeholder. Without question it will take longer than 20 days to 40 days to present a detailed program for universal health care coverage, but it is nonetheless important for the 2010 budget to include a proxy for the rough cost of this initiative when it is initially presented to Congress.

Third, OMB will need to launch a review of health spending and prices across the economy. Rising federal health care expenditures on Medicare and Medicaid are driven by the rising cost of health care across the economy. Overall government spending on health care is less than half of the total health economy, and it has been rising at roughly the same rate as overall health care costs. This means that reducing federal spending without addressing the overall problem of rising health care costs would mean reducing the access to health care for the elderly, the disabled, and the poor—the groups whose health care is funded by federal programs. While the new administration can and should undertake cost containment measures within federal programs, it will be impossible to bring federal spending on health care under control in the absence of policies that address health care costs more broadly.

Similarly, OMB needs to begin a review of defense spending, which will determine the pace of proposed deficit reduction as well as the amount of resources available for domestic initiatives. In the short run, the costs of the wars in Iraq and Afghanistan will continue to drive defense spending, but even before those wars there were spending implications stemming from the aging of the last big set of defense acquisitions—implications that are larger now as a result of intensive use.

Finally, OMB needs to start building a rescission list. OMB can illustrate the president's priorities by asking Congress to remove or reduce appropriations in areas that are inconsistent with the administration's agenda, a step that will also help offset the cost of new initiatives. The president's first budget can also demonstrate fiscal discipline and honesty in budgeting by clearly spelling out the implications of its policies. Prior to the current administration, proposals included detailed estimates of budget authority, outlays, and receipts for a full 10 years. The Bush budgets shortened that to five years, and for many programs only one year. While long-term forecasts may not be precisely accurate, a shorter window masks problematic trends. The new administration should include 10-year estimates in its budget proposals.

The First 150 Days

Amid the rush to pull together a credible and insightful 2010 budget for the new administration, OMB will also need to launch a review of Bush-era Executive Orders and lead the effort to either rescind or modify these E.O.s. President Bush issued almost 300 E.O.s during his administration. Some were well-covered in the press, but many others received scant attention. They remain in place and valid until rescinded or modified by a subsequent Executive Order.[8]

A substantial number of Bush E.O.s will require no action—many provided directives that have expired and others simply carried out routine or benign actions. But others clearly address controversial issues, such as the treatment of foreign nationals detained by the U.S. government, which must be harmonized with the new administration's priorities and positions. The greatest challenge will come in identifying E.O.s with innocuous titles that nonetheless contain social and economic policies on which the new administration differs dramatically from the Bush administration. Some of these involve union membership and dues, the "taking" of property rights, and tort reform.[9]

In addition, OMB needs to begin identifying critical management problems and proposing fixes at federal agencies. Over the past 8 years, inefficient and ineffective federal programs have hit the front pages of the nation's newspapers—from the woefully insufficient response to Katrina to the massive backlog in processing applications for passport renewal. The Clinton administration made progress in heightening awareness within federal agencies of the importance of "customer service" in the broadest sense, effectively managing government programs and increasing the confidence of the American people that their government is working for them. Because there has been a significant erosion of the commitment to effective management and customer service during the Bush administration, it is essential to restore that trust and faith.

Many troubled federal programs can benefit from focused attention and additional resources. Within the first 150 days, OMB should review the status of the most pressing management problems, and then select two or three on which real progress could be made during the first two years of the administration. OMB should select programs that are highly visible and important to the public—such as the Federal Emergency Management Agency, the passport and/or naturalization process, or Transportation Security Administration procedures at airports—along with the 2010 Census, which was added recently to the "High Risk" list of the Government Accountability Office.

A strong OMB deputy director for management, with a solid background in managing large public institutions, should drive this process, with the first task being to convince targeted agencies that this effort is a high priority. That could be a challenge if the new leaders at these other agencies are preoccupied with establishing their own new initiatives rather than confronting the trouble spots they have inherited.

The issue of government performance, however, goes well beyond troubled federal programs. Recent administrations and Congress have repeatedly sought to strengthen the performance and accountability of federal agencies. The Bush administration upped the ante in 2002 when it created the Program Assessment Rating Tool, which requires agencies to complete a questionnaire of at least 25 multi-part questions. OMB then rates each program within the government and posts the results on OMB's website.

The PART process has proved troubling on many fronts. It is extremely time-consuming for the agencies and OMB, and allows considerable inconsistency with respect to the "rating" of the agencies. Some have suggested that PART provides cover to use seemingly objective data in the service of ideological opposition to (or favoritism for) particular government programs. Critics also say the over-emphasis on quantification obscures important values because the one-size-fits-all framework leads to convoluted assessments.

Compounding this problem is Executive Order 13450, issued by President Bush, which created in each agency a "performance improvement officer" with ties (and loyalty) to the White House and OMB rather than to the agency head. It also created a narrowly populated "performance improvement council," which critics contend "has the potential to be the conduit for infusion of political directives and biases into program operation."[10]

The new administration should embrace the idea of holding government agencies accountable through some form of performance-based measurements. The administration should signal that, while it will substantially reform the existing PART program, performance matters.

The First Year

Preparing the president's FY 2011 budget will take many months, beginning with general guidance to the agencies in April or May that sets targets for overall spending levels. Agencies submit their proposed budgets to OMB near Labor Day, OMB gives responses to the agencies before Thanksgiving, and final budget decisions are made by the end of the year so the documents can be written and prepared for transmittal. At each stage, economic assumptions developed by the lead economic agencies (Treasury, OMB, and the Council of Economic Advisers) are used as the basis for projections.[11]

OMB's initial guidance to agencies should include fiscal policy direction and a dollar allocation that reflect the president's objectives. Typically, the so called mid-session review, which is due to Congress in July to update the budget for likely changes in the economy, becomes the basis for making the broad fiscal policy decisions that determine the overall direction of the guidance.

After the agencies present their budget proposals to OMB, there are typically "hearings" at an OMB staff level that eventually lead to a series of budget reviews—called director's reviews—at which agency-by-agency baselines and proposed changes are presented to OMB leadership between Labor Day and November. OMB then returns a "passback" of a revised budget proposal to each agency, usually before Thanksgiving. The details of these proposed budgets reflect the OMB director's consultation with the president and the White House economic team to ensure that the priorities match the administration's objectives. Agencies can appeal passback levels, either to the OMB director or a policy board that also includes the White House chief of staff and/or the vice president.

OMB in the first year also must find the time and personnel to re-evaluate the government's approach to competitive outsourcing. The federal government has traditionally relied on the private sector for needed commercial services used by the government, such as transportation, food, or maintenance services. OMB Circular A-76, first issued in 1966, was based on the premise that inherently governmental activities should be performed by government employees, but that taxpayers would receive maximum value for their dollars if commercial activities were subject to the forces of competition.

What was introduced as a tool for cost-effective management of the government has unfortunately become a way to significantly limit the government, reduce its accountability, and arguably increase, rather than decrease, the cost of government overall. The Clinton administration, pressured by the Republican Congress, required agencies to intensify their efforts to identify commercial activities that could be privatized. Then President Bush made competitive sourcing a top priority, announcing that both civilian and defense agencies had to subject 425,000 positions to competition with outside entities by 2007. This figure represents half of all federal jobs suitable for competition.

Here, as in the case of performance measurement, the new president should recognize that there is some merit to the underlying policy of competitive sourcing, but that the way the program is currently being implemented requires drastic change. First, it is critical that the line be properly drawn between core government functions that should be carried out only by government employees, such as processing Veterans Administration disability benefit applications that involve discretion, and activities that are truly commercial, such as food services in federal facilities. Second, the process for competitive sourcing should be carried out efficiently, and in a way that is not disruptive to ongoing work.

Most importantly, where outsourcing of commercial activities occurs, the agency should retain meaningful oversight over those activities. Too often, when the federal team loses a competition, the agency's workforce is reduced to the point that it lacks experienced personnel who can effectively monitor the outsourced activities. The results: failure to ensure efficiency, prevent fraud and abuse in outsourced contacts, and hold outside contractors accountable.

This problem grew swiftly in size and scope during the Bush administration because of the steady increase in outsourced contracting, including in areas critical to government policy—from security services and reconstruction in Afghanistan and Iraq, to prison management, to enforcing numerous regulatory programs. The 44th president should signal early on that he will reverse these developments and put in place sensible competitive sourcing principles.

Office of the United States Trade Representative

Responding to the Changing Global Challenge

IRA SHAPIRO AND RICHARD SAMANS

Against a backdrop of deep public and congressional skepticism about the benefits of global trade and the collapse of the Doha Round, the Office of the United States Trade Representative must formulate a new and different trade policy—one that takes a strategic approach to making globalization more inclusive and sustainable. This new approach must be developed in league with Congress through a major review of our trade policies and the challenges and economic strategies of other nations. This new approach must build on the recent bipartisan agreement to include enforceable labor and environmental standards in new trade pacts and include a new focus on ensuring that trade rules help combat climate change and do not impede the essential global energy transformation.

The new U.S. trade strategy should increase opportunities for cutting-edge U.S. industries in large markets around the world, and it should consider new trade arrangements, including World Trade Organization agreements in key sectors and wide-ranging agreements with those developed countries that share our commitment to open markets, intellectual property protection, labor rights, and environmental and consumer-protection standards. USTR and the new administration should focus intently on our country's slipping trade position in Asia, as well as be part of an overall effort by the new administration to engage vigorously with China to redress the global economic imbalances exacerbated by China's export-led growth and currency arrangements. The United States should take a leadership role in working to ensure that the least developed countries have the increased trade opportunities that the Doha Round has failed to deliver.

The Office of the United States Trade Representative has the responsibility for leadership in the executive branch for the formulation of U.S. trade policy and the negotiation of U.S. trade agreements.[1] USTR, with just over 200 professionals, is led by the cabinet-level trade representative and is part of the Executive Office of the President. For the incoming administration, the good news is that USTR remains well respected within the U.S. government, by congressional trade committees, by foreign governments, and by the U.S. business community. Some of USTR's most accomplished negotiators have recently retired, but the challenge of international negotiation ensures that talented public servants continue to be attracted to the agency. The USTR continues to operate effectively because the interagency process is well established by statute and practice, as is the extensive network of advisory committees that informs the office.[2]

The fundamental challenge for the new administration, however, is the trade policy that USTR has pursued lacks support among the American people and Congress. Americans generally recognize that globalization is inexorable, but they have growing doubts that it is beneficial to the majority of American workers. They are increasingly hostile to trade agreements, which they view as the U.S. government taking action to serve multinational corporations and their executives amid rising inequality, massive manufacturing job losses, and recession.

To illustrate the erosion of congressional and public support: the North American Free Trade Agreement was approved by the House of Representatives in 1993 with the votes of 102 House Democrats, but in 2005 the Central American Free Trade Agreement passed the House of Representatives with the votes of only 15 Democrats. In 2000, 64 percent of the public questioned said that "free trade with other countries is good" for the United States, with 27 percent saying it was "bad."[3] In 2008, when asked whether "free international trade has helped or hurt the economy," 26 percent said "helped," while 50 percent said "hurt."[4]

The time is right for a new U.S. trade policy, and not just because the public mood demands it, the new president promised it, and the Doha Development Round has collapsed.[5] In fact, U.S. trade policy is increasingly disconnected from the realities of a swiftly changing global economy. Enormous time and energy have been dedicated to negotiating trade objectives, yet the negotiations have proven outdated, commercially insignificant, or just plain futile. Meanwhile, the real challenges to U.S. trade policy are unaddressed, particularly those posed by China, Asia, and more generally, areas where an increasing number of important economic players pursue their own strategies and trade agreements—either disregarding the United States or consciously seeking to disadvantage our economy.

The arrival of a new president with comprehensive domestic economic strategies will reduce some of the acrimony over trade that exists between the White House, Congress, and the American people. Trade will loom less large when the new president and Congress focus on financial market regulation, health care reform, retirement income security, and job creation through increased investments in infrastructure, research and development, and new technologies to transition to a more efficient, low-carbon economy.

But ultimately, USTR will have to formulate, articulate, and pursue a U.S. trade policy that is different from the policy of previous USTRs, Republican and Democratic alike. The United States today shows clear signs of "trade fatigue," but it is a luxury that we cannot afford. A retreat from trade is not the answer. A new and comprehensive trade strategy that supports U.S. economic interests by helping our cutting-edge industries and creating expanded middle classes around the world, lifting tens of millions more people out of poverty, is absolutely essential.

The First 100 Days

The fundamental goal of USTR's first 100 days should be to begin building a consensus for a new U.S. trade policy that will have real and sustained support from Congress. Inevitably, the new trade representative will find this early period dominated by consultations with Congress, as well as meetings with trade ministers from other leading nations, to determine the challenges and opportunities that are available globally in the aftermath of the Doha failure.

USTR is required by Congress to issue three annual reports that will frame the agency's priorities for the reduction of unfair trade barriers around the world. On March 1, USTR must release the USTR Trade Agenda, which becomes an early signal from the new administration of its approach to trade. President Bush's Trade Representative, Robert Zoellick, used this report effectively to present in detail Bush's "competitive liberalization" agenda. This report is an opportunity for the new president to lay out the parameters of his review of U.S. trade policy.

Then, on March 31, USTR must issue the National Trade Estimate Report, which is a comprehensive analysis of the "acts, policies or practices of each foreign country which constitute significant barriers to, and distortions of U.S. exports of good or services."[6] One month later, USTR is required to "identify those foreign countries that deny adequate and effective protection of intellectual property rights." This report, known as "Special 301," also requires USTR to identify "priority foreign countries" that have the "most onerous or egregious acts, policies or practices."[7]

The professional staff at USTR excels at turning out these massive reports, with major input from the affected industries. The reports present early opportunities for the new trade representative to highlight some priorities by focusing on the trade barriers or unfair trade practices, and the offending countries that are of most concern to the United States. These reports will frame the changes required to place U.S. trade policy on more sound policy and political footing. These changes will be numerous, fundamental, and interrelated with changes required in other areas of foreign economic policy.

A New Partnership with Congress

The constitutional authority of Congress to set trade policy requires for all practical purposes that any major, new strategy will have to be developed in close consultation with the leadership of the House Ways and Means Committee, Senate Finance Committee, and other relevant committees and congressional leaders. This is a process that is likely to take at least the better part of the first year in office, yet the groundwork with Congress must begin immediately.

To this end, the trade representative should help the president prepare an announcement during this period that spells out three basic objectives. First, the announcement should direct USTR and other relevant agencies, such as the Departments of Treasury, State, Commerce, Labor, and the Environmental Protection Agency, to develop recommendations for a new, more integrated approach to trade and globalization within his first year in office—based on an evaluation of the historical performance of U.S. trade and foreign economic policy and the strategies of other nations. Particular focus should be given to the interrelationship between trade and the necessary steps to combat climate change around the globe.

Second, the announcement should direct USTR to lead an unprecedented process of consultation with Congress to develop this new strategy. As part of such consultation, USTR should state that it welcomes any initiative by congressional leaders to involve the public and wider House and Senate membership in this process through a coordinated set of hearings in relevant committees. Third, the announcement should articulate a set of fundamental principles on which these recommendations should be based. By articulating a set of "first principles" through this series of consultations, the president and his trade representative could set the direction for the changes in policy they seek, without preempting the robust debate within the administration and Congress that will be necessary to build confidence and buy-in for a new trade policy.

These "first principles" should reflect the new administration's view that global economic integration, including regional integration, can be fundamentally a positive force for economic growth and poverty reduction around the world, but that trade agreements are a means to that end rather than ends in themselves. Like other instruments of economic policy, trade agreements should be evaluated based on whether they contribute to broad-based progress in living standards.

Our trade policy should seek to create economic opportunities by opening markets and establishing fair rules in the major overseas and industry sectors likely to be the fastest growing in the coming years. It should provide the public with confidence that agreements are being enforced and our competitors are playing by the rules. And it should reinforce, rather than clash with, U.S. policy goals in other major areas, in particular poverty reduction, worker rights, environmental protection, and climate change mitigation.[8]

This set of first principles should also reflect the view that trade liberalization often only realizes its full potential to contribute to win-win outcomes for living standards both here and abroad when it is integrated with steps to ease economic dislocation; strengthen labor, environmental, consumer, and other institutions; and ensure that exchange rates are driven by fundamental economic conditions. And the principles should reflect the idea that commensurately greater responsibility for sustaining global growth comes with higher levels of industrialization and global integration.

To be more effective in advancing a positive sum vision of global economic integration, U.S. international trade, aid, and monetary policies should be reformulated in line with these principles, bolstered by a major renovation of the multilateral institutions most relevant to this task: the International Monetary Fund, the World Bank and regional multilateral development banks, the International Labor Organization, and the World Trade Organization.

This new trade policy framework can be formulated successfully only if the partnership between the executive and Congress is rebuilt, the views of domestic constituencies are meaningfully considered, and the new administration's assessment of global prospects are grounded on careful analysis and serious discussions with key trading nations around the world.

The Multilateral Agenda

The United States has long been the leading champion of the multilateral General Agreement on Tariffs and Trade/WTO trading system, founded in the aftermath of World War II, and should continue to be a committed leader of the multilateral system. Multilateral trade liberalization has contributed to increased prosperity around the world. It remains a preferable alternative to bilateral or regional trade arrangements, which can easily result in discrimination against other trading nations, and the rise of regional trading blocks.

Despite an unwavering commitment to the multilateral WTO system, the new trade representative should resist the temptation to commit the president to rescuing the Doha Round—the multilateral trade negotiation initiated in 2001 with the stated objectives of continuing the broad-based liberalization of trade and removing trade barriers to agricultural and nonagricultural market access and services. The collapse of the Doha Round in mid-2008 was not un-expected. It was not a failure that can be remedied by new negotiators or an ex-ercise of U.S. political will by a new president. The promised "development agenda" created high expectations; ambitious liberalization goals generated in-adequate support; and the sensitive issues in the areas of agriculture and food proved simply insurmountable. The concept of a comprehensive round based on a "single undertaking" means that no agreement can be reached unless everything is agreed to. That has proved to be unworkable.

Nevertheless, it is possible that next year there will be the opportunity to reach a more modest Doha outcome that seeks to consolidate many of the concessions made in the run-up to the collapse of negotiations. The new trade representative should indicate that he or she maintains an open mind in this re-spect depending upon whether there is sufficient movement by other parties, since it would not be in the interests of the United States to be characterized as an obstacle to progress in the WTO. The United States still has a powerful in-terest in maintaining a workable multilateral trading system to avoid a world in which trade and investment increasingly gravitate toward regional blocks, probably to our disadvantage and to the benefit of China's growing power and influence.[9] But in the event the Doha talks are not salvaged, the best course for the United States would be to pursue its objectives by other multilateral and plurilateral means, such as through sectoral and free trade agreements and trade preference programs.

Sectoral and Free Trade Agreements
For example, the new trade representative could explore with Congress and other nations the desirability of plurilateral sectoral agreements in some of the fastest-growing sectors, such as energy and environmental industries, medical and health industries, or media and entertainment industries. These sectoral agreements could be modeled after the successful negotiations of the late 1990s on information technology, financial services, and basic telecommunica-tions.[10] Based on the experience of the earlier agreements, a critical mass of na-tions with significant interests in the sector would join because they would not want to be excluded.

As part of the proposed interagency evaluation of how U.S. trade and foreign economic policy can be improved to strengthen progress in living standards at home and abroad, the new administration must reconsider the U.S. approach to negotiating free trade agreements. President John F. Kennedy once described himself as "an idealist without illusions." The current U.S. approach to FTAs is neither idealistic nor realistic, and is sorely in need of change.

During the Bush administration, under the flag of "competitive liberalization," USTR negotiated a dizzying series of bilateral free trade agreements, mainly with developing countries, among them Chile, Morocco, Jordan, Oman, Australia, Bahrain, Colombia, Peru, Panama, South Korea, and a regional FTA with Central America. A commercial argument, grounded in reciprocity, can be made for almost all of them—in virtually every case the U.S. market was more open to our trading partner than its market was to us.

That does not mean, however, that these agreements generated broad-based contributions to living standards in both trading partners commensurate with the political capital required to negotiate and gain political approval of them. A series of random bilateral trade agreements with countries all over the world, many of them small economies, is neither economically effective nor politically sustainable. There is simply no support in Congress for continuing to negotiate in this way.

Powerful international competitive pressures, however, are driving the pursuit of certain FTAs. Trading nations want to lower barriers, but they are opting for preferential arrangements with chosen trading partners rather than reaching multilateral or broad regional agreements that lower barriers to many trading partners.[11] Many trade experts contend this blizzard of FTA negotiations risks further complexity in doing business globally, trade diversion, and even growing mercantilist competition among trading blocks. But the drive toward preferential FTAs is likely to accelerate because of the failure of the Doha Round.[12] The United States cannot simply stand by and allow its competitive position to erode if our competitors prove more adept at negotiating and implementing FTAs than we are.

The Special Case of Asia

The United States faces an enormous challenge in regaining its economic position in Asia, the most dynamic region of the world. Over the past six years, the Asian countries, led by the Association of Southeast Asian Nations, have increasingly embraced the idea of free trade between themselves on a regional basis. The result has been a rapid series of bilateral and regional FTAs involving virtually every country in the region. Most of these agreements and proposed arrangements include East Asian economic integration, potentially leaving the

United States on the sidelines as Asian trading partners lower barriers among themselves.

GATT Article XXIV allows bilateral and regional trade agreements as an exception to multilateral rules, but only if they are comprehensive, covering virtually all trade. The current USTR position seems to be that U.S. FTAs meet that standard, those pursued by other countries do not, and the U.S. will neither challenge the other countries' FTAs nor adopt a more flexible approach to negotiating our own. This is not a tenable policy.

USTR should not let ideology prevent pursuit of potentially beneficial free trade agreements with Asian nations, particularly when these agreements are potentially more economically beneficial and will receive greater political support on Capitol Hill.

The new administration, for example, could reach out to the more advanced countries in Asia as potential partners in a vanguard, global club of advanced economics that agree to pursue deeper economic integration through both free trade and basic consistency of structural, regulatory, and exchange rate policies and institutions. It is possible to envision a group of countries including Australia, Singapore, South Korea, and Japan joining in such an agreement with the United States, featuring liberalization of services, high levels of intellectual property protection, and strong labor rights and environmental standards.[13] The U.S. desire to be more firmly anchored in Asia might coincide with the interest of Asian nations in having a counterweight to China's increasing economic and political clout.[14]

This vision of a plurilateral inner core of countries within the world trading system where trade and investments flow freely, raising median incomes synergistically without undue distortion from disparate institutional environments or deliberate currency management policies, may ultimately represent a sounder organizing principle for FTAs than geographical proximity or bilateral ties. As part of the negotiations to establish such a plurilateral arrangement, the founding countries should also seek to harmonize and upgrade their trade preference rules with low-income countries as well as other features of their often overlapping free trade agreements that serve to complicate business and divert trade around the world.

More than an FTA in a conventional sense, this new arrangement would commit a pioneer group of countries to providing long-term leadership to the multilateral system by deepening their economic integration on a sustainable basis through open product and services markets; comparable labor, environmental, consumer, and investor protections and regulatory capacity; and market-determined exchange rates. By welcoming other countries to join as they develop, this pioneering group would expand over time, unconstrained by regional proximity, thereby providing a more natural bridge to deeper economic integration on a multilateral basis.

Developing Countries. USTR's efforts to negotiate free trade agreements with developing countries have generated enormous controversy on Capitol Hill. This is clearly an area where the new trade representative should be consulting extensively with Congress and assessing the results of existing FTAs. In general terms, the new trade representative should be pursuing only those FTAs with developing countries that can help increase living standards, purchasing power, and import demand among all countries. The idea would be to combine such trade liberalization with trade adjustment assistance and social safety net reform in the United States. Trade is but one tool, along with development and macroeconomic policy, to help broaden the benefits of globalization to more citizens in developing countries.

This is why the new president should require USTR to conduct a thorough economic assessment of whether any bilateral FTA with a developing country is likely to result in an agreement that would contribute significantly to a net (not just bilateral) expansion of trade before deciding whether to request congressional authority to enter into free trade agreement negotiations. In particular, USTR must determine whether improvements should be sought in the country's labor, environmental, consumer, or investor laws and institutions in order to strengthen the likely payoff to broadly rising living standards through expanded trade and investment links with the U.S. economy.

The first test would force a more rigorous discussion within the administration and with Congress about the economic (as opposed to foreign policy) justification for deviating from what should be a general preference for multilateral over bilateral trade liberalization. The second test would require an interagency process, including the Labor and Treasury departments, to take a hard look at the policy-instituting capabilities of the country in key arenas such as labor rights, environmental protection, and consumer and investor safeguards, in order to determine the extent to which capacity building assistance should be mobilized.

The more economically advanced the country, the higher should be our expectation of the quality of its laws and institutional capacity in these areas. Yet there should be no expectation or requirement that these arrangements must be exactly like our own—the only exception being labor law as it relates to the International Labor Organization's Declaration on Fundamental Principles and Rights at Work. These core labor standards are internationally recognized as universal human rights, which means they should be reflected as strongly in the laws of poorer countries as they are in wealthier ones.

Major weaknesses in legal or institutional capacities in any of these areas should become part of the scope of the negotiating mandate the new administration seeks from Congress and agrees to with the negotiating partner or partners. The purpose of such negotiations should be to develop a mutually agreed upon plan of development cooperation to narrow these gaps over time. In particular, if worker rights or certain other basic social, environmental, consumer, or investor protections covered by the negotiating mandate are found to exist in law but not in practice, then these concerns should become an element of the negotiations. A package of relevant multilateral or bilateral technical assistance should be agreed to and funded as part of the overall agreement.

This approach would have the virtue of building directly on the important steps that have already been taken—starting with the Jordan Free Trade Agreement negotiated in 2000—to include respect for enforceable labor and environmental standards in the body of trade pacts.[15] This approach would build on the recent leadership of Reps. Charles Rangel (D-NY) and Sander Levin (D-MI) and the long-standing advocacy of the AFL-CIO, which resulted in the incorporation of ILO core labor standards and related capacity-building assistance in the recent Peru Trade Promotion Agreement. It would ground free trade agreements in a wider, more coherent strategy to strengthen the positive-sum impact of integration on global living standards.

Trade with Least Developed Countries. In the United States and around the world, progressives identified strongly with the Doha objective of a "development round." The idea was to break down trade barriers and eliminate trade-distorting practices that disadvantaged the poorest nations—many of which are found in sub-Saharan Africa—in developing their export potential, particularly in agriculture. The failure of Doha is a setback for the poorest nations that can least afford it, and it must be offset by other imaginative and effective measures. The new administration will want to formulate and implement a coherent and compassionate approach to trade with the world's least developed countries. This is an economic opportunity for the United States over the long haul, but more importantly it is a moral imperative that USTR should make a top priority.

There is significant evidence that the U.S. Generalized System of Preferences trade program and other trade preference programs, such as the Africa Growth and Opportunity Act and the Andean Trade Preferences Act, are beneficial to developing countries. A study of U.S. preference programs from the 1980s shows that GSP-beneficiary countries increased exports of products eligible for GSP treatment by about 8 percent annually.[16] A more recent analysis showed that preferences generated significant positive effects on investment in Central America and export diversification, contributing to income growth in the region.[17]

Nevertheless, GSP programs do not appear to be reaching their full potential because the programs often fail to cover the products that poorer countries have a comparative advantage in producing. Nongovernmental organizations most familiar with the performance and shortcomings of GSP programs advocate for important reforms, including making GSP permanent—providing complete duty-free access for all exports from the least developed countries—because the present pattern of short-term extensions is a disincentive to investments.[18] Such a reform would be an important part of the new United States trade policy, and obviously a crucial piece of U.S. foreign policy toward the developing world. But the new trade representative should also explore whether the European Union, Japan, and other developed nations would coordinate their preference programs with ours so that a number of major trading nations were giving tariff-free access to imports from the least developed countries.

Colombia and South Korea FTAs

The end of the Bush administration is likely to leave for the next president and Congress the problem of what to do with the U.S.-Colombia FTA and the U.S.-South Korea FTA, agreements already negotiated with friendly nations and allies in vital regions of the world.[19] These agreements, if mishandled, could have a very detrimental effect on the U.S. position in Latin America and in Asia because of the expectations that have been raised there.

Rather than risk our relations with these two important countries through further delay, the new president and trade representative should seek to address the concerns that leave many uncomfortable with supporting their ratification. For Colombia, that would require evidence of sufficient progress in not only ending violence but also in investigating and prosecuting those who have engaged in such violence.

For South Korea, that would require addressing the impediments to U.S. beef and auto exports. Without progress on these fronts, Congress is unlikely to support the agreements. The job of the new president and his secretary of state will be to explain to the leaders and citizens of these two countries why these issues are so important to Congress and the American people, while at the same time explaining to Congress and the American people the importance of these trade agreements to U.S. economic and foreign policy and economic objectives.

North American Free Trade Agreement

The next president's framework for trade policy should become part of our dialogue with our Mexican and Canadian counterparts in NAFTA. In the spirit of cooperation among neighbors, USTR should indicate that the United States seeks a full discussion in which the three countries share their perspectives on how well NAFTA has operated, and place on the table their ideas, too, for enhancing the performance of the agreement.

NAFTA has been in effect nearly 15 years. During that time, world trade patterns have been dramatically affected by, among other things, the economic rise of China and the pervasive influence of the Internet. It is perfectly appropriate for the three countries to undertake a serious evaluation of the trade agreement at this juncture. It is entirely possible that Mexico and Canada would be willing to explore steps in a number of other areas that could improve the performance of the agreement without reopening the complicated and highly interdependent framework of tariff and quota concessions negotiated in the 1990s.

These talks could be framed as a strategy to strengthen the competitiveness of North America as a whole vis-à-vis Asia and Europe and to broaden the gains to living standards for Americans, Canadians, and Mexicans alike. It could include a group of topics chosen to be broadly palatable to all three parties, among them strengthening the labor secretariat's capacity to monitor, adjudicate, and provide technical assistance in respect of labor standards enforcement; undertaking a broad assessment of North American environmental challenges with a view toward developing a regional strategy of environmental cooperation; and providing a major increase in funding for border environmental infrastructure needs for which the North American Development Bank was originally envisioned, but never adequately funded to deliver.

Other areas that the three countries should consider might include: improving coordination between regulatory authorities to address food safety concerns; examining border clearance delays that hinder trade; increasing cross-border energy cooperation and investment in refineries, transmission systems, and oil production; strengthening adjustment assistance policies; and perhaps even strengthening guest worker arrangements to ensure they enjoy full legal protection in the United States. The United States, Canada, and Mexico are all major energy, food, and automobile producers; these sectors manifest some of the fundamental challenges facing the global community. Seeking common, mutually beneficial approaches in these areas would be a valuable objective of the discussions among them.

Climate Change

Other than the war in Iraq, nothing has diminished the international standing of the United States as much as the Bush administration's failure to provide leadership on the global challenge of climate change. There is no doubt that providing leadership on climate change will be one of the new president's highest priorities in his first 100 days. Yet it is increasingly clear that it will be impossible to reduce carbon emissions globally without coming to grips with the international trade implications of doing so.

It will be very difficult for the developed world to impose on its manufacturers the additional cost of controlling carbon emissions while allowing developing countries to avoid those costs. The European Union is already debating the application of a border tax adjustment to level the playing field for its industries that are being required to limit emissions. Rapidly developing nations, however, largely lack the institutional capacity to institute the emissions controls necessary to accurately reduce their carbon output; they believe it is unfair to require them to slow their emissions before they have experienced economic growth comparable to the developed world. Reducing energy intensity and the rate of emissions growth is the best outcome that may emerge from international negotiations.

This is a crucial issue, raising novel WTO legal questions, where both new thinking and international negotiation will be required. This is an urgent problem that must be addressed in the first year of the new administration; it cannot drag on for years. At the instruction of the president, the new trade representative should move immediately to engage with his or her counterparts in the European Commission, Japan, China, India, and Brazil in an effort to negotiate the international trade rules that will govern the efforts to reduce carbon emissions.

While the principal focus would be on seeking agreement on the permissible use of border tax adjustments and other similar devices, the discussion should include giving tariff-free treatment to environmental services and goods, a goal already pursued in the Doha Round. Equally important is the need to clarify that subsidies for the development of new technologies and products can be fairly characterized as combating climate change, and thus are permissible under WTO rules, which are hostile to most forms of subsidies. Emphasizing these new trade issues will make it clear that the new president intends to be internationally engaged, but that he has very different priorities from the previous administration and will deploy the resources of USTR and other government departments accordingly.

Trade Law Enforcement

After the WTO dispute settlement system was created in 1994, the Clinton administration made it a priority to launch as many WTO cases as it could identify. The WTO cases litigated by the United States rose dramatically in number. Moreover, to heighten the visibility of the enforcement function, USTR created a separate Office of Enforcement and Monitoring, separate from the Office of General Counsel, to spearhead the effort. And under the radar, USTR officials undertake significant enforcement efforts virtually every day, less visibly than formal WTO dispute resolution cases but still very important.

But more can and should be done. The new trade representative should ask Congress to assign responsibility for enforcement to a Senate-confirmed USTR official, with ambassadorial rank, who would be in charge of the Office of Enforcement and Monitoring. The general counsel would continue to be charged with providing legal counsel and policy advice to the trade representative,[20] but the new assistant trade representative for enforcement and monitoring would be responsible for identifying the areas where the practices of our trading partners are causing harm to U.S. trading interests and formulating a strategy for dealing with those areas—including the initiation and prosecution of WTO cases and building alliances with other countries to combat common problems.

Three areas that would benefit from heightened focus are intellectual property piracy and counterfeiting, the misuse of agricultural sanitary and phytosanitary regulations, and a range of "new mercantilist" practices—including tariffs, discriminatory taxes, and antitrust enforcement—designed to protect other nations' high technology industries and disadvantage ours.[21] This new senior USTR official should be put in charge of significant additional enforcement resources, including more lawyers in the Office of General Counsel. But USTR should ask Congress to appropriate additional funds for enforcement resources attached to our embassies in countries that present the thorniest trade issues, particularly China. This approach is probably the most effective step that could be taken to bolster enforcement, and would be very popular in Congress.[22]

China

The question of whether the United States' economic relationship with China and other rising nations is mutually beneficial will be determined by many policy decisions beyond the realm of trade policy. But a U.S. trade policy that does not more effectively address the challenges posed by China's astonishing rise will not receive or deserve the support of the American people.

The administration should engage with China, along with other leading economies, in a global effort to address the current economic imbalances, including the problem of misaligned currency exchange rates. For too long, China has maintained astronomical growth rates by means of exports and attracting inward foreign direct investment, rather than by domestic spending and consumption.[23] The United States' own savings and investment imbalance has fueled a dependence on Chinese capital to finance U.S. domestic consumption, often of Chinese goods. The resulting economic imbalances are unsustainable for the United States and the European Union, and not in China's long-term interests either.[24]

China's leadership recognizes the problem and is taking some initial steps to boost domestic consumer-driven economic growth. Beijing has also allowed its currency to appreciate 19 percent against the dollar since 2005—under U.S. pressure and due to its own domestic inflationary problems. This is a step in the right direction—and a welcome development for both countries—yet China's currency is still considerably undervalued. China's monetary policy is predicated on the slow appreciation of the yuan in order to manage inflationary pressures and the flow of "hot money" into China in the anticipation of rapid appreciation of the currency, but Beijing needs to move more rapidly to a market-determined exchange rate as part of its emergence as a global trading powerhouse.

The new administration, led by the secretary of treasury, should reduce the incentive for China to continue to undervalue its currency by improving the International Monetary Fund's currency surveillance and macroeconomic coordination functions, a program it initiated in 2006 and then refined in 2007 to focus on bilateral currency exchange rates that cause "external instability." The new president and his treasury secretary should make it clear that they prefer to deal with currency exchange rate issues in joint, cooperative action with China—through the U.S.-China Strategic Economic Dialogue and as part of China's growing leadership role in new global arrangements. But the United States also should work with other nations through the International Monetary Fund, which recently agreed to take on a larger role in global economic imbalances, to pressure China for significant changes in currency alignment and economic policy.

While currency and intellectual property issues often dominate the discussion of China trade issues, the United States should also move vigorously to hold China to all the trade commitments that it has undertaken. Cases in point: China's subsidies to its semiconductor industry; its use of technical standards to discriminate against U.S. companies; and its continued willingness to support state-owned enterprises all present particularly severe challenges to our high-technology industries, and raise serious questions about whether China is adhering to its WTO commitments.[25]

European Union

The United States has long had an enormous trade and investment relationship with the European Union, and many shared common interests like high-wage economies with strong labor and environmental protections. It is impossible to envision the multilateral trading system succeeding without close cooperation between the United States and the EU. Nevertheless, the U.S.-EU trade relationship is a competitive and sometimes prickly one. The largest economic block in the world—the EU-27 includes 490 million people—the EU understandably sees itself as the global trade leader and works actively to shape the global trade environment in a way that both benefits EU companies and reflects EU values.

Given the relatively low tariffs between the United States and the EU, "regulatory harmonization" has been the objective of the U.S. and European business communities for more than a decade. But those regulatory differences often reflect profound differences in approach between the United States and Europe. In comparison to the United States, the European Union takes a tough line on competition policy, is far more hostile to genetically modified foods, adheres to the precautionary principle for assessing risk, and generally regulates more stringently in the environmental area.

While it will be tempting for USTR to pursue the goal of regulatory harmonization with the EU, it should be recognized that progress can be very slow. Harmonizing regulation in the service sector is more promising, because it involves fewer considerations of environment, health, and safety, all of which are sensitive and ideological in Europe. The potential value of a U.S.-EU services agreement should be carefully assessed, as should the value of a U.S.-Japan services agreement.[26]

Certainly USTR should engage the EU in areas of common interest, such as combining efforts to combat China's violation of intellectual property rights, use of subsidies, and other trade practices that are inconsistent with its WTO obligations, and the effort to address the trade aspects of climate change. At times in the past, the EU has undercut a strong position taken by the United States, trying to derive benefits from China by taking a softer line. More recently, however, amid a soaring EU bilateral trade deficit with China, the EU has shown a willingness to take a firmer line.

Latin America

Starting during the Reagan administration with the original idea of adding Mexico to the U.S.-Canada FTA, USTR has devoted enormous time, energy, and resources to the hemispheric trade agenda. President Bush will leave office with the Panama and Colombia FTAs almost certainly unresolved by Congress, but even those trade experts most committed to Latin America agree that the U.S. trade agenda in this hemisphere has exhausted itself. At the same time, Latin American nations have benefited from the global economic demand for commodities; their economies are generally growing and are also receiving increasing investment from China and India. A number of Latin American nations, particularly Brazil, are feeling more confident about their prospects and their options and less committed to accepting the hemispheric leadership of the United States.

The new president and trade representative will have to define U.S. trade policy toward the hemisphere against a backdrop in which the negotiating models that have governed—the Doha Round, the Free Trade Area of the Americas, and the bilateral FTAs in the region—have either failed or are likely to have run their course. The ultimate trade-negotiating goal in the hemisphere would be an agreement between the NAFTA countries and the Mercosur countries (Brazil, Argentina, Uruguay, and Paraguay), led by Brazil, but that is not realistically foreseeable in the early part of the new administration. Dealing with Brazil, never easy, will be a crucial element to moving ahead. With Brazil, and throughout the hemisphere, a focus on key issues of shared interest—the environment, biofuels, and energy—rather than a trade-negotiating model, might provide a new start and the best way forward.

Trade Promotion Authority

Sometime during the first year, USTR will have to confront the issue of whether and how to obtain trade-negotiating authority from Congress, which expired on June 30, 2007. The dilemma can be simply stated. USTR will not be taken completely seriously by other nations unless and until Congress restores trade-negotiating authority. But many members of Congress are hostile to trade agreements, and many more dislike the idea of "fast track" negotiating authority, which they regard as an encroachment on legislative prerogatives. Congress will not restore trade-negotiating authority until it has much more confidence in U.S. trade policy, and that will not happen until a majority in Congress agrees on what the negotiating authority will be used for.

Consequently, USTR should not request trade-negotiating authority until it has completed its interagency review, developed overall recommendations for

U.S. trade and foreign economic policy, and had sufficient time to identify and discuss with Congress its specific trade-negotiating priorities. Moreover, when negotiating authority is requested, USTR should be willing to address long-standing congressional concerns by making significant changes from the past formulation.

For instance, the new administration should consider supporting the creation of a joint congressional committee on trade, which would include the chairmen and ranking members of all the key committees with jurisdiction over issues that appear in trade agreements. The negotiating authority could include the requirement that no trade agreement negotiation should be formally initiated unless this joint committee, or the joint committee and the trade committees, voted to give the negotiation the go-ahead. This mechanism would give Congress an expanded role in choosing U.S. trade negotiating partners, and it would give the president and USTR, as well as U.S. partners, the assurance that a broad cross-section of Congress had endorsed the concept of the negotiation.[27]

In sum, the new trade representative will assume responsibility at an absolutely pivotal moment for U.S. trade policy. A new trade policy is desperately needed, and if the new administration builds a real partnership with Congress, it is possible to envision a trade policy that would be simultaneously more strategic, more realistic, and more idealistic—and certainly more successful in contributing to U.S. economic growth and improved living standards around the world.

Department of Commerce

Proving Ground for Sustainable Economic Growth

JONATHAN SALLET[1]

The Department of Commerce should be the new administration's proving ground for sustainable economic growth. But meeting global economic challenges will require the new secretary to integrate the department's multifaceted expertise into a singular force. The department brings together trade, environment, telecommunications, domestic economic development, among other areas of expertise, and it can help forge successful working relationships with businesses and state and local governments to confront pressing national challenges. The department should begin by strengthening its focus on economic and energy issues, developing a Regional Competitiveness Initiative that utilizes the potential and strength of industry clusters, and promoting better coordination among federal agencies on trade. It should also reinstitute the Advanced Technology Program to provide incentives for creating technologies that further national priorities; change the name of the National Telecommunications and Information Administration to the "National Broadband Agency" and refocus its efforts on deploying nationwide broadband; and lead a new 21st century manufacturing strategy. Longer term, Commerce must focus on ensuring that the 2010 and 2020 censuses are as efficient and accurate as possible.

The Department of Commerce could be—and usually has been—operated as a miscellaneous collection of semi-independent fiefdoms, each pledging primary allegiance to its specialized constituencies. That is not surprising given the department's obvious institutional diversity, which includes trade promotion, export controls, technology development, telecommunications policy, the U.S Census Bureau, the National Weather Service, fisheries management, and more. Moreover, the Bush White House actively sought to weaken key department programs, including the outright elimination of the Manufacturing Extension Partnership and the Advanced Technology Program, at a time when the U.S. manufacturing sector and its workers have suffered and American economic success rests increasingly on technological innovation.[2]

The new secretary of commerce must turn the disparate pieces of the department into a singular strength; together, they contain exactly the expertise needed to confront today's business challenges. Think for a moment about what it will take for U.S. businesses and workers to succeed. The United States needs to transform how our businesses use energy for their economic success in order to improve efficiency and create new jobs in a world where energy independence and environmental sustainability are vital. We must integrate strong science and data-driven policymaking into management of natural resources and global environmental challenges.

The new administration must forge a concentrated approach to globalization that will benefit both U.S. businesses and workers by building on local and regional "clusters" of competitiveness. This means creating a public-private strategy to ensure that the United States maintains a manufacturing base that creates high-paying jobs; catalyzing applied research that businesses, universities, and communities can use to bring new innovations to market; and ensuring that minority enterprises have the opportunity to succeed. It also requires a national broadband strategy to fuel sustainable economic growth and help solve pressing social problems. The fruits of all our research must be able to access strong intellectual property protections.

Expertise in each of these areas—and more—lives within the Department of Commerce. The department brings together historically separate disciplines—trade, environment, telecommunications, and domestic economic development—that can only be effective if they are integrated. Commerce will have to sow the seeds of synergies by promoting testbeds for state and local governments, educational institutions, and American businesses. It is a repository of critical information—none more important than the 2010 census. The department's job is to ensure that information flows freely to those who can use it, and that science and data, not ideology, inform governmental decision making. The department's economic and statistical capacity and world-class analysis of climate change and oceanography will provide the basis for confronting some of the most challenging issues facing the United States.

We live in a time when nothing is more important than the American economy's ability to innovate, which has been our great strength for 200 years. Our comparative advantage in the newly globalized economy will lie in our ability to continue to create new ideas that bring value to workers and businesses, not natural resources or cheap labor. Yet the United States ranks seventh within the Organisation for Economic Co-Operation and Development countries, placing it behind Sweden, Finland, Japan, and others in the percentage of its gross domestic product (2.6 percent) that is devoted to research and development.[3] And today, the United States has no specific innovation or productivity policy.[4] The Bush administration believed that the government should have little role in supporting technological innovation; in fact, our history demonstrates the opposite. The new administration will have to change this mentality by spurring innovation and using applied research and advocacy to develop better governmental policies.

In sum, the department will have to leverage all its resources and work closely with local and regional economies to effectively bolster innovation. The new administration's role will be to facilitate the flow of information and assistance to local governments and U.S. businesses; integrate the various "stovepipes" of expertise needed to build comprehensive federal policies regarding international trade, global climate change, sustainable resources, and national innovation infrastructures; and use federal resources to encourage innovation—the only long-term means of securing a sustainable future for the United States.

The First 100 Days

The new president should immediately strengthen the Commerce Department's focus on energy and climate issues by charging his new National Energy Council (discussed in the White House section of this book) with the creation and implementation of a new strategic plan to tackle climate change and bring our nation closer to energy independence. As part of this effort, the new president should announce executive orders to create a Department of Commerce Climate Initiative and a National Institute for Standards and Technology Greenhouse Gas Initiative, which will provide data and analysis to support this administration-wide climate change effort.

The new plan would be a leadership strategy for an energy-efficient, low-carbon America that builds long-term prosperity and security through an economy that is both "green" and growing. Achieving this grand vision would require unprecedented coordination between the Commerce and Energy departments, the Office of the United States Trade Representative, the Environmental Protection Agency, the Office of Science and Technology Policy, the National Economic Council, and, of course, the new National Energy Council. The new president should announce this initiative as a centerpiece of his economic plan and ask the secretary of commerce to lead the administration's exploration into how businesses of all kinds and sizes can prosper in a sustainable economy.

The new president should subsequently announce the creation of the Department of Commerce Climate Change Initiative through an executive order. The initiative should fuse the expertise of the Commerce Department's National Oceanic and Atmospheric Administration, the National Institute of Standards and Technology, and the International Trade Administration. NOAA should establish a special Task Force on Climate to integrate the information and expertise it gathers through its National Weather Service and its oversight of coastal natural resources into an ongoing study designed to ensure that the nation's policymakers have access to the most current and accurate data on the effect of human activity on climate change.[5]

NOAA should give special attention to coastal regions. Fifty-five percent of the U.S. population lives within 50 miles of a coast and the population densities along the coasts are five times that of the national average.[6] Sea levels are expected to rise anywhere between one-half and two meters during the 21st century. The Intergovernmental Panel on Climate Change reported that by 2080, over 30 percent of the world's coastal wetlands could be completely engulfed.[7] Just a one-meter rise in sea levels could submerge between 5,000 and 10,000 square miles of dry land, with the southeastern United States bearing the large majority of the land lost. For example, the geography and coastal habitats of the Chesapeake Bay, the nation's largest estuary, would be dramatically altered.[8] And given coastal population density, the economic implications are even more daunting.

NOAA is uniquely positioned to provide data to coastal communities that can help them take effective local action, while giving decision makers at all levels of government a keener understanding of global trends. Its National Weather Service, in particular, can provide insight into climate change's potential effects on weather patterns, such as hurricanes in the Atlantic Ocean and Gulf of Mexico and inland tornadoes.

The new president should, at the same time, establish within the National Institute of Standards and Technology a Global Greenhouse Gas Initiative. NIST is the leading expert in creating standards and measurements. NIST should develop and promulgate measurements that will help us understand the greenhouse gas and carbon emissions that cause global warming—a critical next step in creating an effective climate strategy. NIST can also establish a research program on climate change standards, measurements, and processes; use the Institute's National Measurement Laboratories to conduct specified research on materials and manufacturing processes that are more energy efficient and will reduce greenhouse gas emissions; and utilize the National Voluntary Laboratory Accreditation Program to accredit its greenhouse gas production measurements. A critical component of the NIST efforts should be to create certification protocols that empower market mechanisms such as the emerging market in "carbon offsets."[9]

The Department of Commerce will also have to begin preparations for the next round of post-Kyoto global negotiations on climate change, scheduled for 2009 in Copenhagen, Denmark. The International Trade Administration should begin working immediately with the Office of the United States Trade Representative to minimize any conflicts between pending climate change legislation and our multilateral trade obligations and develop a strong positive trade policy.

The Regional Competitiveness Initiative

The Regional Competitiveness Initiative should empower local communities and businesses to work together to achieve a national objective: finding the best formulae for sustainable economic growth and innovation. Geographic regions have a proven track record for facilitating innovation, productivity, and high-paying jobs in growing companies. Yet current economic policy does not effectively utilize the potential of these regional clusters or their ability to work with local businesses.

The federal government should frame and facilitate, through funding and by sharing expertise, regional competitiveness strategies. The secretary should involve multiple departmental agencies in the formulation of this effort, including the Economic Development Administration, which manages Regional Development Accounts and can provide research and technical experience; the Minority Business Development Agency, which can help reach out and provide particular support for minority-owned businesses; the National Institute of Standards and Technology, home of the Advanced Technology Program and Manufacturing Extension Partnership; the National Telecommunications and Information Administration, which can provide leadership on broadband deployment policies; the International Trade Administration, which leads the Working Group on Manufacturing Competitiveness and can provide analysis of U.S. industries; and the U.S. Bureau of Economic Analysis and Census Bureau, which can provide analysis of economic conditions, including income-disparity and its effect on competitiveness. The entire department can, in essence, contribute needed expertise.

The new secretary should direct these agencies to recommend and draft in 90 days a regional innovation strategy that will form the basis of a new Regional Competitiveness Initiative. This initiative should place special emphasis on how the department can facilitate collaboration between local governments, educational institutions, and businesses, through competitive cost-sharing and a longer-term grant program.

A culture of learning and experimentation will be critical to the department's future success. As part of this, the secretary should convene key governmental and business leaders in 2010 to benchmark and share ideas for how the Regional Competitiveness Initiative can best be implemented at the local level and supported by the federal government. The summit should include successful "case studies" from regional competitiveness initiatives such as those implemented in South Carolina, Oregon, Maine, and California, and include a specific focus on energy-efficient and low-carbon technologies. A portion of this summit should be devoted to discussing the feasibility of the Economic Development Administration supporting an initiative for privately run microfinance programs built on the model of Grameen Bank's first location in New York City.

Trade Promotion
Expansion in the size and reach of global trade has made it more difficult for large segments of our industrial and manufacturing sector to compete in the global economy. The new administration will have to implement policies that empower U.S. businesses and industries to compete successfully. The front line

in this global competition is often composed of small businesses that have both the most to gain and the most to lose. Without the scale and international ties of their larger brethren, small- and medium-sized companies need assistance from all relevant federal agencies, working together as a single unit.

The new president should issue an executive order to reconstitute and strengthen the Trade Promotion Coordinating Committee, which is chaired by the secretary of commerce. The executive order should more clearly define the committee's mission, require federal agencies to more effectively share information among themselves and with U.S. businesses, and more effectively allocate personnel in the participant agencies, particularly the State and Commerce departments.[10]

The TPCC and its member agencies operate according to annual national export strategies that change from year to year. Yet there is no systematic means of evaluating the progress and effectiveness of these strategies. Objectives are transformed from year to year without any broad analysis of the previous years' work. Such analyses would not only be useful retrospectively; it would be enormously beneficial if shared between agencies and used to adapt and alter TPCC's objectives and strategies.[11]

Secretarial Initiatives
The new secretary should move quickly to ensure that the department is ready to meet its existing responsibilities and can manage a wholesale integration of its strategic approaches. The secretary, immediately upon taking office, should appoint a deputy secretary to harness the department's interdisciplinary work in support of presidential and secretarial priorities. The deputy secretary should be given the job of ensuring that the department provides the information that governments and businesses need to create effective strategy; integrating the department's activities, especially in areas such as manufacturing where multiple parts of the department have expertise; and innovating the department's approach to creating, facilitating, and supporting economic growth initiatives. Only a departmental official with backing from the president and secretary can be successful in achieving these outcomes.

The new secretary should order a 30-day review of the U.S. Census Bureau's readiness for the 2010 census, with specific emphasis on information-technology tools and the evaluation performed by the Government Accountability Office in the spring of 2008.[12] This evaluation will help ensure that the 2010 census is the most accurate and advanced in our nation's history.

The secretary should also, in the first 100 days, instruct the patent and trademark commissioner to improve the federal government's strategic planning for intellectual property protection. The International Intellectual Property Alliance found that global piracy cost U.S. copyright industries over $13 billion annually in both 2004 and 2005.[13] It is critically important that the new administration send the message that theft is not innovation. Strategic planning for IP protection will be the first step toward executing a comprehensive federal policy regarding the enforcement and protection of legally authorized intellectual property rights.

The secretary should work closely with Congress to implement the U.S. Commission on Ocean Policy's most important recommendations. An ecosystem-based oceans policy is vital to the U.S. economy and the global environment, and the Department of Commerce should begin establishing a strategy to help the nation reach the day when its oceans, coasts, and Great Lakes are "clean, safe, prospering, and sustainably managed."[14] Regional governance issues should be addressed quickly so that other issues can also be addressed and a comprehensive oceans policy can be implemented based on guiding principles proposed by the commission. The secretary, with Congress, should instruct NOAA to conduct a scientifically based review of fisheries issues and fisheries management and report its conclusions within 90 days.

The First Year

The Bush administration terminated the Advanced Technology Program, one of the few civilian efforts that spans the gap between basic and fully realized commercial research and development. The new administration should work with Congress to reinstitute ATP and strengthen it by providing funding of at least $200 million annually.

The department should use ATP to establish its national technology priorities and focus research on energy-efficient and environmentally sustainable technologies. The program will give grants to assist early stage businesses that would otherwise lack access to research and development funding. It should be reconstituted as a cooperative program, anchored by local colleges and universities who would award matching grants to the businesses and manage the program on a day-to-day basis. Individual ATP grants should be awarded through a competitive process administrated by the colleges and universities who join the ATP program.

The new ATP should combine the talents of businesses, community-based educational institutions, and federal leadership to make a lasting contribution to U.S. competitiveness through leadership in technology and innovation. This new partnership approach will allow ATP to use applied research to help the nation meet its most pressing challenges, such as energy efficiency; to provide community support and involvement through colleges and universities; to uti-lize business expertise in setting research and development priorities; and to generate positive spill-over effects in regional economies.

The National Broadband Agency

"Telecommunications" is a 20th century term associated with 20th century pri-orities. In the 21st century, our national priority is to assure that all Americans have access to affordable, high-speed Internet access over broadband networks. Congress should therefore rename the National Telecommunications and In-formation Administration the "National Broadband Agency" to demonstrate its new focus.

The NBA, as the president's principal historical advisor on telecommunica-tions policy, should be given the task of implementing a new initiative entitled "Broadband Access for All," in addition to maintaining its previous responsibili-ties, especially with regard to the nation's transition to digital television and the use of wireless spectrum. This initiative would be designed to provide federal facilitation and funding to efforts led by local governments and non-govern-mental organizations.

The National Broadband Agency would build upon past programs created by Congress and the initiative included in the Farm, Nutrition, and Bioenergy Act of 2008. The farm bill allocated $25 million a year over the next five years to expand broadband access in rural areas. Though a step in the right direction, the farm bill left much to be accomplished in the future. Congress should be-stow upon the NBA leadership of an expanded matching-grant program to fa-cilitate cooperative public-private partnerships at the state and regional levels in urban, suburban, and rural America.[15]

The federal government should fund up to 500 communities annually over a five-year period at $80 million per year to increase critical access to broadband, as well as provide underserved communities with mapping resources and in-centives to build demand. Grants would be used to form public-private partner-ships; 80 percent of funding would come from the federal government and the other 20 percent would come from funds at the state level. Grant proposals would be peer-reviewed, and evaluation and sharing of best practices would be built into the program. Eligible entities would be limited to five years of partic-ipation, with collaboration required among state agencies, service providers, relevant labor organizations, and community organizations.

This initiative would focus on both supply and demand barriers, recognizing that the use of broadband is as important as its deployment. This approach would allow for a wider view of broadband access challenges, one in which social applications of the technology—in the health care and education fields, for example, are part of a comprehensive effort. Recent studies have demonstrated that broadband technologies can be an effective substitute for more energy-intensive activities—through teleworking, for example, or digital downloads of products that would otherwise require shipping and packaging.[16] The NBA should work closely with the administration's larger energy initiative to ensure that an appropriate understanding of broadband technologies for these purposes is included within federal policies.

21st-Century Manufacturing

Commerce houses considerable expertise in the field of manufacturing—a critical area of U.S. competitiveness and economic growth. Manufacturing jobs provide higher pay to workers, but they continue to fall as a percentage of U.S. employment, from 40 percent during World War II to around 12 percent today.[17]

The Manufacturing Extension Partnership currently leads the department's manufacturing efforts. Established in 1988, it consists of regional centers throughout the country that are designed to provide assistance for small- and medium-sized manufacturing companies through knowledge and technologies developed by the National Institute of Standards and Technology. MEP receives federal funding, as well as matching funds from non-federal sources. Funding levels for the program have dropped since fiscal year 1999, as is the case with many tech transfer programs. MEP funding was slashed 63 percent in FY 2004, but restored in FY 2005. The president's FY 2009 budget again sought a significant reduction of MEP funding.

Given the importance of manufacturing to U.S. competitiveness, Congress should create, and the Department of Commerce should administer, a new Advanced Manufacturing Initiative. The initiative should support "green manufacturing" by providing as much as $1 billion a year over 10 years to foster green manufacturing in both small and large industry sectors. Large manufacturers in industries such as steel, chemicals, and automobiles are among the most energy intensive.

The federal government can hasten the transition to a cleaner, more energy-efficient economy by encouraging the development of green manufactured products and processes that would otherwise not have a real chance to come to market. These could include steel for a renewed power grid, fiber-optic cable for new broadband networks, nanotechnology that improves the efficiency of internal processes, and agriscience technologies and "green chemicals." Boosting productivity and positive environmental outcomes is essential to sustainable economic growth, especially at a time when energy costs are incentivizing manufacturers to keep jobs in America.

The initiative should also double the current funding of traditional MEP centers to $180 million a year so that effective partnerships can be built with state and local governments to provide small and medium businesses access to the "best practices" of energy-efficient manufacturing. Without the scale of large manufacturers, small- and medium-size manufacturers may be inhibited in growing. MEP helped to maintain 50,000 American jobs in 2006, but more needs to be done.[18]

Congress should build on the collaborative model of the Advanced Technology Program by establishing, in league with the Regional Competitiveness Initiative, a federal counterpart to successful state efforts such as Michigan's 21st Century Jobs Fund. The new Advanced Manufacturing Fund will support innovative companies that are prepared to invest in new technologies and the creation of advanced manufacturing jobs beyond the boundaries of the "green" manufacturing and MEP efforts. The Advanced Manufacturing Fund, alongside the Advanced Technology Program, will help fill the critical gulf between basic and fully commercialized research.

Longer-Term Agenda

The Department of Commerce's leading initiatives each incorporate the essential qualities that will make the department a proving ground for more effective government—they spark and encourage innovation within the integration of diverse disciplines. As such, they are a form of innovation themselves. They create open ecosystems where learning is essential, experimentation yields further insights, and cooperation between governments and businesses is an important component of private competitive strategies.

The hallmark of such systems is that they are permitted to evolve, and that lessons from one region, sector, or time period are widely shared so that best practices can be adopted, and failure can be the basis for future success. To make this work, the department must be a force for innovation in its own activities and in its management of administration initiatives. That will require more than compliance with rules; it will require the department to incorporate the spark of ingenuity into its management of each effort and to undertake a relentless quest to demonstrate the flexibility and innovation that characterize America's most successful businesses today.

Commerce should shift its thinking over time from a focus on trade to a deeper understanding of worldwide commerce in a globalized setting. Recent events have demonstrated that non-trade factors can have important economic effects that ripple across the world's economies. Growth in demand in one part of the globe, for example, can lead to higher prices and shortages in goods and services in all of the rest. The goal should be to ensure that current trade policies are sized and shaped to advance future U.S. interests. The secretary should create a working group that recommends how the department's trade efforts can best meet this goal.

The recommendations should provide additional support and funding to enhance the department's ability to work with workers and businesses coping with globalization, including service companies. It should instruct the Bureau of Industry and Security to implement—and complete in 12 months—a review of its Control List, which consists of items that are subject to export control licenses. Items should be removed from the Control List that are widely available from foreign sources or are no longer relevant to our security. The department should launch a new trade enforcement program within the International Trade Administration that would work directly with small- and medium-sized businesses, assisting them in identifying trade violations such as illegal tariffs or subsidies. It should also launch a new Export America campaign focused on bringing the products and services of small- and medium-sized enterprises to the attention of our trading partners.

Any reforms to America's manufacturing industry must also address the effects of globalization and free trade. It is important that Commerce do its part through enforcing and further developing effective trade laws that will be beneficial to our own jobs and industries while maintaining our nation's commitment to open markets, as detailed in the chapter on the Office of the U.S. Trade Representative.

The 2010 Census and Beyond

One of the Commerce Department's foremost responsibilities is the management and execution of the U.S. census. The census requires accuracy, both for the dispersal of federal funds and to ensure that, as federal policies are made, every American is counted.

The department must review the Census Bureau's policy regarding "error." As with any broad survey, there needs to be an effective and rational policy concerning statistical inaccuracies. The census is in many ways inherently inaccurate in its attempts to count and record a massive number of constantly moving people. Such errors frequently manifest themselves in the form of field imputations wherein field operators—when faced with empty houses on their field visits—estimate household sizes without concrete information or knowledge of the persons living there. Instances of field imputation were incredibly large in 2000—around 12 million—and they contributed greatly to some inaccurate results.

The Department of Commerce needs to begin an immediate review of their policies regarding error and, in a timely manner, implement an effective and coherent strategy that will help to reduce such problems as quickly as possible. Progress was made in 2000, but there are still important sectors of the population that are inaccurately represented. Such errors have been reported in the African-American, Asian, Hispanic, and gay and lesbian populations.[19]

The department should also explore the effective use of technology to improve the census. It should immediately consider re-implementing an Internet response option for the census questionnaires. Although the Internet was used and cited as a "success" in the 2000 census, the Census Bureau has failed to adopt such a strategy for 2010 even though studies from around the world and in the United States have shown that the Internet is a reliable and effective tool for census studies. The Information Technology and Innovation Foundation found that just a 20 percent response rate for questionnaires filled out on the Internet would save $35 million.

When planning for the long term and the 2020 census, the Census Bureau should look into adopting a "national community survey" whereby census questionnaires would be rolled into a monthly panel survey, similar to how we currently calculate national unemployment rates. Though greater research and investigation needs to be done in this regard, there exists a definite opportunity to implement a cost-effective and accurate strategy.

Department of Labor
Promoting Opportunity While Protecting Worker Rights

EDWARD MONTGOMERY

The Department of Labor should play a central role in the new administration's efforts to expand the middle class and protect the rights of working Americans. DOL can begin to do this immediately by effectively enforcing labor and safety laws already on the

*books and making sure that contracts and grants are awarded to programs with
demonstrated effectiveness and the greatest need. Newly motivated DOL leadership can
then attack other inherited problems by revamping workforce training programs, restoring the unemployment insurance safety net, boosting the department's critical labor law
enforcement capabilities—which include protecting the unfettered right to form and
join unions—and modernizing trade and displaced worker adjustment assistances so
that job loss does not lead to economic ruin for workers and their families. Pragmatic,
effective, and transparent programs in these arenas will help expand the middle class
and remind American workers that they do not have to choose between their health and
safety, and their job.*

The Department of Labor represents the interests of working Americans
and protects their basic rights. The secretary of labor must make sure that
workers' concerns are at the forefront of the nation's agenda and operate the
agency in accordance with its mission: to help workers acquire the skills that
they need; protect workers' basic rights, including the right to organize; help
workers obtain adequate pension and health care benefit coverage and security; and keep workers safe on the job by vigorously enforcing our nation's labor laws.

In 2008, our nation experienced an economy teetering on the brink of a recession, with home foreclosures, health care costs, and gasoline prices all reaching record levels. On top of these immediate concerns was a widening earnings
gap between workers and chief executives, where it takes the average worker a
year to earn what the typical CEO makes in a day.[1] Job and income growth
have been anemic since 2001, averaging about 50,000 new jobs per month or
about one-fifth the rate of job creation seen in the previous eight years, and the
economy actually lost jobs for much of 2008.[2] The Department of Labor
should play a central role in the new administration's efforts to address both
these immediate challenges and the long-term concerns of workers in our dynamic market economy.

The secretary of labor will have to actively use his or her bully pulpit in conjunction with the agency's programmatic and regulatory authority in order to
be effective. But it will also be critical that the 44th president work with Congress to ensure that DOL has the resources and authority needed to accomplish its mission.

The Bush administration's proposed fiscal year 2009 Department of Labor
budget actually contained fewer employees and less discretionary spending
than the department had in FY2001.[3] DOL's budget has been cut an extraordinary 34 percent since 2001.[4] This decline in real funding actually understates

the drop in DOL resources relative to its mission, since spending on training programs would need to be almost 17 times greater than currently proposed—$50 billion rather than $3 billion—to keep pace with the growth in the size of the labor force since the 1979 level.[5] Similarly, the number of Occupational Safety and Health Administration inspectors and staff would need to be 2.5 times greater than currently proposed—5,488 rather than 2,165—to keep pace with the growth in the number of businesses since 1975.[6]

DOL can significantly leverage its programmatic resources and regulatory authority by working in concert with other agencies. The new labor secretary should work closely with the Office of Management and Budget on regulatory oversight and design, and play an active role in the National Economic Council, Domestic Policy Council, and any other interagency coordinating groups that the next administration may establish. To forge a new trade strategy with enhanced labor and environmental protections, for example, DOL must be positioned to work effectively with the departments of Treasury, State, and Commerce, the United States Trade Representative, the Environmental Protection Agency, and the Council of Economic Advisors, among others.

The 44th president will need a new way of doing business that entails greater interagency coordination that leverages private sector as well as state and local efforts in order to develop effective solutions for problems relating to trade, climate change, retirement security, health care, and rebuilding our economy. The labor secretary should play a major role in formulating and implementing this new policy approach.

The First 100 Days

The new labor secretary's first priority should be to clearly signal that the department exists to serve and protect working Americans and to begin building an agenda that matches that mission. Because legislative and programmatic changes take time, the most effective way to demonstrate this new approach will be to swiftly take control of the department's regulatory and enforcement operations as well as the contracting and grant-issuing process.

The secretary will have to actively embrace DOL's law enforcement functions by making sure the worker protection agencies have the personnel and resources they need to uphold the law by aggressively pursuing violators. DOL is probably the largest federal law enforcement agency outside of the Department of Justice. It oversees over 180 laws and their associated regulations, and protects millions of employers' and workers' wages, pensions, health plans, and safety.[7]

The Bush administration, in its final weeks in office, pushed so-called "midnight regulations." The new labor secretary should put an immediate moratorium on issuing new rules and review all recently enacted rules. The secretary should also place a hold on issuing opinion letters and interpretive bulletins until a process for reviewing these orders has been undertaken. This will ensure that these documents afford workers the protections to which they are entitled.

The new department should pay particular attention to final rules that might narrow Family Medical Leave Act protections, scale back the protections that are part of the labor certification process for migrant farm workers, or shift the responsibility for providing personal protective equipment. Rolling back these regulations has been at the top of business' agenda for years, and doing so could adversely affect millions of American workers.

The new secretary must also send a signal to taxpayers that their money will go only to high-quality projects with proven success rather than projects that have inside connections. The new secretary must break from the practice of awarding large numbers of sole-source, or noncompetitive, grants. To begin this process, DOL should establish an immediate moratorium on awarding or modifying discretionary contracts and grants until those in the pipeline can be reviewed.[8] New processes will need to be developed and implemented to ensure greater transparency and integrity in the contracting and grant process.

A strong middle class is critical both to our democracy and long-term prosperity. The Department of Labor, and the new administration more broadly, should consider the effect that its regulatory and programmatic actions have on the economic health of the middle class and the institutions that support it. Unions have been one of the most effective tools for helping to raise worker earnings to middle-class levels, increasing the incidence of employer-provided health and pension plans, and improving worker safety.[9] Since the passage of the National Labor Relations Act more than 70 years ago, it has been national policy to encourage and protect the practices of collective bargaining.[10] Yet the rights afforded by the NLRA have been eroded over the years by National Labor Relations Board decisions, the use of harassment or intimidation that has kept workers from voting for unions, and employer stalling tactics that prevent a first contract from being signed.

The labor secretary and the new administration must begin reversing this trend. A first priority toward this goal should be working with Congress to pass the Employee Free Choice Act. This bill would lift some barriers to unionization by allowing workers to join a union if a majority sign cards authorizing union representation, imposing increased sanctions on employers for firing or harassing workers who want to join a union, and providing arbitration or mediation if negotiations over the first contract stall.

The secretary should also ensure that public money awarded to government contractors produces quality jobs, with good pay and benefits, and that public money awarded to government contractors does not support law breaking, including labor law violations.[11] Starting to level the playing field within the first 100 days would provide a foundation for other governmental and nongovernmental actions to rebuild the middle class over the ensuing months and years.

The secretary will need the active engagement of the career staff of the agency in order to effectively implement this agenda. There is an invaluable wealth of knowledge waiting to be tapped among the career personnel on everything from understanding which programs are most effective to how others might be reformed, and from which enforcement strategies work to the pitfalls associated with current regulations. The secretary should hold departmental and agency town hall meetings for career personnel within the first week to regain trust, energize employees, and begin a dialogue to demonstrate that a new, open approach will make sure that they will get the information they need and that their input is welcome.

It is important that the secretary and incoming agency heads have highly skilled and dedicated executives in the right positions to carry out the mission of each agency. The secretary should therefore initiate careful reviews of the performance of the agency's career executives during the first 120 days after the appointment of a new agency head, with the goal of keeping or building a first-rate leadership team within each agency.

To hit the ground running, the secretary will also need a political leadership team to supplement and direct the career leadership. The secretary will have to immediately select a deputy secretary and chief of staff with expertise managing large, complex organizations, who can think strategically, and who will have the ability to effectively communicate the agency's mission to a broad array of audiences.

The secretary will also need an experienced assistant secretary for administration and management available quickly to help with personnel and the budgeting effort. By the end of January, DOL will have to begin formulating new proposals for the FY2010 budget, and having internal budgetary expertise as well as an effective assistant secretary for congressional and intergovernmental affairs will be a critical part of the initial agency administrative team. Because of the large regulatory and enforcement components to the DOL, having a solicitor on board as part of the initial team will be vital to keeping these functions moving forward.

The First Year

Federal spending must be realigned to support programs that protect workers and expand opportunity. The incoming administration will inherit a sea of red ink with a projected deficit in excess of $400 billion for FY2009, but working families' challenges are too great to maintain the status quo. The Department of Labor must work with the new administration to enhance the skills and improve job placement assistance for displaced workers, rural and inner-city youth, and low-wage adults to make sure there is a ladder into the middle class. It must ensure that our transitioning veterans and their families—some who may have disabilities—get the services they need and deserve to help them find good jobs. The new administration must work to implement health and safety regulations and incorporate core labor standards into our trade agreements. The private pension system needs to be expanded, and the Pension Benefit Guarantee Corporation, which protects the pensions of nearly 44 million American workers and retirees, should be kept solvent. Enforcement of our equal opportunity laws needs to be reinvigorated, and our system for handling claims for injured energy workers reformed.

There are three areas where the labor secretary should immediately seek additional investments and place priority attention: broadening the unemployment insurance system, reforming the trade adjustment system, and improving enforcement of worker protection laws.

Broaden Unemployment Insurance

The secretary should begin to repair and extend the nation's social safety net. We have a dynamic economy where each year about 15 million jobs are created and 13 million are destroyed.[12] Some workers are buffeted by short-term economic downturns, while others face permanent job losses due to trade or technological shifts. The Unemployment Insurance system, since its inception in 1935, has been a federal-state partnership providing temporary financial assistance to millions of workers who lose their jobs—an important counter-cyclical stimulus to the economy.[13]

Yet the Unemployment Insurance system's effectiveness has been slowly eroded by changes in the stability of employment, increases in part-time or alternate work arrangements, and growth in low-wage employment and two-earner couples, among other labor market dynamics. The current program typically provides benefits to a third of the unemployed, and the maximum weekly benefits replace only 35 to 65 percent of statewide average weekly wages.[14] Over 35 percent of recipients exhausted their benefits even during the strong economy experienced in the 1990s,[15] and low-wage workers are currently half as likely to receive unemployment insurance benefits as higher-wage workers, even though they are twice as likely to be unemployed.[16]

The Unemployment Insurance Modernization Act of 2007, introduced by Rep. Jim McDermott (D-WA) and Sen. Edward Kennedy (D-MA), would provide incentives for states to cover those working part-time; revise eligibility standards to make it easier for low-wage workers to qualify based on the use of an alternative base period, which reflects recent earnings rather than those that occurred one or two quarters before job loss; and improve administrative services.[17] The legislations would also increase incentives for states to cover those forced to leave their jobs because a spouse relocates or because of domestic violence, and link Reed Act distributions, or changes in the temporary Federal Unemployment Tax,[18] to state UI modernization efforts in order to meet statutory funding targets for administration spending by state UI and Employment Service programs.[19]

The approximately $7 billion in revenue from the temporary Federal Unemployment Tax surtax provides a source of funding to accomplish these and other potential reform objectives. There are numerous other ideas or proposals that merit consideration as part of this effort, including covering workers while they are receiving training, fixing the federal extended benefit systems, increasing benefit replacement rates, and updating the maximum Federal Unemployment Tax taxable base from its 1983 earnings level.[20]

Reform Trade Adjustment Assistance
Trade Adjustment Assistance programs were established by President John F. Kennedy to compensate those who lose their jobs due to trade liberalization. The current program serves about 100,000 certified workers each year, providing them with retraining funds, income support, relocation assistance, and a health insurance tax credit.[21] The program has been criticized for failing to certify workers promptly, efficiently, or in a transparent manner; for inadequate training due to budget caps on training resources; and for inadequate help with health insurance premiums.[22] The TAA program needs to be reauthorized and extended as the second plank in a comprehensive upgrade in our social safety net.

As has been proposed by Sen. Max Baucus (D-MT) and others, the current TAA program could be improved by expanding training funds, streamlining and improving certification and enrollment requirements, extending benefits to service sector workers, covering shifts in production to non-Free Trade Act countries such as China and India, and increasing the health care premium subsidy.

Enforce Worker Protection Laws

The Labor Department needs to step up its enforcement of worker protection laws and reinvigorate the process for identifying and regulating current and emerging workplace hazards. DOL agencies charged with worker protection typically operate with between 1,200 and 2,400 inspectors and staff, but are called upon to oversee a workforce of 160 million workers in nearly 9 million establishments. The Occupational Safety and Health Administration is expected to carry out 37,700 inspections in FY2009, which would mean that it would take 198 years to get to all private-sector establishments.[23]

While investments in worker safety at OSHA have languished, the budget for the Office of Labor Management Standards grew by almost 90 percent under President George W. Bush, and the number of inspectors monitoring union compliance with DOL regulations has increased by almost 25 percent.[24] The new secretary should work to realign the available worker protection resources with the areas that have the greatest effect on the health and well-being of workers.

The new secretary should continue to encourage firms' voluntary efforts to comply with existing health and safety statues and regulations as well as worker training and outreach efforts. There are simply too many establishments to reach without employers' cooperation and active participation in compliance. DOL should pay special attention to engaging unions and other employee organizations in the compliance and workplace safety process. While voluntary efforts are needed, they are not enough. These efforts must be coupled with targeted, active field enforcement efforts supported, when appropriate, by aggressive actions on the part of the solicitor to pursue claims.

DOL should target its enforcement efforts to where the problems or abuses are greatest. DOL conducted compliance surveys in a series of low-wage industries in the 1990s and found that nearly a third of residential health care facilities and almost two-thirds of garment industry companies in New York City were violating wage and hour laws such as minimum wage and overtime laws.[25] By using these data, DOL was able to successfully target particular sectors and types of employers where violations were likely to be greatest. After updating these surveys to reflect changes in the labor market since the 1990s, DOL should target those low-wage employers or industries where Fair Labor Standards Act enforcement actions could prove highly effective.

OSHA also needs to invest in better data to improve its targeting, since Bureau of Labor Statistics injuries data have been found to undercount injuries by as much as two-thirds due to its reliance on employer OSHA logs.[26] The currently available data do suggest that higher-risk industries are emerging in the service sector that need OSHA attention along with the historically high-risk manufacturing and construction industries.[27] The recent mine tragedies in 2006 and 2007 provide telling evidence of the need for an aggressive underground mine inspection program. The Mine Improvement and New Emergency Response Act of 2006 increased penalties and provided for rescue teams. Nonetheless, the Mine Safety and Health Administration appears to have failed to carry out required inspections or assess fines when violations have been found.[28]

The secretary must in the first year choose a select group of potential high-impact enforcement actions in the service, manufacturing, construction, and mining sectors to send a message that the department is willing to use its authority to help working people. As DOL steps up enforcement of existing rules, it should also examine areas where new rule-making might be necessary or where existing rules need amending. Given the length of time required to develop, propose, amend, and finalize any new rules, these efforts will need to be started early in the new administration if they are to going to have a chance of being implemented.

To reinforce the message that the secretary attaches great importance to worker protections, the secretary should also consider issuing an order to make the Wage and Hour Division of the Employment Standard Administration a separate independent agency reporting directly to the secretary. The labor secretary should put an assistant secretary in charge of this agency to send a strong signal about the importance of enforcing the Fair Labor Standards Act, the Davis-Bacon Act, the Family and Medical Leave Act, and other statutes it enforces. This should be part of a strategy to reduce inequality and improve earnings, since these statutes set guidelines for minimum wages, overtime, pay for workers on federal contracts, and what happens to a worker's job in the event of illness.

Longer-Term Agenda

The new administration should work toward developing a comprehensive assistance program for all dislocated workers. Workers who suffer permanent job loss, whether from trade or domestic competition or technology, typically suffer from protracted periods of unemployment, significantly lower wages in their new jobs, and the loss of health insurance and pension benefits.

Rather than having separate programs for each cause of dislocation, the secretary should strive to consolidate and extend the existing dislocated worker program. The current dislocated worker program provides job placement assistance and training services for only about 300,000 to 400,000 workers each year. Based on data from the Dislocated Worker Survey, this suggests that our current program serves about 1 out of every 7 to 10 affected workers.[29]

The White House should work toward passing legislation with the requisite funding that would allow DOL to expand the improved TAA program discussed above so that all dislocated workers are covered, regardless of the cause of their job loss. The cost of this expansion may initially make it necessary to limit eligibility in this program to those older or long-tenured workers that studies have found suffer the most adverse consequences when their company or establishment closes. Perhaps by limiting eligibility to those with five or more years of seniority, or to those over the age of 45, it would be possible to begin the process of offering a quality universal protection program.

Workforce Investment Act
Economists have amply demonstrated that, with the exception of a period in the late 1990s, there has been a steady trend since the late 1970s of "hollowing out" the middle of the earnings distribution.[30] Employment in low-wage service jobs has expanded rapidly for those with a high school education or less, while higher-paying manufacturing jobs have been disappearing. The 20 million low-wage workers in our economy today are partly the result of stagnating educational attainment and the influx of immigrants and former welfare recipients. Less-skilled workers often find that they need to obtain at least some postsecondary training and/or relevant work experience to advance. These workers need access to child care and transportation services if they are to compete for and succeed in higher-wage jobs.

Unfortunately, the institutions charged with this task are often only weakly linked to employers and the education and training system. The secretary should start a national workforce dialogue to get stakeholder views about reform of the Workforce Investment Act, which guides most federal training programs and expired in FY2003. A set of principles that reflect a review of best practices and effective workforce program design should frame these discussions. The secretary should actively engage workers, employers, the state and local workforce system, members of Congress, and those parts of the administration that regularly intersect with these Workforce Investment Act programs—such as the departments of Education, Commerce, Health and Human Services, and OMB—to devise a comprehensive reauthorization package for these programs.[31]

DOL, in designing these new programs, should look for ways to leverage its funding with state or nongovernmental efforts. The Worker Advancement

Grants for Employment in States, developed by Georgetown University professor Harry Holzer, could serve as a model for how the federal government could structure a low-wage worker strategy. Under this program, DOL would fund a series of competitive grants to states or local areas to scale up their most successful and innovative initiatives for employment advancement efforts for low-wage or hard-to-employ working poor adults and at-risk youth. A key feature of the program should be that whatever funds are available get leveraged by requiring states to provide matching new public or private expenditures on training or various work supports such as expanded child care, transportation services, or job placement assistance.

Another key feature would provide incentives for state-level efforts to devise partnerships involving local worker investment boards, community colleges, employers and industry associations, and workforce intermediaries. The existing One-Stop offices, which provide access to job training referrals, career counseling, job listings, vocational rehabilitation, and other services, all under one roof, would be a natural hub for these efforts and could improve access to these supports for the working poor. DOL should also perform high-quality program evaluations so that best practices can be determined and made available for others to model.

Low-Wage Workers

Improving the skills, and consequently the competitiveness, of low-wage workers complements the goal of improving workers' health and safety. Reducing the size of the pool of exploitable low-wage workers makes it easier to enforce our existing labor laws. Workers who face limited opportunities are ripe targets for minimum wage violations, and are unlikely to complain when exposed to workplace hazards.[32] These problems are simply compounded for undocumented immigrants who survive in the shadows of an underground economy where they hesitate to avail themselves of the protections afforded them under the law. Having a large pool of workers with substandard wages and working conditions undermines wages and working conditions in the rest of the economy. Thus, stepped-up labor law enforcement plus an increase in the minimum wage, mandatory paid sick leave, and the expansion of the Earned Income Tax Credit should all be parts of DOL's low-wage worker strategy.

The secretary needs to establish an active process to consult with stakeholders and experts to identify workplace hazards that need priority action and begin to target DOL staff to develop appropriate safety standards. Today this process is too cumbersome and too unwieldy, placing workers at risk for far too long. The recent failure to address the potential impact of a pandemic flu outbreak and the use of the chemical diacetyl in food are but two such examples. DOL needs a streamlined process for identifying new chemicals or needed changes in exposure limits as an integral part of building an effective system of worker protections.

There are several obvious areas for consideration as DOL develops its new regulatory agenda. Recent changes to the Fair Labor Standards Act that set the salary tests too low for workers classified as executive, administrative, or professional employees ($5,000 above the poverty line for a family of four) have deprived an estimated 6 million workers of overtime.[33] A first step forward would be preserving the original intent of the Fair Labor Standards Act to exempt only those workers who are really in an executive role.

The growth and transformation of the home health care industry also makes it important for DOL to consider a new standard recognizing that those workers offering care, but paid by third-party agencies, deserve to be treated more like employees than as babysitters. Similarly, the misclassification of workers as independent contractors appears to be a large and growing problem in industries such as construction, communications, information technology, trucking, janitorial service, and others.[34] The level of penalties and fines for health and safety violations, especially for willful violations leading to an injury or death, also need to be updated from the levels last set in 1990.[35] Developing appropriate administrative, legislative, or regulatory remedies to these problems needs to be a priority item for DOL.

Securities and Exchange Commission

Restoring the Capital Markets Regulator and Responding to Crisis

DAMON SILVERS

The Securities and Exchange Commission has grown increasingly ineffectual since 2004—an increasingly worrisome development since the agency regulates capital markets that allocate tens of trillions of dollars in resources, shaping the U.S. and global economy. Investors look to the commission to protect their savings, not from risk but from fraud and unfair dealing. The commission does so through enforcing securities laws that require transparency, enforce fiduciary duties, and structure fair and well-functioning markets. The SEC's weakness, however, contributed to the 2008 global financial crisis—a crisis caused by deregulation that has forced the federal government to act as the effective financial guarantor of the securities industry. This rolling crisis all but destroyed the five largest investment banks in the space of just six months. The next SEC chair will face the challenge of this severe, continuing capital markets crisis against the backdrop of an increasingly irrelevant SEC during the last years of the Bush administration. A swiss-cheese regulatory structure is a major contributor both to the crisis and to the paralysis of regulators confronting it. The first priority of a new SEC chair must be to restore a comprehensive regulatory approach to the capital markets involving the coverage of all securities, derivatives, and futures, and all investment vehicles—hedge funds, private equity funds, and sovereign wealth funds—under a strong regulatory regime focused on transparency and real oversight over capital in relation to risk. The next SEC chair should bear this approach in mind as he or she enters the sweeping debate over U.S. financial markets regulation next year in the wake of U.S. housing and global credit crises.

The president of the United States names the chairman of the Securities and Exchange Commission, who fills one of the five seats on the commission for all or what remains of a five-year term. Traditionally, the outgoing chairman departs at the request of the new president. The next chair of the SEC must strengthen the commission in ways that go well beyond simply restoring the effectiveness and morale of the commission as a regulatory agency.

We live in a world of global capital flows and increasingly linked global capital markets. Our competitive advantage in this globalized world is the depth and integrity of our markets—advantages that make individuals comfortable investing in our markets and institutional investors confident they can rely on published market information to manage their assets reliably and safely. The current financial crisis has deeply affected perceptions of the integrity and stability of our markets both in the United States and around the world, and the SEC will need to act to help restore that confidence.

Perhaps most importantly in light of the financial turmoil, the SEC needs to modernize its mandate to match the enormous changes in the securities markets over the past fifteen years. Private pools of capital are powerful players in public markets. Hedge funds and private equity funds continue to grow apace, and derivatives markets continue to expand—to the point where just the $60 trillion in notional amounts involved in just one type of derivative, the credit default swap, are estimated to be larger than the total capital invested in the entire world's public markets.[1]

Finally, the financial crisis exposed the weakness of the SEC's voluntary oversight of the large broker dealers. In 2009 it is very likely that our securities markets will be dominated in the short term by universal banks—combinations of stock brokers and commercial banks whose securities operations have not been the subject of meaningful safety and soundness regulation by the commission. This must change.

Yet the commission's efforts to maintain basic accountability and transparency in these new and growing financial arenas have been thwarted by the courts, which have attacked the SEC's efforts to regulate hedge funds and mutual funds in recent rulings. Worse still, the commission largely turned a blind eye to the explosion of publicly traded mortgage-backed securities that were at the heart of today's U.S. mortgage crisis and global credit crisis. The next SEC chair must work with Congress and the 44th president to modernize the SEC's authority so that the commission can protect both the investing public and the integrity of our markets as a whole.

At the very least, the next SEC chair has to ensure the commission has a seat at the table when Congress and the new administration begin to craft the broad financial regulatory reforms so clearly needed in the wake of the subprime mortgage meltdown. The SEC is the central regulator of the public capital markets, with the expertise and the culture of investor protection that needs to infuse the process of financial reform.

But well-regulated capital markets are about more than the global competitiveness of our financial services industry. Part of the SEC's responsibility is to ensure that investors have the information necessary to allocate capital in an economically efficient manner. Investors' need for information has changed as the world economy has changed, but the commission's disclosure rules have not kept up with that change in areas as diverse as energy and climate issues, human capital formation, and supply chain management. Meaningful transparency must include these new sets of criteria.

As the next SEC chair seeks to strengthen the agency's ability to regulate the capital markets and closes loopholes, he or she must also be willing to look anew at the regulatory structure that has developed both over the life of the commission and during the Bush administration. The test must always be whether a particular regulatory structure or practice benefits investors and the public. The next chair should look to eliminate or revise regulations that do not meet that test, or are an unnecessary hindrance to productive economic activity.

These broad goals will not be easily achieved in part due to the legacy of the Bush years. The history is worth a brief recap. In 2001, President George W. Bush appointed Harvey Pitt to be SEC chairman, who promptly gave a speech to the accounting industry raising the prospect of "a kindler, gentler SEC."[2] Within days, Enron began to unravel. Its collapse in December 2001 was followed by a series of restatements and other accounting problems at a number of telecom and energy companies, culminating in the collapse of WorldCom in the early summer of 2002.[3] During this period, morale among commission staff seriously decayed as regulatory and enforcement initiatives passed to state authorities.

In the wake of these scandals, Congress passed the Sarbanes-Oxley Act, which President Bush immediately signed into law.[4] But Pitt then stumbled badly by offering the chairmanship of the newly created Public Company Auditing Oversight Board—a board mandated by Sarbanes-Oxley and appointed by the SEC—to former FBI Director William Webster, who was then tied himself to an accounting scandal.[5]

On election night 2002, Harvey Pitt resigned as SEC chair. President Bush then appointed William Donaldson, the former chairman of the New York Stock Exchange. Against the backdrop of the blaring headlines about financial scandals and Pitt's mishaps, Congress and President Bush agreed on substantial increases in the commission's budget. Donaldson appointed William McDonough, the respected head of the Federal Reserve Bank of New York, to chair the PCAOB. Donaldson then undertook rulemakings addressing a number of other issues widely viewed as having contributed to the wave of corporate scandals surrounding Enron.

Donaldson, however, found himself increasingly isolated from Republican commissioners Paul Atkins and Cynthia Glassman.[6] The chair's new enforcement efforts rested on the support of the two Democrats, with a significant number of enforcement matters being reportedly approved on 3-2 votes—particularly cases in which SEC staff sought financial penalties against corporations, as opposed to individuals.[7]

Donaldson then resigned in early 2005, as did Harvey Goldschmid, the senior Democratic Commissioner most closely associated with Donaldson's post-Enron reform agenda.[8] President Bush appointed former Republican congressman Christopher Cox as chairman, who quickly belied conservative expectations that he would align with the commission's other two Republicans.[9] As 2007 came to a close, the two Democratic commissioners, Roel Campos and Annette Nazareth, both resigned, leaving a three-member, exclusively Republican commission until Luis Aguilar and Elise Walters were confirmed in July 2008.

The SEC then became a bystander as the subprime mortgage crisis, globalizing markets, the growing prominence and opacity of private pools of capital and sovereign wealth funds, and the continuing technological transformation of both trading and investment all gained pace in 2008. U.S. Treasury Secretary Henry Paulson underscored the increasing irrelevancy of the commission in the spring of 2008 when he unveiled a proposed overhaul of the U.S. financial regulatory arena, which suggested stripping the SEC of much of its oversight powers and deemphasizing the enforcement of the securities laws.[10]

Recommendations

The chairman of the Securities and Exchange Commission is both the chair and chief executive of the commission. The chairman is constantly faced with the challenge of managing outward and inward at the same time. In recent years, the chairman's office has increasingly relied on non-career, politically appointed staff. The result has been a perception of the chair as isolated from the day-to-day work of the agency and a de-emphasis on the effective management of the commission as an organization. This trend should be reversed. The next chair should trim the political staff in his office, draw upon career staff for positions in his office, and develop a clear senior leadership team including the division heads and the general counsel.

The chairman's office should see as its inward-oriented management objective the development of a strategic operating plan for filling the holes in an outdated regulatory system, improving the disclosure regime, revitalizing the enforcement division, modernizing the commission's authority and rules, and looking for ways to make regulation more effective at protecting the public interest and less unnecessarily burdensome for regulated parties. Division budgets and allocation of resources among the divisions should flow from such a strategic plan.

The chair needs to focus on managing downward, but will face an immediate need to manage outward, toward Congress, to repair damage done to the fabric of securities regulation in the Bush years in the areas of securities fraud, regulation of hedge funds and other private pools of capital, and commission jurisdiction over financial instruments designed to mimic securities.

The commission lacks sufficient statutory tools to maintain effective oversight of hedge funds, private equity funds, and sovereign wealth funds to guard against systemic risk issues and to ensure they are not engaged in improper market conduct. These opaque capital pools have grown dramatically over the past 10 years in size and relative importance in our capital markets.[11]

Many have pointed out the problems associated with private equity firms colluding with management in buyout situations at public investors' expense.[12] There is a parallel concern in terms of sovereign wealth funds acting as agents of their sponsoring governments.[13] The next chair should seek additional authority from Congress over these new types of funds, and in doing so look to coordinate closely with regulators and legislators in other financial markets to try and construct a truly global oversight regime.

In addition, the next chair needs to define precisely what a security is and how the SEC should regulate the many new types of securities that financial market entrepreneurs continue to create that are similar or identical to securities but are structured to avoid the commission's jurisdiction. Indexed equity futures, certain types of over-the-counter derivatives, and most importantly, equity-indexed annuities are all sold to less-sophisticated individual investors. The chair's office should seek to bring all investment products linked to publically traded debt and equity securities under its jurisdiction, in whole or in part.

In 2008, the Supreme Court decided in *Stoneridge Investment Partners, LLC v. Scientific Atlanta* and *Board of Regents of the University of California et al. v. Credit Suisse First Boston et al.* (the Enron case) to all but grant investment banks and other third-party participants in securities frauds immunity from claims by investors.[14] In doing so, the Court rejected the long-standing view of the commission that secondary actors who are engaged in fraudulent schemes are liable to investors.[15] The next SEC chair must lead an effort to identify an appropriate legislative solution and call on Congress to act.

Corporation Finance

The Division of Corporation Finance is the heart of the commission's routine regulation of public companies. It is responsible for regulating the securities offering process under the Securities Act of 1933, for overseeing and monitoring periodic disclosures by public companies under the Securities Exchange Act of 1934, and for overseeing the proxy solicitation process under the Securities Exchange Act.[16] The Division of Corporation Finance will immediately face four issues that have been badly mishandled under the Bush administration.

The most urgent is the continuing fallout from the capital markets crisis. The SEC chair and his or her division director need to examine whether there were defects in prospectuses and other filings for publicly traded debt, as well as disclosure deficiencies in the 10Ks and other filings under the Securities Exchange Act by financial services firms, insurers, credit rating agencies, and home builders. The commission also must determine what deficiencies, if any, exist in the division's review processes and staffing assignments.

Currently, institutional investors with more than $100 million in assets are required to disclose their portfolios to the public quarterly. There is no requirement, however, to disclose short positions. With the rise of hedge funds and other actors that are much more likely to engage in short selling, these disclosures should be modernized to give a complete sense of institutional positions. Another particular area of focus should be on the credit rating agencies. During the summer of 2008, under pressure from Congress, the commission released a series of proposed rules to tighten oversight of the credit rating agencies. If these rules have not been finalized when a new chair is appointed, they should be shortly thereafter. The commission should also consider moving toward an oversight system similar to that currently in place for public company auditors through the Public Company Auditing Oversight Board. Such an inspection-based system could be housed in the commission, at the PCAOB, or at a third, independent body.[17]

The corporate finance division also should undertake a broader review of Regulation S-K, which lays out what companies have to disclose to their investors in annual reports, to determine whether disclosures are properly capturing material information in a global business environment where both risks and opportunities are shaped by significantly different forces than those that existed 20 years ago. In particular, the commission should direct the division to immediately act on the rulemaking petition submitted by a number of state treasurers in 2007 seeking expanded disclosure by public companies of carbon-related risks and opportunities.[18]

The division is responsible for the commission's regulation of proxy voting, corporate governance, and executive compensation. Here the commission needs to take action on a number of reforms that have been blocked or weakened during the second term of the Bush administration. First, it should enact a proxy access rule that would give groups of substantial long-term investors a meaningful ability to nominate candidates for public company boards. Proxy access is perhaps the best way to rein in executive compensation abuses, which are symbolic of the ways in which U.S. public companies seem to be run for the personal benefit of their executives rather than to create wealth in a manner that benefits both investors and the nation as a whole. Unlike many solutions to the problems of weak boards and runaway pay, it is not overly rigid and it can be designed to limit its abuse by short-term oriented shareholders.

In 2003, Chairman Donaldson proposed a mandatory proxy access system for all companies but then let it die under pressure from the White House and the business community. More recently, in 2007 the Second Circuit Court of Appeals found the SEC's existing proxy rules allowed shareholders to raise the idea of proxy access using the shareholder proposal process alongside other corporate governance ideas such as majority voting.[19] This approach was briefly in effect in the 2007 proxy season, but was then blocked by a new SEC rule adopted on partisan lines against intense investor opposition.[20]

While either approach is technically feasible, investor opinion seems to have shifted toward the approach of opening up the shareholder proposal process, which allows for more diversity in approaches among companies. Subject to consultations with staff, this is the direction the next chair should take.

Second, the commission should look at strengthening the shareholder proposal process by restoring shareholders' ability to raise issues of risk management, and by looking at whether to require companies to put executive pay packages to a shareholder vote, as is the practice in the United Kingdom and as has been recently proposed in legislation introduced by Rep. Barney Frank (D-MA) and Sen. Barack Obama (D-IL).[21]

Third, the commission should take more of a leadership role in addressing executive compensation abuses. The SEC should require disclosure of executive compensation consultants' conflicts of interest and consider a rule requiring shareholder approval of consultants with conflicts. Additionally, the commission must immediately revise the rules for executive compensation disclosure. In 2006, a last-minute change resulted in only the partial disclosure of the value of equity-based executive compensation in the final rule.[22] While the change did harmonize proxy statement reporting with Generally Accepted Accounting Principles—the U.S. accounting standard—it resulted in confusing reporting and should be reversed.

Finally, the SEC should examine longer-term reform models, such as the principles on long-term value recently released by the Aspen Institute, with the support of the Business Roundtable, the U.S. Chamber of Commerce, the Council of Institutional Investors, and the AFL-CIO.[23] Key ideas here are reducing the role of quarterly earnings and having stock-based compensation be held past the CEO's term in office.

Enforcement

The goal of the new administration should be to replace the boom-and-bust enforcement cycles of the Bush administration with a steady, properly resourced approach that results in genuine investor protection. That means restoring the morale and professional autonomy of the SEC's Division of Enforcement staff, beginning with defining a clear boundary between the division's investigative work and the decision-making responsibilities of the commissioners themselves. Commissioners should not be involved in reviewing the preparation of cases. This practice both undermines the work of the professional staff and dramatically increases the risk of breaches of the ethics rules.

During the past few years, special procedures were put in place governing cases involving corporate penalties against public companies involved in violations of the securities laws.[24] Like criminal penalties against companies, corporate civil penalties both have a potent deterrent effect and incentivize the management of companies to establish programs and procedures that prevent wrongdoing. These special procedures allowed individual commissioners to look over the shoulders of enforcement staff as they were preparing cases where staff were seeking corporate penalties, and made it easy for a minority of the commission to block the imposition of such penalties. These special procedures were designed to resolve a political conflict that had arisen between Republican commissioners who did not believe in corporate penalties, despite such penalties being provided by law, and the staff and the remainder of the commissioners.[25] These special procedures appear to have discouraged the SEC enforcement staff from enforcing the law and have damaged enforcement staff morale. They should be reviewed with an eye toward eliminating them.[26]

The most extensive set of investigations undertaken by the enforcement division in the Cox era involved abuses of employee stock options, and in particular executive stock options. These abuses included both backdating (pretending options were issued on an earlier date when the stock price was low) and springloading (holding back good news and issuing options). The enforcement staff opened approximately 160 investigations in this area alone. Yet in early 2008 the commission announced that it was moving to wrap up about 80 open options misconduct cases, having brought charges in 8 cases out of 160 investigations.[27]

The stock options investigations were associated with some of the most unusual conduct by the commission, including speeches by Commissioner Paul Atkins defending the practice of springloading while staff were conducting open investigations, and letters from the SEC's chief accountant advising companies they did not have to restate to account for springloading executive options, effectively hiding the conduct from investors.[28] The entire course of these investigations needs to be reviewed to determine whether meritorious cases have been dismissed and whether the settlements that are in process or are being reviewed are in the public interest.

The public financial markets, however, are simply too big to allow the SEC's enforcement division to pursue all possible violations of the securities laws with equal vigor and resources. Currently, the division has resources to bring between 600 and 700 cases per year. The division must maintain a sustained program aimed at the criminal margins—unethical penny stock traders, boiler room operators doing high-pressure sales, and marketing frauds directed at senior citizens. But the lesson of Enron, WorldCom, and the subprime crisis is that illegal conduct that can result in major harm or systemic risk must be the number one priority of the division.

Investment Management Regulation

The SEC's Division of Investment Management primarily implements and enforces the Investment Company Act of 1940, which regulates several types of investment companies but most prominently mutual funds. There are two fundamental problems in the mutual fund markets. The first is the weakness of mutual fund governance, where the funds themselves are supposed to be managed in the interests of their investors, but tend to be dominated by the mutual fund's adviser. The second is the opacity of fund fee structures, which makes it difficult for investors to know what they are paying and to compare fees for funds in the same asset class.

In response to the weakness of fund governance, in 2004 the commission enacted a rule requiring the chairpersons of mutual funds to be independent of the fund's adviser.[29] This rule was overturned in 2005 on procedural grounds by the Federal Appeals Court for the District of Columbia, and, despite promises to the contrary, it has not been revisited.[30] There is no doubt about the commission's authority to enact such a rule. The division staff should review the factual underpinnings, including cost-benefit issues, and the SEC should move forward to reissue the rule.

The division also needs to ensure that mutual funds are covered under Sarbanes-Oxley's whistleblower provisions. Unfortunately, the language is ambiguous about whether employees of the advisers to mutual funds are covered. Because mutual funds themselves typically have no employees, the whistleblower provisions are only effective in the mutual fund context so long as they cover the fund adviser's employees. The commission should act to resolve the ambiguity and provide for protections for investment adviser employees in the mutual fund context.

Similarly, the investment management division must simplify mutual fund fee disclosure. The approach should be the same as it was in the area of executive pay—the desired outcome should be a single number reflecting all fees which should be prominently published both in mutual fund prospectuses and in all mutual fund advertising, together with a system for categorizing funds so as to facilitate comparability. This data should be provided to investors at the point of sale.

The commission is now regulating a market where hedge funds invest large pools of capital free of the restrictions historically placed on mutual funds in the area of short selling and leverage. In 2008, the commission placed substantive limits on short selling on financial industry stocks in reaction to the rolling financial crisis, yet short selling continued largely unabated.[31] The investment management division needs to reassess how it determines what an investment company is in order to tighten loopholes that have been allowed to grow.

Trading and Markets Regulation

The SEC's trading and markets division regulates the national stock exchanges and oversees the newly created Financial Industry Regulatory Authority, or FINRA, the regulatory arm for broker dealers and NASDAQ trading.

Part of the division's responsibilities include the oversight of the major integrated financial services companies' broker-dealer operations through the voluntary program for the Consolidated Supervision of Broker-Dealer Holding Companies, or CSE in SEC speak. This is the program that oversaw the safety and soundness of Bear Stearns Cos., Lehman Brothers Holdings Inc., and Merrill Lynch & Co.—all of which collapsed or were acquired under duress in 2008. In the case of Bear Stearns, this was despite assurances by the SEC days before that all the CSE-supervised companies were sound.

In October 2008, SEC chairman Christopher Cox canceled the CSE program. It should be replaced by a program that is adequately resourced, is made mandatory as a statutory matter, and is extended to large broker dealers that are affiliated with commercial banks.

Some of the financial institutions regulated under this program have expressed concerns that they are subject to overlapping and not necessarily consistent regulation by the SEC and other bank regulators. The financial crisis suggests that the relationships between underwriting and risk management are insufficiently policed, and that in particular the involvement of CSE-supervised firms in shadow markets trading, credit default swaps, and other over-the-counter derivatives and lending to hedge funds are underregulated.

The trading and markets division's larger mission, FINRA, today regulates the members of the National Association of Securities Dealers and the New York Stock Exchange, including over 5,000 brokerage firms and over 674,000 registered securities professionals.[32] At the same time, both the NYSE and NASDAQ today are at the core of a global network of exchanges, with the likely prospect of further integration soon to come. The SEC's trading and markets division needs to examine its oversight of the new governance at FINRA as well as the new ownership and governance structures of the NYSE and NASDAQ—beginning with the historic distinctions between broker dealers and investment advisors, which have eroded in recent years.

Specifically, the Federal Appeals Court for the District of Columbia issued an opinion in 2007 overturning commission regulations seeking to better define the boundary between stock brokers, who both give clients advice and actually buy and sell securities for clients, and investment advisers, who historically give advice but do not execute trades.[33] In the aftermath of the ruling, the commission sought a study of the issue by the Rand Corporation, which found that investors increasingly do not understand the distinction between brokers and advisers or the different levels of protection investors have in dealing with each group.[34]

The commission approach in dealing with this situation should be to look at merging the regulation of the two categories while ensuring the merged approach preserves clear fiduciary duties on the part of the new merged regulatory category to investors. One issue to examine in this context is the role of arbitration in resolving disputes between investors and broker dealers. In light of the D.C. Circuit opinion, implementing this approach may require statutory changes.

FINRA is reportedly considering whether their current rule book strikes the proper balance between principles and rules. As a general matter, rules require or bar specific conduct; principles are less certain in application, but can be more flexible and less easily gamed. All regulatory systems are combinations of rules and principles. The commission needs to monitor this process with an eye to the principles that institutions as well as individuals can be the victims of improper conduct, and that any functioning regulatory system needs both robust principles and detailed rules.

Accounting Regulation

Accounting and auditing issues have become increasingly controversial in the aftermath of Enron, the passage of Sarbanes-Oxley, and the establishment of the Public Company Auditing Oversight Board. There has been significant political pressure on the SEC's chief accountant from the business community, congressional Republicans, and Republican SEC commissioners to weaken both accounting and auditing rules and standards. Conversely, there is a widespread belief among investors and the auditing profession that the Office of the Chief Accountant has been substantially weakened and politicized during

Conrad Hewitt's current tenure. This follows the attempt by the chief accountant's office to pressure the PCAOB about the seriousness of its inspections, and to pressure the Financial Accounting Standards Board about off-balance sheet assets in relation to the subprime scandal. The new chair will inherit a series of initiatives designed to weaken oversight of accounting and financial disclosure.[35] These initiatives will have to be halted or in some cases undone.

At the same time, the commission has moved far in the direction of allowing companies to choose which accounting rules they would use. In July 2008, the commission asked for public comment on a proposal that would allow the largest public companies to choose which accounting system they would use, and envisions a complete switch to international accounting standards by 2014.[36] This approach will take the leverage out of the U.S. positions in discussion designed to merge Generally Accepted Accounting Principles, or GAAP— the U.S.-based accounting standard—and the International Financial Reporting Standards, or IFRS. These discussions need to be restarted on a different basis, with a focus on substantive convergence of the two systems and on putting the international accounting standard-setting process on a more independent basis in terms of its funding and oversight, just as the Sarbanes-Oxley Act did for the United States' accounting standard setting.

International Securities Regulation

The International Affairs Office has been seeking to address the problem posed by regulatory arbitrage—foreign markets competing for business with U.S. markets by advertising themselves as lightly regulated—by pursuing a strategy of building alliances among markets that view themselves as strongly regulated. The importance of this strategy is revealed by the 2008 financial crisis. The United States is perceived internationally as having substantially contributed to the development of the global credit market crisis by insufficiently regulating its own markets.[37] The International Affairs Office needs to be involved in crafting an international posture for the commission, in concert with other relevant agencies of the federal government, to promote the development of a robust international regulatory framework.

In doing so, the next SEC chair needs to ensure that two other initiatives of the Office of International Affairs are reassessed. The first is the push toward giving public companies a choice among accounting systems discussed above. The second is proposals for relatively weak standards for mutual recognition agreements with foreign securities regulators, both in terms of regulatory frameworks and enforcement and oversight capacity. In both these areas there needs to be a reassessment, not of the ultimate goals but of the approach being taken to achieve them. The long-term goal should be to preserve the advantages our strong system of investor protections provide U.S. capital markets while using our leverage in international negotiations to create as robust a floor of international regulation as possible.

Interagency Financial Regulation
Bush administration Secretary of the Treasury Henry Paulson, who chairs the President's Working Group on Capital Markets, transformed the Working Group into more of a source of policymaking for the capital markets.[38] As part of this effort, Paulson issued in the spring of 2008 a blueprint for the reform of financial regulation. This blueprint appeared designed in part to dismantle the SEC as an effective regulator by taking away its jurisdiction over investment banks and by explicitly calling on the commission to adopt the weak regulatory philosophy of the Commodities Futures Trading Commission. This lax approach has since been blamed by many for the speculative bubble in energy prices during the summer of 2008.[39] The Paulson blueprint is fundamentally deregulatory in its approach and should not be the basis for a new administration's reform efforts.

The increased prominence of the President's Working Group on Capital Markets raises the question of the independence of the SEC and other independent agencies whose chairmen compose the President's Working Group. The success of the U.S. securities regulation system over the long run rests on the relative lack of politicization of the commission and its affiliated bodies. While the President's Working Group does perform a vital function, the next SEC chair should be aware of the importance of strengthening the commission's status as an independent regulatory agency.

Since the passage of the Gramm-Leach-Bliley Act in 1999, the legal and business boundaries between commercial credit markets and securities markets have blurred, and the old absolute separation of banking and securities markets was dismantled without being replaced by an adequate regulatory substitute.[40] The result was a catastrophic failure to effectively police the moral hazard problem presented by the combination of investment banking operations with insured commercial bank assets.

The impulse to strengthen and rationalize financial regulation is a sound one. But the organizing idea of such a project should be to maintain both a robust, comprehensive disclosure-based system for financial products that are not insured but are marketed to the public, and to police the insured system against moral hazard effectively. The commission should be one center of such a rationalized and strengthened system. There should be two other centers: one focused on the safety and soundness of insured commercial banking activity, and the other on consumer protection in areas such as mortgages and credit cards. The next SEC chair should be a vigorous advocate of strong transparency-based investor protection and systemic risk management that must underlie such an approach.

The relationship between the SEC and the Commodities Futures Trading Commission will be key to this dynamic. During 2008, weak enforcement by the CFTC became a matter of broad public concern in light of apparent speculative bubbles in oil and food markets. There is almost complete integration between the financial futures markets, over-the-counter derivatives markets, and the securities markets. This integration is clearly responsible for the rapid-fire demise of Lehman Brothers, Merrill Lynch, and U.S. insurance giant American International Group Inc. in 2008. Consequently, the SEC's mandate to protect investors against systemic risk has become impossible to execute without integration with the CFTC.

The policy goal in this area should be increased coordination, leading to a merger of the two organizations. But the regulatory philosophy that should guide this process should be one of strong investor and public interest protections. The CFTC is a much smaller agency than the SEC, so at an organizational level the challenge of integrating the CFTC into the SEC is significant but not overwhelming. First steps toward a merger, such as memoranda of understanding governing areas of joint concern, like the commodities operations of affiliates of broker dealers, are an obvious first step and can be pursued through agency action. Ultimately, though, a merger will require congressional action.

Finally, the SEC has had historically difficult relationships with state regulators and law enforcement officials. This need not be so. State regulators have a closeness to the market and resources that should complement the work of the commission. While some level of healthy competition will always be present in these relationships, there should be increased two-way communication and the development of investigation protocols with attorneys general who are particularly active in the securities area.

PCAOB and FASB

The SEC appoints the members of the Public Company Accounting Oversight Board, which oversees the auditors of public companies. The commission currently has a process for advising the Financial Accounting Foundation on its appointments of the members of the Financial Accounting Standards Board, which is responsible for promulgating the Generally Accepted Accounting

Principles that are currently the required rules for financial statements filed with the commission by U.S. companies. Recently, the Financial Accounting Foundation approved a restructuring of FASB that involved decreasing the size of the board. This was greeted with concern by investors.

January 20, 2009, will be the first change in administrations since the creation of the PCAOB, and it is unclear what that will mean for the composition and leadership of the PCAOB. The board has been under pressure in recent years to be less aggressive in the pursuit of its mission of public company audit quality. The commission should make clear its support for the PCAOB and its mission by moving expeditiously to approve PCAOB standard setting and supporting the board in its dealings with foreign regulators.

FASB for the last decade has been working on a change in the basic framework of GAAP that shifts it from a primarily historic cost approach to financial accounting to a primarily mark-to-market, or fair value, approach. This is an area the next chair should be aware of and monitor. The use of mark-to-market accounting has been associated with some of the most serious abuses in our financial system in recent years, such as Enron's use of derivatives, and in its "mark-to-model" form, the subprime crisis. In the financial crisis, mark-to-market accounting appears to have had a pronounced pro-cyclical effect, accelerating the bubble's growth and accelerating its collapse. Yet the application of mark-to-market principles to executive stock options put an end to accounting abuses in that area.

The commission should support mark-to-market accounting where the items involved can be readily priced in existing liquid markets, and where the items involved could be bought or sold on those markets without affecting other elements of the company's balance sheet. It should be wary of applying mark-to-market concepts where these conditions do not apply or where the outcome would be counterintuitive or circular, such as would occur if company debt was marked to market as a liability in a distressed situation. These issues are complex, and are likely to be resolved in tandem with the question of the adoption of international rules. They deserve the full attention of the commission.

DOMESTIC POLICY

Overview

America's Changing Demographics

MARIA ECHAVESTE AND
CHRISTOPHER EDLEY, JR.

America is constantly redefining itself within a framework of deeply held beliefs that value individual freedoms and a social compact that strives—at its most idealistic—to create opportunity for all. But this model is facing a significant challenge: an increasingly aging white majority supported by a growing, racially and ethnically diverse, younger workforce. The question is whether that workforce will have the education, skills, and social safety net required to generate the human capital that America must have to compete successfully in the global economy. The confluence of demography—age, the growing Latino population, and immigration—with political ideology suggests that this will be a challenge. America must overcome its disability from the "color lines" and its obsession with "the other" to ensure our country makes the critical investments needed to ensure that America in the coming decades will lead the world in innovation, creativity, and opportunity.

After the 2000 census, headlines and news stories highlighted the "changing demographics" of our country. Every time the Census Bureau issues an updated report reflecting the aging of America, the increase in the Hispanic population, or the decline in married two-parent families, the headlines convey a sense of alarm regarding these demographic trends—as if changes of this magnitude have never occurred before.

Today's trends may be different in kind, but not in effect. They are just the latest installment in America's continuing effort to define who we are as a nation and what kind of a society we aspire to be. At this critical juncture in America's story, with trillions in national debt, a severely distressed economy, and foreign policy challenges that threaten our standing in the world, it is even more critical to understand fully who we are and who we are becoming.

Is demography destiny for politics and other facets of our society, as some have written?[1] Do all demographic changes require federal public policy responses, or only some of them? Is the impending retirement of the baby boom generation, coupled with longer life expectancies and the resulting "aging of America," the most salient demographic changes confronting our society? Are racial and ethnic changes relevant in profound ways, or interesting only to sociologists and ethnographers? Does it matter that racial and ethnic changes are occurring in part because of immigration, and is this wave of immigration radically different from prior history? Why does the trend of "increased racial and ethnic diversity" strike fear in some Americans and create hope in others?

There are some sobering demographic lessons to examine in California's experience over the last three decades. California is a state with a vibrant economy—the sixth largest in the world—and 37 million people who are multilingual and multiracial/multiethnic, including both undocumented and legal immigrants. Yet, in the face of this economic strength and diversity, California struggles with a badly decaying transportation infrastructure, a declining education system, an overtaxed health care system, and increasing inequality with both great wealth and great poverty. Our nation is now beginning to experience some of the demographic shifts that have already shaped California, and it is important that the next president and his administration learn from these experiences so they can better manage the challenges.

The Changing Face of America

Life expectancy grew from 58 years for men and 60 years for women in the 1920s to 74 and 80, respectively, as of 2005. Forecasts based on U.S. Census Bureau data project that by 2030, life expectancy will rise to 78 years for men and 84 years for women. Longer lives coupled with a slowing birth rate mean that the percentage of the population 65 and older will increase. Indeed, by 2030, 71 million people—about 20 percent of the population—will be 65 and older,[2] as compared to less than 12 percent in 2000. This older population will be 72 percent white, 11 percent Hispanic, 10 percent African-American, and 5 percent Asian.[3]

The racial composition of the aging population in comparison to the population below 65 and in the workforce raises the question of whether we are making the necessary human capital investments to ensure that the future workforce, which is increasingly minority and especially Latino, is sufficiently prepared to participate successfully in a robust global economy. In 2030, 25 percent of white Americans will be 65 or older, while only 10 percent of all Hispanics and 14 percent of African Americans will be that age.[4] Orange County, California, provides an interesting example. In 2002, 27 percent of residents were over 65 (as compared to 14.7 percent in the state as a whole), and of that group, 75 percent were white (non-Hispanic), even though the county was only 51 percent white.[5] The remaining 49 percent were comprised significantly of both Asians and Hispanics.

Extended life also means that chronic and degenerative illnesses are increasingly contributing to causes of death. Even today, 80 percent of those 65 and older are living with at least one chronic disease. Differences in race and ethnicity increase the prevalence of high blood pressure, diabetes, and cancer—the most common chronic diseases. Thirty-nine percent of non-Hispanic whites over 65 reported good health in a 2007 study, for example, but only 24 percent of non-Hispanic blacks and 29 percent of Hispanics.[6] Health disparities among racial and ethnic minorities as compared to white Americans may become even more pronounced as those minorities age, compounding the challenges to the already costly health care system.

Hispanics/Latinos

There are currently more than 47 million Hispanics living in the United States, or about 15 percent of the U.S. population. This highly diverse population traces its origins to 20 different Spanish-speaking nations. It includes both recent immigrants and people who can trace their presence to settlements that predate the founding of the country. The foreign-born share of the total American population was about 11 percent in 2006, but among Hispanics, it exceeds 40 percent.

Even the term for ethnic identity—Hispanic versus Latino—varies by region and age. Grossly generalizing, "Latino" appears to be more popular on both coasts and among the younger generation, and "Hispanic" is more commonly used in New Mexico, some parts of Texas, and Florida, and is used in official government publications. Over time, it is not clear whether these terms will become symbolic with little relevance to socioeconomic status (such as Irish or Italian), or whether they will remain substantive indicators of ethnic and minority group status, as with African Americans. Current trends suggest the latter.

The Latino population is both young and growing; by 2030, one in four American residents will be of Hispanic ancestry. It is the fastest growing minority, increasing four times faster than the total population and 14 times faster than the white population.[7] Immigration fueled growth over the last three decades, but population increases are now due to birthrate.[8] The majority of the second generation (the children of immigrants) is currently in school, but by 2030, they will number 26 million and be a significant part of the workforce.[9]

This population boom has begun to displace African Americans in urban cities, especially Los Angeles, and more recently in Chicago and New York.[10] But immigrants' geographic dispersal has changed, no longer confined to the border states and gateway cities. The greatest percentage increases in the Hispanic population have been in the South and the Midwest. These regions have seen a parallel increase in anti-immigrant sentiment, not just among whites, but also African Americans. The low-wage domestic workforce in new states and traditional gateway cities, especially African Americans and previously settled immigrants (or second-generation Hispanics with low levels of education), see the newcomers as competitors for scarce jobs that will drag down their wages and working conditions.

Hispanics include individuals who are monolingual English, bilingual English-Spanish, monolingual Spanish, and everything in between. Some believe that the critical difference between this wave of immigrants and prior periods of intense immigration is that diverse Hispanic immigrants today have a common language, whether ancestral or native, even if they have nothing else in common.[11] This is different from the past, when immigrants had different ethnic backgrounds and different languages, which, coupled with a commitment to public education as part of the "Americanization" of immigrants, may have accelerated the assimilation process, forging a strong "American" identity.

There are strong disagreements about whether this latest wave of immigrants will be fully assimilated or integrated into American society—at least in the same way and to similar effect. Language is often blamed,[12] yet only 7 percent of second-generation adult Hispanics speak predominantly Spanish, and by the third generation, Spanish dominance disappears entirely, and less than 25 percent are even bilingual.[13] This strongly echoes the experience of past waves of immigrants and belies the views of many who fear that language will prevent Hispanics from fully integrating into American society.

Lower educational achievement levels may, however, make full integration and economic and social mobility more difficult for the foreign born.[14] The achievement gap between foreign- and native-born children is particularly troublesome given the age of the immigrant population. Hispanics' median age in 2000 was 27 as compared to 39 for the rest of the population. And the median age of second-generation Hispanics—a significant part of tomorrow's workforce—is only a little over 12 years old.[15] These facts affect both our economic future and the size and degree of investments needed in education and training.

America has a dirty history of color lines. It may be impossible to convincingly disaggregate the influence of color, language, and human capital to accurately forecast their assimilation. Yet Latinos contain the seeds for a new "model minority"—a model for a multicultural America. Idealism aside, Latinos' successful integration into the United States, and economic and social mobility, will depend in part on whether policymakers aggressively address the challenges facing this new population through investments in education, workforce development, health care, and other areas that provide opportunity for all.

Immigration

The current immigration system, the basic framework of which was enacted in 1965, tilts toward family reunification. Our system allocates the majority of legal permanent visas among various categories of family members using a per-country quota, and a smaller number of permanent visas for employment-based immigration. Two major trends have therefore emerged: family-based legal immigration from Asia and Latin America has increased as families reunite, and illegal immigration rates have risen—both because of the lure of employment and limited employment-based visas, and the long wait for family-based visas.

Approximately 40 million, or one in eight U.S. residents, are foreign-born. Of those, approximately 53.3 percent are from Mexico and Latin America, including the Caribbean, and about 25 percent are from Asia.[16] Immigrants from Asia and Africa tend to have higher levels of education on average than those from Latin America, and Mexico in particular, perhaps because of distance and cost. About 60 percent of Hispanic immigrants are from Mexico; these Mexican immigrants have an average education level of 9.8 years, and only about 48 percent of all Mexicans graduate from secondary school, as compared to 93 percent of Koreans.[17]

About 14.9 million, or 5 percent, of the current U.S. population is of Asian descent, and about 55 percent are foreign born.[18] The U.S. Asian population is incredibly diverse, coming from over 30 countries and speaking scores of languages. The geographic dispersal of Asian immigrants is concentrated in the West, particularly in California, Washington, and Nevada, but also New York, with some significant populations in Texas and Georgia. Asian Americans have higher intermarriage rates than any other minority group, which accelerates the integration and assimilation process.

The academic success of so many Asian subgroups, especially Chinese, Korean, and Japanese children, has led to the seriously inaccurate, sweeping generalizations best typified by the label "model minority." The significant educational achievement of the children of Asian immigrants can be partly attributed to the parents' generally higher levels of education. The overall success of this group masks the challenges faced by subgroups that are not succeeding at the same rates as whites or other Asians, including, for example, Cambodian, Vietnamese, Laotian, Filipino, and Bangladeshi populations.

There are now approximately 12 million people without legal status who are living in the United States.[19] The majority are working, and many are in mixed-status families with children who are U.S. citizens and/or legal spouses. The continued ambiguity of their legal status within the United States affects both their ability to work and their families' economic well-being—often tragically so.

Undocumented workers are concentrated in low-wage jobs with minimal or nonexistent labor protections. The sheer number of immigrants from Mexico and Latin America, especially in communities with little previous experience with immigrants, together with rising economic anxiety across America, means that most anti-immigrant feelings are directed toward Hispanics, though Asians are also targeted by hate groups and others.[20] Recent efforts to identify and deport undocumented individuals have been widely publicized, but most experts agree that deportation is a costly, inhumane, and ultimately unsuccessful strategy for dealing with the presence of so many undocumented immigrants.[21] Nonetheless, the public demands action to fix our immigration system, and the government's failure to do so exacerbates tensions in many communities.

Family Changes

The number of family households—those where all occupants are related by marriage, blood, or adoption—as a percentage of all households has dramatically decreased over the last four decades. In 1970, 81 percent of households were family households, but by 2003 that portion dropped to 68 percent.[22] Married family households with their own children declined precipitously from 40 percent of all households in 1970 to only 23 percent in 2003. The increase in people living alone reflects these changes; the amount rose from 17.1 percent in 1970 to 26.4 percent in 2003, while single-parent households similarly grew from 13 percent in 1970 to 32 percent in 2003. These are not insignificant numbers. Single parents ran 3.5 million households in 1970; that population rose to 12 million in 2003, with 83 percent of these households headed by women. These various trends have been relatively stable since 1996, which some attribute to declining divorce rates and delayed marriage.

Policy Implications

Policy analysts have long argued that aging and increased life expectancy will make our current Social Security, pension, and health care systems unsustainable. Experts may disagree about whether Social Security is a "moderate problem" or "crisis," but these three issues together form a ticking time bomb in need of immediate action by the new administration.

It is easy to paint a stark picture. A growing cohort of disproportionately white retirees is being supported by a declining number of workers per retiree, and those workers are increasingly people of color. The generational divide will exacerbate the racial divide, and vice-versa. Younger Americans will have to carry a greater burden to support retirees because there will be proportionately fewer workers. And as health costs continue to grow too fast and minorities make up a larger portion of the workforce, wages will likely decrease due to the continuing racial disparities in income. These lower-wage workers will increasingly be the ones supporting retirees. The longer we wait to mount solutions, the more challenging racial issues will become in the politics and substance of coping with demographic change.

Racial complications are already playing themselves out in education. The K–16 public education system in California was the envy of the nation just a generation ago. Today, the K–12 system is in shambles, having fallen dramatically in every meaningful quality measure. The state's public higher education system is steadily declining in quality and serving a declining fraction of the age cohort. All of this came about just as schools moved toward the majority-minority student population that they have now.

Declining public support for the education of a less-white student population is contemporaneous with declining investments in infrastructure—although not prisons—and the rise of an effective anti-tax movement. It would be wrong, however, to think that either race or anti-tax sentiment provide a complete explanation. The two go hand in hand. People are less inclined to support a community—and overcome a broad reluctance to taxes and government—in order to benefit those they consider "the other."

The question is how to spur consensus to generate the human capital investments needed for economic prosperity over the longer term—prosperity for our overall fiscal system of intergenerational social compacts, both public and private. A strategy for creating this three-level consensus—policy, political, and moral—must include a strategy for bridging the color lines.

Health Care
Health care needs arising from differences in age, socioeconomic status, insur-

ance status, and region also vary with race and ethnicity. The substance and politics of health care policy solutions should therefore be color-coded in our American fashion in order to be most effective.

Yet given the shortcomings of our education system, and teacher shortages in nursing schools in particular, the health care workforce will not reflect the diversity of the communities we expect it to serve. Research suggests that health care disparities will perpetuate in ethnic and minority communities where there will be gaps in language and cultural competence, as well as an unequal commitment of resources and talent. "Pipeline" programs and expanded professional training programs must therefore be structured to deal with the added demand for health and allied health workers as well as the chronic shortcomings in workforce diversity.

The urgency grows, but creativity in developing new solutions has flagged, in part because of the politically troubled status of race-sensitive affirmative action. The new administration should revisit these pipeline programs and look beyond the obvious option of incremental increases in federal spending to see whether structural changes in the pipeline systems might be more effective at the scale required. Everything from high school programs to the organization of doctor residency training should be on the table for review.

Immigration Reform
Leaders in both political parties have pledged to make immigration reform an important legislative priority. Congress has made a significant investment of legislative time and staff energy to work on several aspects of the problem, but meaningful reform will be politically difficult to achieve. The issue lends itself to demagoguery, and powerful interests across the ideological spectrum are mobilized to press their views.

Most of the push-pull factors driving immigration from Latin America will not materially change in the foreseeable future, with the possible exception of a sufficiently robust workplace enforcement strategy that would reduce immigrants' economic prospects. As for other approaches to curbing illegal immigration, it seems doubtful that a political consensus will materialize for more draconian or repressive border enforcement. Nor will our system tolerate still more harshly punitive treatment of detainees and deportees. Latin American economies are not likely to experience China-style economic growth in the near-term, especially in rural areas. And social ties across the border will make northward immigration both appealing and readily imaginable.

The fact that 12 million undocumented workers and their families are living in the shadows is unsustainable as a matter of politics, economics, and social stability. The large number is indisputable proof of failed policies, but the circumstances of these people also constitute a moral stain on our nation and a toxic potion for our politics. Something must be done.

There is substantial consensus on the elements of a comprehensive reform in its broad strokes—there is a *policy* consensus, although certainly not a *political* consensus, for comprehensive reform going forward before more effective border and workplace enforcement are in place. The most critical immigration policy question for the next administration is whether it will support an enforcement-only first phase of immigration reform, deferring "liberalizing" elements such as earned legal status, a future workflow program, and so forth. There is no clear measure of the relative power of the "enforcement first" and "consolidated reform" factions in Congress and the interest groups. Administration leadership will likely make the difference.

Demographic changes in the United States are heightening the labor market imperatives, but also the potential for conflict. We need workers, and we need for them to have access to the opportunity mechanisms that will make them productive, well-paid contributors to the economy and, in particular, the payroll and income tax systems. But demographic changes are also heightening the potential for ethnic conflicts. Xenophobic or anti-immigrant sentiment is crudely evident in many policy debates and electoral contests.

Organized labor and native U.S. minority workers, including established immigrants, make much of localized employment competition from immigrant inflows. If immigrants are undocumented and subject to unpoliced, exploitative conditions, they can have a serious effect on the low-wage labor market. Comprehensive reform must therefore be coupled with measures to prevent exploitation of immigrants—whether or not they are here legally—and the worst effects on local low-wage labor markets.

Politics
Demographic changes are having a significant effect on competition within and between the major political parties. The GOP faces a huge risk if the growing Latino voter bloc moves toward party identification and loyalty comparable to that of African Americans. The ascendancy of a powerful Latino bloc also makes many African-American political leaders nervous. Mismanaging the intraparty racial dynamics could easily rip the Democratic Party apart through competition for elected positions, appointed positions, legislative priorities, budget resources, political messaging, and more.

If we assume that policies will affect trends in political identity, then we should expect partisan combatants to respond to demographic trends in their positioning on such issues as immigration, health care access, and education in-vestments. This will be true, at least, if strategists focus on where the makeup of the public *will be* rather than solely on what that makeup *has been*. In a time of substantial population flux, it may be that the "soft" influences of voter reg-istration, outreach, and civic engagement will have a disproportionate effect on the composition of the electorate, and hence on the policy agenda.

Overview

Building a Vibrant Low-Carbon Economy

BRACKEN HENDRICKS AND VAN JONES

Reversing global warming and reducing our crippling dependence on imported and pol-luting energy present perhaps the greatest chance for the new president. His choices will shape the economic destiny of the nation and the welfare of the planet for generations. The best way to address our climate and energy crises is to build a more prosperous green economy—strong enough to lift millions of Americans out of poverty and into a stronger middle class. We cannot "drill and burn" our way out of our energy, economic, and environmental problems, but we can "invest and invent" our way out. Averting the social and economic disruption of a warming planet will take a major mobilization of public and private investment, driven by smart policy and newfound political will. The benefits of a green economy will be felt broadly in many industries and sectors of the economy, every region of the country, and every country of the world. To realize this opportunity will take a serious early commitment to pass climate legislation, and re-quire a set of complementary energy policies that spur new technology, create new mar-kets, and prepare a clean energy labor force.

Our nation is at a crossroads: inaction in the face of global warming will in-exorably lead toward a climate crisis of tremendous scale. Estimates of the true costs of inaction with respect to climate change have placed the figure as high as 5 percent to 20 percent of global gross domestic product in perpetu-ity,[1] with an even higher toll in human suffering. At the same time, our overre-liance on oil is the largest driver of our trade deficit, costing American consumers jobs as well as real money at the pump. This is a staggering price to pay for a failure of vision.

If left unchecked, climate change within our lifetimes will create profound disruptions in every area: health of the environment, economic prosperity, public welfare, and national security. The Intergovernmental Panel on Climate Change—the largest scientific body ever assembled—has concluded with certainty that global temperatures are rising and that human beings are responsible. Barring immediate action, predicted temperature rises could create 200 million climate refugees,[2] deny regular access to drinking water to 2 billion people,[3] and result in millions of premature deaths from malnutrition as entire regions of the world suffer substantial losses in agricultural productivity.[4] Meanwhile, increasing wildfires, more severe weather events, new vectors for disease, and rising sea levels will exact a bitter toll on rural and urban communities around the planet. The human face of this preventable tragedy is very real, and the costs in lives and treasure will be enormous if we do not act with urgency and resolve to build alternatives.

Compounding the threat of the climate crisis are the economic and security consequences of our nation's addiction to oil. The United States uses more than 20 million barrels of oil each day, at a cost of $41 million every hour, and imports nearly 13 million of these barrels.[5] With oil prices at well above $100 per barrel and constrained supplies for the foreseeable future, ending dependence on oil must be a top priority to save the domestic automobile industry and protect consumers, as families pay more of their monthly income on gasoline, diesel, and heating oil, and rising energy costs ripple through the economy.

Our petroleum trade deficit reached $270.9 billion in 2006, accounting for 33 percent (the largest single share) of our entire trade deficit and contributing to an economic slowdown.[6] Forty percent of our foreign oil imports originate in unstable or hostile countries,[7] allowing insatiable demand to prop up prices and benefit petro-states such as Iran, Saudi Arabia, and Russia. Clearly, our oil dependence both retards our economic progress and distorts our foreign policy. Some call for more domestic drilling of oil supplies to relieve this crisis, but with only 3 percent of proven oil reserves, and over 25 percent of global demand for petroleum, there is no way to solve U.S. consumers' pain at the pump with domestic supply. Instead, we need dramatically new and more efficient cars and a new generation of low-carbon fuels and clean electricity to support our increasingly mobile society.

Although the scale of this energy and environmental crisis is great, the scale of the opportunity from climate solutions is even greater. Our nation has always prospered when we invested in innovation and technology leadership:

from rural electrification, to new transportation networks such as the transcontinental railroad and interstate highway systems, to public investment in semiconductors and the explosion of the telecommunications and Internet revolutions. Bold public leadership providing incentives for scientific inquiry, new technology deployment, and proper infrastructure have repeatedly enabled the private sector to flourish while building a growing middle class.

Today, the "clean-tech" revolution and the transformation of our aging energy infrastructure are poised to become the next great engine for American innovation, productivity, and job growth. Building a clean energy economy can generate hundreds of billions of dollars of productive new investments on the scale of the greatest periods of past American economic expansion.[8] Leadership in low-carbon energy technology is essential for positioning the U.S. economy to succeed in decades to come.

The New York State Energy Research and Development Authority estimates that for every gigawatt hour saved, the agency's programs create or retain 1.5 jobs.[9] A recent report for the American Solar Energy Society counts 3.7 million jobs directly created in U.S. energy efficiency in 2006 alone.[10] And manufacturing, which has borne the brunt of job destruction, could receive a substantial boost from a strategic, presidentially driven shift to renewable energy. According to the Renewable Energy Policy Project, a $62 billion investment to expand wind capacity by 125,000 megawatts over 10 years to help stabilize U.S. carbon emissions could create nearly 400,000 domestic manufacturing jobs.[11]

The majority of "green-collar jobs" in energy efficiency and renewable energy are also living-wage, "middle-skill" jobs. Despite misconceptions, the green economy will not be built by a small handful of scientists and engineers alone. It will be built by electricians, sheet metal workers, machinists, lab technicians, and other workers in familiar professions.[12] These jobs are well within reach for low-income people, including those with barriers to employment, such as low educational attainment or past criminal convictions.

By connecting the people who most need work to the work that most needs to get done, the new president can fight pollution and poverty at the same time. Doing so will require federal leadership to ensure an employment and training infrastructure that combines vigorous outreach, basic skills education, occupational training, and support. This wave of "green-collar jobs" creates the opportunity for stronger career ladders to rebuild pathways into the middle class.

Also, in less developed countries, assisting in the shift to a clean energy economy can support critical work to help fight crippling energy poverty that leaves millions of people around the world without basic energy services each and every day. While spiraling oil and energy prices have erased a generation of gains in debt relief for many of the world's poorest nations, clean energy could restore economic stability and create productive local industries. Fighting global warming successfully is clearly not only a domestic challenge; it means taking on the task of global development to support the world's poorest and most vulnerable citizens as they build economic opportunity on the foundation of low-carbon energy.

The Challenges

Until 2006, opposition to passing climate and clean energy legislation was arguably based on technical, scientific, or even economic rationales. By 2008, however, the greatest barrier to positive federal action was not a lack of information but a lack of political will. For this reason, it is essential the next administration focus on the opportunity of building a green economy, and place jobs, investment, technological leadership, and environmentally sound policy at the center of an economic agenda for the renewal of American prosperity.

To defeat climate protection, polluters have long used economic scare tactics to split working people and low-income communities of color from environmental coalitions, and this pattern continues to this day. The new administration must be prepared to speak not only to maximizing the gain of a green economy, but also to offer solutions to minimize any pain and dislocation caused by this transition to a low-carbon economy. This will include recirculating revenue from selling carbon permits at auction to offset energy-related price increases for rate-payers and consumers. It will require articulating programs to help dislocated workers and to buffer American businesses from the effects of higher energy prices on their domestic sales and exports.

Indeed, the new president must display global leadership to work at the scale of the problem to capture the magnitude of the benefits. Re-engaging the community of nations on the issue of global warming will be important to help America emerge from the self-imposed isolation of the Bush administration. Addressing climate and the need for global development to reverse energy poverty will help regain the moral authority that was squandered by the unilateral and heavy-handed tactics of the last administration.

Distrust of America today is substantial, increasing the importance of a strong and early diplomatic offensive on climate. To regain the initiative will also require the new president to "hit the ground running" at home, too. On energy and climate policy, it is critical that significant efforts be undertaken in the early days of the administration.

The new administration must pursue three policy tracks simultaneously, as the Bush administration left enormous work undone in the fight against global warming.

The first involves exerting immediate leadership within the executive branch, taking measures to coordinate U.S. climate and energy policy across all federal agencies, and using executive orders, public communications, and other presidential prerogatives to manage carbon, capture energy savings, and promote renewable technologies. This can best be facilitated by establishing a National Energy Council (discussed in the White House section) to ensure this agenda is managed effectively across the government.

The second policy track will require the White House to engage with Congress to pass an array of global warming and energy legislation, including a carbon cap-and-trade bill that limits emissions, but also complementary policies that strengthen standards and drive investment in clean energy. The third track will entail a vigorous diplomatic effort to reclaim U.S. moral leadership abroad through progress on international climate negotiations, clean development, and addressing adaptation and energy poverty.

Executive Branch Leadership

The 44th president will need to galvanize new constituencies for action, including labor, business, urban, farm, civil rights, and other stakeholders. By having a clear message on the economic benefits of action for the poor and middle class, for ratepayers and small businesses, the new administration will be able to answer predictable attacks based on costs, as businesses and markets adjust.

The power of the Oval Office to convene industry and interest groups to create a national consensus for action should not be underestimated. Efforts should include strong signals in the opening days of the new administration, including major national summits and prominent public addresses such as the inaugural and State of the Union, to underscore the centrality of this issue and align with the future and not the past. To ensure that attention is sustained, the next administration must also establish a national energy advisor supported by a strong National Energy Council for developing and implementing global warming strategy, and advancing broader approaches to building a green economy.

This leadership and staffing structure should be publically launched in the early days of the new administration and given direct reporting authority to the president. It should have strong links to economic and national security advisors and clear pathways of communication with all agencies and White House offices, to ensure that a unified strategy is employed across the executive branch. Agencies across the federal government must all play leading roles in solving the climate crisis. The administration's energy and climate strategy must therefore be systematic and include all line agency budgets and programs.

The Department of Housing and Urban Development, for example, can advance community development and housing retrofits that promote energy efficiency. The Department of Labor must ensure a trained green-collar workforce is available. The U.S. Department of Agriculture must use its authority related to biofuels and wind energy as well as farming and forestry practices to sequester carbon. The Department of State must play a central role in jumpstarting international negotiations, and the U.S. Agency for International Development will shape assistance to affected countries that now must account for climate impacts.

Similarly, the Department of Transportation will guide strategies for the expansion of rail and transit, land-use planning, reducing vehicle miles traveled, enhancing air quality, and reducing congestion. The Department of Energy, the Environmental Protection Agency, the National Oceanic and Atmospheric Administration, the Department of Interior, and others will all play leading roles in the policy and science of climate change, and global warming will increasingly organize their work.

Regulatory agencies such as the Federal Energy Regulatory Commission will shape rules and incentives for smart grid infrastructure. The White House Council on Environmental Quality will guide federal environmental policy, incorporating climate concerns into its policy agenda. And the departments of Treasury and Commerce will establish mechanisms for carbon trading and incentives and financing for public infrastructure, efficiency retrofits, advanced manufacturing, and a variety of renewable energy incentives to transition U.S. industrial production toward low-carbon solutions.

Executive orders can play a useful role in immediately implementing policies and using federal powers to make carbon emission reduction a top priority. The White House could instruct agencies that greenhouse gas emissions should be analyzed as a prerequisite to achieving compliance with the National Environmental Policy Act. It could also immediately grant waivers to states such as California under the Clean Air Act to begin regulating CO_2 as a pollutant in automobile tailpipe emissions, a measure that the Bush administration denied in 2007.

Federal agencies internally can do much to accelerate the transition to a clean energy economy as well. The Department of Defense, for example, is the world's largest consumer of gasoline, while other federal facilities purchase 65,000 new vehicles each year.[13] Meanwhile, the General Services Administration controls billions of square feet of buildings around the nation. The presi-

dent can show immediate leadership by instructing all federal agencies to reduce their carbon footprint through improved purchasing and acquisitions, vehicle fleet management, and retrofits to existing facilities.

The president can also convey the importance of federal action by working
with Congress to pass a new initiative: a national Clean Energy Corps. A CEC
would combine service, training, and employment efforts with a special emphasis on cities and neglected rural communities to combat climate disruption.
The work would focus on retrofitting homes, small businesses, schoolhouses,
and public buildings, and preserving and enlarging green public spaces. The
CEC would provide the labor wherewithal to expand investment in transit systems, apply distributed renewable energy production technology to underserved communities, strengthen community defenses against climate
disruption, and upgrade infrastructure. Finally, Clean Energy Corps members
could educate citizens and communities on how they can contribute to ending
global warming.

A Clean Energy Corps would also demonstrate the equity and employment
promise of the clean energy economy. These efforts could pay for themselves
through energy savings, making the CEC program largely self-financing, while
generating enormous demand for new jobs in communities that need them.
Launched as a project to span the course of a decade, the CEC would work
with employers, community organizations, educational institutions, and labor
unions to connect workers to job opportunities in the clean energy economy.
An inspiring goal would be to develop "green pathways out of poverty" for at
least 1 million adults, providing them training, work experience, job placement, and other services needed to gain family-supporting jobs. The CEC
would also directly engage millions of Americans, both young and old, in diverse service and volunteer work related to climate protection.

Working with Congress

Arguably, the highest priority for the new administration is to work with Congress to pass major global warming legislation that reduces economy-wide
greenhouse gas emissions.[14] Designing comprehensive climate legislation will
present many design challenges, including whether emission reductions are
deep and fast enough to respond to growing scientific knowledge, how much
of the economy to include in the scope of regulation, how to manage potential
trade impacts, and whether cost controls are placed on the price of carbon,
which could limit investment in innovation. One indispensable component of
carbon cap-and-trade policy that deserves special mention, however, is the auction of a substantial portion of emissions permits available to greenhouse gas

emitters. Under "cap and auction," the federal government not only limits total emissions but also recovers the value of these emissions by requiring that polluters purchase a permit for every ton of CO_2 they release into the atmosphere.

The Congressional Budget Office estimates that the monetary value of these permits would range from $50 billion to $300 billion each and every year (in 2007 dollars) by 2020.[15] This money can be invested in the public interest to ease the transition to a low-carbon economy. Handing out permits for free to polluting companies, as some have proposed, would amount to a multi-billion dollar giveaway to polluters—increasing income inequality through a regressive wealth transfer as consumer costs rise and certain companies reap windfall profits.[16] Instead, a permit auction would provide resources to help reduce energy bills for low- and middle-income Americans; support clean energy research, development, and deployment; invest in energy efficiency and mass transportation; foster the re-industrialization of America with clean energy technology; and train American workers for good, domestic, "green-collar" jobs.

A well-designed cap on carbon, however, is only one instrument in the policy tool kit to cope with global warming and move toward energy independence. Complementary policies will also need to be enacted by the new Congress to achieve emissions reductions and ensure the transition to a low-carbon economy. These policies will include stronger standards for efficiency and renewable energy, increased research and development funding, and requirements to capture and store carbon in coal-fired power plants. It will also be necessary to invest in training a skilled workforce for green jobs in a changing economy.

Improving energy efficiency and deploying renewable technology at scale will produce massive demand for skilled labor. Investing in worker training, supportive employment services, manufacturing extension programs, and community development programs will be essential to meet our goals. Legislation such as the Green Jobs Act and the Energy Efficiency and Conservation Block Grant program offer an opportunity to connect with people who need jobs most, using public investment not only to prime new industries but to lift people out of poverty.

This legislation not only connects to people's immediate self-interest, but calls them to a larger moral purpose. And it is grounded in neighborhood-level actions—restoring communities with green space and green buildings, restoring bodies with parks and clean air, and restoring families with purpose and paychecks.

Of course, the cheapest and cleanest form of energy is that which is never used. The United States uses nearly twice as much energy per dollar of gross national product as other industrialized countries.[17] To achieve immediate efficiency gains, the next administration should implement a National Energy Efficiency Resource Standard to require utilities to cut energy use by 10 percent by 2020. The vast majority of today's buildings are wasteful and inefficient—each non-weatherized building is an open spigot for pollution and wasted energy dollars.

The 44th president should work with Congress to pass a range of efficiency policies that include new commercial and residential building codes, and authorization and funding to retrofit public buildings to higher standards. Congress also needs to establish incentives for new distributed energy networks, energy-efficient home mortgages, and stronger incentives, better accounting tools, and loan guarantees for greening both market-rate and affordable housing. The added local benefits of these programs in a flagging real estate market will be tremendous, as jobs weatherizing U.S. buildings cannot be outsourced.

Renewable Energy and Transportation
The United States needs to fully deploy our abundant renewable energy resources, including wind, solar, biomass, sustainable hydroelectric, geothermal, and wave-tidal. The next administration should require that 25 percent of our electricity comes from renewable energy by 2025. As the market for renewable energy grows due to technology improvements and economies of scale, the objective should be to drive the price cheaper than traditional fossil-based energy in the market, allowing a sunset on any financial incentives.

Substantial economic, employment, and environmental benefits will accompany large-scale deployment of renewable electricity. Diversifying electricity and fuel supplies hedges against disruptive spikes in energy costs as rising demand for limited fossil energy drives prices ever upward. Renewable electricity also creates more than twice as many jobs per unit of energy and per dollar invested as traditional fossil fuel–based electricity. And electricity and heat account for more than 30 percent of all U.S. carbon emissions—a figure that can be drastically reduced by turning to low-carbon renewable energy.

Jump starting the investments necessary to bring both distributed and utility-scale renewable energy resources online will require improvements to the structure and dependability of renewable energy tax credits. Some of the most effective policy tools to date for deploying new clean energy have been the Investment Tax Credit and the Renewable Electricity Production Tax Credit. Congress, however, has repeatedly let these measures expire and offered short term extensions, creating a volatile and uncertain investment climate for renewable technologies.

Legislation that offers a predictable long-term extension of both these renewable energy tax credits will do much to encourage financing of new projects, drawing new private sector investment into clean energy projects and increasing the supply and affordability of renewable electricity. The federal government should also provide a broader range of financial incentives such as low-interest loans, loan guarantees, and federally backed bonds to help reduce upfront costs, improve access to financing, and decrease investor risk for capital-intensive projects. But the demand side of the energy equation must be addressed as well, through bolder tax credits for energy-saving measures such as home and business efficiency improvements and purchasing energy-efficient appliances.

In an era of escalating oil prices, traffic gridlock, hazardous air quality, and the threat of a global warming tipping point, the new president and Congress must also re-invest in local mass-transit systems, regional and interstate high-speed rail, and other low-carbon means of transportation of both passengers and freight. Expanding mass transit and rail infrastructure promises to create thousands of good construction jobs, increasing transportation choices and strengthening communities.

Equally important will be presidential and congressional steps to increase vehicle fuel-economy standards. In the early years of a cap-and-trade program, the price for carbon will probably be too low to change driving behavior. A price of $15 per ton of CO_2 translates to roughly a 13-cents-per-gallon increase in the price of gasoline—not enough to dramatically reduce gasoline consumption. A further increase in vehicle fuel-economy standards to at least 40 miles per gallon via the Corporate Average Fuel Economy, or CAFE, standard will be needed. Increased CAFE standards, combined with incentives for auto manufacturers to retool factories and for consumers to purchase more efficient and alternative fuel vehicles, will support a resurgence of U.S. automotive manufacturing. A new line of ultra-efficient vehicles, such as plug-in hybrids that get 100 miles per gallon of gas, will support manufacturing jobs—from new battery systems to advanced drivetrains—and help consumers save on their transportation bills.

Investing in Innovation

Next-generation coal-fired electricity power plants face economics similar to cars. The cost of CO_2 emissions would have to reach roughly $30 a ton before it would be economically rational to deploy advanced technology that captures and stores carbon emissions through carbon capture-and-storage technology. It may be several years, or even decades, before carbon prices reach such a price threshold—during which time many new polluting plants would come on line—and we simply don't have that much time.

The solution: Congress and the new administration must work together to freeze carbon emissions by coal-fired power plants, and then begin serious reductions within the next few years. To do this will require the coal-fired electricity sector to follow an emission performance standard that mandates all new plants incorporate path-breaking capture-and-storage technology. In the meantime, the United States should not build new power plants that are unable to manage carbon emissions. Coal can play an important and productive role in our energy mix, but the government and private sectors must collaborate on a full-scale "Manhattan Project" to achieve dramatic breakthroughs in carbon capture-and-storage technology.

But electricity generation alone is not the answer to clean energy deployment. There is much that can be done by improving our broader energy infrastructure—and even the regulatory framework that governs our electric grid—that will go a long way toward putting new clean energy electrons on line to power our economy without worsening the climate crisis. There are a number of regulatory decisions that can be made immediately by the Federal Energy Regulatory Commission and state regulatory agencies to favor renewable energy by granting it priority access to the current grid. Net metering provisions, interconnection standards, rate design, and proper financial incentives all play a critical role in ensuring that a robust market for renewable energy develops and that suppliers can provide renewable energy to interested consumers.

A larger effort will also be required, however, in modernizing and upgrading our transmission infrastructure. One important option is to designate new dedicated renewable energy transmission corridors. The United States is blessed with abundant supplies of renewable electricity—with some of the best wind and solar resources on the planet—but they tend to be concentrated in the interior areas of the country, far from the population and industrial centers where energy demand is highest. Bringing utility-scale renewable electricity online will require a major investment in new transmission corridors linking demand centers with these areas of the country—the desert Southwest for solar and Great Plains for wind—where the greatest renewable potential is located.

In addition, local and regional energy grids must be modernized to create digital smart grids that marry information technology and energy infrastructure to enable state-of-the-art energy efficiency, smart metering, and innovations such as real-time pricing that value the system benefits of energy conservation. Together, building a national grid and catalyzing smart grid technology offer a major leadership opportunity for the new president.

The new administration should also pursue multiple options to reduce dependence on fossil-based transportation fuels. It should commit to producing 25 percent of our liquid transportation fuels from renewable sources by 2025. The majority of renewable fuels should come from next-generation biofuels made from nonfood biomass such as switchgrass, wood chips, and agricultural waste.

To ensure the environmental integrity of biofuels, the administration should implement a low-carbon fuel standard to reduce the total amount of greenhouse gas emissions generated by the production and use of all fuels— so-called lifecycle emissions—by 10 percent within 10 years. A low-carbon fuel standard will also help to ensure that we do not address our dependence on imported oil by pursuing solutions that worsen our climate crisis like exploitation of low-quality oil shales and tar sands. Further, a certification program should also be developed for biofuels with transparent sustainability labeling.

A suite of policies are also available to accelerate deployment of plug-in hybrid and all-electric vehicles, including zero-emissions mandates and consumer tax incentives. To build the infrastructure to supply this energy, a new legislative "pump or plug" mandate should require that 15 percent of gas stations retrofit their facilities to deliver E-85 ethanol, biodiesel, or dedicated electricity charging stations for plug-in vehicles in all counties where 15 percent of registered vehicles can run on alternative fuels. Further, local ownership can provide strong economic benefits to rural communities from producing sustainable bioenergy.[18]

Demonstrate Global Leadership

One great tragedy of the Bush administration was the abdication of international diplomatic and moral leadership on climate change, resulting in the loss of eight years without significant U.S. contributions to reducing greenhouse gas emissions. The 44th president must re-engage with the world and simultaneously rebuild American standing abroad. He immediately will be confronted by the need for international commitments on greenhouse gas reductions. The reason: ongoing post-Kyoto Accord U.N. climate change negotiations that will culminate in December 2009 in Copenhagen.

This successor accord to the Kyoto Protocol will set the framework for new international agreements on reducing greenhouse gas emissions, adapting to the effects of climate change, transferring the global economy to low-carbon technologies, and financing for all of these efforts. This timetable should inform the new administration's broader political and diplomatic strategy.

In addition, a series of bilateral and multilateral talks should transform the

Bush administration's Major Emitter talks from a dodge to avoid binding targets into a serious effort for reductions among those nations most responsible for global warming. These negotiations included not only major industrialized nations, among them the United States, Australia, Canada, and Russia, but also rapidly developing nations such as India, China, and Brazil. With a real commitment to reducing emissions, these talks could prove to be a useful forum.

In all of these negotiations, global warming policies must be connected to trade policy. Climate provisions should be given significant weight in international trade agreements. Industry and labor have expressed concern over the adverse economic effects from trading relationships with countries that lack controls on carbon. These concerns should not be an excuse for weak standards but rather should drive policies that ensure a level playing field for U.S. companies and their workers in a world where carbon has a price.

As domestic legislation moves forward in Congress, trade implications are likely to receive increasing political attention. The new president must have answers to calls for ensuring that the price of carbon emissions in the United States does not become a competitive disadvantage for energy-intensive industries. Some concrete proposals include establishing a border adjustment tariff that adds a carbon price to those goods produced in emitting nations, alongside a program for trade adjustment assistance for displaced workers, such as the trade adjustment assistance program enacted to reduce the adverse affects of the North American Free Trade Agreement of a decade ago.

A new trade adjustment assistance program could provide support for training, health care, and lost wages to ensure that workers do not bear the burden of protecting the environment. A strategy to include climate provisions and broader environmental and labor protections in future trade deals will also help to level the playing field. Lastly, a very small number of businesses are both highly carbon intensive and exposed to strong pressure for outsourcing; for these industries, special relief could be provided through an auction or allocation program. (For more details on these proposals, see the chapter on the U.S. Trade Representative.)

Reduce Energy Poverty
Global warming threatens loss of agricultural productivity in much of Africa, and rising sea levels that could consume delta countries such as Bangladesh. In addition, rising energy prices have already wiped out the gains of debt relief for less developed countries. What's more, the secretary general of NATO has identified climate disruption as a top security challenge, resulting from water and agricultural shortages and migration of refugees.[19]

These global security threats require rapid and forceful attention to two major areas of development assistance. First, increasing the ability of poor countries to adapt to changes in food, water, disease, and public safety must become a top priority for the new administration. Second, we must help poor countries leapfrog pollution and rapidly deploy clean energy technology. A major goal of international development assistance should be to alleviate the crippling energy poverty that denies much of the world's population basic energy services, without increasing carbon emissions. Together these measures can help restore American moral leadership.

Many contentious questions remain, especially how to address ballooning greenhouse gas emissions from China and India—the two largest rapidly industrializing countries in the world. But there is no question that the United States must first get its house in order. With only 4 percent of the world's population, we currently produce 25 percent of global greenhouse gas emissions. From a historical perspective, the United States "owns" a share equivalent to 30 percent of world carbon emissions over the last century.[20] We have an obligation and the capacity to assume leadership in curbing global warming and in providing low-carbon energy technologies to meet the needs of rapidly industrializing countries worldwide.

Overview
Health Care Coverage, Costs, Chronic Illness, and Demographics

KAREN DAVENPORT

Few challenges facing the new president and his administration will be as intricately intertwined with American life as those facing the health care system. America's businesses, workers, and families are deeply affected by exploding health care costs and eroding health coverage. Individuals with chronic illness face daily limitations on their lives, while the cost of their care absorbs a significant portion of our national health care spending. And changes in the makeup of the American population challenge policymakers and health professionals to redouble their efforts to correct inequities in health and health care. These trends of coverage, costs, chronic illness, and changing demographics will occupy the health policy experts of a new administration. Reforms to improve coverage—ideally through expansion of group coverage options paired with financial help for those who cannot afford coverage on their own—are a critical component of cost containment and represent a major opportunity for the new administration. Other strategies include investments in prevention and comparative effectiveness information, improvements in care coordination, and quality and infrastructure initiatives.

Forty-six million Americans lack health coverage altogether, and another 25 million adults under age 65 were underinsured in 2007, which suggests a significant erosion of the financial protection traditionally offered by health coverage.[1] Without adequate coverage, these individuals and families struggle to afford basic preventive care, find receptive providers, and cope with the financial crisis that serious illness can create.

At the same time, the United States spent $2.1 trillion on health care services in 2006, which represents 16 percent of the country's gross domestic product.[2] This spending—whether considered in aggregate or calculated on a per-capita basis—eclipses health spending in all other developed countries. The United States spent $6,401 per person on health care in 2005, the most recent year with complete data, compared to the $2,759 average per capita investment in health care among Organisation for Economic Co-operation and Development countries.[3]

The United States also faces a growing prevalence of chronic disease and changing population demographics, which contribute to our high health spending today and could drive our compromised health status in the future. Roughly a third of Americans have a long-standing condition that requires ongoing care today, and the RAND Corporation estimates that half the population will have a chronic condition by 2020.[4] At the same time, the nation is simultaneously becoming older and more diverse. Between 2005 and 2030, older adults will grow from 12 percent of the nation's population to 20 percent, and racial and ethnic minorities, which currently comprise roughly 30 percent of the population, are expected to grow to nearly half of the population by 2050.[5] Health care needs typically become more complex and costly with age, while inequalities in income, education, and other predictors of health status are closely related to race and ethnicity.

These four issues—coverage, cost, chronic illness, and demographic change—represent the major trends that will drive the new administration's decision making in health care policy and will shape the nature of our nation's health care system for decades to come.

Key Challenges

The presence of 46 million people without health care coverage in the United States has profound consequences for individual health and the nation as a whole. Individuals who lack health coverage are more likely to postpone medical care, go without needed medical care, go without prescription medicines, and use emergency rooms as their regular source of care. At the extreme, approximately 22,000 deaths per year can be attributed to lack of health insurance.[6]

Individuals without health insurance pay approximately 35 percent of the cost of needed health care out of pocket. Insured individuals, whose premiums reflect higher provider payments to cover uncompensated care costs—a phenomenon known as "cost-shifting"—cover much of the balance of these costs. Family health insurance premiums in 2005 were $922 more than they otherwise would have been because of health care costs for those without health coverage.[7]

Most Americans obtain health coverage through an employer, but not all employers offer coverage, and not all workers enroll in health insurance. Indeed, more than 80 percent of individuals without health coverage live in working families. Income is also a key determinant of insurance status—of those without health insurance, approximately two-thirds have incomes below 200 percent of the federal poverty level, which is $40,000 a year for a family of four.

The number of Americans who are underinsured has grown dramatically as employers and individuals seeking to control premium increases have gravitated toward policies with higher deductibles and cost sharing, as well as more restrictive benefits. A recent survey estimated that the number of individuals with health insurance who have significant financial exposure relative to income—that is, who are underinsured—grew by 60 percent between 2003 and 2007.[8] These 25 million adults experience problems accessing health services that parallel those of uninsured individuals. They are more likely to go without prescription medications, delay needed health care, and have problems paying medical bills. One study found that more than 75 percent of people who declared bankruptcy due to medical debts had health coverage at the onset of the bankrupting illness.[9]

Cost Crisis

The United States' health care system faces significant cost pressures. From 2000 to 2006, health care spending grew, on average, almost 8 percent per year. This growth rate is nearly twice the rate of growth in the nation's gross domestic product, and nearly three times the average annual inflation rate over the same period. Health care spending has doubled since 1996 and is expected to double again in the next decade.[10]

These increases pose significant opportunity costs for American families and the U.S. economy. Premiums for employer-sponsored family coverage averaged more than $12,000 in 2007. Workers have been giving up wage increases in order to maintain their health care coverage, and businesses struggle with the effect health care benefits have on their bottom line. Rising health care costs restrict the funds available to American businesses for infrastructure investments, new hires, and general business development.

The United States, according to some analysts, also overspends on health care across a range of dimensions. The consulting firm McKinsey and Company has concluded that the United States pays for an "excessive" $500 billion a year in health spending—that is, health spending that is not accounted for by the country's comparative prosperity.[11] This excess spending pervades the American health care system, and can be attributed to a number of dynamics, including how doctors, nurses, and other health professionals are paid and deployed; process costs related to how the delivery system is structured; administrative complexity related to multiple health insurance companies and other payers; profits accruing to private providers and health plans; and other structural aspects of the system. This analysis suggests that simple reimbursement cuts or other "quick fixes" are unlikely to have a meaningful effect on escalating health care spending.

Chronic Illness

More than 125 million Americans have some form of chronic illness—long-term conditions such as diabetes, hypertension, heart disease, and depression that require ongoing care and often limit what an individual can do. While chronic illness is a particular phenomenon for older adults—some estimates suggest that more than 80 percent of Medicare beneficiaries have at least one chronic condition, with 63 percent experiencing two or more chronic illnesses—millions of working-age Americans also suffer from chronic illness. A recent analysis concluded that at least 56 million non-elderly adults with employer-sponsored health insurance have at least one chronic illness.[12] Chronic illness is a particular problem for women. Nearly 40 percent of women have a chronic condition requiring ongoing medical attention, compared to 30 percent of men.[13]

The growing prevalence of chronic illness, driven in part by obesity-related illnesses such as diabetes, heart disease, and stroke, will drive health care spending in both public and private health insurance. Not surprisingly, people with chronic illnesses are the largest consumers of health care services—and people with multiple chronic conditions rack up the vast majority of health care spending. Within the Medicare program, the 63 percent of beneficiaries with two or more chronic conditions represent 95 percent of all Medicare expenditures.[14] Many of these conditions can be ameliorated or prevented altogether through strategies such as physical activity, nutrition, and anti-smoking initiatives.

At the same time, individuals with multiple chronic illnesses often receive care from multiple caregivers specific to their different illnesses. High-quality care therefore requires a high level of coordination between caregivers. In total, roughly half of all patients with chronic illness do not receive appropriate care.[15]

Demographic Changes
The United States faces long-range cost pressures related to demographic changes, notably the aging American population and the country's growing racial and ethnic diversity. As individuals age, their health care needs are likely to become more complex and more costly. As the population ages, more Americans will experience one or more chronic conditions, and more Americans will need long-term care services that provide help with the tasks of daily living. Our health care system and our health care workforce are simply unprepared for this dramatic growth.

Similarly, as African Americans, Hispanic Americans, Asian Americans, and other groups grow as a proportion of the population, the economic and social impact of these subpopulations' more limited access to health care services and lower health status will become more profound. Racial and ethnic disparities in health status and outcomes occur across a wide variety of measures, including the prevalence of chronic illness, mortality rates from acute illnesses, and life expectancy, while disparate access to health care among minority groups in comparison to whites is well documented. Minority groups will compose nearly half of the U.S. population by 2050. If today's disparities in disease prevalence, health insurance coverage, quality of care, and other factors continue unchecked, not only will the health status of these populations continue to languish, but national health care costs will experience significant growth and the health of the nation as a whole will diminish.[16]

Opportunities

Health system reform—specifically reforms that expand health insurance coverage to all Americans, improve quality, and control health care costs—was one of the major themes of the 2008 presidential cycle. The new administration will have a unique opportunity to lower the current trajectory of health care cost growth while simultaneously pursuing a policy agenda dedicated to expanding coverage to all Americans. Because detailed proposals for how to achieve these goals were hallmarks of the presidential candidates' issue platforms, this chapter will touch on important broad themes for health system reform rather than offer a specific reform proposal.

The cost-control effort should place particular emphasis on building the infrastructure for long-term savings. For example, investments in comparative effectiveness research—inquiries designed to improve our knowledge of which medications, devices, and procedures are most effective and most efficient—will arm providers and patients with the tools they need to make well-informed treatment decisions. Similarly, accelerated adoption of health information technology can improve health care processes and thus improve quality today. New access to health IT and the data it creates will also enhance the scope and significance of comparative effectiveness research.

Greater use of preventive services offers another opportunity for long-term cost savings. Less than half of adults in the United States receive the full complement of preventive services, which results in delayed treatment for emerging conditions and suboptimal management of diseases that can be controlled through secondary prevention strategies, such as drug therapy for high blood pressure. Policy approaches to improving the use of preventive services could range from reducing Medicare's copayment structure for prevention to creating a federal prevention infrastructure that would set national prevention priorities and streamline preventive services within the federal health programs.

Expanded coverage is a worthy goal on its own merits—the financial insecurity, delayed care, and poorer outcomes experienced by people without health insurance create a moral imperative for change. But it is also a key component of cost containment. As long as our health care system excludes 16 percent of the population, promising approaches to cost control—such as improved information, enhanced use of technology, and greater utilization of preventive services—will fail to adequately reduce costs. Reforms that hold the greatest promise for achieving affordable coverage for all within a reasonable time frame build on the vital foundation of Medicaid and the State Children's Health Insurance Program, use the market leverage of the federal government to acquire group insurance rates for individuals and small businesses, and provide financial help for individuals and families who cannot afford coverage on their own.

Chronic Disease

The new administration will need to take a two-track approach to reducing the toll that chronic illness takes on our health financing system and Americans' quality of life. It should address the root causes driving the growing incidence of chronic disease, while improving chronic care management for those Americans who have one or more chronic conditions.

Prevention—including clinical services as well as nutrition counseling, exercise, and other lifestyle modifications—is a critical tool in the effort to reverse current trends of chronic disease. Obesity is linked to a number of chronic illnesses, including hypertension, diabetes, cardiovascular disease, and osteoarthritis, while smoking and other lifestyle factors are correlated with additional chronic conditions. Recent estimates suggest that a modest investment in prevention—averaging $10 per person per year—could realize five-year savings of $16 billion, a return of $5.60 for every $1 invested in effective prevention programs.[17]

With nearly half the population suffering from a chronic illness, and 21 percent having multiple chronic conditions, we must also improve how we deliver care today. This will initially require understanding which treatments and procedures are most effective—information that can be developed, in part, through comparative effectiveness research. Other steps include ensuring that those effective treatments and procedures are followed. This will involve strategies that target individual practices and physicians, policies that ensure coordination across different providers and systems of care, and approaches that involve patients in their own care.

Coordination is particularly important with so many people having more than one chronic condition. Research has demonstrated that treating each condition in isolation results in higher costs and poorer care. The new administration should identify successful approaches to coordinating care for people with chronic illness, such as the Chronic Care Model developed by Ed Wagner, MD and colleagues at the MacColl Institute for Healthcare Innovation, and seek to spread these strategies through payment policies, technical assistance efforts, and other techniques.[18]

Changing Demographics

Contrary to conventional wisdom, the aging of the U.S. population does not presage an overall explosion of health care costs. Most estimates suggest that aging, on its own, contributes approximately 0.5 percent per year to the growth in health care costs.[19] However, the aging of the baby boom generation does pose enormous capacity and infrastructure challenges for the American health care system. Policymakers have paid serious attention to—although taken little action on—the public financing challenges posed by the baby boomers' health care needs in retirement, but far less attention has been lavished on building the health care workforce capacity and service infrastructure to meet these needs.

The supply of geriatricians and, even more importantly, a broad range of health professionals with training in geriatrics are of particular concern. The American Geriatrics Society has estimated that the United States has fewer than 7,000 certified geriatricians, yet needs 14,000, and this discrepancy will grow to a difference of 36,000 between available and needed geriatricians by 2030.[20] The Institute of Medicine, in its recent examination of the nation's looming workforce needs, recently made a number of useful recommendations related to geriatric training and licensing and certification. The new administration should examine federal leverage points that can increase the supply of geriatricians and encourage participation in geriatric training for all types of providers, including physicians, nurses, and various categories of direct-care workers.

The direct-care workforce will also need higher skills, greater flexibility in professional roles, and better quality jobs to induce more workers to provide these services and stay in these jobs. Federal involvement may include new licensing standards for certified nursing assistants and strategies for encouraging states to offer wage pass-throughs and wage floors for personal care attendants and other direct care workers. Other efforts to reduce turnover and improve quality of care may include new approaches to worker training and expanded labor rights for direct-care workers.

The new administration will also need to improve service capacity and financing for long-term care. The Medicaid program continues to pay more—in aggregate and at a per capita level—for nursing home care than for home and community-based services. At the same time, millions of elderly and disabled Americans receive personal care assistance and other long-term care services through the informal, unpaid efforts of family members and friends, while others go without needed services. As the very old become a larger proportion of the nation's population, our long-term care service infrastructure will be strained past the breaking point and the financing system will be overwhelmed unless policymakers place a new emphasis on improving long-term care.

The federal government should also examine how existing models of community-based long-term care can be replicated and spread on a broad basis. Innovations worthy of this emphasis may range from the Green House project, which radically redesigns nursing homes, to self-directed aging communities such as Beacon Hill Village, which enables elderly residents to continue living in an urban neighborhood. Other efforts may include leveraging federal housing policy and transportation funding to help the nation's communities prepare for a higher degree of long-term care needs.

Racial and Ethnic Disparities

We need to accelerate the drive to eliminate disparities in health status related to race and ethnicity as the United States becomes increasingly racially diverse. These disparities are grounded in a number of dynamics, ranging from social circumstances and environmental factors to lower levels of health insurance coverage, cultural and behavioral factors, and unequal treatment within the health care system itself.

Other initiatives—notably health system reform designed to provide afford-able health coverage to all and prevention improvements—will make impor-tant inroads on some of these factors, but they will not be able to erase health disparities on their own. The new administration will need to launch additional strategies to combat disparities in health care and health status. A growing body of evidence indicates that general improvements in quality of care can also reduce racial disparities in care—suggestive examples include improve-ments in dialysis and heart attack care.[21]

A federal initiative around improving care for key conditions with high prevalence among minority communities and known disparities in outcomes, such as diabetes or cardiovascular disease, could build the knowledge base and test the limits of this quality improvement approach. Other investments, such as prevention efforts that target minority communities and improvements in the diversity and cultural competence of the nation's cadre of health profes-sionals, will address other known factors that contribute to health disparities.

Additional strategies may be directed at the social determinants of health that contribute to these profound differences in health status. Efforts outside of the health care system—to decrease social isolation through improving neigh-borhood safety, for example—have been advanced as strategies for reducing the high rates of breast cancer mortality in black women.[22] Targeting deeply rooted causes of health disparities, such as income, education, and discrimina-tion, will require efforts that span a wide variety of federal and state agencies as well as private stakeholders.

Overview

Teaching All Our Children Well

CYNTHIA G. BROWN

All of America's young people need a high-quality education to prepare them for the changing needs of our workforce and increasingly intense global economic competition. Yet our public education system continues to fail many of America's students. Inequality continues to plague our public schools and many children do not get the support and opportunities they need before they start formal schooling. Given the international and domestic challenges that better publicly supported education would help allay, the new administration must increase federal investment in effective programs, redesign those that fall short in meeting their goals, and recommend new programs in important but unaddressed areas. The existing and unmet federal commitments to disadvantaged preschoolers and students in elementary, secondary, and postsecondary education institutions must be honored in the short term. Specifically, the new administration should pursue a new pre-school program to be integrated with Head Start, set standards when an education system should reward teachers with more pay who assume greater responsibilities, make substantial investments in middle schools and high schools with high concentrations of low-performing students, and find ways to increase learning time for all students in low-performing schools.

Most American students need better quality education, but the challenge falls unevenly and most severely on low-income and minority students. Achievement and participation gaps tell the story. Disparities begin before children start school. Minority and low-income children and those from families where English is not the home language have less access to center-based preschool programs. Despite some encouraging gains by the lowest-performing disadvantaged students in the early grades, gaps generally continue and grow throughout public elementary and secondary education.[1] Average SAT and ACT scores of college-bound high school seniors vary significantly by race/ethnicity and income.[2]

This same pattern occurs in graduation rates and postsecondary education. Low-income and minority students are the most likely to drop out of high school. And although enrollment in degree-granting institutions for all students increased by 23 percent between 1995 and 2005, low-income and minority students are the least likely to attend a university or earn a four-year degree.[3] While the black-white gap in college degrees granted seems to be shrinking, the gap between Latinos and whites is increasing.[4]

The United States has the most decentralized education system in the industrialized world. Over 90 percent of the decisions are made and paid for at the state and local level. The federal government has historically stepped in with funding—and requirements for institutions accepting it—to assist disadvantaged students and schools. It has also supported research and evaluation on key issues and programs and disseminated findings. While the proportion of federal support for public K–12 schooling is small, its influence on the framework and operation of schools and the public education system is much greater. The same is arguably true for preschool and postsecondary education, but to a lesser degree.

Strategic federal laws and investments have promoted and accelerated major reforms, primarily in public elementary and secondary education. The civil rights laws of the 1960s and 1970s provided legal guarantees to equitable educational opportunities for racial and ethnic minorities, English language learners, students with disabilities, and students of different genders. Major new funding programs such as the Elementary and Secondary Education Act; the Bilingual Education Act; and the Education of All Handicapped Act, now the Individuals with Disabilities Education Act, worked in tandem with the civil rights laws to provide extra funds to programs serving disadvantaged students.

A new, standards-based framework for public education took hold nationwide in the 1990s that called for high learning expectations for all students. It was made real by the adoption of accountability systems through state legislation and the 1994 reauthorization of the Elementary and Secondary Education Act, alongside the enactment of Goals 2000, which required states to adopt rigorous curriculum standards and new state tests measuring student performance against these standards. The next ESEA reauthorization in 2002, named the No Child Left Behind Act, enacted a tough performance standard requiring that all students be proficient in math and reading by 2014. States were required to assess students annually in grades three through eight, and disaggregate the results for subgroups that traditionally underperform on measures of achievement, including students from minority and low-income families, those in special education classes, and English language learners.

Federal investments in preschool and postsecondary programs have also been substantial and include the Head Start program first enacted in 1965, and various student financial aid grant and loan programs for postsecondary study. Yet these federal programs have never been driven by the same kind of institutional reform agenda that underpins the various iterations of ESEA.

Key Challenges

Unlike other industrialized nations, U.S. policymakers at the local and state levels—as well as the federal level—have done little to ensure that tax revenues for education are directed according to student needs. The presidential and congressional motivation behind the NCLB upgrade of ESEA was to put increased pressure on state and local education policymakers to focus on the educational needs and learning outcomes of disadvantaged students in the K–12 system. The federal government substantially increased its funding for high-poverty schools for a couple of years after the passage of NCLB, but state and local policymakers never leveled the educational playing fields with those funds, and there was no push from the federal government to do so. Consequently, too many of NCLB's various program funds are used to fill in gaps left by local and state funding practices that ignore or inadequately account for differences in student needs and the cumulative effects when needy students are concentrated in certain schools.

There is a three-level problem in the way schools are funded in this country. First, although many states have developed fairer funding systems, often as a result of years of litigation in state courts, school districts still often receive large and unjustifiably different amounts of state funding. Second, almost all large- and medium-sized school districts expend more dollars on personnel and services in schools with fewer low-income students, although this sometimes occurs unknowingly. Districts do not allocate local and state funds to their schools by giving a dollar amount to each school based on numbers of pupils or even by weighting distributions according to student need. They allocate "staff" resources—a type of employee such as a teacher or counselor—per the number of students in a school or per school. Yet salaries for teachers and other staff vary greatly depending on years of service and education level, with the most experienced and qualified staff concentrated in schools with the lowest numbers of poor students. The federal ESEA/NCLB provisions overtly condone this inequitable local practice.

Third, the federal government distributes ESEA Title I money based on poverty, but it does so through a formula that combines numbers of children in poverty with state per-student expenditures. This practice penalizes states with low tax bases even if they tax themselves heavily for education.

Money alone will not ensure that students receive high-quality instruction and support, nor will it translate directly into student achievement, but fundamental fairness dictates that every school be given the same opportunity to succeed. Securing adequate funds is an essential step in operating a successful high-poverty school in which all students learn at high levels. For the most challenging schools, that means extra resources are necessary to expand and enrich the learning experiences of disadvantaged students.

Results for students receiving special education services under the Individuals with Disabilities Education Act have been somewhat better. IDEA, which is both a civil rights and program funding law, has educated millions of students with disabilities to levels rarely seen four decades ago. Yet its federal funding levels fall very short and the program's procedural requirements do not work well for students and parents in low-income families.

There are several policies and practices beyond financial inequalities that impede high student performance levels in American schools. The most important are those that affect the quality of the public school teaching force. Research demonstrates that a very good teacher as opposed to a very bad one can make as much as one full year's difference in the achievement growth of students.[5] Yet reports continue to document the ongoing weakness of traditional teacher preparation programs. Little is done to address the inequitable distribution of effective teachers among high-poverty and high-minority schools as compared to those with fewer proportions of disadvantaged students. Outdated and ineffective human capital systems plague most school systems and do not encourage states and districts to implement evidence-based strategies for increasing student learning and closing achievement gaps.

Teachers have little incentive to choose high-quality professional development or to benefit from it since they generally are not required to demonstrate their learning through student results. Principals do not take teacher evaluations seriously or use them to make tenure decisions because the norm is that everyone will get tenure. Few teachers are compensated for achieving success with their students, taking on additional responsibilities, or working effectively in challenging schools or in shortage subjects.

The back-loaded pension system contributes minimally in the early years of teaching when retention of teachers with fast-rising productivity should be a priority, but offers steep contributions late in careers, when productivity gains have leveled off. The single salary schedule, the tenure system, and the pension system might be tolerable individually, but together they signal that teaching is about compliance, or sticking around and jumping through hoops, rather than performance or helping students learn.

Another major challenge is designing and implementing systems of accountability for results from preschool through postsecondary education. Unheard of three decades ago, fitful progress has been made, particularly with regard to elementary and secondary schooling. But student testing instruments remain relatively crude and are too variable in their design and use; workforce evaluation tools still lack the reliability necessary for employee buy-in; and education officials in all levels of government fall short in the capacity to administer accountability efforts fairly and credibly.

There are many additional policy challenges. Federal and state governments have not invested adequately in free, high-quality preschool for children from low-income families, those whose home language is not English, or those with special needs, despite compelling evidence that high-quality preschool makes an extraordinary difference for disadvantaged children. There have been no systemic efforts to ensure that students get the health and social service supports they and their families need so that students are ready to learn every day.

Standards are also sorely lacking. There is a proliferation of widely varying state academic content standards and performance expectations for students, with few, if any, states establishing college-ready standards for their 12th graders and then mapping backward to preschool. States have also failed to develop detailed and common curriculum tools for teachers based on high standards. And there has been little investment in supporting the next generation of assessments of student learning for both diagnostic and accountability purposes.

There has so far been little systematic effort to ensure that students are receiving high-quality education and developing the skills they need. Instead there has been an inattention to developing commonly needed skills for today's workplaces such as critical thinking and problem solving; flexibility and adaptability; initiative and self-direction; social and cross-cultural skills; and information, communications, and technology literacy.

Once students leave high school, federal and state policymakers have provided inadequate strategies and investments to make postsecondary study available to students whose families lack the necessary financial resources. They have also failed to adequately meet the needs of growing proportions of immigrant students, particularly in terms of access to postsecondary education, and have neglected youth and young adults who did not complete high school.

There also is inadequate investment in education research and development to determine, among other things, the best ways to raise achievement of educationally disadvantaged students to high levels in all core subjects, to find successful pedagogical strategies for working with a variety of student learning styles, and to use technology effectively as a learning tool and assessment vehicle. It is unlikely that federal leadership and actions can "fix" all these problems, but it can accelerate needed reforms through incentives, promotion of data transparency, support for experimentation and innovation, investment in research and development, well-designed accountability requirements, and increased funding for programs that work.

Given the challenges of international competition and the still-gaping achievement differences at home between haves and have-nots, federal leadership in education has been far from sufficient. While federal policies and programs have triggered major changes and improvements in educational quality and equity, much more is required if this nation is to attain the high-quality preschools, elementary and secondary schools, and postsecondary programs that it needs to thrive in the 21st century.

Recommended Agenda

Federal education programs account for only about 9 percent of the expenditures for public elementary and secondary education,[6] but they have a disproportionately greater effect on American schooling. Funding for early childhood education, unlike K–12 education, remains the primary responsibility of individual families.[7] And although it is difficult to quantify federal support for postsecondary education, it was estimated to be about 19 percent of total expenditures in 2003.[8] Given the international and domestic challenges that better publicly supported education would help allay, the new administration must increase federal investment in effective programs, redesign those that fall short in meeting their goals, and recommend new programs in important but unaddressed areas.

Research has consistently demonstrated that high-quality preschool education has significant and lasting effects on children's learning and development, including increased educational attainment and future employment, decreased rates of delinquency and crime, and improved health.[9] Studies have also documented very positive cost-benefit analyses, with the benefits associated with preschool enrollment outweighing the costs at ratios ranging from nearly 3:1 to over 16:1.[10]

The evidence of payoff for such an investment is overwhelming, yet federal law has done virtually nothing to encourage states to join as partners in ensuring that low-income children are able to enroll in excellent preschools. A new federal program that invests in high-quality preschool needs to be integrated with the Head Start program and be designed to also encourage the expansion of quality child care for children ages zero to three.

Equitable Funding
Few policymakers acknowledge that the greatest funding inequities in the country are among states—more so than within states or within districts. Only

the federal government can equalize opportunities for students nationwide. The federal role historically has been to invest in added educational supports for disadvantaged students. Yet it really makes no sense that a low-income student in one state is given $1,000 less in federal dollars than a low-income student in another.

This occurs because three of the four main NCLB Title I formulas are based on the actual per pupil expenditures for that state as well as the numbers of low-income students, with no consideration of local tax effort. For example, the federal government sent two states with similar tax efforts but very different per pupil investments—Massachusetts and California—$2,310 and $1,280 respectively for *each* Title I eligible student in the 2003–04 school year.[11] Hold-harmless and small-state minimum provisions exacerbate these patterns.

The political challenges inherent in fixing these problems are great, but presidential leadership in promoting fundamental fairness in the distribution of federal Title I funds could have an enormously positive effect. The new administration should propose that the basic Title I formula grants be distributed based on state tax effort and the numbers and concentration of low-income students, rather than per-pupil expenditures. Such a change should be phased in over a reasonable, though not extensive, time period.

Finally, the federal government should revise the Title I comparability provision that allows unfair school district resource allocation practices to continue. The comparability provision was supposed to promote equality by requiring that state and local funds for schools be distributed equitably before federal Title I funds are added to schools with large concentrations of low-income students. But it contains a "loophole" that allows differences in teachers' salaries to be excluded from calculations and consequently supports the longstanding and unequal ways that local and state funds have been distributed by districts. This loophole should be closed.

More Effective Education Workforce

Two million teachers are expected to leave their positions within the next decade,[12] which presents both a challenge and an opportunity to overhaul systems of preparing, hiring, retaining, and compensating teachers and principals. The new administration needs to make a major investment in experimenting with innovative initiatives that will increase the supply of highly effective educators. The appropriate vehicle for this is NCLB Title II.

Too little attention is paid to creating the financial incentives necessary to recruit and retain an effective teacher workforce. The new administration needs to significantly expand incentives for states and districts to offer competitive compensation that recognizes and rewards different roles, responsibilities, and results. If a teacher or a principal is taking on more challenging subjects, teaching in tougher schools, or delivering positive results, he or she should be paid more. If a teacher assumes greater responsibilities such as mentoring or becoming a master teacher, he or she should be compensated. We need career pathways for teachers that reward their talents and are tied to classroom practice.

Experimentation with different compensation systems, together with actions that respond to poor performance—including creating a rigorous tenure process and fairly and effectively removing ineffective educators—should make larger state and local investments in teacher and principal salaries more politically viable and maximize the return on such investments. The TEACH Act proposal,[13] introduced by Rep. George Miller (D-CA) and Sen. Edward Kennedy (D-MA), provides a strong design platform on which to build. NCLB Title II also provides funds for professional development. While these funds are supposed to be targeted to high-poverty and low-performing schools, the General Accountability Office has reported that they are generally not spent as intended.[14]

Data and Accountability Systems

As with most everything in the nation's decentralized education system, the quality and robustness of state data systems varies widely and directly affects accountability systems. Because of NCLB, state progress has accelerated and expanded particularly with regard to documenting the performance of subgroups of students, but much more needs to happen. The new administration should prioritize sustained federal investment in data system development, with prescribed elements that must be included as a condition of funding. Wise data-driven decision making and accountability actions from the classroom to the statehouse, executive branch, and Congress will only be as good as the solid and comprehensive data that are available.

It is simply not possible to evaluate results or properly assess student, teacher, and school performance without reliable information. A nationally consistent data system may be a future goal, but in the short term the Department of Education needs to support the building of transparent and easy-to-understand state longitudinal data systems that track individual students' performance over time, connect this data to individual teacher records, and present schools and district resource allocations in real dollars.

Data on teacher and principal performance can be used to improve instruction through well-designed and specific professional development activities. Clear budget information can lead to the distribution of money based on documented student needs and more effective and equitable deployment of the teacher workforce. And both of these improvements could help rectify inequities in student opportunities for learning. Better data systems also make it possible to measure the effectiveness of preparation programs for teachers and principals.

The new administration should also include in its data development program incentive funding for districts and states to undertake school satisfaction surveys of teachers, principals, parents, and students, with public reporting of results. This has been done for two years in New York City, and Maryland has plans for a statewide survey for schools on quality of school leadership, administrative support, professional development, and facility conditions, among other things.

Incentives for Low-Performing Schools
NCLB sets a 2014 deadline for academic proficiency in reading and math for all students and also stipulates reporting requirements on progress for schools, which has publicly highlighted the very large number of underperforming schools across the country. About 4,500 Title I schools were identified in 2006–07 for corrective action or restructuring for failing to meet required student achievement benchmarks.[15] Debate continues to rage about the wisdom and fairness of the NCLB accountability system, and improvements must be proposed as the reauthorization of the law proceeds over the next few years.

Just as contentious, but even more important, is how best to assist low-performing schools. These schools will receive major support from efforts to more fairly fund schools, strengthen the quality of teaching and leadership, provide better curriculum and classroom assessments, and develop more robust data systems to guide decision making. The government should undertake more research on how best to combine and use these supports and initiate incentive programs for states and districts to experiment with new programs and strategies.

A particularly promising strategy is the expansion of learning time for all students in low-performing and high-poverty schools. These schools work to enhance student success by aligning rigorous academic and enrichment content with curriculum standards and student needs. They are typically led by regular teachers and paraprofessionals, and frequently partner with successful community-based or other non-profit organizations to provide enrichment opportunities and support.

The on-time high school graduation rate for American students has failed to top 70 percent for several decades. This is well below current graduation rates in other countries. Rates for low-income, African-American, and Hispanic students are closer to 50 percent. Researchers have found that about 15 percent of the nation's high schools, or 2,000 schools, produce almost half of its dropouts.[16] Almost as distressing are the proportions of students graduating from high school who are not prepared for college and consequently must take remedial courses for no credit as they begin postsecondary study.[17] Students falling off track face severe threats to their future economic independence and advancement. This trend also threatens our nation's overall competitiveness, as students in other nations become better prepared for the jobs of the future.

The new administration needs to propose a substantial investment in middle and high schools with high concentrations of low-income students. This would correct the federal government's historic inattention to these schools since an estimated 90 percent of ESEA and NCLB Title I funds have been spent at the elementary school level. Such investment should foster a college- and career-oriented culture to make high school more relevant to students. The Graduation Promise Act, which was introduced with bipartisan support in both the House and Senate in 2007, provides an excellent framework for meeting this challenge.

A "Grow What Works" Fund

The achievement gap in America is unacceptably large, and the rate at which it is being narrowed is unacceptably slow. Yet small pockets of success can be found around the country. Schools, teachers, and national non-profit and community-based organizations are beating the odds and producing results in the midst of communities that seem mired in failure. To accelerate closing the achievement gap, we should celebrate these practices that are working and support their replication.

Scaling up best practices enables the gains made at one school to take hold across networks of schools, and ultimately, across school districts. To accomplish this, the new president should work with Congress to create a "Grow What Works" fund, as proposed by Rep. Miller. The "Grow What Works" fund would sustain and expand programs demonstrated to produce results in high-need communities, and help identify and document the best practices that can be shared with schools and school districts in order to drive improvement around the country.

National Academic Content Standards

Consensus is developing that a system of 50 different state standards for core academic subjects is counterproductive to strengthening the quality of education nationwide. Researchers have documented that the quality of state standards and designation of proficiency levels varies greatly from state to state, with high proportions of students designated proficient on state-level tests in some states, and relatively few in others. This becomes evident when these state proficiency levels are compared with the results from the National Assessment of Educational Progress—the only nationally administered achievement test that allows for state-by-state comparisons.[18]

Despite growing agreement around the desirability of national standards, major policy questions exist. What is the best way to develop national standards? Who develops the standards and who promulgates them? What is the appropriate role of Congress and the executive branch? How voluntary should state adoption of national standards be? Should complementary student performance standards also be proposed?

There is no consensus on answers to these questions. The new administration should therefore recommend a process for moving forward that can be reviewed and adjusted at regular intervals. The federal government could invest in simultaneous experiments that would be evaluated and publicly reported. It might finance, for example, a competition for a consortia of states to develop common standards and aligned assessments in selected curricula areas. It could create a competitive research and development grant to work with National Assessment and Educational Progress frameworks in one or two core subjects and translate them into well-aligned standards for all grades. Or it could award a competitive grant to a non-profit organization to convene a group of subject experts to develop standards. One thing seems clear: Doing nothing to move toward a more nationalized curriculum standards approach preserves the very unsatisfactory status quo.

Teachers, test developers, and policymakers also all agree that the current state and local tests of student performance are crude instruments that fail to measure the full range of academic and workplace skills that students need to acquire. Both the public and private sectors are investing in cutting-edge research to develop much more sophisticated test instruments, some for school accountability and others for classroom use, that will be delivered in large part through computers and other technologies. Experimentation and implementation costs are too great for most states. The next administration needs to provide incentives and subsidies for states to adopt better performance measures as they come on line.

Curriculum Materials, Classroom Assessments

All states have standards in core subjects, but decisions about curriculum are left to districts and even schools. Some states exercise more control than others, but there are too few curriculum materials across the board, and the training and support in using them are not well aligned with state standards. Most benchmark and interim assessments, which are rapidly growing in classroom use, are also not aligned with curriculum materials and state standards. The new administration should propose a major program of funding for states to develop or procure high-quality curriculum materials that are aligned with state standards, provide such materials and training on them to teachers, create aligned benchmark and interim assessments, and distribute model lesson plans and examples of student work.

Community Schools

In addition, too many American children come to school every day burdened with hunger, health challenges like asthma, and worries about their families' distress. Schools must link to other supportive agencies and organizations in their neighborhoods and communities and open their facilities for much longer hours to these groups so that children are ready to learn every day. The new administration needs to foster and encourage these community schools.

Education R&D

The new administration must commit to increasing the investment in education research and development to ensure that students are taught using strategies and methodologies that have proven effective. Current funding for research and development is estimated to be as low as $50 million annually.[19] Just as in the health arena, where research and development are expected to lead to breakthroughs in diagnosing and treating the most serious illnesses, research and development has the potential to radically affect schools and student learning.

Postsecondary Education

College completion rates in the United States have declined simultaneously with increases in college enrollment. One factor is that college costs have soared, while federal and state investment in postsecondary study has declined. Federal financial aid policies also remain extremely complicated and difficult to access by consumers. Applicants for aid must complete the Free Application for Federal Student Aid form, which requires a great deal of financial knowledge. Low-income and first-generation students are less likely to complete it even though they are eligible for higher levels of aid. The recent reauthorization of the Higher Education Act, which simplifies the FAFSA form, is one step in the right direction.

The new administration should increase resources and focus its postsecondary policy agenda on providing access for a wider variety of students and ameliorating obstacles that currently prevent many low-income and minority students from attending college. It must simplify the FAFSA form. It should also lead a bipartisan effort to repeal federal legislation barring access to college for young people who were brought to the United States years ago as undocumented immigrant children and support enactment of the Development, Relief, and Education for Alien Minors, or DREAM, Act.

Poor academic preparation of students who enroll in college has also contributed to the decline in college completion. According to one estimate, only half of students who receive a high school degree are prepared for college.[20] Many students must enroll in remedial courses,[21] but these students are less likely to graduate from college. The new administration should assist institutions in supporting motivated students in obtaining the necessary skills to complete a college education. It also should explore incentive and accountability strategies that would result in greater actions by postsecondary institutions to improve degree completion rates.

Overview

Immigration Reform Can Be Orderly and Fair

CECILIA MUNOZ

The new administration will have to contend with the fractious issue of immigration both because the nation's security—including economic security—depends on a rational immigration system, and because it may be difficult to accomplish any other domestic policy agenda while the immigration problem remains unresolved. In the short term, the 44th president must shift focus away from destructive workplace and neighborhood raids, and focus instead on abusive employers. This shift should be accompanied by an overhaul of the immigration detention infrastructure, an improved process for processing backlogs for visas and naturalization applications, and a renewed commitment to human rights among the leadership at the Department of Homeland Security. Yet long-term change that ensures that immigration to the United States is orderly

and legal will require the new president to work closely with Congress to ensure that
comprehensive immigration reform is front and center on the legislative agenda.

The debate over immigration policy is one of the most fractious challenges the new president will face. He will need to address the issue not only on its own merits, but also because it creates tension that will infect every other social policy debate in a new administration.

The American public clearly understands that our immigration laws do not function effectively, but undocumented immigrants provide an attractive target for the kind of demagoguery that makes a rational policy debate difficult. So while at one level this is a complex policy debate, it is also a referendum on demographic change, and even race, in an America that is rapidly evolving. Immigration policy, then, is about porous borders and a discomfort with the growing presence across the country of Latinos, who have become the nation's largest minority.

Resolving the immigration issue will determine whether we remain committed to the value of family reunification, which has been the cornerstone of our immigration policy up to now and has acted as a critical economic and workforce contributor. The economic evidence strongly suggests that current and even modestly increased levels of immigration—especially if it takes place legally—are important elements of economic growth, even essential as the U.S. workforce ages. But it is often difficult to reconcile public sentiment with these long-term economic realities, particularly in a time of downturn in the U.S. economy.

Indeed, a rational immigration debate cannot take place productively in the absence of a larger discussion about economic and social justice. The immigrant rights movement sees itself as part of the larger movement toward economic and social justice, but by itself, immigration policy cannot address the larger question of equality of opportunity that is essential to the nation's future.

The immigration issue is, at its core, a civil rights debate. Many of the recent assaults on voting rights—requiring photo identification at the polls, for example—may have been attacks aimed at low-income communities of color, but they were explained to the public as attempts to prevent immigrants from voting. Similarly, attempts to restrict access to public services, such as Medicaid, for undocumented immigrants who are already categorically ineligible for them have led to verification systems that exclude African Americans and other populations who do not always have the right documentation at hand. Assaults on immigrants are often politically palatable Trojan horses that attack a variety of vulnerable constituencies. When any group of Americans feels the need to

carry a passport or birth certificate as a matter of routine to prove that they belong in their own country, the nation has a fundamental civil rights challenge
on its hands.

Challenges

The new administration will have to confront a badly broken immigration policy. It is estimated that 12 million undocumented immigrants live and work in
the United States, and backlogs of those seeking to come legally can be
decades long. There is a severe disparity between the economic phenomena
that drive the migration process—a combination of economic desperation on
one side of the border, and opportunity in the service and other sectors on the
other—and the laws regulating it. It's a little like having a superhighway with
the speed limit set at 30 miles per hour; as a result, people speed.

The nation is embroiled in a passionate debate in which one side argues that
we should spend more than the billions of enforcement dollars we already
spend attempting to round up undocumented immigrants and deport them.
The other side found a voice in a bipartisan coalition in the U.S. Senate, which
has twice in the last two years unsuccessfully attempted comprehensive immigration reform—an adjustment to the speed limit of sorts.

The Senate debate's failure to produce a politically viable and substantively
effective immigration reform has left a vacuum that state and local governments, under pressure from an often angry public, attempt to fill with the limited and crude policy tools at their disposal. The result is often a patchwork of
policies that appear to be aimed at making everyday life as difficult as possible
for undocumented immigrants in the hope that they will pack up and go home.
The harshest of these policies, in states such as Arizona and Oklahoma, punish
employers of undocumented immigrants by revoking their business licenses
and in some cases even punish people for "transporting" immigrants if they so
much as offer a ride to a co-worker.

These state policies have reportedly pushed immigrants either further underground or to neighboring states, often at the expense of local economies
that rely on immigrant labor.[1] The harsh rhetoric about immigrants has had
even more disturbing effects. Hate crimes against Hispanic Americans have
jumped by 23 percent over three years,[2] and the majority of Latinos, regardless
of immigration status, report discrimination and other hardships as a result of
the immigration debate.[3]

This dynamic is clearly unsustainable; it is difficult to imagine the new administration succeeding in any major area of social or economic policy with-

out addressing the immigration issue. Any debate on health reform, for example, could founder on the thorny question of whether to include undocumented immigrants. As the recent debate on reauthorizing the State Children's Health Insurance Program demonstrates, even a dedicated effort to make sure undocumented, and even legal, immigrants are excluded from coverage still attracts vigorous accusations of creating a back door for spending tax dollars to cover "illegals." Anyone paying close attention to the legislative debate in Congress will notice this ominous trend. One side will make every social or economic issue a referendum on whether the other side is sneakily providing benefits to immigrants.

An immigration policy regime must function well without violating the civil rights of those legally here, and while providing due process for the undocumented. The first step toward achieving this goal will be to acknowledge that the Bush administration's strategy, which amounted to an effort to round up and deport 12 million undocumented immigrants or make their lives so miserable that they self-deport, was doomed to failure.

Many of the undocumented have been here for a decade or more, living with their U.S.-citizen and permanent-resident spouses and children and establishing deep roots in our communities. They are not likely to leave and it is unacceptable for them to remain in the shadows, largely unknown to the government and subject to abuse and exploitation. We need to return to Americans' values of pragmatism, fairness, and order. Having 12 million people living outside of the rule of law is corrosive to the foundation of any advanced society. The openness of the United States to immigrants and refugees is one of our nation's most powerful assets, and a strong challenge to leaders of closed, undemocratic societies.

Immigration reform will only succeed if those in the shadows are screened, learn English, pay taxes, and move along a path toward U.S. citizenship. The path itself needs to be created; and it may make sense to require participation, to assuage the public's inaccurate but forcefully held concern that the problem with undocumented immigrants is that they don't want to integrate and abide by the law. Ultimately, attaining legal status and U.S. citizenship is the only natural solution. No amount of additional enforcement can work otherwise.

The second step will be to create a law that is enforceable—that is, a law that provides legal pathways for those who would otherwise enter illegally. Our economy's demand for additional workers is predicted to rise. Low birthrates and an aging workforce, combined with a concomitant demand for services, have produced a steady demand for labor that cannot be fully met by domestic workers. This means identifying how many such workers are needed to fill legitimate labor market needs, and regulating their entry in a way that does not undercut other sectors of the workforce. This approach in effect stretches the current immigration system in order to allow for a legal flow of immigrants to replace the flow that currently takes place illegally.

At the same time, an effective reform must resolve other flaws in the system that contribute to illegal migration, especially the backlogs in the family immigration system and other obstacles to family unity that too often make entering the country illegally the only way to keep a family together.

The third step will be to engage the country in a conversation that leads to developing a coherent policy aimed at fully integrating immigrants into the larger society. This is needed both because the United States does very little to invest in the social and economic integration of immigrants, and because the American public needs reassurance that, at a time of great demographic change, immigrants can and will become fully American. Interestingly, the country accomplishes a great deal of integration with little fuss or effort; immigrants today tend to integrate as fast as they did a century ago.[4] Nevertheless, a coherent strategy that provides resources for English-language instruction, as well as support for economic and social integration, could calm nerves about what immigrants mean to our collective future.

Finally, the best immigration policy ideas cannot be effective without wholesale reform of the agencies charged with implementing them. It is extraordinary that the former Immigration and Naturalization Service, which was famously plagued with backlogs and management troubles, was reformed into three even more problematic agencies: Immigration and Customs Enforcement, or ICE, U.S. Citizenship and Immigration Service, or USCIS, and U.S. Customs and Border Protection, or CBP. These agencies exist within the Department of Homeland Security with no mechanisms to coordinate immigration policy or reconcile conflicts in the interpretation of immigration laws. The immigration court system within the Department of Justice also merits careful review.

Issues of enforcement abuse, tragically inhumane detention conditions for immigrants and asylum seekers, mismanagement of resources, and outrageous backlogs of would-be immigrants and naturalizing citizens do little to instill confidence in an agency on which the success of any rational immigration policy depends.

Opportunities

If there is a national consensus on any one aspect of the troublesome immigration policy debate, it is that the public wants a system of order and control at the border so that immigrants come in with inspection under the rule of law. An effective policy can only be produced through collaboration between Congress and the executive branch; it will start with legislation and a commitment to ensuring that the federal immigration agencies can function.

Even as the new administration prepares for a legislative debate, there are several immediate measures that the 44th president can implement to instill confidence in the public that the issue is a priority and address ongoing abuses. The new president should first minimize destructive workplace and neighborhood raids and focus instead on abusive employers. He should reassert guidelines that immigration enforcement will not be conducted where there is a union organizing effort or an ongoing labor law investigation.

He will need to overhaul the immigration detention infrastructure, addressing gross abuses such as denying adequate medical care and injecting detainees with dangerous psychotropic drugs.[5] Vital due process protections are also necessary to ensure that asylum seekers and immigrants have the full protection of the law, including expanded legal orientation programs, administrative and judicial review, and detention focused on those who are dangerous or present flight risks alongside alternatives to detention programs for others.

As part of a comprehensive overhaul of our immigration laws, the new president should provide his full support to enact the AgJOBS legislation and the DREAM Act, two bills that have languished in Congress for far too long. AgJOBS provides legal status for undocumented farmworkers, enabling them to support their families with dignity and justice. The DREAM Act offers permanent residence to undocumented immigrant children who graduate from high school and go on to college or service in the military, allowing them to pursue their American dream.

And finally, he will have to clear processing backlogs for visas and naturalization applications. This will require selecting leadership for United States Citizenship and Immigration Services, Immigration and Customs Enforcement, and Customs and Border Protection that have credibility and experience in law enforcement and national security, as well as a clear commitment to human rights, civil rights, due process of law, and the welcoming tradition of a nation of immigrants. Indeed, it may require the new administration to create a new position to which these agencies report—one vested with the authority to shape policy toward immigrants and refugees, as well as the agencies implementing that policy.

These steps will be important early signals of what change means on the immigration issue. But getting to the heart of the matter will require the president to clearly communicate to Congress that immigration reform should be a legislative priority early in the new administration. The comprehensive immigration reform bill's failure in the 110th Congress suggests that providing legal status to undocumented immigrant workers and regulating the flow of future immigrants can be part of a larger strategy to strengthen the U.S. workforce, particularly those who work at low wages.

The immigrant rights movement sees its agenda as part and parcel of a broader movement for economic justice. It recognizes that some industries fill their staffs with vulnerable, undocumented workers, and that union organizing drives and other attempts to improve wages and working conditions can be undercut by threats to contact the immigration authorities. The immigration agenda is ultimately a workers' rights agenda, yet this case has not been made effectively in the legislative debate thus far and should be a cornerstone of it for the next administration.

The new president should introduce a major immigration reform bill and work for its enactment ideally in the first year of the new Congress. There are a host of complex pieces of an immigration reform framework that together make up a coherent policy. An effective immigration reform bill should at its core focus on enforcement and legal immigration reform. But it will also have to consider integration for immigrants into life in the United States, look critically at our nation's trade and foreign assistance policies, and reform the agencies with jurisdiction over our immigration laws.

Enforcement

The most important thing to understand about immigration enforcement is that it cannot be effective as long as its goal is to hound 12 million people out of the country. The harshest enforcement measures provide a great deal of hardship but reap minimal results. Mass deportations are financially unfeasible and patently unrealistic. Deporting today's 12 million undocumented immigrants has been estimated to cost over $200 billion.[6]

This cost to taxpayers doesn't begin to account for the resulting devastation suffered by families, communities, small businesses, and local economies. A recent study documents that for every two immigrants apprehended in workplace raids, one child is left behind, creating a new set of challenges for schools, communities, and the social service infrastructure.[7] *The New York Times* estimates that some 13,000 American children have had a parent detained or deported;[8] this is a high price to pay for the extremely modest "success" in removing some .002 percent of the undocumented population, some of whom undoubtedly return. Despite the yelling about enforcement and "amnesty" on the nation's airwaves, the public largely thinks a deportation-only strategy is undesirable and ineffective, and majorities have for years supported bringing undocumented immigrants out of the shadows.

The debate boils down to a fight between expulsion and integration. As long as it is clear that integration means learning English, paying taxes, abiding by the law, and ultimately becoming U.S. citizens, it is both the most rational approach to the problem of the undocumented and the one preferred by most Americans. Unless the current undocumented population has access to legal status, immigration enforcement will be impossible. A pathway to citizenship for undocumented immigrants is therefore a crucial piece of the enforcement agenda.

Legalizing the undocumented will also eliminate the two-tiered system that exists today, where unscrupulous employers seek out undocumented workers to cut corners, not only on wages but also on health and safety practices. Beyond enforcing the laws already on the books, states can amend living wage or minimum wage laws to earmark fines recovered from violators to fund new enforcement, and support legislation that authorizes complaints on behalf of others.

A more difficult challenge will be to design an enforcement regime that can be effective in the future while simultaneously respecting civil and human rights. From 1986 to 2002, the budget for the Border Patrol increased tenfold from $151 million to $1.6 billion.[9] Yet during that same time, since 1990, more than 9 million undocumented immigrants were added to our population.[10] Steady increases in personnel and technology at the border may have delivered political cover for legislators who want to show their commitment to border control, but they have not delivered significant reductions in the flow of immigrants.

Legislation introduced by the new president must codify enforcement choices that actually deter border crossings in the first place, while minimizing harm to human and civil rights. This means concentrating enforcement resources on employers, particularly those who violate labor laws while also flouting immigration restrictions, and reinvigorating labor and civil rights enforcement in every sector of the workforce after years in which this infrastructure has been left to decay.

Legislation must address enforcement at the border and provide adequate budgets, access to new technology, and provisions to enforce accountability and professionalism. The country will always have a Border Patrol; it should therefore be among the most professional and accountable police forces in the nation.

The immigration debate has been moving the country toward some form of verification system that would be used in the workplace to limit undocumented immigrants' access to jobs. Whether Americans know it or not, the immigration debate has long since planted the seeds of an identification system that will affect all American workers at the point of hire. There are many dangerous variations of a verification proposal currently on the table. As currently envisioned by legislators on both sides of the aisle, employers will consult a database to determine whether their employees are lawfully authorized to work.

In theory, the verification system could be as simple as a credit card transaction. In practice, the data must be reliable in order to be effective, and millions of Americans' ability to work will depend on the quality of the data in the system. There must therefore be a system of protection and remedies for those who are unfairly treated. The whole package will require federal agencies to invest billions of dollars, not to mention years of intensive focus, on improving the quality of existing data. Any discussion of a workplace verification system must proceed carefully, incorporating benchmarks and targets for the quality of data before it is fully implemented, and include vigorous provisions against misuse of data and for the protection of privacy so that the system does not disrupt workers' rights.

Legal Immigration Reform

The current immigration system does not deliver on its fundamental promise: to speedily reunite Americans with their closest family members. U.S. citizens and legal permanent residents wait in unreasonably long lines to reunite with their own spouses and children. In some cases, American citizens are completely unable to reunite with their spouses if there is any history of undocumented status. These deficiencies in the system have the perverse effect of stimulating undocumented migration, since family ties are inevitably stronger than the limitations of the law. New immigration legislation will need to provide both orderliness and fairness by adding a number of visas to the system to address these backlogs and to create a functional legal immigration system.

At the same time, the law must adapt to provide some accommodation for those who will be tempted to enter illegally in the future because the law simply provides no legal avenue for them to join the U.S. workforce—even in industries where there is a clear need—unless a worker is part of a U.S. family. This "future flow" issue must be dealt with, or we will find ourselves in another immigration debate in 15 years when a sizeable undocumented population has again accumulated. We will need to establish legal channels to regularize the flow of new workers to reduce future illegal immigration; otherwise the chaos and deaths on the border will continue. We must transform the current illegal flows into programs that provide safe, legal, and orderly ways for future immigrants to come to the United States.

Previous attempts to address the future flow problem through a temporary worker program actually undercut support for immigration reform because many worried that even strong labor protections would not be enforced vigorously enough to protect immigrant and U.S. workers. The new president should therefore consider creating a visa category to bring future workers in with permanent immigration status in numbers sufficient to replace the undocumented stream without growing to a number that could undercut the U.S. workforce. At the end of the day, whatever visa program is instituted must guarantee that workers have the ability to change jobs freely, the right to join unions and enjoy full labor and civil rights protections, the right to bring immediate family members with them, and the opportunity to become U.S. citizens.

This approach must be accompanied by tough labor law enforcement throughout the workforce and additional employment visas, because they will produce a system in which legality is the norm. This means a critical trade off—explaining to the American people that the path to an orderly immigration system in which immigrants come legally means a larger immigration stream in exchange for dramatic reduction in undocumented migration.

Integration

English-language acquisition has traditionally been the fundamental measure of the extent to which immigrants adjust to life in the United States. This is an important measure, not so much because the presence of other languages in American communities so unsettles portions of the public, but because facility in English is essential to immigrants' economic success. The United States does very little to help immigrants make this crucial adjustment. Demand for English language instruction for immigrant adults dramatically outstrips the supply of classes. Many of these services are supplied by community organizations in ethnic communities, often with donated classroom space and volunteer instructors. A national strategy focused on English would go a long way toward addressing this important indicator of integration.

It is also critically important to expand the integration framework well beyond the question of English. Unlike a century ago, the nation is not designing its education strategies for children in a way that addresses the integration challenge for children in immigrant families, who make up some 20 percent of the population of children in the United States.[11] More also needs to be done to expand health care outreach and access to care. Our ability to integrate immigrants is ultimately a question of economic integration as much as it is a social and cultural question.[12]

Sending Communities

The immigration debate far too often focuses on what the United States can do that might attract or deter migration. This ignores the circumstances in other countries that may contribute to migration and assumes that the United States has nothing it can do or say about those external circumstances. Almost no thought or effort is focused on the dynamics of the so-called "sending communities" from which immigrants migrate.

Supporters of trade policies have used immigration as a rationale for more open trade with Latin America. A principal argument in support of the North American Free Trade Agreement is that it would reduce migration by promoting development in Mexico. Yet there is very little evidence that these policies have deterred migration in any way. A critical look at our nation's trade and foreign assistance policies—with an eye toward economic development in sending communities—is long overdue as a contribution to the immigration policy debate.

Agency Reform

Even the most effective legislative policies will fail if the new administration does not pay greater attention to the effectiveness and accountability of the agencies charged with implementing them. Immigration and Customs Enforcement, the agency tasked with enforcing immigration policies, controls one of the few pieces of the federal budget that regularly increases, though there is little to show for it in terms of effectiveness. In fairness, ICE is charged with enforcing a set of laws that is largely unenforceable. Nevertheless, the agency is guilty of major lapses in respect for human and civil rights.[13]

ICE implements a set of detention policies that deny detainees access to counsel and detain children and families in often deplorable conditions that sometimes lead to the injury or even death of detainees while in ICE custody.[14] Its implementation of enforcement policies in the border region has long been criticized for insensitivity to the concerns of residents there. Americans living near the border complain about harassment and community disruption, and have long argued that they deserve—although they have so far been denied—a voice in the development and implementation of the border policies that affect them. A reasonable, enforceable policy must include provisions that assure the accountability of the agency charged with implementing them, including the kind of civilian oversight that is a staple of most urban police forces.

Customs and Border Protection, responsible for admitting over 400 million people each year at our ports of entry, while screening out terrorists and criminals, is also responsible for ensuring that bona fide asylum seekers are not turned away at our borders. An exhaustive study conducted by the United States Commission for Religious Freedom of asylum seekers in expedited removal identified serious shortcomings in the implementation of procedures, endangering asylum seekers who face persecution if returned to their home countries. Recommendations to remedy these flaws have yet to be adopted by CBP. A new administration must take immediate steps to correct these problems and restore protection to vulnerable asylum seekers.

United States Citizenship and Immigration Services, like its counterparts at DHS, is also plagued with problems that hinder its ability to perform its function of welcoming immigrants and refugees and completing the naturalization process for those who seek to become citizens. The agency seems unable to cope with long backlogs and insists that it is able to rely solely on user fees to pay for application processing without requesting additional budgetary support. The perverse result of this policy is an expensive fee structure that continues to rapidly climb, while backlogs grow astronomically longer. What's more, USCIS has been described by *The Washington Post* as treating immigrants with hostility.[15] The new administration will clearly need to turn this around.

Reform of the Executive Office for Immigration Review—the immigration court system—is also long overdue. Concerns regarding the integrity of this court system and the impartiality of its judges have been raised by advocates, federal judges, and members of Congress. Streamlining procedures instituted under the Bush administration have eroded necessary checks and balances and created significant backlogs in the federal courts. Independent decision-making has been compromised as immigration judges fall under the purview of the Department of Justice, a prosecutorial agency with policies and regulations driven by the agency's litigation interests.

Furthermore, the Department of Justice has failed to provide adequate resources to train immigration judges and hire necessary agency staff. A new administration will need to carefully evaluate the immigration court system and consider whether integrity, impartiality, and adequate checks and balances can best be restored by creating an independent court system outside the Department of Justice.

Overview

Government Transparency in the Age of the Internet

ELLEN S. MILLER

The new administration will have the opportunity to embrace government transparency and the potential for citizen engagement offered by the Internet and new communications technologies, making government more open, more responsive, more accountable, and thus more trusted by the American people. Putting online all the public disclosure information that is currently available only to visitors to Washington, D.C., would mark a big change from the culture of secrecy of the Bush administration. The new administration should also expand the amount of data available to the public by working with Congress to reform the Freedom of Information Act and ensure that there are adequate resources to provide the public with information. The new administration should reverse the trend toward the classification of documents; provide timely, accurate information to the public in searchable, sortable, downloadable formats; and require all government agencies to engage the energy of citizens online.

We now live in an increasingly networked global society, one in which people are capable of communicating and collaborating with each other in radically new and powerful ways. Blogs, microblogs such as Twitter, and social networking sites are tools not only for sharing information, but also for organizing. Powerful search engines provide instant access to information. Databases, mashups, and other technologies create the potential for seeing anything—from the performance of a sports team to the happenings on a single city block—with a depth and context previously unimaginable.

The information age has already demonstrated the dynamic power of its disruptive potential. Brick and mortar businesses, Hollywood and television studios, and print media organizations alike are all now competing with their online-only rivals head-to-head on the Internet. Individual citizens have ceased to be solely customers, audience members, and readers—instead they can also be entrepreneurs and restaurant reviewers, creators of content and purveyors of news. In an online world, communication is more evenly distributed. The mass audience—the captive audience—of the era of mass communications is a thing of the past. Everyone can be a publisher, an activist, an organizer.

While government has been slow to adapt itself to this new digital information age, the networked world hasn't waited. Technologists, hobbyists, bloggers, non-profit organizations, and concerned citizens have leveraged the power of the Web to free government information from unwieldy sites, to lobby government to make more information available online, to scrutinize government data and ask hard questions or formulate alternative policies, and to act as watchdogs on everything from congressional earmarks to the administration's firing of eight U.S. attorneys.

The federal government stands to gain from all of the ways that new communications technology empowers the participants in our democracy. First, public scrutiny, once the exclusive domain of the press, is being reinforced by cadres of interested citizens demanding digital access to governmental proceedings and data, and then offering analysis and policy expertise. Second, new tools also hold the promise of an efficient, effective government, better able to manage information, analyze it, and respond to it. Finally, a government open to a networked citizenry creates opportunities for increased civic engagement, offsetting the privileged influence and access accorded to special interests.

We are only now starting to see the potential of technology to boost government transparency and open government at federal agencies. Realizing its full potential promises to create a new balance between citizens and government. As of 2007, there were an estimated 165 million to 210 million American users of the Internet, according to the Pew Internet & American Life Project.[1] But the government has only just begun to grant access to its information. The new administration, working with Congress, can ensure that the federal government becomes as responsive, open, and effective as increasingly networked Americans expect it to be.

Today's Offline Government

There are a number of major obstacles that the new administration will face in creating an open and transparent government. Much government information is not available online, and much of what is online is invisible to search engines, and thus to those seeking it. What's more, a great deal of data is only available through Freedom of Information Act requests, especially since the terrorist attacks on September 11, 2001, after which government agencies began to classify incredible amounts of information that previously was public.

New communications technologies offer ways to overcome all of these obstacles, but they have been adopted only to a limited extent. Let's begin with the public disclosure of information, which is the principle means by which government deters corruption and ensures the accountability of public officials. Often, government agencies simply do not release this information to the public. Case in point: the Office of Government Ethics, which collects personal financial disclosure forms from the president, cabinet officials, and other high-ranking administration officials, does not put any of this information online where the public could find it. Instead, the documents are stored offline, and must be requested by individual citizens by letter or fax.[2]

Or consider the Employee Benefits Security Agency, which oversees the U.S. private pension system. It maintains a database of pension plan documents and disclosures, which can be searched only by visiting the basement office of the Department of Labor's Washington, D.C., headquarters. Specific documents can be requested by mail (there is a copying charge of 15 cents a page), but that assumes an individual knows which document he or she needs to see.[3]

When government does put information online, it's often published in such a way that a user can't find it. The E-Government Act of 2002 had as its goal making the federal government more transparent and accountable—in part by granting access to more government information—but the results have been mixed. A December 2007 joint report by OMB Watch and the Center for Democracy and Technology, "Hiding in Plain Sight: Why Important Government Information Cannot Be Found through Commercial Search Engines," noted that "in many respects, the law has been successful, including encouraging agencies to work together to build websites that allow users to find information by its content and not only where it is housed in the bureaucracy."[4]

But the report also shows how vital government information appears "invisible" to ordinary Americans using the Internet, even though the data exist online.[5] The report found, for instance, that a search for "New York radiation" did not find basic government data on "current conditions and monitoring." Searches for "small farm loans" took users to commercial sites offering loans and information about government loans, but not the federal government site built to assist small farmers with loans.

The government is not always so eager to release information to the public. The Transactional Records Access Clearinghouse, or TRAC—a research center sponsored by Syracuse University—maintains a set of databases that allow subscribers to see, for example, which U.S. attorneys' offices have prosecuted no environmental cases or have most actively pursued narcotics cases. TRAC also has data on which income groups are most heavily audited by the Internal Revenue Service. They obtain this basic data on government actions through Freedom of Information Act requests, and often have to resort to the courts not only to get their FOIA requests filled, but then also to force noncompliant agencies to disgorge records.[6]

In August 2007, the Coalition of Journalists for Open Government issued a report showing "current government handling of FOIA requests is deteriorating" across the government agencies.[7] The National Freedom of Information Coalition highlights some of the worst problems.[8] Government entities did not process two of every five FOIA requests filed in 2006, and FOIA denials increased 10 percent in 2006 alone. The coalition also found that even though governmental agencies are processing 20 percent fewer FOIA requests, the cost of processing those requests is up 40 percent since 1998. The upshot: government action on FOIA requests takes longer and costs more, and requests are often not acted upon, causing longer waits for the public.

While FOIA has failed to provide the public with government information covered by the act, more and more information has been classified as secret and thus exempted from disclosure. OpenTheGovernment.org, a nonpartisan coalition of 33 organizations dedicated to combating unwarranted government secrecy, issues an annual Secrecy Report Card.[9] The latest, in 2007, shows a continued expansion of government secrecy across a broad array of agencies and actions. The report found that the government spent some $44 million declassifying information—and $8.2 billion creating more secrets.

The Bush administration exercised an unprecedented level not only of restriction of access to information about the federal government's policies and decisions, but also of suppression of discussion of those policies, their underpinnings, and their implications. It also refused to be held accountable to the public through the oversight responsibilities of Congress. These practices inhibit democracy and frustrate our representative government.

Such concerns often go unheard by federal officials, in part because the government has created its own Potemkin panels of outside advisors who often have a stake in the status quo. In "The Shadow Government," an investigation of federal advisory committees, the Center for Public Integrity found that a sometimes secret, multi-layered, and unaccountable shadow bureaucracy influences much of the federal government—with precious little oversight and largely no record of their activities.[10]

There are over 900 committees, boards, commissions, councils, and panels that advise the various agencies of the executive branch and the White House and that are meant to offer government expert opinions on various topics. Yet the CPI investigation found that these committees were packed with industry representatives, and that members had been added or removed for political reasons. The committees form subcommittees or working groups where decisions are made behind closed doors. And the committees seal records, if they exist at all.

Launching Government 2.0

The 1966 Freedom of Information Act was conceived in an era when the U.S. Postal Service was the fastest means of exchanging a document and when computers ran on punch cards. Yet the same ideal that animated FOIA—positing access to information as a central democratic concept—is fueling the movement to redefine the way we relate to government. And the Internet and other new technologies provide a mechanism capable of providing the widest possible access, whenever and wherever people want the information.

To seize the opportunities for making more information available to more people in usable formats, and to increase citizen engagement in government actions and policies, a mix of presidential executive orders and legislative initiatives will be required. First and foremost, a presidential executive order should direct the Office of Management and Budget to catalog all of the public disclosure information available offline in the offices of federal agencies that maintain physical public disclosure "reading rooms." All federal agencies should then be directed to publish this information in a searchable format.

Making disclosure requirements more robust is a first necessary step toward building a more productive, inclusive deliberative process. The goal: a participatory dialogue between citizens and government so that each shares a stake in public policy outcomes. When the public can easily see who regulators meet with and why, how taxpayer dollars are spent, or what laws have been introduced or passed, then the first requirement for participation has been met. Basic civic information is the foundation on which deeper participation can be built.

Accordingly, requiring that cabinet secretaries, deputy secretaries, and high-ranking officials in the executive office of the president post their schedules online—including with whom they meet and the subject of the meetings—would be one highly symbolic way of differentiating the new administration from its two predecessors. Both the Clinton and Bush administrations used high-profile secret bodies—the Task Force on National Health Care Reform in the first term of the Clinton administration and the Energy Task Force in the first term of the second Bush administration—to develop policy.

More substantively, the few disclosure initiatives launched over the last 16 years should be expanded. Until passage of the Federal Funding Accountability and Transparency Act in 2006, citizens had no access to timely, accurate, easy-to-use information about federal contracts, grants, and other forms of government spending. In December 2007, the Office of Management and Budget launched USAspending.gov, a new searchable website of federal contracts and financial assistance. In an example of government collaboration with an interested stakeholder, OMB consulted with OMB Watch, which launched a database called FedSpending.org in September 2006 that contains the same data as mandated for release by the 2006 law, and ended up adopting FedSpending.org's user interface and database architecture.

More could be done. OMB Watch has challenged OMB and Congress to expand federal spending information to include information about the award, contractor, and grantee performance and compliance with laws and regulations. Additional data in other databases could also be "mashed up" by government agencies or independent programmers with the information in USASpending.gov, including a database of the lobbying efforts of those seeking federal contracts or their campaign contributions. New tools could be added as well, including maps and census data, providing additional context to government spending.

In January 2007, OMB began collecting from government agencies data on all fiscal year 2005 earmarks—congressionally directed spending measures—that they were funding. OMB released this in a searchable database that includes the recipient of the earmark, the citation authorizing the spending, the amount of money awarded, and other data.[11] OMB should continue to collect and publish this information, and attempt to incorporate congressional earmark disclosure in its data sets.

Most other government bureaucracies, however, do not have a good record of releasing information to the public in a timely or useful manner. Consider the Environmental Protection Agency. OMB Watch, in its October 2007 report on government transparency, suggests ways for the agency to disclose environmental information "that could be implemented by EPA without new legislation."[12] During the Clinton administration, EPA did establish the Office of Environmental Information, which serves as the nexus of the agency's disclosure efforts. Other proposals have "languished," however, according to OMB Watch.[13]

To address this, the new administration should require agencies to develop a comprehensive list of the information sets they maintain and provide easy-to-use online access. The list could be linked with other federal agency databases to develop profiles about facilities and regulated companies. They should make greater use of electronic filing and online data reporting to speed up the collection of information, reduce data errors, and limit republishing costs; they should then identify information gaps and establish processes to make the missing information available.

Legislative action should complement agency efforts, enhance them, and provide adequate funding for them. Sen. Joseph Lieberman (I-CT), chairman of the Homeland Security and Governmental Affairs Committee, was the architect of the 2002 E-Government Act. In December 2007, he introduced the E-Government Reauthorization Act of 2007, saying that the federal government needs to learn from private sector innovations to improve the delivery of government information and services, and to make federal government data more accessible, transparent, and interactive. Sen. Lieberman's legislation would extend the original 2002 law for five years, with the goal of increasing government transparency and directing agencies to implement the sitemap protocol, which enables public search engines to catalog and access governmental data sets.

Often what's crucial is how legislation is implemented. Congress enacted the Open Government Act of 2007, the first reform of the Freedom of Information Act in a decade. David Ardia, director of the Citizen Media Law Project at Harvard Law School, hailed the act for expanding the definition of who is representative of the news media. "This change would significantly benefit bloggers and non-traditional journalists by making them eligible for reduced processing and duplication fees that are available [to members of the media]."[14]

Ardia lists other important provisions of the new law, among them: including information on government contracts held by private contractors; assigning public tracking numbers to all requests; penalizing agencies that exceed the 20-day deadline for responses by denying them the ability to charge requesters research and copy costs; helping FOIA requesters who have to sue to force compliance to collect attorney's fees; and establishing an FOIA ombudsman office at the National Archives "to accept citizen complaints, issue opinions on request, and foster best practices within the government."

However, weeks after signing it, President Bush "cut the heart" out of the act,[15] the Citizen Media Law Project contended, by refusing to fund the FOIA ombudsman's office in the National Archives.[16] To restore it, and to improve the experience of citizens requesting documents under FOIA, the new administration should address the backlogs and timeliness—or lack thereof—of responses to FOIA requests, and develop penalties for government agencies that violate deadlines for responding to requests, allow the public to track responses to FOIA requests online, and ease the release of historical records.

In addition, the burden of proof in FOIA appeals and court cases should be shifted from the private individual or organization requesting the information to the agency withholding it. The new administration should work with Congress to pass the Faster FOIA Act of 2007, which would establish a 16-member commission on FOIA delays to study processing FOIA requests and provide recommendations to ensure the efficient and equitable administration of FOIA throughout government. The FOIA ombudsman office in the National

Archives also should be fully funded, as the Open Government Act of 2007 stipulated. And finally, the Department of Homeland Security should prevent FOIA disclosure only in the narrowest of circumstances; Bush administration memos allowing limited disclosure by DHS should be overturned.

Fighting for Open Government

In 2005, Rep. Henry Waxman (D-CA), then ranking member of the Oversight and Government Reform Committee, released "Secrecy in the Bush Adminis-tration," a report analyzing how the administration implemented each of the nation's major open government laws.[17] It found "a consistent pattern in the administration's actions: laws that are designed to promote public access to in-formation have been undermined, while laws that authorize the government to withhold information or to operate in secret have repeatedly been expanded." In other words, the administration's actions constitute "an unprecedented as-sault on the principle of open government," as Waxman's report concluded.

The report's admonishments of the Bush administration could be read as a "what-not-to-do" list for the new administration. Existing open government laws, including FOIA, should be enforced rather than circumvented. Executive orders delaying and restricting the release of the papers and documents of past presidents to the public should be rescinded. The dramatic increase in the num-ber of classified documents should cease, and adequate resources should be de-voted to declassification of "secret" documents.

A new administration should cooperate with Congress when it exercises its constitutional duty to oversee the executive branch—rather than sue to hide documents from Congress, the new administration should share them. It should also reinvigorate the Federal Advisory Committee Act of 1972 to open up to public scrutiny the insider advice the government gets on policy. Con-gress's intent in passing FACA was to discourage the influence of insider discus-sions on agency decisions, something that continues today with no public disclosure. Reps. Henry Waxman and William Lacy Clay (D-MO) are sponsor-ing the Federal Advisory Committee Act Amendments of 2008, which are meant to improve balance, transparency, and independence.

Opening up the deliberative processes of government, however, can go much further than after-the-fact disclosure. Some recent projects within Con-gress and federal agencies have seen preliminary success in integrating public participation into traditionally closed processes at the basic level of setting in-formation access policy. The U.S. Occupational Safety and Health Administration's eTools, for example, are a series of interactive, Web-based training tools on various OSHA topics, ranging from "Ammonia Refrigeration" to "Youth in Agriculture." The eTools site advertises itself as the place for citizens to "receive reliable advice on how OSHA regulations apply to their work site."[18]

The U.S. Department of Labor also developed and used Web-based tools to educate citizens on the department's rules, regulations, and compliance protocols. A 2003 Urban Institute study found that the program "has become a key component of the department's broad efforts to promote compliance assistance as a means of increasing regulations' effectiveness while limiting their cost to government and to regulated firms."[19]

Another interesting example is a pilot project out of the U.S. Patent and Trademark Office, which set up a wiki (an interactive online bulletin board and editing tool) that allows the public to make public comments on pending patents. PTO's Peer to Patent Project uses "a community rating system designed to push the most respected comments to the top of the file, for serious consideration by the agency's examiners," according to Michael Fix and Katherine Lotspeich, both of whom noted that the project was "a first for the federal government."[20]

The New President

Ultimately, the biggest reform would be to elect a president who understands the potential of an open federal government in the age of the Internet—a president who does not believe that more information in the public domain weakens his ability to effectively govern, but rather enhances it. The new president alone can quickly do more to open government than all the work of reformers and the right-to-know community.

In February, 2008, Steven Aftergood, director of the Project on Government Secrecy at the Federation of American Scientists—where he writes the Secrecy News blog—wrote an essay that makes the case for the next president to turn back the last seven years of secrecy of the Bush administration with the stroke of a pen:

> The next President will have the authority to declassify and disclose any and all records that reflect the activities of executive branch agencies. Although internal White House records that document the activities of the outgoing President and his personal advisers will be exempt from disclosure for a dozen years or so, every Bush Administration decision that was

actually translated into policy will have left a documentary trail in one or more of the agencies, and all such records could be disclosed at the discretion of the next President.[21]

Aftergood points out how the two contestants for the presidency in 2008 specifically criticized the secrecy of the Bush administration. The new president, guided by these sentiments, could radically increase the amount of information publicly available, enhance government accountability, and improve the quality of decision making by involving the public in decisions affecting their lives, which is just what the founders intended. "Whenever the people are well informed, they can be trusted with their own government," wrote Thomas Jefferson in 1789. "Whenever things get so far wrong as to attract their notice, they may be relied on to set them to rights."[22] The American people have more powerful tools than ever to fulfill that mission. All they need is the information.

Overview

Renewing Our Democracy

MICHAEL WALDMAN

America's democracy badly needs repair. The new president boasts a tremendous opportunity to tap the energy of the civic surge of 2008, and in so doing reform government policies long stymied by special-interest gridlock. Vital reforms all push toward greater participation. In voting, the new president should lead the fight for universal voter registration, which would add up to 50 million American citizens to the rolls. He should also fix electronic voting and push for public funding of elections, with an emphasis on boosting the power of small contributors. And he can use the bully pulpit to urge the states to curb gerrymandering after the 2010 census and to move to a national popular vote for president.

The new president faces an overarching challenge: leading a renewal of our democracy. Meeting that challenge will be central to the success of his term and the larger project of building a progressive majority.

The 2008 election cycle was marked by a thrilling upsurge of civic participation and citizen engagement, with millions of new voters, the explosion of small dollar contributions, and a sharp rise in participation. All this could add up to a transformative moment. And yet the basic institutions of American democracy are broken. Voter registration laws are among the most restrictive in the democratic world, even before the recent conservative push to disenfranchise minority, poor, and young voters. Members of Congress are still overwhelmingly funded by large contributions from special interests, and the number of corporate lobbyists in Washington, D.C., has tripled in a decade.

Then there's the legacy of President George W. Bush, who used 9/11 as the pretext for a long hoped-for executive power grab in ways that will take years to unravel. Public trust in government during conservatives' control of the White House and Capitol Hill plunged to its lowest level since Watergate. In all these ways, the very institutions that we will rely on to translate public discontent into lasting progressive change badly need repair.

With imagination and verve, the new president must not only focus on short-term, tangible policy "deliverables" but also on renewing the systems of democracy that empower ordinary citizens and make all other changes possible. If he exerts this leadership, then he will help permanently enlarge the constituency and coalition for progressive politics. Such steps would also make it far easier to enact vital change—combating global warming, enacting health care reform, creating a fairer tax system—all of which will force us to overcome entrenched and well-funded interests that now dominate the system.

Today's new wave of government reform, however, should not try to purify the messy, inevitably rambunctious world of politics. Money will always play a role. Rather, the new administration should seek changes to catalyze the participation of wider numbers of citizens in informed engagement in the political life of the country. We cannot eliminate "special interests," but we can fix the jammed mechanisms of government so that policies once again can be enacted that broadly benefit the public interest. And we can seek to use new digital technologies to boost democracy.

A shift toward wider participation will push politicians and parties to focus on what matters to ordinary people, and will change the realm of what is possible. In short, changing the process of our system will by definition change the power dynamic within it.

An Inclusive Voting System

Voting is the heart of democracy. America's voting system remains decrepit, prone to error, and rife with barriers to full participation. In 2000, the country learned to its surprise that the way we cast and count ballots is far from neutral or precise. According to the best estimate, between 4 million and 6 million votes were lost in that year's presidential election due to faulty lists, disenfranchisement, and other problems at the polls.[1] The federal Help America Vote Act, enacted in 2002, was a partial solution.[2] The number of "residual votes," or votes cast but not counted, fell sharply.[3] But substantial problems remain.

Millions of eligible Americans still cannot vote because they are not on the voter rolls—sometimes because they never registered, but just as often because they fell off the rolls when they moved or have found it difficult to get and stay on the rolls. Election administration remains largely an afterthought. Ballot design varies from county to county.[4] Officials operate under inadequate conflict-of-interest rules. Some are openly partisan. Katherine Harris of Florida and J. Kenneth Blackwell of Ohio chaired their state party presidential drives while supposedly refereeing the contests as secretaries of state. Blackwell oversaw elections while he himself ran for governor.

Or consider that officials routinely purge voters from the rolls with no public notice, no standards, and no accountability. One consequential result: the multiple purges in Florida that prevented thousands of eligible voters from casting ballots in 2000. The 13,000 separate jurisdictions that administer elections vary wildly in skill and neutrality. Information and voter lists must be parceled out to at least 200,000 separate polling places across the country.[5]

Faced with this welter of laws, our government should have found ways to expand voter registration and improve election administration. Instead, conservatives mounted a fierce campaign against imaginary "voter fraud," despite the sheer absence of evidence for in-person voter impersonation (the only kind of fraud that would be prevented by voter ID requirements). Statistically, an individual is more likely to be killed by lightning than to commit voter fraud.

Yet every two years, a rash of new rules threatens to spread, requiring that voters produce a government-issued photo ID, or, worse, a birth certificate or passport. In 2008, in *Crawford v. Marion County*, the U.S. Supreme Court upheld the nation's strictest voter ID law, in Indiana.[6] The Court agreed there was little, if any, evidence of fraud, but then said, in effect, "so what?" The justices did leave a path open for further litigation when more facts are developed.

It would be unfortunate if the contentious issue of voter ID blocks the opportunity for transformative voting change. Many Americans simply lack various kinds of ID—up to 15 percent lack a driver's license, for example, and they are overwhelmingly the urban poor, elderly, and students. The true concern should be to assure that every eligible citizen has any ID that is required, either by accepting many different types of ID, or by assuring that government-provided free ID is genuinely widely available.

The Help America Vote Act recognizes up to a dozen forms of identification. In Michigan, citizens must produce ID, but if none is available, then they can sign sworn affidavits confirming their identity. No eligible citizen should be denied the right to vote due to an absence of proper paperwork. The new president should take as a staring point an 11th commandment: thou shalt not disenfranchise.

He also should recognize that expanding the vote is central both to the country's promise and to progressive strategy. A series of bold policy reforms could change American democracy, beginning with universal voter registration. The most important single step the new president could take would be enactment of a national universal voter registration law. The voter registration systems in the United States were first implemented a century and a half ago to make it harder for newly arrived European immigrants to vote.[7] By one estimate, requiring the government to keep and update accurate voter lists could add as many as 50 million eligible voters to the rolls.[8]

Universal voter registration could transform the practice and outcomes of American politics. It would push campaigns toward mobilizing the maximum number of voters rather than competing for slivers of the electorate. While voter registration is conducted by the states, the prod of a federal law is needed. It should require states to phase in universal registration. There are several ways this could happen. States could compile existing lists such as driver's license databases and state income tax records, or conduct a census, as Massachusetts does now. Part of any state reform should be permanent registration; when voters sign up, they stay on the rolls even if they move (as one in six Americans do every two years). This federal mandate would be accompanied by federal funding to help states make the transition.

At the very least, federal law should institute election-day registration. Why cut off registration in the immediate weeks before an election just when debates, newspaper endorsements, and water-cooler conversations heat up? Already, Minnesota, Maine, Wisconsin, Idaho, New Hampshire, Wyoming, Montana, and Iowa have election-day registration.[9] In 2006 nearly 4,000 Montanans registered on election day, more than the margin of victory for the state's new Sen. Jon Tester (D-MT).

In 2007, North Carolina instituted "same day" registration. Voters can register any day during the early voting period two weeks before election day, but not that day itself. Election-day registration turbocharges turnout. Most estimates show it boosts voting by 5 to 7 percent.[10] States with election-day registration have fewer problems with registration lists on election day than is typical. There is no evidence of increased fraud or chicanery.[11]

The new president also needs to get behind efforts to improve electronic voting. Since 2000, 49 states have moved to electronic voting. These machines have numerous advantages over the old system of paper ballots and "hanging chads," especially for the millions of voters with disabilities. But myriad studies warn these electronic systems are woefully insecure, prone to error, and vulnerable to hacking.[12] Fortunately, protective measures can markedly improve the security of electronic systems, among them: a paper record, verified by the voter, which is technically known as an audit trail; a ban on wireless components; and a requirement for random audits, conducted at the polling site, to make sure that the paper trails actually match the votes recorded in the machines.

Many states have banned the use of touchscreen machines without a paper trail, yet so far no state has enacted all the steps that experts believe are needed to secure the vote. In the 110th Congress, bipartisan legislation introduced by Rep. Rush Holt (D-NJ) and Tom Davis (R-VA) would have required paper trails and taken other needed steps. Despite wide support, it was derailed by a combination of concerns from the disability rights community and disgruntled local officials worried about tight deadlines and new requirements. A new version of federal legislation endorsed by the new president should smooth these political wrinkles.

Federal law is also needed to strike down one last remnant of Jim Crow. Today 5 million American citizens still are legally barred from voting due to a felony conviction.[13] Four out of five of those disenfranchised are out of prison or never served a day of time. Some state officials have moved to reform the practice, such as Florida's Republican governor Charlie Crist, who moved to end felony disenfranchisement by executive action. The next step is a federal law to restore voting rights upon release from prison.[14] Law enforcement and religious communities concur this will help reweave those released from prison into the wider, law-abiding community.

Finally, the new administration should work with the new Congress to strengthen the Election Assistance Commission. The Help America Vote Act created this tiny new federal agency in 2002 to guide states toward improved voting. Unfortunately, the EAC is hobbled by weak laws and politicization of its work. At its birth, Congress neglected to fund the panel, and commissioners had to meet in a Starbucks.[15]

Since then, EAC has taken some good steps, such as offering states useful help in setting up voter databases. Less effective has been its work overseeing the transition to electronic voting, where the agency has allowed voting machine vendors to choose the labs that certify their products for use. Part of the problem is resources. The entire EAC, charged with helping all 50 states and the District of Columbia administer voting, has a budget of $15 million and only 30 employees. The new president's first budget must substantially increase this support.

Campaign Finance Reform

Perhaps the greatest obstacle to change is the political culture of Washington, D.C., itself. No factor is more profound, or pernicious, than the system of financing congressional campaigns.

Of course, the fact that money shouts is hardly news. Mark Twain, not Jon Stewart, quipped, "There is no distinctly native criminal class except Congress." But over the past decade, the system lurched badly in the wrong direction. Congress became mired in crass corruption, as the conservative congressional majority's "K Street Project" made the link between lobbying, fundraising, and policy more explicit than at any time since the Gilded Age of the 1800s. Jack Abramoff and former Majority Leader Tom Delay are gone, and Congress quickly moved forward on reform, passing strong ethics measures in 2007. But the broader gridlock and special interest stasis remains.

Today lawmakers spend much of their time fundraising—often, most of their time. Funds overwhelmingly flow to incumbents. The presidential campaigns this past election year were transformed by small contributors. But in the halls of Congress, the small donor revolution is just a rumor. As of June 2008, less than 10 percent of contributions to congressional campaigns were $200 or less. Meanwhile, the lobbying industry continues to grow in size and impact, tripling over the past decade.

Stale debates on campaign reform long have pitted those who regard campaign contributions as a robust expression of free speech against those who seek to limit the size of gifts. The 2002 Bipartisan Campaign Finance Reform Act, the product of a decade's effort, curbed the worst excesses and helped point presidential candidates and political parties toward raising more money from small donors. But it did not try to grapple with the most common and endemic ways that big money dominates politics.

The 44th president can cut this Gordian knot, slicing through the arguments that have tied up reform for decades. He should insist on robust voluntary public financing. And he should propose that any public funding system boost the power of small individual contributors to Congress, too. The goal cannot be hygienic, to "clean up Congress." Rather, the goal of campaign finance reform (as with voter registration measures) should be to amplify the voice, and thus the power, of ordinary citizens.

The best way to achieve this goal would be to enact the Fair Elections Now Act, which would provide voluntary public financing for congressional elections. This most important step, and most difficult, has eluded success for decades. In 1994, proposals passed both houses but failed to reach President Bill Clinton's desk. Since then, states such as Arizona and Maine have enacted successful public funding systems. Now Sens. Dick Durbin (D-IL) and Arlen Specter (R-PA) have revived a public funding plan for congressional races, the Fair Elections Now Act.

This strong measure needs to be improved in one key way—to encourage a small donor revolution for Congress. Consider New York City's bold 20-year-old election law, under which small contributions receive a multiple public financing match (originally 1:1, then 4:1, now up to 6:1). City politicians rely on networks of small donors, and the system boosts grassroots organizing. A similar innovative approach would revitalize Congress; public funding systems should allow unlimited contributions of $100 or less. We cannot expect to get "big money" out of politics, but we can create incentives to get ordinary citizens and "small money" into politics.

This also needs to happen in future presidential races. An easy first step may be to restore the presidential public funding system, put in place after Watergate in 1974. It worked well for three decades. In the first five elections, three challengers beat incumbents—a level of competitiveness found in no congressional district in America. Now, only less wealthy candidates participate because the amount of public funding is too low. Early in 2009, the new president should prod Congress to increase the tax checkoff to $10, increase the spending limits, and make other changes. This approach already has bipartisan congressional support, including the two candidates for president, Sens. John McCain (R-AZ) and Barack Obama (D-IL).

A final but pivotal piece of reform is the need to strengthen the Federal Election Commission. This agency, at least, works as intended: it was designed to fail.[16] The panel, split evenly between Democrats and Republicans, poked open the loopholes for the soft money system of the 1990s. The commission should be replaced by a far more independent body, with a strong chair or at least an empowered professional staff. In the meantime, the new president should break the decades-long pattern of appointing commissioners for loyalty to party rather than fealty to law.

Use the Bully Pulpit

A democracy movement, sparked by visible change in Washington and led by the words of a new president, can spread most effectively at the state level, where many of the rules governing democracy are crafted. The 44th president can use the bully pulpit to endorse and push two major local reforms that would make citizens' votes count.

The new president could help restore electoral competitiveness by curbing gerrymandering while presiding over the decennial census—and thus the redistricting that will redraw electoral lines in all 50 states. Congress is so riven by stark partisanship in part because few lawmakers face a competitive general election, fearing only a primary challenge. Gerrymandering, of course, is as old as the republic. In the very first election, Patrick Henry tried to draw the electoral map to keep James Madison from getting elected to Congress.[17]

Today, however, computer software helps politicians draw surgically precise district lines to minimize competition and maximize advantage. And the courts refuse to intervene. The U.S. Supreme Court several years ago declined to overturn the crass mid-decade redistricting in Texas, admittedly undertaken solely to squeeze a few more seats in for the political party controlling the legislature. The first election after the last census was the least competitive in American history.[18] A true electoral tide may still swamp incumbents, but it would have to be at S.S. *Poseidon* strength. Routinely, voters don't choose lawmakers—lawmakers choose voters.

Redistricting reform proposals would give some neutral body—say a bipartisan or nonpartisan panel—the task of drawing district lines.[19] Such a system works well in Iowa and Washington state, and one has just been launched in Arizona. Reform efforts have focused on states, yet several federal bills have proposed a national standard. With the 2010 census looming, it is hard to imagine a new president muscling such a bill through Congress with enough time.

Instead, he can use his executive authority to make fairer redistricting far easier in the states by changing the way the next census counts prisoners. Current census rules count prisoners as living in the communities where they reside, rather than where they come from. Yet those prisoners cannot vote. The result, in states such as New York, is that rural districts have far more clout than they would otherwise because the population of prisoners is counted for redistricting. The new president could change that by executive order.

The presidential bully pulpit would be especially effective to create a national popular vote. The Electoral College was a constitutional afterthought that has proven the exploding cigar of American democracy. Four times, the person who got the most votes lost, most recently, of course, in 2000. (That is not a partisan point: if Sen. John Kerry (D-MA) had won 60,000 more votes in Ohio in 2004, he would have won the presidency despite losing the popular vote by two million). Even when the biggest vote-getter actually wins, the Electoral College often forces campaigns to focus on a few swing states rather than campaigning throughout the country.

According to a study by FairVote, in the five weeks before the 2004 general election, both major party candidates spent more on TV advertising in Florida than in 45 states combined. "More than half of all campaign resources were dedicated to just three states—Florida, Ohio and Pennsylvania." Voters in 18 states saw neither a candidate visit nor a TV ad.[20]

A creative way to bypass the Electoral College without resorting to a constitutional amendment is gathering momentum. States sign up for a multistate compact pledging to vote their electors for whoever wins the popular vote—so long as enough other states adding up to 270 electors do so, too. Five states, so far, have agreed to do this. The new president could endorse an end to the Electoral College—as Presidents Lyndon Johnson and Richard Nixon both did the last time it came for a vote in Congress in 1969.

Democracy as a Strategy

For the new president and his administration, a push for government reform and a renewed democracy must be more than a set of issues on a laundry list. It must be central to governing strategy. If it is, then the president can catalyze a broader movement and transformative changes in the country at large. A focus on democracy reforms has several strategic advantages.

First, it serves as a way for the new president to display early mastery of powerful arrayed interests that threaten a progressive agenda. Any chief executive faces such tests from the "permanent government." Successful ones show their ability to overcome such established power centers. President Franklin D. Roosevelt closed the banks on his second day in office—not recommended for all new presidents—but also shocked Congress by vetoing the veterans' pension, the prime special interest bill of its day. Ronald Reagan fired the striking air traffic controllers.

Bill Clinton, by contrast, acceded to congressional complaints about grazing fees and other moves, showing the massed lobbyists and their congressional allies that the new president could be pushed around. A democracy push can instead help "brand" the new president's program as populist, nonpartisan, and attuned to the massive surge in voter engagement. It would signal to young voters, especially, that their exertions had produced change.

The new president must also avoid the mistake made by Bill Clinton in the early 1990s. After Ross Perot won 19 percent of the vote in 1992 on a platform of reform, Clinton and his allies in Congress failed to ruthlessly co-opt Perot's vote and issues. Those independent-minded swing voters have decided nearly every election since. This time, the new president can focus on appealing to the angry sentiments of the "radical middle," which is sick of partisanship and yearning for effective government.

More broadly, and more fundamentally, democracy reforms can form part of a larger political strategy for the new administration. Transformative presidencies succeed, in part, by widening the electorate and altering the political balance of power. Andrew Jackson, for example, massively increased the pool of voting citizens, first by attracting votes, and then by passing laws to repeal the property requirement for voting. Reform spurred more reform.

Lyndon Johnson's support for the Voting Rights Act transformed Southern politics and made possible the election of Jimmy Carter, though the white backlash vote proved more formidable over the long run, moving the South into the Republican column for a generation, as Johnson also predicted. Roosevelt's steps in the first New Deal, such as encouraging unionization through the National Recovery Administration, gave activists tools for organizing, which in turn built pressure for more profound changes such as Social Security.

The new president has always played a unique role in the struggle for political reform. Great presidents find a way to use their singular voice and role as a prod to create a revolution of rising expectations, thus setting in motion forces that push the political system further. The 44th president must avoid overpromising, and many issues inevitably will crowd the agenda. It may make sense to forge a quick bipartisan compact on key reforms, acting even during the transition to reach agreement with legislative leaders. The next president must follow through with an agenda of election reform. If he does, he will put democracy at the center of American politics again—just where it belongs.

Department of Justice

Restoring Integrity and the Rule of Law

DAWN JOHNSEN

The Department of Justice must be restored to its fundamental role as a principled en-forcer and interpreter of our nation's laws. From their first days in office, the next pres-ident and his attorney general should lead a dramatic change in direction and return DOJ to its best nonpartisan traditions: accurate and principled legal interpretation; ex-ecutive branch compliance with all applicable legal constraints; a commitment to trans-parency and accountability to the maximum extent consistent with national security and other vital concerns; respect for Congress and the courts; and vigorous law enforce-ment efforts untainted by politics. DOJ also should reassess and improve its substantive priorities—in counterterrorism, civil rights, environmental protection, criminal law en-forcement, and more—in order to promote an America that is safer and more just.

Under the best of circumstances, a new attorney general confronts a formi-dable range of responsibilities and challenges. Federal laws entrust the Department of Justice with enforcement authority in the areas of federal crime, civil rights, national security, environmental protection, antitrust, tax, and others. Beyond enforcing existing laws, DOJ plays a central role in develop-ing policies in all these areas and also represents the government before the courts. DOJ also provides the legal advice and direction necessary for the presi-dent to fulfill the constitutional commands to "take Care that the Laws be faithfully executed," and to "preserve, protect and defend" the Constitution. Officials throughout the executive branch depend upon DOJ's legal advice to ensure that the government acts lawfully in all that it does. Through its varied work, DOJ also contributes to how we as a nation interpret the Constitution. In sum, the department is entrusted with nothing short of keeping Americans safe from threats at home and abroad while preserving our constitutional de-mocracy and securing equal opportunity for all.

The presidential transition will occur under the most challenging of circum-stances. The Bush administration dangerously compromised DOJ's integrity and thus its ability to fulfill its core responsibilities—at a time when our nation faces extraordinary threats to its security. Improper political considerations and a dangerously expansive view of presidential authority infected the work of the department, undermining both the reality and the perception of DOJ as a

guardian of the rule of law. Among the department's most prominent transgressions, recognized by Republicans and Democrats alike, are repeated claims
of presidential authority to act contrary to statutes and treaties; infamous legal
interpretations of prohibitions on torture and cruel treatment to allow interrogation methods such as waterboarding, stress positions, and extreme sleep and
sensory deprivation; the suspicious and possibly unlawful firing of U.S. attorneys; the exclusion of experienced career lawyers from decision making; the
hiring of career lawyers based on their partisan connections; and law enforcement decisions that may have been improperly motivated by partisan concerns.

Repairing the damage to DOJ in transparent and constructive ways should
be a top priority from the earliest days of the transition. Understandable desires to be forward-looking should not lead to dismissing past unlawful actions
as simply belonging to a previous administration. The United States *government*
is responsible for those abuses, which carry continuing consequences and important lessons.

From their first days in office and even earlier, the new president and attorney general both should send the unequivocal message, backed by action, that
they bring a dramatic change in direction and tone. This message should convey a critical distinction: when DOJ lawyers implement the president's policies
or advise on their legality, they must interpret and enforce the law in an impartial and principled manner. At the same time, the president's policy objectives
should greatly influence much of DOJ's work—in setting priorities for criminal
and civil law enforcement and in devising legislative initiatives. The attorney
general will be a critical part of the next democratically elected administration
and should be responsive to it, by helping to advance the president's chosen
agenda and by safeguarding legitimate and valuable presidential authorities.

Extraordinary change is needed not only to restore the rule of law, but also
throughout DOJ's varied substantive work, beginning with the development of
a comprehensive affirmative vision for making America safer and more just.
The many areas in need of improvement and new direction include crime prevention and enforcement, civil rights, environmental protection, immigration,
and counterterrorism.

Day-One Priorities

The new president must assume office ready to act on several critical day one
priorities—matters of such urgency that they should not wait weeks or months
and therefore should be the subject of intense and detailed work by the president-elect's transition team. First, the president-elect should move as quickly as

possible to identify individuals of the highest integrity and abilities to serve in DOJ's leadership. Even prior to assuming office, he should announce his choices and work with the Senate for their prompt confirmation.

The immediate installation of an attorney general will be a matter of national security for a nation at war and facing terrorist attacks. Beyond the attorney general, the president should strive for day-one appointments of the deputy attorney general, the associate attorney general, and the assistant attorney general who heads the Office of Legal Counsel, which is the office charged with providing principled legal advice on national security and many other pressing issues. The politicization and neglect of civil rights enforcement call for the early appointment, too, of an assistant attorney general for the Civil Rights Division. Other positions that most call for appointments in the early days include the solicitor general, the assistant attorney general for the Criminal Division, and the assistant attorney general for the recently created National Security Division. Prior governmental experience among DOJ's leadership will be of great value. Of paramount importance will be a profound personal commitment to the rule of law and a willingness to tell the president "no" when necessary.

The president will need to work closely with the Senate to ensure prompt confirmation of his nominees. Early attention should be paid as well to the need to move far more quickly than during past transitions to fill some mid-level political positions, such as at the deputy assistant attorney general level, given the extraordinary challenges facing DOJ. The president-elect also should work with the outgoing administration to expedite security clearances for political appointees and key transition staff during the period before he takes office.

Restore Legal Constraints on the President
Central to the success of the next president's new team at DOJ is the restoration of the integrity of the Office of Legal Counsel and the legal theories and interpretations it adopts on behalf of the president and the attorney general. OLC functions as a legal counsel to the top lawyers in the executive branch (including the counsel to the president), all of whom generally send OLC their most difficult and consequential legal questions. By tradition and regulation, OLC's legal interpretations are binding within the executive branch unless overruled by the attorney general or the president. A flawed OLC opinion therefore facilitates unlawful governmental action and at the same time makes it difficult to hold legally accountable anyone who reasonably relied on that opinion—as demonstrated by the Bush administration's use of unlawful interrogation methods and violations of the Foreign Intelligence Surveillance Act.[1]

At the center of much of the controversy over Bush administration counterterrorism policies has been OLC's flawed legal advice—advice premised on an extreme and unfounded view of presidential power used to justify desired counterterrorism policies that conflicted with federal statutes, international law, and the Constitution. Unless and until formally withdrawn or replaced, the Bush OLC's advice will continue to guide practices into the next administration. The uncertainty created by lack of confidence in the quality of OLC advice also can be threatening to national security. The new administration therefore should immediately restore OLC's tradition of accurate, principled, independent legal interpretation.

The current crisis stems from the highest levels and earliest days of the Bush administration, from President George Bush and Vice President Dick Cheney and their top lawyers, Alberto Gonzales and David Addington. From their first day, they sent the message that they wanted appraisals of legal constraints on presidential power to be influenced by the administration's desired outcomes. Counsel to the President Gonzales' message at his first White House Counsel staff meeting was "[t]hey were to be vigilant about seizing any opportunity to expand presidential power."[2] According to Jack Goldsmith, the head of OLC in 2003 and 2004, "Cheney and the President told top aides at the outset of the first term that past presidents had 'eroded' presidential power, and that they wanted 'to restore' it so that they could 'hand off a much more powerful presidency' to their successors."[3] These directives and signals tainted DOJ's legal work to the point that, in Goldsmith's words, key OLC counterterrorism opinions were "deeply flawed: sloppily reasoned, overbroad, and incautious in asserting extraordinary constitutional authorities on behalf of the President."[4]

Restoration of the correct expectations and standards similarly should come early and from the top. Even before taking office, the president-elect should make clear he will demand that all legal interpretations be accurate, impartial, and principled, and all executive branch action lawful. He should affirm that his administration will vigorously fight terrorism and protect the nation's security *and* that it will do so within the law. The problem in part is one of public perception and loss of confidence, so the solution should aim to eliminate both the vestiges and perceptions of abuse. The president therefore should address the public as well as the government and also ensure that others in his administration, the attorney general chief among them, convey the same message, again and again: in public speeches, in congressional testimony, in a national summit of U.S. attorneys, and in daily interactions.

Ultimately, the Bush administration largely failed in its ambition to remake constitutional understandings and expand the president's power to act free from congressional or judicial constraint. This is primarily thanks to the Supreme Court, which rejected key aspects of Bush's plans unilaterally to detain, interrogate, and prosecute those he labeled unlawful enemy combatants.[5] Bush's failure stands as an important caution to future presidents: presidential abuses can diminish power and credibility for future administrations as well as harm the government's reputation at home and abroad.

Notwithstanding the Court's repudiation of some unlawful and harmful policies, many others remain in need of correction. It is imperative that from day one the president replace the Bush administration's extreme claims with his own well-developed, constitutionally sound approach to presidential power. He should disavow the Bush administration's views regarding the president's unilateral authority to act contrary to legal prohibitions. He should make clear that if existing statutes present obstacles that endanger national security, he will work with Congress to fix the problem rather than assert an untenable view of presidential authority to act contrary to law.

End Abusive and Unlawful Policies

Beyond this much-needed profound general shift, the president-elect's transition team—followed later by DOJ, working with other agencies—should move as quickly as possible to identify all flawed executive orders, legal interpretations, directives, and other actions that require remedy, beginning with counterterrorism policies. Transparency should remain an overriding objective, beginning with the immediate revision of Executive Order 12958 to re-establish the presumption against classification that was in place under the Clinton administration but eliminated by President Bush.

At the top of the list, the new president should declare unequivocally that all cruel treatment—including waterboarding, stress positions, and severe sensory deprivation—is unlawful and will not be tolerated. It is long past time to put an end to the government's embarrassing refusal to concede this obvious point. He should immediately rescind Executive Order 13440 on interrogation, declare that no one in the executive branch may rely on OLC legal advice issued during the Bush administration concerning interrogation, and provide clear direction about which interrogation techniques government actors may use. One good source is the Army Field Manual, which Congress sought to impose government-wide in legislation that President Bush vetoed in March 2008.

Guantánamo, secret black sites, and extraordinary renditions to countries known to use torture also are stains on the United States' reputation as a champion for the rule of law and human rights. All should immediately end. With regard to Guantánamo detainees, the president should order an immediate review to determine which detainees should be released and which transferred to secure facilities in the United States for further processing, including consideration of the possibility of transfer to civilian control for trial before Article III courts. The president should order DOJ to work with other agencies and Congress to ensure that any individual detained under the United States' control anywhere in the world is lawfully held and justly treated. That review should also encompass rendition policy, to ensure that the United States does not transfer any individual to a country where there are reasonable grounds to fear risk of torture or other mistreatment.

The Bush administration kept secret many of the details of its abuses and erroneous claims of power. Immediately upon election, the president-elect should seek access to all such information. He should work with the Bush administration to ensure that all presidential and executive branch records are properly preserved, to allow for future accountability. He should scrutinize all presidential directives and OLC opinions issued under Bush, beginning with those pertaining to national security and counterterrorism, so that he will be ready on day one to correct errors and substitute his own policies. The review should reflect consultation with all affected agencies and components of DOJ with relevant expertise, as well as with experienced, respected Republican lawyers, to avoid even the appearance of partisanship.

The First 100 Days

The priorities proposed below are also urgent. Some may not be completed in the first hundred days, but all should be initiated in the first weeks and months. This will require substantial work on the part of the president-elect's transition team.

The new attorney general should thoroughly investigate serious charges of the improper politicization of many aspects of DOJ's work, with an eye toward public accountability for past abuses and reform to prevent future transgressions. The Bush administration's firing of U.S. attorneys continues to undermine the legitimacy of federal law enforcement. And major investigations undertaken jointly by DOJ's Inspector General and the Office of Professional Responsibility uncovered widespread unlawful career hiring practices. A June 2008 report described numerous instances in which top DOJ officials violated federal law and department policy by basing hiring decisions for career positions in the esteemed "honors" program on political and ideological affiliations—for example, by hiring Federalist Society members but excluding exceptional candidates who were members of the American Constitution Society.[6] A July 2008 report disclosed violations in other DOJ career hiring, including in the selection of immigration judges. DOJ political appointees rejected high-quality candidates, for example, who were suspected of being Democrats, in favor of less-qualified candidates, in some instances because those candidates were deemed sufficiently conservative on "god, guns + gays."[7]

The new attorney general, again with the president's express support, should set clear expectations that partisan and other improper political considerations may never again influence personnel decisions or criminal or civil law enforcement. The attorney general should immediately implement appropriate reforms suggested by past internal and congressional reviews. Beyond that, the attorney general should quickly commence and complete a review of any area of DOJ action about which there exists a serious question of improper politicization. Likely candidates for review include: the firing of the U.S. attorneys; hiring practices for career positions; the exclusion of experienced career attorneys from the making of key decisions; allegations that the Civil Rights Division used the administration of voting laws to skew elections in favor of Republicans; and allegations of pressure on U.S. attorneys to target Democrats.

The primary purposes of the reviews should be fourfold: to put an immediate stop to any continuing harm from inappropriate past politicization; to assess and publicly reveal the full extent of the problem; to provide any available remedies; and to devise safeguards against future abuses. The reviews should include career personnel as well as political appointees and should place a high priority on making available to the public all information that appropriately can be shared.

Some specific necessary reforms are already clear. The new attorney general should review and as necessary amend the procedures in place to prevent the kinds of excessive and dangerous contacts between officials at the White House and DOJ that occurred under Attorney General Gonzales. The DOJ leadership should make clear that career attorneys are valued and will resume their central role in the work of the department. In hiring, special consideration should be given those candidates the Bush administration improperly refused to hire due to their political or ideological affiliations. The attorney general also should consider rehiring and consulting with experienced career lawyers who were pushed out of DOJ.

Institutional changes should encourage ethical behavior from all governmental actors. In addition to selecting political appointees of the highest integrity, the new administration should empower career lawyers to be true to their own ethical obligations and also to serve as a check on political leadership.

The Justice Management Division, for example, should be reformed to ensure the effective use of mechanisms to guard against improper politicization.

The attorney general also should put an end to all inappropriate political influences in DOJ's awarding of grants and in its research and data collection functions. In 2005, for example, Bureau of Justice Statistics Director Lawrence Greenfeld was demoted after he vigorously objected to a political appointee's changes in a press release describing findings from a Bureau of Justice Statistics study on racial profiling. And in 2008, ongoing investigations examined actions of the head of the Office of Juvenile Justice and Delinquency Prevention for possible misconduct in connection with grantmaking.

Openness over Secrecy

The Bush administration's culture of secrecy is inconsistent with our constitutional democracy. It impairs Congress's ability to legislate and the judiciary's ability to adjudicate, it encourages unlawful executive action, and it undermines the American public's faith in the fair and impartial administration of justice. The new president and attorney general should implement numerous specific early reforms to promote openness and accountability throughout the executive branch.

The attorney general should return to the rule issued by Clinton administration Attorney General Janet Reno that required a presumption in favor of disclosure in processing Freedom of Information Act requests. Bush administration Attorney General John Ashcroft eliminated the presumption of disclosure and instead authorized the withholding of requested information whenever a colorable legal basis existed for its withholding, even absent any basis to believe that disclosure would harm national security or another strong interest.

In addition, the new attorney general should publicly release all OLC legal opinions that support the government's counterterrorism measures unless their release would endanger national security or other vital interests. Where necessary, DOJ should issue versions of the opinions that redact national security information and share the classified versions with appropriate members of Congress. Over time, OLC should review past opinions upon which the government has relied for official action to evaluate them for possible release (as well as for possible revision), and also issue general standards to govern the release of future opinions.

Of particular concern should be OLC opinions that interpret federal statutes, given the Bush administration's irresponsible practice of secretly interpreting statutes to allow government action apparently prohibited by law (such as torture and warrantless wiretapping). Congress cannot provide adequate oversight of executive branch legal compliance or consider desirable statutory changes if it does not know how the executive branch is interpreting or failing to enforce existing statutes.

DOJ also should work with the president and other relevant agencies to revise the system of classification so that it truly protects national security information and is no longer abused to avoid (or delay) releasing information that safely could be shared with the public. DOJ should do the same with other systems and practices created by the Bush administration to withhold information.

Similarly, the new president and his attorney general should review the use of the state secrets privilege and develop guidelines for its more limited assertion than during the Bush administration. The frequency and breadth of recent assertions have given rise to fears that the privilege is being abused to shield improper governmental action from scrutiny. DOJ's mission is to do justice, not to win cases, so it should not routinely assert the privilege to defeat meritorious claims. To safeguard against abuses by future administrations, DOJ should work with Congress to enact new legislation along the lines of the State Secrets Protection Act, which was cosponsored by Sens. Ted Kennedy (D-MA) and Arlen Specter (R-PA).

Executive privilege is another legitimate tool of secrecy, in both litigation and dealings with Congress, that the Bush administration abused and that demands early reevaluation. The Bush administration denigrated Congress's interest in having access to executive branch information and failed to follow the accommodation process that the Constitution mandates, which requires the president to consider not only legitimate needs for secrecy but also Congress's legitimate needs for information. The new administration should reconsider particular past assertions of executive privilege, such as in Congress's investigation of the firing of U.S. attorneys, and also issue general guidelines to govern future assertions.

Finally, the new administration should respect the profound importance of the government's willingness to admit to the public when it has made a mistake, even at the risk of deep embarrassment or legal liability. Such openness is essential to democracy and the American people's ability to check their representatives through elections. Fundamental to a system of checks and balances is notice to Congress and the courts of questionable executive action. Fundamental to the rule of law is governmental transparency and accountability. The Bush administration repeatedly refused to acknowledge its grave errors. One instructive example is its refusal to take responsibility for the horrific mistreatment of Maher Arar, a Canadian whom the Bush administration erroneously suspected of terrorism and rendered to Syria, where he was tortured for almost a year. In striking contrast, the Canadian government issued a formal apology, paid Arar C$10 million, filed a formal protest with the United States, and issued a lengthy report chronicling the mistakes it and the United States had made.[8]

New Standards and Procedures

The attorney general (and earlier, the president-elect's transition team) should lead a comprehensive effort to develop, and wherever appropriate make public, standards and procedures to guide the work of the department, both within divisions and DOJ-wide. The ultimate aim should be to encourage integrity and excellence.

To begin, the attorney general should immediately implement processes to ensure the proper supervision of DOJ's work. Some of DOJ's recent failings resulted at least in part from poor internal processes, including the lack of adequate supervision. Two cases in point: former Attorney General Gonzales by his own (albeit inconsistent) accounts did not adequately supervise the process that led to the firing of U.S. attorneys; and on critical questions of the legality of some counterterrorism measures, a mid-level appointee, OLC Deputy Assistant Attorney General John Yoo, at times provided legal advice, binding on the executive branch, without adequate supervision and review. The problem ultimately stemmed from demands made by President Bush and Vice President Cheney and their lawyers for legal interpretations that would support their desired ends. Therefore the solution requires the commitment of the president as well as DOJ leadership to the rule of law. It also requires the new attorney general to establish effective processes to reinforce that commitment, beginning with a system of regular and frequent meetings with the DOJ leadership.

The development of standards should draw upon recent work, inspired by DOJ's recent problems and abuses, concerning how future administrations should go about their work faithful to the department's best nonpartisan traditions.[9] One such report came from the National Association of Former United States Attorneys in November 2007. Out of concern over the U.S. attorney firings, the association adopted a resolution that outlined rules of conduct designed to "promote the essential independence of United States Attorneys in their districts and to promote the fair and impartial administration of justice." First among them: "Decisions by United States Attorneys regarding bringing a case should be made without regard to political issues and should be made in an impartial manner."[10]

Another useful report was authored by 19 former OLC attorneys who came together out of concern over the 2002 OLC torture memorandum. They developed 10 principles to guide the formulation of legal advice to guide executive branch action—principles that reflect DOJ's "longstanding practices ... across time and administrations." The first among those principles holds, "OLC should provide an accurate and honest appraisal of applicable law, even if that advice will constrain the administration's pursuit of desired policies."[11] The OLC principles also detail the internal processes vital to promoting accurate legal appraisals, processes that range from when OLC opinions should be publicly released to a requirement that advice be formulated with the involvement of at least one career attorney and two deputy assistant attorneys general. The new administration should adopt these principles, or some version of them.

President Bush's abuse of signing statements and of the interpretation and nonenforcement of statutes also generated important evaluations by former DOJ lawyers, prominent academics, and the American Bar Association.[12] DOJ should issue clear and detailed guidelines for the legitimate use of signing statements and also delineate the circumstances under which it is legitimate for the executive branch to decline to enforce a constitutionally objectionable statutory provision or to interpret the statute in light of the constitutional avoidance doctrine. DOJ should take care not to overreact to past abuses by creating guidelines that deny legitimate presidential authority.[13] Memoranda by Attorney General Benjamin Civiletti in 1980 and OLC assistant attorney general Walter Dellinger in 1993 and 1994 should serve as models.[14] The Bush administration violated but did not publicly disavow and replace these guidelines.

Also among the areas demanding new guidelines is how to conduct election-time criminal investigations. The guidelines currently provided in the election manual issued by the Public Integrity Section of the Criminal Division need revision, because the Bush administration revised them to loosen restrictions on criminal investigations during the period before an election.

New Substantive Priorities

Also in the first hundred days, the attorney general should lead the development of an affirmative agenda that includes replacing the misguided policies of the Bush DOJ. That agenda should be informed by a comprehensive review of the department's priorities—those specific to particular divisions, such as the Civil Rights Division's enforcement of the nation's civil rights laws, as well as issues that cut across components and even agencies, such as highly effective counterterrorism policies that respect civil liberties and human rights. The new administration should develop a detailed affirmative vision of how the department's resources and expertise can best promote a just, humane, and safe America, faithful to its constitutional commitments. It should work closely with Congress on developing and implementing that vision.

Many priorities will emerge or be refined with the input of experienced DOJ personnel, but some will be clear from the outset and should be implemented promptly. High among the priorities that cut across executive branch agencies will be counterterrorism efforts, which will require OLC's assessments of the legality of governmental action and the substantive expertise possessed by the Criminal Division, the FBI, U.S. attorneys, and others. The Supreme Court's rejection of voluntary race-conscious desegregation efforts in the Louisville and Seattle public schools calls for a major effort by DOJ working with the Department of Education to consider what voluntary efforts could be effective and judicially upheld—along the lines of the Clinton administration's "mend it, don't end it" response to the Supreme Court's 1995 *Adarand Constructors v. Pena* decision on the constitutionality of affirmative action efforts.[15] DOJ also certainly will work closely with other agencies on climate change and other environmental protection initiatives.

Other priorities centered at DOJ will cut across divisions. For instance, litigators throughout DOJ will need to identify possible ongoing litigation that raises issues of potential concern, including where DOJ is advancing a position that the new administration might want to reconsider. Effectively combating violence and obstruction at reproductive health care clinics, including through enforcement of the Freedom of Access to Clinic Entrances Act, may involve reinvigorating or resurrecting Attorney General Janet Reno's National Task Force on Violence Against Health Care Providers, the U.S. attorneys' working group on clinic violence, and the work of the Civil Rights Division. And issues of racial justice suggest priorities for criminal justice reform, discussed in greater detail under longer-term priorities.

Many other DOJ priorities will center in particular DOJ divisions. The Civil Rights Division in the Bush administration, for example, moved substantial resources away from traditional civil rights enforcement areas such as race discrimination in employment and in violation of section 2 of the Voting Rights Act. This shift and the politicization of personnel decisions led to dramatic, costly losses of longtime career attorneys. The new administration should bring resources in line with its own priorities. Among them should be the vigorous enforcement of voting rights and employment discrimination protections and the development of new approaches to assuring full access to the polls. Several early legislative priorities are likely to deal with civil rights, including enactment of the Employment Nondiscrimination Act, the Hate

Crimes Prevention Act, the Deceptive Practices and Voter Intimidation Prevention Act, and the Lilly Ledbetter Fair Pay Restoration Act.

DOJ's Environment and Natural Resources Division will also require attention and substantial change. ENRD continues to defend controversial Bush administration actions, sometimes taken against the recommendations of career personnel. The new administration should carefully review past agency action and litigation positions regarding environmental and natural resources statutes. It should also pursue innovative litigation and policy initiatives, such as on the pressing issue of climate change and a possible water project to assess water allocation and quality issues.[16]

The Antitrust Division should evaluate how best to improve its effectiveness, including by possibly reinvigorating horizontal merger enforcement (about which the Bush administration was very lax), initiating cases to protect against the enduring effects of market power, and building U.S. leadership in the international antitrust world. And the Executive Office for Immigration Review warrants thorough review and reform given the pervasive criticism of the consistency and quality of EOIR's adjudication of immigration cases in recent years.

Then there's the issue of judicial nominations. Through his judicial nominees, President Bush continued an effort begun more than a quarter century ago by President Reagan to move the federal courts and the law to the ideological right. This concerted effort to promote radical legal change—for example, to narrow the scope of established constitutional rights while expanding others, such as property rights—has achieved significant success, with a Supreme Court that now is closely divided on many vital issues.

The new president will have the opportunity to appoint a number of federal judges. DOJ's Office of Legal Policy (and earlier, the president-elect's transition team) should promptly begin the work necessary to enable the president quickly to nominate exceptional individuals and secure their Senate confirmation. The attorney general also should lead a DOJ initiative to develop an affirmative legal vision that is faithful to our Constitution and values. It should examine the full range of important legal issues: substantive constitutional law and interpretive methodology; principles of statutory interpretation; labor and employment law; criminal law; antitrust law; corporate law; environmental law; civil rights law; administrative law; international law; and issues of access to justice, such as standing, access to counsel, and attorneys fees. The new administration's views on these core issues should help guide DOJ's varied work, from litigation to judicial selection.

Longer-Term Priorities

Central to DOJ's mission is safeguarding the public's safety and welfare through a criminal justice system that is both effective and just. This responsibility to protect the public's safety, including by depriving persons of liberty and even life, demands much from many DOJ divisions. The attorney general should launch a coordinated set of initiatives that tackle the most fundamental and intractable problems in the criminal justice systems, both federal and state.

Various components of DOJ possess an impressive range of expertise and resources they can bring to criminal justice reform efforts. The Criminal Division, the Civil Rights Division, the Office of Legal Policy, and the U.S. attorneys are obvious central players. In addition, the Office of Justice Programs should convene key state and local stakeholders; the Bureau of Justice Statistics should gather and analyze relevant data; the National Institute of Justice should commission relevant studies; and the Bureau of Justice Assistance should fund pilot projects.

State, local, and tribal criminal justice initiatives provide promising areas of focus. Although crime is largely a state and local responsibility, federal leadership can be enormously influential beyond the federal system through assistance that fosters innovation, supports research, and shares information about "what works" in combating crime. DOJ should explore how it can best jump-start innovative state, local, and tribal efforts—like the COPS program of the 1990s, drug courts, and programs aimed at violence against women and juvenile justice. In recent years such programs have languished due to both a lack of federal leadership and a lack of federal funding. Beyond direct funding for programs and research, DOJ should highlight models of successful programs from around the country, and develop and disseminate best practices and guidelines. DOJ should highlight as well particularly harmful state and local policies that warrant change, such as onerous felony disenfranchisement laws that prohibit people from voting even years after they have fully served their sentences.

Incarceration Rates

Incarceration in the United States is an issue crying out for DOJ attention. After holding steady for most of the 20th century, the federal prison population increased 10-fold in the last 25 years. The United States at all levels of government incarcerates more of its population than any other nation in the world, both in terms of the incarceration rate and in absolute numbers: one out of a hundred adults in the United States is behind bars. Even China, with four times the population, incarcerates fewer.

These numbers are in large part attributable to crimes related to illegal drugs, which account for over half of imprisonments in the federal system. Many of those imprisoned for these crimes have no history of violence. The costs, both financial and social, are astronomical. DOJ should undertake affirmative efforts to decrease prison populations without endangering public safety. Again, states can provide useful models for each other and for the federal government. In response especially to budget crises, some states have successfully reduced incarceration rates without increasing crime. DOJ should study, disseminate, and implement best practices, which include increased and improved use of drug courts and treatment alternatives to incarceration.

Legal Representation

The nation has never lived up to the promise of *Gideon v. Wainwright*, the landmark 1963 case in which the Supreme Court ruled that the Constitution requires the government to provide counsel for people facing criminal charges who are unable to afford private counsel.[17] In practice, the lawyers that states and counties make available to indigent defendants often lack the experience, training, time, and resources necessary to provide an effective defense, as has been repeatedly and vividly documented.[18]

Today the federal government is neither monitoring nor enforcing compliance with *Gideon*. Much can be done, including the reinvigoration of efforts of some past administrations. DOJ should document the condition of indigent defense representation systems in the states, compile existing national and local standards for indigent defense systems and defense counsel, and bring stakeholders—judges, defenders, and prosecutors—together to devise solutions to the problem.

Beyond this, DOJ should advocate for federal funding for state indigent defense systems analogous to funding for state prosecutorial functions. DOJ should adopt and enforce standards for indigent defense systems to accompany that funding, provide training for indigent defense counsel, and evaluate and report on the extent to which indigent defense systems comply with constitutional requirements. DOJ also should look beyond the criminal system and consider ways to address the severe impediments to access to justice that exist in the civil and immigration contexts.

Racial and Youth Justice

DOJ should strive to remedy the terribly disparate racial impact of current criminal law enforcement efforts. Under both the federal and state systems,

African Americans suffer gravely disproportionate treatment at every stage—stops, arrest, prosecution, conviction, and sentencing. The causes and solutions are complex. The consequences, however, are devastating, in terms of shockingly disparate rates of imprisonment, which translate into political disenfranchisement and exclusion from student loans, jobs, and other life opportunities.

Abundantly clear, too, is that the courts will do little to rectify the problem. But that does not mean, as DOJ sometimes has contended, that the racial disparities do not signify a problem of constitutional dimension. The Supreme Court has held that, absent proof of discriminatory purpose, the courts may not directly enforce the Constitution's guarantee of equal protection to remedy even dramatic disparate racial impacts of governmental action—even on matters as grave as who is subjected to the death penalty. The Court, however, explained that this was in part due to institutional competence: its belief that the political branches of government, and not the courts, should determine how best to address such disparities.[19]

The solutions typically should not be race based, but should address the harms of problems such as ever-lengthening prison terms and the failures of the war on drugs. Yet the gross disparate impacts on African Americans, and the perpetuation of the historic harms of discrimination, provide a special moral imperative for concerted attention to problems that harm us as a nation.

In addition, DOJ should pay special attention to how our criminal justice policies harm our nation's youth, diminishing forever their life opportunities. Most obvious are extremely lengthy prison sentences and even life without parole imposed for crimes committed by juveniles. Another recent such trend is to put children convicted of sex offenses on public sex offender registries, in some cases for the rest of their lives, which in turn may be used to limit where they may live or work. An additional counterproductive policy disqualifies those convicted of most drug crimes from eligibility for student loans. A focus on youth obviously should prioritize prevention and reentry, including work through the Office of Juvenile Justice and Delinquency Prevention and through collaboration with other federal agencies, state and local entities, and nongovernmental advocacy groups and service providers.

Some progress in resolving these and other fundamental criminal justice problems can be made in the first months of the new administration—and the effort certainly should begin then. But real change will take far longer. Criminal justice reform should remain a priority throughout the next administration, with the goal of a more just and humane criminal justice system that better protects the public.

Department of Health and Human Services
Delivering Efficient and Effective Health Care for All Americans

JEANNE M. LAMBREW

The new president and his new secretary of the Department of Health and Human Services face a difficult but necessary health care challenge—expanding and improving health care for all of us while also working to reduce the cost of that care for individuals, businesses, and the government. Fortunately, these are not contradictory goals. Our health care system is the most expensive but least effective at promoting health in the industrialized world. Making health coverage affordable would expand it, and covering all Americans would, after an up-front investment, reduce system costs. The new president and his HHS secretary can begin to meet our nation's health care challenge quickly through a series of executive orders and HHS directives, then weigh in with key administrative and legislative reforms in the first year of the new administration, and then implement the long-term policy reforms necessary to deliver cost-effective, efficient, and affordable health care to all Americans.

One of the most critical challenges facing the next president—and by extension, the next secretary of the Department of Health and Human Services—is addressing problems of cost, coverage, and quality in the U.S. health care system. High and rapidly rising costs hurt families, employers, and the federal government, and represent a growing threat to the U.S. economy. Employer-based health insurance premiums nearly doubled between 2000 and 2007, rising at a rate four times higher than wage growth.[1] This growth in costs directly contributes to the rise in the number of uninsured Americans. In 2007, about 47 million Americans lacked health insurance—an increase of 7 million since 2000.[2] Over any two-year period, 82 million people, or about one-third of all non-elderly Americans, experience at least a one-month gap in coverage.[3] Lacking health insurance contributes to delayed care, more serious health complications, and an increased risk of death.[4]

Uninsurance, however, is not the only contributor to preventable disease, disability, and death. The lack of consistent, high-quality health care leads to higher rates of medical errors in the United States compared to peer nations.[5] Among 19 developed nations, we rank 19th in the rate of deaths amenable to health care before the age of 75.[6] Among Medicare beneficiaries alone, nearly a quarter-million deaths over three years may be attributable to low-quality care.[7]

These urgent problems overshadow persistent, neglected, and potentially deadly infrastructure gaps in the system. Our capacity to detect, track, and cure disease is seriously diminished due to chronic underfunding of public health. Case in point: the continuous collection of birth and death information almost halted in 2007 due to insufficient funding, making the United States the only industrialized nation at risk of lapsing in its vital statistics monitoring.[8] Our ability to react and respond to a natural or man-made health crisis is equally inadequate—as seen in the days following Hurricane Katrina and in the haphazard response to the recent national outbreak this past summer of foodborne illness due to salmonella. And preparation for clear, long-term health challenges is neglected. The inexorable aging of the U.S. population will strain what little long-term care safety net exists, while the obesity epidemic threatens to make children's life expectancy shorter than their parents' for the first time in a century.[9]

The Department of Health and Human Services has considerable, if not sole, authority to meet these challenges. The Veterans Administration, the Department of Defense, and Office of Personnel Management also operate health programs for their constituents. The departments of Labor, Treasury, Agriculture, and Energy, as well as the Environmental Protection Agency, have some jurisdiction over health policy. Yet even not counting these other agencies' spending, HHS's budget comprises nearly one-quarter of all federal outlays—second only to the Department of Defense.[10]

The HHS budget for fiscal year 2008 was $707.7 billion ($71.9 billion in discretionary funding), and the department fields 64,750 employees.[11] HHS contains 11 agencies, has 20 offices within the office of the HHS secretary, and runs over 300 programs. In addition to being a dominant force in the executive branch, HHS's programs fund a large share of national health spending. In 2009, for example, Medicare and Medicaid (including the state share of spending) are projected to finance about 35 percent of the $2.6 trillion health system.[12] While Congress sets the parameters for most of HHS's activities, the department itself boasts considerable ability to influence policy through its regulatory, guidance, and oversight authorities. The new secretary of HHS, working with the 44th president, can address the health system's most pressing challenges.

The First 100 Days

The policy actions taken by the new administration in the first 100 days will signal new policy priorities as well as a change in direction from the Bush administration. For the HHS secretary, such actions should fit with the goals of improving health care access, efficiency, and quality. The policies should also involve changes that can occur quickly and with clarity rather than those that require complex policy or a long regulatory process.

An immediate step for the new president is to lift constraints on the expansion of state health insurance programs imposed by a set of administrative policies established by President Bush. Despite a growing uninsured population, the Bush administration implemented a number of executive-branch policies that limit states' ability to expand Medicaid and the State Children's Health Insurance Program. In August 2007, it issued a directive that set new, difficult-to-meet conditions for states' SCHIP expansions.[13] This directive also required states that already expanded coverage to higher-income children to limit eligibility to those who were uninsured for the previous 12 months. As of January 2008, 23 states either had proposed expansions that were blocked or had existing expansions that they may have to scale back.[14]

The department also issued several regulations that dampened Medicaid coverage. A 2007 regulation eliminated administrative funding for outreach and enrollment activities conducted by schools. Although Congress issued a moratorium on this regulation, it will become effective after the next administration takes office. Similarly, HHS's 2006 implementation of a 2005 law created onerous documentation requirements for all applicants to prove citizenship. Some states reported that enrollment in Medicaid declined because of the difficulty of finding and verifying the proof of citizenship as required by the new policy. Enrollment dropped by 14,880 children in Louisiana, between 18,000 and 20,000 in Kansas, and 13,279 children in Virginia.[15]

HHS also issued a number of regulations that constrain federal Medicaid matching payments for specific activities like targeted case management and hospital payments. The estimated total impact of all of these regulations could be nearly $20 billion over five years, according to the Congressional Budget Office.[16] Although some of these rules do not directly affect eligibility, their fiscal impact limits states' ability to invest in sustaining and expanding needed SCHIP and Medicaid coverage for their at-risk citizens.

The new HHS secretary should immediately roll back or amend these policies. Specifically, the new director of the Centers for Medicaid and State Operations should rescind the August 2007, directive. It has no strong policy rationale, has been challenged legally, and runs counter to efforts to promote state flexibility and coverage for low-income children and families. The new administration should also replace the citizenship documentation with a less burdensome policy. It could give states simple options for how to verify citizenship, as were offered in the SCHIP reauthorization bills vetoed by President Bush in 2007, or accept self-declaration with subsequent verification and enforcement policies.[17] Lastly, the new HHS secretary should extend the existing congressional moratoria on other Medicaid regulations while developing reasonable policy to balance accountability with state flexibility. Together, these policies would enable states to strengthen their safety-net coverage for vulnerable children and families.

Strengthen Consumer Protection in Medicare's Private Plans

The administration also needs to swiftly rework one of the mistaken health policy priorities of the Bush administration—encouraging greater private plan participation in public programs, at the expense of consumer protection and the long-term solvency of those programs.[18] The Medicare Modernization Act of 2003 increased funding and flexibility for private plan options in Medicare. It also created a major new Medicare drug benefit run entirely through private plans. The law authorizing both changes left most of the policy regarding consumer protection in private plans to HHS. The regulation and agency guidance issued by the Bush administration, along with parts of the underlying law, are riddled with holes and weaknesses.

Studies have shown that the per-beneficiary payments to these private plans are significantly higher than traditional Medicare, perhaps by as much as 12 percent to 13 percent. Some of this extra funding has been used by private plans to add benefits as an enrollment enticement. But in other cases, plans have scaled back other Medicare benefits to discourage high-cost enrollees. One analyst, for example, looked at a hypothetical woman with a broken hip in California and found that she would pay less than in traditional Medicare in five Medicare Advantage plans, but more if she were enrolled in other local options. These plans typically charge higher hospital and nursing home co-payments than under the traditional program.[19]

Private plans argue that this flexibility allows them to move resources to benefits that enrollees may value more than current Medicare benefits. These changes, however, increase the risk borne by sick beneficiaries, discourage high-cost beneficiaries from enrolling in the first place, and raise program costs. In addition, aggressive tactics have been used to sign beneficiaries up for private plans. Insurance agents have been offered trips to Las Vegas and flat-screen TVs for signing up large numbers of seniors. Unlicensed agents have been used; some agents have claimed that they are "from Medicare."[20] Strong incentives have led to unscrupulous marketing practices, including providing inadequate information about the options, for example by not explaining limits on providers in the network or benefits, or through misleading branding, such as claiming that they were just signing them up for "new Medicare bene-fits."[21]

The new HHS secretary should direct the new administrator of the Centers for Medicare and Medicaid Services to issue guidance to clarify permissible benefit variations. It could set standards for supplemental benefits like those that govern Medigap, the individual-market plans that sell supplemental Medicare coverage. The CMS administrator should eliminate the guidance im-plemented under the Bush administration that allows a plan to raise cost shar-ing above Medicare's levels on services that are not discretionary, such as chemotherapy and hospitalization. Allowing plans to offer substandard bene-fits in these areas undermines the basic protections that Medicare had guaran-teed to its beneficiaries.

In addition, CMS should strengthen both the guidance on marketing as well as the enforcement of it.[22] It should increase its review, standardization, and limitations on marketing material, which today tend to confuse more than in-form Medicare beneficiaries.[23] This is especially true when sellers "cross-market" other products. CMS should limit the use of agents to those who are state licensed and trained according to national standards, prohibit door-to-door marketing for all products (not just private fee-for-service), and increase state insurance regulators' role in enforcement. And CMS should develop methods to ensure that no senior or person with disabilities signs up for a plan without understanding its tradeoffs on benefits, cost sharing, and the scope of provider networks. Many of these proposed policies could and should apply to Medicare Advantage, prescription drug plans, and to private insurers regulated by HHS when possible.

Promote Access, Scientific Integrity, and Data-Driven Policy
Increasingly, U.S. global leadership is due less to our natural resources or manu-facturing strength than to our ability to innovate and compete in an informa-tion-based economy. This extends into the health sector. Our academic medical centers, research institutes, think tanks, and government research agencies, among them the National Institutes of Health and the Agency for Healthcare Research and Quality, are world-renowned. Strong data systems and research help us meet the goal of a high-performing health system. Data allow us to track problems and devise solutions. Research enables us to understand the ba-sic relationships between actions and outcomes. Systematic demonstrations and program evaluations provide insight on what works and why.

In numerous instances, however, the Bush administration proved to be hos-tile to medical and health services data and research. President Bush issued an executive order limiting federal funding for embryonic stem cell research to stem cell lines derived before August 2001—over the objections of bipartisan majorities in a Republican-led Congress and conservatives such as Nancy Reagan. HHS also suppressed health information (by deleting references to condom use from the Centers for Disease Control and Prevention website), distorted results (by giving unmerited weight to discredited studies on the alleged link of breast cancer to abortion), and discouraged research (by ceasing funding for research on sexual behavior and increasing scrutiny of proposals that include the word "gay").[24]

HHS also edited out some of the negative implications of a report on racial disparities, in contradiction to the science.[25] Richard Carmona, surgeon general from 2002 to 2006, stated, "much of the debate was being driven by theology, ideology, preconceived beliefs that were scientifically incorrect," adding, "I was blocked at every turn."[26]

The incoming HHS secretary should take a number of steps in the first 100 days to reinvigorate HHS's scientific integrity and to reinforce the highest ethical standards in conducting scientific research. In addition to issuing a new stem-cell research executive order—discussed in the Office of Science and Technology Policy chapter of this book—the HHS secretary should assert that all programs will be held to the highest standards of medical accuracy and scientific integrity, free from political interference and in accordance with leading ethical guidelines.

To assist in this, the surgeon general should be granted greater independence and authority. This step would include having the surgeon general report exclusively to the HHS secretary rather than to other assistant secretaries or the White House, and would allow him or her to issue reports or calls to action that can only be blocked by the secretary. The surgeon general could also be charged with annually issuing a clearly written, publicly understandable report on the state of the nation's health.[27]

Similarly, the HHS secretary could issue new data access and support policies. Currently, certain government-collected data are kept from researchers' responsible use, such as Medicare data on physician and drug utilization. In addition, data use agreements limit how the data may be analyzed and published, with no clear grounds for denial of access.[28] The secretary could clarify data access and release policies to ensure necessary information sharing while protecting privacy. This could include the protected collection of racial and ethnic information to reduce health disparities.

Another option is to streamline research and data functions through reorganization. Options for creating a new center or agency for comparative effectiveness research, which could assess the relative merits of therapies and research critical to improving affordability, have been proposed by experts, Congress, and presidential candidates. This could be quickly adopted.[29] Additionally, the National Center for Health Statistics could be moved into the Agency for Healthcare Research and Quality to make it the single source for health services research. These changes would not only improve our understanding of health and the system; they also would increase accountability, transparency, and health system performance.

Prioritize Prevention

Preventable chronic diseases are this century's epidemic. About 70 percent of deaths and 78 percent of health care costs in the United States are attributable to chronic diseases, many of which are preventable.[30] By 2020, an estimated 50 percent of Americans will have some sort of chronic disease.[31] In addition, Americans still suffer needlessly from acute but preventable illnesses and injuries. More than one in five children fail to receive recommended immunizations, with higher rates in certain areas, such as Nevada, where the rate is 40 percent.[32] Only half of recommended clinical preventive services are provided to adults.[33] And injuries, many of which are preventable, account for more potential years of life lost before age 75 than cancer or heart disease.

All this carries economic as well as health implications. In 2000 alone, the 50 million injuries that required medical treatment will ultimately cost society more than $400 billion in direct and indirect costs.[34] One study estimates that if all elderly Americans received influenza vaccines, health costs could be reduced by nearly $1 billion per year.[35] Over 25 years, Medicare could save an estimated $890 billion from effective control of hypertension, and $1 trillion from returning to 1980s levels of obesity.[36] Effective prevention could, in some cases such as helping people stop smoking, increase direct medical costs as people live longer. Yet there is an intrinsic value to improved quality of life for these individuals, and their indirect contributions to the economy are generally high.[37]

The Bush administration did little to promote wellness and prevention, despite worsening trends. Its promotion of high-deductible health plans with health savings accounts arguably moved policy in the wrong direction.[38] Inadequate information plus the need to pay for prevention out-of-pocket (or out-of-accounts) also may contribute to less, rather than more, use of proven preventive services. In addition, funding for public health and community-based prevention remained low and inadequate. This was especially true for family planning services, education to limit sexually transmitted diseases,

HIV/AIDS prevention, and other interventions that raise concerns among some conservatives.

The new secretary of HHS should make prevention a priority. A new council, center, or agency could be created to signal its importance and concentrate policymaking authority.[39] The Centers for Disease Control and Prevention, for example, could maintain its traditional public health functions but relinquish its focus on clinical and selected community-based disease prevention efforts. The new organization would be in charge of setting prevention priorities, promoting healthy lifestyles, and developing policy for all HHS programs, including Medicare and Medicaid. It would become the main source of information on prevention, create a list of top concerns and goals, develop a cross-department budget, and issue a blueprint for administrative and legislative actions to advance the priorities.

This prevention blueprint would include policies for expanding the health care prevention workforce, creating incentives to promote prevention, and developing tracking systems for lifelong prevention. Over time, this agency, center, or council could, with congressional authorization, oversee a trust fund to pay for prevention. After all, insurers have little incentive to pay for prevention now that will benefit some other insurer or Medicare later. A Wellness Trust Fund that pools funding and directly pays for high-priority preventive and certain public health services could make disease prevention like other disaster preparedness: a public good.[40]

The First Year

The incoming HHS secretary should lay the groundwork through executive actions, regulations, and recommended legislation for a more accessible, affordable, and high-quality health care system. While most significant changes to the system will require comprehensive reform legislation, progress also could be realized in other areas.

At the top of this first year "to-do" list is to encourage proven, simplified eligibility rules, and regulations for public health insurance programs. The United States does not have a health coverage safety net for all low-income people. A patchwork of federal eligibility options combined with significant state flexibility yields a complicated and gap-ridden web of rules as to who is eligible for Medicaid and SCHIP. While this allows policymakers to target resources to subsets of low-income people, it also adds to confusion and increased administrative costs for both consumers and the government.

One study estimates that the cost of enrolling a child in Medicaid or SCHIP was $280—an amount that could be reduced by 40 percent by implementing simpler application requirements.[41] This complexity also affects participation by discouraging both enrollment and retention in Medicaid and SCHIP. Numerous studies have shown that simplifying the rules and applications for these federal and state programs can increase program participation among eligible individuals.[42]

The secretary could change Medicaid regulation to promote eligibility simplification. Specifically, the regulation that blocks states from receiving 90 percent matching funds for changing their eligibility systems could be modified.[43] This would allow states to access such funds to link eligibility systems in health to other state programs.[44] One of the most efficient ways to find and enroll eligible individuals into Medicaid or SCHIP is to use income information from non-health programs with comparable eligibility rules like the school lunch or food stamps program.[45] To ensure the greatest impact of these funds, their use could be conditioned on states adopting proven simplification practices, such as assets tests or continuous eligibility.

Promote Health Information Technology

Policymakers across the political spectrum agree that health information technology is essential to improving efficiency and performance. President Bush launched efforts to develop standards, and set a goal of equipping the majority of Americans with electronic health records by 2014. This is viewed as a good start, but it is not enough. Disagreement persists over how to accelerate adoption.[46] Some conservatives support letting the market pace the process. Others, including former Republican congressional leader Newt Gingrich, suggest greater government involvement.

As the country's major purchaser of health care, HHS could do what the Veterans Administration did—require its hospitals and providers to adopt basic technology standards as a condition of program participation.[47] Numerous other "carrots" (like loan funds) and "sticks" (like phased-in requirements for use) could also accelerate the adoption of health information technology.[48] The new administration should also appoint a new, high-profile national health information technology coordinator. The post has been empty for two years. This coordinator would be asked to prioritize resolving issues such as the legitimate concerns about medical privacy and whether the federal government should use only open-source software.

In addition, both Medicare and Medicaid could provide financial support for adoption of electronic medical records under certain circumstances. Medicare could use its pilot and demonstration authority to test different models for implementing health information technology in ways that are cost effective. Medicaid could also use its 1115 demonstration authority for this purpose, as it has done in the past.[49]

In addition, the new director of the Centers for Medicaid and State Operations could issue a regulation that ensures that the implementation of electronic medical records for Medicaid beneficiaries qualifies for 90 percent federal matching payments, and that its ongoing operation qualifies for 75 percent federal matching payments, comparable to other information technology in Medicaid. Conditioned on using common technology that builds on the Medicaid Information Technology Architecture, this approach could jump-start federal and state efforts for over 40 million beneficiaries. Lastly, the secretary could collaborate to allow safety-net providers, like community health centers or public hospitals, to use the Veterans Administration's successful VistA information technology system.

React Quickly to Health Emergencies
The United States remains ill-prepared to address health emergencies or crises, whether they are natural or man-made. Our emergency response system is swamped caring for millions of uninsured who have no other portal to the health care system. Between 1994 and 2004, emergency department visits rose by 26 percent while the number of emergency departments dropped by 9 percent.[50] Funding has been dedicated to protect against bioterrorism: nearly $50 billion since 2001 according to one estimate.[51] But this funding has primarily gone to the biotechnology and homeland security industries, with less invested in public health and hospital capacity, and with little attention paid to performance and accountability. The public health system remains plagued by fragmentation, inconsistency of response, and lack of integration with the medical system.[52] This was seen vividly in the haphazard response to Hurricane Katrina.[53]

In addition to working with Congress to increase funding, the HHS secretary could take several steps to increase the nation's readiness to deal with health emergencies.[54] It could continue to streamline and centralize the cross-agency communication and planning authorities in the HHS Office of the Assistant Secretary for Preparedness and Response. Currently, the ASPR both advises the secretary and coordinates federal, state, and local preparedness activities and response.

The HHS secretary could direct ASPR to increase its oversight of states' use of federal funding to achieve preparedness goals. Twelve states, for example, now lack integrated disease surveillance systems, and 10 do not have plans for distributing emergency vaccines, drugs, or supplies.[55] ASPR could link these states' receipt of related federal funding to developing compliance plans, working in collaboration with other federal agencies. ASPR could also ensure that its nascent Emergency Care Coordination Center, created in 2008, has the authority to lead efforts in HHS to address the national crisis in emergency care.

The secretary could also keep reserve funding in the Public Health and Social Services Emergency Fund. This fund usually receives direct appropriations from Congress for time-limited activities, such as the Y2K scare or the very real threat of avian flu. The secretary also has the ability to reallocate (called "reprogram") discretionary funding from other programs to this emergency fund for public health emergencies. The secretary could annually reprogram funding to keep a reserve in this account as well as seek an annual appropriation for it. This would lessen the need to seek emergency supplemental funding or congressional approval for the reprogramming of funds in the case of an emergency.

Longer-Term Agenda

A number of health system challenges are slow burning: their onset, duration, and implications take place over years rather than days. Their solutions tend to be more complicated, often cutting across sectors and traditional policy silos. The political system is also biased against them because reelection to Congress and the White House is often based on what policymakers have delivered for constituents lately; changing a long-run trend line may have little currency in this context. The HHS secretary should both use the bully pulpit to develop cross-agency initiatives as well as employ existing authorities to lay the groundwork for long-term health care system improvements.

Arguably, the most troubling statistics about our health system are those that show systematically worse health access, quality, and outcomes for racial and ethnic minorities. The infant mortality rate for African Americans is 2.3 times higher than for whites.[56] Life expectancy is lower for Hispanics than whites. Native American and Alaskan natives are twice as likely to lack prenatal care as white women.[57] These differences are not just the result of unequal income, lack of insurance coverage, or illnesses. Even controlling for these factors, racial minorities receive less and worse quality of care.[58] Former Surgeon General David Satcher estimates that elimination of such disparities could have prevented 85,000 deaths among African Americans in 2000.[59]

The incoming secretary could make racial disparities the focal point of an HHS-wide quality initiative. A new assistant secretary for quality and value could have the mission of reducing variations in quality along racial as well as socioeconomic and geographic lines. The new assistant secretary could promote training in cultural competency, access to quality patient translation services, lifelong learning to accelerate the adoption of best practices, feedback on practice pattern variation, and financing incentives aligned with disparity reduction.

This type of work could also be achieved by restructuring the existing Office of Minority Health. The HHS secretary might also consider working with the secretaries of education and labor as well as the private sector, including the media and entertainment industries, to identify ways of reducing the discrimination that plays a role in lower quality of care for minorities. Given the broad social determinants of health, the HHS secretary could also urge a cross-department effort to develop a long-run agenda to reduce income inequality—a contributor to racial health disparities.

Advance Integrated Long-Term Care

Even though the United States has the most expensive health system in the world, it underspends on long-term care relative to peer nations.[60] The historic reliance on expensive nursing home care has diminished but has not been replaced with a quality-oriented, soundly financed, community-based alternative. Medicaid, through legislation, litigation, and administrative action, is now beginning to tailor care systems to community care and individuals' needs. Medicaid eligibility, however, is limited. Medicare covers some home health and skilled nursing facility care, but does not pay for the full range of long-term care needs. The private long-term care insurance market finances even less care. This already-inadequate system will be strained as the Baby Boom generation retires, doubling the number of seniors in the next 30 years.

The HHS secretary could use existing tools to expand demonstrations and state options for community-based long-term care services. For instance, demonstrations could assess integrated programs across service areas, such as Medicare-Medicaid dual eligible demonstrations linking health and income support or housing programs. The secretary could also encourage a reconsideration of federalism and long-term care. States have the primary responsibility for community-based long-term care, yet their ability to invest in such programs is constrained by the requirement that they fill in Medicare's gaps for low-income beneficiaries. Fully 40 percent of Medicaid costs are associated with Medicare-Medicaid dual-eligible enrollees.[61] The secretary could explore ideas, such as making Medicare primarily responsible for filling in its acute-care cost sharing (as it does now for the drug benefit's cost sharing) while making states primarily responsible for certain types of long-term care.

Promoting private savings and long-term care insurance should also be examined since the strain on public financing, given changing demographics, will be enormous.[62] In addition, the HHS secretary should explore and expand complementary public program financing and expand capacity to provide care in homes and communities through assisted living, technology to allow home monitoring, and more community health workers and home health aides. Lastly, options for improving palliative care should be developed as a growing number of Americans die from chronic disease.

Support 21st-Century Health Care Workforce

While technology has increased the productivity of workers in most industries, the same is not true in the health sector.[63] Medical advances, along with disease and demographic shifts, have increased the need for health care workers as the content of care has intensified. Technology has also increased the number of jobs: in 2005, for the first time, health care exceeded manufacturing as a percent of all jobs.[64]

But the overall number of health care jobs masks distributional problems. Not all areas of the country have an adequate supply of providers. Moreover, the distribution of providers by specialty does not reflect the distribution of need. For example, the growing burden of chronic and preventable diseases is best met by primary care, yet between 1997 and 2005 the number of medical school graduates entering family practice residencies dropped by 50 percent.[65] Medical fields such as dermatology and radiology have gained in popularity, drawing off physicians.[66] Misaligned financing is partly responsible, with relatively low payment for primary care and long-term care providers. Undertraining and difficult working conditions are also to blame. And, as globalization takes hold, we may attract health care workers from other nations, but this may diminish their own capacity to deal with health crises like HIV/AIDS.

The HHS secretary could take a number of steps to steer the health care workforce toward new and emerging needs. The department's Health Resources and Services Administration operates a number of programs to fill these gaps; they could be reviewed for their efficacy and could probably be expanded. In addition, Medicare is the primary direct and indirect payer for medical education. Although Congress dictates this spending, the HHS secretary could develop recommendations on how to spend it better, possibly by creating an all-payer trust fund for medical education.[67]

Beyond affecting the aggregate supply of health care providers, the secretary could shape the content of the training. Promoting prevention, reducing racial disparities in the quality of care, and adopting health information technology all could be advanced through the education and recertification processes. More radically, the secretary might examine scope-of-practice laws, such as reviewing what health services nurses, physician's assistants, and others are authorized to provide, to see if they need revision to adapt to current and changing demographics and health needs. The United States may need to enlist a new set of health care workers, such as pharmacists and community health workers, to achieve the full use of high-value preventive services.[68]

The need for different as well as more health care providers could rise if the next president succeeds in insuring all Americans. Massachusetts, which recently implemented its universal coverage system, has experienced a surge of unmet needs that revealed gaps in the state's ability to meet them.[69] This could be the most important long-term policy effort of the new HHS secretary should comprehensive health coverage become law during the new administration.

Food and Drug Administration

Protecting Public Health Through Science

VIRGINIA A. COX

American consumers today are understandably skeptical about the safety of their food and medical products, yet the Food and Drug Administration is struggling to keep pace with breakthroughs in science, an expanding global market, and years of underfunding. The new administration can begin restoring FDA's place as a world regulatory leader by providing the resources it needs to do its job, guaranteeing there is a focus on science rather than ideology, ensuring the quality of imported products by increasing inspections abroad, and implementing several specific food and drug safety measures. Once the agency is able to effectively respond to these current challenges, it can begin to focus on strengthening its scientific base so that it can continue to protect and promote the public health through the use of emerging technologies, cutting-edge science, and long-term prevention measures, such as reducing obesity and tobacco use among adolescents.

The Food and Drug Administration today is in crisis, plagued by a lack of funds to do all it needs to do to ensure the safety of our food supply and health care needs, and suffering from eight years of ideological interference with its operations and policies. This is a potential crisis for the American people, too, because the FDA's scope of regulatory responsibility touches the lives of every American every day in multiple ways.

The agency is responsible for ensuring the safety of our foods and drugs, medical devices, vaccines, blood supply, and cosmetics. It also ensures that these products are accurately and truthfully represented to the public. From breast cancer screenings to the West Nile virus, FDA is responsible for the safety and effectiveness of a vast array of products, and deals with a wider range of public health issues than any other regulatory agency.

In fact, FDA is responsible for overseeing approximately one-fourth of all consumer spending in the United States. Its responsibilities are enormous and extend far beyond the U.S. borders, regulating more than 375,000 establishments worldwide in 2006, in more than 100 countries. And the international dimension of FDA's role continues to grow.[1]

The agency must also prepare to handle such nascent complex issues as genomics, nanotechnology, robotics, and regenerative medicine, as well as threats from bioterrorism and virulent new diseases such as SARS and avian influenza. To do all this, FDA must recruit and retain the best and the brightest in the scientific field. This will especially be important during the new administration given FDA's growing responsibilities and depleted resources, including scientists. Additionally, more and more FDA is dealing with clear science and safety considerations, including animal cloning, bioengineered food, and emergency contraception.

In 2006, FDA Commissioner Andrew von Eschenbach commissioned a report to assess the agency's scientific capabilities, and whether the agency could handle its large mission.[2] The FDA Science Board's findings, echoed by many leading authorities, among them the Institute of Medicine, the Government Accountability Office, and various congressional committee experts, concluded that FDA was not equipped to ensure the safety of the nation's food supply, pharmaceuticals, medical devices, or biologics. Moreover, the Science Board said the agency lacked the resources to keep pace with promising technologies relevant to protecting the public health.

In its report, the FDA Science Board recognized that a strong FDA is critical to our public health. "The world looks to FDA as a leader—to integrate emerging understandings of biology with medicine, technology and computational mathematics in ways that will lead to successful disease therapies."[3] But in her testimony before a House committee, Gail H. Cassell, the chair of the Science Board, testified that "FDA suffers from serious scientific deficiencies and is not positioned to meet current or emerging regulatory responsibilities. We conclude that American lives are at risk and that there is an urgent need to address the deficiencies."[4] Remedying this situation will require a quick succession of short-term fixes followed by more thoughtful but no less important long-term reforms.

Confronting this array of challenges will require, above all, independent leadership dedicated to the efficacy of science and committed to supporting the strong scientific work of the FDA staff, who suffered increasing morale problems over the last eight years. Many experts argue that FDA should become an independent regulatory agency comparable to other regulatory bodies such as the Environmental Protection Agency, rather than its current status as part of the Department of Health and Human Services. Whether autonomous or not, FDA must remain an independent, science-based agency and make its decisions without undue political interference.

Bringing that sort of leadership should be a top priority of the 44th president. Many governmental, academic, and scientific experts conclude the agency is not prepared to handle its current or escalating regulatory responsibilities. That's not an option, given the importance of the agency to the health and safety of the American people, but the solutions to restoring FDA's reputation will take time and effort.

The First 100 Days

The new administration inherits an agency that does not have the financial, personnel, or technological resources to handle its broad mission. Before the new president and his transition team begin to make decisions necessary to restore FDA's "gold standard" reputation over the course of his administration, they need to take stock of the dire situation at the agency.

The Bush administration ignored urgent calls for more funding of FDA. In fiscal year 2008, which ended on September 30, 2008, FDA's budget was just over $2 billion, but a large and increasing amount of that budget comes from industry-paid "user fees" that can only be spent to carry out product reviews and closely related safety functions. The agency's appropriations from Congress have been held down for several years, resulting in a loss of over 1,000 scientists at the agency—despite the increasing workload being placed upon it.

By comparison, FDA's sister agencies in HHS, the Centers for Disease Control and Prevention and the National Institutes of Health, have seen their budgets increase fourfold and twofold, respectively, over the last decade.[5] Yet over the past two decades, Congress has enacted 125 statutes that require new FDA action, scientific knowledge, expertise, and resources.[6] In that same time period, FDA's budget has declined by $300 million in inflation-adjusted dollars, a substantial portion of a meager $2 billion budget, including user fees.[7] According to the Science Board, the agency's appropriations would need to be more than doubled for it to be able to do its job.[8]

Congress, at least, is finally taking notice, having called for increases in FDA's budget, especially for duties related to foreign inspections, in 2008. The agency's current budget dedicates approximately $13 million for all foreign inspections in fiscal year 2009. According to a recent GAO report, it would cost the agency over $70 million to inspect just the foreign drug establishments it targeted for its 2007 good manufacturing practice surveillance inspections, including $15 million for China alone.[9]

In addition to funding, another resource problem is how FDA recruits and retains a workforce that can keep pace with emerging science and technologies. According to von Eshenbach, "Demographics of the FDA's current workforce present one of the greatest challenges we face."[10] Less than 4 percent of its workforce is under 30 years of age, and 44 percent are over 50. Almost 50 percent of its managers and supervisors are eligible for retirement in the next five years.[11] Overall budget constraints have caused a serious depletion of experts and scientists from the agency, particularly in drug review divisions, adding to a turnover rate that is twice that of other government agencies.[12]

Even without bleak projections, staff depletions at FDA are extensive. In the agency's food center, for example, staffing is down 20 percent over the past three years, despite an increase in food-borne outbreaks in the United States.[13] Personnel shortfalls in the drug divisions are currently over 500 vacancies.[14] Worse still, efforts to increase staff with qualified candidates are hampered with difficulties. The hiring system is cumbersome; finding qualified candidates is difficult because a competitive pay structure is lacking; and recent HHS regulations removed from FDA its basic human resources function, further reducing its ability to hire and keep dedicated staff.

FDA's technological resources are also outdated and unstable. Many reports are still handwritten, and databases fail periodically or are not integrated with other important systems. This is highly dangerous for an agency responsible for monitoring and tracking millions of adverse drug reactions, the spread of disease, and tons of foods entering our borders. A recent investigation found that many manufacturing plants are not investigated because they are not even found in FDA's database. GAO investigators found that one computer program within the agency estimates that 3,000 plants export drugs to the United States while another incompatible program estimates that number at 6,800.[15] FDA has currently proposed developing new data systems and updating its Adverse Events Reporting Systems. Attention and resources should be focused on building better systems, obtaining current data, and aligning various systems to better monitor and manage the agency's complex workload.

To get a handle on all of these serious issues will require the president to be prepared to nominate an FDA commissioner immediately. The commissioner is a Senate-confirmed position, which means that politics can often prolong the process. The nominee and the transition team should begin setting up meetings with both Senate Republicans and Democrats to address the need to rebuild FDA and outline the nominee's plans to do so. This should be a time for the nominee—who should boast an impeccable science and science policy reputation—to listen to the concerns of the Senate and build relationships so that the new commissioner can begin focusing on key priorities, such as securing more federal funding for an array of necessary functions, as outlined below.

With these critical budget and personnel efforts in place, the new president will then have to put his power and prestige behind FDA's efforts to perform its various jobs with the scientific integrity and dedication to public service that once characterized the agency. FDA in turn should focus on three arenas— protecting the food supply, improving drug safety, and reducing health and safety risks to our food and drugs from abroad.

Protect the Food Supply
FDA is responsible for ensuring the safety of about 80 percent of the U.S. food supply, with the remainder (primarily meat and poultry) regulated by the U.S. Department of Agriculture. FDA regulates approximately $417 billion in domestic food and $49 billion in imported food annually.[16] Recent outbreaks of *E. coli* in spinach and salmonella in peanut butter and a confusing variety of fresh produce have exposed serious problems in food safety, imposing heightened scrutiny and attention from Congress.

Like most of the agency's problems, some of the issues around the adequacy of food-safety protection are directly related to insufficient funding and increasing demands. Between 2003 and 2007, the number of domestic FDA-regulated food establishments increased more than 10 percent while at the same time staffing and funding decreased.[17] Although FDA is responsible for the majority of food oversight, the majority of food expenditures reside at the U.S. Department of Agriculture.[18] Adequate funding alone, however, will not solve these problems. FDA must also develop better strategies and coordinated implementation systems in order to effectively prevent and respond to future outbreaks.

Ideally, resources should be spent on preventing contamination problems. In November 2007, FDA released its Food Protection Plan to address safety concerns and to try to put preventative measures in place. While the plan is a good start, it does not go far enough. GAO, for example, has made several valuable, additional recommendations that should be pursued, including sharing the burden of inspections and quality control with other countries, hiring third parties to help with inspections, and sharing responsibilities with USDA where there is overlap between the two agencies.[19]

Unfortunately, when the Bush administration released its 2009 budget, it did not include funding to implement the overall Food Protection Plan. Dissatisfied with FDA's response to date, both chambers of Congress are currently drafting new legislation to address food safety. The new president and his transition team, working with Congress, should be able to ensure adequate funding is in place in the 2009 budget to implement the Food Protection Plan.

Protecting the food supply is even more urgent due to the potential for bioterrorism in our food supply—which would threaten the health of hundreds of thousands or millions of Americans in one or a series of assaults and wreak havoc on our farmers and food industries. Even a small, controlled bioterrorist incident could cast doubt on the safety of the food supply, causing mass panic and devastating consequences for the economy. Because such threats would most likely be focused on food processing where FDA has responsibility, it is important that Congress provide FDA with adequate bioterrorism funding to protect the food supply from such an attack.

Key steps to take include providing FDA with new statutory authority to implement the Food Protection Plan, putting into place science-based preventive controls for food, implementing coordinated and risk-based inspections, and requiring food processors to register with FDA annually and notify FDA when they find hazards in or threats to the food they manufacture. These provisions will better equip FDA to handle food-borne illnesses and contaminated food supplies.

Improve Drug Safety

FDA's regulatory authority and responsibilities over pharmaceuticals have changed substantially over time, stretching from adulterated ingredients to product safety to product efficacy. With the advent of user fees in 1992 to help fund the agency's new drug review process, FDA has had more resources to strengthen and speed drug reviews, but it still lacks comparable resources to assure postmarket safety. In 2006, in response to growing concern with drug safety, the Institute of Medicine recommended that FDA needed increased funding and staffing alongside clearer regulatory authority, including a robust postmarket safety surveillance system. The report also addressed the need to provide a timelier notice to the public when risk issues arise.[20]

Recent high-profile withdrawals from the market, such as Vioxx, led to widespread perceptions that FDA and the pharmaceutical industry are not doing enough to ensure drug safety. At the same time, there is a concern that consumers do not have access to important life-saving drugs that are needlessly held up. The imperative is to strike the right balance. This concern was partly addressed through recent legislation in the form of the FDA Amendments Act of 2007, which allowed user fees to be used more fully for postmarket drug safety work.

Over time, this may bring a better balance between safety and efficacy reviews. But the new president needs to make sure FDA, which is now in the process of developing a more proactive postmarket surveillance system to better detect adverse events and more effectively monitor the safety of these drugs in the general public, implements these postmarket measures within the first year of his administration. These measures must include FDA's sentinel initiative, which will allow it to tap into large health-provider databases to monitor medical product safety.

FDA also is going to need to develop a better risk-communication system to communicate with health care professionals and consumers about certain drugs. All drugs have risks that must be evaluated against their benefits, and the public must be made aware of those risks and benefits and how to balance the two. Additionally, FDA will need to develop policies around how it addresses safety concerns with certain high-risk drugs that have offsetting benefits only for specific, targeted subpopulations.

The new FDA commissioners will have an opportunity to outline clear policy guidance that can distinguish between the withdrawal of drugs already on the market and enhanced communication or restricted distribution of other drugs. These new guidelines could help resolve important public safety issues, such as the case earlier this decade when so-called adverse event reports about the irritable bowel syndrome drug Lotronex forced FDA to remove it from the market. Tens of thousands of women, however, begged FDA to restore the drug, as it was some patients' only hope of treating the condition, thus allowing them to have a normal lifestyle.

Yet the drug's risk-versus-benefit ratio required careful restrictions on its use, as it clearly is not safe for all patients. In order to find balance, in 2002 FDA allowed for re-release of Lotronex, but with restricted marketing to treat only women with severe irritable bowel syndrome, and also required an aggressive risk management program to educate patients and physicians of risks.

Reduce Risk from Abroad

The growing number of products, especially food and drugs, being imported into this country presents special challenges. It is estimated that approximately $2 trillion worth of products are brought into the United States each year by over 800,000 importers, landing in over 300 ports.[21] As more and more products are manufactured abroad, the expansion of complex supply chains poses new threats to imported products, including counterfeit drugs and contamination of products.

A number of high-profile incidents, involving toothpaste, seafood, pet food, and pharmaceuticals, not only had serious health and economic implications but also highlighted the large gaps that exist in FDA's ability to regulate products from abroad, and the potentially dangerous effects these gaps can have on the public health of Americans. With an increasing number of problems discovered in products coming from China, particularly in pharmaceuticals, there is widespread anxiety over imported drugs and additional congressional scrutiny about FDA's ability to regulate imported products.

A contaminated blood thinner containing the active pharmaceutical ingredient heparin highlights the difficulties of securing the safety and quality of products in a global supply chain. A popular blood thinner commonly used in surgery and dialysis, heparin in 2008 was linked to 81 deaths and hundreds of serious illnesses. The contaminant was finally traced to crude materials that its supplier obtained in China. Heparin is derived from pig intestines, and is produced in various "home" laboratories across China that are often unregulated. Before becoming a finished drug, the raw ingredient is transferred to a consolidator that sells it to a manufacturer that turns it into heparin. That ingredient is then transferred to at least one other supplier, and possibly many other suppliers in many different countries, before entering the United States. The more suppliers in the equation, the more difficult it is to verify from where the product is derived.

The supply chain in today's global economy is highly complex and often unregulated. China contends that it inspects its plants for domestic consumption, but not those exporting products overseas. FDA inspects domestic plants approximately every 2.7 years but only inspects about 8 percent of foreign plants in a given year, resulting in only one inspection every 13 years.[22] A recent GAO report showed that 80 percent of all drugs sold in the United States are made, in whole or in part, overseas.[23] In 2007, FDA conducted routine surveillance inspections of only a handful of several thousand known foreign drug manufacturing plants, and just over 100 of over 190,000 foreign food establishments.[24]

FDA's records indicated that it never inspected the Chinese plant supplying heparin to the United States because of a mistake in its database. The investigation into the heparin crisis uncovered many weaknesses in FDA's databases, as well as its inability to accurately account for foreign establishments that import their products into the United States. While some 566 plants in China exported drug ingredients to the United States last year, the agency only inspected 13 of them.[25]

Congress blames FDA for not putting enough resources into China, but in fact the Bush administration never allocated enough funding to conduct inspections abroad, and only recently allocated just $3.1 million for the establishment of an FDA presence in China. While it is unrealistic to assume that all foreign food, pharmaceutical, and device plants will be inspected—and even less realistic to believe that all packages can be inspected at the borders—much more must be done to improve the current inspection process abroad.

FDA needs to be able to certify that products are safe before they enter the United States. China has recently put policies in place to register drug manufacturing plants, yet Chinese officials currently only inspect those plants in which products are made for the Chinese market. The agency is in the process of setting up offices in China and other countries, and must be able to utilize third parties to certify foreign manufacturing plants.

The Bush administration in 2008 did ask Congress to amend the law to grant the agency greater authority to inspect foreign food and drug firms that export products to the United States, but the new administration will need to develop and implement a comprehensive risk-based approach to overseeing foreign inspections. It also must work with foreign governments and other agencies to coordinate inspections, synchronize databases, and integrate systems where applicable.

Long-Term Priorities

Advances in science have created new technologies to produce more complex and sophisticated foods, pharmaceuticals, devices, and biologics. Consequently, the agency must have the expertise to understand the new science, and be able to put policies in place to ensure that end products are safe and effective for consumers. There are four particular areas where FDA should focus its attention in the upcoming few years: animal cloning and bioengineered foods, nanotechnology, genomics, and drug and diagnostic development.

FDA is currently reviewing the science behind the safety of food products derived from cloned animals to ensure that cloned-animal products are not different from those of normal animals, particularly in ways that could impact public health. In 2002, the National Academy of Sciences published a report on the safety of cloned animal products, which found no evidence that food products derived from cloned animals presented any safety concerns.[26] Still, there continues to be much debate about the social, religious, and ethical implications of animal cloning, as there continues to be with bioengineered foods, too. During the administration's first term, FDA must conclusively assess the safety of cloned-animal products and their effect on human health through an independent, scientific process.

Nanotechnology is another example of an emerging technology that may have a significant effect on the way FDA regulates products. Nanoparticles are molecules of nanometer scale that are engineered to increase product performance and consumer appeal. But because this technology can change the physical properties of the particles, some worry whether they're safe, and whether there's enough information to approve the use of this technology. FDA is aware of some products under its regulatory umbrella that use nanoparticles, particularly some cosmetics and sunscreens.

From a scientific and marketplace perspective, the future of nanotechnology looks very promising. Safety concerns, however, are already being raised around the globe about potential health concerns and long-term effects of exposure to nanoparticles in products for sale and as those products decay. Over the next several years, FDA will need to investigate such engineered particles, and then establish guidelines for evaluating the safety and efficacy of each product containing nanomaterials.

The sequencing of the human genome has also brought forth new technologies and more possibilities in drug development. One in particular is the use of genomic information to match certain drugs and their responses with individuals—allowing for a whole new field of personalized medicine. This process, called pharmacogenomics, has the potential to bring better medical therapies directly to patients, and to revolutionize the science of medicine. So-called novel cell and gene therapy products are being researched as well. While these discoveries bring great hope, they have not created new therapies. FDA must be sure that its own scientific review and regulatory processes assure safety and effectiveness but do not hinder innovation.

While new developments are happening across scientific fields, FDA is concerned that drug development is decelerating. The number of new breakthrough therapies in the pipeline is clearly tapering off. There also is growing concern that new treatments available through advances in science may not reach fruition because of costs associated with product development. To address this gap, FDA created the Critical Path Initiative to help modernize the drug-development system by creating a process to identify new critical therapies, to prioritize innovation, to work with the nongovernmental scientific community, and to streamline processes. This program boasts some support in Congress, but it has not received the funding it needs to be effective. The new administration should provide a more detailed and focused plan to jump-start this critical initiative.

Expand Consumer Options

A revised pathway to approve generic drugs in 1984 has allowed the agency to make hundreds of new, lower-cost drugs available to consumers. When that law was passed, however, biotech drugs made from living cells (as opposed to the various compounds that pharmaceutical drugs are composed of) had not become a reality, and thus were not included in FDA's new authority. Today, however, biotech drugs are a rapidly growing segment of the drug marketplace, making up some of the more expensive and increasingly important medications available to patients.

Further, some of the earliest patents for these gene-therapy-based drugs are beginning to expire. President Bush's 2009 budget calls for new authority for FDA to approve so-called follow-on biologics, or generic versions of biologic drugs. If FDA is given this authority, then it must be backed by matching resources and scientific expertise to enable it to approve these drugs. In addition, as more and more generic drugs hit the market, and as many more gene-therapy-based new drug applications arrive at FDA, the agency needs more resources to handle the workload.

The White House should continue FDA's effort to seek user fees for the testing and approval process for generic drugs, as it does now with pharmaceutical drugs and medical devices. More and better targeted funding will clearly be needed to ensure FDA has the expertise to determine that new biotech drugs coming to market are safe, and that any biotech drugs slated to go generic are also safe.

Reduce Tobacco Use

When the new president takes office, Congress may well have passed the first legislation to provide FDA with the authority to regulate tobacco products. If this authority is granted by Congress, then the agency will be charged with regulating the manufacturing, marketing, and sale of tobacco products. FDA has fought for such authority for years, but this will be entirely new regulatory territory for the agency—with the potential to save millions of lives and improve overall public health significantly. The legislation moving through Congress in 2008 as this book went to print had a user-fee component that is expected to provide sufficient resources for FDA to carry out an effective regulatory program, without competing with other programs for appropriations.

Such a law would substantially change the advertising and sale of cigarettes and other tobacco products to children. It also would allow FDA to deliberately begin a process of identifying and removing from cigarettes their most harmful ingredients, and it would give cigarette manufacturers, for the first time, a legal process for developing and marketing a "safer" cigarette, if such a product can truly be crafted.

Prevent Obesity

Much of FDA's mission is focused on *protecting* the public health, but it also is responsible for *promoting* public health. Unfortunately, given increasing demands and stagnant resource levels, the agency has not aggressively advanced healthy options for consumers. Given its authority over nutrition and food labeling, as well as over weight-loss drugs, a fully funded FDA under the new administration would have an enormous opportunity to address the obesity epidemic in this country. A recent Centers for Disease Control and Prevention report showed that poor diet and lack of exercise caused an estimated 400,000 deaths in 2000. CDC estimates that 64 percent of all Americans are overweight, including 30 percent whom it classifies as obese.[27] Most disturbing is the increasing rate of childhood obesity and the dramatic health effect that weight has on young people.

FDA has taken several steps to address obesity, but so far it has not seized the opportunity to provide sound prevention strategies to address this growing health crisis. The agency helpfully requires nutrition labels on all food packages and defines terms like "low fat." But the agency has not had the capability to date to devise prevention strategies for obesity, such as better nutrition guidance for young people and the development of effective weight-reduction therapies. This should also be a long-term priority of the new administration's re-energized FDA.

Department of Housing and Urban Development

Meeting 21st-Century Metropolitan Challenges

BRUCE KATZ AND HENRY CISNEROS

Federal housing policy since the 1930s has responded to market trends, changing political circumstances, and the shifting philosophies of the day. The pressing housing challenges facing the nation at the start of the 21st century require federal housing policy to renew itself once again. Left unchecked, current housing trends threaten to undermine national economic, social, energy, and environmental priorities. The new president and his new secretary of housing and urban development need to reform HUD's outdated housing programs, building on the energy and innovation that is emerging from state and local leaders across the country. That means immediately tackling the housing and foreclosure crises and helping New Orleans and surrounding communities finally put the ravages of Hurricanes Katrina and Rita behind them. HUD should also expand the supply of affordable housing, make housing part of the solution to climate change, and create a new White House Office on Metropolitan Policy.

All of these steps are meant to be federalist rather than federal, fully acknowledging the pre-eminent role of state and local governments in setting the rules of housing production. Many housing constituencies would rather protect their piece of a shrinking pie at HUD than strike out for new, uncharted territory. Yet the new president and his HUD secretary must forge a new national compact on housing so that federal policies can align with the changing demographic, economic, and environmental realities of today's metropolitan regions.

The Department of Housing and Urban Development should be a steward of national housing policy. HUD runs a vast array of programs and policies designed to enhance the affordability of housing for renters and homeowners. Through the Federal Housing Administration and the Government National Mortgage Organization, or Ginnie Mae, the department helps stabilize and extend the reach of the housing finance system. HUD also works to ensure equitable treatment in the housing market through its oversight of the fair housing and fair lending laws. Finally, HUD is an advocate for the renewal of cities and urban places and, in earlier decades, was associated with positive efforts to revitalize downtowns and transform neighborhoods of high poverty.

Unfortunately, HUD's effectiveness in carrying out these missions has dramatically diminished in recent years and needs to be restored. Today, HUD stands as one of the prime exemplars of a legacy government—an overly compartmentalized agency administering programs and policies more suited to an earlier era, with information systems that impede rather than facilitate customer service and accountability. For the most part, HUD has failed to keep pace with broad demographic, economic, technological, and environmental changes that altered the wage structure for low-skilled workers, the spatial geography of poverty, and the production and financing of housing. In many respects, the department is no longer even at the center of the housing debate, given its inadequate response to the mortgage foreclosure crisis.

What's more, the Department of Treasury oversees major housing-related tax expenditures, such as the mortgage interest deduction and the low-income housing tax credit, and income-boosting efforts such as the Earned Income Tax Credit, which plays a fundamental role in making housing affordable to low-income Americans. And recent legislation has removed HUD's regulatory responsibilities for the two housing finance giants, Fannie Mae and Freddie Mac. In urban policy, too, the department has failed to adapt to the changing landscape of our cities and metropolitan areas, with traditional policies ill-equipped to address the decentralization of employment opportunities, the suburbanization of poverty, and the altered economic role and function of central cities.

In short, 40 years after its inception, HUD lacks ambition, vision, and relevance. The department is a shell of its former self, diminished in size—with about 9,300 employees, down from 13,300 in 1990—lacking in capacity, unable to respond to or recognize the imperatives of our times.[1] To restore HUD's relevance, the new administration should quickly recreate it as a strong and smart department capable of addressing two crises inherited from the Bush administration. HUD should be a central player in the broader effort to mitigate the harm to individuals and communities from the mortgage market meltdown and modernize the nation's flawed housing finance system. The new administration must also bring a new level of focus and leadership to accelerate the sluggish and inequitable recovery of New Orleans and the Gulf Coast in the aftermath of Hurricane Katrina.

But in the longer term, the nation needs to tackle the structural housing challenges that directly affect our ability to grow a productive economy, build a strong and diverse middle class, and thrive in sustainable and energy-efficient ways. This will require pursuing a balanced housing policy that focuses equally on expanding opportunities for both renters and homeowners. This will require the new president to create an Office of Metropolitan Policy within the

White House to reflect the new metropolitan reality in the United States and drive new, integrated solutions to the multidimensional challenges faced by cities and suburbs. This office would encourage collaboration across jurisdictional lines and enable metropolitan leaders to "join up" housing, transportation, and other policies to address critical issues like competitiveness, congestion, and climate change.

The First 100 Days

The new HUD secretary must focus on four central tasks in the first 100 days. He or she must staff up the department with smart leadership and committed employees, respond vigorously to the home mortgage crisis as well as the persistent challenges in New Orleans and other parts of the Gulf Coast, create new budgets for fiscal years 2009 and 2010 that reflect the new administration's housing policy priorities, and establish a White House Office of Metropolitan Policy.

It is a long-standing principle in government that "personnel are policy." This is particularly true in federal agencies such as HUD that deal with issues generally receiving little attention in presidential campaigns, national media, or public discourse.

Six appointed positions, all subject to Senate confirmation, stand out for their immediate importance. The deputy secretary oversees the "administrative side" of the department, such as its accounting and information systems, contracting and outsourcing questions, and hiring practices. Difficult challenges include ensuring that HUD's workers have the skills and training necessary to excel in today's housing markets and that HUD's accounting and information systems are state of the art.

The assistant secretary for housing/FHA commissioner oversees the Federal Housing Administration as well as the supply of privately owned housing constructed in the 1960s and 1970s with federal assistance. The FHA commissioner will oversee the agency's modernization and restoration as it acts to stabilize the mortgage market, both by aiding struggling borrowers and expanding lending opportunities for new buyers.

The assistant secretary for public and Indian housing oversees at least 1.9 million units of affordable housing managed by public and Indian housing authorities, alongside nearly 1.9 million vouchers that ease the affordability burden of low-income renters.[2] This office will inherit a public housing system in transition and will be a central player in the rebuilding of New Orleans given the contentious issues surrounding the reconfiguration of public housing in that city.

The assistant secretary for fair housing and equal opportunity supervises the enactment and enforcement of legislation to prohibit discrimination and provide equal opportunity within the housing sector and in HUD programs. Housing discrimination persists despite progress since the enactment of the Fair Housing Act of 1968, with 17 percent of all adults in the United States reporting some form of housing discrimination, according to one recent survey.[3] The preponderance of high-cost loans among racial minorities amid the current mortgage crisis also underscores the importance of this position to ensure greater scrutiny of unfairness in the marketplace.[4]

The assistant secretary for community planning and development oversees a series of "block grant" programs, among them the Home Investment Partnerships, or HOME program, and the Community Development Block Grant program, which enable states and localities to expand and preserve the supply of affordable housing and address homelessness. With nearly $4 billion in new resources deployed to these programs by Congress this past summer to mitigate the impact of foreclosures on neighborhoods, this assistant secretary should play an important role in converting vacant or foreclosed properties back to productive use. And the assistant secretary for policy development and research provides critical guidance on policy and budget issues.

The new HUD secretary must take proactive steps to recruit the "best and the brightest" to HUD to fill all of these critical positions. Fortunately, the secretary can draw from a deep and broad talent pool, reflecting the growth in capacity at the state and local levels and the maturing of private and non-profit institutions and intermediaries. Given the ethics challenges that have plagued HUD in recent decades, it is imperative that individuals designated for top positions be of the highest integrity and character. In the initial period of the new administration, there may be merit in supplementing the political team with a group of loaned executives from the public, private, and non-profit sectors.

Crisis Management

The new president and his HUD secretary inherit two housing and community crises. The new administration will confront the continuing fallout from the mortgage crisis and a period of loose and reckless home lending. Nearly 2.8 percent of home mortgages—over 1 million in total—were in foreclosure at the end of the second quarter of 2008, with millions more at risk in the coming year.[5]

The mortgage meltdown hit individual homeowners and their communities sharply but unevenly. The concentration of high-cost and subprime loans among minority borrowers is undoing prior progress in narrowing racial wealth disparities.[6] Foreclosures are also concentrated in older industrial regions such as Detroit and much of Ohio, where communities are already battered by broader economic restructuring, as well as newer markets such as Las Vegas and much of California, where real estate speculation and the proliferation of exotic and risky mortgage products led to unsustainable real estate bubbles.[7]

The mortgage meltdown and foreclosure crisis led to a series of escalating and increasingly bold actions by Congress, the Bush administration, the Federal Reserve, and major financial institutions to stabilize the housing market and mitigate the effects of the mortgage crisis on individual borrowers and, to a much lesser extent, hard-hit communities. Initially, HUD and the Treasury Department convened the "HOPE NOW" alliance of major mortgage lenders and investors to help borrowers modify loans and reschedule payments. And the FHASecure program enables homeowners with good credit to refinance if their payments skyrocketed after low teaser rates.

But these programs are limited in scope. Just about half of the 1.5 million HOPE NOW beneficiaries have received the option of a loan modification.[8] FHASecure has enabled about 325,000 borrowers to refinance since September 2007, a fraction of those in jeopardy.[9] Emergency congressional actions included in the 2008 stimulus legislation also expanded the level of homeownership counseling, and temporarily increased the size of the loans that FHA can insure and that Fannie Mae and Freddie Mac can purchase.

Congress then enacted its sweeping housing legislation in late July. The new law enables a broader group of affected borrowers (perhaps as many as 400,000) to avert foreclosure and refinance to more affordable, FHA-insured loans. The new law also gave states and localities $3.9 billion in flexible resources to pay for the purchase and rehabilitation of foreclosed properties to help to stabilize neighborhoods and home prices, based on a proposal and analysis by the Center for American Progress.[10]

Finally, the law provided a permanent increase in loan limits; modernized the regulation of Fannie Mae and Freddie Mac, creating a new stronger regulator—the Federal Housing Finance Agency; and gave the Treasury Department substantial authority to shore up Fannie Mae and Freddie Mac. Treasury in September 2008 placed the two government-sponsored entities in conservatorship, and now effectively controls these mortgage giants.

Oversight of the GSEs will remain in the hands of Treasury and FHFA, but a broader interagency effort is essential to ensure an effective response to the mortgage crisis and oversee the swift and effective implementation of related pieces of the 2008 housing legislation. The failure of HUD to play a meaningful role in the response to the mortgage crisis to date does not mean the new administration should adopt a similar model. HUD's programs and perspectives are vital tools that must be brought to bear in designing an immediate response alongside long-range reform of the mortgage market.

The president-elect should therefore form a mortgage crisis working group as soon as possible after the election. This group, which will ultimately be headed by the secretary-designates for Treasury and HUD, should assess the state of play in the mortgage crisis, the efficacy of public- and private-sector actions taken to date—particularly implementation of the recently enacted housing law—and any additional legislative and administrative reforms and public-private initiatives that are needed to respond. This working group should provide a series of recommendations that will ultimately form the basis for the president's State of the Union Address in January 2009. The recommendations of the mortgage crisis group should fall into three main categories.

First, the group should recommend a package of regulatory and counseling efforts to avoid a recurrence of the current crisis. Although HUD is not a bank regulator, there is a clear need for better regulation to curb irresponsible and predatory lending practices through measures that include restrictions on balloon payments and prepayment penalties, and require stricter underwriting scrutiny of prospective borrowers. States including New York, Ohio, and North Carolina have taken the lead here, and the federal government should follow suit, while encouraging other states to follow and find innovative further solutions. On the consumer side, HUD should lead a national effort to counsel and educate prospective borrowers.

Second, the group should assess what additional steps are necessary to restore the positive role of FHA and increase the supply of stable and affordable loans. According to the Government Accountability Office, the market share of FHA-insured loans (in terms of numbers of loans) decreased by 13 percentage points between 1996 and 2005, while the share of riskier subprime loans jumped by nearly the same margin. Lower-income and minority homebuyers veered toward the private market, captivated by minimal down payments, low teaser rates, and speedy transaction times.[11] FHA's market share has grown dramatically amid the mortgage crisis because of the complete disappearance of the private subprime market. And the new legislation giving it an important role in restructuring at-risk mortgages also gives it renewed centrality to the mortgage system.

But FHA faces new challenges, including a lack of adequate expertise and capacity to handle mounting responsibilities and a risk-adverse bureaucratic culture, which make it difficult to operate in a rapidly shifting market-driven environment. Establishing state-of-the art regulatory requirements to prevent predatory lending in its programs, modernizing its lending practices, and up-grading its personnel and procedures are now desperately needed to comple-ment congressional actions on loan limits and mortgage refinancing.

Finally, the working group should recommend aggressive actions to help communities address the fallout from foreclosures. In September the Bush ad-ministration allocated $3.9 billion to affected communities. Yet the impact of this and any future funding will depend on HUD's ability to serve as an active partner in community recovery rather than a passive distributor of block grant funds.

As with past HUD successes, such as its implementation of the public hous-ing redevelopment effort (HOPE VI) in the 1990s, the new secretary should provide the technical assistance necessary to inform the work of state and local governments and their partners as well as gather and disseminate best practices from across the country. This effort should concentrate on ensuring that inno-vation can be constantly identified and replicated.

The HUD secretary should also use the funding incentives to promote state and local reforms that modernize the laws governing foreclosure. Recent Brookings Institution research, for example, recommends the amendment of state landlord-tenant laws to allow renters whose landlords enter foreclosure to continue living in their homes unless a new owner intends to occupy the prop-erty. Legislation could also enable foreclosed homeowners to continue living in their homes as renters.[12]

Other Brookings research recommends state reforms that enable and pro-mote the creation of land banks and other "property recycling entities" as insti-tutional vehicles to take over, manage, and develop foreclosed or abandoned properties.[13] Efforts in Genesee County, Michigan, and elsewhere demonstrate that land banks can be useful tools for revitalizing communities facing wide-spread vacancies on account of foreclosure, dwindling population, downtown abandonment, or other reasons. Land banks also play an important role in transforming vacant properties into affordable housing.[14] While the recently passed housing law embraces land banking as a valuable tool for struggling communities, state and local legal reforms dramatically increase the likelihood of their proliferation and success.

Rebuilding New Orleans and the surrounding Gulf Coast is the other crisis the new HUD secretary will confront. It has been more than three years since hurricanes Katrina and Rita destroyed over 200,000 Louisiana homes—about 82,000 of them rental homes.[15] As residents continue to return to the region (the City of New Orleans has recovered about 72 percent of pre-storm house-holds), serious shortages of quality and affordable housing remain. Rental prices have skyrocketed since the storm; the fair market rent for a 2-bedroom apartment increased over 46 percent since 2005.[16] At the same time, vacancy and disrepair have scarred even affluent neighborhoods. And three years after the storms, a substantial number of African-American and poor residents remain widely dispersed across the nation, still living particularly in the Houston, Dallas, or Atlanta metro areas and other parts of the South.

With Community Development Block Grant funding, the Louisiana Recovery Authority operates the "Road Home" program to compensate Louisiana homeowners for their losses, provide grants for infrastructure repair, and offer incentives for small-scale rental property owners who provide affordable rental units. Beyond funding, however, the federal response lacks a strong, guiding hand. The problem lies partly in President George W. Bush's 2005 executive order establishing the Office of the Federal Coordinator for Gulf Coast Rebuilding within the Department of Homeland Security. The executive order failed to provide this office with a budget or significant implementation authority with regard to recovery—two serious systemic weaknesses.

Although the office is perceived to be an important advocate by the New Orleans community, it currently lacks the power necessary to motivate smart, sensitive, and timely decisions by line agencies. HUD, for example, failed to maximize the flexibility of the Community Development Block Grant funds, imposing time-sapping hurdles on localities and firms, delaying smart restoration and revitalization. The federal government largely employed a hands-off approach that failed to mobilize resources and enhance the capacity and expertise of local actors.

Consequently, the new president should by executive order shift the Office of the Federal Coordinator for Gulf Coast Rebuilding to the White House, and then appoint a powerful federal coordinator to build on and enhance the recovery efforts in New Orleans and the Gulf Coast. The current location of the office within the Department of Homeland Security is an impediment to meaningful implementation of its assigned duties. The 44th president should also delegate to the federal coordinator enhanced powers to oversee and coordinate the activities of the principal agencies involved in the recovery, particularly the Federal Emergency Management Agency, HUD, and the U.S. Army Corps of Engineers.

The 2009 and 2010 Budgets

The preparation of the "next year" budget is the first formal vehicle for placing the new administration's imprint on housing policy. It sends strong signals to Congress and key constituencies about the new president's program priorities and innovative ideas. The pressure to set priorities for next year is paramount, as program spending for fiscal year 2009 will be governed—at least through March—on a continuing resolution by Congress.

Thus, there will be immediate pressure on the incoming HUD secretary to declare program priorities for both the remainder of FY2009 as well as the coming fiscal year.

The new secretary should work with the Office of Management and Budget and the White House to develop budget submissions that reflect the priorities of the new administration and telegraph the kinds of legislative reforms that will be sought in the first year.

The secretary's initial spending priorities should help close the gap between wages and prices by calling for an additional 100,000 housing vouchers in the first two fiscal years, as well as funding a new $500 million grant program to expand the preservation of older assisted housing. To ensure that federally sub-sidized housing catalyzes the revitalization of distressed neighborhoods, the secretary should call for a restoration of the successful HOPE VI program to pre-2001 levels. And to help align housing policy with the goals of climate change and energy security, the secretary should seek funding to create an Office of Sustainable Housing, headed by a senior advisor subject to Senate confirmation.

These early budgets will be crafted in exceptionally difficult fiscal circum-stances with many competing priorities. Nonetheless, they also should begin to remedy some of the serious shortfalls in funding for HUD's core programs, es-pecially at a time when many communities served by these programs are suf-fering also from the foreclosure crisis and the broader economic downturn. The FY 2008 appropriation for Community Development Block Grant, for-mula grants, for example, was 17 percent below the FY 2003 appropriation level, even before adjusting for inflation. Similarly, the FY 2008 appropriation met just 84 percent of the public housing authorities' operating needs.[17]

HUD estimates that there is a capital repair backlog for public housing of $18 billion.[18] HUD should couple its requests for restoring shortfalls in funding with recommendations for programmatic reform, particularly around encour-aging metropolitan collaboration and governance on issues that transcend parochial borders.

A New Office of Metropolitan Policy

The new president and his HUD secretary will need to take a new and more in-tegrated approach to the challenges facing urban and metropolitan America. Forty years of HUD "urban" policies reflect assumptions about the function

and needs of cities and suburbs that are substantially outdated. "Urban" policies have focused almost exclusively on central cities and alleviating challenges—such as the lack of quality housing—within neighborhoods of distress
and concentrated poverty. At the same time, more substantial federal programs
and policies overseen by the Department of Transportation and the Environmental Protection Agency operate without any regard for their impact on cities
and metropolitan areas.

Yet the economic geography and spatial landscape of America have altered
considerably, and federal policy must do so as well. As recent Brookings reports
demonstrate, the top 100 metropolitan areas alone now house two-thirds of
the U.S. population and generate three-fourths of our gross domestic
product.[19] These metropolitan areas, cities and suburbs together, have become
the engines of national prosperity since they serve as the gateways of international trade and migration, and harbor the private and non-profit institutions
that are at the cutting edge of innovation.

Moreover, metropolitan areas look markedly different than the ones that existed in the mid-1960s when HUD was created. The populations of these areas
and those employed in them are now widely dispersed, with only 22 percent of
the jobs in the top metropolitan areas located within 3 miles of the central
business district.[20] More poor people now live in suburbs than cities, indicating
a wholesale shift in demographic patterns.

Federal policy needs to shift from an outdated focus on "urban policy" to an
expansive, asset-driven perspective of "metro policy." Metro policy would seek
to create a new compact between the federal government and its state and local
counterparts to enable metropolitan areas to achieve their fullest economic, social, and environmental potential. To that end, metro policy would seek to
strengthen and leverage those metropolitan assets—innovation, infrastructure,
human capital—that drive national prosperity by developing integrated solutions to address the multidimensional nature of metropolitan challenges such
as competitiveness, traffic congestion, unaffordable housing, or excessive
greenhouse gas emissions.

The White House Office of Metropolitan Policy would design next-generation federal policies that empower major cities and suburbs to collaborate on
problem-solving, and "join up" related issues of domestic policy, such as economic and workforce development, transportation, energy, and housing. The
new office would also have responsibility for designing and implementing a
new performance partnership with metropolitan areas. This partnership would
give individual metropolitan areas, starting perhaps with the top 100, a transparent picture of the nature and scope of federal investments and policies that

affect these communities. The federal government could, for example, create an annual Metropolitan Investment Review to disclose the level of all federal tax and spending resources distributed to a particular metropolitan area and its major cities and counties.

Creating a new White House office is an effective strategy for organizing a new interagency effort that requires high-level leadership to force change across agencies. It may not be necessary for such an effort to remain within the White House over time, but placement in the White House at the start helps to ensure bureaucratic resistance is overcome. This new White House office would work closely with key cabinet agencies, among them HUD, EPA, and the departments of Transportation, Labor, Commerce, Treasury, and Education. The new office also would actively engage the true metropolitan experts—local corporate, civic, and government leaders—in the design and implementation of new, cutting-edge policies.

First Two Years

One of the most important tasks for the new HUD secretary is to provide a clear and compelling vision for the department, set priorities for the delivery of that vision, and assess the capacity of the federal government to move from plan to action. The "vision thing" has been sorely missing from HUD since 2001, with the result that public and even congressional discourse often lacks the context or empirical rigor necessary for smart, evidence-based, and outcome-driven decisions. This vision should boast three elements.

First, most federal housing discussions generally start and end with issues of housing supply or finance, yet the crux of the housing challenge in the United States is the growing disconnect between wages and prices. Given globalization and technological innovation, U.S. workers at the low end of the education spectrum experienced little or no wage growth over the past few decades. Workers without a high school diploma saw their real average hourly wage drop between 1973 and 2005, the last year in which full data was available, and those with no more than a high school diploma saw no growth at all.[21]

Despite the housing market correction, housing prices remain unaffordable for a substantial portion of the workforce in major metropolitan areas. This imposes particular burdens on the third of Americans who rent. Since 2000, gross rents (which include utility costs) have grown faster than inflation, while the median renter's monthly income has declined 7.3 percent. As a result, average gross rents as a share of renter income today stand at 30.3 percent, up from 26.5 percent in 2000. In 2006, about 46 percent of the 36.5 million rental households in the United States were spending 30 percent or more of their income on rental costs.[22]

The inadequate supply of low-cost housing also plays a role in the affordability crunch. Although the overall housing supply is still expanding, its growth is not keeping pace with population and household growth, so that the net stock of low- to moderate-cost rental units is steadily shrinking. One reason for the lag is the disproportionate focus on the building of for-sale homes during the homeownership boom that began in the early 2000s.[23] Local zoning laws, land-use controls, and other regulatory barriers also limit total housing production, raise the costs of new units, and often prevent the production of low-cost units. Threats to the continued affordability of housing financed under federal assisted-housing programs in the 1960s and 1970s, shrinking support for public housing and housing vouchers, and HUD's single-minded focus on completing new accounting systems and oversight reforms amid a dramatic housing market crisis have all exacerbated the situation.

Second, there is a spatial mismatch between the location of affordable housing and employment and educational opportunities in metropolitan areas. As metropolitan areas sprawl outward and jobs become increasingly dispersed, fewer low-wage renters can find housing near their work. While employment growth is fastest in the low-density counties on the fringes of America's metropolitan areas, affordable housing—and affordable rental housing in particular—remains disproportionately located in inner-city and older suburban neighborhoods.

Nationally, 45 percent of all renters and two-thirds of poor renters live in central cities.[24] The stratified and unbalanced nature of metropolitan housing patterns places enormous strains on urban and suburban households as commutes lengthen and gas prices rise. Given the distended nature of metropolitan communities, the true "affordability calculus" should include the combination of housing and transportation costs, which now average near 60 percent of income for working families in metropolitan areas.[25]

Finally, residential housing, retail, commercial and industrial buildings, and the transportation networks that link them all together, are major contributors to energy consumption and global warming. Residential buildings alone account for 20 percent of U.S. carbon emissions, with the vast majority coming from detached single-family houses. The average American home generates 20,000 pounds of carbon emissions annually due to the energy it uses, causing strain on both the environment and the residents who are forced to pay for rising utility costs. The transportation sector accounts for another third of carbon emissions, in part because sprawling development patterns separate jobs and houses and, without adequate transit systems, necessitate car travel. Commercial and industrial operations account for the remainder: 18 percent and 28 percent, respectively.[26]

Legislative Proposals

The White House should form a housing legislation working group, to be led jointly by the secretaries of HUD and Treasury, and include high-level representatives from OMB, the White House policy councils, EPA, and the departments of Transportation, Energy, Veterans Affairs, and Agriculture. The working group will develop legislative reforms to submit to Congress in 2009 and 2010. The next several years promise to be a productive period for housing legislation if upcoming opportunities are appropriately leveraged. Reforms can build on the actions that have already been taken to respond to the mortgage crisis and restore the role of FHA.

Moreover, several non-housing legislative vehicles may have greater impact on the supply, location, and carbon footprint of housing than traditional housing legislation. Major tax legislation is highly probable in 2009 or 2010, and the new Congress will likely take up significant climate and transportation bills. The working group should be mindful of these opportunities, and offer a vision for legislation that acts on each of the priorities indicated above.

New legislation, whether on the spending, tax, or credit side, can enhance the affordability of rental and for-sale homes. The next major tax bill should supplement incomes through an expansion and improvement of the Earned Income Tax Credit, which already reduces the number of households with severe housing cost burdens by about 18 percent. Extending the credit to childless workers and other neglected groups and expanding participation would further reduce the number of working families paying unaffordable housing costs, particularly if combined with a modest increase in the federal minimum wage.[27]

The new authorization and appropriations legislation should also substantially increase the number of federal housing vouchers awarded competitively to local and regional entities that are able to implement innovative programs linking vouchers with effective support services and quality schools. And the new tax legislation should expand the low-income housing tax credit program by at least 20 percent. Low-income housing tax credit resources should be reallocated to provide more credits to states where rental housing is in short supply, and fewer credits to states with sufficient or excess supply.

The new administration should also consider new tax vehicles to stimulate the production and preservation of rental and for-sale housing that is affordable to lower-middle- and middle-income workers. That should include exit tax relief to facilitate the preservation of older assisted housing. Also desirable would be tax benefits to stimulate the supply of employer-assisted housing, a new shallow subsidy workforce housing tax credit, modeled on the low-income housing tax program, to boost supply in high-cost markets, and the introduction of a mortgage interest tax credit to benefit homeowners who do not itemize their deductions.

All of these tax reforms should be coupled with federal efforts to encourage (through increased incentives and rewards) state and local governments to lower regulatory barriers to the production and preservation of quality, affordable housing. Federal action should also strive to broaden the kinds of communities that offer affordable housing, to enhance the access of low-income households to employment and educational opportunities, and to promote the potential for appreciation of property values.

This new legislation should recommit the federal government to strengthening public housing, including the transformation of severely distressed public housing by restoring funding for the HOPE VI program to the levels in place prior to the Bush administration. Legislation should also make distressed assisted housing eligible for the kind of transformative redevelopment practiced under HOPE VI. In many metropolitan areas, the assisted housing stock is in more dire need of federal funding than the public housing inventory. HUD should work with Congress to set priorities for the selection of projects, and then ensure that residents who relocate either in the short or long term have the opportunity to maximize their choice in the private rental market and move to quality neighborhoods.

The legislation should focus the production of new affordable housing in communities of economic opportunity in broad metropolitan areas rather than concentrating subsidized housing in distressed urban neighborhoods. Recent analysis reveals that central cities received almost 57 percent of all metropolitan low-income housing tax credit units built between 1995 and 2005, even though they are home to only 38 percent of metropolitan residents. And one out of every seven tax-credit projects sited in a central city is located in a neighborhood of extreme poverty.[28]

To end this practice, income limits on low-income housing tax credits should be adjusted so that the credits support two distinct types of housing developments: mixed-income housing in revitalizing communities where the broadest possible mix of incomes is needed, and affordable housing in opportunity-rich communities where more of these housing units should be targeted to low- and moderate-income levels within mixed-income neighborhoods.

In addition, the next surface transportation law should directly link transportation and housing by requiring metropolitan planning organizations to prepare regional housing strategies that complement the regional transportation plans already mandated by federal law. These housing strategies should ensure that all communities in a metropolitan area, including the prosperous ones, participate in the production of housing for families with a broad range of incomes.

Finally, new legislation should require cities and counties receiving funds from the Home Investment Partnerships, or HOME program, and Community Development Block Grant programs to implement housing programs in concert with regional housing strategies. Localities should not receive funding until metropolitan planning organizations certify that their housing efforts are in compliance with the regional housing strategies.

New climate and energy legislation offers a vehicle in 2009 and 2010 to improve the energy efficiency of housing and catalyze sustainable development patterns in several ways. This legislation should ensure that green-building standards and energy efficiency standards account for older and rental housing, and that existing standards apply only to new construction. Well-executed policy would also enable individual Americans, owners of federally insured and subsidized multifamily properties, and public housing authorities to apply savings from lower energy costs to pay for retrofitting their homes.

Congress should also amend the Real Estate Settlement Procedures Act, or RESPA, to increase transparency about energy efficiency and energy costs by requiring the documentation of utility costs for two years prior to sale and the uniform disclosure of energy-related improvements or repairs. Specifically, a RESPA amendment could require that regional multiple-listing services across the country include information to educate buyers about whether different homes are Energy Star or green certified. Increasing the availability of "green" mortgages could also communicate the value of energy-efficient homes to buyers and make new tools available to support informed consumer choices.

New legislation should also create an Office of Housing and Sustainability within HUD, directed by a senior advisor to the secretary, whose appointment should be subject to Senate confirmation. Such legislative action should enable the department to have the expertise necessary to ensure that housing experts have a "seat at the climate table" and are able to add practical value and insight to energy solutions in the residential sector. The new office should remove regulatory barriers to energy reduction, provide new financing and other regulatory tools to encourage energy savings, and identify best practices to lower the carbon footprint of HUD-supported housing stock. If it hopes to transform private behavior, the federal government must lead the way.

Finally, HUD should advance legislation that would create a "sustainability challenge," a flexible, competitive program in which metropolitan areas would submit proposals for plans to reduce greenhouse gas emissions and lower their carbon footprints. Applicants might propose to concentrate mixed-use facilities and mixed-income housing around transit stations, institute congestion pricing, or expand commuter rail. The Office of Housing and Sustainability would evaluate proposals in collaboration with DOT, and provide successful applicants with additional resources as well as new powers to align and leverage disparate federal programs.

To advance and complement these systemic legislative reforms, HUD should seek a substantial increase in funding dedicated data collection, performance measurement, program evaluation, and overall accountability. Such funding should be provided in a reliable, predictable way, perhaps through a mandatory set-aside from the major housing programs. We envision, at a minimum, a doubling of the policy development and research budget to enable the fundamental modernization of the systems used to collect housing data and assess housing trends in the United States. Such funding could be used, for example, to create a combined housing and transportation affordability index so that housing consumers can ultimately assess the transportation costs of disparate housing location decisions.

The enactment of major housing legislation in 2009 and 2010 will require the department to focus intensely on implementation in subsequent years. The immediacy of housing issues and the congressional window for legislative activity dictate that the first two years focus on crisis management and lawmaking, and the final two years focus on implementation of priorities and more systemic agency restructuring.

Department of Education

Restoring Our Nation's Commitment to an Equitable Education for all Americans

JUDITH A. WINSTON

The quality of our nation's public schools, colleges, and universities—alongside equitable access to all of these educational institutions—is a critical cornerstone of our national security, our economic prosperity, and our ability to compete globally. Although the role and scope of federal involvement in education is limited by our Constitution and the principles of federalism, the new president and his Department of Education must play a central role in ensuring that a high-quality, affordable, and accessible education is available to all at every level from preschool through college. The department can achieve this goal by leveraging limited federal education funds to build strong partnerships with state and local governments, and with institutions of higher education, business, social entrepreneurs, and other non-profit groups, in order to expand significantly our nation's educational research to improve teaching and learning—especially for the nation's poorest children. Key to this effort will be assembling a strong management team at the department to target funds to schools educating the poorest students while working to expand the federal education budget to support strong, consensus-based, non-punitive education reform accompanied by effective educational accountability policies.

Congress established the Department of Education in 1979 with a limited purpose and mission: to strengthen the federal commitment to ensure access to equal educational opportunity for every individual; supplement and complement the efforts of states and local school systems to improve the quality of education; encourage the increased involvement of the public, parents, and students in federal education programs; and promote improvements in education through federally supported research, evaluation, and dissemination of information.[1]

Critics today of the department's elementary and secondary school policies often complain that the federal government "overreaches," adopting laws, regulations, and policies that improperly intrude on state and local education matters, or fails to provide the fiscal resources necessary for states and school districts receiving federal education dollars to carry out effectively their many prescriptive obligations. These criticisms, however, overshadow the fact that most policymakers embrace the education reform goals of the No Child Left Behind Act, the major federal education law governing elementary and secondary schools.[2] NCLB requires states to develop educational standards and assessments and make steady progress in raising student achievement in key subject areas as a means of holding states, school districts, and schools accountable for what children learn in the classroom. Concerns about NCLB are primarily about who should pay for federally conceived reform efforts under NCLB. The debates center on the perception (if not the reality) of an overly prescriptive federal system of accountability, the imposition of one-size-fits-all sanctions, and the failure of the federal government to provide adequate funding.

College and university policymakers also balk at what they perceive to be overly prescriptive conditions for receiving federal funds to maintain eligibility for student financial assistance programs and institutional research grants. This resistance is often present even if the purposes underlying the federally imposed prescriptions are not in and of themselves objectionable.[3] The challenging priorities at the higher education level, however, center more on how to make postsecondary education accessible and affordable for poor, middle-class, and minority students and, more recently, how to make higher education institutions more accountable for results.

The vehicles for achieving these goals will be the two largest grant-in-aid programs administered by the department: the No Child Left Behind Act, which dictates the federal role in primary- and secondary-school education; and the Higher Education Act, which governs grants to postsecondary education programs and student financial aid programs. Congress is required to reauthorize both NCLB and the HEA every five years. In August 2008, Congress did reauthorize the HEA, but chances are high that the new president and Congress will be involved in the next reauthorization of NCLB in 2009.[4]

When enacted into law and then implemented by the department, both NCLB and the HEA will likely include major changes in policy and direction that will dominate the policy agenda of the department for the next five years or until they are reauthorized again.[5] The new president and the secretary of education, then, will have an unprecedented opportunity to formulate new directions in policies and practices by influencing the legislative language of NCLB, and the regulatory and nonregulatory interpretation of the newly enacted HEA.

Equally important, however, is a commitment by the new president and the Department of Education to vigorously enforce the antidiscrimination civil rights protections guaranteed to every child. The students who have traditionally been "left behind" in the quest for high-quality education and equal educational opportunity are those who have the fewest resources to pursue these rights. Therefore, these students depend upon the good faith of those charged with enforcement of the civil rights laws to ensure they are not denied equal educational opportunity because of their race, national origin, gender, disability, or English language skills.

The First 100 Days

The new president and the secretary of education should make it a priority to strengthen substantially the policy and implementation of NCLB, and assemble a strong senior leadership and management team to do so. The most critical positions beyond the secretary are the deputy secretary, the undersecretary, the general counsel, and the assistant secretaries who will administer the elementary-secondary schools programs, the higher education programs, the civil rights compliance and enforcement efforts, and congressional and legislative affairs. The Office of the General Counsel is responsible for the department's ethics programs, and should begin immediately to work closely with the secretary and White House personnel to ensure that all appointees recognize and disclose potential conflicts of interest.

The secretary should examine the department's organizational structure as well to determine if a more efficient and collaborative organization—one that eliminates excessive "stovepiping," or the various subdepartments' tendencies to not work together, and establishes cross-cutting policy and programmatic teams—can be implemented quickly without detracting from the important substantive work ahead.[6] In this context, the new secretary should direct the undersecretary to focus on education reform, covering the pre-kindergarten years, K–12 grades, and higher education.

This office would be responsible for driving transformation and improvement of the institutions that educate our young people in a so-called "preschool through 16" model. The secretary should establish a few unified priority areas that would enhance coordination and collaboration across the department on critical education reform issues, among them teacher quality, improving the linkage between K–12 and postsecondary education, and the delivery of quality education services among students receiving special education and English-language learners.

The secretary also should begin immediately to develop an open dialogue with critical stakeholders at all levels of government and leaders in the education, business, and non-profit communities. The objective: to develop and implement a consultative and collaborative framework for productive federal-state and public-private partnerships to push education reform initiatives. The new president and the secretary of education also should build consensus on policy priorities for NCLB reauthorization and execution.

In the first 100 days the secretary and his top aides also will need to develop budget proposals working with the Office of Management and Budget to address prior year flat funding and underfunding of currently authorized education programs for fiscal year 2009, which ends September 30, 2009. Increased funding is crucial. President Bush's FY2009 budget proposal included only $59.2 billion for the department, freezing its budget at the FY2008 omnibus level. Funding for 47 education programs was eliminated, and the federal government's investment in education programs was reduced by more than $3.2 billion under this proposal.[7]

What's worse, NCLB was underfunded again by President Bush.[8] He proposed only a 2.9 percent increase for a total of $14.3 billion—even though the authorized funding level is $25 billion and the proposed increase lower than the rate of inflation. The budget ignores also the significant increase in eligible Title I children—educationally disadvantaged and poor students—because of the number of families who have fallen into poverty under the Bush administration's eight years in office. The need to boost federal funding for NCLB is also evident in the cumulative $85.6 billion shortfall in funding over the six-year life of NCLB.

Especially egregious is the poor funding for special education of children with disabilities under President Bush's FY2009 budget. Funding would have increased only 3 percent to $11.3 billion under the Bush budget proposal.[9] The proposed level represented only 17.1 percent of the national average per-pupil expenditures toward meeting the excess cost of educating disabled students. Indeed, the proposed amount was less than half of the amount (40 percent) promised by Congress when the Individuals with Disabilities Education Act was enacted in 1975. The funding proposed to support special education was $10.2 billion short of the FY2009 authorized level of $21.5 billion.

The First Year

During the first year of the new administration, the department should: strengthen education accountability measures; propose increases in the program budgets of those programs that enhance state and local capacity to use technology more effectively; collect and analyze data to improve teaching and learning based on measurable results; and strengthen the federal education research function.

More specifically, the Department of Education should complete work on the new administration's NCLB reauthorization proposal, addressing detailed changes and initiatives in a variety of arenas. One focus should be on teacher quality, distribution, incentives, performance, and evaluation. Only by improving the overarching teacher-student experience in a quality management setting can we expect our teachers to perform to the best of their abilities.

Another focus should be on efforts to strengthen state capacity in P–16 data collection and analysis. Multiple, reliable measures of student progress and achievement are essential in determining whether progress is being made, and in ensuring the department can hold states and local school districts accountable for teaching and learning. To craft different strategies for schools needing improvement requires the ability to conduct effective data-driven decision making.

A third focus should be the more effective and transparent use of the secretary's waiver authority to stimulate innovation and research to improve teaching and learning.[10] Federal education law permits the secretary to waive certain statutory provisions and regulations to provide states and school districts with flexibility to meet the unique learning needs of their students and to provide the opportunity to implement innovative practices.

School districts, for example, may be granted a waiver to implement effective alternatives to the annual burdensome testing regimens prescribed by NCLB for measuring student achievement and academic progress. Or, the waiver may permit otherwise-restricted professional development grant funds to be used not only to improve math and science teaching but also literacy and writing when a needs assessment suggests overall student achievement may be improved.

The secretary can also employ his or her bully pulpit to drive high school reform at state and school district levels that includes accountability for low graduation rates and meaningful educational growth requirements for all students regardless of race, ethnicity, gender, English-language skills, or disability. In particular, the secretary and the department should devote significant federal attention to so-called "dropout factories," or those high schools with exceedingly low graduation rates and their feeder primary schools. Finally, the secretary will need to more intelligently fund research that is useful and readily disseminated to principals, teachers, and teacher-training institutions. This type of non-punitive federal support for states and school districts is essential to help school administrators and teachers better engage with their pupils.

Two equally important tasks will be a renewed emphasis on children with disabilities and pre-kindergarten children. The new administration will need to develop proposals for the 2009 reauthorization of the Individuals with Disabilities Education Act to ensure that the civil rights and due process protections of disabled children receiving special education continue to be rigorous and aligned with the achievement and accountability goals developed in the reauthorization of NCLB. Similarly, the new administration will need to strengthen the commitment of the federal government to support and advocate for universal early childhood/pre-K education as a means of insuring the greatest return on the investment in the nation's schools. Research demonstrates the long-term positive effects that early childhood education can have on students and adults over time.[11]

Finally, the new administration will need to close the college achievement gap as a means of ensuring that all children have the opportunity to meaningfully participate in the 21st-century American economy. The goal must be to improve the department's national data collection system for measuring college enrollment, which is a challenging measure within the P–16 pipeline, to enable researchers to evaluate programmatic success. But the new secretary of education should also consider engaging the public broadly, through regional and town hall meetings among other methods, to discuss the appropriate federal role and responsibility in the achievement of excellence and equity in the nation's schools and colleges. These "road shows" would highlight the collaborative partnership framework the department intends to use in pursuing its education reform goals.

Postsecondary Education

The new administration and secretary of education will also need to complete the regulatory and nonregulatory implementation of HEA. The new secretary must concentrate on enhancements in the context of negotiated rulemaking and nonregulatory guidance with other stakeholders, addressing changes to or enhancement of policies in a range of areas. A top priority must be teacher recruitment, preparation, and professional development.

Professional development must be focused on incentives that can improve teaching and learning and are reflected in student achievement outcomes. For example, Title II of the HEA is one vehicle that may be utilized for this purpose. It currently funds "teacher quality enhancement grants for states" to improve student achievement and the quality of the teaching force through improved teacher preparation and professional development.[12] States are explicitly authorized to use funds to develop and implement mechanisms to ensure that school districts can effectively recruit highly qualified teachers and reward principals and teachers whose students are making significant progress in academic achievement.

The mechanisms that may be used include performance-based compensation systems.[13] Among other things, Title II funding could be significantly increased for this purpose, and the legislation should be amended to encourage states and districts to develop incentives and other options for rewarding teacher performance to increase student achievement beyond traditional pay increases for seniority and additional certification.

On the financial front, a number of reforms are in order. The best place to begin would be to simplify the student financial assistance application process—as mandated by Congress when HEA was reauthorized in August 2008—since today it is too complex for many incoming college students and their parents to grasp. In addition, the developing student loan credit "crunch," precipitated in large measure by the recent mortgage-lending debacle, limits the availability of capital at favorable rates—making student lending less profitable and causing a number of student-lending companies to withdraw from the market or discontinue loans to students in community colleges and some four-year colleges. Lenders are eliminating or reducing student lending even though the government guarantees student loans at nearly full value.

The Bush administration and Congress in 2008 took some important steps to help ensure students will have continued access to college financing, such as expanding the capacity of the Direct Student Loan Program to make direct loans to students and enacting the Ensuring Continued Access to Student Loans Act to help lenders raise money to make new loans.[14] Yet continued instability in the credit markets will require the department to continue to monitor the situation closely, take administrative action where necessary, and encourage further legislative initiatives if required.

In addition the department needs to reduce the cost of student loans and make loan repayment more manageable, including the creation of more opportunities for loan forgiveness for entering critical occupations or for volunteering for community service or mentoring in public schools. For students attending non-elite colleges and community colleges in particular, the department needs to expand access to low-cost student loans,[15] including the Direct Student Loan Program. The department should also explore opportunities to ease the administrative burden of operating the Direct Student Loan Program for smaller institutions, and enact a tuition tax credit program to reduce the burden and costs of postsecondary education.

Equally vital but often overlooked is the role the department could play to support, strengthen, and encourage effective working partnerships among pre-K through grade 12 school systems, community colleges, and other institutions of higher education and businesses that are geared to the 21st-century workplace. Programs and initiatives in this arena would seek to improve college readiness and work-life success by aligning high school graduation standards and coursework to prepare students effectively for postsecondary education and career development in today's global competitive economy.

Specifically, the department could support efforts to ensure that state standards at all elementary and secondary levels create a trajectory that matches high school graduation requirements with state university admission standards. The department should strengthen student access to challenging and advanced mathematics and science courses, including increases in the quality, quantity, and diversity of the mathematics and science teacher workforce, and the development of evidence-based studies that contribute to the understanding of how students effectively learn mathematics and science. The department should lend significant support to a related effort central to our national security interests and global competitiveness: an expansion of foreign language programs at both the secondary and postsecondary levels.

Finally, the department needs to recognize the high degree of mobility among college students by supporting the development of better data and management systems that can readily manage the efficient transfer of credits from one institution to another.[16] More seamless coordination as students move from high school to community colleges to four-year colleges and universities to productive work opportunities would enrich our postsecondary education system, and would create new information-sharing collaborations and joint ventures with the private sector.

Equal Educational Opportunities
The civil rights compliance and enforcement authority of the Department of Education is traditionally a critical responsibility of the federal government. Title VI of the Civil Rights Act prohibits race, national origin, and color discrimination by recipients of federal financial assistance. Title IX of the Education Amendments of 1972 prohibits sex discrimination in education programs. And Section 504 of the Rehabilitation Act of 1973 and the Americans with Disabilities Act prohibit discrimination against disabled students.

During the Bush administration, the department's Office for Civil Rights was variously described as "missing in action" or pursuing a "negative agenda" that discouraged legally permissible efforts to enhance racial and ethnic diversity in our educational institutions.[17] The lack of strong leadership at the top and the insular position of OCR within the department, marginalized the involvement of the office in education reform policy. This is exceedingly unfortunate since the implementation of NCLB provided the leverage to form cross-cutting departmental teams addressing civil rights-related compliance issues under NCLB,[18] HEA, and the Individuals with Disabilities Education Act.

These important tasks under the new administration will require more effective use of resources. In fiscal year 1996, OCR had a budget of $55 million and a full-time equivalent staff of 744. Ten years later, OCR had a budget of $91 million—an annualized increase of more than 7 percent even taking inflation into account—and yet OCR maintained a smaller full-time equivalent staff of 630. The results of this downsizing are evident in the results of OCR's compliance reviews, which are major OCR-initiated investigative tools to uncover and resolve discriminatory practices in education programs, and in its civil rights enforcement efforts generally. In 1996, OCR initiated 146 compliance reviews and resolved 173. In 2006, it initiated nine compliance reviews and resolved only 72.[19]

OCR should also enhance its capacity to provide technical assistance to help school districts understand legally available voluntary options to eliminate racial and ethnic isolation in schools, and diversity in colleges and universities. Accordingly, the department should issue guidance to school districts on allowable voluntary school integration programs to help them respond to the Supreme Court's Seattle and Louisville cases—*Parents Involved in Community Schools Inc. v. Seattle School District* and *Meredith v. Board of Education*—which substantially narrowed the ability of school districts to voluntarily desegregate schools, reduce racial isolation among students, and increase racial and ethnic diversity in schools and classrooms.[20]

In addition, the secretary should reverse departmental guidance documents that disregarded NCLB's civil rights provisions and decreed that supplemental service providers that receive funding derived from Title I allotments are not recipients of federal funds and therefore not bound by federal civil rights statutes, including Title VI of the Civil Rights Act, Title IX of the Education Amendments, and section 504 of the Rehabilitation Act.[21, 22]

These two actions would guide school districts in understanding how to increase diversity in schools and classrooms within the complicated legal framework established by the Supreme Court, and help to ensure access to equal educational opportunity for all children in schools and programs receiving federal funds.

The new president and secretary of education should also undertake a full-scale management audit of the work of OCR to determine how its resources are utilized, and the extent to which it has effectively carried out its civil rights compliance and enforcement authority. The new administration should also require OCR to undertake compliance reviews of practices that may disadvantage students who are disabled or members of racial and ethnic minority groups.

Specifically, the department needs to ensure access to comparable and equitable services for disabled students, students of color, and English Language Learner students in public charter schools. Equally important to disabled students, students of color, and ELL students is access to quality supplemental education services and the range of services available under NCLB to such students through supplemental education services providers.

OCR also has an obligation to ensure all students have access to Advanced Placement courses and specialized curriculum offerings and programs such as the International Baccalaureate program, college preparatory courses, and Gifted and Talented programs offered as part of the regular program or after school. In addition, access to guidance and counseling on college admission, financial aid, and careers for all students regardless of race, ethnicity, sex, English-language ability, and disability should be a top priority.[23]

This last step is critical to ensure that the inappropriate tracking of minority children into lower-expectation classes and the overrepresentation of children of color in special education and disciplinary actions is swiftly corrected. This focus should also ensure that labeling children as limited-English speakers does not postpone accountability requirements under NCLB.

Finally, in the area of special education, states and school districts are obligated to implement appropriately prescriptive federal rules under the Individuals with Disabilities Education Act, NCLB, the Americans with Disabilities Act, and Section 504 of the Rehabilitation Act of 1973. The opportunity for conflicting or inconsistent interpretation and application of the policies underlying each of these provisions is great, and disabled children are potentially harmed by such conflicts or inconsistencies. The potential for confusion within schools is also significant.

Longer-Term Agenda

Among the most far-reaching long-term solutions now under debate in educational circles are those offered by University of California, Berkeley law professor Goodwin Liu.[24] He concludes that disparities in school funding among states are significant, and are less the result of the willingness of states to spend and more a matter of capacity.[25] Therefore, he argues that only federal intervention will address this barrier to equal educational opportunity in the least-wealthy states, which also happen to be the states with a large percentage of poor and minority children most in need of educational services.[26]

Professor Liu provides a compelling analysis of interstate educational inequality that is demonstrably reflected in "educational standards, resources, and outcomes showing that the disparities disproportionately burden children who are poor, minority, or limited in English proficiency."[27] At the federal level, a first step toward ameliorating these disparities is to reform the Title I funding formula for states, which determines the amount of federal funds that flow to school districts with high levels of poor children, a disproportionate number of whom are minority and educationally disadvantaged students.

Professor Liu proposes to eliminate the "state expenditure factor," which ties each state's Title I allocation to the state's average per-pupil expenditure—a practice that exacerbates already existing interstate education funding disparities.[28] In lieu of the state expenditure factor, Title I funds would be allocated "in proportion to each state's share of poor children," with a cost-factor adjustment related to geographic differences.[29]

The second step proposed by Professor Liu: the creation of a national foundation plan of federal aid to ensure a decent floor of education resources in all states.[30] The Liu Foundation Plan is far too complex to be adequately described here, but briefly the plan would involve pupil-weighted formulas, minimum state effort, and a federal matching rate, among other factors. In a simulation of possible approaches, Professor Liu estimated in 2006 that an effective foundation plan would require an additional $30 billion in education funds annually—over and above the $13 billion then appropriated for Title I allocations to the states.[31]

Third, Liu would create a federal fund and other incentives to support nongovernmental organizations in the development of national education standards. These standards would be made available to states for voluntary adoption.[32] The idea, he says, would be to "combine the idea of a common core of knowledge and abilities essential to full membership and participation in society with state and local flexibility to design curriculum, instruction, and assessments geared toward the common core."[33] The new president should link his proposal for achieving funding equity and encouraging and supporting externally developed national standards with a bold initiative such as Liu's in order to upgrade the teaching profession and ensure that high-quality teaching is rewarded and that teachers are treated and compensated as the professionals they are.

In addition, the department needs to increase the supply and quality of public school teachers to raise substantially both student achievement across the board in core subject areas and students' ability to engage in critical thinking. And the department needs to support, fund, and encourage the development of teacher performance and accountability systems that provide substantial incentives to new teachers and senior teachers to improve student achievement outcomes that are measurable and can be replicated across disparate demographic areas.

Ensuring the availability and quality of universal early childhood/pre-K education should be another long-term goal. Our nation needs to guarantee that all children (notably including English-language-limited students and poor children of parents with limited education) are ready to learn when they enter first grade. And we must ratchet up the reform of both the middle school and high school curriculum that prepares students for college-level work and ensures the availability of related services, such as in-school guidance counseling and supplementary college prep opportunities, so that high school is a launch pad to college and career success. The Gear-Up Program, for example, ensures that all students are engaged in coursework of a high quality aligned with college admission, college-level preparation, and global economic and workforce developments.

Another long-term priority for the new administration is to expand efforts to substantially reduce high school dropout rates and develop strategies for bringing high school dropouts back into the education system, particularly in light of the disproportionate number of African-American, Latino, and English Language Learner students who are failing to complete high school.[34] And at the other end of the educational spectrum, the department needs to sharply reduce the financial barriers that stand in the way of students seeking postsecondary education opportunities but who face rising college costs. These barriers are among the greatest challenges threatening students and families, especially in a weakened economy in which job losses are increasing and family incomes stagnating.

U.S. Department of Transportation

Green Reforms for Environmental
and Consumer Safety

JOAN CLAYBROOK

The transportation sector consumes 70 percent of our nation's oil and is the circulatory system of our economy. It is therefore essential that the new president and his secretary of transportation develop a national transportation plan to address the massive demands of infrastructure maintenance, environmental protection, and public health concerns. In the air, that means installing new technologies to keep the aviation sector safe and efficient, and overhauling oversight procedures at the Federal Aviation Administration. On the ground, it means tackling the misallocation of federal funds, which now tilts heavily in favor of highways over other surface transportation. And it means enacting stalled vehicle and truck safety rules to reduce highway fatalities and working closely with the Environmental Protection Agency to better coordinate fuel economy standards and greenhouse gas emissions from vehicles.

Americans' quality of life depends on a safe, reliable, economical, and environmentally sound transportation system, and America's economic strength depends upon getting products to market and workers to their jobs safely and efficiently. The new president's challenge will therefore be to enhance personal mobility and economic competitiveness in the global marketplace, while addressing the problems of rapidly rising energy costs, global warming, and the changing demographics of transportation users, including more older and younger drivers. The transportation sector, for example, consumes more than two-thirds of the oil used in the United States.[1] With oil prices so volatile, industries producing and depending on transportation are in serious financial trouble because of the extraordinary cost increases.

Transportation issues also involve safety. In 2002, over 42,000 people were killed and nearly 3 million more were injured on our roads and highways at a cost of more than $230 billion.[2] Large truck crashes kill 5,000 Americans each year, including more than 700 truck drivers.[3] Little, if any, progress has been made in the last decade to reverse this public health epidemic. Transportation infrastructure also is in disrepair across the United States, straining to meet the demands of increased use. Thousands of bridges are unsafe, trains are running at full capacity, and streets are riddled with potholes and crumbling sidewalks. This lack of investment sends the message that America is not taking care of its assets.

Our country also needs an aviation sector that is safe and efficient. Unfortunately, recent mass flight cancellations, lapsed inspections, rising fuel prices, an aging workforce of air traffic controllers and inspectors, and outdated air traffic control technology jeopardize this goal. Domestic airline travel is essential in a country as large as the United States to transport consumers, business travelers, and cargo. Yet in recent years, the combined effects of 9/11, huge fuel price increases, and adjustments to deregulation have thrown the airline industry into a tailspin. Recent mergers, price increases, cuts in service, give-backs by union workers, and security demands have all drastically degraded airline travel. This perfect storm of problems is battering both the airline industry and consumers. The Federal Aviation Administration has not provided adequate leadership.

The new administration's policies must better connect economically important regions, invest in efficient freight transportation coordination, and create "green-collar" jobs. National transportation policy can do all three, but only if it is no longer guided by a "spoils system" that benefits the well-organized, well-funded, and most politically connected sectors that succeed in influencing legislation or regulation.

Surface Transportation

The Safe, Accountable, Flexible, Efficient Transportation Enhancement Act: A Legacy for Users, which in 2005 authorized $286 billion in tax spending for transportation projects,[4] will expire in October 2009.[5] Securing its reauthorization should be a top priority for the new administration.

The reauthorization act will require more than $624 billion over six years to make significant improvements to transportation infrastructure, including highways, bridges, rail, and transit.[6] At the same time, Congress will consider separate climate protection laws. The convergence of highway reauthorization and climate issues, addressed by many of the same key players in the Senate, represents a major opportunity to link transportation and climate concerns. The reauthorization act will need to provide both surface transportation and climate benefits, which will require a fundamental shift away from a largely highway-based transportation system and toward cleaner transit options such as rail service. Our nation is already experiencing an explosion in demand for transit options and rail service, which has seen ridership up 12.3 percent from 2006.[7] Congestion can be cut and underserved areas can enjoy improved access to jobs by using smart metropolitan area planning. But federal policy has yet to respond to these changing demands, continuing instead to emphasize highway investment over more efficient transportation methods that produce fewer greenhouse gas emissions and consume less energy, because road builders, road material suppliers, and automakers have blocked reallocation of highway funds to transit projects.

A continued emphasis on motor vehicles produces serious health and safety consequences. Motor vehicle crashes are the leading cause of death in the United States for Americans ages 2 to 34, and having more vehicles on the road makes transportation more dangerous for cyclists and walkers.[8] It also contributes to air pollution and fosters asthma in children. Never before has there been such a great urgency to reshape the nation's transportation policies to achieve climate, energy, and safety goals, while also keeping vital infrastructure operational.

Short-Term Priorities

The National Surface Transportation Policy and Revenue Study Commission made it clear that significant additional funds will be needed to deliver the dramatic investments needed in the surface transportation system. The commission estimates that the Highway Trust Fund, which is financed by gas tax receipts, will have a $4.5 billion deficit by 2009.[9] And with higher gas prices, reduced driving, and fuel purchases, the amount of gas taxes going into the fund will decrease.

Determining funding sources for the Highway Trust Fund and creating a national infrastructure bank that expands federal transportation investments should be a top priority. Congress must re-examine current revenue sources in terms of equity and identify new ones that require all stakeholders to pay their fair share based on use. The current allocation of federal transportation funds—80 percent for highways and 20 percent for transit[10]—should also be rebalanced to assure that the delivery of transit systems is competitive in the 21st century. Allocations must provide the necessary level of investment to maintain our existing infrastructure, including bridges and highways, while also promoting national energy, environmental, and safety goals. But increasing funding and exploring new funding sources for developing highway alternatives are also crucial.

Long-Term Priorities

Congress and the new administration must respond to the dramatic need to repair existing infrastructure—as evidenced by the August 2007 Interstate 35 bridge collapse in Minneapolis—while also preparing surface transportation systems to accommodate future needs. The National Surface Transportation Policy and Revenue Study Commission report, released in January 2008, calls for a $225 billion annual investment for the next 50 years to upgrade our existing infrastructure to a "state of good repair." The United States is spending less than 40 percent of this amount today.[11]

A modernized U.S. transportation system should link ports with regional economies, connect airports with transit systems, and invest in critical national corridors by financing regional high-speed rail and upgrading existing freight and passenger rail services. Only long-term commitment and investment can keep the United States competitive in a global market and bring relief to vehicle-dependent consumers who have been struggling with soaring fuel costs.

The new administration in its first year should also develop and begin to execute a long-term, national surface transportation strategy that meets safety, economic, environmental, and national security needs. A detailed, national transportation plan is the best way to address the massive demands of infrastructure maintenance, environmental protections, and public health concerns. While these needs can be met in the interim through annual appropriations bills, developing a plan covering capital-intensive systems will be a long-term commitment.

The national plan should be multimodal and embody a significant shift away from a highway-centric surface system, with a focus on expanding regional public transit and significant future investments in Amtrak passenger rail. Passenger and high-speed freight rail networks are essential components of a balanced, efficient, and healthy national transportation system. A sound funding strategy for the future should also provide significant capital funds to repair and expand rail infrastructure, including intercity freight, along with passenger and commuter services for both rural and urban areas.

According to a study by the Oak Ridge National Laboratory, intercity passenger rail transportation consumes 17 percent less energy per passenger mile than air travel and 21 percent less than automobiles. Intercity passenger rail also produces significantly fewer carbon dioxide emissions per passenger mile than vehicle or airplane travel. The study also found that heavy trucks require 12 times as much energy as rail to transport freight and about 88 percent of primary rail corridors are operating below capacity.

The new administration should hold states, metropolitan groups, and local governments accountable for diversifying effective transportation options and reducing energy consumption and greenhouse gas emissions. Metropolitan and local government planners should be allotted greater responsibility and authority to build additional rail, transit, and road capacity, with clear direction from the federal government that these investments must achieve national energy, environmental, and mobility goals without a bias for any one mode. The administration should reward states and local governments that make the most progress toward meeting articulated national goals by granting them additional money for transportation project development. Incentives delivered on the local level can also create more sustainable infrastructure and generate more green-collar job opportunities.

Auto and Large Truck Safety

Two agencies within the U.S. Department of Transportation shape its highway safety policies. The National Highway Traffic Safety Administration is responsible for new passenger vehicle, light truck, and large truck safety performance standards, and state grants to improve traffic safety. The Federal Motor Carrier Safety Administration has authority over the safety of large carrier trucks and commercial vehicle operation on the highway. FMCSA oversaw more than 690,188 carrier companies in 2007, which had more than 5.4 million licensed commercial drivers.

Motor vehicle crashes kill over 42,000 people and injure nearly 3 million annually.[12] After reaching a low point in 1992, traffic fatalities have been rising ever since.[13] In 2006, almost 5,000 people died in crashes involving large trucks, including more than 700 truck drivers.[14] Large truck crashes comprise about 12 percent of highway crash deaths, though only about 3 percent of registered vehicles in the United States are large trucks.[15] In total, traffic crashes cost our economy $230.6 billion in 2002, the last year for which data are available.[16]

The Federal Motor Vehicle Safety Standards adopted by NHTSA in the 1960s and 1970s have been credited with saving thousands of lives in the past 30 years:[17] Airbags alone have saved more than 25,000 lives since 1975,[18] and seatbelts over the years have saved more than 226,000 lives.[19]

NHTSA has since become a reactive agency that lacks safety initiative and only takes major regulatory action when mandated by Congress. Even then, it produces minimal rules that are often agreeable to industry interests. NHTSA has not upgraded many vehicle safety standards since initial issuance decades ago. Recently proposed standards for rollover protection and roof crush are glaringly weak and fail to require car manufacturers to make use of the best available technologies or replicate real-world crash events through comprehensive dynamic testing like other previously issued crash protection tests.

FMCSA similarly has been resistive in issuing vital truck safety require-ments. It addressed major congressionally mandated rulemaking actions such as truck driver hours of service or new entrant driver training only after long delays and a number of successful court challenges by national safety organiza-tions. This reluctance to act has resulted in weak, unjustified rules, which place industry interests over truck safety.[20]

The new administration must reclaim safety as the highest priority in both NHTSA and FMCSA. Both agencies have congressionally mandated major rules pending that are years behind schedule and totally inadequate. They need to be revised and finally issued because they will save thousands of lives a year. The reauthorization of SAFETEA-LU in 2009 is a key opportunity to signifi-cantly increase starvation-level safety program funding.

Short-Term Priorities
About 10,500 people are killed each year due to motor vehicle rollovers.[21] The proposed roof crush injury prevention rule is noticeably weak. Another final rule from NHTSA, required by SAFETEA-LU to prevent rollover ejections, is due on October 1, 2009.[22] The Department of Transportation should incorpo-rate these two rules into a new comprehensive rule that embraces rollover roof crush, ejection mitigation, and safety belt performance standards with a dy-namic test to evaluate occupant protection in real-world crash situations.

Each year, more than 100 children are killed by accidental backovers.[23] The Cameron Gulbransen Kids and Cars Safety Act of 2007 requires NHTSA to is-sue a final rule to expand the driver's rearward field-of-view to cover the entire path behind backing vehicles.[24] NHTSA needs to issue rules that maximize lives saved and utilize existing state-of-the-art safety technologies.

Then the public needs to know about these new technologies. The New Car Assessment Program developed in 1979 is one of the most important con-sumer aids available to new car buyers, but it needs to be updated and ex-panded. It requires manufacturers to put stickers on new cars that list safety information about the vehicle's make and model. But the information provided by NCAP is minimal when compared to how other countries fully inform con-sumers. The United States fails to include information on vehicle aggressivity and compatibility, pedestrian safety features, child restraints, rollover injury prevention, and rear crash or vehicular crash avoidance ratings. The Depart-ment of Transportation should require the New Car Assessment Program to add these categories, and in order to avoid consumer confusion, the rating sys-tem should eliminate the five-star rating in favor of an A-F grade for vehicles.

Trucking too, needs to become safer. Some lawmakers—at industry urging—have suggested increasing the allowable large truck weight limit on federal highways from 80,000 pounds to either 97,000 or 100,000 pounds. Bigger, heavier trucks endanger the public, as they are harder to control and damage roads and bridges, many of which are already in poor condition. Increasing the allowable size and weight of trucks exacerbates congestion. The DOT also concluded in a 2004 study that 97,000-pound, six-axle trucks are less fuel-efficient than currently permitted 80,000-pound, five-axle trucks by more than 10 percent.[25] The new administration should work with Congress to block any legislation that would allow heavier trucks on federal highways.

The government should also reduce the allowable length of truckers' daily, weekly, and monthly driving and working hours. NTSB studies have concluded that truck driver fatigue may be a contributing factor in as many as 30 to 40 percent of all heavy truck crashes.[26] It issued rules in 2003 and 2005—both struck down by the U.S. Courts of Appeals—that would allow truckers to drive up to 14 hours a day and work and drive 98 hours in an eight-day period.[27] A reasonable hours-of-service rule, along with mandatory electronic on-board readers that monitor driving time behind the wheel, should be a top priority because they would help prevent driver fatigue.

Long-Term Priorities
The Department of Transportation should prioritize long-term changes that will improve vehicle safety for drivers, passengers, and pedestrians. European and Japanese manufacturers already meet their nations' vehicle safety standards designed to prevent injuries to pedestrians struck by motor vehicles. Yet NHTSA has never even issued such a standard. Annual pedestrian deaths have remained near 4,800 this decade[28]—a number that could be greatly reduced if NHTSA issued a pedestrian safety standard requiring vehicle exteriors to have more energy-absorbing designs, while eliminating sharp edges and points.

Incompatibility—when one vehicle inflicts more damage upon another in a crash due to a vehicle's size and design—can lead to devastating consequences, particularly to passenger car occupants in crashes with larger passenger vehicles such as light trucks. Although NHTSA and vehicle manufacturers have conducted crash compatibility research, the agency has not issued a proposal for rulemaking. The agency instead invited manufacturers to develop a voluntary program to reduce crash incompatibility, but this has not been effective. This is not surprising since voluntary industry standards rarely work because there is no obligation to comply and the public is excluded from developing the standard.

Poorly designed seat structure also leads to many debilitating injuries each year. The NHTSA's rear-impact testing documents that seat backs commonly collapse in rear-impact collisions, which turns front seat occupants into backward-moving projectiles, endangering everyone in the rear seat. NHTSA should develop a new safety standard requiring integrated seating systems with upper safety belt anchors installed on the seat instead of the door frame, and improved design and performance for occupant safety belts, such as inflatable belts, load limiters, automatic retractors, and rollover-triggered gyroscopic functions.

In addition, too many states lack some of the most basic and important life-saving laws that would reduce motor vehicle deaths and injuries. Annual motorcycle crash deaths have been increasing since 1997 and now total over 4,800 a year,[29] and more than half of those killed in motor vehicle crashes are unbelted. Motor vehicle crash deaths are directly attributed to lack of uniform state adoption of mandatory motorcycle helmet and primary enforcement seatbelt laws. Only 26 states and the District of Columbia have primary enforcement seatbelt use laws, and 20 states, including the District, have all-rider helmet laws.[30]

Nearly 8,000 people died in crashes involving 16- to 20-year-old drivers in 2006 alone.[31] Graduated driver licensing programs introduce teens to the driving experience gradually by phasing in full driving privileges over time and in lower-risk settings. GDL laws have been successful in reducing teen driver crash rates, but too many states have incomplete GDL laws. Only Delaware has an optimal GDL law with five criteria that make their roads safer: a six-month holding period, 30 to 50 hours of supervised driving, nighttime restrictions, passenger restrictions, and cell phone restrictions.[32]

One of the major causes of motor vehicle crashes is impaired driving; in 2006, 41 percent of all fatal crashes were alcohol-related.[33] The new administration needs to compel states to adopt critical impaired driving laws, including mandatory blood alcohol testing in all fatal crash situations; sobriety checkpoints; strict child endangerment laws; open container laws; and mandatory ignition interlocks for first-time offenders. These measures would all reduce alcohol-related deaths. The new administration also needs to seek strategies that accelerate uniform state adoption of laws that require seatbelt and motorcycle helmet use, tougher drunk driving penalties, and comprehensive GDL programs.

FMCSA should also work to abolish ongoing practices that endanger truckers' safety and the safety of other drivers sharing the highway. Under current rules, each new motor carrier company can operate for 18 months primarily upon receipt of just a paper application.[34] During this period, FMCSA does not perform a full safety compliance review or require any safety proficiency examination. FMCSA should revise the new entrant program to ensure that new motor carriers undergo a safety audit, including a safety proficiency exam, prior to receiving temporary operating authority.

Truck drivers are exempt from the Fair Labor Standards Act and are usually compensated by a pay-per-mile travel system, which encourages unsafe driving practices since the direct economic motivation is to drive faster and farther, despite fatigue. Instituting an hourly rate for drivers would help eliminate these unsafe driving practices and help ensure that all truckers earn living wages sufficient to cover fuel costs, truck maintenance, and personal expenses, while creating improved economic stability within the trucking industry.

Air Transportation

Flying is one of the safest forms of travel in the United States, but air transportation systems will need a complete overhaul to keep these high levels of safety amid increasing demand and with more than 8,000 planes in airline carriers' fleets and almost 225,000 general aviation aircraft in service.[35] This is especially the case for current air traffic control systems, which are less advanced than a child's Xbox video gaming device.[36]

The largest aviation issue over the next decade will be the implementation of a new air traffic control system called the Next Generation Air Transportation System, also known as NextGen. This program will enhance travel safety, improve congestion management, and help conserve fuel. Unfortunately, some 20 years and billions of dollars have been wasted in failed attempts to upgrade the existing antiquated system.

American Airlines, Delta Airlines, and Alaska Airlines canceled thousands of flights and stranded tens of thousands of passengers in order to inspect the bundling of wires in Boeing MD-80 wheel wells in April 2008. The move brought the nation's air travel to a near standstill. Even though this represents a single disruption in travel, it demonstrates the need for the Federal Aviation Administration to enhance its carrier oversight. If the FAA's aircraft inspections had been properly managed on schedule, these delays would have been minimal.

The government's failures in aviation were highly publicized in 2008, causing Congress to more closely scrutinize the FAA. Yet the agency has been without an administrator since September 2007. Congress shelved the nomination of Acting Administrator Robert Sturgell to the full-time, five-year term because his perspectives on safety issues too closely match the current status quo in an agency that requires a major overhaul.

The FAA needs stricter oversight, fuel-saving initiatives, better workforce management, and action on safety measures and consumer protection, such as alleviating congestion and delays at airports. Until this needed retooling takes place, there will be a growing human toll as well. Delays are stranding passengers and high fuel costs are weakening airline financial viability and increasing costs to consumers.

Short-Term Priorities

Some FAA whistleblowers recently charged that the FAA has developed a cozy relationship with the industry it is supposed to regulate, citing Southwest Airline's delinquency in airline repairs as a key example. The past year's debacle of lapsed inspections across airlines shows the need for the FAA to take back control of the regulatory harness from the carriers.

The FAA needs to strengthen oversight in its inspection process. Timely and rigorous inspections must be an absolute priority without the blind acceptance of a carrier's assurance that maintenance checks are being performed properly. This change should include establishing an independent team of aviation and safety experts to conduct reviews of the FAA's oversight responsibilities.

To further create a culture of safety, the agency must sharpen protections for whistleblowers. The latest saga resulted in the suppression of some FAA employees due to anonymous complaints lodged against them that were never substantiated. The FAA should review how these complaints are handled.

The FAA also needs to oversee the implementation of an "airline passenger bill of rights" to ensure that passengers are not stranded on the tarmac without proper accommodations for extended periods of time. In a much publicized event, hundreds of passengers were stranded at JFK for nearly 10 hours during an ice storm in 2006. The House and Senate in 2008 debated legislation to address these delays. A final version must include access to food, water, restroom facilities, and the right for passengers to deplane should a delay last more than a reasonable amount of time.

Pilot fatigue is a major concern that the FAA has placed on the backburner. The National Transportation Safety Board's most-wanted list for transportation safety improvements includes developing a fatigue awareness and countermeasures program for air traffic controllers, as well as working-hour limits for crew, pilots, mechanics, and controllers. These issues have been on the most-wanted list for more than 10 years and demand immediate attention.[37]

Long-Term Priorities

The new NextGen traffic control technology is critical for air travel growth, safety, and fuel economy. NextGen will cost $15 billion to $20 billion.[38] In the late 1980s, the FAA pushed hard for a microwave landing system, but the agency took so long to approve the technology that NextGen has overtaken it.[39] The proposed NextGen would include satellite communication between planes by broadcasting their positions to other planes and ground control. This initiative has received a positive response from the aviation industry and the FAA, but current forecasts have this project operational around 2025—far too long from now.

A key element of NextGen is the En Route Automation Modernization system, which generates display data for air traffic controllers in real time, showing routing of planes when dealing with congestion, weather, and other developments that require fast data processing for more flexible flight paths. The FAA needs to meet its goal of having ERAM fully operational in all air route traffic control centers by the end of 2009.

According to FAA data, the last three months of 2007 saw an average of 2.5 runway incursions per day.[40] This is an alarming problem that can be largely eliminated through the use of technology to transmit immediate warnings of possible collisions directly to the cockpits of planes involved. NextGen includes an Automatic Dependent Surveillance Broadcast system, which would use global positioning to signal pilots and controllers with real-time display of surrounding air traffic. This would vastly improve awareness of potential runway incursions, but installing this segment will require priority funding.

The FAA can also improve runways by installing perimeter taxiways that would allow planes to land quickly without sacrificing safety. Taxiing takes a significant amount of time and prevents landing planes from utilizing runways. Moving taxiing planes to separate areas reduces delays and runway crossings that could lead to dangerous incursions by landing aircraft. This change would also reduce excess spacing between landing planes, further speeding up the process. More funds in the FAA's Grants in Aid for Airports should be allocated to address this issue.

Fuel Economy

The last three years have seen sharply rising and record-breaking gasoline, diesel, and crude oil prices. Ignoring the warning signs, U.S. auto companies and the federal government failed to encourage competitive, fuel efficient vehicles, and now the industry is in deep financial trouble. Congress rushed through a $25 billion bailout with no conditions to save this sector.

Two-thirds of U.S. oil consumption is used by the transportation sector,[41] and rising fuel costs affect all modes of transportation. Dramatic price shifts in transportation fuels have caused near chaos for consumers driving personal vehicles, for the shipping industry relying predominantly upon large trucks for goods delivery, and for the freight and passenger arms of the airline industry.

Short-Term Priorities

The new administration will have to integrate fuel economy standards into a national climate policy. A successful transportation energy program must not conflict with the policies, actions, or goals of climate change policy. Navigating the relationship between fuel economy standards and vehicular greenhouse gas emissions standards will require close coordination between NHTSA and EPA.

The top priority for NHTSA's fuel economy program, established under the Energy Independence and Security Act of 2007, will be to ensure that Corporate Average Fuel Economy standards do not preempt state regulation of greenhouse gas emissions.[42] NHTSA should push Congress to cancel the dual-fuel program, which give automakers producing dual-fuel vehicles a credit against fuel economy requirements. The new administration should, however, provide incentives to consumers to purchase hybrids and electric cars.

NHTSA also must be administratively independent from the automotive industry and set more ambitious fuel economy targets of 35 mpg by 2016 and 43 mpg by 2020 that go beyond the statutorily mandated 35 mpg by 2020 that is already out of date. Vehicles also should be required to have real-time on-board fuel economy indicators to educate drivers about how driving habits influence fuel economy.

NHTSA also needs to provide as much information as possible to help consumers decide what vehicle is right for them. It should focus on establishing a comparative fuel economy labeling scheme for consumers that includes information about relative greenhouse gas emissions. NHTSA and the Environmental Protection Agency should also develop a lifecycle analysis of transportation fuels and develop an easily compared carbon content rating for consumers. And the agency should study the effects of biofuels and alternative transportation fuels. Publishing results of such studies will help consumers make informed decisions and address concerns about potential corrosion and fuel system component damage attributable to nontraditional fuels.

Gasoline prices increased 160 percent between the summer of 2001 and 2008, but the price of diesel has increased more than 210 percent.[43] The effect of this sudden and dramatic price surge for diesel, in particular, has created an increasingly large number of struggling trucking companies. Independent drivers are acutely affected since they must pay fuel costs up front. Many drivers face out-of-pocket expenses of more than $1,000 for a 250-gallon standard fill-up.

The Energy Independence and Security Act of 2007 directed the Department of Transportation to work with the National Academy of Sciences to issue a report assessing technologies and costs associated with the development of large truck fuel economy standards.[44] The new administration must develop this report in order to ensure that large trucks are held to more stringent fuel economy standards, which will ultimately save the industry money and improve air quality.

Long-Term Priorities

Freight rail offers environmental benefits, is cost-effective, and uses significantly less fuel than large trucks to move the same amount of freight. Railroads are on average three times more efficient than trucks for freight hauling. A truck-to-rail shift encouraged through subsidies would also ease demand on the trucking industry, which currently does not have the workforce needed to handle projected freight demand.

Airlines will spend $40 billion on jet fuel in 2008. Projections for 2009 are $61.2 billion—four times what the aviation industry paid five years ago.[45] An immediate savings in fuel costs can be achieved by flying at slightly slower speeds. Southwest Airlines recently applied this strategy. By adding an average of one to three minutes per flight, Southwest is projecting an annual savings of $42 million in fuel this year.[46] All airlines should adopt this plan as a quick method to lower costs and help the environment.

Environmental Protection Agency

Restoring Scientific Integrity, Sound Regulation,
Fair Enforcement, and Transparency

CAROL M. BROWNER

The Environmental Protection Agency during the Bush administration was continually plagued by White House interference. EPA staff were repeatedly forced to ignore or squelch their own science-based conclusions about a number of important matters, including the damaging effects of climate change on the quality of our air and water. Courts rejected the lax pollution regulations encouraged by the White House as being outside the requirements of the law and failing to provide important protections for the American people. The public was denied access to information about pollution in their communities—including the residents of lower Manhattan after the 9/11 attacks. Furthermore, the budget for enforcement was slashed. The new president and his new EPA administrator must restore scientific integrity at the agency, enact sound regulations that maintain the integrity of the laws and the science, and enforce our nation's environmental laws. Fortunately, EPA boasts the tools and a committed staff to return the agency to its important work on behalf of the American people, which includes ensuring clean air, clean water, healthy communities, and the reduction of greenhouse gases.

Since its inception, the Environmental Protection Agency's mission to safeguard Americans from the hazards of pollution has been based on a set of core principles: science; sound regulation; fairness in enforcement; and recognition of the public's right to know about the quality of the air we breathe, the water we drink, and the land on which we live. Reliance on these principles has meant steady progress toward cleaner air, water, and land, and ultimately healthier communities. The interdependence between a healthy environment and a healthy economy has been demonstrated over and over, disproving the notion that we cannot both protect our environment and grow the economy.

Unfortunately, the past eight years represent a complete disregard for the mission of the agency. After the failure of the Bush administration to take serious steps to address climate change over the past eight years, the new administration must move decisively and energetically to reduce greenhouse gas emissions, enhance energy efficiency, and secure alternative energy sources.

Between November 4 and the Inauguration in January, the president-elect's transition team will need to ensure that the new administration can immediately begin to develop and implement a new energy and environment plan on day one. In particular, the team should develop a broad outline of the new administration's plans to transition the country to a low-carbon economy, and be prepared to nominate three key officials at the EPA: administrator, general counsel, and chief scientist, all of whom need to be confirmed by Congress immediately after the new president is sworn in.

To inform the president-elect's energy and climate change plans, the transition team should also convene a bipartisan group of the nation's governors and mayors, as well as Native American, scientific, business, faith, and non-profit leaders, to help identify the most important priorities in tackling climate change. Our states, cities, and tribal nations now boast a broad portfolio of regulations and initiatives on climate policies, and scores of U.S. businesses have implemented far-reaching voluntary climate change programs. Learning from these leaders will be invaluable in shaping federal efforts in this arena, and working with them will help forge a bipartisan coalition in Congress to act on the new president's comprehensive policy proposals.

Day One

On day one in office, the new president must clearly demonstrate his commitment to the role of science, sound regulations, fair enforcement, transparency, and public engagement in addressing our nation's environmental and energy challenges by taking a number of key steps. Immediately following his swearing in, the new president should sign an executive order that covers all executive branch rulemaking activities and lays out the interagency rulemaking review process that the new White House will follow (as detailed in the Office of Management and Budget chapter of this book). The president should explicitly direct EPA to begin a review of how best to use its existing authority to reduce greenhouse gas emissions, increase energy efficiency, and expand alternative energy sources.

In addition, the new president should direct EPA to reconsider the Bush administration's 2008 denial of the "waiver" sought by California under the Clean Air Act to require the sale of more fuel-efficient cars in their state. Numerous other states have indicated their support for the "California car."

On Inauguration Day, the 44th president should also create a new National Energy Council whose structure and work would be modeled after that of the National Economic Council. This new White House council would include the secretaries of most cabinet agencies and the heads of the Council on Environmental Quality, the National Economic Council, and the National Security

Council. The council would be led by a national energy advisor with authorities comparable to the national security advisor and the national economic advisor, as detailed in the White House section of this book.

First 100 Days

The EPA and its new administrator must develop an agenda that signals to Congress and the public that the agency's work will once again be guided by its core historical principles—reliance on science, sound regulation, fairness in enforcement, and a recognition of the public's right to know. EPA professionals must be permitted to perform their jobs as directed by the laws. They are experts in their fields and bring many years of experience to the work of the agency.

The new administration must reverse the Bush administration's record of interference and indifference to scientific findings and reports. A survey of EPA scientists, released in April 2008, found that 889 of nearly 1,600 respondents reported having experienced political interference in their work during the previous five years.[1]

With respect to climate change, the Bush White House interfered repeatedly with EPA and other agencies' reports on the likely environmental and public health effects of global warming. In 2003, the White House edited EPA's *Report on the Environment*, deleting and modifying sections on climate science.[2] In October 2007, the Office of Management and Budget edited testimony on the public health effects of climate change by Julie Gerberding, director of the Centers for Disease Control and Prevention, eliminating six pages of written testimony.[3]

In December 2007, the White House refused even to open an email containing EPA's proposed findings and recommendations developed pursuant to the Supreme Court's 2007 *Massachusetts v. EPA* decision regarding greenhouse gas regulations.[4] Ultimately, the White House changed the document, and in June 2008, EPA released a highly edited version of its original proposal in which large sections of analysis in support of regulating greenhouse gases had been removed.[5]

In March 2008, EPA announced a proposal to change the national ozone standard. The proposed standard ignored the recommendations of EPA's scientific advisory committee, which found that a lower standard was necessary for the protection of human health.

The new EPA administrator should issue a public statement reaffirming that science will guide the work of the agency and that the agency's scientists and staff will be allowed to do their jobs in an appropriate, professional manner. The administrator should pledge that recommendations of the agency's scientific advisory boards will be given full consideration in agency decisions. EPA should expand its partnerships with the external scientific community through the creation of scientific centers of excellence focused on emerging risks such as climate change impacts.

Sound Regulation

EPA should announce its intention to fully exercise its existing authority under the Clean Air Act of 1990 with respect to greenhouse gas emissions pursuant to the Supreme Court decision in *Massachusetts v. EPA*. The first step in that process is to determine whether an air pollutant "cause[s], or contribute[s] to air pollution which may reasonably be anticipated to endanger public health or welfare."[6] In order to do this, EPA should make a finding based on the science and, if that results in a determination of "endangerment," proceed to rulemaking under the Clean Air Act and in accordance with the Supreme Court's decision.

The EPA administrator also should direct EPA staff to determine, based on the science and the law, whether mercury is a neurotoxin and thus a hazardous air pollutant. The Bush administration removed mercury from the list of hazardous air pollutants and proposed a pollution reduction scheme that would have had the effect of leaving some communities with inadequate protection from mercury pollution. In February 2008, a federal court rejected the Bush administration's efforts as both insufficient to protect human health from exposure to mercury and in violation of the Clean Air Act.[7]

Much of the Bush administration's approach to air pollution centered on the Clean Air Interstate Rule. In July 2008, CAIR was unanimously rejected by a federal appeals court on the basis of flawed reasoning in its establishment of pollution standards and its distribution of pollution allowances.[8] The Bush administration has requested a rehearing, and Congress has introduced legislation in support of CAIR. Under a new administration, EPA should withdraw the request for a rehearing and commence rulemaking for a new program to replace CAIR. The agency should work with states, cities, nongovernmental organizations, and the business community to fashion a program that will achieve air pollution reductions appropriately and legally.

In accordance with provisions of the Energy Independence and Security Act of 2007, EPA has the responsibility to review the impacts of the new Renewable Fuel Standard. The agency must complete this lifecycle analysis if the

Bush administration has not done so by the end of its term, evaluating the effects of ethanol and other biofuels production on industry, agriculture, and our natural forests, land, and water resources.

Early in the new administration's term, EPA should take steps to reassert its historical authority to protect our nation's wetlands and streams. Bush administration actions put 20 million acres of wetlands and thousands of miles of season streams at risk to pollution, dredging, draining, and filling.

In January 2003 and June 2007, EPA and the Army Corps of Engineers issued a staff directive and new policy guidance that limits protection for isolated waters based on a very narrow reading of two Supreme Court decisions in 2001 and 2006.[9] The guidance has created ongoing confusion as to what is and is not covered by the Clean Water Act.[10]

The new administration should withdraw the 2003 staff directive and the 2007 guidance and then issue new guidance to guarantee that the historical scope of jurisdiction is maintained. EPA and the White House should simultaneously announce their support for congressional passage of the Clean Water Restoration Act, which will reaffirm the long-standing interpretation that isolated and seasonal wetlands and streams are subject to the Clean Water Act.

Additionally, the new administration should clarify EPA's position on the role of cost-benefit analysis in standard-setting procedures under the Clean Water Act, with specific regard to the regulation of "cooling water" associated with power plants and manufacturing facilities. The Clean Water Act requires industry to install "the best technology available for minimizing adverse environmental impact," but in 2004 EPA issued a regulation stating that compliance could be waived if the cost of compliance to business would be significantly greater than the benefits to water resources.

A U.S. Court of Appeals ruled in January 2007 that EPA could not use cost-benefit analysis to regulate cooling water under the Clean Water Act.[11] The Bush administration subsequently filed a brief with the Supreme Court, and the case will likely be argued during the first year of the new administration.[12] Both in the court and in the agency's rulemaking authority, the new administration should reaffirm the historic interpretation of the Clean Water Act to protect our nation's water bodies.

The new administrator should also withdraw EPA's current "water-transfer" rule, issued in June 2008, which allows polluted urban and agriculture wastewater to be pumped into less polluted waters, including public drinking water supplies, without requiring a permit or environmental impact assessment. The agency should reaffirm that all transfers of water are subject to review and impact assessments pursuant to the Clean Water Act, and those that result in the discharge of pollutants should be subject to appropriate limitations and restrictions to protect the health of the receiving water.

Fairness in Enforcement

The Bush administration dramatically reduced EPA enforcement activities. The Criminal Investigation Division now employs fewer than 200 investigators, which is a violation of the minimum number of enforcement personnel required by the Pollution Prosecution Act, signed in 1990 by President George H.W. Bush. During the second Bush administration, criminal enforcement cases dropped by more than a third, as measured by the number of prosecutions, new investigations, and total criminal convictions. The number of civil lawsuits settled declined by more than two-thirds between the late 1990s and 2006.[13] The new EPA administrator should immediately direct staff to conduct a review of all pending investigations, enforcement actions, and previously halted investigations to ensure that the appropriate legal actions are being pursued in accordance with the law. EPA should develop a budget proposal that will allow for appropriate staffing levels.

The agency should reassert its authority to regulate power plants under the New Source Review provisions of the Clean Air Act, which require older facilities to install modern pollution control equipment when they upgrade their facilities. In 2003, the Bush administration issued new guidance on New Source Review that significantly relaxed the permitting process for existing utilities. In separate studies, the Government Accountability Office and the congressionally appointed National Academy of Public Administration found that EPA's 2003 decision was not grounded in scientific evidence and that the new rules present an increased threat to human health.

Similarly, EPA should review the current compliance and enforcement of Clean Water Act regulations for concentrated animal feeding operations, or CAFOs. In 2005, the U.S. Court of Appeals ruled in *Waterkeeper v. EPA* that only those CAFOs that discharge or intend to discharge livestock effluent are required to obtain National Pollutant Discharge Elimination System permits, which are used to put in place appropriate pollution control requirements. Thereafter, EPA developed a new CAFO strategy for this permitting regime. The new administration should review this strategy to ensure that all CAFOs required to obtain a permit have done so, and to identify whether those CAFOs already possessing permits are in compliance with their permit requirements.

The Public's Right to Know

EPA must provide the public with access to timely and relevant information about the quality of the air we breathe, the water we drink, and the land on which we live. Over the past eight years, the Bush administration took steps that have reduced the quality of information collected and the ability to access this information. The Bush administration increased tenfold the reporting thresholds for the Toxics Release Inventory; limited content, hours, independence, and accessibility of EPA libraries; and allowed data quality to deteriorate, maintaining inconsistent databases in spite of repeated challenges from the U.S. Chamber of Commerce and others under the Data Quality Act of 2001.[14]

The new EPA administrator should commit the agency to fully communicate contamination dangers to the public following disasters, including what the agency knows and does not yet know about contamination at a site. After the terrorist attacks of September 11, 2001, residents and rescue workers did not receive accurate information regarding contamination in the area. Moreover, EPA initially deferred responsibility for ensuring site decontamination. Ultimately, in 2002 and 2006 the agency did conduct contamination testing and cleanup of individual units surrounding the site.

One of EPA's most important "right to know" programs is the Toxics Release Inventory. Since 1988, the EPA annually provides information to the public gathered from approximately 23,000 facilities regarding their emissions of 650 toxic chemicals. In December 2006, the Bush administration increased the reporting threshold for toxic releases from 500 pounds to 5,000 pounds per year. In the first year since this rule change took effect, the threshold changes have resulted in a decrease of more than 600 facilities reporting.

Twelve states subsequently sued EPA, arguing that the agency failed to adequately justify the increase in the reporting threshold.[15] Congressional legislation to reinstate the lower threshold has been introduced in both the Senate and the House, and has been placed on the Senate legislative calendar. In the event that the legislation does not pass in the 2008 Congress, the new EPA administrator should immediately move to reinstate the lower threshold. Additionally, EPA should increase the usefulness of Toxics Release Inventory reporting by decreasing the lag time between data collection and publication; currently EPA does not release the annual report for more than a year after the information has been collected.

For individuals who do not have computers, EPA's library systems provide an important way to access agency information and databases. The Bush administration sought to close the libraries and cut the library budget by 80 percent from 2006 to 2007. In response to concern from the public and Congress, in February of 2008 EPA agreed to reopen some of the library facilities, albeit with limited content. A GAO 2008 investigation of the library closings faulted

EPA for restructuring the library system without considering input from the staff and the public.[16]

In the new administration, EPA should conduct a full review of its library system, including an outreach program to agency staff and the public, to determine whether and how the libraries can fulfill their purpose of providing the public access to agency materials. The agency should consider all mechanisms for enhanced access and "user-friendly" formats. To ensure quality data and reporting of greenhouse gas emissions, the new administrator should review development of the program mandated by Congress in 2008 to ensure compulsory reporting by emitters of greenhouse gases, and should establish a method of collection to ensure accuracy and ease of reporting as well as public access to the information.

EPA has a long history of relying on federal advisory committees to engage the public and experts in the work of the agency. In keeping with the Federal Advisory Committee Act amendments of 2008, the agency should evaluate whether EPA's use of advisory committees meets FACA requirements for transparency, disclosure and accountability, and where necessary taking actions to improve performance.

The First Year

Over the first year, the EPA administrator should work with the Office of Management and Budget to develop an agency budget that restores the resources needed to implement its existing environmental priorities and to undertake expanded work on energy efficiency, renewable energy sources, and climate change. Under the Bush administration, EPA's budget was cut dramatically since 2004, amounting to overall reductions of nearly one fifth the agency's annual budget. Certain programs were particularly hard hit by budget cuts, including scientific research, state and tribal assistance grants, libraries, and environmental justice.

Case in point: even as EPA announced a review of environmental justice activities in its programs, the agency's environmental justice budget was cut by 28 percent and then 40 percent in the 2008 and 2009 federal budgets. Funding for these programs should be restored and the scope of their activities should be reviewed to ensure that the agency is receiving adequate support to carry out its mandated responsibilities.

As the new president deals with climate change, energy efficiency, and the development of the next generation of biofuels—alongside the traditional environmental challenges facing the nation—EPA should request a budget increase to provide support for both research and program implementation in these areas. For example, the first-year efforts on climate change mitigation and adaptation will require budget allocations, as will the agency's responsibilities in the biofuels program mandated by the Renewable Fuels, Consumer Protection, and Energy Efficiency Act of 2007.

The new administration's budget must include increased funding for drinking water and wastewater infrastructure upgrades. Our nation's water management systems are aging, and the funding shortfall for needed infrastructure upgrades has grown to over $11 billion annually. Every year, there are 75,000 sanitary sewer overflows in the nation, and 3,700 people fall ill from these overflows each year.[17] In many parts of the country, drinking and wastewater management systems are more than 100 years old.

Without additional investment, these systems will fail to meet even basic federal water quality regulations in the coming decades. To address these problems, the new administration should increase funding for both the drinking water and wastewater state revolving loan programs. To better inform the agency's budget recommendations, EPA should undertake a new, comprehensive review of the nation's wastewater and drinking water infrastructure needs, which were last evaluated in 2002. As part of this review the agency should take into account climate change impacts on drinking and wastewater systems.

The new administration should work with Congress to adopt a dedicated funding mechanism for EPA's Superfund program. The tax that historically funded the Superfund program expired in 1995; funding now comes from general revenues. Funding for the program has been declining, as the program must focus on sites that are large and complex and also include natural resource damages. New funding sources should be identified and developed, based on the nature of the sites now in the program.

Other budget areas which may require reinstatement of funding levels or additional resources include: labs and libraries, the Office of Children's Health Protection, the Integrated Risk Information System, information collection and management programs, and the Science to Achieve Results program, which supports scientific research at universities and which has experienced budget cuts on the order of 30 percent from year to year.

Climate Change and Energy

The new EPA administrator should appoint an internal staff committee to evaluate, oversee, and coordinate EPA's actions on climate change. This committee should undertake a review of each law under its jurisdiction, to determine what authorities exist and how best to use them to mitigate greenhouse gas emissions and address adaptation to the impacts of climate change.

EPA, for example, will need to develop regulations for carbon capture-and-storage technology, including permitting and monitoring of these facilities. Historically, EPA's regulation of underground formations has been developed under the Safe Drinking Water Act. The agency should determine whether the existing Safe Drinking Water Act and other authorities are adequate to ensure the effective permitting, operation, maintenance, and safety of carbon capture-and-storage facilities. EPA should also be closely involved in any government research and pilot programs for this technology. In addition, the agency should be a leader in the administration-wide effort to develop climate change adaptation plans. As part of this effort the agency should create a "blue ribbon" scientific panel to assess the ongoing effects of climate change on human health and the environment. This panel should produce biennial reports to inform Congress and the American people about what is happening and what is likely to happen in the coming years due to climate change.

Under the new administration, EPA should expand its work on energy efficiency as well. Both producers and consumers should be encouraged to develop energy efficiency as a resource in its own right and as a way to prevent pollution and mitigate climate change. To promote adoption of energy-efficiency programs by utilities in the power sector, EPA should encourage state public utilities to decouple utility earnings from volume of sales and should assist states with programs to provide incentives for energy-efficiency gains. The 2006 National Action Plan for Energy Efficiency, facilitated by the EPA and Department of Energy, presents a set of recommendations on regulatory policies and rate designs to encourage efficiency at the utility level. EPA should take the next step by supporting implementation of these programs at the state and local levels.

To encourage energy efficiency in end-use electricity consumption, EPA should modify its Energy Star labeling program to promote "total appliance" energy efficiency. EPA's voluntary Energy Star labeling program provides information to consumers on energy use by home and office appliances. As the program currently stands, Energy Star labels indicate that an appliance has low energy use while on standby. Energy Star's qualification requirements should account for energy use while an appliance is turned on, as well as when it is on standby. This shift to "total appliance" qualification standards would be in keeping with international trends and would provide a more accurate measurement of appliance efficiency.

To encourage energy efficiency in vehicle fuel consumption, EPA should publicize and promote the advanced vehicle technologies developed by the National Vehicle and Fuel Emissions Laboratory. As the vehicle fuel economy standards established by the Energy Independence and Security Act of 2007 come into effect, the laboratory will be instrumental in ensuring compliance from the auto industry.

The new Renewable Fuel Standard that was established by the Energy Independence and Security Act of 2007 will require EPA regulation to ensure that the increase in biofuels production does not lead to unacceptable environmental consequences. EPA should establish performance standards for biofuels production, requiring certification of responsible water, fertilizer, and pesticide management, as well as a minimum greenhouse gas emissions reduction from a gasoline baseline, in order for the biofuels to be counted toward the Renewable Fuel Standard mandate.[18]

Green building design, which should be a top priority of the new administration, is characterized by improved energy efficiency, water efficiency, indoor air quality, and sustainable land use patterns. The deployment of green building design throughout the nation presents a tremendous opportunity for protecting public health and environmental quality. EPA should work with all relevant government agencies and business leaders to promote green building design for our nation's schools, businesses, and homes. The agency should develop green building standards for all government-owned facilities, contributing the agency's expertise on indoor air quality, water efficiency, and energy efficiency to a comprehensive green building design program in coordination with the Department of Energy.

The Energy Independence and Security Act of 2007 includes numerous provisions to encourage the construction and use of green buildings in the residential, commercial, and government sectors. EPA should move forward expeditiously with implementation of this act by developing guidelines for school siting, working with the Department of Education to provide grants for green school building design, and conducting a study of the effects of green school design components on indoor environmental quality in schools that serve kindergarten through 12th grade students. The act also directs EPA to create a program of competitive grants to local governments for green building demonstration projects and prohibits federal agencies from leasing buildings that have not earned an EPA Energy Star label.

Environmental Quality

EPA also must move aggressively to utilize its authorities under the Clean Air

Act to protect the public's health. Many of the Bush administration's efforts under the Clean Air Act disregarded scientific facts and legal requirements. The National Ambient Air Quality Standards program requires the agency to review six air pollutants every five years to determine, based on the best available science, whether current standards are adequate to protect the public's health. The pollutants are: ozone, particulate matter, carbon monoxide, sulfur dioxide, nitrogen oxides, and lead.

EPA should work with states, local governments, businesses, and the public to determine how best to protect individual water bodies and implement the Clean Water Act's Total Maximum Daily Load program, including regulations adopted by EPA in July 2000. The TMDL program recognizes that no two water bodies are identical and that the standard required for a given pollutant may vary from one body of water to another. Under the TMDL program, each water body is considered in its entirety. Environmental authorities must determine what the problems are and where the pollution is coming from—discharge pipes or runoff.

As part of its work under the Clean Water Act, EPA should expand its programs at the watershed level, including those in the Chesapeake Bay, the Everglades, the Great Lakes, the Mississippi River, and the San Francisco Bay Delta. The watershed programs allow EPA to work with all stakeholders in the hydrologically defined watershed to reduce pollution more effectively and efficiently.

The agency should also review its current programs on wetland mitigation and water pollution trading, and should adapt these programs to ensure appropriate protections for our nation's waters. The agency should strengthen permitting requirements to ensure that compensatory wetlands are adequately filtering water and performing the functions of the wetland systems they have replaced. In March 2008, EPA issued revised regulations governing this program; these regulations should be evaluated to ensure their effectiveness in achieving the goals of the program.

Similarly, in its water-pollution-trading program, the agency should put in place safeguards against the trading of toxic water pollutants that accumulate in place rather than being dispersed throughout the water body. The agency should also evaluate what measures could improve the effectiveness of this program in achieving pollution reductions.

Finally, climate change also will have an increasing impact on our water resources—rivers, lakes, streams, wetlands, and estuaries. EPA should work together with the Army Corps of Engineers to develop a climate adaptation plan for managing our water resources in the face of increased droughts, storms, and storm water surges.

The new EPA administrator also must reaffirm the agency's commitment to ensuring that environmental justice concerns are considered in all of the agency's work. Across the country, low-income and minority communities continue to suffer disproportionately from the pollution of our modern industrial economy. The agency should conduct an agency-wide assessment of current environmental justice performance in EPA programs.

In June 2008, EPA administrator Stephen Johnson called for an environmental justice review of all EPA programs in 2009. The new administration should adapt the proposed review as necessary both to ensure that it will provide sufficient information and guidance and to include an evaluation of climate impacts on environmental justice in the United States.

Longer-Term Agenda

Over the course of the new president's first term of office, EPA should look ahead to support new programs that will support the mission of the agency. In all its activities, EPA should work with the business community to find the most efficient and effective solutions to the environmental challenges facing our nation.

Enhanced scientific capability is both a short- and long-term necessity. The agency's scientific agenda must serve several functions: it must inform the regulatory work of the agency, contribute to the analysis of pollution risks, and provide an enhanced understanding of emerging threats. EPA should work with universities and other research institutions to improve the dialogue between policymakers and the research community.

Similar to the Department of Energy's existing Energy Lab program, EPA should create centers of excellence at institutions across the country focused on particular issues including climate change adaptation, energy efficiency and green technology, children's health, and environmental justice. The agency should produce a biennial report on the results of its science research programs to present to the president and Congress.

To ensure that EPA joins other federal departments and agencies in embracing government transparency, the agency should make public access to information more user-friendly and expand the available information to include "real-time" monitoring information. The administrator should revive EPA's detailed environmental monitoring program, known as EMPACT, which was discontinued in 2001, and should provide access to this information through the "Window to My Environment" EPA web program that is currently in place.

EPA also should connect data on local environmental indicators with the agency's performance standards.

Scientific research, access to information, and real-time monitoring are all crucial to support data-driven decision making.[19] But as this information infrastructure is built, there also must be accompanying changes in the decision-making process. In particular, this means developing systems to link key data to decision makers, clearly justify priorities and regulatory decisions using the best information available, and incorporate and respond to input from the public.

Clean Water

EPA has two important water authorities: the Clean Water Act of 1977 and the Safe Drinking Water Act of 1974. While they are separate laws, they are mutually reinforcing; together, these statutes prevent pollution from entering our rivers, lakes, and streams, making the delivery of safe drinking water easier. The combined trends of growing populations and higher drought frequencies will affect our ability to protect the quality of our water. Population growth, and the associated changes in land use, can harm wetlands and increase polluted runoff into lakes and streams.

The goal of the Clean Water Act is water that is "swimmable and fishable." While we have made real progress in reducing the pollution that comes from point sources such as wastewater treatment facilities and industrial pipes, we still have more than 20,000 water bodies that are identified by state authorities as polluted and in need of cleanup. A large portion of the remaining pollution comes from urban and agricultural runoff. In addition, climate change will affect our fresh water supplies, including salt water intrusion into fresh waters, alterations in the availability of water due to drought, and wetlands degradation with resulting impacts on groundwater.

To inform the agency's activities under the Safe Drinking Water Act, EPA should conduct a new, peer-reviewed study on the effects of hydraulic fracturing activities on underground water supplies. Hydraulic fracturing, used in oil and gas exploration, directly affects our nation's water supplies but is largely exempt from federal regulation under the Safe Drinking Water Act, due to a 2004 EPA study which found that hydraulic fracturing did not present health or environmental risks under the act. The study was the subject of concern both within and outside the agency as to its scientific independence and rigor. A new assessment should be conducted by EPA to more credibly evaluate the risk of drinking water contamination due to hydraulic fracturing.

Superfund

EPA should initiate a comprehensive public review of the Superfund program. To speed the pace and ensure the long-term safety of cleanups, the new administration should consider alternative mechanisms to manage resolution of liabilities, costs of cleanups, and long-term operation and maintenance at sites. For those sites with multiple "potentially responsible parties," the agency should consider a dedicated fund to help cover the share of cleanup costs of defunct companies.

EPA should consider the creation of a trust generated from the settlements of nature resources damages. The revenues generated could be used to address site-specific remediation needs as well as climate change adaptation plans. The agency should explore the concept of a trust fund/insurance pool to manage the long-term cleanup liability of both National Priorities List sites and brownfield sites.

The agency should also improve the information and financial systems for tracking clean-up progress and costs. As well, the agency should clarify the goals and processes of post-construction monitoring of former Superfund sites, and improve public access to the five-year post-construction reports by displaying the reports on the EPA website.[20]

For sites on the National Priorities List, EPA should measure cleanup progress on a quarterly basis, and should publish a web-based Superfund Annual Report each year disclosing this information to the public. The annual report should cover all National Priority List sites, and should summarize both site-level and program-level progress updates.[21]

Chemical Safety

To improve health and environmental protections from chemical exposure, the new president should send Congress a proposal for reauthorization of the Toxic Substances Control Act of 1976. The legislation should clarify the legal risk threshold required for EPA regulation of toxic chemicals and require more detailed hazard characterizations of new chemicals.

Prior to the reauthorization of the Toxic Substance Control Act, EPA should establish a mandatory testing program for the 2,200 chemicals that are produced or imported into the United States in excess of 1 million pounds per year. EPA has the authority to expand and codify the voluntary High Production Volume Challenge program currently in place under Section 4 of TSCA, which requires testing of chemicals that may result in significant human or environmental exposure.[22]

Mandatory High Production Volume data development would help to fill in the current information gaps in the Chemical Assessment and Management Program, or ChAMP, announced in March 2008, which relies heavily on HPV data for its risk findings. In order for ChAMP to be more effective and relevant, EPA should also update the TSCA Inventory to better reflect the universe of chemicals currently in commerce. Finally, EPA should make all data used for ChAMP risk assessments publicly available and should include peer-reviewed third-party data in its evaluations, where available.[23]

Endangered Species

To better protect endangered species, EPA must take into account the Endangered Species Act when implementing other federal environmental laws. In 2004, EPA issued a regulation that it could approve pesticides without consulting scientists and experts from federal wildlife agencies. In 2006, a federal court overturned this policy, but since then EPA has still been reluctant to fully examine the effects of pesticides on ecosystems and endangered species. The new EPA administrator should formally consult with the Fish and Wildlife Service and the National Marine Fisheries Service on the possible harmful effects of pesticides monitored by EPA on endangered species before registering pesticides.

Department of Agriculture

Tackling Food and Energy Crises Amid Global Warming

JAMES R. LYONS

The U.S. Department of Agriculture is at the intersection of some of the most critical and vexing issues facing the nation and the world. From the first days in office, the new president and his secretary of agriculture should lead efforts to address the global food crisis, food safety, and the development and production of biofuels, as well as play a lead role in building strategies to address climate change and reverse the Bush administration's harmful natural resource and environmental policies. The department's other high-priority concerns should include managing wildfires and repairing their ecological damage; improving nutritional standards to help reduce obesity and health care costs; restoring rural infrastructure; protecting the nation's water quality, roadless lands, and biodiversity; promoting agricultural trade; and maintaining America's farms and family farmers.

The U.S. Department of Agriculture's programs and policies affect nearly every American. The department protects food safety; provides nutritional guidance; supports rural communities; promotes food and fiber production; contributes to agricultural trade and international food assistance; and protects water quality, wildlife habitats, and the environment. The USDA Reorganization Act of 1994 eliminated 13 agencies in USDA and refocused the department's work under six undersecretaries. The purpose of this effort was to improve efficiency while significantly reducing expenditures at a time of high budget deficits.

Despite USDA's broad reach, its budget and workforce are in decline. The new president and his administration will therefore have to work to maximize its abilities by improving government coordination and collaboration, minimizing redundancy, and finding synergies in policies, budgets, and programs. USDA can eliminate program redundancies by creating one federal food safety agency and encouraging closer coordination, such as between USDA and the Department of the Interior and the Environmental Protection Agency on matters affecting water quality and watershed protection. The department can also maximize the benefits associated with new energy policy initiatives through, for example, a "home-grown" energy initiative that would use agricultural waste to produce energy for farms and return electricity to the grid to help meet the energy demands of rural communities and reduce CO_2 emissions.

The First 100 Days

The cost of rice, wheat, and corn rose 83 percent worldwide over the past three years, creating a global food crisis. These increases were caused by many factors. High energy prices raised food production and transport costs. Institutional investors moved more of their capital into commodities futures markets. More corn was diverted to ethanol production. Higher protein diets are on the rise in fast-growing developing countries such as India and China. Other contributing factors include extended droughts in Australia, North Africa, and Ukraine alongside a reduction in aid from the United States to promote agricultural production in developing countries.[1]

Elevated food costs are difficult for many Americans to handle. But rising costs are proving even more challenging for developing nations, where food riots in dozens of countries have generated social unrest and security concerns, and for international food organizations, which are working to feed the world's poor.

High food prices increase international pressure on the United States to reduce or eliminate tax credits for ethanol production and renewable fuel standards, which were adopted in conjunction with the Energy Security Act, and to permit lands currently enrolled in the Conservation Reserve Program to be converted back to commodity production. The international community also wants the United States to increase the amount of food assistance it provides to help avert starvation and malnutrition in food-limited parts of the world.

The new administration immediately should hold a cabinet-level discussion on the global food crisis given its complexity and far-reaching effects from economic, social, and national security perspectives. The new president should come to this meeting with the understanding that while increasing food exports and reforming current food assistance programs is essential, these steps provide only a short-term solution. He will also have to acknowledge that domestic efforts to promote energy security by promoting the use and production of ethanol may be contributing to the global food crisis. And he must recognize that the United States will have to commit to long-term investment in improving agricultural production in developing countries in order to reverse funding declines over the past 25 years.

Partnerships with a number of large, private foundations committed to improving global agriculture such as the Bill and Melinda Gates Foundation, Google Foundation, and the Rockefeller Foundation, as well as international financial institutions such as the World Bank, and international nonprofits with expertise in food aid and agriculture, can and should help USDA and the new administration prioritize investments that will yield the highest benefits.

Reform the Food Safety System

Responsibility for the nation's food safety system is divided between two agencies. The USDA's Food Safety and Inspection Service is responsible for the safety of meat, poultry, and processed egg products. The Food and Drug Administration is responsible for the safety of virtually everything else.

The current food safety system, and its associated complex of legislative authorities, needs to be reviewed, restructured, and simplified. Americans' health and food safety would ultimately be better served by combining the two agencies' food safety responsibilities into one food safety and inspection system within one agency in the federal government. If this is not politically or bu-reaucratically possible, then the new administration should improve the cur-rent food inspection system by requiring joint training of inspection personnel, adopting scientifically based inspection systems such as the Hazard Analysis and Critical Control Point systems, and eliminating redundant inspections.

According to a 2007 Government Accountability Office analysis, FDA could authorize USDA inspectors to inspect 1,451 facilities on their own that are cur-rently regulated by both agencies.[2] But this has not yet been done. At a mini-mum, the new president should work to grant USDA and FDA the legal authority to mandate food recalls for products that fail food safety standards and close food processing facilities when they find significant standards viola-tions. Despite the high public visibility, health risks, and potential economic consequences of tainted or unhealthy foods, recalls are voluntary and cannot be compelled under current law.

The new administration should also work with Congress to mandate that food processors and marketing and retail outlets be required to implement a trace-back system that would permit inspectors to determine the origin of foods or food ingredients when a food safety hazard arises. The outbreak of sal-monella in the summer of 2008 that was first associated with tomatoes and then with jalapeños illustrates the need to require the use of existing technolo-gies to ensure food safety and reduce the likelihood of inadvertent or inten-tional contamination of the nation's food supply.

Wildfire Prevention and Ecological Restoration

Devastating wildfires affected large portions of the western United States dur-ing the summer of 2008—part of a continuing pattern of increased wildfires across large portions of the American landscape that caused deaths, increased property damage, raised air quality concerns, and cost taxpayers billions of dol-lars in fire-fighting costs. As a result, 48 percent of the Forest Service's fiscal year 2009 proposed budget will have to go toward wildfire management, leaving lit-tle money to address its other public lands management responsibilities.

The Clinton administration in 2000 developed a strategy for reducing prop-erty damage and firefighting costs due to wildfires, which was endorsed by a bipartisan group of western governors. This strategy is in sharp contrast to the Bush administration's efforts, which continually sought to increase logging and waive environmental reviews for forest projects under its Healthy Forests initia-tive. To the contrary, the path to minimizing fire damage must include aggres-sive efforts to reduce fire-prone fuels near at-risk communities and increase partnerships with state and local governments to ensure that future development doesn't occur in ways and places that exacerbate fire risks for people and their property.

State and federal natural resource agencies will also need to improve their collaboration in order to repair the damage to millions of acres of public lands by wildfires in recent years. Reforestation, watershed restoration, road rehabilitation, and habitat improvement work can help minimize further environmental damage to scarred landscapes. These investments offer opportunities for public-private collaboration, can produce jobs for workers in rural communities whose income may have been affected by previous disasters, and can include large-scale volunteer projects for AmeriCorps and other service organizations. Ecological restoration projects can also increase carbon sequestration as a means of helping to address global warming concerns.

"Home-Grown" Energy Initiative

Congressional efforts to promote U.S. energy independence led to increases in biofuels production, primarily through subsidies for corn ethanol. While these efforts have accelerated the production of ethanol, recent studies question the net benefit of corn-based ethanol from a climate change perspective, and there is pressure, due to increased food and feed prices, to bring more environmentally sensitive conservation lands back into agricultural production.

USDA, in conjunction with the other relevant departments and the new National Energy Council (see the chapter on this new council in the White House section of the book), should convene a group of experts who can guide investment in a renewable energy strategy that includes, but is not limited to, biofuels production. This strategy should include opportunities to produce fuels from other cellulosic sources, from animal and other waste products, and from woody biomass such as from forest fuels reduction and removal. These approaches could reduce pressure on food production systems and commodity prices, while driving rural economic growth from materials that are often treated as waste.

Fuel production from woody biomass, if appropriately managed, could also provide a marketable use for woody debris in and around fire-prone communities and other areas of high ecological value at high risk from wildfire. These strategies, in conjunction with efforts to bring to scale other renewable energy technologies such as wind, solar, and animal waste anaerobic digesters, could redefine "farming" in certain parts of the nation. Where wind patterns permit, for example, windmills could be "planted" with corn, allowing wind energy to be reaped from the wind turbines, corn to be harvested for food production, and the corn stover (stalks and waste) to be used for cellulosic energy production.

Accelerated investments in research and development for next-generation biofuels could revolutionize energy production and boost the United States' capacity to meet domestic energy needs, all while continuing to meet U.S. and foreign food aid obligations and export objectives. The new administration must, however, commission a comprehensive assessment of the most rational energy strategies to pursue before committing significant resources to any particular energy alternative. This assessment must consider each energy source's effect on food prices, environmental and climate concerns, and economic factors.

Roadless Area Priorities

Americans want to see new leadership in efforts to protect environmental quality and improve our quality of life. During the Clinton administration, the USDA was a conservation leader in advocating for protecting the remaining National Forest roadless areas; improving the water quality of the nation's lakes, bays, and rivers; protecting key watersheds and their biodiversity; and preserving America's unique wild lands.

The new agriculture secretary should make a clear statement on reversing the Bush administration's anti-environmental policy decisions by recommending that the president issue an executive order to reinstate the January 2001 policy to protect remaining National Forest roadless areas and bring to a close the protracted debate over roadless area protection.[3] There is strong public and gubernatorial support for protecting roadless areas, and this action would be well received by most Americans.

The USDA's 2010 budget should seek funding for the backlog of private land conservation projects and the implementation of the conservation measures related to high-priority water quality and watershed needs laid out in the 2008 farm bill. The new administration should also convene a task force to identify critical watersheds and subsurface aquifers, beginning with those on public lands in the West that support public water supplies for major population centers, such as the Mount Hood watershed for Portland, Oregon. The secretaries of agriculture and the interior, in conjunction with the administrator of EPA, should then announce an administration commitment to repair resource damage and minimize further adverse effects on high-priority watersheds and subsurface water sources.

The First Year

Obesity has become an epidemic in the United States. The percentage of Americans who are overweight—60 percent according to the Centers for Disease Control—exceeds that of most developed nations. Obesity in children and young Americans is linked to an increase in the rate of Type II diabetes, and Type II diabetes can result in health problems and rising health care costs when left untreated.

USDA can help improve Americans' health and reduce our health care costs by setting standards for a healthy diet that emphasize current understanding about the connection between nutrition and human health and are not compromised by special interests. To do so, the department should work with independent experts from the nutrition, health, and medical professions to review and revise the USDA nutritional guidelines and develop standards for diet and exercise that are specifically designed to combat trends in obesity.

The revised nutrition standards should be incorporated into USDA nutrition programs and food guidelines, such as the federal school lunch program. Education and extension programs, and other USDA nutritional programs, should be used to disseminate this information as a part of a campaign for healthier Americans.

USDA programs should be evaluated to ensure that they are not working at cross purposes to achieve these healthy nutritional goals. This should apply to standards for USDA nutritional programs such as food stamps, school lunches, after-school meals, and related programs, as well as farm programs that might promote the production and use of foods or food additives such as high fructose corn syrup that add to an unhealthy diet. USDA's organic certification program should also be evaluated to ensure that it promotes a healthy American diet.

The department should also help improve opportunities for exercise and access to the outdoors, which, according to Richard Louv, author of *Last Child in the Woods*, provide physical, social, and psychological benefits.[4] The Forest Service, in conjunction with the National Park Service and the Department of Housing and Urban Development, should encourage greater protection of open space, parks, trails, and recreational access when designing and developing federally supported housing and urban areas. These new design standards for healthier communities would go a long way toward promoting greener and healthier communities.

Climate Change Readiness

The secretary should initiate a review of the consequences of climate change for U.S. agriculture, conservation, and forestry programs, and lead efforts to develop mitigation and adaptation strategies to address the effects of global warming. GAO gathered a wide range of scientists and federal land managers in 2006 to assess the potential effects of climate change on marine resources, forests, freshwater systems, and grass- and shrublands. An overall finding was that "federal land and water resources are vulnerable to a wide range of effects from climate change, some of which are already occurring."[5] Animal, plant, and human diseases could spread with increasing temperatures, requiring new strategies for prevention and treatment. Extreme weather events are predicted, and with them, the likelihood of increased flooding and extended drought in some regions.

The new secretary of agriculture should help frame the administration's climate change initiative and legislative recommendations early in 2009 by requesting that the National Science Foundation or an independent scientific panel review the findings of existing scientific research to determine the nature and extent of risk to domestic agriculture, rural communities, food supplies, and natural resources, and to recommend specific agency responses. This review should be informed by studies undertaken by a number of states and would benefit from collaboration with the National Association of Departments of Agriculture and the National Governors' Association.

USDA may, as a result of this review, need to begin responding to the effects of global warming by accelerating research into drought-resistant seed sources for key food and fiber crops; increasing assistance in the development of water conservation strategies for drought prone areas; adding support for energy audits and conservation measures for farms and rural communities; reviewing current research on biofuels, especially corn-based ethanol; and evaluating the effects of increased warming on flora and fauna, and the wildfire risk to national forests. This research might also consider ways to use current USDA conservation programs to promote greater carbon storage in agricultural soils and forests as a means of mitigating temperature rise and achieving other conservation goals.[6]

Farm Safety Net and Price Supports

Critics of current farm policy argue that programs benefit a relatively small percentage of U.S. farmers—only 25 percent of farmers currently receive commodity payments. They argue that program payments continue to go to farmers who don't need the income support, while other producers see little or no benefit. At the same time, programs such as the conservation assistance programs, which provide broader benefits, are oversubscribed and underfunded—as many as three-fourths of farmers and ranchers are turned away because of a lack of funds.

The new administration could elect to reduce program benefits to farmers who do not need the added financial support given the growing public criticism of U.S. farm programs, controversy over U.S. farm subsidies in the context of negotiations over international trade agreements, and the rapid rise in commodity prices and associated global food crisis. Any savings from cutting benefits could be redirected to other priority needs, such as promoting conservation projects, helping farmers adapt to the effects of climate change, or accelerating investments in research to promote cellulosic ethanol production.

These systems clearly need review given that the current farm safety net and price supports were created more than half a century ago, and much has changed since then. The new agriculture secretary could convene an independent review panel to determine what an appropriate farm safety net is and what kind of support modern American agriculture might need as it operates in a global economy.

Help Minority Farmers

Claims of longstanding prejudice and discrimination in lending practices and unfair treatment of minority farmers by USDA resulted in the Pigford lawsuit in the late 1990s. Yet this lawsuit and settlement did not resolve matters. Provisions in the 2008 farm bill provided for a moratorium on related farm foreclosures and gave $100 million to settle outstanding claims. To end this difficult and painful chapter in USDA history, the new secretary should bring together representatives of the affected parties and make clear that prejudice or discrimination will not be tolerated at the USDA.

To help move past this contentious issue, the secretary should also take two immediate actions. The secretary should establish a debt settlement initiative to resolve outstanding farmer debt involving discrimination claims, which are likely to exceed the $100 million authorized by Congress. And the secretary should propose additional funding in the fiscal year 2009 budget for the Small and Disadvantaged Farmers Program, covered in Sec. 1501 of the farm bill. These funds would provide support for programs to assist African-American, Hispanic, and Asian-Pacific American farmers in the United States whose numbers continue to decline. The 2008 farm bill increased funds for this program to $15 million, and as a sign of good faith and to provide needed support to minority farmers, the secretary should recommend funding at the fully authorized level.

Resolve U.S. Agricultural Trade Issues

The Doha round of World Trade Organization negotiations ended in July 2008 without achieving its primary goal of a new trade pact to help developing countries lift themselves out of poverty. A principal cause for the demise of the

Doha negotiations was controversy over the extent to which U.S. and EU farm programs distort trade. In addition, a long-standing dispute with Brazil over the cotton program led to a finding by the international body that administers WTO guidelines that said the U.S. cotton program violates current trade rules. A subsequent ruling permits Brazil to retaliate against U.S. exports in order to recover damages resulting from U.S. cotton subsidies.

The United States has a vested interest in resolving this dispute and continuing to capitalize on the strong demand for commodity exports. Markets in China, India, and other developing countries will continue to grow, and the United States is well positioned to capitalize on these markets, bringing added benefit to U.S. farmers, agribusinesses, and rural economies, and helping to address the U.S. balance of trade. Resolving this dispute could position U.S. agriculture to fully capitalize on new and emerging global markets for U.S. agricultural products.

Restoring Rural Infrastructure

The deterioration of America's infrastructure is not limited to cities and their suburbs. Rural roads, bridges, and utility and communications connections are all suffering from a lack of maintenance and inadequate upgrades. This failure to invest in upkeep could have alarming consequences. Many dams and levees built by the Soil Conservation Service and the Army Corps of Engineers, for example, have long outlived their engineered life spans.

USDA should launch an assessment of rural infrastructure reinvestment needs in anticipation of the new administration's input into the reauthorization of the Surface Transportation Act. This reinvestment would offer the added benefit of creating new rural employment opportunities, particularly in communities that have transitioned from natural resource extraction-based economies such as timber and mining to a broader economic base. Many workers' skills from these sectors of the economy can be applied to rural infrastructure projects; engineers dedicated to building roads for logging, for example, can now refocus their efforts on road and bridge repair.

Longer-Term Agenda

The new secretary of agriculture should direct the chief of the Forest Service and the director of the Bureau of Land Management to develop new, coordinated, and comparable approaches to public land management planning to bring nearly two decades of dispute over the national forest planning rules to closure. The secretary of agriculture should also suspend current forest planning rules—if final rules are promulgated by the Bush administration—and, in coordination with the secretary of the interior, direct that this joint rulemaking be completed within one year.

Public lands management is currently a crazy quilt of agencies with differing philosophies, missions, policies, and procedures. Better coordination and collaboration between these agencies would improve customer service, reduce costs, and simplify rules and procedures. There is still a strong need to encourage more collaboration among the agencies that manage the American landscape.

The Forest Service and Bureau of Land Management experimented with this approach late in the Clinton administration as the agencies shared roles and even "transferred" management authority to the agency best positioned on the landscape to guide land management. Given limited budgets and staffing shortages, more efficient strategies for public land management should also be explored, including managing federal assets on a watershed or ecosystem basis, coordinating budget development for highly valued landscapes and important national resources such as the Greater Yellowstone Ecosystem, and simplifying fee and permit systems.

Address Farm Labor Shortages

Farm labor shortages are affecting large and growing sectors of the U.S. agricultural economy, particularly fruit and vegetable growers. Shortages of pickers and other farm workers have forced farmers to destroy large parts of recent fruit and vegetable crops at a time when food prices are escalating. Temporary workers, primarily from Mexico and Latin America, have traditionally filled this void.

But the current debate over immigration reform has stymied efforts to resolve agriculture's need for farm labor. Immigration reform must ensure that agricultural workers are permitted to enter the country when labor-intensive crops are harvested and that migrant laborers are provided adequate shelter and health care, as well as compensated fairly for their work. Failure to address these issues in the context of immigration reform could severely reduce available workers and result in the loss or destruction of millions of dollars of crops.

Protect National Forest Lands

The Bush administration's rush to lease oil and gas reserves in the western United States could have a substantial, negative effect on air and water quality, wildlife habitat, and recreational assets in national forests. Environmental reviews were abbreviated or circumvented by Bush appointees who placed priority on getting potential energy tracts leased. Since the Forest Service has jurisdiction over land management issues, but no control over subsurface leasing, USDA should conduct a review of potential land and resource management conflicts arising from the Bush administration's "oil and gas rush."

This review should provide the basis for determining which leases should proceed and which warrant further review and/or buyout. The review should be coordinated with the Department of the Interior and criteria for review should be made consistent between both departments. The agriculture and interior secretaries should agree to transfer authority for the management of subsurface rights under national forest system lands to the Forest Service to simplify their administration.

Develop Distributed Energy

USDA, in order to capitalize on interest in low-carbon emitting "green" energy technologies and renewable energy sources in general, should undertake a pilot program to develop alternative energy systems for farms, ranches, and rural communities. The goal would be to create self-sustaining energy sources using distributed technologies that can operate "off the grid" and produce energy that can be returned to the grid.

It is not inconceivable that local farms could produce sufficient energy from renewable sources such as wind, solar, animal waste, biomass, and biofuels to sustain their own operations as well as support the energy needs of associated rural communities. An "Energy Independence Initiative" could borrow from new, distributed energy technologies—biofuels, wind, geothermal, solar—currently being employed on a small scale in the United States and in China and other developing nations. Rural electric cooperatives, with technical assistance and incentives, could provide the funding to promote this kind of investment as an alternative to coal-fired power plants and petroleum-based energy development.

Promote Family Farms

In many respects, the "family farm" has become a myth in American agriculture. Almost 60 percent of farms rely on alternative, non-farm sources of income to survive. Farmers and their spouses often must work two jobs to make a living, keep the farm in operation, and pay for health care and other essential costs. USDA should therefore conduct an evaluation of the factors necessary to better support family farms, such as improved access to credit, technical assistance, marketing assistance, or reduced cost for health care coverage, in order to find the most effective and efficient strategies to stem the continuing decline in America's family farms.

Some solutions might include creating a program to "pool" family farmers as a means of approaching health care providers to seek reduced health care costs. Others might include new marketing strategies for high-value farm products and added investment in the beginning farmer program.

Consumers and farmers are increasingly looking to local markets to reduce costs, ensure greater product freshness, and support local agriculture. The buy local movement has become a marketing strategy for some states, farm groups, and supermarket chains. In addition, advocates concerned about maintaining farm lands as a part of their landscape and carbon footprint are seeking ways to promote local farm production. The growing popularity of community-supported agriculture—where individuals "purchase" an interest in a farm or pre-purchase products from that farm—is one outgrowth of this trend.

USDA, through the Agricultural Marketing Service, promotes farmers' markets to increase marketing opportunities for local farmers and to reduce their transportation costs. The farmers' market coupon programs that provide special supplemental nutrition to needy mothers and their children, senior citizens, and food stamp recipients could be expanded to provide farmers' market coupons to foster healthier diets. USDA, working with the National Association of State Departments of Agriculture, should make "green" strategies an increasingly important part of its marketing efforts. The department should explore opportunities to link production and consumption strategies, and to connect farmers' markets and "buy local" marketing opportunities with local farmland protection efforts, the smart growth movement, and efforts to promote a healthier American diet.

Department of the Interior

Natural Resources Serving Society

JOHN LESHY

The Department of the Interior will be a key player in the new administration's efforts to control carbon emissions, forge a sound energy policy, and adapt to climate change. That should be its immediate priority. The department's near-term priorities should include expanding the young National Landscape Conservation System, revitalizing the government-to-government relationship with Indian Tribes, launching a multi-pronged initiative to protect biodiversity, and partnering with the states to forge management policies for critical water resources challenged by a destabilized climate. Over the longer term, the department must put management of publicly owned natural resources on a fiscally sound basis, improve the scientific credibility of its decisions, revitalize the nation's world-renowned systems of national parks and wildlife refuges, expand the national wilderness and wild and scenic river systems, and make better use of its lands and resources to promote environmental education, a conservation ethic, and volunteerism.

Historically dubbed the "Department of Everything Else," the Interior Department is a mélange of programs and responsibilities. It manages far more land and natural resources than any other cabinet department—about 500 million acres, or about one of every five acres in the United States. The department also manages subsurface minerals on hundreds of millions of other acres. The lands under Interior's management include the nation's 84 million acres of "crown jewels" in the National Park System, 95 million acres of rich biological resources in the National Wildlife Refuge System, and the 260 million acres of so-called "public lands" managed by the Bureau of Land Management, which makes BLM, despite its relative obscurity, the largest single land manager in the country. All told, Interior's lands are a major setting for recreation and environmental education, and a primary source of vital natural resources such as fossil fuels and water.

Interior is a dominant presence in the West. The department manages between 28 percent and 83 percent of the lands in 11 different western states and Alaska. Interior's Bureau of Reclamation operates water projects in 17 western states, supplying municipal water to 31 million people and irrigation water to 10 million acres of farmland. Beyond the West, Interior manages land in every state and hundreds of millions of acres of submerged land on the Outer Continental Shelf that rings the country. Its Minerals Management Service administers and collects some $11 billion per year from federally leased oil and gas offshore and onshore, making MMS the third leading revenue collector in the government (after the Internal Revenue Service and Medicare).

The department also leads in natural science expertise. Its U.S. Geological Survey conducts basic geological, hydrological, and biological research. Interior's Bureau of Indian Affairs is the focal point of the national government's relationship with more than 500 federally recognized Native American Tribes throughout the country. It holds legal title to more than 50 million acres of Indian reservation land, natural resources, and money held in trust for tribes and several hundred thousand individual Indians. Finally, some of Interior's important regulatory responsibilities extend far beyond federally owned assets. Its U.S. Fish and Wildlife Service is the primary enforcer of the Migratory Bird Treaty Act and Endangered Species Act, and its Office of Surface Mining administers the Surface Mining Control and Reclamation Act.

Key Challenges

The new administration's Department of the Interior will have three key challenges: to reform national natural resource policy to forge a sustainable energy policy and deal responsibly with climate destabilization; to protect America's public land treasures for the future and engage the growing progressive forces in the western United States where most of these lands are found; and to restore Interior's credibility and leadership role in natural resources science and management and rebuild funding for key Interior programs.

Climate destabilization poses formidable new challenges to the nation, and Interior will be instrumental in the new administration's efforts to adopt a greenhouse-gas-sensitive national energy policy. Interior's broad expertise and substantial information-gathering apparatus in the earth sciences—geology, hydrology, and biology—must play a key role. Interior's lands should serve as a vast demonstration project for how to manage natural resources in the face of this daunting problem. Federal lands will likely be the locus of renewable resource development such as solar, wind, and geothermal and associated energy transmission infrastructure, as well as significant biological sources of carbon sequestration and suitable sites for geological carbon sequestration.

Interior-managed lands and waters will also play an important role in climate-change adaptation strategies, including serving as sanctuaries for species imperiled by shifting habitats and other climatic changes. And Interior's responsibilities regarding water will become even more vital. New climate models as well as studies of climate history are leading to a widening agreement among scientists that many regions, particularly fast-growing areas in the Southeast and Southwest, will face major water disruptions. In the Colorado River Basin—an important water source for 30 million people in seven U.S. states and Mexico—the years 2000–2007 were the driest by far in more than a century of record. Droughts will likely be longer and deeper, and warmer temperatures will reduce snowpack—an important source of water storage throughout the West—and accelerate spring runoff.

The Bush administration exercised almost no leadership in this area. State and local water management agencies have admirably filled the vacuum and begun to develop a number of progressive strategies for addressing what soon may be a crisis. The new administration, and particularly the Interior Department, needs to sustain this momentum.

Interior also plays a key role in current energy supply. Interior-managed lands, including lands on the Outer Continental Shelf, now account for about 40 percent of domestic natural gas production and one-third of domestic crude oil production. About half of U.S. coal production now comes from federal lands managed by Interior, mostly in Wyoming, up from 10 percent three decades ago. The dams managed by Interior's Bureau of Reclamation produce significant amounts of hydropower, and several Interior agencies are responsible for ensuring that licenses issued by the Federal Energy Regulatory Commission for non-federal hydropower projects on the nation's rivers adequately protect fisheries and other natural resources. Interior's lands might also be a major source of uranium fuel for nuclear power plants if that technology regains favor. Interior must carefully craft its policies in these areas to facilitate the transition to the new energy era.

Federal lands managed by Interior also contain many of the nation's crown jewels. Besides the well-known national parks and historic sites, these lands include watersheds vital to the nation's supply of clean fresh water, some of the nation's best fishing and hunting opportunities, coastal wetlands, key wildlife habitat, and inspirational wild lands. The Bush administration substantially neglected the nation's great systems of parks, refuges, wild and scenic rivers, and wilderness, as well as the fledging new National Landscape Conservation System that was established during the Clinton administration. These systems need attention, nourishment, and expansion.

Most of these areas are in the American West, which has long been the most rapidly growing region in the country and now has a higher percentage of its residents living in urban areas than any other region in the country. Its burgeoning metropolitan areas are sprinkled across a landscape of splendid natural amenities, much of it managed by Interior. In recent decades the western regional economy has broken its historical dependence on producing commodities such as trees, minerals, and beef. While that transition was underway, irritation and conflict marked the relationship between westerners and the federal government. Interior—the most visible federal presence in the region—was in the crosshairs.

Those tensions have subsided considerably. Westerners have deepened their appreciation of the vital and generally positive contributions Interior makes to the quality of life in the region. Western states have become more progressive, and even historic adversaries like ranchers and conservationists now find common ground on a number of issues. Climate and water disruption and the need to reorient energy policy make cooperation ever more important. The new administration has a huge opportunity, and responsibility, to formulate strategies and policies to constructively partner with this "New West."

The last eight years have been difficult ones for the department. Despite its enormous reach and the grassroots popularity of many of its programs, funding for most of its important programs has been constrained. What's more, Interior has abdicated its leadership role in natural resource policy, and has instead become mostly a lapdog for the oil and gas industry and other development interests. The science underpinning the department's important responsibilities has been subjected to rank political manipulation—most notoriously, a political appointee with no scientific training routinely rewrote Fish and Wildlife Service biological findings under the Endangered Species Act—and the department's neglect of the larger public interest carried more than a whiff of scandal, with its deputy secretary from 2001 through 2004 serving a jail sentence for obstruction of justice by lying to investigators about his contacts with convicted felon and former lobbyist Jack Abramoff.

The Bush administration sought to paper over this decline with empty platitudes about "consultation, communication and cooperation in the service of conservation." Morale in the once-proud department has plummeted. A rebuilding effort is sorely needed, starting with vigorous leadership and recruitment of new talent and recognition that dollars spent at Interior have a tremendous multiplier effect, touching the lives of many millions of people.

The First 100 Days

The Bush administration watered down or jettisoned numerous Clinton-era reforms that had modernized environmental controls on hard-rock mines and livestock grazing on federal land. It overturned carefully balanced decisions such as one protecting wildlife and delicate tundra ecology while developing the oil and gas resources in the National Petroleum Reserve in northwest Alaska, and another phasing out noisy, polluting snowmobiles in Yellowstone, the world's first national park.

Some Bush-era decisions truly defied common sense. The administration claimed, for example, that Interior lacked the authority to disapprove mines proposed on federal land no matter how disastrous the environmental impact, or designate "wilderness study areas" on public lands in order to preserve Congress's option to add them to the National Wilderness Preservation System. The new administration should thoroughly review policies and positions adopted during the past eight years, promptly decide which ones need to be reconsidered, and initiate a process for doing so.

The Interior Department should give careful consideration to the Bush White House's energy-related policies, and work to reorient energy policy involving federal lands. The Clinton administration leased millions of acres of federal land onshore and offshore for oil and gas development, but took care to avoid special places inappropriate for industrial development. By contrast, beginning with an executive order issued in May 2001, the Bush administration made energy production the dominant use of federal lands and consistently overrode the concerns of state and local governments, ranchers, hunters, anglers, and others in its relentless drive to turn federal energy resources over to the energy industry.

The 44th president should send clear signals that private energy companies are no longer in command. Federal lands will remain an important source of fossil fuels to bridge the transition to a new energy policy. These include submerged lands offshore, which sometimes pose fewer conflicts with other resources than onshore land. Overall, the administration should work closely with affected states and other interests to limit fossil fuel development to areas of high potential where serious conflicts with other important resources are manageable or avoidable. It should also tighten regulation to ensure that energy companies operating on federal lands are responsible for thorough cleanup and reclamation. And it should take the lead in crafting new policies regarding energy-related uses of federal lands, addressing such issues as how much to charge non-federal entities for permission to use sites on federal lands for solar, wind, and carbon sequestration projects.

Expand National Landscape Conservation

Interior and the public have increasingly recognized that the Bureau of Land

Management's 260 million acres contain some superb scenic, historic, cultural, and recreational sites that provide inspiration, education, and outdoor scientific laboratories, not to mention tourism dollars for local economies.

Since the 1970s, a little more than 10 percent of BLM lands have been protected as national conservation areas, monuments, and wilderness. The Clinton administration created a new National Landscape Conservation System within BLM for these specially designated lands. Some of the Clinton monument proclamations were initially controversial in more conservative parts of the West, but they and the NLCS quickly gained wide acceptance. The Bush administration, initially hostile to the NLCS, has now endorsed a proposal, expected to become law in late 2008, that will make the NLCS permanent.

Yet the NCLS remains a work in progress. Many other BLM areas—ranging in size from a few acres to large landscapes—are worthy candidates for inclusion. The system should take its rightful place alongside the national park, national forest, and national wildlife refuge systems. The new administration, to that end, should promptly announce an initiative to fill out the NLCS, inviting nominations from governors, tribes, historic and cultural preservation groups, hunters, anglers, and other recreationists, conservationists, tourism representatives, and local business interests. Interior should work with Congress and all affected interests to decide what areas to include. Congress could add areas through legislation, or the new president could add them through the Antiquities Act.

Revitalize Relations with Tribes

The new administration should create a task force of Interior and other federal officials and tribal representatives to explore ways to revitalize the government-to-government relationship between federal agencies and tribes. After eight years of neglect, federal Indian policy needs overhauling.

One example is unresolved tribal legal claims to water. Interior should work with the tribes and the Congress to facilitate their resolution. The department has had considerable success over the last couple of decades working with tribes and states to resolve tribal water rights claims without resorting to expensive, divisive, lengthy, and uncertain litigation. There is, however, a good deal left to do. Nearly two dozen tribes are currently in settlement discussions. The biggest obstacle to resolving these claims is typically money, as proposed settlements can cost dozens to hundreds of millions of dollars, mostly borne by the federal government. At the same time, the federal government continues heavy subsidies for non-Indian agricultural irrigation, which typically relies on water rights junior to the Indians' rights.

New legislation and court decisions also make it appropriate to reexamine a 1995 executive order spurring federal agencies to use best efforts to identify and protect features of Indian cultural and religious value found on federal lands. Interior should also make sure tribes are informed and make intelligent choices about whether to use Indian lands for solar, wind, and other energy-related developments. The new administration should also work to bring to closure long-standing litigation over Interior's historical mismanagement of Indian trust funds. A federal judge recently determined that the United States owed Indians $456 million. Both sides have appealed; the Indian beneficiaries believe the government's liability greater.

The First Year

The rich variety of life on Earth is shrinking at an alarming rate, with profound economic, ecological, sociological, ethical, and human health implications. Climate disruptions will probably accelerate this loss by altering habitats and changing the timing of seasonal events such as snowmelt and insect emergence. The new administration must deal with the problem both domestically and internationally, with Interior playing a key role. Interior's Fish and Wildlife Service has the lead responsibility for implementing the Convention on International Trade in Endangered Species of Flora and Fauna, a global effort to protect biodiversity. Interior's expertise ought to be brought to bear to ensure that efforts to address carbon emissions around the globe involve intelligent use of carbon offsets to protect biodiversity.

Federal lands will likely be ever-more crucial reservoirs of biodiversity, but they are not always well located to play that role; gaps exist in their coverage of biodiversity "hot spots" and key migration corridors. The new administration should convene a group of experts to examine these issues systematically, and craft strategic guidance to federal land and water agencies on how best to preserve biodiversity against the challenge of climate destabilization.

The new administration will also need to review Endangered Species Act policies. The Clinton administration put in place a number of administrative reforms to make the ESA work better, including broadening the focus beyond single species and enlisting the voluntary cooperation of state and private landowners. By contrast, the Bush administration gave the ESA lip service but did not back up its words with effort or dollars, instead working strenuously behind the scenes to ignore or evade ESA responsibilities.

The new administration should reinvigorate efforts to make the ESA more effective and user friendly, using the tools of habitat conservation planning and adaptive management and promoting stronger partnerships with state wildlife agencies and private landowners through the use of financial and other incentives. For instance, various proposals have been made to extend valuable tax credits to private landowners who enter into agreements with the government to protect and recover endangered species, one small part of which was included in the 2008-enacted farm bill.

Concerns remain whether, as currently written and funded, the ESA can stem the loss of biodiversity in a climate-disrupted world. Species particularly sensitive to climate destabilization are being brought under its protection. Interior recently listed the polar bear, imperiled by Arctic melting, as a "threatened" species under the ESA, and is currently engaged in a court-ordered reconsideration of its 2005 decision not to list the sage grouse, whose habitat extends over millions of acres in 11 western states occupied by the energy industry and cattle ranchers.

Yet some experts think the Act could be overwhelmed if its processes are heavily relied upon as a primary means of tackling greenhouse gas emissions. Numerous problems with the Act, including its focus on single species, its "emergency room" dynamic, its complex bureaucratic processes, and its lack of clarity with respect to habitat protection, have spawned repeated efforts in Congress to reform the Act over the past 15 years, all of them unsuccessful.

The ESA focuses attention on the need to safeguard the planetary web of life upon which we all depend. The new administration must fashion ways of preserving the ESA as a powerful symbol and an essential tool for protecting biodiversity.

Address Water Supply Problems

The new administration must work with Congress and federal, state, tribal, and local water officials and others to craft measures to help areas at risk to manage vital water supplies while coping with drought and other water supply disruptions. It can bring many tools to bear to meet this challenge. It must bolster the U.S. Geological Survey's hydrologic expertise and systematic information-gathering capabilities. It must also re-examine the Bureau of Reclamation and the Army Corps of Engineers' policies with an eye toward cushioning the effects of climate disturbances. The Bureau and the Corps should take energetic steps in collaboration with state authorities to promote more efficient use of water, wastewater recycling, groundwater storage and recovery, and conjunctive management of ground and surface water. They should also facilitate voluntary transfers of water from lower- to higher-value uses, and adjust operations of federal water projects to better protect aquatic ecosystems.

The Interior department should craft clearer policies to govern the use of federal lands for groundwater storage and supply projects; pipelines and other water conveyance facilities; and solar, wind, or other energy projects to help provide the large amount of energy needed to move water to where it is needed. Interior can play a major role in promoting better water management by exercising its power to formulate binding environmental conditions for Federal Energy Regulatory Commission-licensed hydropower projects, and by helping to resolve conflicts among the states over water bodies, including groundwater basins, with interstate dimensions.

All of these water issues implicate Interior's responsibility for endangered species. The Endangered Species Act is increasingly shaping the management of river systems throughout the country, as the nation's 80,000 dams and associated water diversions have drastically reshaped aquatic environments and put a number of species, such as many wild salmon runs, in peril.

National Park and National Wildlife Refuge

Despite its iconic stature and overwhelming popularity, the National Park System has suffered mightily in recent years. President George W. Bush took office promising full funding for the system, but his administration never came close to achieving that goal. His administration meanwhile undertook such misguided initiatives as weakening rules that protect air quality in national parks. To hide these failures, the Bush administration announced an ambitious Centennial Initiative in 2006—a 10-year revitalization program to end with the 100th anniversary of the National Park Service in August 2016. The Initiative calls for up to $2 billion in new federal funds, the second billion requiring a match of $1 billion in private money.

The new administration should embrace the general idea of a centennial initiative, but should at the same time create a blue-ribbon commission to examine challenges the system faces as it heads into its second century, including appropriate criteria for expansion, the system's role in urbanized areas, the role of public-private partnerships, and how best to assess and meet deferred maintenance needs.

The National Wildlife Refuge System, which receives more than 40 million visitors a year, includes about 100 million acres—an area the size of California—in 550 units scattered throughout the 50 states. This system too has suffered from neglect, lack of funding, and threats from inappropriate uses. It now faces the challenge of adapting to a destabilized climate because many refuges are located on barrier islands, in coastal wetlands, and in other climate-sensitive habitats. A similar blue-ribbon commission should be created to chart the future of the refuge system, including exploring ways to make its funding base more secure.

The new administration should also launch an initiative to expand the role of federal lands in promoting environmental education, a conservation ethic, and volunteerism. Recent studies have documented a shocking degree of "nature-deficit disorder" among the nation's youth. This all-too-common "denatured" childhood has many pernicious health, educational, cultural, and political effects. Interior can play a significant role in reversing this trend. Lands managed by the department are within easy driving distance of the overwhelming majority of Americans, and they offer outstanding opportunities for stimulating educational experiences.

The initiative would revitalize Theodore Roosevelt's vision of a "prophylactic dose of nature" to bring more balance to modern life and inculcate a conservation ethic. It should include measures to promote volunteerism on the federal lands, from senior citizens helping out in visitor centers, to volunteer crews doing trail maintenance and cleanup, to students and others helping with surveys of wildlife and cultural and historic resources. Such public involvement would benefit the agencies, the lands, the visitors, and the volunteers themselves.

Strengthen Fiscal Policies

The new administration must systematically review federal policies regarding whether and how much to charge for the use of federal lands and resources by miners, ranchers, recreationists, timber companies, utilities, and others. This includes restoring credibility to the oil and gas royalty collection program, achieving full funding of the Land and Water Conservation Fund, and securing reform of the Mining Law of 1872.

Federal policy on these fiscal matters is an incoherent hodge-podge, having evolved haphazardly over the years. It lacks a consistent rationale for the kinds and levels of rents, royalties, and fees charged, and the methods of calculating them. Some exploiters of valuable federal resources such as hard-rock miners pay no rental or royalty at all. Federal agencies charge other users much less than state or private landowners charge in comparable settings. In recent years, federal agencies, spurred by legislation such as the Federal Lands Recreational Enhancement Act of 2004, have begun charging fees for camping and other recreational uses of federal lands, creating controversy and proposals for legislative reform.

Adding to this confusion, revenues generated by such fees are used in widely different ways. Some go directly into the federal Treasury; others are earmarked for various purposes, such as the Land and Water Conservation Fund, but remain subject to congressional appropriation; and still others are put in true revolving funds where, for example, revenues from recreation fees are recycled to local land managers.

Clear, consistent rationales on these matters are essential for public confidence in the management of these publicly owned resources. The new administration should promptly convene a blue-ribbon task force to comprehensively examine federal land royalty, rental, and fee policies, comparing them as appropriate to policies followed by state and private landowners, and making recommendations for reform. This task force also should scrutinize fee-setting for such important emerging federal land uses as wind and solar generation projects, energy transmission facilities, groundwater storage and recharge projects, and carbon sequestration projects. Some potential fee reforms can be implemented administratively; the Mineral Leasing Act, for example, sets a minimum but not a maximum royalty rate for fossil fuels. Others, such as levying rents and royalties on hard-rock miners, require legislative action.

The department must also work with Congress to restore full funding for the Land and Water Conservation Fund. The LWCF, established in 1965, is supposed to receive about $1 billion annually from federal oil and gas receipts for distribution to support federal, state, and local conservation projects throughout the country. President Bush came into office promising to fully fund it, but LWCF appropriations declined by 70 percent between 2001 and 2008. The LWCF enjoys wide popular support, and it can effectively defuse and fairly resolve many natural resource conflicts.

In recent years, Interior's royalty collection program, which in fiscal year 2007 collected more than $11 billion from more than 2,000 companies producing from 30,000 leases on federal and Indian land, has been the target of substantial criticism from Interior's Inspector General and the Government Accountability Office. These agencies have charged that Interior's supervision is inadequate. Legislation may be necessary to restore the program's credibility and to ensure that the American people are receiving their fair share of the profits that private companies reap by exploiting enormously valuable public resources.

The Deep Water Royalty Relief Act of 1995 is of particular concern. It directed the department to waive royalties for companies producing oil and gas from deep water in the Gulf of Mexico in order to encourage development of deepwater extraction technology. Following its enactment, Interior began including a term in Outer Continental Shelf leases that limited such royalty waivers when the price of oil rose above certain levels, reasoning that higher oil prices eliminated the need for the incentive. Some OCS lessees persuaded a federal judge, in a decision now on appeal, that Interior lacked legal authority to cap royalty relief based on the price of oil. With oil prices at record levels and a large amount of oil and gas being produced in the deepwater Gulf, tens of billions of dollars are riding on the outcome of the court appeal. The House twice approved bills aimed at securing more payments from the federal lessees, but the Senate has so far taken no action.

Another law badly in need of reform, the Mining Law of 1872, governs precious metal mining on several hundred million acres of federal land. It was crafted in the wake of the California Gold Rush, yet is remarkably still on the books. The mining industry views the law as giving it a "right to mine" that trumps all other uses and values of the federal lands. Miners remove minerals with few environmental controls, pay no rental or royalty fees, and sometimes leave the government to clean up gigantic messes at taxpayer expense. After many years of trying, a comprehensive reform bill passed the U.S. House in the fall of 2007. The reform never made it through the Senate in 2008, but the new administration should vigorously pursue modernizing this old law in the new Congress.

Longer-Term Priorities

Long-term priorities should include working with Congress to expand the National Wilderness Preservation System and the National Wild and Scenic Rivers System, re-examining and improving the processes that govern planning and environmental assessment on federal lands, working to reconfigure Bureau of Land Management landholdings to meet emerging needs, and re-examining federal wildfire policies.

The Wilderness Act, which will celebrate its 50-year anniversary in 2014, created a system of federal lands managed primarily to protect their primeval conditions, without roads or commercial intrusions. Congress makes the final decision whether to put lands in the system. So far somewhat more than 100 million acres have been included. Up to 100 million more acres are eligible for inclusion, but await congressional consideration. The Wild and Scenic Rivers Act, which will mark its 50-year anniversary in 2018, protects designated river corridors from dam-building and most other forms of intensive development. Some 11,000 river miles have been designated. Another few thousand miles are currently being studied for inclusion. The new administration should work with Congress and set ambitious goals for enlarging these great national systems.

Many Interior Department decisions are channeled through a resource-management planning process, by which federal land managers essentially

"zone" federal lands under their jurisdiction for different kinds of uses and facilitate them through the environmental impact assessment process of the National Environmental Policy Act. Concern has grown in recent years that,
rather than achieving better decisions, these processes have resulted in ritualis-
tic paper-shuffling. Rather than trying to improve them, the Bush administration took steps to jettison them entirely for broad categories of federal land
decisions, by diluting planning requirements and making aggressive use of so-
called "categorical exclusions" from the National Environmental Policy Act.

The Interior Department should work with the Forest Service, the President's Council on Environmental Quality, and other interests to craft and implement sensible reforms of the planning and environmental assessment
processes. Making them work better is especially timely because new climate
policies will likely require that federal land management agencies consider climate change mitigation and adaptation strategies in their decision making.

Interior should also work to reconfigure the Bureau of Land Management's
landholdings to meet emerging energy and economic needs. A considerable
amount of BLM-managed land is held in awkwardly shaped or scattered tracts,
shot through with in-holdings or otherwise configured in ways that make management to serve national needs difficult. A tool with particular promise is the
Federal Land Transaction Facilitation Act, enacted in July 2000. It authorizes
BLM to sell scattered, difficult-to-manage tracts that have value for economic
development and other useful purposes, and use the proceeds directly, without
having to wait for appropriations from Congress, to buy in-holdings and other
lands with higher conservation values. The Bush administration, unfortunately,
pushed to use the proceeds from FLTFA sales for other purposes. The new administration should work to reauthorize FLTFA, which expires in 2010, and
keep the Act's conservation orientation.

A final longer-term priority is to reform federal wildfire policies. The number and destructiveness of forest and grassland fires has increased dramatically
in recent years, especially in the arid West. The causes include a century-old
policy of fire suppression, homebuilding in isolated locations, drought, and destructive invasions of pests such as the pine bark beetle and exotic species such
as cheatgrass. Climate change will likely exacerbate this problem.

The Bush administration sought, with some success, to capitalize on people's fear of wildfires to weaken environmental protections and promote logging as a fire protection measure. The federal fire-fighting budget meanwhile
continues to skyrocket. The new administration should work with state and local governments, the insurance industry, and others to craft a more balanced
approach to the challenge of wildfires.

A range of tools need to be brought to bear, including more fire-resistant construction, "firewise" landscaping, fuel-load reductions like brush control and thinning, avoiding construction in certain fire-prone areas, and prescribed or controlled burns. The Forest Service should take the lead on this issue, as about half its total budget is now devoted to firefighting, but Interior shares considerable responsibility because many of its lands are involved.

Federal Communications Commission
Preparing the Way for Ubiquitous Broadband

LARRY IRVING

America is at a watershed moment for the telecommunications industry. We are shifting from a regulatory structure based on managing spectrum scarcity to a period of spectrum abundance driven by technological innovation. The new administration's highest priority will be to develop and implement a national broadband strategy that ensures every American household has affordable access to a broadband network of at least 100 megabits per second by the year 2012. Providing a ubiquitous broadband network is a national imperative, but ensuring consumers have nondiscriminatory access to the network, as well as the content and applications they desire, are also critical goals.

There has been an unprecedented increase in media concentration over the past decade, which has reduced the number and quality of local voices and elevated commercial interests at the expense of the public interest. The new president and the Federal Communications Commission should restore the primacy of the public interest standard and our national commitment to diverse voices and diversity of ownership. The FCC should also prioritize including all of our rapidly diversifying population in the mainstream of the technological revolution so that women and members of minority and immigrant communities are not just consumers of technology, but also owners, producers, and creators of content, applications, and facilities.

The Federal Communications Commission was created in 1934 during President Franklin D. Roosevelt's first term, and was charged with ensuring that broadcast licensees served "the public interest, convenience and necessity."

Broadcast regulation historically assumed that the electromagnetic spectrum is a scarce public good and only a limited number of licensees are possible in any community. The commission adhered to a three-legged stool in support of the public interest standard: localism, diversity, and universal service. The commission required licensees to serve the discrete and specific interests of local communities; meet the diverse needs of the public and contain a multiplicity of voices; and serve all Americans, irrespective of income or geography.

Successive commissions considered localism, diversity, and universal service integral to our nation's communications policies until the early 1980s, when Mark Fowler, the first FCC chairman of the Reagan administration, launched the first in a series of attacks on the public interest standard. Fowler's efforts to "deregulate" broadcasting and telecommunications entities and licensees were merely the opening salvos in an almost three-decade long battle to define and redefine broadcast and telecommunications regulation. Broadcasting and telecommunications industries, which traditionally had been monopolies or oligopolies, were facing new competition as a result of technological and marketplace changes. The FCC during this time initiated a more market-oriented focus to reflect those changes and bring the benefits of increased competition to consumers of broadcast and telecommunications services.

Under Fowler and a succession of chairmen, however, "the marketplace" was not just a factor to be considered, but the primary factor. Commercial interests, not the public interest, assumed primacy in commission decision making. The Clinton-era commission chairs Reed Hundt and Bill Kennard fought to reinject public interest into the FCC by trying to ensure that every American had access to advanced telecommunications and information technologies, particularly the Internet, and that no American was left on the wrong side of the emerging "digital divide." Hundt and Kennard understood that innovation and competition are enhanced by the public interest standard. They also understood, as did the framers of the 1934 Communications Act, that both service providers and consumers benefit when all Americans have access to new telecommunications and information technologies.

Hundt and Kennard's efforts, unfortunately, were rolled back during the Bush administration, which oversaw a deeply partisan and dysfunctional FCC during its tenure under the chairmanships of Michael Powell and Kevin Martin. Most recently, there have been complaints by other commissioners that Powell and Martin operated outside of the norms of transparent and open rulemaking. The new administration and the commission will have the responsibility for shepherding the United States into the broadband Internet era, transitioning to digital broadcasting, overseeing a new era of wireless and satellite technologies, and countless other innovations.

Communications policy under the new administration will not be driven by spectrum and bandwidth constraints. The emergence of capacious, ubiquitous broadband networks will provide an opportunity for a more democratic media, increased consumer choice, and enhanced international competitiveness. The commission will no longer manage a scarce spectrum resource, but spectrum and bandwidth abundance. It must therefore ensure the return to primacy of our historic commitment to service in the public interest and the attendant values of localism, diversity, and universal service.

The First 100 Days

Almost immediately upon taking office, the FCC and the new administration will be confronted with the most drastic overhaul of our domestic broadcasting system in history. On February 17, 2009, less than a month after the new president is inaugurated, every television station in America will cease transmitting in analog and those analog signals will be replaced by digital ones. Congress mandated the transition in order to free spectrum for auction and for use by public safety officials. The transition to digital will result in better video and audio signals for most Americans, and increased programming options from most stations, but Americans who own televisions manufactured before March 1, 2007, will not be able to secure an over-the-air television signal unless they sign up for a subscription television service, such as cable or satellite television; buy a new digital television; or purchase a converter. The government authorized a program to provide coupons for $40 toward the price of a converter box, but it is unclear whether this program will be adequate to ensure that all Americans—particularly low-income and rural Americans who rely more heavily on television to receive news and emergency announcements and are also less likely to be able to afford the cost of conversion—have television access after February 17.

This digital transition could result in massive consumer frustration and dislocation. The FCC, Department of Commerce, industry associations, and others have attempted to inform the American public about the impending switch to digital. Congress has authorized and funded both an education campaign and a billion-dollar program to provide consumers with converter boxes. Yet it is not clear whether most Americans understand how dramatic the change is. Over 21 million Americans rely solely on over-the-air television, and these

Americans are disproportionately low income, rural, or speak Spanish as their primary household language.

The new administration and FCC must quickly conduct broad education efforts to prepare the American public for the transition to digital television. They must ensure that every American knows and is prepared for the impending digital television transition. And agency and administration officials must inform people why the transition was mandated—to ensure that public safety officials have adequate spectrum and other electronic resources in the event of a national disaster, act of war, or terrorism.

Officials must also ensure that the voucher program is flexible enough to ensure that every American who needs or wants a converter box is able to obtain one prior to the transition. If the voucher program runs aground in the early days of the new administration, it will be difficult to convince the public or the broadcasting and consumer electronics industries that the new FCC and the new administration are competent when it comes to technology. Moreover, although most of the preparatory work for the transition will have been undertaken during the Bush administration, Congress will have no patience with whoever is serving as chair of the FCC on February 18, 2009, if millions of Americans are unable to obtain a television signal in their homes.

National Broadband Strategy

The new administration and the FCC's highest priority will be to articulate and implement a comprehensive national broadband strategy. Investment in broadband infrastructure will drive significant improvements in democratic discourse, education, health care, energy reduction, environmental monitoring, economic and job growth, and national competitiveness. Over the past eight years, the FCC has failed to promote policies that increase investment in and availability of broadband networks. Broadband penetration rates in America are unacceptably low. Only slightly more than 50 percent of American households subscribe to broadband, and according to recent surveys, African Americans, rural Americans, and Spanish-speaking Hispanic households currently subscribe to residential broadband at distressingly low levels.[1]

The new administration should within the first 100 days articulate a broadband vision, and then over the next six to nine months develop a comprehensive national broadband strategy to achieve that vision. The president should set a goal of making sure that all Americans by 2012 have access to an affordable network that provides, at a minimum, 100 megabits per second. To achieve that goal, the president should launch a mapping initiative to determine pockets of broadband abundance and broadband paucity, and develop policies and practices designed to assure universal broadband access and promote universal broadband connectivity.

The mapping initiative would be a public-private partnership undertaken by the FCC in conjunction with the Commerce Department's Census Bureau and National Telecommunications and Information Administration. It would expand on successful state efforts, such as the Connect Kentucky initiative, the California Broadband Task Force, and others. An annual Census Bureau survey reviewing consumer usage of the Internet, particularly broadband networks and technology adoption, would supplement the mapping initiative.

The FCC must include consumer organizations and affected industries, content and application creators, and equipment manufacturers in the design and implementation of the mapping initiative. A critical component of the initiative will be to devise metrics and analyses that by the end of 2009 would establish a baseline of broadband penetration and utilization in the United States. The mapping program should be more granular than previous and current commission studies of broadband penetration. In mapping broadband deployment and availability, the commission should use more granular census block metrics so that policymakers and the public have the most specific information possible.

The commission should work with other federal agencies that have experience in reporting pricing information to ensure that proprietary information not only is treated appropriately, but that prices and pricing trends are adequately and accurately reported, in order to protect competition and competitors. The commission should also, in conjunction with the State Department and the Department of Commerce, promote the development of international metrics based on our domestic mapping efforts so that appropriate and accurate international comparisons can be made, possibly beginning in 2010 or 2011. A global mapping initiative should help to bridge international technology and broadband gaps and could identify solutions for common problems, particularly in deploying infrastructure in rural and geographically dispersed areas.

Yet today, as we transition to the emerging Internet, domestic policymakers are entangled in an intense debate over the appropriate level of regulation necessary to ensure fair treatment for content providers, application creators, and entrepreneurs on existing networks. The Federal Communications Commission promulgated four "Network Neutrality" principles in 2005 intended to ensure that consumers have access to desired content and applications, and broadband providers do not disadvantage new, innovative content and applications. The four principles, which encourage broadband deployment and preserve and promote the open and interconnected nature of the public Internet, state that consumers are entitled to: access the lawful Internet content of their choice; run applications and use services of their choice, subject to the needs of law enforcement; connect their choice of legal devices that do not harm the network; and enjoy competition among network providers, application and service providers, and content providers.[2]

The commission should add fifth and sixth principles requiring nondiscrimination and disclosure of any "traffic management" efforts or activities by broadband providers. While traffic management can be an appropriate tool to address network congestion, consumers and application and content providers should receive notice of data traffic management by providers prior to signing a contract with the broadband provider. The FCC must vigorously enforce the above principles and quickly and aggressively penalize broadband providers that are found to be in violation of the above principles with meaningful fines and other financial penalties.

The new administration will also have to address wireless broadband. It should explore the option of using the so-called "white spaces"—the vacant space between television channels—as an unlicensed "innovation space" for additional wireless spectrum. By preserving large areas of prime unlicensed spectrum across the nation, the new administration can assure and promote innovation in wireless uses, applications, content, and devices. The innovation space would serve as a test bed for entrepreneurs and as a competitive spur for licensed wireless operators to develop new wireless technologies and applications.

The broadcasting industry opposes any use of this spectrum, citing concerns that it will interfere with television signals. New, smarter radio technologies can and will solve that problem. Some existing mobile companies want the commission to auction the "white space" spectrum to bring more money into the U.S. Treasury and, not coincidentally, to provide additional opportunity for those companies to obtain more spectrum.

The First Year

The concept of universal service has been at the core of America's communications policy since the FCC's inception. The FCC now supports four Federal Universal Service programs. The Low Income program provides discounts on telephone installation and monthly telephone service to qualifying consumers. The Schools and Libraries Program, also known as the e-Rate program, provides affordable telecommunications services for all eligible schools and libraries, especially those in rural and economically disadvantaged areas. The commission manages a rural health care program that uses telecommunications networks to improve health care quality. The largest of the commission's universal service programs, the High Cost Fund, supports companies that provide telecommunications services in areas where the cost of providing service is high, principally in rural America.

The High Cost Fund, in particular, requires significant near-term scrutiny. The program currently rewards inefficiency, provides subsidies to carriers irrespective of the financial needs of the carriers' customers, and is a vestige of a past era of the telecommunication industry. The High Cost Fund still primarily funds basic telephony even as America moves toward broadband technologies. The High Cost Fund also treats wireline companies in a disparate and, arguably, preferential manner at a time when more and more Americans are moving to Internet-based and wireless technologies. As of June 2008, more than 15 percent of American households relied solely on wireless phones for telephone service.[3]

If we truly want to bring the benefits of America's best telecommunications and information technologies to all corners of America, particularly rural America, we cannot continue spending in excess of $6 billion annually on an inefficient and antiquated program. It is neither prudent nor politically possible to abolish the program, but the next administration should be able to transform the program over a period of about four years into an initiative that supports investments in broadband infrastructure; promotes efficiency; protects against government waste, fraud, and mismanagement with periodic audits and other measures; and is Internet Protocol based, though technologically neutral, so that it is scalable for future technological innovation.

The Federal Communications Commission and the Federal State Joint Board, which is comprised of federal and state commissioners, should in the first year develop a new, broader-based, but technologically neutral funding mechanism for maintaining existing Universal Service programs at the current levels. The commission should begin to transform the High Cost Fund into a rural broadband fund designed to construct wireline and wireless projects in unserved areas—as identified by the national mapping program. Twenty-five percent of the fund should go to broadband construction projects in the first year, 50 percent in the second year, 75 percent in the third year, and 90 percent in the fourth year. Ten percent of the High Cost Fund would remain available to assist high-cost telecommunications providers for a brief transitional period, not to exceed three years, in order to ensure that no American is left without affordable telephone service. After that three-year period, if needed, up to 10 percent

of the rural broadband fund could be used to assist low-income rural subscribers to pay for a defined level of telecommunications services.

Companies that receive construction funding from the newly transformed
High Cost Fund would be subject to several requirements. The FCC would require the networks to meet a threshold standard of minimal speed and bandwidth to be determined by the Joint Board and the commission. A private
entity, by itself or in conjunction with a state or local government, would have
to provide at least 50 percent of construction costs. And to the extent possible
and practicable, the network would assist schools, libraries, rural health clinics,
and community colleges in the service area to connect at a lower-than-
commercial rate.

Many Americans access the Internet, and particularly the broadband Internet, at public libraries. The schools and libraries program has been an unquali-
fied success, with more than 95 percent of classrooms and 99 percent of
libraries now connected to the Internet, but the program still can be improved.
A particular area in need of improvement is the application process for libraries. More than 40 percent of public library systems do not receive E-Rate
funding largely because the application process is too complicated or the dis-
count is too low to invest the time in the application process.[4]

It is important that the commission ensures that the program's administrators have adequate information to prevent waste, fraud, and abuse, but it is
equally important that small, rural libraries not be constrained from applying
for much-needed funding because of a daunting, overly complicated application process. Libraries will need additional funding as they upgrade their Internet connections to broadband connections. The E-Rate program should be a
primary asset for bringing broadband to libraries, but it can only succeed if the
application process does not deter libraries, particularly libraries in smaller
communities, from applying for E-rate funding.

Media Concentration and Diversity

Diversity of broadcast voices and ownership are bedrock principles of America's broadcast laws. Broadcast law has been premised on the expectation that
content regulation is not necessary because of the robustly diverse marketplace
of ideas available on broadcast stations. Yet in recent years, legislative and regulatory changes in multiple ownership rules governing the number of broadcast
outlets one entity can own locally or nationally have rolled back commission
regulations designed to increase minority ownership. Increases in prices for
broadcast outlets have combined with these legislative changes to cause an un-
paralleled concentration of ownership of broadcast properties.

Ben Bagdikian, in his seminal 1983 book *The Media Monopoly*, decried the merger and acquisitions activities that resulted in 50 companies dominating the media marketplace. He also predicted that further consolidation would dramatically shrink the number of media owners in coming years. Only 25 years later, the pace of media consolidation has far surpassed even what Bagdikian imagined; eight companies effectively dominate the American media landscape: Time Warner, Comcast, Viacom, Disney, News Corporation, NBC Universal, Yahoo, and Google. These eight companies own the six largest broadcast networks, the largest television and motion picture studios, dozens of cable networks, hundreds of broadcast outlets, and book and magazine publishing companies.

Much of the deregulation of media ownership rules was predicated on the assumption that the Internet would provide a new, alternative source of information for the public. Yet the dominant media companies are dominant online as well. According to Comscore, Yahoo, Google, News Corporation, and Time Warner comprise four of the five most popular online companies, own 7 of the top 10 online video properties when measured by videos viewed, and 9 of the top 10 online video properties by unique visitors.[5]

Media concentration, as Consumers Union has noted, reduces the level of local programming, particularly local news; limits free expression; consolidates homogenized culture; and may promote indecent and objectionable content on the air.[6] Perhaps most problematically, the changes in media ownership regulations that created historic levels of media concentration also caused a dramatic reduction in the number of broadcast outlets owned by minorities; ownership levels for women also remain unconscionably low.

The new administration must review critically the commission's multiple ownership policies. It should request that Congress roll back the newspaper-broadcast cross-ownership rules. The new administration and FCC also must ensure that no further relaxation or modification of multiple ownership rules are permitted or initiated until the commission determines whether the existing ownership rules serve the public interest or whether they have resulted in unacceptable concentration of ownership.

The commission also must develop a more reliable database of minority ownership. The Government Accountability Office concluded in a recent report that minority ownership of media properties remains limited, but just how limited is hard to tell due to deficiencies in commission data collection, inadequate data quality procedures, and problems with data storage. The GAO report further concluded that "though smaller owners, including minorities and women, have opportunities to enter the media industry by way of Internet-based and niche publications, these groups continue to face long-standing challenges to the ownership of radio and television stations."[7]

Free Press analyzed ownership levels of television properties in a recent report and found that women own only 67 television stations, or less than 5 percent of all stations, and racial minorities own only 44 stations, or 3.3 percent.[8] The numbers for radio station ownership are similarly abysmal, with ethnic and racial minorities owning only 7.7 percent of full power radio licensees. Full power stations are what are traditionally thought of as broadcast stations. The FCC also has "low power" stations that serve a smaller geographical area and provide more of a niche programming service.

The new administration should work with Congress to pass legislation reinstating the minority tax certificate program, thereby permitting broadcast stations that sell to minorities to defer capital gains taxes so long as they invest the proceeds in other media properties. Tax certificates, in existence from 1978 to 1995, were one of the most effective tools for increasing minority ownership. They addressed a principal impediment to minority ownership—decreased ability by minority entrepreneurs to access the capital needed to purchase broadcast property. Reinstating tax certificates should be accompanied by a fuller assessment by the commission of how to increase minority and women's ownership of full power broadcast stations.

Wireless Bill of Rights

Wireless service has exploded in popularity in recent years with approximately 260 million subscribers—85 percent of the population.[9] A recent study concluded that Americans would find it harder to abandon their cell phones than the Internet, television, or traditional landline phones.[10] Yet Americans are very dissatisfied with the service they get from cell phones. The Better Business Bureau says that of the 3,900 industries it tracks, the wireless sector has received more complaints than any other for three straight years.[11] Several states, in response to consumer complaints, have begun crafting so-called wireless bills of rights, designed to ensure that consumers receive an acceptable level of service from wireless providers.

Wireless companies that serve a national consumer base and some members of Congress agree that a national wireless bill of rights will better serve the interests of both consumers and the wireless industry. A national solution would allow carriers to adhere to one set of rules, and consumers would be assured of carrier performance, irrespective of where they live or the status of legislative or regulatory efforts in their state.

The new administration should work with the FCC, state regulators, and members of Congress to develop legislation establishing a Wireless Bill of Rights. It would primarily protect residential and small business subscribers and address issues such as disclosure, choice, privacy, public participation and enforcement, accuracy of bills and redress, nondiscrimination, and safety. Enforcement would occur at the state level. States that have already passed such regulations should not be pre-empted by federal standards so long as they had been passed and enacted prior to January 1, 2009.

Public Safety Wireless

The new administration will have to work with the FCC to ensure that all local, state, and federal public safety professionals have access to interoperable communications devices that will allow them to communicate across jurisdictions in times of national or regional emergency.

It is an urgent national priority that first responders be provided with all necessary and appropriate tools and resources to ensure effective communications in the event of an act of nature, such as Hurricane Katrina, or acts of terrorism, such as the 9/11 attacks. Lives have been lost and rescue efforts have been delayed in the past because various law enforcement and public safety personnel could not talk to one another at a time of local or regional crisis. Technology is available that could solve that problem. The most recent FCC auction for the "D Block"—designed to provide spectrum for shared private and public safety uses, and intended, in part, to help solve the problem of public safety interoperability—failed to secure bids at the reserve price due to conditions that FCC placed on the spectrum.

The new commission must develop a plan for rebidding the D Block spectrum at the earliest practicable date. The auction should identify a partner to build the new network and secure sufficient funding to assist in delivering the interoperable communications to first responders. The commission should allocate all auction proceeds to the creation of a Public Safety Trust. The most recent auctions raised $19.6 billion—well in excess of the $12.5 billion to $15 billion estimated by the Congressional Budget Office. Building a public safety network will require billions of dollars of investment; it is therefore entirely appropriate for the FCC to commit all proceeds from the auction to the Public Safety Trust.

State and local governments would only be able to access funds from the trust if they meet certain requirements, such as complete compliance with new interoperability standards or solutions that meet the criteria of being both forward-looking and backward compatible. Funds would be used only for technology, infrastructure, and other critical needs to achieve interoperability such as use of commercial broadband networks. State and local governments should be required to match the federal funds—at least doubling the resources applied to the effort—in order to be eligible for the grants.

Longer-Term Priorities

The FCC must improve its enforcement capabilities and transition to a 21st-century agency. The GAO stated, after investigating the FCC from November 2006 to December 2007, that the commission is incapable of tracking complaints about telecommunications service and resolves only a fraction of them. The GAO also concluded that "These limitations make it difficult to conduct trend analysis, determine program effectiveness, allocate commission resources, or accurately track and monitor key aspects of all complaints received, investigations conducted, and enforcement actions taken."[12]

The commission should be a model agency in using technology and making its processes accessible and visible. The new FCC should ensure that the general public is able to participate in commission proceedings without having to hire a lawyer. The administration should request that Congress require the commission to append a one-page consumer impact statement and a one-page economic impact statement to every completed rulemaking. Many of the commission's actions are based on theories or premises as to how industry will perform or consumers will benefit as a result of the commission's actions. Statements reflecting the anticipated effect on consumers and industry will give commissioners a metric to gauge the effectiveness and efficacy of their actions and would give legislators and the public an additional metric for gauging agency performance.

Innovation Agenda

The FCC's role must change as technological advances and marketplace innovations usher in an age of spectrum abundance. Rather than merely assuming that spectrum abundance will occur, the FCC must assist in creating an environment for the creation of such abundance. It must also ensure that, where spectrum is constrained or market power exists, dominant companies do not discriminate against competitors or new market entrants, whether they are application providers, content providers, or facilities-based competitors.

The commission should preserve entrepreneurial opportunities by creating and retaining unlicensed spectrum bands; continue federal funding for unserved or underserved areas and populations; improve the technology infrastructure or provide increased access for residents of underserved areas; and ensure that public-private partnerships are created that will help bring new technology to places where market forces alone might not be sufficient to attract investment. The commission must also continue to review its policies and market developments with an eye to ensuring increased diversity of opportunity for participants from emerging communities, particularly racial and ethnic minorities and new immigrant populations.

The FCC is not currently organized to handle the new paradigm of rapid technological advances. The commission still organizes itself around stovepipes at a time when market players are increasingly flexible and multifaceted. All telecommunications companies, including wireless and satellite, increasingly are essentially data providers. Organizing company regulation based on companies' historic origins will make less or no sense in coming years, and could serve to constrain consumer welfare and industry creativity and investment.

The FCC must therefore be reorganized to reflect rapid industry and technological changes. The commission will have to strike a critical balance between constraining and preventing discrimination by dominant companies and promoting robust, cross-platform and inter-platform competition.

Federal Trade Commission

Consumer Protection and Competition for a 21st-Century Economy

JOAN Z. BERNSTEIN AND
ANN MALESTER

The Federal Trade Commission must play a key role in assuring that the marketplace is safe and fair for consumers and that the U.S. economy remains healthy and globally competitive. The new administration should appoint a chairman who will use the FTC's broad jurisdiction to reexamine antitrust and consumer protection doctrine in order to make the agency more effective in dealing with the latest forms of marketing, emerging technologies, and globalization. The FTC should speak out on important consumer issues and make greater use of its rulemaking authority to set national consumer standards, especially in emerging areas such as data privacy. It should reinvigorate its enforcement agenda and empirical research to target anticompetitive business conduct in key economic sectors such as health care, energy, and technology. The FTC must also address information technology needs and critical internal management issues, such as developing and retaining human capital. Because the FTC has a small budget but broad jurisdiction over much of the economy, strong and innovative management will be vital to its success.

T he Federal Trade Commission is unique in being the only federal agency with broad jurisdiction over both consumer protection and competition is- sues. Consumer protection enforcement ensures that companies do not de- fraud or mislead consumers, while competition enforcement ensures that companies do not use anticompetitive conduct or mergers to gain market power in order to charge supracompetitive prices or reduce innovation. To- gether, these law enforcement activities protect the operation of the free mar- ket and are critical for the U.S. economy to remain healthy and globally competitive.

Many questionable business practices require a blend of consumer protec- tion and competition enforcement analysis. Case in point: one important ques- tion the FTC had to address when analyzing Google Inc.'s proposed acquisition of DoubleClick was whether the transaction would adversely affect non-price attributes of competition, such as the level of protection afforded to the vast ar- ray of consumers' private information that the combined company would be able to access. Answering that question required both consumer protection and competition expertise. The FTC also needs to assess private consumer protec- tion measures, such as industry-wide self-regulatory programs, to assure that they pose no risks of anticompetitive effects through industry collusion. The commission's broad jurisdiction allows it to effectively tackle these types of issues.

The FTC also has broad jurisdiction to hold hearings, conduct workshops, and write reports. Armed with an innovative agenda derived from sound strate- gic planning, the agency can use its broad powers to investigate a wide range of emerging economic issues, both in terms of fact development and intellectual leadership. The commission produced a generic drug study in 2002,[1] for exam- ple, that led to legislative changes intended to increase the availability of generic drugs in a timely manner. In the consumer protection arena, the FTC, partnering with federal health officials, addressed the role of food advertisers in this country's childhood obesity crisis.

The FTC could have used these same tools more aggressively to study and develop an enforcement agenda to address fraud in the subprime mortgage market. Producing such studies and reports is a particularly crucial role for the FTC as new economic models of competition emerge and global competition challenges U.S. companies to develop new products and services and market them using innovative technologies.

The FTC developed strategic plans in the 1990s for both consumer protection and competition enforcement based on hearings that addressed the "Global, High-Tech Marketplace." Using the information learned from those hearings, the agency's strategic planning enabled it to successfully target the most critical problems, anticipate new areas of concern, and leverage its resources through key alliances with other federal and state agencies. The hearings accelerated the understanding of consumer protection issues on the Internet, for example, and led to new competition guidelines for joint ventures. The FTC's capacity to develop strategic plans based on the results of public hearings for both enforcement and policy agendas gives it a distinct advantage over other agencies in exposing and correcting market problems.

The FTC is governed by five commissioners, appointed for staggered seven-year terms, with no more than three from the same political party. The agency's rules require that at least three commissioners support any initiative, including pursuing litigation or rulemaking. The exchange of ideas among these presidential appointees and the need to build consensus typically leads to better-accepted precedents than if a single person made all of the decisions. The governing structure of the FTC also ensures that the agency's enforcement decisions do not swing widely based on the ideological bent of one administrator. All of these advantages will enable the FTC to take a leadership role in renewing competition and consumer protection policies and contributing to a sound understanding of new economic challenges.

The First 100 Days

Appointing a chairman is the most important decision related to the FTC that the new administration will make. It is critical that the 44th president appoint someone who offers significant leadership skills in three core areas: substance, management, and decisiveness. He or she must have substantive knowledge of the agency's mission and be able to provide intellectual leadership to revitalize competition and consumer protection doctrine. The chairman must have management skills to build support for a strategic plan among fellow commissioners and to motivate, energize, and direct the staff in carrying out that plan. And the chairman must be able to set priorities, communicate them effectively, and, together with the agency's senior management, implement them expeditiously.

History has demonstrated that chairmen with these attributes have had remarkable success in strengthening and revitalizing the agency. Two examples stand out: Miles Kirkpatrick, in the early 1970s, completely transformed a lackluster FTC into a vigorous and respected law enforcement agency;[2] and Robert Pitofsky, two decades later, restored the FTC's historic use of public hearings to examine broad market trends and then charted a course for future policies and enforcement in both competition and consumer protection. One result was a comprehensive consumer protection program that addressed the emergence of the Internet, globalization of the marketplace, and the growing problem of consumer privacy.[3]

The hearings also provided an in-depth analysis of the effect of global competition on U.S. markets and the importance of competition in promoting innovation, which guided the agency's antitrust agenda in subsequent years.[4] The work of both these chairmen set a dynamic course for the FTC that lasted well beyond their terms in office.

Develop a Strategic Plan

The agency must develop a clear and detailed strategic plan for allocating its resources to ensure that it does not spread itself too thin or lose sight of its top priorities. Without sufficient guidance, the agency's staff can waste efforts pursuing cases that are later not approved by the commissioners. The process should be transparent and inclusive of all of the commissioners, as well as the agency's staff.

The FTC has many tools, such as undertaking economic studies, conducting hearings and workshops, and accessing its vast consumer complaint database, to identify both existing and emerging problems.[5] An effective strategic plan should identify the key challenges the agency faces, including human capital needs, such as the loss of a significant number of experienced staff and the need for new types of specialists in various high-tech areas; identifying new directions in law enforcement and how best to organize staff to undertake them; and conducting an overall evaluation of the technology resources needed to carry out the agency's mission.

It should also draw on advice and recommendations from stakeholders outside the agency, including consumer organizations, industry members, state attorneys general, congressional representatives, and other governmental agencies. Once in place, such a strategic plan will enable the FTC to better work with Congress to implement its legislative agenda and to obtain the resources necessary to carry out its plan.

Overhaul Competition Analysis

The predominance of the Chicago School of economic thinking in antitrust analysis has led to an overly limited view of the types of conduct that can harm competition.[6] Although the Chicago School provided a much-needed correction to less-than-rigorous antitrust analysis, it appears to have overshot the mark and led to an approach that is undoubtedly too permissive. The Chicago School approach, as currently applied, tends to assume that the market is always self-correcting without fully appreciating the anticompetitive effects that may flow from market imperfections.

Leading experts in antitrust and economic thinking have begun to articulate proposals that would enable enforcers to challenge more effectively anticompetitive conduct that emerges as technologies, industries, and business behavior change over time. Some experts propose reinvigorating merger enforcement by restoring presumptions based on market concentration and making those presumptions more difficult to rebut.

Other experts have suggested changes to the Department of Justice and Federal Trade Commission *Horizontal Merger Guidelines*[7] to require a more careful, thorough, and fact-based analysis of whether the likelihood of new entry or specific business justifications actually would resolve competitive concerns. Yet others propose issuing new guidelines to govern the analysis of vertical mergers, and some urge legislative action to overturn recent court holdings that may lead to consumer harm.[8]

A strategic planning process can help identify which of these proposals are paramount and should be addressed right away. The agency also will need to build stronger empirical support for the antitrust theories it decides to pursue, particularly in the face of an increasingly conservative judiciary. Because of its ability to hold hearings, issue reports, forge consensus along the ideological and political spectrum, and develop a new enforcement agenda, the FTC is the right place to lead a renewal of antitrust thinking.

Revitalize Consumer Protection

Chicago School thinking also has constricted consumer protection analysis and limited consideration of emerging economic theories such as behavioral economics. The Chicago School believes in solving consumer protection problems by giving consumers more information, and more accurate information, so they can make decisions for themselves. But this is not always the right answer in a world where consumers often have *too much* information. Research in the areas of financial privacy and credit disclosures has shown that consumers either do not understand or are unable to sift through an overload of information and may throw up their hands in confusion.[9]

Information disclosure is most effective when it is based on sound empirical data that demonstrate consumer understanding. Marketing research conducted by outside experts should play a greater role in the FTC's efforts to develop regulatory and enforcement remedies that incorporate disclosure or other notice to consumers. Such research would inform the agency about how consumers process various kinds of information and which communication techniques or media are most effective.

This analysis also would assist the commission's in-house consumer and business education efforts by strengthening the agency's ability to target and educate its intended audience and measure the outcome of its education campaigns. The FTC, to the extent information disclosures are found lacking, needs to lead the way in finding other solutions to stop deceptive or abusive practices through rulemaking and law enforcement.

The financial services industry is one area in particular that needs more comprehensive attention from the FTC. The current crisis in the financial markets, and resulting widespread injury to consumers, is due in some measure to the lack of clear and consumer-friendly information and to abusive practices by industry members in the areas of mortgage lending and credit card offers. The FTC should clarify the scope of its authority over certain financial services organizations, including those that provide services to banks and other financial institutions. The agency also needs to consider a comprehensive approach to addressing the myriad deceptive and misleading practices affecting consumers. Where disclosure is not an effective remedy, the FTC should consider treating such practices as abusive or unfair, and banning them altogether.[10]

Bolster Staff

The commission has been losing talented staff to private law firms due to enormous salary discrepancies, a longstanding frustration with the risk-averse culture that has enveloped the agency, and too many layers of bureaucratic review. It can address at least part of this problem by reallocating some of its resources and enhancing the benefits of working at the agency.

The FTC should begin by reducing the layers of managers. The staff often express frustration with the lack of resources devoted to key policy initiatives and congressional directives. At the same time, some staff recommendations move through the agency much too slowly, often because there are too may layers of review. Along the lines suggested by Paul C. Light, a well-regarded expert on public service, the FTC should consider reducing the layers of managers and shifting those resources downward to the staff level where the agency's real work is done.[11]

The agency must make better use of the resources allocated to economic analysis. The FTC has a large staff of economists in a separate Bureau of Economics whose contributions do not match their cost to the agency. Many on the staff are very talented, but the Bureau of Economics as a whole provides insufficient support to the attorney staff in building a solid economic basis for enforcement recommendations and in testifying in support of the FTC at trial. The commission typically looks to outside economists to testify at trial, but has had limited resources to devote to this crucial aspect of litigation support. Many of the FTC's economists actually consider it their job to find reasons why the FTC should not bring enforcement actions, while others spend time on research that is unrelated to ongoing investigations and does little to further the agency's mission.

Some of the resources currently allocated to the Bureau of Economics should be used to hire top-ranked economic consultants to testify in specific cases in support of the agency in order to maximize the agency's chances of prevailing in litigation. The remaining resources should be used for staff economists to be slotted into positions in the Bureaus of Competition and Consumer Protection to work as a team with the attorney staff investigating competition and consumer protection issues and to conduct economic research directly related to the agency's priorities.

The FTC also must hire skilled litigators and expand litigation training. It will have to do more than bring lawsuits to protect U.S. consumers; it has to win cases. This will be a tough job given the conservative judiciary, which has resulted in increasingly conservative precedent. Truly skilled litigators can significantly enhance the FTC's likelihood of success. The agency will need to devote substantially greater resources to litigation training for staff attorneys such as the training offered by the National Institute of Trial Advocacy. It will also need to hire additional experienced litigators, or enter into contracts with such litigators if bringing them on staff is not feasible.

The FTC can better attract and retain employees by taking full advantage of the Federal Student Loan Repayment Program.[12] This program allows agencies to repay federally insured student loans, up to a maximum of $10,000 for an employee per calendar year (up to a total of $60,000 per employee). The goal of this program is to help federal agencies hire and retain top-quality employees. The FTC so far has not taken advantage of this program in any meaningful way despite the fact that it is competing for attorneys with law firms that pay significantly more.

Increase IT Resources

It is very difficult for the FTC, as well as many other agencies, to keep up with the information technology revolution, both in terms of hardware and software and human resources with the necessary skills. The commission may soon be hampered in its ability to challenge anticompetitive transactions because the merging parties will provide the required documents and information in a massive electronic "data dump" that agency staff will not be able to handle during the limited time afforded by the Hart-Scott-Rodino statutory deadlines.

Outdated technology also limits the FTC on the consumer protection side by hampering its ability to monitor the National Do Not Call Registry and to find out about and challenge increasingly sophisticated consumer scams and misleading advertisements. Databases are, in some instances, running on outdated software; other technological tools cannot be effectively used because of insufficient processing power or server capacity. Each year, new technological challenges are presented, whether involving malware, mobile marketing, or spam, which require the purchase of software and/or hardware, and require knowledgeable, trained IT staff. As bad actors move farther away from any paper trails, it is increasingly critical to provide IT forensic support. The commission will need to make a significant investment in both IT equipment and human resources.

Longer-Term Challenges

The most important long-term challenge for the FTC is to become a national and global leader in protecting consumers' privacy. Online behavioral advertising is becoming an increasing concern as Americans conduct more of their lives online. Companies track consumers' activities online—including the searches consumers conduct, the web pages they visit, and the content they view—to deliver advertising targeted to an individual's interests. The FTC so far is relying on industry self-regulation to protect consumers rather than taking the lead itself.[13] The agency should take a more proactive approach, targeting bad actors through law enforcement actions and seeking congressional authority to issue a rule addressing the practices of concern.

Such a rule would provide transparency to consumers by requiring disclosure and affirmative consent for certain practices dealing with information collection and use. It could also limit or entirely prohibit companies from collecting certain types of sensitive data and restrict how they use other types of information. This rulemaking process would allow the agency to consider which entities should be covered by these restrictions, and whether a proposal to create a "Do Not Track" system that consumers could opt into would be a technologically feasible and effective way to protect consumers.[14] Given the increasingly global nature of fraud and deception through the Internet and electronic commerce, the FTC should also aggressively use the powers it obtained under the U.S. SAFE WEB Act[15] to coordinate privacy initiatives with its international partners.

Pursue a Legislative Agenda

The FTC chair should, during the administration's first year in office, continue the commission's recently initiated efforts to develop a legislative agenda to deal with problematic areas where only legislative solutions would be effective, such as eliminating the FTC's jurisdictional limitations, clarifying and redefining the role of various agencies, supplementing the FTC's law enforcement remedies, and broadening its rulemaking authority.[16] The commission also should continue working with the appropriate members of Congress and their staffs both to rebuild its relationships with Congress and to implement its legislative agenda. This approach will enhance the credibility and prominence of the agency with Congress and the general public, and make it more likely that legislative changes will withstand industry lobbying.

The FTC is limited in its ability to protect consumers from unfair and deceptive practices as well as anticompetitive conduct in important sectors of the market place because of restrictions on its jurisdiction. The agency should encourage Congress to enact legislation that would eliminate exemptions for common carriers, insurance companies, and not-for-profit organizations. It should also work with the heads of the other agencies that play a role in regulating industries, such as the financial service industry, in order to better coordinate efforts to protect consumers and address emerging problems. Similarly, the FTC's authority over the tobacco industry has been hampered by the ambiguity that surrounds the role of the federal health agencies, to the detriment of efforts to protect American consumers, especially children and adolescents. Legislation may be needed that more clearly delineates each agency's role in these types of industries.

The FTC's law enforcement efforts are also sometimes thwarted by legal hurdles that make it hard for it to obtain monetary penalties from wrongdoers or those assisting wrongdoers. The agency should therefore consider seeking legislative authority to obtain civil penalties for violations of Section 5 of the Federal Trade Commission Act—which prohibits business practices that are harmful to consumers because they are anticompetitive, deceptive, or unfair—that involve particularly egregious practices. It should also seek the authority to obtain relief from third parties engaged in aiding and abetting wrongdoers.

The commission already possesses generalized rulemaking authority under the Magnuson-Moss Act,[17] but the process is slow and cumbersome. In contrast, congressionally authorized rulemaking undertaken pursuant to the Administrative Procedures Act, although not perfect, has resulted in more expeditious, targeted solutions to complex industry practices. The agency should seek APA rulemaking authority to deal with ongoing concerns that are not easily addressed through traditional law enforcement, such as consumer privacy and data security. The FTC should also consider seeking parity with the bank regulatory agencies by obtaining the authority to issue rules under the Fair Credit Reporting Act.[18]

Corporation for National and Community Service

Supporting Civic Action to Solve America's Problems

SHIRLEY SAGAWA

The new president should focus the Corporation for National and Community Service on four long-term goals: growing AmeriCorps-style national service to make opportunities universally available to young adults who want to serve; making service learning a common experience for all young people growing up in America; leveraging service by volunteers of all ages, including baby boomers, to solve pressing problems; and positioning the corporation as a lead agency for promoting social entrepreneurship, fostering cross-sector solutions to national challenges, and building non-profit capacity. Key steps to achieve these goals include appointing a presidential commission to examine cross-sector solutions to America's problems, creating a new fund to grow innovative results-based organizations, and making a substantial federal investment to expand national service targeted to solve specific problems and engage key populations.

President Bill Clinton in 1993 merged two agencies—ACTION and the Commission on National and Community Service—to create the Corporation for National and Community Service. Over the past 15 years, the corporation has administered AmeriCorps, the Learn and Serve America service-learning programs, and the Senior Corps—the agency's three main programs. Although the authorization for this agency and its programs expired in 1997, it has continued to receive appropriated funds despite political attacks that jeopardized the agency in its early years.

AmeriCorps, which provides its members with education awards in return for full-time or substantial part-time service, experienced a funding crisis in 2003 due to administrative miscalculations. But strong advocacy from leaders in the non-profit sector resulted in a restoration of funds the following year.[1] Support from President Clinton and President George W. Bush, as well as key congressional supporters, kept the agency at a budget of roughly $1 billion over the past decade, with AmeriCorps reaching a peak of 75,000 members in 2004. Effective leadership by Bush-appointed Corporation for National and Community Service CEO David Eisner in recent years put the agency on firm footing, resulting in clean audits and its designation as one of the best small agencies to work for in the federal government.

The Corporation for National and Community Service is now poised for growth. Presidential candidates of both parties have strong track records in support of national service, and a February 2008 poll found that 85 percent of Americans support the idea of expanding national service to 1 million members.[2, 3]

The new president should build on the Corporation for National and Community Service's strengths and focus on four long-term goals: growing AmeriCorps-style national service to make opportunities universally available to young adults who want to serve; making service learning a common experience for all young people growing up in America; leveraging service by volunteers of all ages, including baby boomers, to solve pressing problems; and positioning the corporation as a lead agency for promoting social entrepreneurship, fostering cross-sector solutions to national challenges, and building non-profit capacity.

Strong support for national service so far is due in large part to AmeriCorps' strong track record of "getting things done" for communities in a variety of fields, including education, youth development, housing, health care, energy efficiency, community development, and environmental conservation.

Habitat for Humanity, for example, engages AmeriCorps members to serve as construction liaisons, volunteer recruiters, and teachers to help Habitat families develop self-sufficiency skills. In Michigan, AmeriCorps members have assisted Habitat for Humanity by collaborating with churches, businesses, and other nonprofits throughout the community to eliminate substandard housing, and by developing a "ReStore" retail store that sells donated household and building supplies. Before AmeriCorps teamed up with Habitat for Humanity in Michigan, Habitat affiliates had been unable to increase their production beyond one house per year. Now, Michigan Habitat chapters, with the help of AmeriCorps, have built 500 homes since 2000, generated over 28,000 volunteers, and expanded the state's property tax base.

Community Health Corps, another AmeriCorps program, brings together diverse members and trains them in enrolling patients into free or low-cost health insurance plans, helping them navigate through the health care system, educating them to manage chronic conditions, and linking them to other services such as housing and employment. As an added bonus, the experience leads 85 percent of corps members to pursue future employment in the health care field.

At yet another AmeriCorps program, Equal Justice Works, members bridge the "justice gap" that denies low-income people access to legal services by recruiting volunteer attorneys; each member recruits an average of 92 lawyers. The organization's work has been particularly important in areas affected by Hurricane Katrina. Before the hurricane, there were fewer than 20 public interest lawyers in the state of Mississippi. With the support of AmeriCorps, Equal Justice Works added an additional eight. These attorneys and the volunteers they recruited assisted more than 3,000 hurricane survivors, helping them cut through red tape and financial disruptions resulting from the disaster. This work cost the government less than $25 per client.

Other innovative AmeriCorps programs include Case Verde Builders and Sports4Kids. Case Verde Builders enlists low-income youth to serve in a youth corps that has built over 90 quality energy-efficient homes for low-income families. The youth earn their General Educational Development, or GED, high school-equivalency certificates while they serve and learn green building techniques that will lead to good jobs. Sports4Kids restores recess for the entire student body—fighting obesity with exercise, teaching children to play without conflict, and making it easier for them to focus in their afternoon classes—all by just placing one AmeriCorps member in a school.

These programs are highly effective at strengthening communities, providing services to Americans who need help, and getting their members interested in lifelong service. A 2008 longitudinal study from the Corporation for National and Community Service contrasted AmeriCorps members with a comparison group comprised of individuals who applied for, but did not serve in, the program. It found that, after eight years, the AmeriCorps members were significantly more civically engaged and more likely to pursue public service careers in the government and non-profit sector than their counterparts. They were also significantly more likely to be happy and satisfied with their lives.[4]

The Corporation for National and Community Service also uses national service dollars and AmeriCorps members to support organizations started by social entrepreneurs, including Teach For America, JumpStart, Public Allies, and National Student Partnerships. AmeriCorps' flexibility, because it is not limited to a single issue area or service delivery design, offers a unique opportunity for innovators whose models do not fit with existing federal programs in their fields. AmeriCorps' results orientation, which requires all programs that receive grants to establish measurable outcomes in three different areas, may contribute to the success of these path-breaking organizations.

The First 100 Days

The Corporation for National and Community Service should move quickly to work with the White House to prepare a legislative proposal to reauthorize the corporation and move toward the long-term goals of making national service opportunities universally available to young adults; establishing service learning as a common experience for young people; leveraging service to solve pressing problems; and positioning the corporation as a lead agency for promoting social entrepreneurship, fostering cross-sector solutions to national challenges, and building non-profit capacity.

The new president should prioritize pushing for the long-overdue reauthorization of the National and Community Service and Domestic Volunteer Service Acts. This legislation should not simply extend the programs; it should lay the groundwork both for promoting universal national service and service learning, and increasing the use of volunteers of all ages to solve important problems. It should also expand the corporation's role in support of cross-sector partnerships and social entrepreneurship. The 44th president can work with Congress to draft the legislation so that it engages key demographic groups such as disadvantaged youth and baby boomers who can benefit from service experiences; refocuses efforts on high-priority issues; expands and refocuses established programs such as VISTA and the National Civilian Community Corps; invests in high-performing and innovative programs; and reengages alumni, all in an effort to accomplish the larger goals.

The corporation has in the past struggled with management challenges that have hampered its ability to achieve its substantive priorities. In order to get a quick start on this national service agenda, the new president will have to fill key positions early on with highly qualified individuals—particularly the chief executive officer, managing director, and chief financial officer positions.

Engage Americans

The AmeriCorps program was originally designed to target college-bound or college-educated young adults. Subtitle C of the National and Community Service Act provides Segal education awards to participants in AmeriCorps programs specifically to attract and retain members from these groups.

When originally enacted, the National and Community Service Act of 1990 included a separate title for youth corps, which typically engage disadvantaged youth and young adults in service through full-time programs that also provide education and job training. In 1993, this title was folded into Subtitle C, and benefits, such as GED training, were included to make it possible for a diverse range of individuals to serve. But the best practices for youth corps programs are sometimes at odds with Subtitle C requirements. For example, while youth corps often provide members with an hourly wage and bonuses for exemplary behavior or penalties for violations, Subtitle C requires programs to establish an annual living allowance without regard for these factors.

At the same time, programs hoping to engage baby boomers and other older adults as members have found that the Segal education award provided to those who complete a term of service is of little interest to this group. Older adults might prefer alternative awards, such as travel vouchers, health care services, or gas cards. Some have proposed allowing older adults to transfer their education award to a child of their choice, although this option both breaks the link between opportunity and responsibility, and may be of less interest to seniors than awards that benefit them more directly.

Those who are interested in using national service to encourage low-income youth to pursue college educations have proposed that pro-rated Segal education awards also be made available to school-aged youth who serve 100 hours or more through a designated program, such as Summer of Service, or school-based programs that engage students as tutors or peer leaders who encourage other students to apply to college. College Summit has achieved significant success encouraging a college-going culture in schools serving low-income students; a critical part of this effort has been peer leaders, who might take the program to even higher levels if they could receive education awards based on the outcomes of their efforts.

Modifying the National and Community Service Act to allow variations of this sort would make the Corporation for National and Community Service's programs more flexible and potentially even allow it to more effectively achieve national goals.

Improve Student Learning

AmeriCorps has been effectively contributing to school improvement over the past 15 years by providing schools with teachers, one-on-one help for students, afterschool enrichment programs, and role models who improve the school climate.[5] AmeriCorps members who serve in EducationWorks run clubs, summer camps, and youth leadership programs through urban schools. Students served by this program on average increase their attendance over the previous year by 20 days. Teachers report that 90 percent of students improve academically and more than 80 percent have better classroom behavior.

Experience Corps places older adults in schools, where they provide one-on-one and small group attention to students needing extra help. Ninety-seven percent of teachers agree or strongly agree that Experience Corps members improve students' learning environment, and three out of four report that students made significant academic progress as a result of the program.

Teach For America is one of AmeriCorps' most visible grantees. It brings together a group of diverse, outstanding college graduates who make two-year commitments to teach in low-income urban and rural communities around the country. Teach For America attracted more than 18,000 applicants in 2007, including more than 8 percent of the graduating classes of Dartmouth, Harvard, Princeton, Spelman, and Yale. An independent study found that students of Teach For America teachers make on average 10 percent more progress per year in math than similar students in classrooms with certified and veteran teachers.

Yet these school-based programs operate on a small scale relative to the need. National service must grow to make members available to any struggling school or school district that identifies important ways these resources can improve its educational program.

Programs to reengage disadvantaged youth through service, education, and job training can also contribute to addressing this national challenge, and should be expanded. YouthBuild participants, for example, spend half of their time learning construction trade skills by building or rehabilitating housing for low-income people; the other half of their time is spent in a YouthBuild classroom earning a high school diploma or equivalency degree. More than half of YouthBuild students who complete a program cycle receive their GED or diploma, and 76 percent are placed in jobs or go on to higher education.

Years later, YouthBuild alumni stay on track. According to a Brandeis University study of 900 YouthBuild completers, 75 percent were either in postsecondary education or in jobs with an average wage of $10 an hour within seven years after graduation.[6] Establishing an Upward Pathways program based on the YouthBuild model would allow local programs to branch into additional high-demand fields that offer pathways out of poverty.[7] Based on this strong track record, national service could be effectively targeted to address other issues on a larger scale, such as environmental and energy conservation, urban and rural community development, and community health care.

Citizen Teachers, Mentors, and Tutors

AmeriCorps members should recruit and supervise volunteers who are trained to teach new skills to America's most vulnerable children and their families. These volunteers could end waiting lists for mentors and tutors in low-income neighborhoods; help illiterate adults to read and non-English speakers to learn English; teach music, writing, and art, and financial and technological literacy; and lead real-world apprenticeships and service learning projects.

The Citizen Schools National Teaching Fellowship can provide a model for what this program would look like. Citizen Schools teaching fellows, many of whom are AmeriCorps members, staff afterschool programs that expose disadvantaged middle school students to career options through "apprenticeships" led by business and community leaders. Under the supervision of these community volunteers, the students build working model solar cars, litigate mock trials, publish children's books, manage stock portfolios, launch websites, and gain the self-confidence that comes from saying, "I did that."

The middle school students who are part of these programs outperform their peers on school-related indicators, including attendance, on-time promotion, reduction in disciplinary incidents, grades in English and math, and standardized test scores in English. And they are more likely to enroll in top-tier, college-track high schools.

Support High-Performing Organizations

Current law requires that one-third of Subtitle C funds go to state service commissions based on a formula that regrants to programs within the state; the remaining two-thirds of funds go to state commissions and "national direct" organizations, typically national nonprofits, based on competition. Programs must reapply every three years, competing with new and other existing programs for funding.

This funding structure limits the corporation's ability to provide longer-term growth funding to those established programs that have proven results. New legislation should authorize the corporation to partner with a select set of longstanding grantees with strong track records that have the potential for considerable growth.

Such partnerships should include providing substantial grants on a competitive basis for a period of 5 to 10 years, predicated on meeting specific agreed-upon benchmarks and the availability of appropriations. Greater weight should go to organizations that agree to open new sites in designated underserved areas, with such sites receiving lower matching fund requirements.

AmeriCorps*VISTA and *NCCC

Volunteers in Service to America, originally proposed in the 1960s as the domestic Peace Corps, places adults in full-time positions with the goal of reducing poverty. All VISTA members are part of AmeriCorps and can receive the Segal education award. For many smaller organizations that cannot use large numbers of members, VISTA is a more effective alternative than AmeriCorps grants.

Its flexibility allows the corporation to respond quickly to emerging priorities and form partnerships with national nonprofits that are not interested in running full-scale AmeriCorps programs. VISTA should be expanded dramatically from 6,500 slots to 25,000 and should provide greater emphasis on "cost-shares," which allow non-profit organizations to pay for VISTA slots.

The National Civilian Community Corps has a unique niche as the only program whose members are recruited and supervised directly by the corporation, and as one of the few residential programs for diverse young adults. The NCCC is modeled on the Depression-era Civilian Community Corps and the military; its members are deployed to assist community organizations with a variety of education, environmental, public safety, and other projects. It played an important role in recent years responding to urgent needs, including the aftermath of Hurricane Katrina. The NCCC should be reauthorized with a clear focus on disaster response.

In addition, the new president, in order to streamline the corporation's role in disaster response, should transfer the Citizen Corps and other volunteer management and donation coordination from the Department of Homeland Security to the corporation.

Draw on AmeriCorps Alumni

More than 540,000 individuals have served in AmeriCorps as of 2008. These individuals represent an important national resource. Yet the federal government has invested very little in making the best use of these committed individuals. New legislation should fund the creation of a "national reserve" of Ameri-Corps and other national service alumni who are willing to be called upon for additional volunteer service to meet urgent national needs, provide easier paths for AmeriCorps alumni to enter the federal civil service, and offer small competitive grants to those alumni starting innovative new service programs.

Expand Student Service

Learn and Serve America is a corporation program that promotes service learning through grants and projects in kindergarten-through-12th grade schools, community groups, and colleges and universities. The new president should work with the corporation to expand and revise the Learn and Serve America K–12 and higher education programs. Most Learn and Serve America grants go by formula to state educational agencies, which regrant the funds in small amounts to schools and a limited number of community organizations. While these grants no doubt have helped to seed valuable new programs, they could have a greater effect if the corporation could make strategic choices to provide support to the states and to national non-profit organizations with the best plans to use funding to expand high-quality service learning. At the higher education level, funds should be awarded based in part on the institution's track record of supporting service, which should include requiring service transcripts, matching Segal education awards, offering service learning through required courses, and using a higher percentage of work-study funding for community service jobs.

The 44th president should also help establish and work with Congress to fund a new Action Entrepreneur Experience program for middle school, high school, and higher education students. Helping youth and young adults de-velop a sense of purpose increases their chance of educational success. The Ac-tion Entrepreneur showcase, modeled on the science fair experience, would enable students to identify a real problem facing their school or community and propose a strategy to address the problem by organizing volunteers, creat-ing a program, advocating for policy change, or other activities. By tying this experience to specific educational standards and school curricula, students would sample the experience of being a social entrepreneur and learn a variety of strategies for community problem solving.

The corporation should also establish a Summer of Service program within Learn and Serve America. Summer of Service would be a rite of passage before high school during the developmentally important period when youth are in the process of making decisions that may well determine who they will be as adults, for better or worse. Young people who drop out of school often begin down that path in middle school, when they question the importance of academic learning, which they may perceive as unimportant for their futures. Providing youth experiences that help them connect classes to the real world can prevent dropouts, increase motivation, and build young people's skills.

A new program to make a "Summer of Service" a rite of passage for youth transitioning from middle school to high school is needed to fill this gap and help make service learning a universal experience.[8] Providing modest scholarships to these students would help them envision themselves in college and could contribute to an increase in college-going in the future.

Support Innovative Programs

Program restrictions and limited appropriations for innovative initiatives have resulted in inadequate support for new programs, particularly those targeting older adult volunteers. The new president should ask Congress to give the corporation greater authority to support innovative efforts. For instance, baby boomers are a key untapped group that can offer their time and talents in second careers and volunteer jobs in the social sector. Innovative programs could also respond to emerging issues, such as use of technology to solve intractable problems and improve the capacity of social sector organizations.

The corporation should also expand support for local organizations to use service credits. These mutual service communities match individuals who need help with others who can provide assistance in exchange for credits they can use to request services themselves. These programs have proven particularly effective in helping older adults continue to live independently.[9]

Build Non-Profit Capacity

Non-profit organizations play an increasingly important role in delivering government-funded services, particularly for low-income communities. Unfortunately, too many nonprofits struggle to achieve their goals because they have limited access to the technology and expertise they need to achieve greater results.[10] The federal government, rather than helping with these challenges on a large scale, often presents its non-profit grantees with cumbersome requirements and funding restrictions that cut against organizational health and capacity.

The new president should create by executive order a Commission on Cross-Sector Solutions to America's Problems, to be led by the new White House Office of Social Innovation and supported by the corporation. The commission should be comprised of a politically balanced group of open-minded influential leaders representing a variety of backgrounds, as well as the heads of federal agencies that engage with nonprofits. After seeking public input, it would make recommendations regarding ways to improve the relationship between non-profit organizations, philanthropy, business, and the federal government in order to solve critical problems facing the country.

The commission should address ways to improve government policies to foster non-profit accountability; build nonprofits' capacity and the quality of services they deliver; streamline the process for non-profit organizations to obtain federal grants and contracts, eliminating unnecessary requirements; remove barriers that prevent smaller nonprofits from participating in government programs; partner with nonprofits after a disaster to help nonprofits rebuild or scale up quickly after a crisis; and make more data available about the non-profit sector, as the federal government already does for the business and government sectors.

The corporation, in conjunction with the commission, would provide funding for grants to support research on the sector and model new ways for the government to solve social problems by supporting social entrepreneurship.

A Community Solutions Fund Network

Social entrepreneurs are finding solutions to the nation's most pressing problems that could be applied across the country. Although they are creative about using and obtaining private sector resources, few of these organizations— including those with consistent, effective track records—are able to obtain growth capital that will enable them to expand beyond a modest level. Many communities similarly have limited private-sector philanthropic resources and are unable to expand or replicate what is working.

The new administration should respond to these challenges by setting up a network of "community solutions" funds that would use federal dollars to stimulate contributions from businesses, private philanthropy, individual citizens, and state and local public agencies toward specified outcomes. These funds would enable local communities, state-level funders, and national funding institutions to provide large, long-term grants to organizations whose programs achieve demonstrated results and are targeted to meet unique community needs.

Funders that operate consistently with the best practices of venture philanthropy would be certified as Community Solutions Funds and become eligible to compete for national leveraging capital. Decision making by the funds would be based on four key principles: impact-based results, cross-sector strategies, leverage, and long-term focus.

A network of funds, rather than a single national fund, would enable communities, states, and national funding organizations to create and control Community Solutions Funds targeted to specific needs. One city might develop a fund focused on neighborhoods with high concentrations of poverty, or a state might create a fund to assist rural communities. Multi-state funds could focus on specific issues, such as education or child care, or on specific populations such as low-income immigrants or people with disabilities. In addition to being more responsive and flexible than a large national fund, a network of funds will leverage more private sector resources and provide an opportunity for organizations to learn from one another, pilot and spread innovations, and advance the field's knowledge faster.

A federally chartered non-profit organization overseen by the Corporation for National and Community Service should oversee the Community Solutions Fund Network. The corporation's history with outcome-based funding and support for social entrepreneurship, as well as its cross-issue focus and mission, makes it an appropriate oversight agency.[11]

Create Interagency Council

National service has proven to be an effective strategy for solving important problems, but is rarely accessed by public problem solvers from other fields. In past administrations, these ties have been fostered through presidential leadership—such as President Clinton's America Reads program, or President Bush's focus on faith-based organizations and mentoring children of prisoners. The new president will also have priorities that could be addressed, in part, by national service.

The new president should issue an executive order to create an interagency council to deploy national service volunteers in support of key federal initiatives and connect national service with related programs such as the Peace Corps and service corps at the departments of Agriculture and Interior. The goal of the council should be to create linkages among service programs, such as common recruitment or leadership training opportunities, and to promote the use of service as a means of addressing important national problems.

The First Year

The new administration's priorities for the first year should tie closely with and build on the goals established during the process of reauthorizing the Corporation for National and Community Service. These first-year priorities should include deepening ties with the newly established interagency council, establishing the Commission on Cross-Sector Solutions by executive order, funding innovative model programs, investing in research into service-related solutions, and redesigning the grant-making process.

Once the new interagency council is established, the council and the new administration should work closely to foster deep substantive ties between national service and other important national priorities. Although many national service programs have goals that are related to other agencies' work, these interagency connections have not been mined to improve program quality. The corporation should partner with the Department of Education, for example, to promote service learning and draw on the department's expertise to strengthen national service in schools. The council should also engage service programs across the federal government to share best practices and build recruitment and other partnerships.

Taking national service to scale might involve providing 1 million opportunities to meet demand, and will likely be costly. The corporation should therefore support experiments with innovative lower-cost options, rather than force every program to conform to a lean cost structure that does not recognize program and regional differences. Such options could include fellowships whose costs are matched by private sector sponsors, professional positions designated as hard-to-fill, and individual slots allocated on a long-term basis to nonprofits that agree to fund half the cost.

The corporation can also invest in new solutions by developing a research agenda that strengthens national service programs' ability to achieve substantive outcomes. Corporation-funded research has explored nonprofits' capacity to use volunteers, underrepresentation of disadvantaged youth in service learning programs, and other important issues. A next generation of research should focus on ways that national service can address key issues, including dropout prevention, reconnecting youth who have dropped out to education, and other priorities.

Over time, the corporation will also have to redesign the grant approval and oversight process to allow for substantial scale, including the use of technology, business customer tools, and other innovative methods. The corporation should explore new systems to monitor quality and accountability. The current systems have been largely effective at rooting out weak programs. Yet at full scale, especially with significant numbers of individual or small group placements, such a system may be too cumbersome and expensive. Online rating systems, customer satisfaction surveys, and spot checks may be useful at identifying problem hotspots. Providing "risk assessment" ratings to programs based on their track records and other factors may also enable better targeting of oversight.

NATIONAL SECURITY POLICY

Overview

Containing the Terrorist Threat

JESSICA STERN

Terrorism has increased since the "war on terror" began. Even if attacks in Afghanistan and Iraq are excluded, the extreme jihadi terrorist movement is now spreading around the globe.[1] During this same period, Al Qaeda evolved from a commander-cadre organization based in Afghanistan into a hybrid organization made up of self-recruited or locally organized cells, many of them linked, if only virtually, to resurgent leadership groups in Pakistan.[2] Largely because of these developments, the president-elect should begin preparing now for the possibility of a major terrorist attack during the transition period or early in the new presidency. The new president, however, needs to be sure that our counterterrorism policy is not based only on a desire to avenge wrongs or reduce fears, but instead to reduce terrorism, which is a national security problem and a military threat that cannot be obliterated with large-scale military action. Terrorism can only be contained, which means U.S. national security for the foreseeable future will require an effective counterterrorism strategy that involves the patient deployment of all instruments of national power, with special emphasis on intelligence, information operations, and covert action. Containing the threat of terrorism requires much more than military action. It requires undermining the terrorists' narrative and reputation using the tools of counterinsurgency, adapted to the Internet age.

The president-elect should begin preparing now for the possibility of a major terrorist attack during the transition period or early in his new presidency. Muslim extremist terrorists attacked the World Trade Center for the first time in February 1993, during President Bill Clinton's second month in office, and for the second time in September 2001, during President George W. Bush's first year. Al Qaeda also bombed the USS *Cole* in October 2000, immediately before a presidential election, and released a video in October 2004, immediately before that year's presidential election.

435

Al Qaeda leaders will presumably want to put the next president on notice that they remain a significant threat, and they know that the interregnum of the transition period could increase the impact of an attack. The president-elect needs to develop contingency plans now for how he would respond to such a strike, should it occur. Transition teams should work closely with current officials to ensure the kind of intelligence failures that occurred in the transition to President Bush's first term do not recur.[3]

Terrorism is psychological warfare, and the new president must be prepared psychologically to fight it. The objective of terrorism is first and foremost a feeling. Terrorists aim to terrorize their enemies into acting in ways that harm their own interests, always trying to provoke the enemy government into over-reacting, or reacting in ways that damage the government's legitimacy or prestige. The new president must avoid the temptation to act quickly—especially if there is uncertainty about who is responsible for the next attack. Bellicose actions or rhetoric, which might assuage the pain of the American public in the short term, could have an enormously negative impact on the security of American civilians.

Terrorism cannot be obliterated with large-scale military action. It can only be contained, which will require recognizing that terrorism and asymmetric warfare will remain the most important threats to U.S. national security for the foreseeable future. An effective counterterrorism strategy must involve the patient deployment of all instruments of national power, with special emphasis on intelligence, information operations, and covert action.

The Challenges Ahead

The most significant foreseeable future threats to the United States and its allies will emerge from below the level of the state or will make use of nonstate actors. Our enemies will be hard to find, mutable, and globally spread, forming constantly changing alliances. And yet, many strategic analysts continue to view the September 11, 2001, strikes as an anomaly, rather than a harbinger, and to some extent, our military posture reflects that misapprehension.[4] The high-tech and high-cost weapons our military is still acquiring are more suited for conventional threats of the past and a potential far-off future, but not the protean enemy we face today.[5]

The global extremist jihadi movement exploits groups and individuals who feel humiliated or endangered by modern societies.[6] The terrorists seek out areas of weak governance, whether inside cities or between states. And yet, the new president will inherit a system still oriented toward meeting threats that emerge from strong states rather than weak ones—and from static national powers, rather than transnational groups.

Containing terrorism instead will require a global response based on shared intelligence—both within and between countries—and enhanced transnational law enforcement cooperation. It will require a capacity to shift rapidly military and intelligence priorities. Much of the intelligence required will come from below the level of the state, making America's image with global publics as important as its relationships with leaders. And yet, the new president will confront resentment, fear, and rage against America, reducing our ability to persuade other countries and groups to share intelligence or share responsibility for promoting effective governance.

Several attributes of contemporary political life suggest that terrorism is likely to spread and increase, both in quantity and severity. The possibility of secondary proliferation from nations such as Iran and North Korea and the growing capacity of private nuclear-supplier groups increases the risk that terrorists will acquire weapons of mass destruction. The rapid pace of globalization is itself a risk factor, given the number of contemporary terrorist groups that describe globalization and American hegemony as a significant threat to their cultures. Terrorist attacks are now easier than ever to undertake with ever-larger capacities to devastate and terrorize neighborhoods, communities, and cities.

Substate terrorist groups are difficult to detect, target, or deter. Global communications and transportation facilitate terrorists' ability to network with other groups, and increase their access to weapons, expertise, skilled operatives, sympathizers, and finances. The very freedoms afforded in liberal democracies can shield some of these risky activities. Monitoring terrorists' online conversations and entrapping them in chat rooms is likely to be more effective than stealing information from national governments. The ability to sift through massive amounts of open-source information will become increasingly important over time.

Globalization enhances terrorists' access to weapons, information, and finances, as well as the tools for recruitment and mobilization. It also allows local groups to describe their grievances in terms that appeal to global audiences, potentially broadening their fundraising and support base.[7] This process works both ways: transnational groups with global agendas are supporting or outsourcing operations to state-based groups with local agendas. Extremist jihadi terrorist groups have learned to recruit from a pool of potential supporters across the globe, forming fluctuating alliances of convenience with groups or individuals with widely disparate agendas. The networks they form sometimes work together, and sometimes compete.

Case in point: when Abu Musab al-Zarqawi created Al Qaeda in Iraq, his goals were not identical to those of Osama bin Laden and Ayman al-Zawahiri, the two most important leaders of "Al Qaeda Central."[8] Zarqawi's goal of exporting the Iraqi jihad to the West was consistent with Al Qaeda Central's goals, but his effort to provoke a sectarian civil war in Iraq was not. Or consider the merging and shifting alliances among an array of insurgent and terrorist groups operating in Iraq, from nationalist groups promoting Iraq's territorial integrity to Islamist extremist groups promoting a Sunni Shari'a-based state.

This scene—with groups cooperating or merging one day and competing or splintering the next—has the immense potential to complicate intelligence collection. But it also creates opportunities to use the groups against one another. This requires timely and accurate intelligence, with the expertise required to distinguish useful information from deliberate disinformation or misinformation. To acquire that kind of intelligence requires penetrating the groups, which would entail exposing our agents to far greater risk.

For terrorists and insurgents, an attractive ideology is central to success. The Al Qaeda movement exploits what Zawahiri referred to as the "humiliation of globalization." It aims to destroy a status quo that its adherents believe is humiliating to the global Muslim community. Jihad is an attractive way of expressing dissatisfaction with a power elite, whether that elite is real or imagined, and whether power is held by totalitarian monarchs or by liberal parliamentarians. And we should not assume jihad is a Middle Eastern or European problem. The idea is spreading here in America as well. Examples include: a cell planning to attack JFK International Airport and to ignite an underground fuel pipeline; a group of ex-convicts plotting to attack synagogues and government facilities; a cell preparing to attack the army base at Fort Dix, NJ; and an individual planning to attack a shopping mall in Rockford, Illinois, with hand grenades. All of these plots were thwarted by U.S. government officials.[9]

There is an appeal to an identity of victimhood: if I am a victim of someone else's bad actions, then I have an excuse for not meeting expectations, my own or others'. There is an appeal to righteous indignation. There is an appeal to avenging wrongs visited on the weak by the strong. The narrative will be more seductive if moral questions seem to have easy answers, if good and evil can be easily distinguished, if perpetrators and victims stand out in stark relief, and if they never trade places, as they often do in the real world. American actions sometimes play right into the hands of terrorist ideologues, whose success depends not only on the appeal of the narrative they weave, but also their ability to illustrate it with facts, or at least pictures that appear to be facts. Iraq, alas, has been producing many of the pictures the terrorists need, Abu Ghraib the most chilling example.

Mobilizing in-country recruits who can provide logistical support or carry out their own operations has become increasingly important for Al Qaeda because enhanced border protection and intelligence collaboration have made it harder for terrorists to travel into the West. Al Qaeda has responded to this challenge by constantly shifting its shape to evade law-enforcement detection and by altering its mission—from narrow to broad, and from regional to global—to appeal to new audiences. Al Qaeda's rhetoric is focused on the plight of Afghans, Chechens, Palestinians, or Bosnian Muslims.

At other times it articulates a mission so broad (to "fight the new world order" or to "lift oppression from all mankind") that it appeals to an extraordinary variety of individuals and groups from across the political spectrum—from antiglobalization groups on the far left to neo-Nazi and Christian Identity groups on the far right.[10] Al Qaeda's propagandists discriminate among their audiences, sometimes promulgating a narrow mission to appeal to a specific group.

Terrorist groups have also established dominance on a critically important battlefield—the Internet—where our military is not well-equipped to fight. Pro-jihadi Internet warriors are now tailoring their message to recruit operatives in the West, raising new questions about surveillance and privacy. In 2007, for example, Zawahiri began targeting African-American soldiers, speaking admiringly of Malcolm X, and at great length about how America is taking advantage of black Americans in the war in Iraq, in a new kind of slavery.[11]

In some ways, however, Al Qaeda's evolution into a movement has diminished its capacities. According to CIA Director Michael Hayden, Al Qaeda in Iraq and Saudi Arabia is largely defeated.[12] A number of Islamic scholars and extremists, who earlier supported the movement, have turned against Al Qaeda. The targeting of Muslim civilians and contradictory demands by various Al Qaeda factions have reduced support for the movement.[13]

But other developments suggest that Muslim-extremist terrorism is far from defeated. Al Qaeda in the Lands of Islamic Maghreb and Al Qaeda's North African affiliate both have expanded their reach and target set to include Western and U.S. interests.[14] In this still-evolving age of terrorism, risks of both underreaction and overreaction are genuine as democratic societies seek to balance security and liberty. Under national security emergencies of this kind, presidents and prime ministers are prone to arrogate power, and governments are prone to weaken transparency and oversight of detention procedures. We need to find a balance between policies that reduce the threat of terrorism to-day with those that prevent recruitment of the next generation of terrorists.

A central challenge in this effort will be to protect the way of life that the terrorists seek to destroy, including religious and other freedoms, while ensuring that governments are not foreclosed from taking actions required to protect their citizens. Domestic and international legal structures must be adapted to respond to these new threats, which come from below and beyond the level of the state.[15]

Fighting Terrorism

The president-elect needs to prepare now for the possibility of a significant terrorist attack during the transition or early in the new administration. Terrorists aim to make us overreact out of fear. Our fear serves their interests, especially if it induces us to act in ways that undermine our moral or political authority. A new president has never held such a challenging job. Even with the best possible advisors, he will be prone to overreact if he feels that the people he was elected to protect are in danger. Terrorists believe, and they are often right, that frightening the enemy into using excessive force will serve their interests.

Preparing the new president for the possibility of a terrorist attack early in his tenure means preparing him not to react out of fear. Waging war against nation states in response to terrorism perpetrated by nonstate actors is unlikely to reduce terrorism. First, there are very few military targets in a counterterrorism campaign. Second, terrorists live and fight among civilians, making it difficult to avoid civilian casualties. The terrorists' goal is to create a kind of autoimmune response, to frighten the enemy into undermining its own interests through attacks that harm civilians. "An operation that kills five insurgents is counterproductive if collateral damage leads to the recruitment of fifty more insurgents," the Counterinsurgency Field Manual warns.[16] The same adage applies to terrorism.

The incoming president will want to know how well the government is organized to detect, interdict, defend, and recover from a catastrophic attack—and should be briefed by the Bush administration before the elections on all of these contingencies. He will want to prepare his own set of contingency plans as part of his presidential transition planning well before the elections.

The new president must also have an offensive strategy ready the day after he wins the November 4 election—a strategy that attacks terrorists' reputations. Terrorists have a story to tell the world, and they use violence as a form of theater to improve their reputation among existing supporters and to attract the attention of potential supporters, who are more likely to be worried about paying the rent than about the supposed humiliation of the global Muslim community at the hands of the West.[17] The theatrical aspect of terrorism is critically important for us to understand.[18] We cannot deter suicide terrorists by threatening to kill them. A more effective strategy is to focus on what terrorists value most—their reputation.

Zawahiri has repeatedly emphasized the importance of jihadi media, declaring "more than half of this battle is taking place in the battlefield of the media." Al Qaeda runs its own news organizations and has regular video-news conferences that are displayed on YouTube, and there are now thousands of pro-jihadi websites. Zawahiri has initiated a new practice of responding to readers' questions, in a kind of terrorist version of "Meet the Press."

Moreover, as David Galula explained in the seminal book on insurgencies, populations can be divided into an active minority who favor the cause of the insurgents, a neutral majority, and an active minority against the insurgents. Both the terrorists and the counterterrorists aim to win over the neutral majority.[19] The side with the more compelling narrative, and the greater capacity to provide for the social welfare of these undecided Muslims, will win more recruits. This does not mean that the United States should sacrifice its own national security interests to placate the terrorists or to assuage frustrations in the global Muslim community. It means that we need to weigh the public diplomacy impact of every policy remedy we contemplate.

The one overarching theme in the multiple narratives articulated by the global extremist jihadi movement is that the West disrespects Islam, and that under the guise of spreading democracy, America is leading a crusade to dominate, and ultimately destroy, the global Muslim community. Polling suggests that Muslim publics are beginning to agree.[20] Nearly 80 percent of those polled in four Muslim-majority countries believe that our actual goal in the Middle East is not to spread democracy but to weaken and divide the Islamic world.[21] In polling in 35 predominantly Muslim nations, Gallup found that 7 percent of Muslims approved of the September 11 attacks.

These "radicals" were distinguished from the "moderates" by their greater level of fear of being dominated by the West and their stronger feeling that the West disrespects Islam.[22] This trend is dangerous. At the same time, in the last year, a number of religious leaders who once supported Al Qaeda have publicly turned against the organization. The terrorists believe that the doctrine of takfir (the practice of declaring a self-identified Muslim an unbeliever) gives them license to murder Muslims whom they see as insufficiently pure, and that is beginning to affect adversely the image of the global jihadi movement. Al Qaeda and its affiliates have killed tens of thousands of Muslims in Iraq, Algeria, Afghanistan, and elsewhere.[23] A number of polls suggest that support for Al Qaeda among ordinary Muslims is waning.[24] We need to capitalize on these developments.

To do so, the new president should convene a Presidential Commission to develop a counternarrative and a strategy for disseminating it. The commission should be given a very short timeline to complete its recommendations, with a maximum of six months. It should take advantage of work already underway by other organizations, but should focus specifically on reaching at-risk youth. A counternarrative would emphasize that the vast majority of people killed in Al Qaeda's global jihad are Muslim, and would highlight why former jihadis changed their minds.

Our goal should be to maximize the split between the population and the terrorists. Members of the commission should include: Muslim youth from around the world with varying types of expertise; former Islamists who turned away from the movement, for example, the founders of the Qulliam Foundation in London; clerics who can develop detailed arguments about why the jihadi position is wrong; and the world's most successful youth-marketing experts. Madison Avenue advertising gurus should not lead this effort; it should be led by individuals who know how to access at-risk youth, with support from such gurus, among others.

The commission also needs to study how Al Qaeda and related groups spread their ideology, and then develop a plan for reaching the same audience with an effective countermessage. Several grassroots efforts are presently under way in Great Britain, for example, among them something called the "Radical Middle Way," which is attempting to spread a mainstream interpretation of Islam in a way that is relevant to youth.[25]

The new president must also press other nations to create similar commissions, especially in countries that are high risk, as well as a multilateral commission under the auspices of the United Nations and international nongovernment organizations. In the Netherlands, for example, cities have been sponsoring conferences that bring together Muslim groups—including youth groups, specialists on Islam, and officials at all levels of government—which provide a useful model.

Developing a successful counternarrative will require many efforts, in many different arenas, with experts from all over the world. This is a case where more is better. To kick off this effort, the new president early in his tenure should launch a listening tour to hear the concerns of the global Muslim community, publicized especially on youth media in local markets abroad. The president in these listening tours should respond directly to the perceptions of America that come out of reliable polls.

Contain Blowback from Iraq

The United States will presumably begin drawing down troops from Iraq early in the new administration. When U.S. troops leave, at least some of the insurgents and jihadis will decide to stay in the same line of work. Those who elect to remain in the terrorism business will take the networks and military skills they have acquired in Iraq to new "jihads" around the globe.

An unfortunate side effect of the war in Iraq is the excellent training the insurgents have received. Former Baathist military and intelligence officials have now established networks with criminals and foreign jihadi "volunteers," some of them from Western countries. They have been training against the best-equipped military in the world. Moreover, if Iraq erupts further into civil war, psychologically bruised and politically humiliated refugees are likely to become attractive recruits to terrorist organizations.

The new president should initiate meetings now with neighboring states to prepare a strategy for dealing with the inevitable "blowback" from the Iraq war. Working groups need to be established with neighboring states to develop strategies for dealing with refugee flows and with flows of "decommissioned" insurgents who are seeking new jobs, some of them, undoubtedly, as global jihadis. For instance, might it make sense to "buy" the services of out-of-work insurgents through jobs programs? Religious ideology has turned out to be a relatively uncommon reason for Iraqi youth to join the insurgency, while lack of training and jobs is far more important. Job creation may turn out to be the best long-term counterterrorism strategy, at least for the vast majority of detainees.

At the same time, the hardcore, ideologically committed jihadis are unlikely to be rehabilitable. Efforts should be put in place now to monitor the movement of insurgents who leave Iraq. This will require both bilateral and multilateral intelligence efforts, with special emphasis on inevitable efforts by the Islamist extremists to set up virtual training camps on the Internet and seek financing and recruits online.

Create a Reserve Intelligence Force

Because the threats we will face in the coming years will emerge rapidly, from areas we cannot yet predict, we need to create a far more flexible intelligence capability. The new president should create a reserve intelligence force that can be scaled up and scaled back as needed. After September 11 it became clear that we could no longer afford to retain intelligence officers who specialized in cold war–era threats. We needed, instead, analysts and spies who specialized in the Middle East and South Asia, who were fluent in languages such as Pashto, Urdu, and Arabic, rather than Russian.

But that doesn't mean we will need these specialties indefinitely. In the coming years we are likely to find ourselves suddenly needing other kinds of area and technical specialists to analyze new threats, emerging from different parts of the world, which we cannot yet predict. We need to have a way to bring specialists in rapidly and to send them back to the private sector as soon as their expertise is no longer needed. Government employees will require the ability to manage outside experts.

Talk to the World

Since the invasion of Iraq on mistaken and false premises, America's image has fallen, not only among Muslims but also among our long-term European allies. Polls show that European publics view America as unreliable, untrustworthy, and threatening to their security.

Consequently, the new president should launch a major campaign, with a series of speeches in global capitals, to persuade the international community that we mean to be a cooperative, fair player. He will also have to make clear to a domestic audience that the motivation for promoting multilateral cooperation is protecting American civilians, not an ideological dedication to international law and norms. The goal is to secure the military, intelligence, and law-enforcement cooperation we require to prevail in the fight against transnational threats.

The same strategy should apply in predominantly Muslim states, where polling makes clear that ordinary Muslims object to what we do, not who we are. While terrorists have many grievances against Western societies, only some of which are related to U.S. policies, it is important for us to make clear that we distinguish between terrorist organizations' grievances—with which we may or may not agree—and their actions, which we categorically oppose.[26] Many national leaders, for example, including President Bush, have endorsed the idea of a Palestinian state, but that does not mean that those leaders endorse terrorist groups that kill Israeli civilians, purportedly to promote Palestinian statehood. Clarifying this distinction could enhance our credibility in the global Muslim community, even if it has little effect on the terrorists.

Similarly, meeting with our enemies today, including nations such as Iran that are major supporters of terrorist organizations, is an opportunity to collect information while simultaneously building confidence. We should not assume that talking to governments that support terrorists will persuade them to change their policies. The goal is to threaten our enemies' Manichean world-view, and if possible, to encourage further divisions within.

There will be times when it would be imprudent to engage directly with individuals who are declared enemies of the United States or its allies. But our declared policy should be that, under the right circumstances, we are prepared to listen, even when we disagree.

Such an approach is clearly required to resolve the Palestinian-Israeli conflict. The perception that the United States blindly supports Israel at Palestinians' expense remains a critically important grievance among non-Palestinian Arabs, according to polling.[27] Sixty percent of Arab respondents said that the most important thing America can do to improve its image among Arab publics is to broker Arab-Israeli peace.[28]

Choose Prudence over Precaution

The one thing we can predict with relative certainty is that our difficulty in predicting the probability and severity of terrorist strikes will increase over time. Law enforcement and intelligence officials, for example, have repeatedly intercepted components of nuclear weapons sold on the black market. But what percentage of actual sales of usable nuclear weapons materials (as opposed to non-fissile radioactive isotopes or counterfeit materials) have been caught? Have any end users capable of acquiring the expertise to fashion a nuclear device actually managed to purchase fissile materials? If such sales were made, will any of those capable end users actually attempt to use the device? And if they do, will it fizzle or detonate?

We don't know the answers to these questions. The position that "experts" take on the probability of nuclear terrorism may tell us as much about the expert's personality or psychology as it does about nuclear terrorism. When probabilities are uncertain, but expected costs are high, policymakers often deliberately choose to err on the side of precaution.[29]

While expected utility analysis (multiplying the probability of an attack and its expected cost) is generally the best approach for coping with risk, including catastrophic risk, it does not apply to decisions under uncertainty (where probabilities cannot be assigned to outcomes) or ignorance (where even the possible outcomes are ill-defined). Moreover, expected utility analysis of games against nature does not apply to strategic contexts, when the problem entails a game against other minds, as in terrorism or war. The analysis of risk, uncertainty, and ignorance becomes even more complicated where there is learning, for example, when new information keeps coming in.[30] The complexity peaks when uncertainty is a feature of the possible policy remedies as well as the problem.

Precautionary approaches are particularly seductive to politicians, because not acting often appears to be more dangerous than taking action.[31] The problem with precautionary policies such as preventive war is that they can lead us to ignore the new risks introduced by our policy responses. If the side effects of the remedy are more debilitating than the original ailment, it may be better to do nothing.[32] In the aftermath of 9/11, having just experienced a "false negative" error in regard to the risk of terrorism, it was difficult to avoid a precautionary approach to what appeared to be occurring in Iraq.

Precaution, in this case, appeared to dictate a preventive strike against Iraq's alleged weapons of mass destruction facilities, because of the risk that those WMDs would end up in the hands of Al Qaeda.[33] Beyond precaution, Bush administration officials sought to justify an invasion of Iraq, and they appear deliberately to have exaggerated evidence of Iraqi WMDs. Prudence would have dictated considering the countervailing risks introduced by the proposed remedy, and the likelihood that the terrorist threat to Americans would actually increase if the United States invaded and occupied a Muslim-majority state.

Indeed, it is especially important to consider countervailing dangers in regard to terrorism because terrorists aim to induce overreaction on our part. They provoke governments to choose a precautionary approach because it helps them mobilize new recruits. The strategy of counterinsurgency dictates prudence, in the sense that it takes very seriously the countervailing dangers introduced by the way that our enemies exploit any military excess on our part to mobilize new recruits against us. In short: our fight against terrorists will be far more effective if it incorporates the more prudent policies of counterinsurgency.

There are unavoidable tradeoffs between the short-term military necessity of killing or capturing the terrorists today and the long-term goal of containing the movements that give rise to them. Containing the threat of terrorism requires, as the U.S. Counterinsurgency Field Manual explains, "synchronized application of military, paramilitary, political, economic, and psychological actions," attacking the "basis of the insurgency rather than just its fighters."[34] The global extremist jihadi movement is a particularly complex insurgency, which means the new president will have to modernize our response for a new kind of unconventional enemy.

The best tools for this long war will often be the simplest ones. Our Air Force will need more unmanned aerial vehicles.[35] Rather than high-tech imaging devices, our intelligence services will need more old-fashioned human intelligence. Our armed forces will need scrupulously to avoid collateral damage, requiring extraordinary discipline and courage because protecting civilians from harm often puts soldiers at significantly greater risk.

Every military operation we contemplate must be considered through the filter of this question: Will the long-term propaganda or military value to the terrorists exceed the benefits to our side? An effective strategy for containing terrorism requires understanding that we are fighting a seductive idea, not a state. Military action minimally visible and carefully planned and implemented may be necessary to win today's battles. But the tools required in the long run to contain the terrorist threat are neither bombs nor torture chambers. They are ideas and stories that counter the terrorist narrative—and draw potential recruits away from the lure of terrorism.

Overview

The Costs and Benefits of Redeploying from Iraq

LAWRENCE KORB

The cost of continuing the war in Iraq makes the United States less safe from its real terrorist enemies around the world. Our nation's overall security interests are not served by the open-ended occupation of Iraq, and our military presence ensures the flames of Islamic extremism will only burn brighter around the Muslim world. Redeploying our armed forces from Iraq over the course of 2009 should set the stage for political compromise and reconciliation among Iraq's ethnic and sectarian groups, and for greater regional involvement in bringing peace and stability to Iraq. But redeploying our armed forces from Iraq to other bases around the region and back home must be handled carefully, and must be accompanied by focused political, diplomatic, and counterterrorism steps to ensure the best outcome from the Bush administration's massive strategic blunder. Closing out a war that should never have been fought after about six years of multiple civil conflicts within Iraq will not be easy, but U.S. security interests cannot be held hostage to a dysfunctional Iraqi government. The costs of remaining in Iraq indefinitely far outweigh any potential benefits.

The new president will have to make a number of critical and interrelated military and political decisions on Iraq the moment he wins the presidential election in November in order to implement them swiftly come January 2009. In the military realm, he must answer the following three questions. First, how many American troops will remain? Second, for how long? And third, what will be their mission until those troops that remain are redeployed?

Politically, the 44th president must also answer three policy questions. First, how can he best pressure the Iraqi government to meet the 18 benchmarks agreed upon by the U.S. and Iraqi governments in late 2007 to bring about political reconciliation? Second, how will the U.S. and the Iraqi governments coordinate their military operations? Third, how will the U.S. government work with the Iraqi government and neighboring countries to ensure that Iraq remains a unified country with diplomatic, economic, and humanitarian links around the region?

In making these decisions, the new president must first determine what U.S. national interests our military and political policies should serve in Iraq. These interests can be placed into five categories. First, the United States must prevent Iraq from becoming a launching pad for terrorist groups with a global reach, such as Al Qaeda. That is what happened in Afghanistan in the 1990s after the Soviets were forced to leave and the United States turned its attention elsewhere. We cannot make that mistake again in Iraq.

Second, the United States must restore its credibility, prestige, and capability to act diplomatically and politically around the globe. Because the Bush administration misled the American people and the world about the need to invade Iraq, U.S. credibility among its own citizens and the global community is at an all-time low. Moreover, the abuses of Abu Ghraib and Guantánamo have further undermined our moral standing in the world.

Third, the United States needs to improve stability in the entire Middle East region. Foreign fighters from Syria, Jordan, and Saudi Arabia have streamed into Iraq to support the insurgency and have established a branch of Al Qaeda in Iraq. Millions of refugees from Iraq have flowed into the neighboring countries, particularly Jordan and Syria. Kurdish groups such as the Kurdistan Workers Party, or PKK, conduct terrorist attacks in Turkey, provoking ground and air military actions by Turkey in the Kurdish area. And Iran, anxious to ensure that Iraq does not again become a hostile neighbor or that the United States does not use Iraq as a base to undermine its regime, provides funding for military equipment and training to several Iraqi Shia militias.

Fourth, U.S. policy must seek to limit and undermine Iranian influence in Iraq and around the region. Iran's reach around the Middle East is growing apace precisely because of the U.S. invasion and occupation of Iraq. By top-pling the regime of Saddam Hussein, the Bush administration removed a major threat to Iran, in effect making it more powerful. By allowing a majority Shia-led government to take power in Iraq, Iran now has a new ally. And by claiming the right to invade Iraq before it developed a nuclear weapon, the Bush administration in fact empowered those in Iran seeking to develop a nuclear weapon.

Fifth, it is in the interest of the United States for Iraq to remain a single state. Carved out of the Ottoman Empire, Iraq's three groups—the Shia, the Sunni, and the Kurds—have been held together only by force, first by the British occupation and then by Baathist dictators. The great challenge will be to ensure that Iraq's three main groups willingly choose to remain as a single state rather than breaking up into three or more pieces.

The new president must also recognize that he will not have any good options in dealing with this unnecessary diversion from what the Bush administration calls the "War on Terror." Regardless of the military, political, and diplomatic choices the next chief executive makes on Iraq, there is no guarantee that all or even some of the anticipated outcomes will be achieved either in whole or in part.

Military Decisions

In January 2009, the United States will have around 140,000 troops on the ground in Iraq, down from a peak of 168,000 in November 2007. They will be composed of 14 combat brigades and their support personnel. Secretary of Defense Robert Gates had hoped that the number would drop to 100,000.[1] But on September 9, 2008, President Bush announced that he intends to leave about that number in Iraq.[2] The exact number of troops will depend upon the security situation on the ground, which in turn will depend upon three other factors.

First, what will become of the so-called Anbar Awakening? This Sunni movement to protect Sunni neighborhoods and fight the Al Qaeda in Iraq terrorist group is underwritten by the United States, which provides payments of $300 per month to about 100,000 members of about 125 Sunni militia groups alongside training, logistical help, and sometimes weapons. These local proxy armies, also known as Concerned Local Citizens or Sons of Iraq, serve as police forces and as eyes and ears for U.S. troops.

But the Shia-dominated Iraqi government is not comfortable with these Sunni-dominated groups. Consequently, the central government refuses to integrate the vast majority of them into the Iraqi Security Forces. The issue is how long these groups will continue working with U.S. forces if the ruling Shia leaders refuse to share power. In fact, there is evidence that they are already losing patience, and the central government has begun to arrest some of their leaders.

Second, how long will the Mahdi Army of radical Shia cleric Muqtada al-Sadr refrain from attacking U.S. forces? In August 2007, for reasons that are not yet clear, Sadr ordered his fighters to lay down their arms for six months. In February 2008, he extended the ceasefire for six more months, then mobilized his militia for a short time in late March 2008 in response to Iraqi Prime Minister Nouri al-Maliki's attack on Basra.

Sadr then called a ceasefire again, and in June hinted he may resume the fight. Some U.S. officials believe he engages in these periodical ceasefires in order to purge the unruly elements from his 60,000-strong militia. Others believe that Sadr is continuing to train and arm his militia and is simply biding his time. Others note that some Mahdi Army fighters are ignoring Sadr's call and are instead forming new, more lethal special groups.

Third, how well will the Iraqi Security Forces perform? Even with the surge, the United States did not have sufficient troops to "clear, hold, and build" the entire country. Therefore, it must depend upon the 600,000-member-strong ISF to keep areas secure after U.S. or allied troops move on to another area. If these troops do their job, then the United States can reduce its footprint. But if, as has happened all too frequently, they remain loyal to their tribe or sect, security will not be maintained. Case in point: when the Maliki government ordered the ISF to take control of Basra in April 2008, at least 1,300 members of the ISF defected to the Madhi Army or refused to fight.

Because the costs of maintaining up to 140,000 U.S. troops in Iraq far outweigh whatever benefits might be gained from remaining there in larger numbers for at least another decade, the new president must decide whether to withdraw, and if so, how rapidly.

The costs can be placed into the following categories: human, financial, security, and diplomatic. By January 2009, over 4,000 American servicemen and women will have been killed—an estimate based on the current rate of casualties in Iraq—and another 30,000 will have been wounded, 5,000 of them severely. By the beginning of 2009, anywhere between 200,000 and 1 million Iraqi civilians will have died, alongside at least 8,000 Iraqi members of their own armed forces and militias.[3]

Financially, the United States will have incurred about $1 trillion in direct costs to fight the war in Iraq, with much of this money borrowed from abroad. In real dollars, the direct costs of military operations already exceed the costs of the 12-year war in Vietnam and are more than double the cost of the Korean War. Maintaining U.S. forces in substantial numbers will continue to cost well over $100 billion a year, and is likely to result in thousands of Iraqi deaths and hundreds of U.S. casualties each year.

Overall U.S. national security is worsening and will continue to do so as long as the United States keeps substantial numbers of troops in Iraq. The quality of the U.S. Army, which has borne the brunt of the occupation in Iraq, has declined dramatically since the invasion. Since the American people have turned against the war, many are discouraging their sons and daughters from joining the Army. Consequently, to meet its recruiting targets, the Army has been forced to lower its educational and aptitude standards for new recruits dramatically, and has been forced to take in thousands of people each year with criminal convictions, including felonies.

Since the beginning of the war in Iraq, the number of new Army recruits with high school diplomas dropped to 71 percent from 94 percent in 2003, and the proportion of recruits who require waivers for criminal records jumped to 11.2 percent from 4.6 percent over the same period. Since 2003, suicides (115 in fiscal year 2007), divorces (approximately 20 percent of married troops in Iraq are planning divorces), and desertions (nearly 4,700 in fiscal year 2007, the highest rate since 1980) are also up dramatically.

Moreover, the Army continues to lose more and more of the best and brightest as West Point graduates leave the Army after completing their obligatory service in numbers not seen since Vietnam. More than half of the West Point class of 2002 (who completed their obligated service in 2007) got out. Finally, the Army has had to spend increasing amounts on enlistment and reenlistment bonuses. Before the war in Iraq the Army spent $157 million a year on bonuses. That number now stands at around $1 billion.

What's more alarming is that the ability of the United States to respond to other crises is severely hampered as long as so many of our military forces are bogged down in Iraq. Already, the security situation on the ground in Afghanistan continues to deteriorate as a result of insufficient troops. Because of the way we have treated our NATO allies in the lead up to the war in Iraq, they have refused to pick up the slack in Afghanistan. On September 9, 2008, Bush announced that because of the commitment to Iraq, the Pentagon could send only 4,500 troops to Afghanistan, far short of the 20,000 additional troops our commanders say are needed right now.

Admiral Mike Mullen, the chairman of the Joint Chiefs of Staff, summed up the situation when he said that, "in Afghanistan we do what we can, in Iraq we do what we must."[4] Mullen and other military leaders also acknowledge that we do not have sufficient ground forces to deal with crises elsewhere around the globe because of the extensive commitment to Iraq. For example, at the height of the surge, all four brigades of the Army's 82nd Airborne division, the Army's strategic ground reserve, were deployed either in Iraq or Afghanistan.

Finally, as long as U.S. forces remain in Iraq in large numbers we will continue to "prove" Al Qaeda's propaganda that we came to a Muslim country to get control of the oil and undermine their religion and culture. Our invasion and continuing occupation remain an excellent recruiting tool for groups such as Al Qaeda in Iraq, Al Qaeda central in Afghanistan and Pakistan, and Al Qaeda offshoots around the world.

If President George W. Bush had honestly informed the American public of all of these costs before the invasion, it is unlikely the public would have supported it. Francis Fukuyama, one of the neo-conservatives who originally supported the war, put it well when he said that if President Bush had told the American people that more than 4,000 Americans would die, 30,000 would be wounded, and we would spend $1 trillion so Iraq could have an election, he would have been laughed out of the ballpark.

But we did invade and occupy the country, which means the new president must consider the benefits of remaining as well as the costs of leaving. There are several potential costs of an American withdrawal that need to be recognized—costs that conservatives in favor of remaining in Iraq indefinitely frame in almost apocalyptic terms—but costs that have to be balanced against benefits.

Here are some of the questions the president needs to consider. When we leave, could a full-scale civil war break out that could spread throughout the region? Could Al Qaeda in Iraq reconstitute itself and then use Iraq as a launching pad for international terrorist attacks? Could the moral authority of the United States be weakened because (as former Secretary of State Colin Powell told President Bush) we broke Iraq and so we own it?[5] And could leaving before the Iraqi government can govern the entire country embolden global terrorist networks to attack us or our allies in other places, including the U.S. homeland?

The new president must ask whether any of these doomsday scenarios are really possible. Iraq, after all, belongs to the Iraqis, an ancient civilization with its own norms and tendencies. It is entirely possible, perhaps even probable, that in the absence of a cumbersome and clumsy U.S. occupation that now allows Iraq's political leaders to avoid making hard political choices, Iraqis will make their own bargains and compacts to head off the genocide that many anticipate.

Opponents of the war in Iraq have far more confidence in the abilities of the Iraqis to responsibly manage their affairs than the advocates of remaining indefinitely. The United States did destroy Saddam Hussein's regime in Iraq, but after five long years of multiple civil wars chances are good that Iraq's fractious political parties will bargain among themselves more earnestly if U.S. armed forces are not on the ground acting as referees. Additionally, our continued diplomatic and political involvement—accompanied by a much reduced and clearly temporary military presence—will demonstrate we are not abandoning Iraq.

Moreover, the American withdrawal will finally compel the region to face up to its responsibilities in Iraq, forcing the country's neighbors and the Muslim community worldwide to decide whether a civil war with all its dramatic consequences is in their collective interest. Faced with that stark reality, it is quite likely the Saudis, Iranians, Jordanians, and others will seek to mediate, as opposed to inflame, Iraq's squabbles—especially as the United States launches a diplomatic "surge" while it executes a phased withdrawal.

Political Decisions

After focusing on the military costs and benefits of leaving Iraq, the president must turn his attention to the political dimensions: namely, how best to get the Iraqis to meet the political benchmarks necessary to bring about political reconciliation, and how to delineate the rules governing the U.S.-Iraqi military relationship when the U.N. mandate expires at the end of 2008.

No matter how long the United States remains in Iraq, there will be problems when we leave if the Iraqis do not complete a meaningful reconciliation process. This is something that both President Bush and Prime Minister Maliki recognize. In fact, to move the process along both Bush and Maliki agreed in November 2006 to a series of 18 benchmarks to measure progress toward reconciliation. These benchmarks, which were put into Iraqi legislation in March 2007, specified 18 steps that were to be completed by the end of 2007.

Because many of Bush's supporters argued that Maliki could not meet the benchmarks as long as security continued to deteriorate in Iraq, especially in Baghdad, the president escalated the American military presence by increasing the number of American combat brigades to 20 from 15 and the number of American troops to 168,000 from 130,000. This increase in American combat brigades, a dramatic increase in the number of air strikes, the Anbar Awakening, and the Sadr retreat led to an improved security situation beginning in late 2007.

Yet the Maliki government has made comparatively little progress in meeting these benchmarks. As of the summer of 2008, only two of the 18 political benchmarks had been fully met. Nor were Iraqi forces able to take over secu-rity in the 18 provinces as Bush and Maliki had agreed to in Jordan in Novem-ber 2006. If anything, the Maliki government regressed politically in 2007, squandering the sacrifices made by our men and women in uniform, including more than 1,000 additional American deaths, and another $150 billion in U.S. taxpayer dollars.

The only hope of getting the Iraqi government to take these difficult politi-cal steps is to signal the end of our military commitment with a date for with-drawal. Even a conservative such as Tom Cole (R-OK), a member of the House Armed Services Committee, believes that the only thing that will compel Iraq's various factions to work together is the threat of a U.S. withdrawal.[6]

Yet even if the new president begins to withdraw our forces as soon as he comes into office, it cannot be completed safely overnight. Therefore, the new administration needs to ensure that there is a satisfactory arrangement govern-ing the role and responsibilities of U.S. forces. The new president will inherit ei-ther a so-called Status of Forces agreement signed by the United States and Iraq governing the role of the U.S. military presence in the country, or a temporary extension of the U.N. mandate for U.S. forces to remain in Iraq. The new ad-ministration will have to chart any military redeployment plans based on these political and diplomatic agreements.

Neither a Status of Forces Agreement nor a new U.N. mandate, however, obviate the need to manage the strategic redeployment of U.S. troops so that political considerations and military considerations dovetail according to the best interests of U.S. diplomacy and national security. For that to happen, sev-eral key steps need to be taken.

Next Steps

In order to minimize the damage to U.S. security interests, the 44th president must take a number of steps immediately upon taking office. He cannot post-pone making decisions or allow our policy to continue to drift on the false hope that victory is just around the corner.

First, he must set a specific timetable for a phased withdrawal of all American troops and their critical equipment from Iraq, accompanied by an announce-ment that the United States will not maintain any permanent bases there. This phased withdrawal can be safely executed within 10 months to 12 months, and can be accomplished by not replacing units as they complete their one-year tours of duty. This timetable would allow sufficient time to dismantle all of the major bases, such as Camp Victory in Baghdad and the Balad and Tallil Airbases, as well as return most critical U.S. military equipment to the United States.[7]

As this redeployment begins in 2009, a smaller number of U.S. forces would continue to rotate into the region to take up missions in Kuwait, Turkey, and Afghanistan. These forces will enhance regional security by taking up critical missions outside of Iraq, and will enable U.S. forces to strike terrorist targets in Iraq if necessary. These forces will include an Army brigade and a tactical air wing in Kuwait, a Marine expeditionary force, and an aircraft carrier battle group afloat in the Gulf.[8]

In addition, four to five Army combat brigades should be sent to Afghanistan to complete the mission of defeating Al Qaeda and the Taliban on the real central front in the war against Islamic extremists. This military redeployment would not only relieve the strain on our overextended ground forces, but would put the Iraqi political leaders on notice that they cannot count on us forever and must instead begin to make the hard political choices necessary to bring about political reconciliation. If they do not make these compromises as we redeploy then it will be clear they are unable to make them at all.

Some analysts outline grim scenarios for Iraq and the Middle East if the United States withdraws its military forces in a year. These arguments, often offered by many of the original (and now discredited) proponents of the Iraq war, essentially argue that the United States cannot leave Iraq because it will result in sectarian cleansing, a new base for Al Qaeda, and a regional war.

Yet all of these consequences are already occurring even with close to 140,000 U.S. troops in the country—and with no capacity to expand the number of U.S. troops for a full-fledged occupation of the entire country.

Because faulty assumptions and bad analysis got the United States into this war, it is important to examine the arguments for continuing U.S. military operations in Iraq with no end in sight. First of all, Iraq's violence is already quite deadly, with tens of thousands of Iraqis killed in sectarian cleansing and terrorist attacks since 2003. Deep ethnic and sectarian fragmentation among Iraqis means that no single force will be able to truly gain an upper hand in the country.

In addition, the absence of heavy weapons—such as tanks, attack aircraft, and artillery—would likely limit the casualty rates and ethnic violence in Iraq. In short, the absence of a U.S. military presence means that a military stalemate among the Iraqis could lead to political compromises.

Second, the notion that Al Qaeda might take over a portion of Iraq is farfetched. Foreign jihadist fighters make up only a small portion of the overall insurgency, less than 10 percent according to most intelligence estimates. In addition, at least 80 percent of Iraqis (the Shia and the Kurds), as well as a growing number of Sunnis, would not allow Al Qaeda to gain a foothold in the country because they see these groups as inimical to their own culture and interests.

Third, direct military intervention by neighboring armies is highly unlikely. Syria, Saudi Arabia, Kuwait, and Jordan lack the military capacity to launch an invasion, and face other overriding security concerns. The United States can deter threats of invasion from Turkey and Iran by remaining in the region. Furthermore, with a more effective strategy for the region built on collective security measures and intensified diplomacy, the United States can help countries in the region more effectively advance their own interests in a more secure Iraq and Middle East.

Finally, the United States should combine a credible military redeployment plan with pragmatic regional security and diplomatic efforts. The main goal of these regional security and diplomatic initiatives is to ensure that the costs of intervening to exploit Iraq's internal divisions are much higher than the benefits gained from working collectively to contain, manage, and ultimately resolve Iraq's internal conflicts.

Leaders around the world, and in the Middle East in particular, fear that the forthcoming U.S. military withdrawal from Iraq will lead to terrible consequences for their own countries' interests. It is time for the United States to capitalize on these fears to get our allies, Iraq's neighbors, and other Muslim-majority countries of the world to do more to help stabilize their own backyard.

Discussing the implications of the U.S. redeployment from Iraq with all the countries in the region will help manage the transition. Maintaining a U.S. military presence in the region as well as initiating these regional security diplomatic efforts will guard against the threat that neighboring countries will increase destructive interventions into Iraq's internal conflicts.

Regional diplomacy also involves getting other countries to act in their own self-interest in regional stability by working with the United States and other world powers to dismantle global terrorist networks such as Al Qaeda. Indeed, countries in the region must prepare for an additional threat—the "boomerang" effect of foreign jihadists returning to their home countries after U.S. forces redeploy out of Iraq.

When the United States invaded Iraq, the country became a magnet for Islamist militants from across the globe and a live training ground for global terrorist groups. Now there are growing signs that these terrorists are heading to other countries in the region. This is the greatest external security threat facing not just Saudi Arabia, Syria, and Jordan, but also Egypt and the Arab countries of North Africa.

Increased terrorist threats can be managed and contained more effectively without a large presence of U.S. ground forces in Iraq, but will require a modified approach that employs the full potential of U.S. intelligence and law enforcement capabilities cooperating with regional actors. The United States should formalize a regional network of government security forces to combat global terrorist networks such as Al Qaeda. It may not be practical to include all countries at this stage given the mutual tensions and animosities, but announcing the intent to support an inclusive effort would put countries such as Iran and Syria on notice.

To facilitate such dialogue, even though conditions may not be ripe for decisive diplomatic action, the United States should encourage regular meetings between defense and interior ministers of countries in the region, with a system for direct communication, coordination, and intelligence sharing. Over time, as the positive effects of the U.S. strategic realignment take hold, new opportunities to rebuild counterterrorist alliances are sure to arise.

The United States must also boost collective efforts to assist Iraqi refugees. An estimated 2.5 million Iraqi refugees have fled to neighboring countries, among them Jordan, Syria, Iran, and Egypt, creating social, economic, and potential political problems in those countries—in addition to the hardships faced by the refugees themselves. A more coordinated effort must be made to alleviate the refugees' situation, and to help their host countries cope with them—starting with a small working group consisting of the United States, the United Nations, Syria, and Jordan.

The United States should appoint a high-level coordinator for Iraqi refugee affairs to work with the United Nations and countries in the region on Iraqi refugees. This coordinator could build on the discussions at the April 2007 U.N. refugee conference in Geneva, and coordinate the actions of U.S. agencies such as the departments of State and Homeland Security to ensure that the United States is fulfilling its moral obligation to Iraqi refugees.

The United States should get other countries to do more by increasing the number of refugees it accepts. Washington should raise the total number of political refugees allowed into the United States annually to 100,000 from the current level of 7,000. The United States should use the growing refugee crisis as an argument for garnering greater support to resolve Iraq's internal conflicts.

In addition, the United States must encourage economic linkages between Iraq and its neighbors as another way to help get Iraq's neighbors to play a more constructive role as U.S. forces are redeployed around the region. With greater economic ties come greater reasons to help Iraqis solve their internal conflicts.

Finally, the new administration must support longer-term regional security cooperation. By developing more productive ways to jointly address the common threats faced by countries in the region, the United States could plant the seeds for more constructive and responsible actions by those countries. The list of security challenges in the Middle East is long and daunting. But by more constructively and directly helping countries address these issues head-on through diplomacy, the United States can build a more sensible strategy for addressing difficult regional security issues such as Iran's nuclear program.

Overview
Reducing Global Poverty Is a
Moral and Security Imperative

GAYLE SMITH

The new president has an opportunity to fashion and leverage a defense, diplomacy, and development triad that creates a world where a majority of capable states and open societies share common goals, where democracy delivers, and where the trend toward extreme poverty is reversed. To accomplish this, he will have to make global economic development a priority and equip the United States to act by institutionalizing White House leadership, modernizing a dysfunctional foreign aid system, crafting a new relationship with Congress on the management of foreign aid, and securing the support of diverse stakeholders for a development agenda.

The new president will inherit a country less secure in a world divided by sharp disparities between the world's rich and poor, between nations actively engaged in fast-paced globalization and those left behind, and between people who have tangible reasons to believe in a secure and prosperous world and those who daily confront evidence that violence is a more potent tool for change than hope. These challenges can be conquered neither by a singular reliance on our military power nor simply by dint of our diplomacy. Because

stark economic poverty is at the root of these dualities, the most powerful anti-
dote is sustainable economic development.

Security imperatives and moral convictions have led the United States to help
improve the lives of the world's poor throughout our modern history. In his inaugural address in 1961, President John F. Kennedy highlighted this commitment of the American people: "To those peoples in the huts and villages across
the globe struggling to break the bonds of mass misery, we pledge our best efforts to help them help themselves, for whatever period is required—not because the Communists may be doing it, not because we seek their votes, but
because it is right. If a free society cannot help the many who are poor, it cannot
save the few who are rich." As he launched an ambitious postwar development
plan, General George Marshall explained, "Our policy is directed not against
any country or doctrine but against hunger, poverty, desperation, and chaos."

The vision of JFK and the Marshall Plan is no less convincing today than it
was during the last century. But the challenges now are far greater. Institutional
disarray and lack of a clear direction have left the United States ill-equipped to
deploy foreign aid as an effective tool in this increasingly divided world.

Consider the facts: 1 billion of the world's people still live on $1 or less per
day;[1] 2 billion have no access to basic energy supplies;[2] over 10 million children
die before their fifth birthday each year, mostly from preventable diseases;[3] and
roughly 25 percent of children in the developing world do not finish primary
school.[4] Economic disparities within and between countries, meanwhile, are
on the rise. In Latin America, for example, the poorest 40 percent of households receive less than 14 percent of total income while the richest 10 percent
take in an average of more than 36 percent.[5] Globally, the income of the
world's richest 5 percent is 114 times more than that of the poorest 5 percent.

While we may see gains in economic growth in some countries, new realities will undercut progress. Adaptation to climate change, for example, will
cost developing countries an estimated $50 billion each year.[6] The increased
trade that comes with globalization, meanwhile, will not soon yield meaningful results for the world's poor. Though they account for more than 40 percent
of global population, the world's poorest countries represent less than 3 percent of world trade.[7]

The new president will face a host of global challenges that cannot be defeated by military power or dissuaded by skillful diplomacy. Climate change is
expected, for example, to strike its most devastating blow against the developing world, where 75 percent of the population live in rural areas and depend on
agriculture for their livelihoods.[8] Experts believe that the world's 40 poorest
countries could lose 10 to 20 percent of their grain-growing capacity due to

water shortages, and the cycle of drought has already intensified across sub-Saharan Africa.[9] The developing world's ability to either adapt to climate change or mitigate its effects, meanwhile, is sharply constrained by structural poverty. As leading former military officials have noted, "Climate change can act as a threat multiplier for instability in some of the most volatile regions of the world, and it presents significant national security challenges for the United States."[10]

The cycle of conflict is also intensifying in the developing world, where the risk of war increases in direct proportion to the levels of poverty. Africa is estimated to be losing $18 billion per year—or an annual average loss of 15 percent of gross domestic product—to conflict.[11] This translates into $284 billion since 1990—or one-and-a-half times the continent's expenditure on health and education.[12] This history leaves much of Africa trapped in a vicious cycle where poverty breeds conflict that fuels poverty. Meanwhile, conflict has triggered the authorization of 26 new UN peacekeeping missions around the world between 1988 and 1995[13]—and 29 peacekeeping and support missions since then[14]—driving up U.S. expenditures on humanitarian assistance to the extent that we today spend more on relief than we do on development.

Against this backdrop, the world is now "more threatened by weak and failing states than we are by conquering ones," as President George W. Bush noted in his 2002 National Security Strategy. Experts classify some 52 states as weak or failing because their governments are unable to protect their borders, provide basic services to their citizens, or claim the legitimacy needed to ensure political, social, and economic cohesion.[15] The threats posed by these states are potent. In Pakistan, a weak state provides an environment for the spread of extremism. Across Africa, weak states provide safe havens for terrorist networks, arms dealers, criminal syndicates, and money launderers. In Somalia, state failure provides the backdrop for conflict, chaos, and regional crisis. And perhaps most significant, weak and failing states dash the hopes of billions of the world's people.

Opportunities and Challenges

The Bush administration called for, and Congress legislated, a dramatic increase in foreign assistance over the past eight years with strong bipartisan support. A new milestone was set in 2008 when 186 members of Congress—from both sides of the aisle—wrote to President Bush urging him to increase the fiscal year 2009 International Affairs Budget consistent with the 2006 National Security Strategy, which states that "Development reinforces diplomacy and defense, reducing long-term threats to our national security by helping to build stable, prosperous, and peaceful societies."[16] President Bush responded by increasing the FY09 International Affairs Budget to $39.5 billion, a 16-percent increase over the previous year.

Support for two major Bush administration aid initiatives was also strong. In January 2004, the United States established the Millennium Challenge Corporation, a grant-making federal agency, and pledged $4.8 billion in support of development grants to the best-performing countries in the developing world. Sixteen countries have signed MCC compacts and 22 are in line, making efforts to adhere to the social, judicial, and political reform indicators set forth under the program.[17] The MCC was challenged by budget battles and the noticeable gap between stated goals and implementation, but it garnered support from both Republicans and Democrats. Bipartisan support for PEPFAR—the President's Emergency Program for AIDS Relief—is even more robust, with both parties in Congress supporting initial outlays, as well as President Bush's 2008 call to double program funding.

Much of the pressure to increase the foreign aid budget comes directly from the American people. A 2007 Gallup poll found that 56 percent of Americans were "dissatisfied" with the current role of the United States in global affairs.[18] Another poll showed that 65 percent of Americans—and the majority of both Republicans and Democrats—support increasing global poverty-reduction expenditures to 0.7 percent of U.S. GDP.[19] Doing more to improve the lives of the poor is one way that Americans believe we can restore our global image—and a key way for the new president to prove that he is an effective and representative global leader.

The growing understanding that weak states and poverty combine to create the conditions in which extremism can flourish has also driven aid increases. Leading foreign policy experts in both parties and several high-level commissions have come to the same conclusion drawn by the Center for Global Development's bipartisan Commission on Weak States and National Security, which states that, "the roots of this challenge—and long-term hope for its resolution—lie in development."[20]

Funding may have increased in recent years, but the new president will face a system in disarray. In 2007, the congressionally mandated HELP Commission, which was established to review and make proposals to reform U.S. foreign aid, reported that of the over 100 government officials (both civilian and military), aid practitioners, foreign policy experts, academics, and private-sector representatives consulted, ". . . not one person appeared before this commission to defend the status quo."[21]

Our foreign aid system is broken. U.S. foreign aid programs and funding are arrayed across more than 24 government agencies, departments, and initiatives, each with its own goals, priorities, and procedures. No single individual or agency has the authority or the responsibility to oversee or coordinate these myriad programs. The United States has no global development policy or strategy, and foreign aid is instead guided by a Foreign Assistance Act that was written in 1961 and has since grown to 2,000 pages in length and been amended to include 33 goals, 247 directives, and 75 priorities.[22]

America's foreign aid agency—the U.S. Agency for International Development—has been sidelined and weakened and its professional staff eroded to the point that there are more people serving in U.S. military bands than there are development experts in the executive branch. During the Vietnam War, USAID had a permanent staff of 15,000. Today, it numbers some 3,000,[23] and USAID is forced to rely heavily on outside contractors to manage programs in over 150 countries.

Segregating foreign aid accounts among different agencies alongside the absence of either a strategic plan or high-level coordination significantly hampers development progress. Kenya, for example, witnessed a marked increase in U.S. foreign aid and now receives over $500 million annually. But in the FY08 budget request, 90 percent of this was marked for HIV/AIDS funding, and less than 1 percent was set aside for other development programs.[24] The net result is that there is next to no funding available to either counter the conditions that gave rise to Kenya's destabilizing post-electoral crisis or consolidate the gains that may be achieved through the fragile post-crisis political agreement.

In recognition of the resulting capability gap, the Bush State Department in 2006 launched "Transformational Diplomacy," a plan designed to reorganize U.S. foreign aid. It has received poor reviews from both Capitol Hill and development experts. "Transformational Diplomacy" set out to rationalize foreign aid and ensure its coordination within the executive branch, but the new Deputy Undersecretary for Foreign Aid has no formal jurisdiction over aid programs run by the military, the MCC, or several other agencies. The plan moves development planning from the field to Washington, and it further weakens USAID while leaving over half of all nonmilitary official foreign assistance programs to be designed and executed by other government agencies.

"Transformational Diplomacy" is a good phrase with good intentions, but it has failed to fill the development vacuum. This vacuum is now being filled not by civilian agencies, but by the Department of Defense, which has dramatically increased its own development programming and been on the receiving end of what is proportionally the largest allocation of development dollars within the executive branch. With its focus on the "Global War on Terror" and a new mandate to aid states in stabilization, reconstruction, and development, the Defense Department's development budget has soared from 5.6 percent of the executive branch total in 2002 to 21.7 percent, or $5.5 billion, in 2005.[25]

This shift risks increasing the imbalance between aid allocated in response to immediate national security challenges by the military and aid programmed by civilian agencies to address the conditions that allow these challenges to arise. This shift is already evident. During its second term, the Bush administration created AFRICOM, a unified African military command mandated to undertake economic development efforts and coordinate U.S. interagency efforts in support of economic development across Africa. The need for a more robust approach to development in Africa is warranted, but leadership by the military marks a dramatic shift from past practice, places development in the hands of a department that lacks professional development expertise, and fuels the perception that the United States is conflating development and the "Global War on Terror."

Recommendations

The new president has an opportunity to fashion a defense, diplomacy, and development triad in pursuit of the long-term goal of leading in a world where a majority of capable states and open societies share common goals, where democracy delivers, and where the trend toward extreme poverty is reversed. To accomplish this, the new president will have to reorient the executive branch's approach to development, elevate and modernize the foreign aid system, craft a new relationship with Congress on the management of foreign aid, and ensure the support of diverse stakeholders for a development agenda.

He will first have to articulate to the American people the powerful rationale for U.S. support for global economic development. As a matter of policy, he must work with Congress to ensure that the United States is able to deliver assistance that can buttress our immediate foreign policy goals and aid that can target the root causes of instability, crisis, and inequity. The 44th president must also establish clear global economic development priorities that focus and direct the allocation of resources on key objectives, including building the capacities of governments and civil society, supporting the creation of effective and transparent institutions, and promoting equitable and sustainable economic growth.

Across the span of successive administrations, the United States has allocated the bulk of its foreign aid to support real-time national security challenges, and invested far less in ameliorating the conditions that have given rise to those challenges. Between 1980 and 1990, for example, the United States provided over $5 billion in economic and military assistance to Pakistan. Yet following the cold war and throughout the next 10 years, assistance dropped to just 10 percent of the amount expended during the previous decade.[26] After September 11, assistance spiked once again, and from 2002 to 2007 the United States provided Pakistan with over $10.5 billion in assistance.[27]

The largest recipients of U.S. foreign assistance today are Iraq, Egypt, and Pakistan. The United States provides over 45 percent of total foreign aid to 10 countries, but only 6 percent to the world's 10 poorest countries.[28] The United States will continue to require and utilize aid to buttress immediate foreign policy and security goals, but we must also have the ability to invest foreign aid in support of the long-term development goals that can contribute to a safer and more prosperous world over time.

Establish White House Foreign Aid Structure

During the presidential transition phase after the election, the President-elect should identify a third Deputy National Security Advisor for long-term strategic planning. In a White House facing the pressures of competing global and domestic crises, 24-hour news coverage, and a four-year election cycle, there is little time for thinking about and planning for the long term. A designated deputy NSA mandated to think and plan ahead will allow the incoming administration to make up for the time lost by the Bush administration on issues such as climate change, and allow the new administration to get out ahead of future threats such as resource scarcity and new global pandemics.

The new president should also create a directorate, led jointly by the National Security Council and National Economic Council, to initiate and oversee the coordination of all foreign aid agencies, initiatives, departments, and programs. Given the growing role of non-governmental organizations, philanthropic groups, and corporations in humanitarian and development efforts overseas, the directorate should ensure that the U.S. government is in regular consultation with these prominent partners.

As the first step toward formulating a government-wide policy on development and crafting a whole-of-government development strategy, the new president should issue a presidential directive providing initial guidance to the multiple agencies, departments, and offices that are now pursuing their own individual agendas. The guidance should neither be so vague—by pointing to, for example, "reducing global poverty"—as to be meaningless, nor so prescriptive that it undercuts the ability of professionals on the ground to make informed decisions. The presidential directive should be the precursor to a National Development Strategy that should be drafted annually.

U.S. Global Economic Development Agency

During his first term, the new president should work to create a new U.S. Global Economic Development Agency—an independent, cabinet-level agency focused on global poverty-alleviation goals. Because development is a field distinct from either defense or diplomacy, it warrants its own department and leadership and a seat at the foreign policy table. Military and security assistance would remain under the jurisdiction of the departments of Defense and State, but humanitarian and development aid would be centralized under the new department. This new department would focus on long-term goals: building capable states, reducing extreme poverty, and creating the conditions under which social entrepreneurship and open societies can thrive.

Great Britain, which has been the most forward-leaning of any donor country in meeting global development challenges, created an independent development agency in 1997 called the Department for International Development. DfID is led by a cabinet-level minister and is guided by the distinction between the security of states and human security, which is the ability of people, across and within borders, to break the bonds of extreme poverty. The security of states falls under the purview of the Foreign Office, and DfID focuses on human security.

Critics of this idea argue that a new department would weaken the hand of the Secretary of State and that the rationalization of foreign aid can be realized by building on the Bush administration's "Transformational Diplomacy" agenda and/or by creating a unified national security budget that merges the aid or "150 Account" with defense and other national security spending. However, the Bush "Transformational Diplomacy" policy has done little to reorganize or rationalize foreign aid programs, and the State Department is not operational and is thus not equipped to manage the development portfolio.

Vesting a cabinet-level agency with the ability to focus on long-term goals such as supporting the creation of stable states, the alleviation of poverty and disease, and institution-building frees the Secretary of State to focus on numerous and immediate diplomatic and national security pressures. It also recognizes that development and diplomacy are entirely different tasks that are undertaken on the basis of different time horizons, require distinct expertise and different capabilities, and entail separate and contrasting approaches.

Coherent Aid and Trade Policy

Modernizing foreign aid will require more than plans for moving the institutional boxes around. As the reorganization of national intelligence and the creation of the Department of Homeland Security have shown, institutional realignment is not, in and of itself, sufficient, and can in fact prove counterproductive.

Reform requires greater policy coherence, including between our aid and trade policies and between our foreign and domestic policies. The United States today, for example, collects more in tariffs from MCC countries than it provides in support of their development projects. As is well known, though not reflected in new Farm Bill legislation, U.S. cotton subsidies have a direct and net negative effect on the ability of poor West African and other countries to engage in the global cotton trade.

Our robust food aid program, meanwhile, pits the need to utilize an American grain surplus against the need to stimulate local markets in the developing world and reduce costs. The new international development directorate, led jointly by the National Security Council and National Economic Council, would help to minimize these and other policy contradictions by coordinating U.S. economic engagement with the developing world.

Engage New Actors and Approaches in Global Development

New capital, new actors, and new ideas have dramatically changed the global development landscape in recent years. Private philanthropy has injected a source of additional nongovernmental capital into the aid mix, while the private sector has also increased its engagement by supporting development programs and, among the most forward-looking of companies, transforming their business models to achieve developmental outcomes. The nongovernmental sector has spawned a new generation of business-oriented organizations that are investing in social entrepreneurs who are delivering real results, and new technologies are also registering success.

This new, expanded, and dynamic landscape offers the new president the opportunity to coordinate U.S. efforts with those undertaken by other influential actors, to use U.S. assistance to seed innovation, and to leverage U.S. aid in support of new development models. While the effectiveness of these new efforts on the development scene needs to be evaluated over the long term, the new president can use a variety of policy tools and resources to encourage greater innovation and experimentation, as well as foster cross-sector partnerships between social enterprises, corporations, philanthropists, and government.

To tap into the ideas and energy of these new actors in the global development arena, the new president should host during his first year in office a Global Development Action Summit to enlist their support, lay the ground for effective coordination and collaboration, and identify the most effective ways that the United States can bolster the most effective initiatives.

The new president has an opportunity to expand and enhance America's standing and security around the world, and to revitalize a potent foreign policy tool that, when coupled with defense and diplomacy, provides the United States with the means to meet the immediate challenges of today while also reducing the challenges of the future. This opportunity cannot be pursued or achieved without clear policy goals and leadership, or without repairing the broken and fragmented foreign aid and development system.

America's experience in Iraq and Afghanistan has taught us that a singular reliance on the military is inadequate for the tasks we face. The lack of progress toward functional democracy in some of our largest aid recipients, such as Egypt and Pakistan, makes clear that the pursuit of short-term imperatives without a parallel focus on long-term goals neither enhances global stability nor delivers on our security. And if the "Global War on Terror" has taught us anything, it is that it is not enough to show the world that we are *against* terrorism, but it is also imperative to make clear to the world that we stand *for* democracy.

Overview

Securing America from Nuclear Threats

JOSEPH CIRINCIONE

The cold war is long over but the cold war weapons remain. The 44th president must finally disarm this deadly legacy, protecting America from nuclear threats old and new. This will require a threat assessment unbiased by ideology, an integrated and comprehensive strategy, the full power of presidential persuasion, and the cooperation of many nations large and small. With the right strategy aggressively implemented, the president could prevent nuclear terrorism, block the emergence of new nuclear states, reduce toward zero the risk of nuclear weapons use, and restore powerful global barriers to their spread. By confronting and subduing this planetary threat, the new president will help restore America's global leadership and fulfill a presidential ambition first envisioned by President Harry Truman and promoted by presidents John F. Kennedy and Ronald Reagan: a world free of nuclear weapons.

The most serious national security threat facing the United States and most other nations is a terrorist attack with a nuclear weapon. Though the risks of such an attack are fairly low—the ability to acquire or build a nuclear bomb remains very difficult—the consequences would be enormous. A single, compact nuclear device with the yield of the Hiroshima bomb could instantly devastate a mid-sized city.

This nuclear 9/11 would kill hundreds of thousands of citizens, trigger trillions of dollars of economic loss, terrorize the nation, and alter the political structure of the country. This is why nuclear weapons are the most deadly weapons ever invented—the only true weapons of mass destruction. Preventing a nuclear 9/11 is the highest national security priority.

This terrorist threat, however, is one of four interrelated nuclear dangers confronting the country and the world. The second is the danger from existing arsenals. There are 26,000 nuclear weapons held by nine nations in the world, 96 percent by the United States and Russia alone. Thousands are still on a cold-war posture, ready to launch within 15 minutes, greatly increasing the risk of unauthorized or accidental launch. Tensions between nuclear-armed nations risk regional nuclear wars with global impact.

The third is the danger posed by new states acquiring nuclear weapons. The risk is not primarily that a new nation such as Iran immediately would use a nuclear weapon, nor that it would transfer the weapon to a group it could not control. The true danger is the regional reaction as neighboring states seek to match the new, threatening capability. The Middle East could go from one nuclear-weapon state (Israel) to four or five—a potential apocalypse fueled by the region's unresolved territorial, religious, and political tensions.

The fourth danger—a collapse of the nonproliferation regime—is perhaps the most worrisome medium-term danger. If global arsenals remain at cold-war levels and if new nuclear nations emerge, then many states will conclude that the weapon states' promise to reduce and eventually eliminate these arsenals has been broken. Some of the 183 non-nuclear states may therefore feel released from their pledge not to acquire nuclear arms. The collapse of the interlocking network of treaties, export controls, and security pacts that has effectively slowed, if not altogether prevented, the spread of nuclear arms could lead to a "cascade of proliferation," as a high-level United Nations panel warned.

Each of these threats is deadly in its own right. Together they represent an unacceptable national security risk for the American people and for the world. Yet these dangers are neither inevitable nor innate. Policies applied consistently and firmly can reduce and even eliminate many of these dangers. Choosing the right policies and their sequencing will be among the most difficult challenges facing the 44th president.

Challenges

The new president will face an immediate dilemma: how to make early decisions on nuclear issues that must be addressed, issues the president promised to address during the campaign, and issues the new president should address. The "must do" issues will be driven to the president's inbox by external events or administrative deadlines. They include implementing the agreement to end the North Korean nuclear program; building a coalition to prevent an Iranian nuclear weapons program; assessing budgets for the U.S. nuclear weapons and weapons complex; reviewing funding and strategy for antimissile weapons; and preventing the lapse and expiration of the U.S.-Russian Strategic Arms Reduction Treaty, or START.

The "promised to do" list consists of policy pledges made during the campaign. They possibly could include compiling an inventory of all nuclear weapons and materials on earth and securing them from terrorist acquisition within the first term; achieving deep reductions in U.S. and Russian nuclear arsenals; extending the warning time for the launch of U.S. and Russian missiles; ratifying the Comprehensive Nuclear Test Ban Treaty; and banning all intermediate- and medium-range ballistic missiles globally.

The "should do" list includes those actions and policies necessary to implement the "must do" and "promised to do" lists, or those required to shore up the weakened nonproliferation regime. Specifically, the new president will need to initiate nuclear policy and nuclear posture reviews; begin negotiations for a treaty to verifiably end the production of weapons material; launch a serious effort to reform the nuclear fuel production process; and prepare for the 2010 Nuclear Non-Proliferation Treaty Review Conference.

The new administration must have in place a process for integrating all of these related policies. Decisions on one will affect prospects for successfully resolving others. Case in point: creating an effective, bipartisan campaign to ratify the test ban treaty early in the first term, including moves to reduce U.S. and Russian weapon stockpiles, will help ensure a successful NPT Review Conference at which the support of other states can be garnered to restrict any new states' weapons programs, which, in turn, will reduce the stores of nuclear material that terrorists might steal or acquire.

Realistic Threat Assessment

The new president's strategy must be grounded in a realistic assessment of the threats. The national security analysis developed during the Bush administration identified the greatest threat as the nexus of outlaw states, terrorists, and weapons of mass destruction. It advocated a strategy of regime change, with military force as the leading instrument of American statecraft. Neither the assessment nor the strategy was correct.

The nation waged an unnecessary war in Iraq while Al Qaeda flourished, programs to prevent nuclear terrorism languished, and states lost confidence in the nonproliferation regime. Meanwhile, command and control of existing nuclear arsenals—including U.S. weapons—deteriorated, as was dramatically demonstrated by the unauthorized 2007 cross-country flight of a U.S. B-52 bomber armed with six nuclear weapons no one knew were on board.

The rise of apocalyptic groups such as Al Qaeda who openly declare their plans to acquire nuclear weapons now threatens to marry a terrorist demand with the generous global supply of nuclear material. Experts surveyed by Senator Richard Lugar (R-IN) in 2004 pegged the risk of such an attack at 20 percent during the next 10 years. The threat comes not primarily from hostile nations, but from nuclear weapons and materials wherever they exist, independent of a state's geopolitical orientation.

An estimated 60 tons of highly enriched uranium, enough for over 2,400 nuclear weapons, is stored at civilian facilities in over 40 countries, ranging from Argentina to Vietnam. Much of it is protected with little more security than that given to library books. With less than 50 pounds of this material, and with the expertise of sympathetic or hired experts, a well-organized group could create a nuclear truck bomb that could destroy a city. The key is to prevent any group from getting this material. Every step after that is easier for the terrorists to take, and harder for nations to stop.

A Systematic Approach

While the terrorist threat is the most immediate threat, a coherent strategy to reduce all nuclear dangers would simultaneously address all the major problems. Preventing nuclear terrorism must be addressed at the source by preventing terrorists from getting the weapons or materials. All states need to be convinced to maintain robust standards for securing, monitoring, and accounting for all weapons-usable nuclear materials in any form. As much of this material as possible must be eliminated.

Preventing any new nuclear-weapon states is also paramount. All non-nuclear weapon states must reaffirm their commitment never to acquire nuclear weapons and support new global mechanisms for holding accountable states that break that pledge. These arrangements should evolve to prevent the construction of new national nuclear fuel facilities that could be used to produce nuclear weapons. New international arrangements must be created for assuring all states a guaranteed supply of the fuel and services necessary for nuclear energy.

Stopping all illegal transfers of nuclear technology and devaluing the military and political saliency of nuclear weapons are the next steps. All nations must establish and enforce prohibitions against individuals, corporations, and states assisting others in secretly acquiring the technology, material, and expertise necessary for manufacturing nuclear weapons. And all states must honor their pledge to end the explosive testing of nuclear weapons and diminish the role of nuclear weapons in national security policies. Weapons stockpiles can be safely reduced to low numbers as these weapons are unnecessary for any purpose other than preventing a nuclear attack by another nation.

Finally, committing to resolve the conflicts that give rise to proliferation is a special obligation of the United States and the other nuclear-weapon states. The nuclear powers need to work together to resolve the regional conflicts that compel some states' pursuit of nuclear weapons for security, prestige, or regional advantage. Only by resolving these underlying conflicts can the proliferation imperative be blunted.

A Realistic Plan

The new president should aim to change from the existing U.S. posture focused on deterring the use of the large number of weapons held by the former Soviet Union to one focused on the threats from the smaller but still deadly arsenals. U.S. nuclear policy should establish as its primary strategic objective the prevention of any new actors—states or terrorist groups—from seeking or acquiring nuclear weapons, and then reducing toward zero the risk that those that still have these weapons will use them.

The most effective means for doing so is to establish the elimination of nuclear weapons as an organizing principle of U.S. national security strategy. The United States should reaffirm its commitment to achieving a world free of all

nuclear weapons, and then orient its policies accordingly. The verifiable elimination of these weapons is uncertain, and is likely to take many years. But the
new president must begin a series of practical steps toward reducing and eliminating many of the current threats.

Accordingly, he should establish during the presidential transition a working
group of top experts (both those likely to hold positions in the administration
and those likely to remain outside the administration) to detail the timing and
sequencing of policies necessary to achieve this reorientation. On day one of
the new administration the 44th president should articulate the broad strategic
goal of a world free of nuclear weapons in the inaugural address. He can then
elaborate on his vision in a major policy address during his first 100 days, both
to engage the American people early in this effort and to detail the practical
steps he will take to enhance American security in the near term.

Top experts from both parties should be prominently enlisted to validate the
policy vision, involving visits to the White House or a national summit. This
should be part of a sustained effort to build and maintain bipartisan support for
the new strategy. This will not be difficult. Indeed, this bipartisanship should
refer back to the two powerful visions offered by presidents Kennedy and Reagan. John F. Kennedy's pronouncements are well known, including his entreat,
"We must abolish the weapons of war before they abolish us," and "The risks
of disarmament pale in comparison to the risks of a continued arms race."

Only more recently have we begun to appreciate the depth of Ronald Reagan's commitment to nuclear abolition. His pursuit of antimissile systems was
genuinely to render nuclear weapons "impotent and obsolete." As President
Reagan told Soviet leader Mikhail Gorbachev, "My dream is to see the day
when nuclear weapons will be banished from the face of the earth."

There is substantial bipartisan support already, demonstrated by the efforts
of four veteran cold warriors: George Shultz, Henry Kissinger, William Perry,
and Sam Nunn in their Hoover Institute project for "a world free of nuclear
weapons." An overwhelming majority of former top national security officials
now support this aim. Almost 70 percent of the men and women who formerly
served as secretaries of state or defense or as national security advisors now
support the goal, including James Baker, Colin Powell, Madeleine Albright,
Frank Carlucci, Warren Christopher, and Melvin Laird.

The public is also in strong support. Public opinion polls show that 84 percent would feel safer knowing that no country—including the United States—
had nuclear weapons. This support is equally evident among Republicans and
Democrats. Consistent and overwhelming majorities support agreements that

negotiate the verifiable reduction and elimination of nuclear weapons. To capitalize on this public and expert support, the new president should undertake four key initiatives in the first year of office.

First, he should push for a comprehensive program to secure and eliminate nuclear weapons and materials by the end of the first term in office. Second, he should negotiate with the Russians to verifiably reduce each nation's total nuclear arsenal to no greater than 1,000 nuclear weapons and extend the warning time for the launch of each nation's ballistic missiles. Third, he should start a bipartisan process to support ratification of the Comprehensive Test Ban Treaty in 2009 or early 2010. And fourth, he should develop a comprehensive strategy to remove the threat of long-range ballistic missiles.

The first two steps can be done by executive initiative; the latter two require congressional and international support. But all should be done in close consultation with Congress and key allies. To accomplish these goals, the new president should appoint a senior official with sufficient authority to lead the counter-nuclear terrorism effort. He should also permanently dismantle the nuclear-weapon capabilities of North Korea (if the Bush administration has not yet done so) and order an immediate review of more effective policies to contain the nuclear program in Iran.

The November 2007 National Intelligence Estimate on Iran found that "Tehran's decisions are guided by a cost-benefit approach rather than a rush to a weapon irrespective of the political, economic and military costs." U.S. policy should be formulated to find the right combination of intensified pressure and reasonable incentives to encourage each country to, as the NIE concluded on Iran, "achieve its security, prestige, and goals for regional influence in other ways."

The president should then convene a high-level interagency group to formulate a coherent approach to the 2010 review conference for the Nuclear Non-Proliferation Treaty. The administration will have to coordinate policy initiatives, international diplomacy, and presidential statements to ensure the success of this key international gathering. "Success" would mean demonstrating the commitment of the United States and other nuclear-weapon states to the elimination of nuclear weapons, and securing the commitment of the non-nuclear weapon states to enforce tough new restrictions on nuclear-weapon technology transfers and breaches of nonproliferation agreements.

Relevant policy initiatives should include: kickstarting the moribund negotiations to end the production of fissile materials for weapons; starting negotiations to ensure that all nations are allowed the peaceful use of outer space free of weapons; developing assured supplies of nuclear fuel without the construction of new uranium-enrichment or plutonium-reprocessing facilities; and increasing the budgets for the International Atomic Energy Agency to support critical inspections and verification efforts.

The new president should also signal these new national priorities by adjusting the budgets for nuclear weapons and antimissile weapons. He should no longer shortchange pressing conventional military needs by lavishing funds on obsolete or untested programs, or on expanding production facilities for nuclear weapons, development of new nuclear weapons, and research on new delivery vehicles for nuclear weapons pending reviews of U.S. nuclear policy and posture.

Budgets for antimissile systems should be integrated into the budgets of the military services to empower the appropriate military authorities to make the critical budget trade-offs. Normal testing and procurement rules—waived by the Bush administration—should be reapplied, and the Missile Defense Agency—created by the Bush administration as a permanent lobbying force—should be dissolved in order to restore proper oversight to these poorly managed programs. The joint chiefs of staff should be formally asked to give their recommendations for reasonable budgets for antimissile systems, and for the priorities within these budgets. Following the lead of President Reagan with Russia and President George W. Bush with Libya, the 44th president should negotiate new agreements to limit or eliminate threatening missile programs, including making the U.S.-Russian ban on intermediate- and medium-range missiles a global pact.

Concurrently, the president should have the relevant officials engage in sustained dialogue with allies and friends on nuclear policy. It is essential that other nations deeply affected by U.S. policies have input into the formation of these policies. No nation should ever have a veto over U.S. national security policy, but consultation with friends and allies is critical to getting the policy right, ensuring broad support, and protecting U.S. security. The new president can expect considerable international enthusiasm for these new policies, demonstrated by the June 2008 endorsement of a world free of nuclear weapons by three former British foreign secretaries, Douglas Hurd, Malcolm Rifkind, and David Owen, and the British former NATO secretary general, George Robertson.

Finally, the 44th president should consider whether some of his nonproliferation initiatives could be implemented unilaterally. He should consider announcing plans to reduce U.S. forces to 1,000 weapons and extending the warning time for the launch of U.S. ballistic missiles, urging Russia to do the same.

Other decisions can be taken unilaterally without any expected or required reciprocal action, such as declaring that the sole purpose of U.S. weapons is to deter and if necessary respond to a nuclear attack. The president could also order a change in U.S. nuclear targeting policy to eliminate preset plans for large-scale attacks on other nations, replacing them with the ability to promptly develop and launch a tailored response to any nuclear attack on the United States, its military forces, or allies.

A Chance to Make History

The 44th president will come into office with the chance to make nuclear history. He will be in a strong position to take advantage of this unique policy moment. With new leaders in many of the world's major nations, with many nations in agreement on the nature and extent of the nuclear threats, and with new policies already vetted by several high-level, bipartisan organizations, there will be a rare opportunity to make bold, sweeping change.

There are key U.S. allies willing to help in this historic task. Indeed, some are not waiting. The government of Australia has appointed a new high-level panel to promote the elimination of nuclear weapons. The government of Norway has committed substantial funding to the same goal. And significantly, British Prime Minister Gordon Brown promised in early 2008:

> Britain is prepared to use our expertise to help determine the requirements for the verifiable elimination of nuclear warheads. And I pledge that in the run-up to the Non-Proliferation Treaty review conference in 2010, we will be at the forefront of the international campaign to accelerate disarmament amongst possessor states, to prevent proliferation to new states, and to ultimately achieve a world that is free from nuclear weapons.

The new president of the United States should do no less. He can change the nuclear strategy of the United States and, by doing so, change the nuclear policies of the world.

Overview

Prepare Our Homeland for the Worst, but Prepare Smartly

P. J. CROWLEY AND STEVE RICHETTI

The transition to a new president and a new administration will involve both risk and opportunity. It is possible that some kind of terrorist-related event could occur around the time the new president takes office. At the same time, seven years after 9/11 and almost three years after Hurricane Katrina, the new administration can review what has been done, make urgent adjustments, and establish clear and sustainable standards and requirements. The challenge begins with redefining what homeland security is and what being prepared entails. This will require refocusing priorities based primarily on what is at risk and ensuring that governments at all levels have the capacity to do what society expects.

The new president and his administration must assemble a new leadership team, work constructively with the outgoing Bush administration during the transition, meet with appropriate stakeholders, and talk candidly with the American people about risks to the homeland. It should produce a first-ever Quadrennial Homeland Security Review and should use it to improve interagency coordination, define appropriate missions, and adapt existing structures. Longer term, the new president should push the private sector to make the systems that we rely upon every day more resilient, strengthen medical readiness in the event of a pandemic or biological event, and deploy more effective detection capabilities to prevent dangerous materials from being smuggled across or within our borders.

Seven years after 9/11, America is not as safe as it should be. The Bush administration squandered an opportunity to sufficiently strengthen our national defenses and improve homeland preparedness in the event that we are tested again. In fact, given that major terrorist attacks have occurred around presidential transitions globally in 1988, 1993, 2000, and 2001, the new president should be prepared for an early challenge by Al Qaeda, one of its affiliates, or independent actors inspired by bin Laden but working on their own.

The new administration's transition will involve a period of increased risk, but it is also an important opportunity to reevaluate various threats and risks to the homeland, and then mitigate them. The Bush administration's political rhetoric—that we are defeating terrorists in Baghdad so we do not have to confront them here—is wrong. Recent plots uncovered in New York, New Jersey, California, and elsewhere demonstrate that the threat remains real. But terrorism is not, as the Bush administration portrayed it, an existential threat to the United States. Radicals who resort to terrorism rely on the nation state to overreact, which the Bush administration did in many ways—overseas with the invasion of Iraq, and at home with its declaration of unlimited executive authority and erosion of government transparency, accountability, and the rule of law.

President Bush's preference for a "war on terror," a concept that is counterproductive and unsustainable, produced a homeland security strategy built solely around counterterrorism, to the detriment of broader capabilities that could deal with a wide range of contingencies, regardless of cause. This mindset contributed to the national tragedy following Hurricane Katrina. Since then, despite the call to create a "culture of preparedness,"[1] there is still no agreement as to what the country should prepare for: a catastrophic hurricane that will inevitably happen, a pandemic that could happen, or nuclear terrorism that is unlikely to happen but would permanently alter the country if it did. Governments at all levels are moving toward an "all-hazards" approach, and appropriately so, but there are so far few clearly defined national standards that describe what being prepared actually means.

The federal government restructured—multiple times. And there is a constructive change of mindset both within Washington, D.C. and outside the Beltway, although this remains very much a work in progress. But as Clark Kent Ervin details in a subsequent chapter, the Department of Homeland Security is not yet the integrated, competent, and confident department it needs to become. Born in the wake of 9/11 and in the midst of a divisive political campaign, it is an amalgam of 21 (formerly 22) separate agencies still in search of unifying missions and a common culture.

Unlike the Pentagon, there is a much smaller cadre of professional staff to manage DHS's day-to-day operations. Too many senior level positions are held by political appointees, and the department is overly dependent on contractors. Risks for the incoming administration include the lack of sufficient "corporate knowledge" and continuity to guide initial decisions. Limiting factors include the lack of regulatory authority, bureaucratic clout, management systems, planning capacity, effective leadership, and poor employee morale.

What's worse, homeland security and preparedness budget mandates remain underfunded despite 9/11 and Hurricane Katrina. The homeland security budget is literally dwarfed by the defense budget. Including both annual and supplemental funding, the federal government is spending 10 times more on offense than defense. At the current "burn rate" of $12 billion per month for overseas operations, the federal government is spending twice as much to protect Iraq today than the American homeland.

The new administration, to be successful, will need to resolve a number of conceptual, programmatic, and resource issues. In particular, it will need to define the scope of homeland security, outline a clear set of homeland security priorities, and build the Department of Homeland Security's capacity to match these goals.

Defining Homeland Security

The existing National Strategy for Homeland Security defines homeland security strictly in terms of combating terrorism; it is a "concerted national effort to prevent terrorist attacks within the United States, reduce America's vulnerability to terrorism, and minimize the damage and recover from attacks that do occur."[2] The strategy acknowledges the importance of an effective response to natural or man-made disasters, but this responsibility is explicitly positioned outside the homeland security realm.

But is this right? Seven of the 10 most costly hurricanes have occurred in the past four years, supporting the science that points to more severe and perhaps more frequent extreme weather patterns due to global warming.[3] These disasters certainly rival any likely terrorist attack in economic and social impact. The 2003 Northeast blackout and 2007 Minnesota bridge collapse, together with the breached levees in New Orleans, underscore how "brittle" our national infrastructure is today. A pandemic outbreak would tax and probably overwhelm the existing public health and health care systems that already struggle every day. Each of these threatens our way of life in some way and can create the same cascading effects and economic and social costs that we experienced after 9/11.[4]

Six years ago, six "critical mission areas" served as organizing principles for the federal government as it developed the concept of homeland security: intelligence and warning, domestic counterterrorism, border and transportation security, protecting critical infrastructure, defense against catastrophic terrorism, and emergency preparedness and response.[5] Curiously, the Bush administration later shifted away from specific missions to broader operational concepts, such as keeping dangerous people and materials out of the country and long-term sustainability. Concrete strategic objectives make the most sense and should be clearly delineated by the new administration. They need to be revised, however, to incorporate broader requirements, such as promoting "resiliency" within systems and structures that we depend upon every day.

The new administration will also have to review whether security is the right lens through which to address immigration, and more specifically, hemispheric economic migration. The Department of Homeland Security—for political rather than security reasons—actually pulled resources away from counterterrorism to combat illegal immigration over the past couple years—a legitimate but distinct challenge that has little to do with the threat of terrorism posed by Al Qaeda and its supporters.

Setting Priorities

DHS is not governed by a clear set of priorities, which makes true risk management difficult to achieve. This is further exacerbated by a governing philosophy that wrongly presumes that state and local governments and the private sector can and will do what is necessary with only broad guidance and minimal investment from the federal government. Governments and the private sector cannot protect everything from every potential hazard. Priorities need to be established.

The federal government identified 18 critical infrastructure sectors without specifying why they are critical. Certain sectors such as aviation and transit systems are the most frequent global terrorist targets. Are they a higher priority than industrial chemicals that have been used as improvised weapons in Iraq? What are the implications of daily cyber attacks that may not injure people, but can compromise personal information, financial networks, and confidence in government institutions? Are maritime facilities a target of, or more likely the vehicle for, a future attack?

The Bush administration advanced 15 national scenarios to help state and local governments plan effectively for strikes by nuclear, biological, chemical, radiological, or conventional weapons; attacks involving a cyber network or industrial chemicals; and natural disasters, an infectious pandemic, or a case of food contamination. Credible scenarios were created about what terrorists *might* do, but what are their actual capabilities likely to be? What should be addressed first: the hazards that we face today, the dangers that we will surely confront tomorrow, or the threats that are least likely, but will have the greatest impact? Again, judgments need to be made and guidance provided to stakeholders around the country.

The existing philosophy that homeland security is broadly "self ordering" has failed. The Bush administration, presuming that market forces would produce better security, left the country vulnerable to the lowest corporate security denominator. In this just-in-time world, market incentives and social needs are not perfectly aligned. By every indication, security spending has leveled off following a brief spike after 9/11. Publicly traded companies have prospered on Wall Street by squeezing overhead to a bare minimum. Efficiency has trumped security. Businesses that do exercise enlightened self-interest risk, place themselves at a competitive disadvantage. Increased government regulation, oversight, and accountability will be necessary in key areas, not to skew markets, but to create a level playing field where consistent national standards apply.

What is needed? Federal leadership and a true partnership with state, local, and private sector players are indispensable. Our nation's strategy should not just enhance our ability to counter the terrorism threat; it should help promote far-reaching systemic improvements that prevent harm where possible, minimize the potential for social and economic disruption, and enhance our ability to recover and respond from any catastrophic event, regardless of cause.

Building Government Capacity

Homeland security has been inadequately funded from the outset.[6] The Department of Homeland Security, without adequate resources and personnel, was hesitant to assume responsibility, set national standards, regulate the private sector where necessary, and aggressively push the country to adopt a higher level of security and preparedness.

Budgets have grown, but they have not always translated into additional resources and capabilities to make the country safer. There are plans to add 92,000 troops to the Army and Marine Corps, for example, but the also-stressed Coast Guard had to shift resources away from drug interdiction and other missions to meet expanding maritime security responsibilities. DHS is expected to implement new chemical security standards and oversee the compliance of several thousand facilities nationwide with a skeleton staff. The Transportation Security Administration utilizes 43,000 security personnel to physically screen airline passengers, but only 450 agents to check air cargo that travels on the same airplane.[7]

The clearest example is undoubtedly the Federal Emergency Management Agency. When Hurricane Katrina struck in 2005, FEMA lacked professional leadership, sufficient staff, communications, logistics and contracting systems, and regional structure. Despite growing responsibilities, it had only 2,100 employees on the books, and fewer than that actually on the job.[8]

FEMA is projected to grow to 4,500 employees by the end of fiscal year 2009, a welcome step, but it will still be one of the smallest agencies within the federal government. While there is an ongoing debate regarding FEMA's independence, more attention needs to be given to FEMA's business model. Unlike the military, which invests its operational capability in subordinate commands,

FEMA has a weak regional structure, despite the fact that disaster response is primarily a state and local responsibility. The National Response Plan failed during Hurricane Katrina because it was a top-down product imposed on a bottom-up process—written in Washington, D.C., with minimal input from the field and completely untested. Unfortunately, DHS has repeated this mistake while developing the National Response Framework, the National Response Plan's successor.

The federal government must "provide for the common defense," but states and communities play an increasingly critical role in funding and staffing homeland security initiatives, particularly in light of the Bush administration's broad cuts in federal support to states and cities. Yet the current economic crisis is shrinking local tax bases, forcing security requirements to compete with other priorities such as education and health care. Despite Katrina, the Bush administration proposed cutting first responder support by 26 percent for fiscal year 2007; eliminating grants that help metropolitan medical personnel cope with mass casualties; and reducing the number of firefighters and state grants directed toward improving planning, training, and intergovernmental coordination.[9] Urban area security grants to New York and Washington, D.C.,[10] the two cities attacked on 9/11 and most likely to be struck again, were cut by 40 percent in 2006.

The new homeland security strategy promotes "intelligence-led policing."[11] Yet in many cities, there are fewer police—the foot soldiers of the home front—on the streets today than six years ago. This includes New York City, where the police force has been reduced by 5,000 officers since 9/11.[12] The Bush administration cut support for the Community Oriented Policing Services Program, the principal program that supports police manning at the state and local level.[13]

No city in the United States has the public health capacity to handle a pandemic or significant nuclear and biological event. More than 5,000 hospitals split roughly $415 million in federal funding to prepare for national emergencies.[14] But according to the Center for Biosecurity at the University of Pittsburgh, at least $5 billion up front and another $1 billion per year is necessary to ensure that hospitals have the planning, personnel, equipment, and supplies to deal with the patient load that would follow the outbreak of a serious disease or attack involving a weapon of mass effect.

At a time of heightened threat, the need for federal initiative and resources is clear. Responsibility for homeland security is shared, but it cannot be outsourced. The American people expect government, primarily the federal government, to do everything possible to protect the United States from risk. As the existing national security strategy makes clear, "Defending our Nation against its enemies is the first and fundamental commitment of the Federal Government."[15] Most would add detecting pandemics, responding to hurricanes, and maintaining bridges from sudden collapse to that list.

The Transition and First 100 Days

Major attacks associated with elections or leadership transitions have become a staple of Al Qaeda and its supporters, as evidenced by incidents in Spain, Great Britain, and Pakistan since 2004. Given the current political and international environment, the incoming administration must act with a sense of purpose that some kind of event is likely. In a phrase, it is not just being ready on day one; it is aggressively taking charge on day one.

Five objectives are critical during the first 100 days: ensuring a smooth transition; forming the new national security and homeland preparedness leadership team; establishing constructive relationships with key stakeholders; putting the threat of terrorism in the proper context; and laying a foundation for long-term priorities.

The new administration must be prepared to work closely with the outgoing Bush administration on a smooth transition, engage Congress effectively so that leadership within relevant security agencies is in place rapidly, quickly assess the threat environment, and identify specific actions that put governments at all levels in the best position to prevent or minimize the effects of a terror attack. And it must avoid an "anything-but-Bush" attitude, the flip side of the destructive mindset that handicapped the Bush administration throughout its first term. But further adjustments, without question, will be required.

Repairing relationships among stakeholders, particularly with Congress, and establishing credibility that homeland security will be a policy priority and not just a political prop will be key to laying the foundation for changes that will need to occur early in the new administration. The Bush administration failed to establish consistent and meaningful collaboration with state and local governments and the private sector. Words need to be followed by actions, and actions need to be supported by resources and real accountability.

The new president needs to put the terrorist threat in proper context. This will require a balance between expecting another attack and not fearing it. A radical group will undoubtedly attempt something and perhaps inflict some level of damage despite the best efforts of governments here and around the world. If that occurs, the United States will take appropriate action, but should not overreact and play into the hands of the terrorists, as the Bush administration did. Rather than conducting its affairs in total secrecy, the new president should pledge that his government will be honest with the American people, more transparent, and more willing to publicly debate policy options.

Assemble Core Homeland Security Team

The secretary of homeland security should be named early in the transition and confirmed on Inauguration Day along with other key cabinet members. Given the expectation that the new administration could be challenged early in its term, congressional leaders should be closely consulted in order to successfully undertake an accelerated confirmation process. The president should also visit DHS headquarters during the first week in office, address department employees, and make clear that defending the homeland in this hemisphere will be as important as defeating adversaries abroad.

Sandy Berger, in a different chapter, outlines a modernized structure for the National Security Council and support staff. A related decision will involve what to do with the Homeland Security Council and the homeland security advisor. Clark Ervin suggests that the new administration retain the existing arrangement, which includes a separate homeland security structure, advisor, and staff to the president. This would ensure a certain level of visibility regarding homeland-related issues and a dedicated bureaucracy in the event of a disaster, but it could also work against the development of properly integrated and coordinated policy options.

The president-elect must give this considerable attention. A hybrid structure where the homeland security advisor and staff are integrated within both the National Security and Domestic Policy councils is likely to be most effective because it would avoid the construction of a separate and overlapping bureaucratic rival.

Meet with Mayors and Governors

Significant developments are occurring at the state and local levels. Every state but one has established a fusion center, integrating first preventers, first responders, emergency managers, federal officials, and private sector and nonprofit players in one place to enhance information-sharing, planning, and operations. Some major cities have comparable operations as well.

The challenge is both horizontally and vertically integrating these capabilities into a rational national network, establishing consistent standards, improving the flow of meaningful information while protecting public privacy, and sustaining this capability over time. Local governments face growing resource constraints—particularly regarding police—as budgets grow and the local tax base shrinks. The new administration should incorporate their recommendations regarding capital investments, grant funding, and operating costs into its early action plan. Frequent consultations with gubernatorial and mayoral advisory councils will pay dividends.

Consult with the Private Sector and American People

The 44th president should meet with chief executives from companies in industrial sectors such as chemicals, rail, aviation, telecommunications and information technology, food and water, and key importers, where risks are significant, aggressive action is expected, and resistance might be anticipated. The new administration's objective should be to establish a new relationship with the private sector, along with a promise to more fully integrate the private sector into planning at the national, regional, and local levels. Continued emphasis on information sharing and promotion of best practices within sector security coordinating councils will enhance program continuity.

The new president should also consider an early Oval Office address to the nation regarding long-term risk to the homeland. It would acknowledge, in part, the heightened threat that is anticipated because of the transition and the steps being taken to protect the nation. The 44th president should also pledge that the federal government will release more information related to the threat and what is being done to counteract it. He can also signal a willingness to engage key publics within the United States and around the world, beginning the long process of reversing U.S. isolation and making the battle of ideas about them and not us.

Increase Homeland Security Budget

The new president's fiscal year 2010 budget should include roughly $20 billion in new funding for homeland security, or the equivalent of two months expenditure in Iraq. The increases should be centered on urban area security and emergency management grants, law enforcement, chemical security, air cargo security, Coast Guard manning and modernization, medical readiness, biosurveillance, and food safety.

Funding can be offset by an expected reduction in force levels in Iraq, which would reinforce a fundamental shift in strategy. An alternative would be to identify urgent funding in a supplemental request associated with ongoing military operations.

The First Year

One or more national security issues will define the next presidency—terrorism, proliferation, intelligence, immigration, global economics, natural disasters, public health and health care, and and/or infrastructure. Homeland security and preparedness touch each of these areas in significant ways. As the new president extracts the military from Iraq, the homeland should be restored as the "central front."

The new administration, in its first year in office, should release a new homeland strategy, mitigate significant infrastructure vulnerabilities, strengthen national preparedness, and increase support to state and local governments. Then it needs to adapt policies and structures so that they line up with a revised strategy that places greater emphasis on our homeland.

Much of this work will center on the first-ever Quadrennial Homeland Security Review—a long-term analysis of the threat to the homeland and the strategy necessary to deal with it. Some decisions will require action during this first year, before the Quadrennial Homeland Security Review is completed. One issue is what to do with FEMA. As James Lee Witt outlines in a related chapter, one option is to remove it from DHS and elevate the agency to cabinet status. This should be done only if preparedness is elevated to a "core" homeland security mission.

If the new president decides to retain FEMA within DHS, then its director should be able to provide independent professional advice to the president, just like the chairman of the joint chiefs does on behalf of the military. Regardless of where it sits on the wiring diagram, FEMA requires more full-time manpower, a stronger regional structure, and increased funding, particularly for pre-disaster mitigation planning.

Given the increased risk associated with the presidential transition, specific steps need to be taken to address lingering critical infrastructure vulnerabilities. Al Qaeda's strategy is well defined: strike in or near major urban centers, at well-known critical infrastructure that we rely upon every day, and where large numbers of people work or gather in order to disrupt the national or international economy and ultimately our political process. In light of this ongoing threat, there are specific areas where urgent attention is warranted.

Chemical security also remains a significant vulnerability today. DHS is implementing interim Chemical Facility Anti-Terrorism Standards, or CFATS, which expire in October 2009. Permanent and expanded federal regulatory authority is needed. Even though Congress granted DHS authority over thousands of chemical facilities across the country, DHS may not have the capability to effectively implement its new regulations. It had a budget of only $50 million for fiscal year 2008, and has thus far committed barely 100 employees. Many of them are pulled from other duties to conduct a national screening process, tier facilities based on risk, review vulnerability assessments and security plans, and oversee the development of a third-party validation process to ensure compliance.

The global aviation system remains a favored terrorism target, as the 2001 shoe bomb, 2006 London liquid bombs, and 2007 JFK Airport infrastructure plots reveal. Many security upgrades have made a repeat of the 9/11 suicide hijackings much more difficult, but it is unclear if aviation security is staying ahead of a changing threat, particularly with regard to bomb detection technology and air cargo. More than 75 percent of the Transportation Security Administration's $5 billion budget and most of its workforce is devoted to aviation security, primarily passenger screening at airports. But only $104 million is committed to securing air cargo that can travel on the same airplanes. Even though Congress has mandated 100 percent screening of air cargo by 2010, it is unclear if TSA will be able to meet this deadline. A longer timeline and new approach may be required.

Transit systems are particularly vulnerable because they are designed to be accessible to the public. The most effective security measure is the cops and police dogs on the transit beat, supported by a robust and integrated information-sharing system through which meaningful intelligence and analysis is developed and moves in both directions between the local and federal levels. Real capabilities and networking are improving at all levels, but are unlikely to be sustained without both attention and resources from the federal government.

Quadrennial Homeland Security Review

Congress recently established a requirement for a QHSR, roughly equivalent to the Quadrennial Defense Review that the Pentagon has developed since the mid-1990s. The QHSR is a long-term analysis of the threat to the homeland and the strategy, capabilities, structures, and resources necessary to deal with it.

The White House should use the QHSR to make significant mission and organizational refinements at DHS. It should also use the QHSR to enhance both effective policy development within DHS and interagency planning and cooperation across the federal government. The report is due to Congress by December 2009.

The new administration must also clearly define or redefine what it means by homeland security and what the right priorities are. Priorities should reflect a balance between security and preparedness and should include counterterrorism and information sharing; border and transportation security; citizenship, immigration, and enforcement; national preparedness, disaster mitigation, and emergency response; critical infrastructure protection and resiliency; and public health, disease control, and medical readiness.

The new administration can decide what the appropriate structure is after deciding what the right balance is between security and preparedness. Two areas of emphasis should be greater integration at DHS headquarters, including fewer direct reports to the secretary, and a more robust regional structure outside of Washington, D.C.

Chemical and Aviation Security

The White House should send chemical security legislation early in its first term to Congress. The legislation should replace the existing interim chemical security law and establish permanent federal authority to regulate chemical facilities; combine overlapping authorities regarding freight rail transportation and port security into a single framework, including drinking water and wastewater treatment facilities; and provide incentives for promoting and adopting more secure alternatives—generically called inherently safer technology—that reduce the likelihood that industrial chemicals can be exploited as a weapon. The legislation should also provide significant protections for chemical facility workers and make clear that federal regulation does not preempt states from taking further action.

Bombs represent the primary threat to aviation today. The Department of Homeland Security's Science and Technology Department should accelerate development efforts for improved detection technology for liquid explosives. The Transportation Security Administration can, with appropriate resources, double air cargo inspection using existing capabilities. Research should continue on cost-effective onboard technologies for commercial passenger aircraft to defeat shoulder-fired missiles. No-fly lists should be closely scrutinized and passenger redress procedures streamlined. The deployment of Secure Flight, the long-delayed modernization of the passenger screening system, should be accelerated.

Intelligence-Led Policing and Emergency Preparedness

Only a handful of cities—New York being by far the best example—actually have a robust intelligence and counterterrorism capability.[16] The new administration should launch an initiative to increase federal support for improved intelligence-gathering, analysis, and information-sharing centered on major cities. The new administration can also link this initiative to the expansion of joint terrorism task forces under the FBI and the integration of DHS personnel in state and local fusion centers.

Given the prospect of more significant disasters fueled by global warming and potential additional terrorism attacks, the new president should also announce a transformation of FEMA at the start of the hurricane season. This can be the first step toward improving emergency preparedness.

FEMA requires a stronger regional structure, an improved logistics and contract management capability, better relations with the National Guard and the U.S. Northern Command, and a larger full-time staff. More effort should be devoted to pre-disaster mitigation, whether it be for hurricanes along the East and Gulf coasts or wildfires on the West Coast. The president should also pledge to close the existing $24 billion equipment shortfall within the National Guard, which affects disaster response.

Longer-Term Agenda

Over the new president's complete term in office, he will need to put homeland security and preparedness on a more sustainable footing, with actions based on a realistic, forward-looking, and focused strategy. These actions should be supported by resource allocation and a structure that will keep the country safe and prepared for a wide range of potential dangers.

Across its full term in office, the new administration should develop national homeland security systems, make networks and infrastructure more resilient, match resource allocation to our national and homeland security strategy goals, and reduce the potential for radical groups to obtain the most dangerous technologies.

Much more needs to be done to repair and update our national infrastructure, which is essential to keeping our nation safe and competitive. This includes creating a "surge capacity" so that our public health system and health care systems can effectively detect the emergence of a deadly outbreak, whether it involves a naturally occurring disease or biological weapon. If a nuclear weapon in the hands of a radical group is the ultimate homeland security nightmare, greater international cooperation is required to secure existing materials and reduce the overall global supply. The new administration should complement this by continuing to develop improved detection capabilities to limit the ability to transport radiological substances to this country.

Less than 5 percent of shipping containers flowing through U.S. ports are physically inspected, despite the risk of billions or even trillions of dollars in economic losses worldwide that the exploitation of global supply chains could create. Supply chain security is voluntary, and government oversight cursory. In light of estimates that global trade will quadruple over the next 20 years, more needs to be done to manage post-disaster cargo flows to minimize the system disruption that attackers hope to generate.[17] The lack of adequate supply chain security is a systemic weakness that a deliberate attacker could exploit.

Infrastructure Resiliency Initiative

The new president should establish a long-term government-wide effort to repair and upgrade national critical infrastructure within the first year in office, given recent experiences with the bridge collapse in Minnesota, the Northeast blackout, Hurricane Katrina, and the concentration of energy production and distribution facilities in locations vulnerable to storms and single-point failures. The approach would be similar to the Reinventing Government Initiative during the 1990s.

Similarly the new president needs to undertake a serious review of our country's medical readiness. The existing health care system is struggling to deliver care on a daily basis, much less in a crisis situation. In the event of a biological attack or pandemic, it is very likely that the public health system in almost every major city would collapse due to a lack of adequate hospital beds, vital equipment, medical staff, vaccines, or basic access to health care.[18]

Local authorities may not be able to effectively contain the effects of an attack or an outbreak of disease while waiting for outside federal assistance to arrive. Virtually all exercises to test local authorities' ability to deliver emergency health care in a crisis and distribute needed vaccines and antidotes have failed. A major initiative on medical preparedness would complement the administration's broader emphasis on access to affordable health care.

Surveillance of Dangerous Materials

The federal government devotes significant attention to detecting dangerous substances, particularly within urban areas, but these efforts must be improved and strategic tradeoffs made. The incoming administration will inherit open questions regarding the efficacy of radiation portal monitors that have already been deployed and developed. A $1.2 billion contract to purchase the next generation of technology—advanced spectroscopic portal radiation monitors, or ASPs—is on hold due to compromised testing results.

There is also an unsettled debate regarding the utility of gamma imaging of shipping containers. Congress has mandated 100 percent screening, which the Bush administration and major trading partners resisted. The new administration will have the opportunity to evaluate the results of improved container security testing currently underway at selected overseas ports under the Secure Freight Initiative, and then work with Congress on an appropriate long-term strategy based on those findings. More broadly, existing nuclear forensic projects at the Department of Defense and the Department of Homeland Security should be consolidated under the Department of Energy.

Overview

National Security, Human Rights, and the Rule of Law

HAROLD HONGJU KOH

The United States is built on human rights and the rule of law, and our commitments to these ideals define who we are as a nation and a people. Although the United States has been recognized for generations as the world's human rights leader, the Bush administration has done grievous damage to this reputation in the name of national security. A string of well-publicized policies have seriously diminished the United States' global standing as a human rights leader and left our nation less secure and less free. The next president needs to reassert our historic commitments to human rights and the rule of law as major sources of our nation's moral authority. Even before his Inauguration, the new president should unambiguously signal his intention to move decisively to restore respect for human rights in national security policy with a package of executive orders, proposed legislation, agency shakeups, and concrete foreign policy actions.

Since September 11, the United States has gone from being viewed as the major supporter of the global human rights system to a regular outlier. Seven years ago, the world viewed us with universal sympathy as victims of a brutal attack. But the Bush administration responded with an infamous series of unnecessary, self-inflicted wounds, which have gravely diminished America's global standing. Consider first the prisons at Abu Ghraib and Guantánamo and the cruel treatment of detainees that included torture, indefinite preventive detention of "enemy combatants," and the denial of habeas corpus, which the Supreme Court recently outlawed. Then consider this list: military commissions; warrantless government wiretapping and data mining; evasion of the Geneva Conventions and international human rights treaties; and attacks on the United Nations and its human rights bodies, including the International Criminal Court. The Bush administration justified these policies with a constitutional vision based on claims of unfettered executive power, which violates the Founding Fathers' vision of checks and balances in national security affairs.

The Bush administration's insistence on defining our human rights policy through the lens of the "war on terror" clouded our human rights reputation, gave cover to abuses committed by our allies in that "war," blunted our ability to criticize and deter gross violators elsewhere in the world, and made us less safe and less free. These policies were repeatedly rebuffed by a conservative Supreme Court.[1] Moreover, they yielded strikingly few convictions or visible benefits to our national security, while costing tens of millions of taxpayer dollars to maintain Guantánamo as an offshore prison camp.[2] Most troubling, these policies undermined America's global reputation for truthfulness, along with its commitment to human rights and the rule of domestic and international law.

The new administration must move swiftly to reverse these counterproductive policies through executive orders, proposed legislation, agency reorganization, and foreign policy action. The new president should immediately announce clear principles pledging that our national security policies will respect human rights and remain faithful to the rule of law. He must also clarify that a vigorous antiterrorist policy does not require punishment without due process, but rather justice for terrorist suspects that is credible in the eyes of the world.

As difficult as the last seven years have been, they loom far less important than the next eight, which will determine whether the pendulum of U.S. policy swings back from the extreme place to which it has been pushed, or stays stuck in a "new normal" position under which our policies toward national security, civil liberties, international law, and human rights remain wholly subsumed by the "war on terror."

Key Challenges

The new administration faces major challenges in undoing the damage of the last seven years. The scale of activity that has damaged civil liberties has been so extensive and extreme that it will be difficult to undo over time, and even more difficult to undo quickly. Even a recognized policy fiasco such as Guantánamo—which President George W. Bush, his secretaries of state and defense, and his attorney general now all concede should be closed—has lingered, in part because of the complex interagency and diplomatic negotiations needed to avoid sending detainees who never should have been brought to Guantánamo in the first place to locations where they could be subject to even crueler treatment.

The new administration must also reshape public perceptions after the Bush administration's trumpeting of a "new paradigm" where civil liberties must inevitably be trumped by national security concerns. The Bush administration repeatedly offered the absence of a major terrorist attack on U.S. soil since September 11 as proof that their infringements of law and civil liberties were somehow necessary. Those who have criticized the government's extreme practices have been branded as unpatriotic, naïve, or soft on national security.

Yet all three branches of government participated in the warping of sound constitutional process. Journalistic accounts confirm that a dysfunctional process arose within the executive branch, which excluded all but the most extreme voices. This "groupthink" drowned out moderate government voices and a cloak of secrecy kept extreme policies from being reviewed effectively by good lawyers.[3]

The two other branches of government have too rarely been part of the solution and too often have been part of the problem. A compliant Congress repeatedly has blessed unsound executive policies by enacting nominal, loophole-ridden "bans" on torture and cruel treatment, and rubberstamping, without serious hearings, presidentially introduced legislation ranging from the Patriot Act, to the Military Commissions Act, to the most recent amendment of the Foreign Intelligence Surveillance Act.

The lower courts, where 9/11 litigation has been concentrated, have accepted many of the government's most extreme claims regarding state secrets and immunity. And the Supreme Court, even when setting welcome limits on executive overreaching, has acted late and through sharply divided decisions.

It was civil society that led the resistance to the Bush administration's extreme tactics on each of these issues. The new administration should reassure the American people that it genuinely respects their rights and promise that national security policies will be decided through transparent processes designed to bring diverse viewpoints before key policymakers, rather than by closed and secret "war councils." The new president will need to signal these commitments in his public statements by telling the truth about America's and other nations' human rights records; promoting the accountability of all who commit gross abuses; and preventing ongoing human rights abuses abroad and at home, even if they are committed by the United States or its allies.

Recommendations

During the transition period, the new administration's Justice Department, State Department, Defense Department, intelligence community, and White House teams should work closely with their Bush administration counterparts to identify the steps needed to close the prison camp at Guantánamo as soon as possible.

Each detainee's case should be individually reviewed to determine whether the detainee falls into one of four categories: those who have committed crimes against the United States and should be brought to U.S. soil—and imprisoned in supermax facilities, if necessary—for prosecution in regular federal or military courts; those who cannot be properly tried for crimes against the United States and should be extradited for prosecution at home or in a third country; those who have committed no crime against the United States and should be repatriated home for release; and those who have committed no crime against the United States but must be given asylum or resettled in a third country, rather than returned home to face a substantial risk of torture or persecution.[4]

Immediately after the 2008 election, the incoming State Department transition team should ask the outgoing administration to appoint a high-level confidant of the president-elect as a special envoy in matters regarding detainees who will not be prosecuted in U.S. courts. That special envoy should be dispatched abroad to advise those nations whose citizens comprise significant parts of the Guantánamo population that the strength of their diplomatic relations with the new administration will depend upon their willingness, where possible, to repatriate their citizens *before* the Inauguration and to provide meaningful and enforceable diplomatic assurances that the repatriated detainees will not be subjected to torture or cruel treatment. This promise should be made in writing and monitored by visitations from U.S. diplomats, the International Committee of the Red Cross, and human rights non-governmental organizations.

At the same time, the Defense Department should begin shutting down facilities on Guantánamo to demonstrate that the United States will no longer inappropriately use the naval base as an offshore prison camp. DoD should bring its Office of Detainee Affairs under the supervision of a senior legal counsel position on human rights and humanitarian law, which would be created within the Defense Department's General Counsel's Office. The new administration should create a similar legal counsel position within the General Counsel's Office at the Department of Homeland Security.

The Justice Department should appoint a point person to deal collectively with Guantánamo habeas counsel, and file judicial statements of interest seeking delay of pending habeas petitions in those cases where diplomatic release has been secured. Incoming attorneys to the White House Counsel's office, the Defense Department's General Counsel's office, and the Justice Department's Office of Legal Counsel should also be given access to all classified legal opinions issued by those offices to determine which opinions should be withdrawn based on inappropriate legal theories.

Executive Orders

The new president should, immediately upon taking office, issue four key executive orders. He should order the relevant agencies to begin formally closing the prison camp at Guantánamo by a certain date. He should direct compliance by all U.S. officials with the Geneva Conventions and the Convention Against Torture, which are ratified treaties that are part of U.S. law. He should unequivocally ban the use of torture and cruel, inhuman, or degrading treatment—including waterboarding—by any person employed by or under contract to the U.S. government anywhere in the world. And he should clarify that the vaguely worded Authorization for the Use of Military Force Resolution first adopted in September 2001 was not intended to override existing legislation or infringe upon or modify preexisting legal rights.[5]

As part of that package of executive orders, the new president should also establish a National Security Law Committee as part of the current National Security Council structure.[6] This new entity would serve as the decision-making body for national security related legal issues such as surveillance policy, detention and interrogation practices, and rules of engagement. The attorney general would chair the NSLC, which would include the secretary of state, the secretary of defense, the national intelligence advisor, and the director of homeland security.

The 44th president should also create an independent commission, modeled on the 9/11 commission, to investigate—and, if appropriate, recommend accountability measures to address—torture, human rights abuses, and other legal violations committed or authorized by U.S. government officials in the past seven years. Finally, he should publicly forswear future executive or legislative efforts to avoid habeas corpus by moving detainees to offshore locations through extraordinary rendition to "black sites." As the Supreme Court recently made clear, "the political branches [do not] have the power to switch the Constitution on or off at will" by moving detainees around to various "law-free zones."[7]

These executive orders should send the unequivocal message that the United States does not accept double standards in human rights. Like much of international law, the Geneva and Torture Conventions are not about our adversaries and who they are; they are about us and who we are, and how we are obliged to treat all detainees: with basic humane treatment, as a matter of universal principle. If we truly believe that human rights are universal, we are obliged to respect them, even for suspected terrorists.

National Security Legislation

The new president should ask Congress to create a bipartisan, bicameral standing committee on liberty and security legislation. At the earliest opportunity, the new president should work with these congressional leaders to introduce "national security charter" legislation to support a continuing fight against terrorists, while at the same time defending the basic rights that form the foundation of our society.[8] This legislation should be considered in thoughtful hearings—similar to those conducted when the Foreign Intelligence Surveillance Act was first adopted in the late 1970s—that are aimed at evaluating the policies adopted since September 11 and recommending appropriate reforms.

New national security legislation should repeal the Military Commissions Act or revise it drastically to repair the inadequacies in that law's procedures identified by the Supreme Court in its 2006 decision in *Hamdan v. Rumsfeld*.[9] It should also revise classified information procedures to enable more effective terrorism prosecutions in standing civilian courts.

Any new national security legislation should resist authorizing a new system of preventive detention or creating a special "terror court" of the kind being urged by some commentators.[10] A recent empirical report by former prosecutors extensively reviews more than 120 international terrorism cases pursued in the federal courts over the past 15 years and concludes that the existing federal civilian courts can be adapted to the task of trying terrorist suspects.[11] The Supreme Court has now twice indicated that rulings of regularly constituted courts are more likely to survive judicial scrutiny than those of ad hoc courts.[12]

These sources make clear that our standard for American justice should be the due process of law required by the Constitution and international law—not "at least it's better than Guantánamo." The new administration's goal should be to end debacles like Guantánamo, not set its worst features in concrete. Any tailor-made "terror court" would plainly fail the most relevant test of "credible justice"—justice that potential allies in the Mideast might find convincing.

Few abroad will likely respect the judgments of an extraordinary court designed secretly to punish a particular class of suspect—particularly those of the Muslim faith—for crimes that could not be prosecuted in a standing, open, regularly constituted court. Nor should we promote a system of preventive detention that is likely to become a breeding ground for terrorists—as occurred in the British prisons for the Northern Irish—particularly if those courts will never have any credibility abroad and may eventually be found unconstitutional. As a nation, we should not accept that indefinite detention without trial, abusive interrogation, and other practices have somehow become necessary features of a post-9/11 world. We should appoint good judges and give our standing civilian and military courts their proper role in the system of separation of powers, not further damage our reputation abroad by trying to appoint antiterror judges or create tribunals that will be widely perceived as rubber stamps for executive action.

The arrival of a new Congress along with the new president in 2009 should also create an occasion for revisiting the foreign intelligence surveillance amendments of 2008. Unlike the controversial legislation enacted hastily in 2008, the previous version of FISA was enacted after extensive hearings and a bipartisan legislative process following President Richard Nixon's resignation during Watergate. Similar legislative hearings should be held early in the new Congress, with greater emphasis on examining the effect of widespread data mining and government surveillance on privacy protections, and less emphasis on narrow demands for immunity by telephone and Internet service providers. Such hearings should evaluate, on a 30-year record, the proven strengths and weaknesses of the Foreign Intelligence Surveillance Court as a specialized judicial institution designed to protect both privacy and national security concerns.

Supporting International Laws and Institutions

The new president should recall the words of our founders in the Declaration of Independence and pay "decent respect to the opinions of mankind" by supporting, not attacking, the institutions and treaties of international human rights law. Despite the Bush administration's vocal opposition to the International Criminal Court during most of its second term, it pursued a policy of de facto acceptance of the Court's existence, passively supporting the prosecutions of high-level leaders in Sudan and war criminals in Uganda and the Congo.

The new administration should make support for the ICC official at the earliest opportunity. The new secretary of state should withdraw the Bush administration's May 2002 letter to the United Nations "unsigning" the U.S. signature to the Rome Treaty, which created the International Criminal Court, and restore the status quo ante that existed at the end of the Clinton administration.[13] The new administration should also reengage diplomatically with the contracting parties to the ICC to seek resolution of outstanding U.S. concerns and pave the way for eventual U.S. ratification of the Rome Treaty. And it should publicly support the efforts of the ICC prosecutor to convict those most responsible for the genocide in Darfur and provide prosecutorial and intelligence resources to the prosecutor's staff, much as the U.S. government provided for the prosecutorial staff at the International Criminal Tribunals for Yugoslavia and Rwanda.

The new president should declare his commitment to preventing future genocides and mass atrocities by adopting the recommendations of the Genocide Prevention Task Force of the Holocaust Museum, co-chaired by former

Secretary of State Madeleine Albright and former Secretary of Defense William Cohen.[14] He should further signal his support of accountability for human rights violations by moving the office of the State Department's ambassador-at-large for war crimes into the Bureau of Democracy, Human Rights, and Labor. This move should also clarify that the ambassador's mandate includes both genocide monitoring and prevention coordination.

At the same time, the new administration should broaden the mandates of the antitrafficking and war crimes units of the Justice Department's Criminal Division. The attorney general should appoint a point person in the Justice Department's Civil Rights Division to monitor—and where appropriate, support—accountability efforts of human rights victims in Alien Tort Claims Act and Torture Victim Protection Act cases. A similar position existed during the Carter and Clinton administrations. The transition team for the Civil Division of the Justice Department should survey pending human rights cases against former U.S. government officials to ensure that overly expansive claims of state secrets or immunity have not been asserted.

Finally, at the earliest opportunity, the 44th president should signal his willingness to endorse universal human rights standards by moving forward the long-overdue ratifications of key international law treaties, particularly the American Convention on Human Rights; the U.N. Convention for the Elimination of Discrimination Against Women; the International Covenant on Economic, Social, and Cultural Rights; and the Convention on the Rights of the Child, which only one other nation in the world has not ratified. And he should signal our readiness to resume a leading role on human rights issues by promoting and ratifying the new U.N. Conventions on Disability Rights and Against Forced Disappearances, seeking a seat on the new U. N. Human Rights Council, and engaging with the U.N. secretary-general and high commissioner for human rights to develop and promote a common human rights agenda for the next decade.

Overview

Public Diplomacy Can Help Restore
Lost U.S. Credibility

DOUG WILSON

International respect for America is at an all-time low. An often helter-skelter approach to public diplomacy over the past 25 years has rendered one of America's most valuable foreign policy tools weak and ineffective. U.S. public diplomacy efforts have been ad hoc and filled with public relations gimmicks. Effective public diplomacy works to understand and help shape foreign public opinion and effectively integrate it into the policy-making process in order to help realize our national security and foreign policy goals. To accomplish this goal, the new president will have to work to restore, recruit, and retain a quality corps of skilled public-diplomacy practitioners and give these men and women the credibility they need to engage with skeptical or hostile foreign publics. He also will have to put new exchange and communication tools to use to convince public opinion leaders around the world to listen to the United States, to help the world better understand our values and motives, and to give us and our policies the benefit of the doubt. The 44th president must select a knowledgeable professional to serve as undersecretary of state for public diplomacy. The new undersecretary should conduct a comprehensive review of public diplomacy missions and determine how best to build upon historically successful approaches with 21st-century strategies and communication tools.

The United States Advisory Group on Public Diplomacy for the Arab and Muslim World concluded in a 2003 report that "a process of unilateral disarmament in the weapons of advocacy over the last decade has contributed to widespread hostility toward Americans and left us vulnerable to lethal threats to our interests and our safety."[1] That statement was right on target, and its truth has been reinforced time and again—not just in the Muslim world, but globally—in the five years since it was written.[2]

The real problem goes even deeper. The Advisory Group's report, like many recent efforts, is responding piecemeal to the increasingly anti-American attitudes of foreign opinion leaders and publics. The reality is that, for the past 25 years since the cold war, the U.S. government has had an erratic, helter-skelter approach to public diplomacy.

A lack of understanding of what public diplomacy actually is has only worsened this misguided approach. Many equate public diplomacy with cold war–era propaganda. Those skeptical of smart power dismiss it as "books and ballet." Others define it solely in terms of government-financed radio networks or cultural exchange programs. Since 9/11, a series of short-tenured, high-profile public diplomacy chiefs have turned to Madison Avenue for answers ranging from flash polling to campaign-style rapid-response message spin to myopic "Muslim-only" public relations efforts to help win hearts and minds in the Middle East.

The focus of public diplomacy must be long-term. To be effective, public diplomacy must help U.S. policymakers communicate U.S. values and motives to shape foreign public understanding and then integrate foreign public opinion into the policymaking process in order to help realize our national security and foreign policy goals. To achieve this goal, the new administration must take a holistic approach to reinventing public diplomacy and to the tools necessary to help public opinion leaders around the world better understand our policies and values—convincing them to listen to us and then give our policies the benefit of the doubt.

The executive branch should certainly use the new tools of Internet communication and public opinion research and analysis. But these must be applied in combination with already-proven elements of effective public diplomacy programs: radio broadcasts, educational and cultural exchange programs, next-generation leadership initiatives, and day-to-day dealings with foreign press. These efforts must clearly align and integrate with broader national security and foreign policy goals and be implemented by qualified practitioners to ensure their success.

To make public diplomacy once again a valuable and effective tool of foreign policy, the new administration should focus on five priorities: convincing a new generation of talented men and women that investing in a public diplomacy career will be rewarding and meaningful; giving them the institutional and professional credibility they need to engage with skeptical or hostile foreign publics; ensuring that public diplomacy specialists are at the table at all stages and at the highest levels as foreign policy options are being developed; understanding the new array of Internet-based communications tools and how best to integrate them into a 21st-century public diplomacy operation; and ensuring the necessary funding for these and the educational, cultural, and next-generation leadership exchange programs that, taken together, will be key tools of public diplomacy practitioners.

Restoring, recruiting, and retaining a quality corps of skilled public diplomacy practitioners is central to the success of this effort. This conclusion is reinforced by the central premise of the U.S. Advisory Commission on Public

Diplomacy's June 2008 report on current U.S. public diplomacy efforts.[3] Blogger Matt Armstrong put the essence of the report in a nutshell: "This is the first report to point out that there is no one overseas whose primary job responsibility is to interface with foreign audiences."[4]

The new administration must attract and retain people with the cultural, communications, and linguistic skills to be effective interlocutors with those who serve as critical public opinion gauges and gatekeepers: leaders in foreign media, education, science, business, labor, religion, communities, and politics. Recruitment and retention efforts should also reflect the diversity of American society. Trained professionals must understand not only the politics but also the histories, values, and social forces that shape the views of those who live in the societies in which they will operate. They must use their special skills and talents to communicate essential messages about the United States—our history, values, people, and policies—to opinion leaders within those societies. Most important, what they hear and learn must be incorporated into the U.S. policy-making process at all levels, from the field to the White House.

American public diplomacy practitioners, above all, must be credible interlocutors in the eyes of the target audiences with whom they interact. United States Information Agency public diplomacy professionals received high praise during and immediately after the cold war for promoting American values and helping earn and sustain the trust of foreign publics. The effectiveness of their efforts could be seen from the rise of the Solidarity movement in Poland to the conferences that provided one of the few sustainable channels for dialogue between India and Pakistan during the second half of the 20th century. That was due in large part to the semi-independent status they enjoyed as diplomats who were not—in the eyes of foreign opinion leaders skeptical of or hostile to the U.S. government—completely "tainted" by State Department employment.

Soon after the end of the cold war, the USIA was dismantled and parts of it were stuffed into the State Department. Career public diplomacy practitioners whose expertise had been critical to identifying, training, and educating postwar leadership cadres around the world saw their credibility overseas diminish and their input reduced and subsumed into a larger bureaucracy. Demoralized, many have since retired or jumped ship. Potential successors have turned to more lucrative, attractive, and meaningful careers.

The First Year

The 44th president must begin revitalizing U.S. public diplomacy during his first year in office by restoring its credibility at all levels of the policy-making process. This should begin with appointing a respected and experienced public diplomacy professional as the undersecretary of state for public diplomacy and public affairs, and then asking the new undersecretary to coordinate a formal review of the public diplomacy mission and structure.

The undersecretary of state for public diplomacy and public affairs resides within the Department of State and is responsible for implementing U.S. public diplomacy programs, including educational and cultural affairs, public affairs, and international information programs. The last several individuals to hold this office have been advertising executives or media figures who were well-known or close to the White House, but had little direct knowledge of or experience in public diplomacy. Appointing an undersecretary with in-depth knowledge of U.S. public diplomacy and respected standing will be a key first step toward restructuring diplomacy efforts and raising global perceptions of the United States.

Once key staff are in place, the new president will have to initiate a formal and comprehensive review of the public diplomacy mission and structure. This review would be led by the undersecretary of state for public diplomacy and public affairs. The review must focus on fundamentals, including mission, personnel, budget, tools, and structure, and must involve public- and private-sector leaders. The overall goal should be developing a plan for how to restore public diplomacy as a valuable tool of U.S. foreign policy by building upon historically successful approaches and integrating 21st-century strategies and tools.

The administration should conduct and complete this review within the first nine months of its first year in office. The review should be framed by the five priorities discussed earlier: recruiting and retaining talented public diplomacy staff; giving staff the credibility they need to be effective; making sure public diplomacy specialists are involved in foreign policy decisions; understanding the best ways to utilize the array of new Internet-based communications tools; and determining how best to combine new tools with existing educational, cultural, and leadership development programs.

The review process will delve into how public diplomacy works with and within many facets of government, and any recommendations moving forward must reflect a cross-departmental effort. There should therefore be a formal mechanism to involve key members of Congress and congressional staff; other cabinet and subcabinet agencies beyond the State Department, including the Department of Defense, the United States Trade Representative, and the Department of Commerce; USAID; current and former public diplomacy career professionals; and private sector business, academic, and citizen-diplomacy leaders—particularly those with experience and expertise in educational and citizen-exchange programs, public opinion research, and Internet-based communications.

Department of Defense

The Challenge of Transition During Wartime

RUDY DELEON

The coming presidential transition, with the United States fighting two wars, will pose an unprecedented challenge at the Pentagon. The new secretary of defense must immediately reach out to the joint chiefs of staff and seek their counsel on how to implement the new president's direction to change course in Iraq and Afghanistan and create a strategy that improves American security and safety. In the first 100 days, the priorities will be repealing the Bush doctrine of preemptive war and assisting the new White House team as it creates a new national security strategy that integrates a strong U.S. military posture with robust diplomacy, economic assistance, and cooperation with allies. Reaching out to our allies, reducing the operational tempo for U.S. ground units, vigilantly seeing to the medical treatment of America's wounded warriors, and restoring Pentagon spending discipline are also among the top priorities for the new secretary of defense during the first year of the new administration.

More than 3.2 million people—active duty, guard, and reserve—constitute the all-volunteer "total force" U.S. military, comprised of the Army, Navy, Marine Corps, Air Force, Coast Guard, and the civilian workforce of the Department of Defense. They fulfill the constitutional responsibility "to provide for the common defense" of the American people. Our men and women in uniform and their spouses, children, and parents are our most valuable national security asset. In serving our nation they endure unwelcome separation from their loved ones, work long hours under burdensome circumstances, and often risk death or serious injury.

Even in peacetime, the change of senior civilian leadership at the Pentagon is a monumental management challenge during a presidential transition. In

2009, this will happen while fighting two wars, and with 250,000 servicemen and women deployed around the globe. This will pose an unprecedented challenge that allows for no "honeymoon."

In January 2009, the new president will inherit a ground force drained by fighting two wars for six years, with Army and Marine Corps ground force readiness sapped by continuous operation. These untenable deployments have placed families in military communities under enormous stress. More broadly, local communities are vulnerable in domestic emergencies because many of their most capable citizens and their equipment have deployed to combat zones with their National Guard units.

The overextension of our Armed Forces also means that our military equipment is spent or broken due to continuous operations. This dire situation, however, will prove difficult to correct due to annual defense budgets that already exceed $700 billion in military budget and supplementary spending, with fiscal checks and balances in neglect.

The new president and his secretary of defense will also have to grapple with the excessive reliance on private security firms during President George W. Bush's administration—contractors that sometimes act inappropriately and independently of U.S. armed forces. What's worse, this contracting process for U.S. combat operations in Iraq lacks accountability, and has been very inefficient and wasteful.

Amid all these challenges, however, there is another key problem that plagued the Bush administration—severely strained civilian-military relations between the White House and the Pentagon—that the new administration can quickly resolve. The micro-management of military planning by the White House and other senior Bush administration officials led directly to the strained state of the Department of Defense today, although initiatives by Bush's Secretary of Defense Robert Gates and Chairman of the Joint Chiefs Michael Mullen to improve civil-military relations and the presentation of military advice should be noted. The new president and his secretary of state can immediately build on those initiatives, in turn allowing our armed forces to recover and redeploy to more effectively defend our nation and our national interests abroad.

The First 100 Days

Suite 3E880 is the Pentagon office of the secretary of defense. The nominee (known as SECDEF in military parlance) of the new president is traditionally confirmed on Inauguration Day afternoon. That will place a newly arrived

SECDEF in charge, along with only a small cadre of aides. The new secretary of defense will nevertheless have to deal with the normal responsibilities and decision making of the job.

In the absence of a full civilian Pentagon management team, the SECDEF will need to rely extensively on the chairman of the joint chiefs, the chiefs of the military services (acting as both joint chiefs and chiefs of their military branches), and the senior enlisted advisors. These military leaders are professionals of high caliber and capability, and they have been preparing for the change of administration. Their advice and counsel will be exceptionally important as the SECDEF implements the new president's national security objectives.

During the first 100 days, the new secretary of defense should focus on a number of key priorities. First and foremost is the urgent need to change course in Iraq and Afghanistan. The United States has been fighting in Iraq and Afghanistan for more than six years. There are about 165,000 troops deployed in those two countries, but they cannot remain in their current status for an indefinite period. The highest priority for the new secretary is to work with the chairman of the joint chiefs and the military chain of command in formulating a policy for the new president designed to draw down U.S. combat troops beginning early in 2009, and continuing through a strategic repositioning.

The new secretary will need to request military advice from the chairman and joint chief on how to implement the new president's policy for Afghanistan and Iraq, how to define the strategic objectives for both missions, and how to match them with a strategy that improves American security and safety, as discussed in detail by Lawrence Korb in the Iraq Overview chapter of this book.

There is also the urgent need to draft a new national security strategy at the direction of the new president and in partnership with the other members of the National Security Council. A new national security strategy should be developed that integrates a strong U.S. military posture with diplomacy, economic assistance, and cooperation with U.S. allies. To carry out this program, America needs to use all of its tools, and that means building more capabilities at the State Department, the U.S. Agency for International Development, and other executive agencies to match and complement current missions supported almost exclusively by U.S. military personnel.

This new capacity from the non-defense agencies is extremely important for the success of humanitarian and peacekeeping deployments. The new U.S. national security strategy for protecting the United States should include counterterrorism and counterproliferation of weapons of mass destruction. It must also include plans to prevent and contain instability caused by weak or failing states, and diplomatic initiatives to shape the international environment to prevent conflict and promote stability.

One immediate step in this direction is to repeal President Bush's doctrine of preemptive war. Under international law and United Nations Article 51, a nation has the right to self-defense. Many nations, including the United States, have exercised this right in protection of their citizens, homeland, and allies. In an era where the proliferation of technology for weapons of mass destruction is a potential danger to free and open societies, particular attention must be given to identifying and isolating those threats before they are allowed to cause casualties and fear.

But the 2002 Bush administration national security strategy doctrine of preemptive war and regime change increased the threat to American security. The war in Iraq, a clear example of the Bush doctrine, has overwhelmed our nation's military readiness by keeping a high percentage of America's most capable forces occupied and limited to one region. America must be ready to stand up to adversaries—both national and transnational, and symmetric and asymmetric— but the Bush administration's aggressive policy of preemptive war is counterproductive to the nation's interest, draining the readiness of U.S. ground forces and the U.S. Treasury, and fracturing America's relationship with its allies.

Every president has a duty to protect the country and act if the nation is threatened. But the use of American military power should never be our nation's first nor preferred approach to solving national security dangers. The Bush strategy of preemption must be promptly repealed. This in turn will allow the new president to reverse the Bush administration's dismissive treatment of the U.N. Security Council and U.S. allies in the run-up to the Iraq invasion, which deeply angered our friends around the world and accounts in part for the rise of anti-Americanism worldwide. American security policy should reach out immediately to U.S. allies to rebuild trust and strengthen key alliances. As Admiral Mike Mullen, chairman of the joint chiefs, told the Senate Armed Services Committee in mid-2008:

> We do not—and should not—face these challenges alone. Today, more nations are free, peaceful, and prosperous than at almost any point in history. While each has its own heritage and interests, most share our desire for security and stability. Increasing free trade, regional security partnerships, treaties, international institutions, and military-to-military engagements and capacity building strengthen the bonds between us and other nations. Our engagement with allies and friends demonstrates our leadership and resolve to fulfill security commitments, and works toward the

common good. Most often, it is by taking collective action—and not going it alone—that we increase our ability to protect our vital interests.

Increased attention must also be paid to the members of the North Atlantic Treaty Organization. NATO was the centerpiece of American security during the cold war, but now faces entirely new challenges in dealing with out-of-area problems, such as Iraq and Afghanistan. Managing relations between NATO and economically vigorous Russia must also be a central focus for U.S. defense policy. To meet these new requirements, the U.S. military will have to train more regularly with forces of other nations, as well as conduct joint command-and-control operations at senior levels.

At home, the secretary faces an immediate obligation in his first 100 days: helping our wounded warriors. Improvements in battlefield military medicine have increased the survival rates for U.S. military personnel wounded in action. But the commitment to treatment and rehabilitation must extend beyond the exceptional performance of military medical personnel in the combat zone. To ensure our wounded warriors are treated with the care deserving of their sacrifice, the SECDEF will want to engage the joint chiefs and surgeon generals of the military departments on the status and treatment of wounded U.S. military personnel.

Department of Defense liaisons with the families supporting their loved ones and interactions with primary care medical providers will be extremely important so that the new secretary may personally review critical cases. Finally, an aggressive post-traumatic stress disorder screening program for all returning service members will ensure that the current returning generation of veterans is not left out in the cold. A recent RAND report, commissioned by the U.S. Army, found that nearly one in every five veterans is suffering from depression or stress disorders and that many are not getting adequate care. We must begin planning for their needs now.

Drawing up a new defense budget for fiscal year 2010, which begins in October 2009 but must pass Congress well before then, will require particular attention. During the eight years of the Bush administration, defense budgets increased dramatically. From a baseline in FY2001 of $303 billion to the current FY2009 budget request of $515 billion, baseline Pentagon spending increased by almost 70 percent. The $515 billion 2009 baseline budget for the Pentagon includes military personnel, training and supplies, family housing and military construction, and weapons research and procurement.

In addition to the baseline budget, however, the Bush administration requested an additional $200 billion in emergency supplemental appropriations to cover the war costs in Iraq and Afghanistan. In FY2009, total Pentagon spending will exceed $700 billion. Adjusting for inflation, the Bush military budgets including Iraq and Afghanistan exceed all other periods of U.S. wartime spending except for World War II.

The new secretary starts work on the FY2010 budget with U.S. forces in combat and needing critical supplies and equipment until they are repositioned. Post-Iraq, U.S. ground forces will need substantial fiscal support to restore readiness and training. Those funds must be provided. But a first step in restoring budget checks and balances is to halt the misuse of the supplemental funding process—under the Bush Administration funding for the wars in Iraq and Afghanistan were not accounted for in the regular budgeting process—and limit those budget requests to essential combat costs.

A much-needed second step is the restoration of the planning, programming, and budgeting system within the Pentagon. This is the formal budget system within the Pentagon, managed day-to-day by the comptroller. The challenges are enormous. The SECDEF should begin the budget review by requesting the military advice of the joint chiefs to help focus and prioritize areas of defense investment and management savings. In particular, the joint chiefs should offer recommendations on areas where priorities can be altered, savings identified, and resources reallocated to more urgent tasks. The immediate goal of the FY2010 budget should be to reprioritize spending and start rebuilding the budget checks and balances that are essential to Pentagon fiscal accountability.

Equally essential to this initial budget project will be to create a new readiness initiative. The cycle of high operational and continuous deployments of U.S. military personnel is exhausting and eroding the readiness and capability of U.S. ground forces. The Pentagon should fully implement the readiness proposals offered by Rep. John Murtha (D-PA) and Sens. Jim Webb (D-VA) and Chuck Hagel (R-NE). First, units deployed to combat must be fully equipped and certified as trained and ready before deployment. Second, for every 12 months our soldiers spend in the field, they will have 12 months at home with their families and receive the appropriate training they were often not given earlier when going into combat. The Marines will have a similar standard, appropriate for the maritime service.

It is important to recognize that the Bush Pentagon budgets, dominated by the war in Iraq, are fundamentally different from the Reagan administration defense budgets and programs of the 1980s. The Reagan program did produce similar deficits. But after the implementation of the Reagan defense program and budget, the military had modern equipment, was fully equipped, and readiness levels were highly favorable. The legacy of the Bush budgets is different. At the end of eight years of record spending, U.S. ground forces will return with their readiness consumed. As Army General Dick Cody recently testified to Congress:

> Army support systems, designed for the pre-9/11 peacetime Army, are straining under the accumulation of stress from six years at war. Overall, our readiness is being consumed as fast as we build it. If unaddressed, this lack of balance poses a significant risk to the All-Volunteer Force and degrades the Army's ability to make a timely response to other contingencies.

To correct these problems swiftly, the secretary of defense should assemble an independent group that, in conjunction with the Army and Marine Corps military leadership, provides a readiness assessment on U.S. ground forces and recommends a strategic approach that will repair, reconstitute, and reset ground units after their current deployments to Iraq and Afghanistan. This should be done in tandem with the new secretary's fundamental push in the first 100 days to build a team of leaders under him.

Building a team of leaders for critical Pentagon assignments will require a group of committed recruiters. Personnel reviews, conflict-of-interest checks, background reviews, and Senate confirmation will require urgent action for a new defense team to start fixing the Pentagon. The most key positions include the deputy secretary of defense, who is delegated full power and authority for the SECDEF for any and all matters; the undersecretary of defense for policy, who formulates defense planning guidance and forces policy, DoD relations with foreign countries, and interagency process; the undersecretary of defense for acquisition, technology, and logistics, who oversees policy on DoD acquisition system, R&D, developmental testing and evaluation, logistics, environment, and military construction; the comptroller, who is responsible for DoD financial management activities, which includes a base budget of $515 billion; and the undersecretary of defense for personnel and readiness, who devises policy on recruitment, career development, pay and benefits, and military readiness.

The secretary will also need to move quickly to fill other key top positions at the Pentagon in order to undertake a number of initiatives not just in the first 100 days, but also in the first year of the new administration. The undersecretary of defense for intelligence will be needed to review accountability, oversight, and the chain of command for intelligence planning and special operations. The general counsel, the chief legal officer of the DoD, the assistant secretary of defense for legislative affairs, and the assistant secretary of defense for public affairs will all need to be in place soon after the Inauguration.

In addition, the secretaries of the Army, Navy, and Air Force will all require specialists in acquisition, personnel, financial matters, and legal policy to ensure the new administration's key defense plans are implemented with speed and assurance. In the first 100 days, however, organizational changes should be avoided because they would distract from the critical job of tackling the top issues. There will be time later on to restructure the organization.

The First Year

America's military strength is rooted in the professionalism and capability of its armed services. But the foundation of America's national security and our highly capable military is the health of the American economy. The costs of Iraq and Afghanistan alone may soon exceed $1 trillion. Combined with the 2001 and 2003 tax cuts of the Bush administration, war-funding supplemental appropriations are increasing the U.S. deficit and contributing to a weakening economy.

The Bush administration's Pentagon budgets were dramatic, totaling more than $4.5 trillion over eight years, but their focus was dominated by the operations and supplies associated with military activities in Iraq and Afghanistan. While sufficient resources to keep our troops ready, trained, and equipped for any contingency will remain a national priority, our economic resources are not unlimited. Prudent planning and accountability will demand a rigorous review of all national security budget requests.

Specifically, supplemental spending requests that were misused by the Bush administration must stop. The first-year agenda for Pentagon planners must be to ensure that all the tools of review and management are in place to keep the Pentagon fiscally accountable to Congress and U.S. taxpayers. To do that, the new SECDEF in Suite 3E880 at the Pentagon will need to conduct a Quadrennial Defense Review, examine Army recruiting, and confront the overuse of our National Guard troops.

Quadrennial Defense Review

The Quadrennial Defense Review, or QDR in Pentagon speak, is a congressionally mandated review of national defense strategy conducted by the secretary of defense that serves as a long-range planning guide for the department and as justification for the armed services' individual budget requests to Congress. The QDR is comparable to what the business world would call a strategic review and business plan, a top-to-bottom assessment of all operational issues, revenues, and expenditures.

The QDR must commence at the direction of the new secretary of defense, and only after senior civilian members of the team have been confirmed and are in their new positions. Because of the operational importance of the QDR to the Pentagon, the review must be the product of the department's senior civilian and military leaders, and must reflect the national security priorities of the new president and administration. Absent that dedicated leadership, the QDR becomes the domain of the powerful staff influences within the Pentagon who are advocates for the status quo.

The QDR must review all defense programs in conjunction with FY2011 and the Future Years Defense Budget. The FYDB is the five-year road map for Pentagon spending. The QDR should include a thorough review of the Pentagon investment program to ensure that budget decisions are aligned with the new administration's priorities. This review is unlikely to produce significant budget savings over the next five-year period because of the need to "reset," or restore ground forces after disengagement from Iraq and Afghanistan. Yet the QDR will likely result in a significant budget realignment to meet the national security objectives of the new administration.

The review should include all weapons programs, joint combat and network systems, intelligence and information assurance, a full examination of space programs, and missile defense research and development. The procurement and R&D component of the current budget is $183.8 billion, more than one-third of the defense baseline. Appropriately, this portion of the QDR will be particularly important because significant budget realignment and redirection is likely.

Related to this area, the QDR must also examine the availability of critical technical personnel, especially government executives who serve as program managers for these Pentagon programs. The government needs highly skilled people who can understand the technology, make high-tech trade-offs to get taxpayers good returns for their investments, and send the right equipment to our troops. The career civilian workforce is the best source of candidates for these positions, but their ranks were reduced by congressionally directed budget cuts. With this technical expertise sitting to protect the taxpayers' interest, significant dollar savings are likely.

Army Recruiting

The new secretary should review strategy and standards for recruiting and retaining Army personnel and limit the number of moral waivers that are permissible. In order to meet recruitment goals, the Pentagon is accepting a higher percentage of recruits who would previously have been disqualified from service because of the lack of a high school diploma, a previous criminal record, drug or alcohol problems, or a health condition.

Since the invasion of Iraq, the percentage of Army recruits with a high school diploma has decreased to 71 percent from 94 percent. Before the war began, 4.6 percent of Army recruits required a waiver for a criminal record; today, that figure has risen to 11.2 percent. The success of the all-volunteer military force is based on the high aptitude, exceptional work ethic, and integrity of young military recruits.

While a General Educational Development test in lieu of a high school diploma may be an acceptable benchmark of academic commitment, the other areas where waivers have been granted represent serious concerns. Deviating from these high-performance standards because of the short-term expediency of recruiting during an unpopular war may fundamentally change the characteristics of the U.S. Army and should be avoided.

In addition, the new secretary should ask the joint chiefs and the Pentagon's civilian personnel experts to review and propose the repeal of the "don't ask, don't tell" policy on homosexuals, which today arbitrarily eliminates from military service potential recruits of high caliber, aptitude, and ability. This discrimination against capable Americans is not in the country's national security interest. The current policy serves no useful purpose except to exclude talented American men and women from serving their country. With an all-volunteer force, and during time of war, this is inexcusable.

National Guard

Our National Guard and Reserves were originally designed to supplement active duty forces as a contingency capability in a "total force." The high operational tempo of current military missions, however, today results in the Guard serving in all operational contingencies. In the last decade, the National Guard and Reserves have evolved into an essential element of the military's operational forces. In the field they are virtually indistinguishable from regular forces. In addition to combat missions in Iraq and Afghanistan, National Guard units have carried out peacekeeping missions on the Sinai Peninsula, and in Bosnia and Kosovo. This creates a new and different operational climate for the Guard and Reserves.

The National Guard, in their responsibility to the states in which they serve, is also a critical resource during a domestic crisis. There is no alternative to the nation's continuing and increased reliance on its reserve components for missions at home and abroad, as part of an operational force. The new president, his secretary of defense, and other Pentagon officials will have to deal with the likelihood of longer and more frequent deployments even as the National Guard retains both its military and domestic responsibilities. This balance has served the national interest since the days of the Continental Army and is essential to the continued effectiveness of the National Guard.

Longer-Term Agenda

In addition to issues that must be addressed in the administration's first 100 days and first year, a new administration will need to turn to other priorities. There are myriad issues that need to be addressed over the course of the new president's first term of office, but top among them must be improving and rationalizing the current contracting system. A blue-ribbon group of former Pentagon acquisition officials concluded in late 2007 that military contracting was plagued with systematic problems and failures. Pentagon auditors told Congress that $8.2 billion disbursed by the U.S. Army to contractors in Iraq cannot be properly accounted for in their ledgers.

The investigators found that acquisition and contracting procedures were inadequate to support U.S. military forward deployments in Iraq and Afghanistan. As the blue-ribbon group concluded, "the most notable characteristic of the testimony is a nearly unanimous perception of the current problems, their gravity, and the urgent need for reform."

This panel-of-experts report is the starting point for examining acquisition and contracting needs. Solutions begin with dedicated training for government personnel responsible for contract negotiation and management. This critical function and these important improvements have the potential to save dollars. This is particularly the case in the Pentagon's acquisition process, which has not kept pace with important market-based trends.

Among the long-term critical functions and improvements the Pentagon needs to tackle are technology advances that integrate military "platforms," such as aircraft, ships, and ground vehicles, with redundant information networks, and critical next-generation integrated systems, which require the operational and intelligence communities to come together to work toward common solutions on next-generation systems. Similarly, the Pentagon needs to ensure there is integrated planning, programming, and budgeting—including intelligence programs.

To achieve this end, the current separation of the requirements process (under the joint chiefs of staff) and the acquisition process (under the Pentagon's defense acquisition board) should be eliminated. Moving in this direction, though, will also require that the Pentagon address the several problematic components of our military-industrial base. The Pentagon's capability to manage and integrate large acquisition programs needs to be improved.

The solution lies in the combination of a strengthened Pentagon acquisition workforce and greater reliance on not-for-profit independent advisory bodies, such as the RAND Corporation, the Institute for Defense Analysis, the MITRE Corporation, and other federally funded centers. In addition, the Pentagon needs to return to industry prime contractors that are exclusively concerned with system engineering and program management, yet at the same time develop a new policy on mergers and acquisitions among defense contractors that ensures a healthy defense-industrial base, a robust and innovative workforce, fair competition, and low cost.

Technology Planning

Ensuring our armed forces remain at the forefront of technology will require the quick initiation of some long-term goals by the new secretary of defense. There is growing concern that the future supply of U.S. scientists and engineers will be inadequate for the defense industry, a critical educational issue identified by the National Academy of Sciences report "Rising Above the Gathering Storm." Moreover, many experts believe that too little emphasis is being given to technology-based activities on which advanced military weaponry is dependent.

While it is true that the military must compete for technical talent in the highly competitive commercial market, some of these obstacles can be overcome through mutually beneficial military-commercial dual use projects. New initiatives are possible that can broaden the traditional Pentagon R&D contractor base, especially working with small businesses, including high-technology start-up companies. These companies and the American defense workforce they employ are a critical national security asset. The preservation of these advanced technology skills in the engineering, manufacturing, and system integration areas is a national priority. The Pentagon and private sector must work together to preserve and regenerate these critical skills for the future.

Then there is cyber security. The role of information technologies in the global economy and in critical national security missions makes it imperative that the Pentagon expand operational planning to protect critical communications infrastructure in the cyber world. This should be one of the new secretary's highest priorities in the first year of the new administration given the asymmetrical information technology threats to our national security.

Another important technology focus for the Department of Defense during the new president's first term of office must be promoting environmental security and energy conservation. The continued annual U.S. (and allied) increase in petroleum imports poses an unprecedented U.S. security challenge. With domestic oil production peaking and reserves uncertain, the United States must maintain assured foreign supplies. As in no other area, U.S. security concerns and foreign policy must be integrated to secure these objectives.

The high energy demands of military bases and combat forces also make the United States military vulnerable to extreme weather and instability in oil-supplying countries. In the 21st century, energy conservation must become a necessary component of our national security posture. As one of the largest organizations in the world, the Pentagon is in a position to lead other national and corporate institutions in the area of environmental security and energy conservation.

Similarly, climate change will present a number of national security challenges in the future. For the U.S. military, these trends will translate into more stabilization and humanitarian operations abroad and a greater need for natural disaster responses at home. Some scientists now believe, for instance, that temperature changes can trigger conflict. In Somalia, for example, warlords exploited the prolonged instability in the region caused by mass migration of populations fleeing the disastrous effects of climate change.

The United States and its allies must be prepared to participate in international efforts to relieve such humanitarian crises. Therefore, to meet the coming challenges of climate change, the secretary of defense should integrate national security consequences of climate change into the National Security Strategy and the Quadrennial Defense Review.

Department of State
Rebuilding and Repositioning America's Diplomatic Strength

GREGORY B. CRAIG

Iraq, Afghanistan, and Georgia will still dominate the political debate in Washington, but the new president and his secretary of state will confront a range of other national security challenges—an energy crisis, a looming crisis in Iran, an increasingly unstable

Pakistan, complex political emergencies in Sudan and Somalia, and the ongoing Arab-Israeli conflict. There will also be many new challenges to global human security—climate change, increased scarcity of critical resources, weak and failing states, and a global food crisis—alongside a number of modern, transnational threats that transcend state borders, such as terrorism, nuclear proliferation, global pandemics, and illicit trade.

The new president and his administration will face numerous constraints in meeting these challenges. America's moral standing is at its lowest in modern history, our alliances with traditional and new allies are in urgent need of attention and repair, and a crippling budget deficit will limit the range of options. More troubling still, the White House will inherit a weakened Department of State that has for the last eight years abdicated the lead on U.S. foreign policy to the Department of Defense, failed to effectively adapt its core capabilities to the challenges of the 21st century, and overseen the erosion of the size and skills of the professional Foreign Service. The 44th president and his secretary of state will need quickly to reverse the sharp decline in the department's standing, its resources and its morale. The opportunities are there, among other things, to forge a new bipartisan consensus between the new administration and Congress, create a regional security arrangement to combat the Taliban and Al Qaeda in Afghanistan and Pakistan, and launch an International Peace Corps to demonstrate anew U.S. global leadership at its best.

It is likely that Russia's decision in August 2008 to send its army, navy, and air force into neighboring Georgia will be yet another urgent item on the new administration's crowded foreign policy agenda when it takes office in January 2009. The invasion should have been anticipated but was not, and could have been prevented but was not. It represents a failure of U.S. diplomacy in the past and—at the same time—a challenge to U.S. diplomacy in the future. Getting Russian troops out of Georgia and replacing them with international peacekeepers will be an early test of the new administration's ability to work effectively with our friends and allies in Europe and to engage successfully with the Russians. It will also be a true measure of the new State Department's capacity, its energy, and its imagination.

This is only one reason, however, why the new administration must move swiftly to reposition the State Department, to revitalize its capabilities and rebuild its capacity in order to address the full range of national, human, and collective security challenges facing the United States. For many reasons that are largely self-evident, the Department of Defense has assumed a prominent role in shaping U.S. foreign policy. DoD has elevated post-crisis stabilization to a level of priority commensurate with war-fighting, acquired new authorities and capabilities, seen the dramatic expansion of its share of the foreign-aid budget, and provided its regional commands with new mandates—to prevent crises, to support economic development, and to coordinate interagency activities within regional theaters. But even as the Pentagon has expanded its role in the conduct of U.S. foreign policy, its leadership has repeatedly called for greater civilian engagement from the executive branch, even going so far as to enshrine this appeal in its June 2008 National Defense Strategy. As Defense Secretary Robert Gates put it in a November 2007 speech at Kansas University:

> The Department of Defense has taken on many burdens that might have been assumed by civilian agencies in the past. [The military has] done an admirable job, but it is not replacement for the real thing—civilian involvement and expertise. Funding for non-military foreign-affairs programs remains disproportionately small relative to what we spend on the military. There is a need for a dramatic increase in spending on the civilian instruments of national security—diplomacy, strategic communications, foreign assistance, civic action, and economic reconstruction and development. We must focus our energies beyond the guns and steel of the military. Indeed, having robust civilian capabilities available could make it less likely that military force will have to be used in the first place, as local problems might be dealt with before they become crises.

During its eight years in office, the Bush administration adopted two initiatives aimed at strengthening the State Department's role as the lead agency in the making of U.S. foreign policy. Neither achieved the desired result. In 2004, the State Department created the Office of Crisis Response and Stabilization, which was designed to enable the department to get out ahead of and better manage crises and complex transitions, to deploy a small Active Response Corps, and to coordinate across agencies. Then, in 2006, Secretary of State Condoleezza Rice launched "transformational diplomacy," an initiative whose purpose was to reposition the diplomatic corps so as to provide more coverage of China, India, other developing countries, weak states, and countries in transition. The initiative included efforts to expand the language and other capabilities of the diplomatic service, and consolidate U.S. foreign assistance. Most recently, the State Department, with the full support of DoD, proposed the creation of a Civilian Stabilization Initiative that would establish a Standby Reserve Corps of 2000 government professionals.

The department's "transformational diplomacy" effort is widely perceived to be a modest failure. State's inspector general found that the 280 positions that were repositioned under transformational diplomacy were not supported with adequate resources, and the creation of a new foreign assistance bureau to manage foreign aid gave U.S. support for economic development a lower rather than higher profile. And the new Office of Crisis Response and Stabilization, while staffed by talented professionals and equipped with a sharp analysis and strategy, has not been sufficiently staffed, funded, or positioned to enforce co-ordination across the range of relevant executive branch agencies.

The new president and his secretary of state must also act quickly to address the fact that America's professional foreign service is in dire straits. Resources did not match the requirements of the Bush administration's foreign policy, and the demand is currently for 300 positions in Iraq, 150 in Afghanistan, 280 in areas of emerging importance, and almost 150 to meet new language and functional requirements. The department is short over 1,000 positions for domestic and overseas assignments, and an additional 1,000 for training and temporary needs. This means positions are either empty or being filled by junior officers without the skills or experience required.

USAID, which during the Vietnam War had 15,000 professional employees, now has fewer than 3,000. Recruitment is down, and, in a 2007 survey by the American Foreign Service Association, 44 percent of respondents said that because of "recent developments," they are unlikely to remain in the foreign service for a full career. Neither the Bush administration nor Congress made a priority of reconciling the demands on the State Department with its abilities, though the Bush administration did, in its fiscal year 2009 budget, request an additional 1,000 State Department positions.

The Transition Period

There will be only 74 days between the general election on November 4, 2008, and the Inauguration on January 20, 2009. In that short space of time, the president will have to form a White House team, appoint the cabinet, draft and deliver the inaugural address, present the new administration's legislative agenda, and send a budget to Congress.[1]

Given the enormous national security challenges facing the new president, neither major-party candidate should wait until November 5 to start planning for the transition. Neither campaign should assume that it is either arrogant or presumptuous for a candidate—before being elected—to begin thinking and planning about how to govern. Particularly in matters of national security, and at a time when the United States is heavily engaged in two major wars, it is both negligent and potentially dangerous to wait until after the voters have spoken before addressing, in stark and practical terms, the next phase of America's quest for national security. Ideally, the national security transition team should include a small number of senators and representatives with relevant foreign policy experience, such as members of the Senate Foreign Relations or House Foreign Affairs Committees.

The new administration should focus on several key priorities as it organizes its transition for the State Department. The top priority for the State Department and the rest of the new president's national security team should be to put together a strategic plan for the new administration's first 100 days that will answer the most fundamental questions of what to do first and how to do it. As former Secretary of State James Baker said: "One reason I think that the Reagan administration succeeded in its first term as well as we did was that we had a really definitive, well thought out, right-here hundred-day plan. We went back, and we looked at the plans of everybody all the way back to Truman. What were their first goals, priorities and objectives. We drafted a hundred-day plan and we stuck to it."

The second priority of this team should be to identify credible candidates to serve in the key national security positions. The single most challenging and time-consuming aspect of the State Department transition will be identifying and getting in place the right people for key jobs. To the maximum extent possible, the process of identifying key individuals to take over key jobs should be complete when the election actually occurs.

The new secretary of state must have a keen knowledge of foreign affairs, diplomatic expertise, and the stature to play the lead role in foreign policy. But given the range, complexity, and diversity of challenges facing the new administration, the new president also needs a secretary who is a doer, who will actively work for results, and who is nimble enough to manage diverse relationships around the globe. It is also critical to identify a deputy secretary who has the management experience and leadership qualities to manage the department and ensure its ability to implement policy. And the transition should identify candidates for the undersecretary positions.

The secretary should consider elevating the undersecretary of global affairs. In the past, the global bureau has been charged largely with managing the State Department's role on functional issues, such as global health and the environment. Because of the current challenges of globalization, the global bureau needs to play a much more active role, leading the department's aggressive efforts on key global issues, such as climate change, and begin planning ahead for looming challenges, such as resource scarcity, that will dramatically affect our security in the near future.

The transition team also should focus time and attention on the staffing and role of the Office of Policy Planning. The new secretary of state should consider expanding its role from that of think tank for the department to an active, deliberate planning office that works collaboratively with the Department of Defense, the National Security Council, and other government agencies to conduct the practical strategic planning needed to prepare the United States for future security challenges.

The First 100 Days

When the new president is sworn in on January 20, 2009, it is likely that the United States will still have 130,000 troops in Iraq and 35,000 troops in Afghanistan, and still be pressuring the democratically elected government in charge of Pakistan to deal with Al Qaeda hiding in safe havens in the country's Northwest Provinces. Indeed, the new administration will need to worry about the Taliban operating a headquarters in the Pakistan city of Quetta, and the threat of Islamic extremists taking over the Pakistani nuclear arsenal.

Sadly, too, the United States will still be engaged in a global war against international terrorist networks. Our single greatest fear will still be the prospect of another attack like that which occurred on 9/11, and our single greatest nightmare will still be weapons of mass destruction in the hands of suicidal terrorists. We will still be confronted with the prospect of an Iran with nuclear weapons. Israel will still be under daily rocket attack from Gaza or Lebanon or the West Bank. We will still be dependent upon foreign sources of energy, and we will still be paying billions of dollars to buy energy from governments who are hostile to the United States and who work every day for our nation's demise.

What's more, we will still be searching for ways to reduce our own greenhouse gas emissions while working to construct a sustainable global initiative that will do the same throughout the world. Russia will still have an energy stranglehold on the economies of Europe and will still be dominated by an authoritarian leader with unrivaled popularity among the Russian people and who will still be consolidating his rule at the expense of the Russian people's freedom. China will still hold trillions of dollars of U.S. debt, will still have trillions of dollars in cash reserves, and will still be expanding its economic influence throughout the world. The dollar will still be weak, and our trading relationships will still be grotesquely out of balance.

In the face of these realities, the new president will inherit a set of policies that have divided Americans, turned much of the world against us, and stretched our nation's capacity to the breaking point. Against this backdrop, he will have little time to reflect on what to do and how to do it. The world will be waiting to see what his top priorities are, and the American people will be on honeymoon for only so long.

The new president and his Secretary of State need to quickly communicate to the American people the following basic truths about America's current predicament. First, we must work more closely with our friends and allies in pursuit of common objectives. We cannot go it alone any longer. Wherever and whenever possible, we should seek ways of cooperating with those who share our interests and objectives.

Second, we must look more to the tools of diplomacy and development to pursue our interests. Military force can only do so much for our national security. There are other, more effective ways of exercising influence in this world. One way is to strengthen our diplomacy throughout the world, and to be more active and engaged diplomatically on every front. Using the armed forces is a last resort, and they are most effective when they are held back.

Third, we must renew America's support for democracy and the rule of law, among countries as well as within countries. And fourth, the strength of the U.S. economy domestically is absolutely central to the ability of the United States to lead internationally, which means the new president will need to devote time and political capital to the task of creating jobs, increasing investment, and growing the economy.

This list of challenges and the profound impediments to overcoming them are daunting, yet there are a number of opportunities that the new president and his Department of State must immediately seize to overcome some of these challenges.

End Occupation of Iraq

The election will give the incoming team an opportunity to change course in Iraq. Within the first 100 days of the new administration, the new president must give notice to the U.S. military, the Iraqi leadership, and the entire region that the United States' military involvement in Iraq is coming to an end. After meeting with our nation's military leaders, the new president should announce a plan for the phased withdrawal of American combat troops. And after meeting with our nation's most experienced diplomats and consulting with our closest friends and allies, the new president should initiate a vigorous two-track diplomatic effort with the stakeholders inside Iraq and simultaneously with Iraq's neighbors—the Iranians, Syrians, Turks, Jordanians, and Saudis.

Setting the stage for U.S. withdrawal from Iraq the State Department will need to lead one team of U.S. diplomats to work with the Sunni, Shia, and Kurdish communities inside Iraq and a second team to deal with the neighbors, who should be convinced that they each have an interest in avoiding civil war inside Iraq. Within the first 100 days of the new administration, the new president should go to the U.N. Security Council, the Arab League, and the European Union and ask the members of these organizations to join the United States in an unprecedented effort to provide aid and investment aimed at rebuilding the Iraqi economy.

Restructure Efforts in Afghanistan

The 44th president will also have an opportunity to strengthen our resolve and redouble our efforts to prevail in the effort to defeat terrorism and the Taliban in Afghanistan, and to rebuild that devastated nation. It is necessary but not enough to ask our NATO allies to send more troops. The new president should also initiate new and more vigorous efforts—with the support of other nations that consume the most narcotics—aimed at eliminating the poppy crops in Afghanistan. Such an initiative would require the support of many other nations, a smart strategy, and a massive commitment of resources.

Chasing the Taliban and eradicating Al Qaeda will require a regional strategy. The new president should ask the governments of Pakistan and Afghanistan to create a new central command structure and regional authority—composed of U.S., NATO, Pakistani, and Afghan troops working together—with the legal right to conduct operations on both sides of the Pakistan-Afghanistan border. The new president and the Secretary of State should work with the government of Pakistan to engage the tribal leaders in the Northwest Provinces on nonmilitary issues, to support and subsidize their political leadership, to make common cause with them on a variety of issues (not just against Al Qaeda), and to strengthen the region economically and politically by building schools, training teachers, strengthening infrastructure, and subsidizing basic agriculture.

Maintain Contact with North Korea

During the first 100 days of the new administration, the president should send a special presidential envoy to Pyongyang to deliver a simple message: the envoy should make it clear that the efforts of the Bush administration in 2008 to resolve the standoff over North Korea's nuclear weapons program through the so-called Six Party process involving all of North Korea's neighbors, as well as the direct bilateral talks the outgoing administration finally engaged in, are still on track. It is important for the new administration to make clear to the North Koreans that further development and improvement of the relationship between North Korea and the United States is high on the new administration's agenda, and that the new administration's core objective is to make further progress on the nuclear issue.

The North Koreans should know that direct, high-level bilateral talks between the two governments is a modus operandi acceptable to the new administration. The presidential envoy should stop in Seoul on the way to and from Pyongyang for consultations and briefings. In addition to discussions in Seoul, it will be important to include Japan and China as partners.

Restore U.S. Standing in the World

The 44th president should immediately take high-profile actions aimed at restoring the standing of the United States throughout the world. He should give a speech in a major European capital to show that the United States is trying a new approach to the world. He should give a speech in a major Muslim capital—perhaps in Cairo or Beirut or Jakarta—that rejects the clash of cultures and civilizations, that pays respect to mainstream Islam, and that calls for a new era of dialogue, understanding, and tolerance. He should close the military detention center at Guantánamo Bay. And he should take the symbolic act of signing the Kyoto Protocol on global warming.

The new president should also announce his support for the creation of an International Peace Corps modeled on the successful American Peace Corps, an idea proposed by the Crown Prince of Jordan five years ago. The new president should take a leadership role in creating the new organization by introducing legislation that authorizes U.S. involvement in such a project. He should convene an international conference with other leaders to discuss and approve the idea.

End the Partisan Gridlock

During the first 100 days, the president should take concrete steps to bring Americans together to end the partisan bickering about America's role in the world that has characterized relations between the two political parties as well as the two branches of government. The resulting gridlock has done enormous damage to U.S. standing abroad and to our own capacity to initiate needed reforms at home.

To that end, on the national security front the new president should invite Congress to join in the creation of new institutions aimed at promoting genuine consultation and dialogue on the most pressing issues of the day between the new president's national security team and the foreign policy leaders and decision makers from both parties in Congress. To outline a process of consultation is not enough. A mere promise to meet and to talk every month runs too much risk of being viewed as lip-service to bipartisanship without the real substance. For there to be genuine bipartisanship in the new administration's national security policy, it will be necessary to institutionalize the consultation—to create councils composed of top members of Congress who will meet on a regular basis with top decision makers from the executive branch.

These councils would meet on a pre-fixed schedule or as needed in the event of a national emergency. They would discuss items on an agenda prepared by an independent staff, at a meeting place that is neither in the executive nor the legislative branches of government. The idea of reaching out to include the other party in such consultations, of working to achieve genuine bipartisanship in the formulation of national security policy, is not a new idea, nor is it pie-in-the-sky dreaming. Informal arrangements of this nature were successful during the 1940s and 1950s, when Republicans and Democrats alike, members of the "Greatest Generation," came together to meet the communist threat not only with plans that unified the nation but also with an international strategy aimed at mobilizing the entire non-communist world. Leaders from both parties and from both branches of government were, as Dean Acheson put it, "present at the creation" of the post-war world.

In the first 100 days, the new Secretary of State should develop a plan, in consultation with the leaders of Congress, for mutually agreeable institutions and mechanisms to promote the bipartisanship that is so desperately needed if the United States is to be successful in reasserting its leadership around the globe.

End the Genocide in Darfur

It is hard to know what realistically can be done in Darfur without knowing what the conditions on the ground will be when the new president takes the oath of office. It is reasonable to expect, however, that the international force sponsored by the United Nations will not yet have been fully deployed, and that the refugee camps on the border between Chad and Sudan will still be the target of constant attack by janjaweed as well as by rebels. Within the first 100 days of the new administration, the president should join with key leaders from Great Britain, France, Germany, Scandinavia, Italy, and Japan to meet with representatives of the United Nations, the African Union, and of those non-governmental organizations operating on the ground in Darfur to assess the situation.

This meeting should be convened by heads of state but should be continued by the Secretary of State at the ministerial level to develop a realistic plan to protect the population of Darfur. This plan must be implemented by this coalition with or without the blessing of the Sudanese government. The new administration can not let 100 days go by without taking some significant action aimed at ending the genocide in Darfur. The new administration should also reach out to China, urging Beijing to use its standing with the Sudanese government to press for change, and to initiate a broader discussion about shared U.S. and Chinese interests in an economically and politically stable Africa and possible options for collaboration.

The First Year

The single most important part of any president's job is to protect the American people.

For that reason, the new president should devote personal time and attention within the first year of the new administration to develop a new global strategy of cooperation and consultation aimed at establishing a more effective international system to combat terrorism. As a start, the new president should convene a working conference attended by American friends and allies from all over the world, including moderate Arabs as well as Europeans, the Japanese, Mexicans, and Russians.

The purpose of the conference would be to develop a series of comprehensive plans to combat and prevent terrorism throughout the world. The new policy must be more than adopting a posture of regime change or declaring a global "war on terror." Any effort to defeat terrorism requires new systems to coordinate the work of police, military, and other relevant governmental agencies, to work across national boundaries, to share information quickly, to cut off funding when necessary, to train police and security forces to work together more effectively, to conduct special operations, and to coordinate the work of law enforcement and paramilitary services.

Special attention should be paid to creating an international legal framework that is acceptable to sovereign and independent legal authorities but that is also effective in capturing, trying, and convicting terrorists. There also needs to be new focus on the war of ideas, how best to attack extreme jihadist ideology by replacing Wahabi imams with more moderate Muslims in the mosques, and undermining the power of the madrassas by building public schools to provide alternative, free, mainstream instruction.

The president should convene the first multinational working conference to combat terrorism, and that conference should become an annual event to be held in a different capital city every year. The effort to develop a series of global and comprehensive plans to combat terrorism should begin during the first year of the new administration, but it is a long-term undertaking.

Reduce the Threat of Nuclear Proliferation

During the president's first year in office, the new administration should launch a major initiative aimed at strengthening the nonproliferation regime and securing nuclear materials around the world. The threat of nuclear attack—either from a rogue state or from some stateless person or entity—is simply too great to ignore. Although the new president should take strong action during the first year of the administration, this project will require a long-term commitment of time and attention.

During the past 10 years, the spread of nuclear weapons to non-nuclear states—Pakistan, India, and North Korea, with Iran close behind—coupled with the increased availability of nuclear materials generally has increased the threat of nuclear attack. What was once a nightmare—the idea of nuclear weapons in the hands of rogue states—is now almost a reality. The technological barrier to acquiring a nuclear capability is now relatively low. And the ability to deter suicidal terrorists from detonating any such device is now virtually nonexistent.

The more nuclear weapons material that is out there and unprotected, whether in the form of unsecured materials in a nuclear weapons state or whether in the form of enriched uranium being produced as part of a "peaceful" nuclear energy program, the greater the danger to the United States and its allies. If terrorists acquire nuclear weapons, they will use them. At the top of the new Secretary of State's list of priorities should be an action plan aimed at strengthening the international nonproliferation regime, preventing the spread of nuclear weapons, and forestalling the diversion of nuclear materials by nonstate actors.

Address Global Climate Change

This effort must begin at once but will require a commitment that, to be successful, must be sustained over decades. The president, national security advisor, secretary of energy, and the new national energy advisor will lead the interagency effort on climate change, but the role of the State Department is central. First, the department must lay the diplomatic ground for post-Kyoto negotiations, including with China and India. Second, the department will be tasked to lead the U.S. response to the growing impact of climate change, particularly in the developing world. Third, in its efforts to rebuild U.S. relations with our traditional and new allies, the department will be in the forefront of introducing the new administration's climate policies to the world.

The new administration should take two immediate steps to put climate change into diplomatic play. The secretary of state should send a detailed cable to all diplomatic posts setting the new administration's policies and strategy, and solicit feedback from our civilian representatives in the field. And climate change should be included as a key segment of the first round of the department's chiefs-of-missions conference after the new administration takes office.

In the first year of the new administration, the new president should address the American people to discuss the national security challenge posed by climate change. Internationally, the new president should propose an enforceable international framework aimed at reversing global warming without hindering economic development. Such an effort would begin with the United States symbolically signing the Kyoto Protocol, but it must be followed by the United States sending high-level representatives to participate in the next international summit on climate change in Copenhagen in December 2009. To prepare for this international initiative, the new president should ask the secretary of state to develop a robust diplomatic strategy. The secretary of state should rely on the undersecretary of global affairs to lead an interagency task force that achieves that purpose.

Engage the Middle East Peace Process

During the first year of the new administration, the new president should go to the Old City of Jerusalem and give a speech reaffirming America's commitment to the absolute security of Israel and to the creation of a viable Palestinian state that can be home to millions of Palestinians willing to live in peace with their Israeli neighbors. With support from European and Arab governments, the new president should announce his willingness to engage personally in serious political, economic, and diplomatic efforts aimed at reaching agreement between Palestinians and Israelis that will result in a viable state for the Palestinians and genuine security for the Israelis. This affirmation should be accompanied by a pledge to convene, during his first six months in office, an international summit in a neutral location.

This effort should be seen as beginning in the early days and weeks of the new administration and at its inception should involve the president personally. Responsibility for following up should lie with the secretary of state, the national security advisor, and the assistant secretary for Middle East affairs. Given the various other demands on the president's foreign policy team, the president should consider appointing a senior American diplomat who is experienced, knowledgeable, and known to the region as a full-time presidential envoy with the authority to speak for the government of the United States, and routinely to interface with all the interested parties, including with members of a support group of outside governments.

This envoy should be supported by an interagency team tasked to provide the diplomatic, economic, military, and aid support needed to achieve success. The new administration cannot wait until the seventh or eighth year to make progress on this front.

Engagement with Iran

Iran is the single biggest beneficiary of the U.S. decision to invade Iraq, to overthrow Saddam Hussein, and to rebuild the Iraqi nation. Iran's oldest adversary was removed. Those Shia leaders most closely aligned with pro-Iranian forces now run the Iraqi government. And while the United States remains preoccupied in Iraq and struggling to field enough troops in Afghanistan, Iranian influence in the region has increased.

The new president, during the first year of the administration, should seek ways to engage the Iranians directly, to discuss common interests, and to warn them of the consequences of continuing support for terrorism and going ahead with plans to develop nuclear weapons. Neither the United States nor Iran want to see the Taliban return or the poppy trade flourish inside Afghanistan. Neither wants to see Al Qaeda succeed in the region, whether in Iraq or in Afghanistan. Neither wants to go to war with the other by accident or mistake, or because of petty posturing in the Persian Gulf. Neither wants to see Iraq descend into nationwide civil war that would, almost certainly, inflame the region. Such a local civil war would rapidly become regional. It would draw in the Saudis in support of the Sunnis and the Iranians in support of the Shia. The Turks, too, would move. They would like nothing more than an opportunity to destroy the Kurdish nationalist movement once and for all.

A process of engagement between the United States and Iran would involve the promise of many economic carrots as well as the threat of many sticks. It should also be accompanied by close consultation and coordination with allies. There would be a regional dimension to the exchange that would be self-evident. Iran's role as a regional power would be recognized. The Iranian revolution would be recognized and legitimated. Iran's importance to the region—economically, politically, militarily—would be acknowledged.

The United States would seek to persuade the Iranians that their best way forward is to subject all aspects of their nuclear program to monitoring by the International Atomic Energy Agency, and to terminate Iran's support for terrorist groups in the region. There would be no mistakes as to meanings or intentions. This process of engagement would not solve all disputes, but it would certainly clarify where the parties stood and what they were prepared to do to pursue their interests. Within the first year of the new administration, the president should work to put such a process in place with the Iranians, perhaps using the good offices of the United Nations, the Swiss, and the European Union, and perhaps using Geneva as a venue.

To do this, the new president would rely primarily upon the new secretary of state, the State Department's team of experts, and the U.S. intelligence community. The new president also would be well advised to seek advice from those leaders who have in the recent past dealt directly with the Iranians on nuclear issues and other matters.

Department of Homeland Security

Rebuilding to Create What Should
Have Been from the Beginning

CLARK KENT ERVIN

It is only a slight exaggeration to say that the critically important Department of Homeland Security, created in the aftermath of 9/11, has itself become a disaster. The new president must therefore make it a priority to transform it into the model government agency that it should have been from the beginning. The new administration immediately should fill key DHS vacancies with counterterrorism and natural disaster preparedness experts, as well as skilled managers with experience supervising large bureaucracies. Appointments should be made strictly on the basis of competence, with no regard whatsoever for party or ideological affiliation. The new administration will also have to work with Congress to increase the department's budget in order to close security gaps. By the end of the first year, or as quickly as possible, DHS should begin screening 100 percent of air cargo for explosives; all airport personnel should, like passengers, be screened at checkpoints for deadly weapons; the department's intelligence unit should be strengthened; and 100 percent of counterterrorism grants to cities should be allocated on the basis of risk. By the end of the first term, technology should be installed at every airport checkpoint that can significantly improve screeners' ability to spot concealed weapons; technology should be developed and deployed at our seaports to screen all incoming cargo for radiation; our borders should be strengthened by complet-

ing the U.S. VISIT system by adding an exit feature; and consideration, at least, should be given to ending the visa waiver program. Finally, consideration should be given to radically restructuring and downsizing the department so that it focuses only on counterterrorism, leaving other functions, including natural disaster mitigation, response, and recovery, to other agencies.

The Department of Homeland Security during the six years since its creation became the poster child for government dysfunction. The Government Accountability Office continues to categorize many of the department's key programs and operations as "high risk." Tens of millions of dollars in contracts and grants that were intended to make America safer have been wasted. And although we have devoted the bulk of our counterterrorism efforts since 9/11 to securing the aviation sector, government investigators can still sneak bombs, guns, and knives through checkpoints with relative ease, suggesting that sophisticated terrorists can do so too.

Our airports are impregnable fortresses compared to our seaports, land borders, mass transit systems, and critical infrastructure. The department is surely better prepared to respond to a natural disaster or a terror attack than it was before Hurricane Katrina, but few would go so far as to claim that it is anywhere close to being as well prepared as it should be the next time disaster strikes.

DHS also consistently ranks at or near the bottom of government agencies in terms of employee morale and job satisfaction. This is no idle concern since experience has shown that poorly motivated employees are poorly performing ones. When the job is protecting us from the very real threat of future terror attacks, DHS workers' motivation is a real national security concern.

The First 100 Days

The department is so dysfunctional that some will call on the new administration to do away with the Department of Homeland Security altogether, arguing that it is broken beyond repair. In the parlance of the Vietnam War, the only way to save this village is to destroy it. Others will urge the new administration to radically restructure DHS. There is considerable support, for example, for taking the Federal Emergency Management Agency out of DHS and making it a stand-alone entity again that reports directly to the president. FEMA's response to Hurricane Katrina was, in large part, so slow and inept because it was submerged within DHS' labyrinthine bureaucracy, some will argue. A direct line to the president would ensure that FEMA gets the authority, flexibility, and resources it needs to get the job done.

There will also be pressure to subsume the Homeland Security Council within the National Security Council. Rather than reporting directly to the new president, a homeland security adviser would report to the president through the national security adviser. This restructuring would work against the tendency to distinguish between "national security" and "homeland security" and to favor, in terms of authority and resources, the former at the expense of the latter. For all its apocalyptic talk that terrorism is an existential threat to America, the Bush administration focused the bulk of its attention and government resources on fighting the traditional wars in Iraq and Afghanistan, and preparing for potential traditional wars with other nation states, such as Iran, North Korea, and China. Bringing "homeland security" within the structure and vocabulary of "national security," some argue, would help to refocus efforts on securing the nation against the relatively new threat of terror attacks here at home by stateless enemies.

Still another dramatic proposal would divest DHS of all of its non-counterterrorism related functions such as FEMA's natural disaster response; the Coast Guard's coastline patrol for drug runners, distressed mariners, and oil spills; and Immigration and Customs Enforcement's raids on illegal aliens unconnected to terrorism. At the same time, many of the counterterrorism functions performed by other government agencies would be transferred to DHS. This could include the FBI's responsibility for counterterrorism investigations, and the Centers for Disease Control and Prevention and the Environmental Protection Agency's work on bioterror. Such reorganization would address the concern that DHS does such a poor job of countering terror because it is only one of several different jobs the department has to do, and key counterterrorism responsibilities presently lie elsewhere.

The new administration should resist the temptation to try any of these approaches anytime soon. If recent history is any guide, there is a heightened risk of an attack on the homeland early in the new administration. The first bombing of the World Trade Center in February 1993 occurred at the start of the Clinton administration; 9/11 happened early in the Bush administration; the Madrid bombing came on the eve of Spanish elections in 2004; and the London bombings were foiled at the start of the Brown government in the summer of 2007.

The last thing the new government needs in its first perilous year is to mire itself in yet another major restructuring of its counterterrorism apparatus. The new administration should, however, take the following four "big picture" steps during its first 100 days.

Leadership

The new president should nominate experienced leaders to guide DHS through its critical post-startup years. The secretary of homeland security should not be a political crony or a lawyer or judge without experience and expertise in counterterrorism and national security. The new president should turn to an apolitical, independent-minded, well-known, and highly successful leader steeped in counterterrorism and national security.

A marquee subject matter expert should be paired with a deputy secretary who is a skilled corporate operator well versed in managing complex systems and integrating mergers and acquisitions—a Fortune 500 chief operating officer, for example, or a senior executive at one of the major management consulting firms.

In addition to the secretary and deputy secretary, key positions at DHS to be filled include those of undersecretary for management, assistant secretary for policy, inspector general, and the heads of key components such as the Transportation Security Administration, Customs and Border Protection, Immigration and Customs Enforcement, the Coast Guard, and FEMA. Assuming the new president maintains the position of homeland security adviser, filling that position will also be critical.

Funding

The new administration should acknowledge that DHS is underfunded and that it has been from its start. The new president should make it clear that he will use every tool at his disposal to persuade congressional appropriators to give the department the money necessary to keep the country safe.

The new president should commission a "crash" 60-day review of the department's budget. The questions that will need answers include: How much money is being spent now and for what exactly? What is the correlation, if any, between each line item of expenditure and enhanced security? What other factors besides security considerations, if any, are driving DHS expenditures and why? And where is the country most vulnerable?

The new president should indicate from the beginning that he intends to request and push for a "significant" increase in the DHS budget, but to wait for the results of the review before settling on a specific figure. The president should also be willing to fund the necessary increases with cuts to the Pentagon's budget. Our strategic edge over every other nation in the world must be maintained, but we can ill afford still more defenses against nation states when we have so little in the way of defenses here at home against stateless terrorists.

Openness and Accountability

The 44th president should make it clear that a new era of openness and accountability will prevail in government generally, and at the Department of

Homeland Security particularly. DHS leaders have all too often taken a "head in the sand" mentality with regard to the nation's security gaps.

When undercover investigators sneak weapons through airport checkpoints with ease, the Transportation Security Administration's response is that the checkpoint is only one of many security layers. Even though most experts agree that our number one threat is nuclear terrorism, machines that the department claimed could more accurately distinguish between deadly and harmless radiation turned out to be no improvement over existing technology. DHS assured congressional appropriators that the machines detected highly enriched uranium—the kind of uranium used in nuclear weapons—95 percent of the time. Yet GAO auditors found that detection rates were never higher than 50 percent, and sometimes as low as 17 percent. Not only would scarce homeland security dollars have been wasted without the auditors' insistence to the contrary, the nation would have been under the illusion that it was better protected than it actually was against an existential threat.

The president should stress that the department will be honest about what it is and is not doing to address these security vulnerabilities with Congress, government investigators, and, where doing so does not compromise security, the public at large. Only by acknowledging security gaps can the government begin the task of addressing them. The new administration should hold accountable any official who knowingly or negligently compromises the nation's security by ignoring security gaps or minimizing them, including, under appropriate circumstances, prosecution. The message to DHS employees should be that their jobs will not be endangered by failing to acknowledge security gaps; their jobs will be endangered by failing to acknowledge such gaps and not doing everything within their power to address them.

The new secretary should make a conspicuous point of urging all personnel to cooperate fully with all inspector general and GAO inspections, audits, and investigations. On a regular basis, but no less frequently than quarterly, the homeland security secretary should meet with the IG to be personally apprised of important findings and to monitor the department's progress toward implementing recommendations. The IG and the comptroller general should not be viewed as pests or antagonists, but as indispensable internal and external management consultants, respectively, who are full partners in making the department operate as effectively, efficiently, and economically as possible.

Regulation
The secretary should signal that the days of bending over backward to make security measures as painless as possible for industry are over. Every effort should be made to obtain relevant private sector input before policies and programs

that affect them are implemented. After all, about 85 percent of critical infra-structure in this country is owned or operated by the private sector, and secu-rity measures should be established in ways that, to the extent possible, harmonize the twin imperatives of securing the nation and facilitating commerce.

Yet when there is irreconcilable conflict between security and commerce, the nation needs to put security first. Chimerical programs such as C-TPAT, the Customs Trade Partnership Against Terrorism, which gives shippers the benefit of a reduced chance of inspections before verifying that they have rig-orous security programs in place, should be ended immediately. The chemical industry should no longer be allowed to call the shots on regulations. The de-partment should use the full extent of its existing regulatory authority to, if need be, force industries that are deemed critical to the nation's security to ade-quately prepare for terror attacks. If existing regulatory authority is insuffi-cient, additional regulatory authority should be sought from Congress.

Other Changes

There are several relatively small tasks in addition to the four major changes that the new secretary of DHS could take on in the short term that would make the department more effective. Part of the reason that the department has been less than the sum of its parts is that key legacy agencies retain consid-erable autonomy over their own finances, information technology networks, and procurement systems. This promotes duplication, a lack of interoperabil-ity and other inefficiencies, and works against the goal of integrating DHS' dis-parate parts into a cohesive whole.

The department's chief procurement officer, chief financial officer, and chief information officer do not "control"—have the power to hire, fire, and set the budget of—their counterparts at the Transportation Security Adminis-tration, Federal Emergency Management Agency, Immigration and Customs Enforcement, Customs and Border Protection, and the Coast Guard. These critical administrative personnel at the component level are controlled by their respective component heads. With a pen stroke, the new secretary can and should change this.

"Controls," or guidelines, should also be put in place to ensure that no more precious contract dollars are wasted. The new secretary should, for example, forbid procurement officers from using no-bid contracts. Such contracts are never justified. Even if procurement officers are certain that only one contrac-tor can satisfy particular requirements, there is no harm in opening up the con-tract for bid. Perhaps there are other, previously unknown contractors who can supply the good or service equally well and at lesser cost.

There should be incentives built into every contract for good performance, such as timeliness, staying within budget, and delivering the promised result, and financial or other penalties for poor performance, including, under appropriate circumstances, criminal prosecution. Contractors who consistently miss the mark should be barred for a period of time from bidding on new contracts. And to counter the corrupting influence of the "revolving door," bids from former DHS insiders should be disfavored, other things being equal.

The number of procurement officials should also be significantly increased. DHS can never match private sector salaries, but DHS should seek congressional authority to pay bonuses and offer other attractive benefits to attract and retain such personnel. Competent DHS contracting officers in sufficient numbers are critical to ensuring that contracts are structured and managed in a way that most benefits the taxpayer.

DHS has too few employees managing contractors, and it has too many contractors managing core department functions. Chair of the House Committee on Oversight and Government Reform Rep. Henry Waxman (D-CA), in a spring 2007 speech, said that DHS leaders conceded at a hearing that they had "no idea" how many contractors worked for the department.[1] The GAO has chided DHS for contracting out "inherently governmental" functions,[2] and it is no wonder. According to the *The Washington Post*, "At the Department of Homeland Security, contract employees help write job descriptions for new headquarters workers. Private contractors also sign letters that officially offer employment. And, they meet new congressional hires on the first day of the job. About the only thing they do not do is swear-in DHS employees."[3]

Some contractors at DHS do indeed oversee other contractors. To ensure that the sole interest in mind is that of the taxpayer, the department should have more employees and fewer contractors. Contractors should not be performing inherently governmental functions, and no function is more "inherently governmental" than overseeing contractors.

The homeland security secretary should, in public speeches, congressional testimony, op-eds, and news media interviews, repeatedly stress during the first 100 days that there is no such thing as 100 percent security. We cannot make ourselves invulnerable to attack, but the next administration should do everything it can to minimize the risk of a terror attack, concentrating on catastrophic ones. The ultimate goal must be to vitiate terrorists' ability to pose an existential threat to the nation, and as both President Bush and Sen. John Kerry (D-MA) conceded in moments of candor during the 2004 election, to reduce terrorism to the "nuisance-level" threat posed by crime.

The new administration should also stress that countering terrorism is not the job of government alone. Private sector companies that own or operate critical infrastructure must do their part to secure these key assets from terrorist attack. Even the average citizen has a role to play—being willing to pay higher taxes to support increased security expenditures, if necessary; putting up with even tighter security measures at airports, seaports, land borders, and other potential targets; alerting the authorities when they spot suspicious activity, but not profiling people on the basis of racial or ethnic identity or appearance; and holding their elected leaders to account for their records on security issues.

The First Year

Terrorists continue to target aviation because airplane attacks can kill large numbers of people, cause huge damage to the entire economy, and provide especially dramatic images that rivet international attention. The new administration should accordingly place particular emphasis on further securing this sector.

Congress passed a law in 2007 that was intended to implement most of the then-outstanding 9/11 Commission recommendations. One of the recommendations was to screen 100 percent of cargo carried on passenger planes by 2010.[4] The Bush administration's homeland security secretary, Michael Chertoff, suggested that the airlines will continue to do at least some screening themselves. But the whole point of the law was that airlines cannot and will not police themselves. Allowing cargo to be placed in the hold of passenger planes unexamined is a gaping security hole that will one day be exploited by terrorists to deadly effect. If passengers' checked luggage can be screened efficiently, so can any cargo carried aboard passenger planes. The Transportation Security Administration should screen all passenger plane cargo by the end of the next administration's first year in office.

The administration should also prioritize instituting physical screening of all airport personnel who access secure, or "sterile," areas—the areas in airports that are past security checkpoints, tarmacs, hangars, and loading docks. Badges and random screening are inadequate substitutes; TSA should at least subject airport personnel who access sensitive areas to the same security measures as ordinary passengers.

Intelligence and Counterterrorism

The new administration will have to further improve the department's ability to obtain, analyze, and use intelligence. It goes without saying that DHS can hardly be effective at protecting the nation from terrorist threats if it is uninformed or ill-informed as to what the threats are.

The administration must give the DHS intelligence unit, called Intelligence and Analysis, or IA, the authority and resources that it needs to be the center of the government's homeland security-related intelligence efforts. Shortly after the department's inception, the Bush administration tasked the Terrorist Screening Center, an FBI-led multiagency entity, with the job of consolidating and maintaining various agencies' terrorist watch lists. It then gave the job of synthesizing intelligence concerning threats to the homeland gleaned from the entire 16-member intelligence community to a CIA-led multiagency entity, now called the National Counterterrorism Center.

DHS' Intelligence and Analysis unit should be in control of these efforts, not just represented at them. An IA official reporting to the secretary of DHS should lead each of these intelligence efforts, and the budget should be set and managed by DHS. If any agency is to be in charge of terror watch lists and homeland security-related intelligence, it ought to be the Department of Homeland Security.

The new administration will have to utilize the results of the budget review mentioned earlier to work with Congress to significantly increase the amount of counterterrorism grants to eligible cities under the Urban Area Security Initiative. DHS should redouble its commendable longstanding efforts to persuade Congress to allocate all of these funds on the basis of risk, in addition to making more funds available. This would mean that all, not just most, of the funding would go to the nation's biggest and most prominent cities.

The department should authorize cities to use these grants to pay for ongoing operational expenses such as personnel costs for law enforcement personnel, and not only one-time investments in costly technology. The New York Police Department spends millions of dollars each year for its 1,000-person strong counterterrorism force without much, if any, help from the federal government, even though another attack on "the nation" will likely mean, in practice, another attack on New York City. Protecting such a city should therefore be as much a national responsibility as it is a local one.

The Longer-Term Agenda

Certain critical steps in the areas of aviation security, maritime security, and land border security will take longer than the first year to accomplish, and should be part of the new administration's longer term objectives during its first term.

The Department of Homeland Security should, beginning with the largest airports, install better detection technology at every checkpoint at every airport. DHS will have to determine which of the two cutting-edge detection technologies—"backscatter" or "active millimeter"—has proved in pilot tests to be most effective at spotting concealed guns, knives, and bombs hidden on passengers' bodies. The machines are costly—approximately $100,000 to $150,000 each—and installing them will require expensive and time-consuming modifications to airport checkpoints. It should be possible, however, to deploy them to every airport checkpoint in the country by the end of the administration's first term.

The department, in partnership with industry and academe, should undertake a crash effort to develop technology that can accurately distinguish between harmless and deadly radiation at our nation's seaports. Once developed, the technology should be deployed at every seaport in the nation, starting with the largest and busiest first, whereupon all incoming cargo would be scanned to prevent weapons of mass destruction from entering the country. Because such a weapon could kill millions of people and bring the national and international economy to its knees, there should be no higher priority.

Borders

The department should complete the U.S. VISIT program by adding an exit feature at every legal port of entry. DHS currently tracks foreigners who arrive at ports of entry, but has not yet implemented a system to record exits. If we learn after the fact that a terrorist was inadvertently admitted into the country, there is no way to know whether he or she is still within our borders or might already have exited the country.

The new administration should consider ending the visa waiver program. The citizens of 27 countries (mostly in Europe) can enter the United States without undergoing the now extensive post-9/11 visa issuance process. Their only encounter with the U.S. government is when they arrive at the port of entry (usually, an airport) and are given the "once over" by a CBP inspector who can generally speak only English and has only seconds to check the visitors' name against the terrorist watch list, take fingerprints, and maybe ask a question or two.

By way of contrast, citizens from the rest of the world have to apply for a visa in person at U.S. embassies or consulates, be interviewed by an American consular officer trained in fraud detection techniques and generally familiar with the local language and culture, provide extensive biographic information, have their fingers scanned, and have their names checked against the terrorist watch list. The more rigorous visa process is not a guarantee against admitting terrorists to the country, but the more would-be visitors are scrutinized, the greater the chances that terrorists among them might be discovered.

DHS secretary Chertoff acknowledged the danger posed by the program, but took only half steps to address it, such as requiring European travelers to complete an online biographical questionnaire 48 hours before traveling to the United States.[5] There is no question that ending visa waivers would be a very controversial move. Without intensive diplomatic groundwork beforehand, the global reaction would likely be hugely negative at a time when we urgently need to repair our relationship with the rest of the world and not further damage it.

Because it is a reciprocal program, doing away with the visa waiver program would mean that Americans would likewise have to get visas to visit countries whose citizens presently do not need visas to visit us. If, however, the United States explains the rationale clearly and often enough to the rest of the world, and if we make it equally clear that we Americans are willing to go to the trouble of applying for visas ourselves, the reaction is likely to be less negative and more limited in time.

That said, we are mindful of the political reality that the new president will face. He will have his hands full with repairing ruptured relations around the world. So thought should be given to this move, given the clear risk that visa waiver travel poses. It would be reasonable for the new president to conclude that the diplomatic cost outweighs the security benefit. But, certainly, the visa waiver program should not be further expanded. The new administration should find another way to reward countries for their support that does not undermine our security.

Organizational Changes

The new administration over the course of its first term should consider recommending to Congress that DHS be radically restructured to make it the lean, focused, counterterrorism agency it ought to have been from the beginning. Part of the department's problem is that it has many responsibilities that have nothing to do with counterterrorism, while other agencies outside DHS play significant homeland security-related roles.

Restructuring homeland security responsibilities would in practice mean, for example, spinning off Citizenship and Immigration Services, the part of the old Immigration and Naturalization Service that processes citizenship and temporary residence applications, as well as the Secret Service, which basically provides protection to the president and other high-ranking government officials and investigates money laundering.

This reorganization would also mean transferring to DHS from the Agriculture Department, Health and Human Services, the Environmental Protection Agency, and the Centers for Disease Control all responsibility for preventing and preparing for bioterrorism.

The truly hard part, of course, would be deciding what to do with components such as Immigration and Customs Enforcement, Customs and Border Protection, FEMA, and the Coast Guard, which have multiple missions. One option would be to split each of these entities in two, with the smaller component staying in DHS and focusing only on the counterterrorism mission and the larger one going elsewhere and focusing on everything else. A smaller version of ICE would concentrate only on trying to identify terrorists among the illegal immigrant population. A smaller version of CBP, stationed at our airports, seaports, and land borders, would focus only on trying to keep terrorists out of the country, along with weapons of mass destruction that they might use against us. A smaller version of the Coast Guard would focus only on patrolling our coastline for signs of terrorists and terrorist activity, and evaluating seaports' security programs.

A counterterrorism-focused DHS must be comprehensive to be most effective. It must include a component, for example, that prepares for and responds to the human and material consequences of terror attacks. A smaller version of FEMA would, then, focus only on those aspects of disaster prevention and disaster response, if any, that are unique to terrorism.

Before any radical changes are implemented, however, department leadership and the White House, in the person of the homeland security adviser, should consult widely and deeply, reaching out not only to those who support these ideas, but also to those who oppose them. If, in the end, the considered judgment is that implementing these changes would enhance DHS' counterterrorism ability, even then they should be implemented incrementally over the course of several years. The nation is paying the price for the haste with which DHS was cobbled together; we can ill afford to downsize it as precipitously and thoughtlessly.

Federal Emergency Management Agency

Rebuilding a Once Proud Agency

JAMES LEE WITT

The experience of the Federal Emergency Management Agency over the past eight years requires reassessing and rebuilding the agency from the ground up. Serious organizational, legal, relational, and leadership issues challenge FEMA's ability to achieve its mission, and demand both cultural change within the agency and decisive action to restore public confidence. Early priorities include rethinking its place in the Department of Homeland Security, empowering the FEMA regional offices to better support the agency's customers, and strengthening relationships with state and local counterparts. FEMA also needs to provide more resources and less restrictive funding to support state and local all-hazards emergency management capability. By the end of the first year, the new administration needs to institutionalize cultural change within the agency, professionalize and depoliticize agency activities, and show leadership within the emergency management community—particularly in the area of mitigating hazards.

Over the longer-term, FEMA will need to professionalize emergency management as a discipline, review agency staffing levels to provide better customer support, and further reduce bureaucratic red tape in the delivery of agency services and programs.

The Federal Emergency Management Agency has a committed team of employees, an influx of new resources, a nation more attuned to the threat of natural and man-made disasters, and the attention of Congress and other stakeholders who want to see the agency succeed. Yet the blundered response to hurricanes Katrina and Rita, the degradation of state emergency management capabilities, and unacceptable lapses in judgment (such as staged press conferences and ignorance of public health concerns related to formaldehyde in FEMA travel trailers) all confirm a need to reform the agency from the ground up.

These reforms fall into four general groupings. First, there are organizational issues that must be addressed by reevaluating its place in the Department of Homeland Security and by reforming agency structures. Second, there are legal and structural issues, including the need to re-evaluate FEMA's legislative authorizations, regulations, and policies to provide the agency with more flexibility to address the needs of a catastrophic event. Third, how the agency communicates with and supports its customers at the federal, state, and local levels needs to be re-evaluated to ensure that FEMA better addresses the needs of its own employees, and to reverse the loss of talent and expertise within its ranks.

Finally, FEMA needs to address its own leadership issues so that the agency once again leads the emergency management community by promoting best practices and providing both encouragement and incentive for others to follow. In short, FEMA needs to be rebuilt quickly and aggressively to ensure its effectiveness and restore public confidence in the agency.

Since hurricanes Katrina and Rita, FEMA has undergone a number of internal changes designed to better position the agency to more effectively respond to disasters, including reforms to its logistics capabilities and its catastrophic event planning and preparedness. In addition, certain disaster preparedness functions stripped from the agency by DHS in 2003 have been returned, thanks to congressional action. These reforms may provide some improvements in agency capabilities, yet the jury is still out as to whether they will be effective over the long term.

The reason: none of these changes has been tested under the stresses of a large event. What's more, the reform effort to date has been piecemeal, and thus insufficient to get at the core of the problems facing the agency. Unless more comprehensive progress can be made, our nation will remain susceptible to the same problems and issues that have plagued federal disaster relief in recent years.

First 100 Days

FEMA can regain its status as one of the most successful and admired federal agencies, as it was early in this decade, but it will take a concerted effort from the new administration, support from Congress, and participation from stakeholders at all levels. The 44th president needs to quickly re-establish the reputation of the federal government in emergency management. This will require an ambitious agenda from the very start, designed to "shake up" the culture of the agency, repair relationships, and begin restoring confidence in the agency's direction and capabilities.

The first, and probably most important, step is to immediately begin the process of moving FEMA out of the Department of Homeland Security. When FEMA was first incorporated into DHS in 2003, it was done with the best of intentions. The result, however, was highly problematic. FEMA's all-hazards mission suffered as assets and funding were redirected to the terrorism mission of DHS. Preparedness functions were stripped away and positioned elsewhere in the department. Many of the people at DHS overseeing FEMA were neither career emergency managers nor experienced with disaster response and recovery. And the agency was "demoted," from an independent agency with cabinet-level status reporting directly to the president, to a mere office within DHS.

As Michael Selves, president of the International Association of Emergency Managers, said before Congress in April 2007, "After being consolidated into DHS, FEMA not only lost resources and experienced personnel—most importantly, they lost authority to make decisions and direct federal efforts during disasters. Bad decisions—like subordinating the role of the FEMA Director, reducing funding, and removing preparedness—led to the problems encountered during Hurricane Katrina."[1]

There are two primary means of correcting this mistake, neither of which will be easy or without controversy. In either case, it will be critical to meet with and involve key stakeholders, including Congress, state emergency management officials, local governments, non-governmental organizations, and other federal agencies involved in disaster response and recovery efforts.

The first option is to create a new independent agency via Executive Order. This is how FEMA was first created in 1979 by President Jimmy Carter, who administratively consolidated disaster responsibilities into a single agency, pulling assets and responsibilities from across the federal government.[2] As in 1979, the next president could also consolidate authorities currently residing within DHS and elsewhere, as appropriate, into a newly created agency by a different name.

The new executive order will need to outline the management and reporting requirements of the agency within the executive branch, re-establish a direct and unfettered reporting relationship of the new entity head to the president, and provide the organization cabinet-level status. These changes will remove structural delays in decision making when a disaster occurs and provide the new agency director with sufficient political "weight" within the administration to gain the cooperation of other federal departments and agencies needed to support disaster response and recovery.

Opting for an executive order, however, may be more complicated now than it was in 1979. Language passed by Congress in the Hurricane Katrina Recovery Act of 2006 can be interpreted to designate certain functions to FEMA, which could complicate their removal from DHS. Key congressional staff are currently exploring the issue of creating an independent agency, but they have not reached an agreement.

The second option is work with Congress to remove FEMA from DHS. This is the ideal legislative fix; pulling emergency management-related authorities and resources out of DHS and defining how the two agencies can best work together when needed. Congress, for example, could define through legislation how FEMA's incident-management capabilities can be accessed and directed during terrorist or other homeland security-related events.

If neither option above is achievable, then a third and much less desirable option is also available—strengthen FEMA within DHS and give it the full authority and responsibility necessary to achieve its mission. This option is not ideal, in that the FEMA administrator will continue to be beholden to the DHS Secretary and budget process, and may not be able to fully exercise its authorities without DHS involvement or interference. Changing FEMA's culture will also be more difficult.

If this third option becomes the only option, then key reform initiatives would need to be considered in this effort. First, Congress would have to update Homeland Security Presidential Directive 5 ("Management of Domestic Incidents," February 28, 2003) and Directive 8 ("National Preparedness," December 17, 2003) to reflect the requirements of the Hurricane Katrina Recovery Act of 2006. To Congress' credit, the Act clarifies and strengthens the role of the FEMA administrator and outlines responsibilities and authorities that reside with the agency. Yet Presidential Directives 5 and 8 do not yet reflect those changes.

Second, the new president would have to move the DHS Office of Operations Coordination into FEMA, reporting to the FEMA administrator. This is necessary because the Office of Operations Coordination establishes a de facto incident-management function that, alongside its proposed Integrated Planning System, establishes the capability for the DHS secretary to directly plan for and manage incidents irrespective of FEMA and the authorities established by Congress as being in the domain of the FEMA administrator.

Once fixing FEMA's place in DHS is underway, the new administration will need to change its culture, refocusing the agency from being largely a deliverer of programs to a provider of assistance for identified needs. FEMA needs to restore its focus on customer needs and not on programs. This will require a three-pronged approach: involve FEMA's employees in the redefinition of the agency's mission; empower personnel to make decisions; and re-engage with state and local stakeholders. Short-term working groups, tasked to rethink how FEMA supports its clients as well as its own employees, should be established and then empowered to make recommendations to the agency head for implementation, thus building ownership and accountability. This will also improve morale, which could help stem the flight of personnel from the agency.

Empowering FEMA's regional offices is also needed to make the agency more effective. The FEMA regions lead the delivery of all the agency's programs and are the day-to-day "face of the agency" for customers. Under DHS, however, FEMA consolidated authority in Washington, D.C., and reduced the ability of agency employees to make decisions on their own to address often unique needs at the state and local levels. This approach unfortunately contributed to lengthy delays in resolving time-sensitive issues affecting disaster operations, reduced the ability of state and local emergency managers to receive timely guidance and support, and led to dissatisfaction among many FEMA employees with their work. This has not always been the case. During the 1990s, the FEMA regions were empowered much more than they are now, and satisfaction with the support provided by the agency was much higher as a result.

The new FEMA administrator should refocus the agency's headquarters operation on broad and overarching policy issues, and re-empower FEMA's regions for service and program delivery. FEMA's field personnel need to be given the flexibility, resources, and tools to do their job to meet identified needs. They should also be included in policy discussions so that policies and procedures coming out of Washington, D.C., have relevance in the field. In accepting these responsibilities, FEMA's regional personnel should be held accountable for measurable improvements in state and local preparedness, capability, and customer satisfaction. And FEMA personnel should be judged against specific performance benchmarks.

To contribute to "field relevance," state and local emergency management directors should be consulted regularly by FEMA, and a more robust advisory group of these directors should be utilized to inform the development of new programs, policies, regulations, and priorities. FEMA should also establish a fellowship program to allow state and local emergency managers to obtain practical experience at the federal level and work with FEMA headquarters and the regional offices.

These types of actions are critical because, fundamentally, all disasters are local events. The federal government can provide valuable support to make a disaster response and recovery effort successful, but it is the local firefighter, police officer, emergency manager, or elected official that will actually manage an incident and spur recovery. While the support role of the federal government is described in the Stafford Act, which defines FEMA's role in disaster-related work vis-á-vis state and local governments, in recent years this has often taken a backseat to federal desires and requirements.[3] The focus on supporting and not supplanting state and local efforts must once again be made a central tenet of FEMA's mission and culture.

Another priority for the first 100 days should be rebalancing efforts to strengthen federal, state, and local capabilities. For the emergency management system to work, all the components of the network need to have the baseline resources and capabilities to perform their respective roles and work together effectively. But in the wake of hurricanes Katrina and Rita, most new resources and assets made available for emergency management have been directed to supporting the federal government's needs, and not to building baseline state and local capabilities.

The primary means of the federal government supporting the development of state and local capabilities is the Emergency Management Performance Grants program. EMPG funds are provided on a 50 percent nonfederal cost-share basis, and are utilized to develop, maintain, and strengthen state and local emergency management programs. Most commonly, these EMPG programs contribute toward expenses and activities associated with emergency management personnel costs, planning, exercising, equipping, and training personnel, maintaining emergency operations programs, and educating the public.[4]

While overall funding for EMPG programs throughout much of this decade has increased, funding levels have been largely unpredictable. Bush administration requests for this funding were substantially below the need (and below the amounts eventually approved by Congress). These fluctuations have made states reluctant to hire new staff or make long-term commitments sufficient to build their capabilities.

More importantly, EMPG funding provided over the past several years was offered with significant additional strings attached, designed mostly to redirect resources toward preparedness for, and developing capabilities to respond to, terrorism events. These strings included planning for National Preparedness Scenarios, which are almost entirely concentrated on national security incidents, assessing threats and administering allocation of funding for Homeland Security, developing public-private partnerships for Homeland Security, planning for the deployment of the Strategic National Stockpile, and implementing other terrorism-related programs and responsibilities.[5]

All of these are additional requirements above and beyond what is required to prepare for, and react quickly and decisively to, all-hazards events. As a result, emergency management practitioners have been left with significantly less funding for all-hazard capability building than in the past.[6] The new administration needs to make EMPG funding a much higher priority, support the full funding of the EMPG program at levels already authorized by Congress for 2009, and maintain or increase EMPG resources predictably in the years thereafter.

The First Year

Over the first year, FEMA will need to develop legislation, policies, and regulations to address the specific requirements of a catastrophic disaster event. The experience of hurricanes Katrina and Rita demonstrated that the existing structures that generally provide support for smaller or "garden-variety" disasters do not always apply when dealing with hundreds of thousands of evacuees; billions of dollars of damages to public buildings and infrastructure; the long-term incapacitation of entire jurisdictions and regions; and the decimation of community tax revenue streams, economic systems, and social structures. The Stafford Act provides significant flexibility for creative approaches in addressing disaster needs. But its toolbox is incomplete and its application is dependent on the will of the people in power at that time.

What is needed now is a catastrophic annex to the Stafford Act, which can be triggered once certain lofty measures of disaster impact are met. As a starting point, a "catastrophic disaster" should be defined as any major disaster in which such designation has been requested by the governor of the state in which the disaster occurred, and in which one or more of the following has occurred:

1. The governmental system over a sizable, multi-jurisdictional area has been mostly or entirely incapacitated, either by the direct effects of a presidentially declared disaster or a subsequent and related financial crisis, and the state cannot effectively replace that capacity due to the scale of the disaster and available resources.
2. The affected state is expected to lose more than 10 percent of its tax-related revenues for any fiscal quarter as a result of the event in the fiscal year in which the disaster occurred or in the subsequent fiscal year.
3. Federal costs are expected to exceed $1,500 per capita (adjusted annually according to inflation) in the state that was affected by the disaster.

This definition would establish high enough thresholds that it would not produce unnecessary costs, yet it would provide for use of the catastrophic annex when it was necessary. Once triggered, certain automatic adjustments would help reduce uncertainty, allow responders to focus attention on critical needs rather than bureaucratic paperwork exercises, and encourage rapid response and recovery efforts. The benefits of a catastrophic annex to the Stafford Act would eliminate the nonfederal cost share for Public Assistance—both emergency work and permanent restorative work—as well as Individual

Assistance and Hazard Mitigation programs and state management and administrative costs attributable to the event.

A catastrophic annex would also extend key timelines for the delivery of disaster relief programs and disaster unemployment assistance, and would make the cost of so-called straight-time, force-account labor eligible for reimbursement if it is directly tied to the disaster effort. It would also provide increased funding caps for Community Disaster Loans, which are to assist local governments who have lost tax revenues and cannot cover operational costs, and funding for operations related to the housing and care of displaced populations, both within the affected states and in other states where evacuees are housed.

Moreover, a catastrophic annex would establish "gap funding" out of the president's Disaster Relief Fund to support the front funding of relief efforts of other federal departments and agencies when their existing budgets are insufficient to meet immediate disaster-related needs. This provision would last until Congress can approve supplemental funding (institutionalized through legislation and regulation, as appropriate). Providing such clear authority, Disaster Relief Fund expenditures would also provide technical assistance to support long-term local, regional, and state recovery planning and coordination.

Furthermore, the passage of a catastrophic annex to the Stafford Act should encourage the application of "common sense" flexibility in the delivery of disaster relief programs (as long as it is not expressly prohibited by law or regulation) and the rapid issuance and/or revision of guidance and policy to meet disaster needs. Concurrent with the development of the catastrophic annex, FEMA should provide leadership on two areas of great importance: long-term recovery planning and support, and hazard mitigation.

For decades, state and local emergency managers paid far too little attention to preparing for the complexities of long-term recovery under the premise that it will "take care of itself." And the federal government buried its head in the sand by saying that planning and long-term recovery (as opposed to immediate repair work) is difficult, highly complex, and not a primary federal responsibility. Hurricanes Katrina and Rita showed the flaw in that approach—a lack of recovery planning results in longer recovery timelines and increased costs. It must be a national priority to help states and local governments to be ready for long-term recovery.

FEMA also needs to rethink its policies and regulations and, where necessary, work with Congress to ensure that the agency has sufficient authority in the area of disaster recovery planning and can authorize the use of funds from the president's Disaster Relief Fund after a large or catastrophic event occurs. A predisaster program should be considered as well, funded on a cost-share basis, to support state, regional, and local recovery plan development, including the establishment of stakeholder coordination networks that can help shape priorities to be engaged after the fact to guide recovery efforts.

FEMA needs to recapture the mantle of leadership of reducing our nation's risk before disasters occur, thereby reducing suffering, property damage, and taxpayer expenditures over the long term. In the 1990s under President Clinton, the agency successfully made the case for hazard mitigation, demonstrating that each dollar invested in mitigation saves, on average, four dollars in avoided losses later on.[7] It focused personnel and resources toward mitigation planning and implementation efforts, and instituted "Project Impact," an initiative designed to build disaster-resistant communities through public-private partnerships, public education efforts, and the involvement of stakeholders.

With relatively modest federal investment, FEMA was able to work with communities in all 50 states to assemble stakeholders, help them understand the risks they face and what can be done to address them, prioritize actions, and target resources (mostly nonfederal) toward cost-effective mitigation measures. The initiative was considered highly successful at the time, and it is not clear why Project Impact was terminated at the start of the Bush administration.

To restore risk reduction as the centerpiece of its activities, FEMA needs to redirect some of its internal resources to more fully staff and support mitigation planning, predisaster mitigation programs, and mitigation recovery efforts. It should work both within the agency and with other federal departments to encourage the consideration of risk and incorporation of mitigation in all that they do. This effort will be far more successful once FEMA is restored to cabinet-level status, giving the FEMA administrator more influence. In the 1990s, other agencies knew that if they were not responsive when FEMA asked for their help, the next call they would receive would be from the president himself. FEMA also should work with the Office of Management and Budget and Congress to restore funding to Project Impact sufficient to allow for at least four Project Impact communities to be selected in each state each year, starting with at least $300 million per year initially, with increases for the program as it regains momentum.

Another priority for the first year should be to initiate a top-to-bottom review of FEMA's programs, regulations, and policies related to disaster relief, looking for ways to make them less paperwork-intensive, more timely, and more flexible. Given the importance and complexity of this effort, this review will likely run into the second year of the next administration's term in office. The review should involve state and local emergency managers and officials, and should focus on identified problem areas, such as planning requirements coming out of FEMA and DHS in recent years that are widely considered to be burdensome at the local level where emergency management organizations are often resource-poor and understaffed.

Other problems this review should examine are policy changes and guidance related to the agency's recovery programs, which routinely take months or even years to make, despite often immediate disaster-related needs. Similarly, the Hazard Mitigation Grant Program is so complex and paperwork-intensive that it is common for individual projects to take 12 months to be developed and approved (and even longer in larger disaster events), limiting options to incorporate cost-effective mitigation into reconstruction efforts.

This review should identify those activities and programs where responsibility to implement can be devolved to states that can demonstrate that they have the capability to manage them, followed by a robust audit and evaluation process to ensure accountability for the use of taxpayer dollars.[8] Programs such as the Public Assistance and Hazard Mitigation Grant programs could be provided through block grants, eliminating layers of review and red tape that currently slow the provision of assistance. The opportunity to assume control and gain greater flexibility in the administration of these activities will also provide a "carrot" to encourage states to invest in their own emergency management capabilities. The review should also look at how targeted incentives may be applied to encourage improved performance.

Recommendations coming out of this review, including possible legislative changes, should be developed for consideration by the FEMA administrator, OMB, and Congress, so FEMA can dedicate sufficient staff and management support to the effort to address the associated workload.

There are, of course, other priorities. One is the need to expedite the transition of FEMA's regional director positions and many of the headquarters senior management slots to career positions, filled by qualified emergency management professionals. Another is to encourage stand-by contracts for equipment, supplies, recovery services, and personnel support, including the provision of guidance on how to contract for such services consistent with federal requirements. This will address two of the biggest problems in recovery— poorly constructed, noncompetitive contracts or contracts with unreasonable costs that slow recovery efforts and federal reimbursements. It will also help affected states and jurisdictions to access needed resources quickly after a disaster without having to take personnel off high-priority tasks to navigate the procurement system.

Longer-Term Agenda

The president will also want FEMA to begin to address a longer-term agenda. Particularly important is the need to encourage greater professionalization of the emergency management discipline. The agency can improve training and developmental opportunities for its employees, which will help retain employees and increase their expertise. Nationally, FEMA should encourage and support educational and degree programs in emergency management, the expansion of training opportunities for state and local emergency managers, and the development of performance and accreditation standards.

To begin addressing these priorities, FEMA needs to reach out to the higher education community to develop degree and certification programs for emergency management. In addition, the FEMA administrator needs to recognize that the demand for training far outstrips the agency's capabilities and facilities to provide it. FEMA should therefore work with the private sector to have it develop training programs complementary to its offerings, as well as deliver FEMA-approved training more broadly to stakeholders in the field.

The agency also should look internally at the needs of its employees. Because it has lost a substantial amount of experience through retirements and the departure of dissatisfied career professionals over the last seven years, substantial effort needs to be put into retaining the people who remain, and building the capabilities of the "next generation" of emergency management professionals. Employee cross-training would create a culture that allows people to make decisions and take risks, if they are being done for the right reasons (and not punishing them for failure), build employee morale, and produce a higher-performing workforce.

Finally, the new administration needs to fully staff the agency to authorized levels and place greater emphasis on direct technical support activities for its customers at the state and local levels. FEMA could then both build capacity in the field (where the service is actually delivered) and change the emphasis from FEMA headquarters in Washington, D.C., to FEMA's ten regional offices. Steps such as increasing staff in the FEMA regions and requiring that personnel seeking promotions to senior posts in the agency have regional experience can refocus resources toward a fully functioning national emergency management system at the federal, state, and local levels. FEMA's greatest asset is its people. Without them, the agency will fail. But with their support and expertise, it can and will become the agency that our nation expects and deserves.

Department of Energy

Implementing the New Energy Opportunity

RONALD E. MINSK AND
ELGIE HOLSTEIN

Upon taking office, the new president will need to immediately address our economy's dependence on oil as a primary fuel source, and the potentially catastrophic planetary consequences of large-scale international reliance on fossil fuels. In the first 100 days of the new administration, the new energy secretary will need to recommend to the president a series of executive orders to jump-start our nation's transition to a low-carbon economy—placing the federal government at the center of efforts to put our economy on a path to a more sustainable and secure energy future. The themes reflected in the executive orders will be echoed in a DOE-led campaign to explain to the American people the need to become more energy-efficient. It will also educate the public about the many ways in which citizens can play a role in building the new energy economy, beginning with ways to save money by using energy more wisely. The new secretary of energy will also need to create strategies for developing the next generation of alternative energy sources, managing our strategic petroleum reserve, and administering our nuclear weapons complex. More broadly, DOE also must initiate new energy-efficiency standards for our everyday appliances and our homes and office buildings in order to more swiftly reduce our use of energy.

Even after repeated oil price shocks to our economy, America's dependence on oil continues, and with each passing year the world's remaining reserves become more concentrated in the Middle East. Today, our nation's economy and its consumers are once again suffering from a dramatic run-up in oil prices, which doubled in less than one year.[1] At the same time, there is a clear international scientific consensus that the continued growth of greenhouse gas emissions from the unrestrained use of fossil fuel poses an immediate threat to global ecology and to international economic and social well-being.[2] It is time to acknowledge that our nation's energy policies, as they have developed over the past 35 years, have failed in several key respects. While our energy systems and infrastructure are highly reliable and cleaner than at any point since the birth of the modern environmental movement, we have not addressed the two most significant energy-related problems we face.

We have completely failed to meaningfully address our nation's dependence on oil despite repeated warnings, previous energy shocks, and volatility in world oil markets that have been readily apparent since the oil embargo of 1973. And although we learned about the dangers of climate change more recently than we learned about the dangers of oil dependence, we have declined to take a leadership role among nations seeking to address the climate crisis.

The challenge of converting to a low-carbon economy is massive, but so are the opportunities that the transformation will create. Acting now will put us on the path to a cleaner, healthier, and more sustainable future, and enable us to create new job opportunities and economic growth that will accompany the development of transformative energy technologies. If we do not capture these opportunities, other countries will. And if we do not help lead the fight for solutions to both climate change and oil dependence, our citizens, and many others around the world, will pay a terrible price.

The First 100 Days

The secretary's first undertaking should be to play a leadership role in the development of a new comprehensive energy plan, and then initiate a public education program to explain the nature of our energy problems, how the new administration intends to address them, and what consumers can do to accomplish national energy objectives. The new president and his senior advisors will be deeply involved, even before the Inauguration, in shaping a new energy strategy, the details of which are examined in other chapters of this book. Here, we identify several ideas that can be part of an initial strategy, both to set the direction for early action by the administration and to contribute to the development of the longer-term energy plan.

This comprehensive energy plan should be drafted in the first 60 days and include a balanced set of proposals to increase the supply of energy—especially renewable energy—and to reduce demand growth. One clear unifying theme of the plan should be a focus on policies to regulate and reduce greenhouse gas emissions. Developing a written energy plan is important for several reasons. First, the scope of our energy challenge is immense, and to be plausible, any response will require a proportionate, multi-faceted response. Second, preparation overseen by the White House will ensure both presidential and cabinet "buy-in," which will be critical as opponents seek to modify or derail the plan. Third, it can help identify key technology challenges, a process that will assist in the development of the department's energy-related research agenda and budget. Finally, the plan will also outline the new administration's goals and priorities with respect to the entire panoply of energy-related programs and issues, and assign responsibilities, as appropriate, to multiple departments and agencies.

The policies established in the plan should be reflected in the president's first budget. To that end, the secretary should work with the White House to ensure passage of any new legislative proposals by the end of 2009. During the transition the incoming secretary of energy should prepare a series of executive orders defining an aggressive energy and climate agenda for the operations of the federal government.

As the largest consumer in the nation, with a presence that extends throughout the economy, the federal government is well situated to lead by example with respect to improving its energy efficiency and promoting responsible and sustainable energy practices. Recognizing the value of setting a good example and the opportunity to make sound energy-related investments by the government, each of the past several presidents has issued executive orders directing the government to achieve specified levels of energy savings within specified time frames.[3] President George W. Bush's most recently issued executive order on the subject, Executive Order 13423, raised the target for energy savings in federal facilities to 3 percent from 2 percent annually through 2015 (or 30 percent by 2015),[4] but revoked a previous executive order that required agencies to reduce their greenhouse gas emissions from buildings by 30 percent between 1990 and 2010.[5] Executive Order 13423 also directed agencies with 20 or more vehicles to reduce their fleet fuel consumption by 2 percent annually.[6]

Immediately upon taking office, the new president should issue a new executive order updating the targets for renewable energy consumption goals and the levels of energy efficiency required by all government agencies with respect to their electric power consumption, consumption of transportation and other fuels, choice of vehicles, and level of greenhouse gas emissions. He should also direct agencies to purchase, whenever possible, the most fuel-efficient vehicles, including plug-in hybrid electric vehicles once they become available. Until these energy-efficient vehicles become available, the order could also direct agencies to purchase only one of the three most efficient models in each class of vehicles, unless the cabinet secretary certifies that none of the available cars meet the agency's requirements.

In addition, the new president also should seek to use the purchasing power of the federal government to help accomplish its energy goals. The government's procurement system should offer additional "energy points" in the award of contracts for products and services. Bidders would receive the points to the extent they can demonstrate that they have achieved, or have plans to achieve, greater energy efficiency and use of renewable energy in their own operations and in the products and services they seek to provide. By requiring some of the largest government contractors and suppliers to adopt efficiency and renewable energy goals in their own operations, the government would not only be saving energy and stimulating renewable energy demand itself, but it would also be leveraging efficiency and the use of renewable energy in its private sector supply chain. Finally, the president's budget should provide sufficient funding to the department's Federal Energy Management Program, allowing it to adequately assist other agencies to meet their obligations under the order.

The Strategic Petroleum Reserve

The Strategic Petroleum Reserve, a government-owned crude-oil reserve established in the mid-1970s in the wake of the 1973–74 oil embargo, is our nation's first line of defense against oil supply interruptions.[7] Since 2000, the Bush administration expanded the SPR from 540 million to 700 million barrels of oil.[8] Although the Energy Policy Act of 2005 directed the Department of Energy to expand the capacity of the reserve to 1 billion barrels and to fill it to that level,[9] in May 2008 Congress passed legislation suspending filling of the SPR through the end of 2008.[10]

The congressional ban on filling the SPR will expire shortly before the new president takes office. Before adding any additional oil to the reserve, however, the new secretary of energy should initiate a process to develop clear guidelines for its use. Spending billions of dollars to fill the reserve without any clear sense of how and when it might be used risks a significant waste of government resources. There is general agreement that the reserve should be available as a response to supply interruptions, and not used in response to price spikes driven by market fundamentals. As we have seen over the last 18 months, however, the effects of supply interruptions can be indistinguishable from the effects of routine, if jarring, market volatility. Yet, while it is generally regarded as appropriate to use the reserve in response to supply interruptions, presidents have typically indicated that they would not,[11] and in fact legally cannot,[12] release oil from the SPR in response to high prices.[13] Therefore, establishing clear guidelines for the use of the SPR presents a significant challenge.

The reserve is already large enough to serve as a "strategic" reserve that can respond to physical supply disruptions related to acts of war or terrorism. The Department of Energy now can release up to 4.4 million barrels of crude oil per day for three months—roughly 22 percent of U.S. daily consumption—after which the release rate declines as the reserve is emptied.[14] This is an amount sufficient to respond to nearly any terrorist event or war that temporarily interrupts oil supplies. Case in point: during the Gulf War in January 1991 the first Bush administration placed 33 million barrels of the reserve's oil on sale, but the market purchased only 17 million.[15]

Today's reserve, however, is far too small and probably could never be made large enough to respond meaningfully to a catastrophic loss of oil resulting from a crisis involving a long-term interruption in the flow of oil. Likewise, the reserve is never likely to be large enough to work well as an economic reserve that could moderate the price of oil over a sustained period of time, even if policymakers wanted to insert the government directly into oil markets in such a fashion. Moreover, the effect on markets of such intervention might well be a reduction in private stocks because of fear that government decision makers might at any time decide to flood the market with oil from the reserve. In addition, exporters worldwide might be expected to reduce their sales to compensate for prolonged release of oil from the reserve.

Of the five major price oil price spikes we have experienced over the past 35 years, three have been related to Organization of the Petroleum Exporting Countries decisions to constrain supplies; one was the result of the loss of OPEC capacity associated with Iraq's invasion of Kuwait and the Gulf War; and the fifth was related primarily to surging demand for oil in developing markets. Yet as easily as we can release oil from the reserve in response to demand-induced price increases or OPEC's exercise of market power, demand can continue to grow or OPEC can simply cut output further.

Because worldwide demand may be stronger, or OPEC's pockets may be deeper than our reserves, we could drain the reserve before OPEC runs out of money or worldwide demand for oil slackens. Given the complex issues regarding its proper use, the secretary of energy should initiate a process to establish criteria for use of the reserve. Of particular importance is a review of Organisation of Economic Co-operation and Development nations' reserve policies and how well those policies work in coordination with each other. Subsequently, the DOE secretary should initiate a study to determine the appropriate size for the reserve, and based on the outcome of that process, offer new recommendations regarding the size and operation of the reserve to Congress.

Energy Technologies, Energy Education
The new secretary should ask the national labs, academic research institutions, the National Academy of Sciences, and others to conduct a review of critical energy technologies. The purpose of the review would be to identify those energy-related technologies that have the potential to transform national and international energy markets, including those technologies that could play a

role in helping achieve major reductions in greenhouse gas emissions. The review will detail the technical and economic hurdles to the commercialization of such technologies, and then make recommendations regarding the type of research and development or additional incentives that could help overcome the barriers. The conclusions would be presented to the new president and his chief energy advisors to incorporate into the government's research agenda, budget, and policies as appropriate, and, to the degree possible, to incorporate into the national energy plan.

This review should be accompanied by a DOE-led effort to improve our nation's energy literacy. Despite the fact that some of our energy problems have festered for over three decades now, many Americans still lack a clear understanding of the combined challenges of oil dependence and climate change. Accordingly, shortly after the completion of an updated energy plan, the department should initiate a national campaign to both improve energy literacy and to explain and sell the new plan.

Improving energy literacy is important because unless the public has a better understanding of the nature of our energy problems, it will be difficult to enlist their support for policies that may involve new choices, tradeoffs, opportunities, and priorities. This campaign could help inform the country about opportunities to purchase "green power" from renewable sources; take advantage of time-of-day or real-time electric rates; and save money by using compact fluorescent bulbs and more efficient heating, ventilating, and air conditioning equipment, water heaters, and other major appliances. The campaign also will disseminate information to help all Americans take advantage of new programs and incentives that encourage the use of energy-wise products and renewable fuels. Less flashy but still very practical benefits to be highlighted by the campaign include those associated with adding insulation and better windows to homes, the availability of state and federal tax credits for the purchase of energy-efficient products and equipment, and the other opportunities that will arise in a world of new and transformed energy technology.

The First Year

The transition to a low-carbon economy will require significant innovation in the private sector in order to commercialize transformative technologies necessary to meet our energy-related goals. Yet today we lack the trained technicians, scientists, and engineers and the research base to meet our future needs. Taking steps to fill this gap over the next decade is a clear first-year priority for the new secretary of energy.

The energy sector of the economy employs over 1 million people, half of whom are over 50 years old and eligible to retire within the next decade.[16] Among those retiring will be the engineers and scientists needed to develop the innovations that will transform the energy sector. Further complicating the picture is the fact that fewer students are training to enter the industry. Enrollment in petroleum engineering and geosciences programs, for instance, has fallen by 75 percent over the last 25 years.[17] With declining enrollments, many university programs that trained students for the energy industry have themselves closed, complicating the effort to rebuild the industry's workforce.[18]

To meet this shortcoming, Congress should establish a scholarship program through the Department of Energy to fund annually 1,000 undergraduate and 500 graduate students studying engineering, geosciences, and other energy-related fields. Emphasis should be placed on training chemists who might develop advanced biofuels; physicists who might develop new materials that store energy; and engineers who are necessary to design and build an advanced electrical grid, advanced wind turbines and solar cells, and more efficient cars. Geologists, too, remain important as they can assist in the responsible development of traditional fuels that will be necessary to support our economy until we more fully develop advanced and sustainable fuels. If we fail to train the next generation of technical experts in the energy field, we will be unable to transform our energy future. Such a program would cost less than $100 million annually and would require new legislation.

Nuclear Weapons Complex
The Department of Energy's nuclear weapons complex has a storied history of innovation, scientific excellence, and dedication to national security. With the end of the cold war, the complex responded competently to the new challenges of maintaining the safety, security, reliability, and performance of the nation's nuclear weapons stockpile, without actual nuclear testing. Today, however, the complex faces many problems that must be addressed if it is to continue to meet its national security responsibilities. Those problems include aging facilities, the need to preserve key skills and knowledge, and the challenge of rising costs in the face of constrained budgets.

The complex's most significant problem, however, and the one that intersects with all the others, is the uncertainty regarding both the future size of the nation's nuclear arsenal and the type of weapons it will comprise. By almost any measure, the size and composition of the stockpile already ensures that the United States will have a fearsome deterrent for many years to come. But decisions about how that stockpile is managed, and how it may change in the future, will play a major role in determining the organization and require-ments of the weapons complex.

Congress and the Bush administration differed sharply with regard to some of the administration's key initiatives involving the complex. Congress, for ex-ample, denied funding for construction of the Reliable Replacement Warhead. The current fiscal year 2009 budget request, which the incoming president must rework, seeks five times as much funding for nuclear weapons activities than for its nuclear nonproliferation work—a request unlikely to be fully funded by Congress.

For more than two years, the National Nuclear Security Administration, the semiautonomous organization within DOE that manages the weapons pro-gram and complex, has studied alternative approaches to the management and reorganization of the nuclear complex. But even those efforts are unlikely to produce a workable pathway to the future absent a coherent plan that puts the administration of the weapons complex in the larger framework of the nation's national security needs, including its nonproliferation and international weapons-reduction goals.

To address such issues, the new energy secretary, together with the secre-taries of defense and state and the president's national security advisor, should organize an effort to define a new, long-term nuclear weapons stockpile strat-egy. The strategy should reflect the new administration's policies and the reali-ties of the nation's post-cold war deterrence and nonproliferation objectives. In addition, DOE should produce a long-term plan for reconfiguring the weapons complex to meet the needs of the strategy while cutting costs, reducing dupli-cation, and decommissioning unneeded facilities.

Reform Alternative Fuel Subsidies

The U.S. government for years has subsidized the production of corn-based ethanol because promoting the production of domestic biofuels was viewed as an important national policy. While it remains so today, the rationale for the current level of support is less compelling. Over the past six years, gasoline prices jumped significantly,[19] far above the historic cost of producing ethanol. Because ethanol is a substitute for gasoline, the price of ethanol is closely re-lated to the price of gasoline. The price of ethanol, therefore, has risen in recent years along with the price of gasoline, thus eliminating the need for a subsidy to make corn-based ethanol production profitable.

Two other developments also contributed to the creation of robust demand for ethanol. First, refiners switched from MTBE, or methyl butyl tertiary ether, to ethanol to meet certain Clean Air Act requirements when they began to face legal liability associated with MTBE's potential for contaminating drinking water. Second, the Energy Independence and Security Act of 2007 included a renewable fuel standard requiring oil companies to use 36 billion gallons of alternative liquid fuels annually by 2022.[20] Yet, despite that government mandate and the other incentives for using ethanol, which together effectively guarantee a market for the product, the government continues to support its already profitable production with a fuel blender's credit of 45 cents per gallon of corn-based ethanol.[21]

Based on a forecast by the Energy Information Administration of ethanol production, the subsidy could cost over $5 billion in 2010, and $7.5 billion in 2015,[22] or more than double the energy technology research and development budget for the entire Department of Energy in FY2008.[23] It is difficult to justify such a large subsidy to the manufacturers of a product for which the government has guaranteed a market. The general rationale for creating any production subsidy is that without it, a product important to the nation would not otherwise be produced. Ethanol and other alternative liquid fuels clearly do not meet this standard, given the fuel mandate in the 2007 energy law.

Nevertheless, there remains a concern that if oil and gasoline prices fall, they might undermine the economic viability of ethanol. Accordingly, the government should replace its subsidies and tax credits for alternative liquid fuels with a government-backed insurance program. The government should offer producers a guarantee that it will purchase all of a producer's alternative fuel production at a specified price, effectively insuring that their operations will remain profitable irrespective of the market price of gasoline. The government could offer to purchase all ethanol at the price of about $60 per barrel of oil equivalent, with minimal risk and minimal, if any, cost. Should prices fall below that level, the government would either pay the difference between the floor price and the market price, or resell the product directly into the market. As of July 2008, the Energy Information Agency and the futures market all project that the price of oil will not fall below $70 a barrel for the foreseeable future, in which case, the program would cost the government nothing.[24]

In exchange for a government guarantee that such alternative fuel businesses will always remain profitable, they should be required to make a payment to the government when prices are above a specified threshold. In short, the government would guarantee that the production of alternative fuel could always be profitable in exchange for a portion of those profits when they rise above a certain level. Were the government to charge a premium of 15 percent of the price above $120 per barrel of oil equivalent, the program would likely generate some revenue for the government.

This initiative will require legislation, and it will be controversial because it would effectively end the subsidies of several billion dollars to ethanol producers. But such a move would provide critically needed transparency to fuel subsidy programs, save taxpayers billions of dollars (some of which could be invested in developing new, low-carbon advanced biofuels from non-food sources), and ensure the profitability of alternative fuel production, so long as producers are willing to participate in the program. This program, if enacted, would eliminate alternative fuel producers' concerns that their production would become uneconomic due to falling oil prices.

Modernize U.S. Electric Grid

Modernizing the nation's electric grid represents one of the most potentially significant infrastructure improvements that can be made by a new administration. Today, the grid is an outdated, balky relic of the last century.[25] Fortunately, technologies already exist to make it not only more reliable, resilient, and secure, but also more of an engine for new economic growth that promotes energy efficiency and renewable sources of electricity.

In a number of areas of the country, the electric transmission system is overburdened, and as congestion grows, additional costs are imposed on the economy.[26] DOE estimates, for example, that congestion charges in 2008 will add $8 billion—about $40 a person—to electricity costs in the eastern grid, which serves all states east of the Rockies except for Texas.[27] The system also provides uncertain protection from cascading blackouts, which may be triggered in one place and spill over into multistate regions.[28] An outdated grid also represents a lost opportunity to stimulate the construction and use of large-scale renewable energy facilities, as well as distributed generation, or localized electricity generation, often from renewable sources. It also inhibits the use of energy-saving technologies such as "smart" meters that can track time-of-day energy use, locally generated power sold back into the grid, etc.

To address these problems, the new administration should double the funding for DOE's grid R&D activities, including those designed to produce breakthroughs in electricity storage and transmission efficiency. As part of that effort, DOE should identify basic research needs that could establish a basis for another wave of technological innovation applicable to the grid.

DOE should also engage utilities and states (including state utility commissions) in the development of policies designed to encourage the development and use of both software and hardware systems supporting a modern grid. The Federal Power Act should be amended to require the Federal Energy Regulatory Commission to offer rate incentives for investment in "smart-grid" technology. Furthermore, the Energy Policy of 2005 granted the federal government the authority to approve the siting of certain transmission lines in designated "national interest electric transmission corridors" where transmission congestion or constraints adversely affect consumers. Congress should expand FERC's backstop transmission line permitting authority in order to allow it also to approve the siting of high voltage transmission lines serving areas designated as having significant potential to generate renewable energy.

Finally, to promote the development of an advanced electrical grid, the next president should propose that Congress require that, after a specified date, utilities may only install advanced electrical meters, capable of metering time-of-day or real time pricing and offering other functionality as determined appropriate by the department in promoting new services, energy efficiency, and renewable energy using an advanced electrical grid.

Longer-Term Agenda

The necessary transformation to a low-carbon energy economy cannot occur without technological innovation. Yet the approximately $70 billion spent by the government over the last 30 years on energy-related research, development, and demonstration projects has failed to deliver the transformative technology that will drive the energy revolution.[29] Today, expenditure of DOE's research funds is not guided in a coordinated fashion, is not designed to develop commercially viable technologies, is not coordinated with relevant research in other government agencies or the private sector, and is too heavily reliant on direct financing. DOE needs to completely reform the manner in which it establishes research priorities and funds research.

The foundation of a revised approach to research should be an interagency council empowered to develop and guide implementation of the government's energy research, development, and deployment agenda. The structure and mandate of this new council is discussed in detail in the White House section of this book.

Similarly, the new secretary should develop a series of prizes, with substantial financial rewards, to spur the development of transformative energy technologies. There exists a long-standing history of using prizes to induce clearly defined technological achievements, from Charles Lindbergh's solo trip across the Atlantic Ocean in pursuit of the $25,000 Orteig Prize to Burt Rutan and

Paul Allen's design of SpaceShipOne, which won the $10 million Ansari X Prize for building and launching a spacecraft.[30] Prizes have several appealing features, including that they have no cost in the absence of a winner and motivate innovators to innovate while eliminating paperwork or bureaucracy for the government. For those reasons, parties as diverse as Newt Gingrich and the National Academy of Science have promoted the use of prizes.[31] An earlier prize sponsored by DOE and other parties in the early 1990s, the Super Efficient Refrigerator Contest,[32] facilitated the development of a highly efficient refrigerator, thereby saving millions of dollars of power and significantly reducing power plant emissions.

Prizes could be awarded, for instance, to help overcome particularly complex threshold problems in the development of transformative vehicles, such as the development of an onboard reformer to produce hydrogen for a fuel cell. The secretary also should initiate a competition to develop, manufacture, and market an ultra-high-efficiency car, or a non-petroleum-fueled automobile. The first automobile manufacturer to sell 1 million qualifying vehicles will be eligible for a significant cash prize, with a smaller prize for the second-place finisher. The competition would accelerate the development of ultra-high-efficiency and/or non-petroleum-fueled vehicles. Accelerating their development will ensure not only that we reap the benefits of a highly efficient or a non-petroleum-fueled fleet sooner, but also that the United States achieves a position of technological leadership allowing for the creation of more manufacturing jobs and opportunities for increased exports of our newly developed technology. Such a program would require legislation.

The DOE also should play a lead role in accelerating development of appliance efficiency standards. The department's current appliance efficiency standards require a range of household and commercially used appliances, including refrigerators, furnaces, air conditioners, and washing machines, to achieve certain levels of efficiency.[33] The efficiency standards, which apply to all newly sold appliances, are designed to remove the most inefficient products from the marketplace while leaving a range of efficient appliances available to consumers.

Better efficiency standards are important, however, because they would address several shortcomings in today's marketplace that facilitate the purchase of inefficient appliances. First, bulk purchasers of appliances, such as builders or landlords, mostly buy inexpensive and inefficient appliances while others incur the operating costs of the appliances. Second, quick purchases by consumers frequently made in response to failure of old appliances often result in the purchase of the cheapest product.

Current law requires DOE to establish initial standards for certain appliances and to review existing standards on a regular basis.[34] Under the Bush administration, the program stagnated. For instance, over the past seven years, the department issued exactly two new standards, one of which, the furnace standard, effectively failed to meaningfully increase the standard above the least efficient appliances currently in the market.[35] Moreover, DOE failed to meet numerous statutory deadlines for the issuance of other standards, and currently is subject to a consent decree that requires the issuance of approximately 20 new standards before 2012.[36] In addition, the Energy Independence and Security Act of 2007 requires the issuance of new standards for about 10 products.[37]

The new secretary of energy should quickly issue revised appliance efficiency standards. He or she should ensure that the program is adequately funded and staffed, and establish as a goal the issuance of new standards as quickly as possible—without waiting for the deadlines established by statute. The more quickly we can introduce more efficient appliances into the market, the sooner we will achieve the critical savings created by this program.

When increasing attention to the program, the secretary also should direct the department to develop standards that provide the greatest economically justified savings possible, once again to maximize savings to the economy. And as new standards are developed for household appliances, the department should determine if the appliance is one that would benefit from an ability to engage in two-way communications with electricity management software or real-time price signals sent by a utility. For instance, a consumer could choose to set a dishwasher or clothes dryer to initiate a cycle only during off-peak hours or when either prices or load fell below a specified level. For those appliances, DOE should require that the appliance incorporate technology necessary to facilitate such communications and controls.

Improve Residential Energy Efficiency

Nearly 40 percent of all electricity consumed is consumed in residences.[38] Yet this obvious opportunity to reduce residential power consumption lacks enough initiatives to support improvements. Much of the focus on increasing energy efficiency in homes is focused on lighting, which accounts for less than 9 percent of residential power consumption, and on the use of efficient appliances. But many other opportunities to increase household energy efficiency, including those that involve the construction of the house and the installation of even more efficient appliances, are never undertaken simply because homeowners are unaware of the opportunities and their potential payback.

Many of the unrecognized opportunities to improve residential energy efficiency could be identified through household energy audits. Energy audits assess how much energy a home uses and identify measures that can increase its efficiency. In addition to evaluating the efficiency of a home's heating and cooling systems and major appliances, auditors often use blowers that identify leaks in a structure alongside infrared cameras, which also can reveal leaks and areas with insufficient insulation. By identifying places that a home is losing energy and suggesting improvements, audits can help homeowners save energy and money.

To promote the use of energy audits, Congress could establish a tax credit equal to 50 percent of the cost of a certified home energy audit, subject to a maximum credit. The Department of Energy could establish minimum requirements for a certified audit, including one that the auditor provide the homeowner with a list of energy saving investments and their payback period. While such a tax credit would not require that homeowners actually take steps to improve the efficiency of their homes, it would identify for them cost-effective measures to cut their energy consumption. With that critical information in hand, consumers would hopefully make investments in efficiency, especially those investments that offer them relatively quick paybacks.

Department of Veterans Affairs
Seriously Caring for Our Wounded Warriors

GAIL R. WILENSKY

The Department of Veterans Affairs must help the men and women of the U.S. armed forces make a successful and seamless transition from active duty to veteran status. Significant attention should be paid to the care of the severely wounded, but transition challenges exist for all 800,000 service members who have served in Iraq and Afghanistan and since left the military. More progress needs to be made on the successful treatment of traumatic brain injury and post-traumatic stress disorder. The number of newly discharged veterans also emphasizes the need to revise and restructure the disability evaluation system—by automating the process and simplifying the rules with clearer and more consistent decision making. In the long term, the new administration will need to reconsider the role of the VA—as an agency primarily focusing on the diseases and injuries related to military service or as an agency providing primary care and outpatient services to traditional VA users in partnership with academic health centers. The expansion of health care coverage to most or all Americans may further change the role of the VA.

The United States has not faced the challenges associated with reintegrating wounded and non-wounded combat troops into a peacetime society since the Vietnam War period. And the country has never had the experience of integrating a returning military that looks like the present military—all volunteer, older, more female, and with large numbers of National Guard and Reservists, although the bulk of deployments is still carried out by active duty personnel. New breakthroughs, such as the remarkable success in lowered mortality rates, also led to new challenges for the military and veterans' health care system in providing the coordinated care necessary for treating severely injured individuals.

The VA operates programs that provide health care; financial assistance, primarily involving disability compensation; and burial benefits to veterans and their families. The VA historically cared primarily for veterans who have service-related disabilities or are indigent; most who receive care through the VA were not career military, since career military retirees have typically used the military's Tricare program. In 1996, the Veterans Healthcare Eligibility Reform Act provided a uniform health care benefit package to all veterans, regardless of service connection or income—although the secretary of veterans affairs was given the authority to limit enrollment eligibility if necessary.[1] The only group currently closed to enrollment is category 8 veterans—non-service connected veterans above a certain income level—who did not enroll prior to 2003.

VA users come from a variety of military experiences, but many of the World War II veterans use the VA as their exclusive source of care. Further, some of the pioneering changes introduced in the VA during the 1990s, such as the use of electronic patient records and bar coding to guarantee the safe dispensing of drugs, greatly improved the quality of care being provided by the VA, and thus its attractiveness.

About 3 million veterans are currently receiving health care on a regular basis through the VA, and about 5.5 million received some care in 2007; another 2 million are enrolled but do not use services. The number receiving services includes some 300,000 veterans who served either in Iraq or Afghanistan out of a total of about 800,000 who served there and subsequently left the military. The users, or even those enrolled, are only a fraction of the approximately 25 million total veterans, most of whom receive care paid for by private insurance and/or Medicare or Tricare.[2]

VA spending in 2007 was almost equally divided between money spent on health care ($32.2 billion) and money spent on pensions and compensation ($34.6 billion), although the estimated spending for 2008 shows a sharp increase for pensions and disability compensation to $41.7 billion, versus $34 billion for medical care.[3] Bush administration requests for 2009 again show an increase in total funding to $94 billion, with $47 billion in discretionary spending, mostly for health care.[4]

The substantial increases in funding reflect both the increased demands being placed on the VA and frustration with periodic reported shortfalls in the availability of needed care. VA health benefits, unlike pensions and disability, are paid for out of the discretionary budget rather than as a mandatory payment or entitlement. Changes to how health benefits are financed could therefore have significant budgetary consequences, particularly if enrollment was again opened to category 8 veterans, which would lead to a potentially large increase in users.

The new administration will face challenges on each side of the VA. Foremost among them will be the transition issues for those moving from active duty or reserves to veteran's status, including the "Wounded Warriors" program—case management for the very severely injured. This will be particularly important due to the very public focus on deficiencies in care for some returning wounded from Iraq and Afghanistan.

Equally important will be assistance for all who leave the military as they transition back to their peacetime activities, including making contact with recently discharged combat veterans who have not contacted the VA. Their transition will focus attention on the need for more and better ways to treat the signature injuries of the Iraq war—traumatic brain injury and post-traumatic stress disorder.

The newly discharged veterans will also heighten the need to consolidate and rationalize the disability evaluation process—although this is much bigger than just a transition issue. Timely processing of disability claims will continue to be a political "time bomb" for the new administration. Automation strategies need to be explored and implemented wherever feasible, modernizing what is now a heavily paper-based system. Continuing attention also needs to be given to modernizing and improving the information technology system, including transforming the existing electronic health record system into a web-based system and ensuring that the electronic systems in the VA and Department of Defense can work together more effectively.

There are several long-term issues that will also need VA attention. The most important will be to clarify the role of the VA in an evolving U.S. health care system, including the role of the VA if insurance coverage is expanded to all Americans.

The First 100 Days

The VA secretary is obviously the most important person to have in place early on. The new president must appoint a secretary who is comfortable and effective working with veterans' groups and the Congress, and able to provide policy and administrative leadership to a very large and sprawling enterprise. If the new secretary is not administratively and operationally savvy, in addition to having good political skills, the new administration should appoint a deputy who can take on the operations management of the department. A background in veterans' issues, or at least a proven track record administering a large organization, is also essential. This is not a place for the substantively unsophisticated—or the uncommitted.

The deputy VA secretary and undersecretaries will also be important to a smooth transition. Yet the undersecretaries are selected using a different, lengthier process from other political appointees. A commission appointed by the secretary interviews candidates and makes at least three recommendations for each position to the secretary and the White House for nomination. The new president, in consultation with the secretary, chooses a candidate who must then be confirmed by the Senate.

The various assistant secretaries are also important to have in place as quickly as possible, particularly those for policy and management. Because there tend to be fewer political Senior Executive Service appointments in the VA, the focus should be on getting the limited number in leadership positions on board quickly. The undersecretary for benefits is currently unfilled; if the position remains unfilled at the end of the Bush administration, filling it quickly will be especially urgent. Disability claims processing is an area that continues to be regarded as "challenged," and not having a confirmed person at its head exacerbates existing problems.

The VA has a particular need for consulting special interest groups as it transitions. The veterans service organizations, or VSOs, as they are called, particularly the "big six"—the American Legion, the Veterans of Foreign Wars, the Disabled American Veterans, American Veterans, the Vietnam Veterans of America, and the Paralyzed Veterans of America—represent an unusually powerful constituency. It is important for the new secretary to establish contact early on and build an effective outreach strategy and personal relationship with them. What makes this particularly challenging is that the various VSOs frequently have competing agendas even though they are all focused on improving veterans' well being.

The VA secretary also needs to articulate a limited number of themes for the first term. Although the VA has made major strides in improving operations, more needs to be accomplished within the first two years of the new administration. The VA should set three critical goals: continue to improve the effective delivery of care and support to U.S. veterans, improve the transition process from active duty to veteran status, and clarify and reassess the philosophy and purpose of the disability system.

Active Duty to Veteran

For each of the most important operational issues surrounding this transition process, an assessment should be performed to identify the "root causes" of each problem. The most important operational issues relating to the transition include claims processing, case management, traumatic brain injury and post-traumatic stress disorder, information technology, and the GI bill of education and vocational rehabilitation benefits.

Reducing claims processing times has been an important objective of the VA for the past several years. Because claims processing drives the system by establishing eligibility for VA services, anything that slows this process generates a lot of adverse publicity and frustration, even though a substantial portion of the backlog in disability judgments can be attributed to veterans reopening and/or refiling claims.

The recent decision to provide five years of free care for all veterans who have served in a combat theater since November 11, 1998, makes the linkage less critical for the receipt of medical care, at least in the short term. Nonetheless, the need to move away from the current heavily paper-based system to an electronic system is urgent and would both facilitate access to information and expedite the process. The VA should undertake a short turnaround external audit of the claims system to provide the secretary with options and any financial or legal constraints regarding their adoption. Even though the Government Accountability Office has done a series of reports on this issue, including one as recently as February 2008, the new secretary may find that a fresh look would be helpful.[5]

Resolving some of the claims-processing challenges may require agreement on the more fundamental changes that need to be made to the VA disability compensation program. These issues will likely be highly charged, and agreements will need to be made as to how much change is politically feasible, as well as what the financial implications will be of any changes in the compensation philosophy and strategy, such as whether and how much to compensate for quality-of-life losses.

In addition, the VA will need to assess the value of the "recovery coordinators" who were hired as a result of the so called Dole-Shalala recommendations to help patients and their families navigate through the various care processes and make sure they receive the care appropriate for their injuries. The evaluation should establish whether they are providing useful services, and also whether the concept is working as intended. Particular focus should be given to whether the recovery coordinators are providing the needed coordination between DoD and the VA, and also whether it is clear who has overall responsibility for each individual veteran at key stages in the veteran's recovery process.

The VA in particular should pay substantial attention to how effectively it is addressing traumatic brain injury and post-traumatic stress disorder. Although these two are distinct disorders, a number of service members have both, and each can result from the same trauma. They are not new injuries, but the number of soldiers who are at risk is very large. A recent Rand Corporation report concluded that 300,000 of the 1.64 million soldiers deployed to Iraq and Afghanistan since October 2001 may have experienced PTSD or major depression, and 320,000 have experienced probable TBI.[6]

Continued investments need to be made in the treatment and prevention of these disorders, as well as in research into their overlap and linkages. This is one of several areas where better coordination with the Defense Department is vital, particularly with regard to the prevention of the injuries.

For more than 10 years, Congress has pressured the VA to assess its information technology and work with DoD to improve both its IT systems and, more importantly, the interoperability between the two systems, including joint development of an inpatient record. The VA, which has received considerable favorable attention for its pioneering use of electronic medical records, is in the process of modernizing its Veterans Health Information Systems and Technology Architecture, or VistA, for maintaining electronic health records; it will be moving to a Microsoft Windows–based system over time.

This means that the VA will not be relying on its own homegrown system in the future, as it has done in the past, which may provide it with greater flexibility and potentially more interoperability with other systems. A report assessing the progress of joint DoD-VA IT efforts is due in 2008. As of late 2007, interoperability between DoD and the VA was primarily limited to ancillary services on the outpatient record for such areas as lab, pharmacy, and imaging services. An update should be done in the first quarter of 2009 assessing further progress both internal to the VA and with respect to progress on interoperability. Establishing a functional exchange of information, with or without full interoperability, is as much a matter for DoD as it is for the VA.

The last key area of assessment should be of the variability of benefits received and the adequacy and effectiveness of the Montgomery GI education bill, as well as support for vocational rehabilitation programs. After months of discussion, a new GI bill was included in the War Supplemental bill signed into law on June 30, 2008. The new benefit, provided to veterans who have served at least 90 days of active duty since 9/11, will cover the cost of education at any public institution capped at the cost of the most expensive public college or university in the state. A book supply and a monthly living stipend are also provided. Reservists will receive a percentage based on the length of their active-duty service. The VA will begin implementing the program mid-2009 with benefits transferable to both spouses and children. It should be possible to assess the new educational benefits bill before the end of the next presidential term to determine whether it is producing the desired results.

Defining Disability

The VA will have to appoint a senior-level group to revisit narrow issues regarding rule definitions that govern the disability assessment process, as well as consider broader philosophical questions about the underlying purpose of the disability system. Some of the specific issues that should be considered are the need for limits on the number of claims, along with the number of reviews; strategies to circumvent the separation between the Veterans Benefits Administration and the Veterans Health Administration; the potential for "over-classifying" PTSD/TBI in ways that prevent people from getting well; and progress on a VA pilot project that started in November 2007 to test the feasibility of a single disability determination.

At a broader level, the goals, objectives, and strategies of the Dole-Shalala Commission appear to be different from those articulated by the Veterans' Disability Benefits Commission.[7] An assessment of these differences and the preferred positioning needs to occur during the first 100 days. The Dole-Shalala Commission proposed transition payments to assess the level of training and assistance needed to have injured veterans reach the highest functional level possible and support veterans during the resulting training process. After the completion of the training, a follow-up assessment would be needed to determine whether any continuing loss in earnings capacity would be likely, and if so, the amount needed to compensate for the loss in earnings.

The Dole-Shalala Commission also proposed compensating for a quality-of-life decrement, or whether the veteran experienced a loss in earnings capacity. The Disability Benefits Commission focused on average impairment, which a person with a particular disability would experience without any reference to the capabilities and future earning power that someone with appropriate training and assistance could achieve. The commission also viewed compensation as appropriately reflecting loss in quality of life.

The First Year

The assessment of problems in claims processing, case management, TBI and PTSD, and information technology undertaken during the first 100 days should reveal various problems that need to be remedied. To the extent that corrective strategies can be identified during the presidential transition, some solutions could be ready for Inauguration Day executive orders, but others will need more deliberation. For the problems that can be remedied administratively, officials should develop timelines regarding milestones and other measurable endpoints and should assess these on a quarterly basis until completed.

Most or all of the changes involved in claims processing improvements should be administrative, although the budgetary implications may require a several-year transition process. Among the issues for resolution will be whether the acquisition of high-speed scanners is the most effective way to convert the paper-based application process to a digitized system or whether another strategy should be adopted, and whether a call center strategy should be adopted that would allow easy access to the digitized data.

Equally important is agreement on the workflow process and its relationship to the existing efforts that take place in the 57 regional offices around the country. If legislation is needed to expedite the move to an automated processing system and to a consolidated workflow process, it should be ready for submission no later than the end of the first year. The affected congressional offices and/or the Veterans Service Organizations may resist these developments; the VA should therefore make the effort to work with the affected groups during the first year.

Following the assessment of recovery coordinators during the first 100 days, the VA should modify the concept of the recovery coordinator to address whatever weaknesses have been uncovered, or bring the needed complement of coordinators to the level appropriate for the existing severely wounded veteran population. The appropriate roles for all case managers beyond those for the severely wounded will also need to be assessed. There is still much that is unsettled regarding the proper mix of individuals needed to provide support to the various levels of wounded veterans. New legislation is not needed, but coordination with the Department of Defense will be critical.

Developing the next generation of VistA electronic health records, moving to Health-e-Vet, the improved web-based system, and creating an interoperable inpatient record system with DoD should not require new legislation. The GAO did recommend in a 2007 report that the VA and DoD make a detailed project-management plan describing the technical and managerial processes that are needed to finish the project. This recommendation needs to be implemented and monitored so that previous slippages are less likely to occur or will be more easily identified earlier in the process if they do occur, and can be remedied in an appropriate and timely manner.

Revamp Disability Determination Process

The Senior Disability group working with the VA secretary should develop a legislative package outlining proposed changes in the disability assessment process. This should follow the review during the first 100 days of recommendations from Dole-Shalala, the Veterans' Disability Benefits Commission, the numerous reports by GAO over the past two years, and an assessment of the pilot project that is establishing a single comprehensive disability exam for use by the VA and DoD.

There is not sufficient data to date to make a decision about whether the ongoing pilot establishing a single disability assessment by the VA and DoD is workable. GAO has raised questions as to whether current evaluation plans will be able to provide a credible mechanism for measuring consistency, timeliness, and accuracy of decisions against the current process. But hopefully any such deficiencies will be corrected before, or if, the pilot is expanded in 2008.

Joint determination of a disability rating by the two departments has the potential to reduce much of the variation that has existed to date in disability ratings across the services and between the military and VA. DoD's determination of less than a 30 percent disability rating has been a particularly contentious issue since anyone who receives a rating of at least 30 percent is entitled to Tricare, whereas those who have a rating less than 30 percent are considered medically unfit for the military, but are not eligible for Tricare by virtue of their disability.

Outside of the pilot, DoD and the VA make separate determinations about a service member's disability. Defense focuses on whether service members are fit or unfit to perform military duties. Their decision determines not only Tricare receipt for the member and his or her family, but also military compensation. The VA's disability rating system determines the amount of VA compensation the veteran receives and also eligibility for a variety of other benefits. DoD and the VA each have complicated rating systems that take months (at least) to complete.

Service members can challenge the rating, which means a decision can take years to resolve. It is probably not surprising that under such a complex system, ratings differ by military service and by VA regional offices. Typically, ratings by the DoD are not only different than the VA ratings, but are also lower. These different outcomes occur despite the use of the same outdated rating schedule by both the DoD and the VA.

If the joint determination pilot is unsuccessful, further consideration may be given to the Dole-Shalala recommendation to have the services determine medical fitness and the VA act as the sole arbiter of disability. While this separation would resolve DoD/VA variability, the variability across the VA still needs to be reduced, although as GAO has noted, the VA has already instituted an aggressive quality assurance program for this purpose and plans to begin quarterly monitoring of compensation and pension determinations.

More fundamental than variability is developing greater clarity in the relationship between physical or mental impairments and work. The VA's basic approach in determining earnings losses associated with various disabilities has been described as embodying a post-WWII mentality that neither reflects the scientific advancements nor the social and economic changes between disabilities and work. Given the move from a labor and manufacturing-based economy to a service and knowledge-based economy, many of the disabilities that may have significantly impaired earnings in an earlier era are no longer likely to be relevant with proper training and education. Yet impairments associated with PTSD or TBI, which were less relevant in earlier periods, clearly may be less amenable to training and education and will have to be a part of whatever new determinations are used.

The VA is attempting to update its criteria for evaluating brain injuries, but the more fundamental challenge is to determine the purpose and function of the disability payment. This includes both "real," or expected, loss in earnings capacity post-training and education, and decrements in quality of life, irrespective of the earnings loss. Decisions in these areas will also help clarify the future roles of the Montgomery GI Bill and vocational rehabilitation in meeting these goals, particularly for military returning from Iraq and Afghanistan.

Longer-Term Agenda

The VA has traditionally relied on services provided by physicians, nurses, pharmacists, and other health care workers that are direct employees of the VA, although many of the physicians are also affiliated with academic health centers and partly paid by them as well. Prior to the 1990s, the VA relied on the "bricks and mortar" approach of providing most services through the VA hospitals. Since that time, there has been an increased reliance on community-based outpatient clinics, or CBOCs, for services that can be provided in an outpatient setting. The increasing use of CBOCs and continued expansion of CBOCs has allowed the VA to reach veterans in more convenient geographic settings and at a far lower cost than would be incurred building new hospital facilities.

The VA has been much slower to take the next step: to integrate the purchase of services from the private sector when it experiences temporary increases in demand or is otherwise unable to easily and expeditiously meet the demands of enrolled or newly returned combat veterans. The VA has the authority to purchase care from the private sector, but it has been timid about using that authority. This reticence is partly because of cost considerations and perhaps even more because it signifies a move toward more integration between direct care and purchased care, a concept that has been foreign to the VA. In late 2005, the VA began what it has termed Project HERO—Healthcare Effectiveness through Resource Optimization—which would integrate private services, but it continues to be slow in moving forward with its use, even though a contract has been awarded with contractors to be paid at Medicare rates.

Moving more aggressively in this direction would allow the VA to respond better to shifts in the geographic locations of its population, the changing demographics of the veterans, and other shifts in peak-load demands. This would be similar to what the military has done with its use of direct care augmented by purchased care within the Tricare system. It will also help alleviate the need to rebuild or recapitalize a system of antiquated hospitals, which would be a hugely costly and largely unnecessary expense, especially if partnering with existing facilities would provide comparable or even superior care.

Yet using purchased care in combination with direct delivery care requires the services to be integrated at various levels, including clinically and financially—a problem that the military has not yet completely resolved. It is particularly important that the VA, which has been a leader in patient safety, electronic patient records, and the use of clinical protocols, brings these characteristics to its private-sector partners rather than producing a fragmented system of care for the veteran.

A slightly different but related issue has to do with whether the VA's focus going forward should be on expanded primary care or secondary and tertiary care. This question relates to the VA's role in an evolving health care system where increasing amounts of care can be provided outside of the traditional hospital setting and various types of care that the VA might not have readily available might be purchased from the private sector. It would also be affected by any federal attempts to provide universal health insurance coverage.

One choice would be for the VA to focus on specialized areas where it has established recognized expertise, such as spinal cord injuries and post-stroke rehabilitation. An alternative direction would be for the VA to focus on primary care and care that can be provided in CBOCs or free-standing surgery centers, and partner with academic health centers for much of the other secondary or tertiary care that needs to be provided in inpatient settings. Moving in this direction would allow the VA to concentrate on expanding its CBOCs to include specialty services and same-day surgeries, but not preclude it from continuing in areas where it has developed specialized expertise, such as in rehabilitation and spinal cord injuries.

Redefine VA Role in Health Care

The new administration should consider the role of the VA in a world where most or all citizens have access to health insurance. The VA has traditionally provided services to a relatively small share of the veteran population—those with service-related disabilities and low-income veterans who do not have other insurance. Even within this grouping, only a relatively small share of the veterans within most of the priority categories of service-related disabilities are enrolled in or actually use the VA. It is not clear what will happen if access to insurance coverage is assured to all or most of the population through new federal legislation, but it could clearly affect the choice of those who have been using the VA. It is possible that some of these populations would choose to receive their care elsewhere. This would modify the role of the VA, although it would obviously depend in part on what else is available and at what cost to the individual.

The VA's role in a post-health-reform world raises another complex issue that goes beyond the department. Many individuals now have access to multiple sources of insurance—employer-sponsored insurance with access to Tricare and/or priority access to VA, VA and Medicare, VA, Medicare, and Tricare.

Sorting out how to best integrate these multiple sources of care, both clinically and financially, or at least ensuring that users are paying in the proper order, will require rethinking the appropriate roles of all of these various government and private programs.

The VA's role and its interaction with the Department of Defense in a world where all those in the military have chosen to be in the military may also present new challenges. These are not issues that will be fully resolved in the new administration, but any short-term changes by the VA, particularly any major construction decisions, need to be consistent with these longer-term challenges.

The Intelligence Community
Making the Newly Created Bureaucracy Work

JEREMY BASH[1]

From stopping terrorism to preventing the spread of nuclear weapons, few areas of government have a greater impact on U.S. security than the 16 agencies that comprise the intelligence community. It is also the arm of government that has changed the most over the past eight years. Following the recommendations of the 9/11 Commission, Congress overhauled the community in late 2004, establishing a Director of National Intelligence to oversee all 16 agencies. Three years into this new structure, there are signs of progress, such as improvements made to analytic standards and greater coordination among agencies in spying and information sharing. But much more needs to be done to establish the "unity of effort" called for in the 9/11 Commission recommendations. Further, controversy surrounding domestic wiretapping, interrogation techniques, and the overreliance on private contractors will require the new president to establish a clear legal framework for intelligence operations that protects America's security while upholding our values.

The past eight years were marked by enormous change in the U.S. intelligence community. Missions expanded, budgets soared, reorganizations took place, and legal authorities dramatically shifted. In 2004, in response to the 9/11 Commission's long-awaited findings, Congress enacted the Intelligence Reform and Terrorism Prevention Act, which fused 16 intelligence agencies with different rules, cultures, and databases under a single "intelligence commander," the Director of National Intelligence.[2] This new DNI structure remains a work in progress. The new president and his director of national intelligence will inherit this revolution in progress, which means they need to grasp how these changes to the intelligence community fundamentally affect our nation's security.

During the cold war, our classic espionage activities were arrayed primarily against the Soviets and their allies. Today, the range of challenges is much more diverse, requiring more than a "one size fits all" approach to espionage. Whether the mission is to thwart the next improvised explosive device, predict the next missile launch, or divine the intentions of a regime's leadership, intelligence work is integral to almost every decision affecting America's national security. The modern American intelligence community emerged at the dawn of the cold war to battle an adversary, the Soviet empire, which no longer exists. That adversary brought a large amount of conventional force to the field of battle. A Soviet tank column, for example, would be easy to find, but hard to stop. Today, in contrast, most of our adversaries may be easy to stop, but exceptionally difficult to find. Killing or capturing Osama Bin Laden or one of his Al Qaeda deputies will not require a large amount of force. But it will require pristine intelligence.

At the same time, policymakers also continue to lean heavily on the intelligence community to collect and analyze regime secrets of traditional potential threats, or "hard targets," such as China, Russia, Iran, North Korea, Cuba, and Syria—countries that maintain aggressive counterintelligence postures.

Over the past eight years, the intelligence community had to become highly proficient in areas in which it has not traditionally excelled. Information sharing is one such area. The intelligence community's culture historically rewarded "stovepiping," or compartmentalization, in order to enhance the security of information. To help connect the dots, agencies are now asked to work together to create all-source intelligence products. The most prominent example is the National Counterterrorism Center, NCTC, which was established by the 2004 law and which is the government's all-source center for all counterterrorism analysis.

The intelligence community continues to struggle with language proficiency and cultural diversity. We still face an enormous shortfall of operators and analysts proficient in Arabic, Farsi, Urdu, Pashto, and Dari, as well as Chinese, a language spoken by one out of every five people on the planet.

On the domestic intelligence front, the FBI is attempting to shift from an "arrest and convict" culture to a "detect and prevent" culture. The Bush administration also increased greatly its reliance on administrative subpoenas and national security letters—government demands to businesses for certain records and data—alongside clandestine informants, domestic wiretapping, and data mining. These changes to domestic intelligence authorities are not well understood by most policymakers or the public at large.

More broadly, the failure of the intelligence community to assess with accuracy Iraq's weapons of mass destruction program in the 2002 National Intelligence Estimate led to major reforms in analytical tradecraft. Finished intelligence products, including the President's Daily Brief, now include information from all 16 agencies, not just the Central Intelligence Agency, as well as a growing number of articles written jointly by more than one agency. Analysts are now required to discuss the quality of sources, explain dissents, caveats, and alternative views, and subject their findings to so-called "red cells," or subject-matter experts who challenge the assumptions of the analysis and offer written critiques for policymakers. These reforms were most prominently seen in the recent National Intelligence Estimate on Iran's nuclear program, which came to a different conclusion about that program than previous intelligence assessments.

Cyberspace and space are two intelligence arenas that are undergoing perhaps the most revolutionary changes. Due to their sensitive nature, little can be said in an unclassified format about intelligence operations in cyberspace and in outer space. Yet it is clear that we face adversaries who recently demonstrated capabilities indicating increased sophistication to detect and exploit vulnerabilities in our information architecture. This is a major priority for the intelligence community as it could well be the terrain on which intelligence battles are won and lost in the not-too-distant future.

In addition to these emerging requirements, the intelligence community must support U.S. forces operating in Afghanistan, Iraq, and around the world. A large number of intelligence professionals from both military and civilian life are deployed forward to enhance force protection, support military operations, and hunt high-value targets. Intelligence agencies have to demonstrate proficiency at "persistent surveillance" of the battle space, using hovering aircraft, for example. They also need to be able to track people, vehicles, and small shipments, be able to train indigenous security forces, and in some cases strike a target with lethal force.

Many of these battlefield roles—traditionally thought of as military roles—are now handled by intelligence agencies. Some within the intelligence community argue that this has led to the "militarization of intelligence" and distracted the civilian agencies from their main mission of producing long-term, strategic, policy-relevant assessments. As long as the U.S. military remains deployed in Afghanistan, Iraq, East Africa, the Philippines, and elsewhere, assisting in warfare will surely continue.

Today, the intelligence community is among the largest federal enterprises. Based on unclassified data, spending on intelligence has roughly doubled in the last decade, with more than $47 billion spent on the National Intelligence Program in fiscal year 2008.[3] This sum is larger than what is spent on the Department of State (about $39 billion), the Department of Homeland Security (about $37 billion), and the departments of Justice and Treasury combined (about $35 billion). As a point of comparison, the United States spends on intelligence about the same as Japan, Russia, and Germany individually spend on their entire defense budgets.[4]

As a result, management of the entire intelligence enterprise has become increasingly complex. It is one of the only arms of government that conducts operations on land, in air, at sea, under water, in space, in cyberspace, in both hostile and friendly countries, abroad and inside the United States, often in secret, and many times under fire.

One by-product of this intense growth and complexity is the increasing use of private contractors to carry out intelligence programs, which is problematic on multiple levels. First, the trend toward contracting creates a "brain drain" of professionals out of the intelligence community and into the private sector. Why should a CIA officer work for the government when he can have the same job for twice as much pay working for a contractor? Second, contracting can cost the U.S. taxpayer more money than full-time government employees. According to the Office of the Director of National Intelligence, contractor employees in the intelligence community cost $207,000 on average in direct labor costs, versus $125,000 for federal employees of those same agencies.[5]

Third, policymakers have less control over contractors. The result too often is that contractors are doing the government's work but are not accountable to policymakers. Concern over the use of private contractors to conduct interrogations led the House Intelligence Committee to include a provision in its FY2009 authorization bill prohibiting the CIA from spending money "for payment to any contractor to conduct the interrogation of a detainee or prisoner in custody or under the effective control of the Central Intelligence Agency."[6]

Reorganization

The Office of the Director of National Intelligence (DNI) was created in 2005. By law, the DNI has two principal roles. The first is to serve as the principal intelligence advisor to the president. Under President George W. Bush, this portfolio required the director to brief the president and vice president in the Oval Office five or six days a week. It also required the director to attend National Security Council and Principals Committee meetings, and to speak authoritatively to policymakers on "what our intelligence community knows."

The second role is to manage the 16 intelligence-community agencies, with particular emphasis on the big "three-letter agencies," comprised of the CIA, National Security Agency, Defense Intelligence Agency, National Geospatial-Intelligence Agency, National Reconnaissance Office, and the FBI. Although this DNI structure has not yet matured to the point where it is able to solve some of the community's most stubborn problems, there are at least three areas where the DNI's impact can most clearly be seen.

The first is the creation of so-called mission managers. The directors under President Bush appointed mission managers for counterterrorism, who also serves as the director of the national counterterrorism center; counterproliferation, who also serves as the director of the national counterproliferation center; counterintelligence; Iran; North Korea; and Cuba and Venezuela. Each mission manager is responsible for analyzing all-source intelligence against the target, developing collection requirements, and tasking collectors.

Individual mission-managers are now responsible for the so-called "integrated tasking" of collection assets based on a single set of analytic-driven intelligence gaps. What this means in practice is that a single individual analyzes what information is unknown about a particular target, such as Iran. These "unknowns" are called "collection gaps." An example of a collection gap may be whether Iran is providing lethal support to Shia militants in southern Iraq, or the number of centrifuges currently spinning at Natanz. The Iran mission manager would then bring all of the collection agencies together and direct each agency to collect information to fill those gaps. Previously, an individual agency might develop its own collection plan without coordinating with other agencies. This led to duplication as well as gaps.

In some areas, such integrated tasking worked better than in others. The concept appears to have worked well when arrayed against a discrete event, such as North Korea's detonation of a nuclear device in October 2006. In that instance, the community was able to quickly provide policymakers with an evaluation of the type of the detonation (nuclear), the location (P'unggye), the yield (less than a kiloton), and the method of analysis (air samples).[7] The intelligence community's assessment of the weakness of this nuclear test arguably strengthened the U.S. hand in discussions with North Korea, which agreed within a month to restart the six-party talks.

One area where integrated tasking is still deficient is in the realm of counterterrorism. The National Counterterrorism Center conducts analysis on terrorist groups, but it does not have the authority to task CIA officers or FBI counterterrorism agents working against those terrorist groups. Under law, the director of national intelligence is empowered to direct all intelligence-community assets, but in practice the National Counterterrorism Center director has no direct authority over CIA case officers or FBI special agents. Those officers are controlled by their own agency heads. If the next DNI wants to empower the NCTC director with tasking authority, he or she will have to make clear to all agencies that the NCTC director's collection tasks must be honored.

A second area where the DNI's impact is seen is in the upgrade of analytic tradecraft. Under the direction of the deputy director of national intelligence for analysis,[8] the Office of the DNI instituted several changes to the way analytical products are written. These reforms were instituted, in large part, to avoid failures like the one that occurred when the intelligence community in 2002 concluded that Saddam Hussein had chemical and biological weapons, and would have a nuclear weapon "during this decade."[9]

Since the passage of the 2004 law, finished intelligence products must adhere to specific analytic standards. Under these standards, all products must be objective, independent from political considerations, and timely, and they must be drawn from all available sources of intelligence and exhibit proper analytic tradecraft standards. Specifically, these tradecraft standards require that any finished intelligence product properly describes the quality and reliability of sources, expresses uncertainties or confidence in judgments, distinguishes between intelligence and underlying assumptions, and incorporates alternative analysis where appropriate.

Today, finished intelligence products now contain more information about the quality of sources. Alternative views are highlighted and incorporated into the analysis. On major products, such as NIEs, the judgments are given to outside experts to evaluate and challenge the findings. In addition, more of the finished products are now the product of collaboration among multiple agencies, as opposed to articles written by a single agency.

Third, the Office of the DNI made a concerted effort to harmonize policies and practices across the intelligence community in the realms of information sharing, handling of U.S. person information, security practices, and information technology. The DNI's office now harmonizes security clearance policies, yet the office has yet to issue formal guidance on ways to eliminate redundant practices and reduce the backlog of clearance applications. Likewise, in the information-sharing realm, the DNI has yet to provide effective guidance to ensure that computer systems across the community can adequately communicate with each other. The office is also trying to develop a centralized advanced research and development capability—much like the Department of Defense has its Defense Advanced Research Projects Agency, or DARPA—to serve a range of intelligence customers.

Assessments of the Office of the DNI are mixed. Last year, the DNI itself launched a 100-day plan and a 500-day plan, but unfortunately these plans were highly bureaucratic, dealing more with management and organization issues rather than filling specific intelligence gaps. Despite these glossy publications, progress is still lacking in chronic problem areas such as language proficiency, cultural diversity, runaway costs for big programs, turf battles, collection gaps, overclassification, and overreliance on contractors.

More recently, President Bush in July 2008 signed a revision to Executive Order 12333, the long-standing EO governing the authorities and responsibilities of the various intelligence agencies. The EO appeared to leave undisturbed many of the core civil liberties protections in the previous order. It did, however, empower the DNI to be the final arbiter on issues such as information sharing, levying analytic tasks, and declassification. As a result of this EO, the DNI will now be able to prevent one agency from refusing to share information with another. How this will work in practice remains to be seen.

The Office of DNI also has to deal with other independent departments and agencies within the U.S. government. The Department of Homeland Security plays a critical role in intelligence collection, analysis, and in particular "indications and warning," the analytic discipline of alerting policymakers about imminent threats to the homeland. DHS is responsible for collecting intelligence at ports of entry, and in the aviation and maritime domains. Due to long-standing restrictions on domestic collection, DHS's intelligence functions often trigger intense scrutiny from Congress and the media.

In addition, the FBI created the National Security Branch in September 2005, in response to a presidential directive. Under this new structure, the NSB places under one executive assistant director the counterterrorism, counterespionage, counterproliferation, and analysis functions of the bureau. The NSB is one of the 16 agencies within the intelligence community, but the DNI only contributes half of the funds for counterterrorism and counterintelligence agents (with the other half coming from the Department of Justice). Because the DNI does not control the entire NSB budget, the DNI's ability to direct the work of the NSB is somewhat limited.

New Legal Authority

Against the backdrop of these expanding requirements, budgets, and reorganizations, the Bush administration and Congress made major changes to the legal authority governing intelligence. Some of the most difficult and sensitive questions have arisen in the context of surveillance, detention, and interrogation of terrorism suspects. The rules and practices of the intelligence community in these three areas changed dramatically over the past seven years.

Shortly after 9/11, President Bush authorized the NSA to secretly wiretap communications involving Americans without an order from the Foreign Intelligence Surveillance Court. Around the same time, President Bush established a CIA program, which he publicly revealed in September 2006, to capture, detain, and interrogate high-value Al Qaeda targets in secret CIA-run prisons. Some of these prisoners accused their captors of torture. In 2008, CIA Director Michael Hayden acknowledged that the CIA waterboarded three prisoners who were in CIA custody.

These programs had a few features in common. In both cases, agency officers were asked to conduct operations for which there was little precedent within the agency, minimal oversight, and a dearth of legal guidance. Both were very closely guarded secrets, carefully overseen by the White House and the vice president's office, and briefed only generally to a few in Congress.

In both of these cases, the Justice Department's Office of Legal Counsel rendered secret opinions that the contemplated activities were lawful—advice that subsequent officials came to believe was wrong. Both programs triggered litigation, investigations, and subsequent legislation. In addition to secret presidential orders, Congress and the courts were altering the legal landscape, too, as Harold Koh outlines in his overview on human and civil rights in a national security age elsewhere in this book.

Why, given all of the other priorities, would this legal arena require the new president's focus? The short answer is that these activities tend to cause tremendous turbulence in the intelligence enterprise. They cause the public to doubt the trustworthiness of public institutions. They cause friction between Congress and the president. They trigger unnecessary and costly constitutional battles. And they threaten to undermine the reputation of the United States in the eyes of those we seek to influence.

These issues also consume an enormous amount of policymakers' time, from the president on down. In addition, resolving these issues is vital to provide clarity to intelligence operators in the field. The last thing we want is for the intelligence community to have convoluted guidance from Washington about what they can and cannot do. Finally, how we resolve these legal and moral issues will have an important impact on our reputation in the world and our ability to achieve broader national security objectives.

The First 100 Days

Because intelligence is so vital to national security decision making, and because the intelligence community has changed so dramatically over the past eight years, the new president should place a high priority on developing a strong relationship with his intelligence community. The 2004 intelligence reform law authorizes outgoing executive branch officials to prepare a detailed, classified, compartmented summary of specific operational threats to national security; major military or covert operations; and pending decisions on possible uses of military force. Early in the transition, the president-elect, his vice president-elect, and their senior national security advisors should carefully review these summaries and decision memoranda with the outgoing officials who authored them.

The 2004 law also urged the president-elect to submit to the FBI the names of candidates for "high level national security positions through the level of undersecretary of cabinet departments as soon as possible after" election day. In the case of the U.S. intelligence community, the president-elect should designate nominees that must be confirmed by the Senate Select Committee on Intelligence with enough time for security clearances to be approved by Inauguration Day. These posts are: the DNI; principal deputy DNI; general counsel of the DNI; chief information officer of the DNI; director of the CIA; general counsel of the CIA; inspector general of the CIA; director of the national counterterrorism center; assistant secretary of treasury for intelligence and analysis; assistant secretary of state for intelligence and research; and assistant attorney general for the national security division.[10] In addition, the president-elect should similarly designate a nominee for the post of undersecretary of defense for intelligence, who must be confirmed by the Senate Armed Services Committee.

In choosing a DNI, the new president should look for several essential qualities. The individual should understand the changes that have taken place in the community and know how to harness this revamped community to provide timely information to the president and senior policymakers. He or she must be willing and able to provide objective and apolitical advice, even if that advice conflicts with the new administration's policy objectives. This individual should be steeped in counterterrorism, counterproliferation, and the ongoing military operations in Iraq and Afghanistan. And he or she should be familiar with current espionage operations and covert action programs. The DNI must also have outstanding relationships on Capitol Hill. Congress sets the budget for the intelligence community and reviews all significant intelligence programs, including covert action findings. The DNI will be the president's "ambassador" to Congress on these critical issues.

For an incoming president, there is no substitute for regular, in-depth briefings from intelligence officials on key analytic issues, as well as ongoing operations. These briefings will allow the new president to understand the community's strengths and weaknesses and to ask questions, which can form the basis for tasking collectors. These briefings should occur several times a week, perhaps (though not necessarily) daily. They should involve the president, the vice president, and the national security advisor, as well as other key officials whose advice may be required, such as the secretaries of defense, state, and homeland security.

The intelligence community will respond to the president's requirements. Operators will move satellites to take imagery of an adversary about whom the president wants to know more. Case officers will ask their assets to risk their lives and report on matters about which the president has a question. The community will respond, if the president asks. It is equally important for the 44th president to send the signal that he appreciates intelligence professionals and will reward their risks, but most importantly, will listen to what they say. Maintaining a regular intelligence briefing and frequent consultations with senior intelligence officials will be the most tangible way to signal interest by the new president.

At a minimum, the new president in the first 100 days will have to direct a review of all covert action programs that are currently underway. He inherits covert action findings from all predecessor administrations. Unless he makes changes, these programs will remain intact. Particularly in the area of counterterrorism, it will be vital for the new president to ask his national security advisor and his senior director for intelligence programs to develop, along with the CIA, a comprehensive review of all covert action activities.

Here are some key questions the 44th president should ask: Are these covert programs achieving their objectives? Are these programs being properly deconflicted with other operations, particularly those undertaken by DoD? Is it necessary that these programs remain covert, or should some of them be conducted with overt or clandestine resources?

And do these programs have strong direction, oversight mechanisms, and checks to ensure that they are legal, consistent with American foreign policy objectives, and a wise use of taxpayer money?

Strengthen DNI

The DNI office made some strides in creating the "unity of effort" called for in the 9/11 Commission Report. Yet the DNI is in some peril of becoming just another layer of bureaucracy between the front lines and the policymakers. The office has grown rapidly, and its 100- and 500-day plans were full of bureaucratic jargon. Some have suggested that the core of the DNI's identity crisis is whether he is a doer or a coordinator. Perhaps the best model is that of an orchestra conductor. The DNI is responsible for ensuring that all instruments of intelligence—human-source, signals, and imagery—work together, and he has the authority to demand more output from a certain element to satisfy requirements.

The new president should relax the DNI's responsibility to participate in the daily intelligence briefings. Instead, he should ask the DNI to focus on his job as "intelligence conductor." If the 44th president can strengthen the DNI's role in driving "integrated tasking," or directing all the agencies at once to collect against intelligence requirements, then he will go a long way toward strengthening the community's output.

Reallocate Resources to Terrorism

The intelligence community's presence in Iraq today stands at historic levels, mostly in support of the U.S. military and U.S. embassy missions. But this intelligence "surge" is not without its costs. Personnel assigned to other parts of the world have been sent to Iraq. Budgets for other programs have been cut to pay for Iraq. Precious satellite and other reconnaissance resources are being utilized to support the war in Iraq, when those resources could be used to locate high-value targets along the Afghanistan-Pakistan border.

The new president must determine how to conduct a "strategic redeployment" of intelligence assets from the Iraq war to the global war against terrorist networks, where greater intelligence assets are needed. Specifically, he should review whether intelligence officers in Iraq can be reassigned elsewhere in the Near East and South Asia to track members of Al Qaeda, Hezbollah, and other terrorist leaders.

The new president also should end the practice of paying for counterterrorism programs with "emergency" supplemental budgets. This practice has forced counterterrorism programs to compete with Iraq war funding, which is also paid for by "emergency" supplemental spending. Terrorism is no longer an unforeseen emergency. Supplemental funding also prevents operators from planning more than one year in advance, and such funding evades thorough scrutiny of the congressional oversight committees. Funding for counterterrorism should be brought within the base intelligence budget starting in FY 2010. This will help ensure that such programs are well resourced, well managed, and not in competition with Iraq funding.

A Clear Legal Framework for Intelligence Operations

The 44th president must have a clear plan to put rendition, detention, and interrogation operations on a solid legal footing. He must close the books on those operations that have resulted in detainee abuse, including, in some cases, torture. The practices of sending detainees to regimes with abysmal human rights records or holding them indefinitely in secret prisons and subjecting them to "enhanced interrogation techniques" is now toxic in the public's mind and complicates our ability to achieve broader objectives.

To be clear: There is value in conducting lawful interrogations of high-value terrorist targets under clear rules of engagement. The U.S. military and the FBI have done this for years. The issue is whether the CIA should have a separate detention program and be granted wider latitude to conduct coercive interrogations against certain high-value detainees. In no instance should the CIA, or any government agency, be permitted to engage in torture. However, in its defense, the agency has always sought and received legal opinions from the Office of Legal Counsel at the Justice Department permitting the agency to employ certain "techniques." The agency is not a rogue; its operations were approved by DoJ and the NSC principals.

The White House should subject these programs to a period of intensive review. The president should personally be briefed on all aspects of the CIA's program, as well as a classified review of what their value has (or has not) been. Then, he should order his attorney general to withdraw the flawed opinions written by the Office of Legal Counsel and replace them with revised opinions to define the new parameters of the program, putting them squarely in compliance with U.S. and international law. Abusive tactics, such as waterboarding, should be banned.

Other interrogation techniques should hew closely to the established procedures used by the U.S. military and the FBI. To the extent that any authorized techniques deviate from military or FBI practices, those techniques must comply with U.S. and international law, be carefully scrutinized by the Justice Department, and be briefed to the full congressional intelligence committees.

The First Year

One systemic problem is that the intelligence community is overly focused on providing tactical intelligence. Case officers, for example, are collecting information on the placement of roadside bombs in Iraq and Afghanistan at the expense of strategic intelligence work, such as analyzing plans and intentions of adversaries who pose strategic threats to the United States. The new president should insist that tactical intelligence requirements be filled primarily by the military service elements engaged in warfare and working in conjunction with special operations forces.

In tandem, the new president and his DNI need to shift the intelligence community back to the basics of spycraft. America today has too few spies—people who actually spot, assess, recruit, and handle people to steal the closely guarded secrets of their governments or organizations such as Al Qaeda. Spying is risky, costly, and very difficult. Our spy service remains predominantly male and white. Our officers lack the cultural diversity and language proficiency necessary to penetrate the plots and learn the intentions of our adversaries.

The new president must focus on recruiting, clearing, and training officers who can blend in with our adversaries. This requires devoting additional resources to recruiting ethnically diverse Americans, conducting better outreach to underrepresented groups, such as Iranian Americans, and abandoning outmoded security procedures that disqualify individuals with relatives abroad.

During the first year, the new president should reward non-political intelligence assessments—the proverbial "truth to power." The Bush administration sparred with intelligence professionals when their judgments did not mesh with its own policy approaches. It cherry-picked and selectively declassified information for political purposes. The 44th president should send an early signal that the politicization of intelligence ends when he takes office.

Transform the FBI

Since its inception 100 years ago, the FBI culture has mostly rewarded gun-toting special agents who investigate crime after the fact and collect evidence to arrest and convict criminals. In an era of terrorism, the FBI culture must transform to one that focuses on detecting and preventing terrorism plots before they materialize. Its agents must be as proficient at analyzing terrorism threats as they are at raiding a house and dusting for fingerprints.

The FBI's National Security Branch now handles counterterrorism and counterintelligence missions under one senior FBI official. This reorganization followed the establishment in February 2005 of a Directorate of Intelligence to focus on intelligence gathering and analyzing. The FBI academy adjusted its training curriculum to focus on developing counterterrorism intelligence. The bureau has also deployed Field Intelligence Groups, or field teams comprised of linguists, analysts, and special operators who develop lists of individuals to target for investigation, analyze information collected, and produce intelligence reports to headquarters. These initiatives have helped transform the FBI into an intelligence organization, but that transformation is not complete.

The new president should consider two needed reforms. First, he should direct the FBI to study the feasibility of creating a career track for intelligence officers. This track would be separate from the special agent track. Intelligence officers would be charged with developing assets (informants) and collecting information about terrorist cells or proliferation networks operating inside the United States. These collectors should receive training similar to the training offered to CIA case officers. Investigations would have to comport fully with U.S. laws and the Fourth Amendment. This career path should be as valued and as prestigious within the bureau as that of a special agent enforcing criminal laws.

Second, and perhaps more importantly, the FBI should strengthen the existing career track for intelligence analysts. Currently, there are not many managerial positions for intelligence analysts. Intelligence analysts should have the same opportunities as special agents to head divisions, run field offices, lead major investigations, and join the senior ranks of the bureau.

New System of Satellites

Satellites are a major component of the classified world. They help us hear the enemy, see the enemy, and conduct other sensitive operations. Today, our "overhead architecture" is plagued by cost overruns, missed timelines, and lack of an integrated plan. These programs are some of the most sensitive and expensive systems in the intelligence realm.

This is one area where we must learn from the private sector. The private sector has had to deliver commercial satellites on faster timelines and for far less money than the government. The new president should appoint a team to reassess our overhead architecture and build a flexible system with cost controls and shorter acquisition cycles. This team should include scientists, engineers, and acquisition specialists with experience in the commercial satellite field. The new president must also signal his commitment to the industrial base that provides the know-how to keep America's competitive advantage in this area.

Clear Rules for Domestic Surveillance

Congress has passed numerous laws governing domestic electronic surveillance. Some of those laws "sunset" (expire) in 2009. Others will require re-examination even before their sunset dates. These include such laws as the Foreign Intelligence Surveillance Act Amendments Act, which was passed in 2008. The 44th president should carefully consult with the NSA, the FBI, jurists, technical and legal experts, and private-sector experts such as telecommunications executives and network security engineers.

The goal should be to establish clear rules for domestic surveillance that uphold the constitutional rights of Americans while protecting our government's ability to conduct lawful surveillance of terrorists and other adversaries. The president should carefully consult with the intelligence and judiciary committees in Congress and propose a bill to readdress FISA well in advance of the sunset dates.

Address the Cyberthreat

Beginning in the spring of 2007, the Bush administration began paying greater attention to cybersecurity after neglecting it for most of the preceding seven years. It rightly concluded that our nation's vulnerabilities in the cyber realm are so serious that they require major new investments of resources. A cyberattack could do more economic damage to our country than the 19 hijackers did on 9/11.

What's more, cyberthreats often cannot be easily attributed to a particular attacker. For example, when Estonia suffered a wave of cyberattacks in 2007 against its banks, government ministries, emergency services, and parliament, it suspected a Russian hand behind the attacks. But such attribution was impossible to prove.

This is a complex issue. Defending against cyberattacks relates not only to our technical capabilities, but also the panoply of legal and constitutional issues associated with surveillance. The new president should continue the work begun by the Bush administration's cybersecurity initiative, which seeks to protect government networks from intrusion and which will begin the research necessary to broaden protection to the private sector.[11] He should appoint an official at the National Security Council to coordinate the government's various cybersecurity efforts, which now are spread among the DNI, the Homeland Security Department, the Defense Department, and the FBI.

And the 44th president must work aggressively to obtain buy-in from the private sector, civil liberties advocates, and key members of Congress on how to protect our national infrastructure, which is so reliant on the Internet. As the House Intelligence Committee proposed in its FY2009 authorization bill, the president should convene an advisory panel comprised of representatives from Congress, executive branch agencies, the privacy and civil liberties communities, and the private sector. The panel's goal should be to make policy and procedural recommendations for information security for the government, critical infrastructure protection, and the authorities, roles, and responsibilities of various executive branch agencies, such as DHS and DoD.

Regulate Use of Contractors

Overreliance on private contractors undermines accountability and erodes the government's ability to retain a competent professional workforce. The new president must task his new director of national intelligence with conducting a top-to-bottom review of the use of contractors in the intelligence community and strengthen controls on their work. Specifically, the new administration must clearly define which intelligence functions constitute "inherently governmental functions" and prohibit agencies from outsourcing those functions. For example, the CIA should be prohibited from outsourcing interrogations to private contractors.

In addition, agencies should be prevented from outsourcing entire programs, such as a particular database system. If the contractor fails to perform or, worse, the company goes belly up, then the government must ensure that some expertise or continuity remains within the government. Finally, the agencies should be directed to provide the DNI with an accounting of the full cost of government employees within their agency—including the full value of their retirement benefits and training—so that cost-benefit decisions about whether to outsource those functions are made with complete information. In some instances, it might be less expensive to hire a contractor. In many cases, it may not.

Notes

A note regarding the Preface by John Podesta and Introduction by Mark Green: the views expressed in these passages are solely those of the respective authors and their respective organizations.

Progressive Patriotism:
How the 44th President Can Change Washington and America

1. M. Waldman, *A Return to Common Sense* (Sourcebooks, Inc., 2008), p. xvi.

2. While the rest of this book went to the printer just before the General Election, this Introduction was completed November 5, hence the awareness that it's President-elect Obama who will be sworn in January 20, 2009.

3. R. McElvaine, "61% of Historians Rate the Bush Presidency Worst," History News Network, http://hnn.us/article/48916.html.

4. Noted in D. Polman, "The American Debate: Democratic Era Coming? Possibly Not," *Philadelphia* Inquirer, November 2, 2008.

5. R. Kuttner, "A Conversation with Doris Kearns Goodwin," *The American Prospect*, December 19, 2007.

6. F. Schwarz, "Restoring the Rule of Law," testimony before the Senate Judiciary Committee, September 16, 2008. See also, M. Green, "What Should Happen Now? A Truth Commission for Bush," HuffingtonPost.com, June 2, 2008; N. Kristof, "Rejoin the World," *New York Times,* November 2, 2008, p. 12.

7. See chapter by Edleman & Glover, p. 99; also, Reich, "Is the Game About to Stop?," *The American Project*, April 2008, p. 44; S. Greenhouse, "Starting Out Means a Steeper Climb," *Nation*, May 12, 2008, p. 22.

8. G. Anderson, "Buffet Speaks," *CNN Money*, March 8, 2004.

9. R. Parker, "Why the New Deal Matters," *Nation*, April 7, 2008.

10. Quoted in G. Kessler, "Both Candidates Embrace Diplomacy," *Washington Post,* October 26, 2008, p. A16.

11. J. Meacham, "It's Not Easy Being Blues," *Newsweek*, Oct. 27, 2008.

12. "For Much of the Country, a Sizeable Shift," *New York Times,* November 6, 2008, p. P1.

THE WHITE HOUSE

National Economic Council

1. See Kenneth Juster and Simon Lazaraus, "Making Economic Policy: An Assessment of the National Economic Council" (Washington, DC: Brookings Institution, 1997), pp. 10–19, for a summary of the different approaches going back to the Kennedy administration. See Jonathan M. Orszag, Peter R. Orszag, and Laura Tyson, "The Process of Economic Policy Making During the Clinton Administration," in Jeffrey A. Frankel and Peter R. Orszag, eds., *American Economic Policy in the 1990s* (Cambridge, MA: MIT Press, 2002), for a history of economic policymaking back to Kennedy. See also I. M. Destler, "The National Economic Council: A Work in Progress" (Washington, DC: Institute for International Economics, 1996).

2. Juster and Lazarus, "Making Economic Policy."

3. Thomas Friedman, "The Transition: Plans and Policies; Aides Say Clinton Will Swiftly Void G.O.P Initiatives," *The New York Times*, November 6, 1992.

4. *Remarks announcing the appointment of Laura D'Andrea Tyson as chair of the National Economic Council and an exchange with Reporters* (Weekly Compilation of Presidential Documents, February 27, 1995).

5. See Ron Suskind, *The Price of Loyalty: George W. Bush, The White House, and the Education of Paul O'Neil* (New York: Simon and Schuster, 2004). See also Ron Suskind, "Why Are These Men Laughing?"*Esquire*, January 2003. See also Alan Krueger, "Economic Scene; Honest brokers separate policy from sausage for the White House," *The New York Times*, November 9, 2000.

6. Executive Order no. 12835 (January 25, 1993), PDD/NEC-2.

7. David Sanger, "Bush Plans to Stress Effects of Economics on Security," *The New York Times*, January 16, 2001.

8. Orszag, Orszag, and Tyson, "The Process of Economic Policy Making During the Clinton Administration."

National Energy Council

1. World Energy Outlook 2007; Energy Information Administration, *Annual Energy Outlook* (U.S. Department of Energy, 2008).

2. "How Can We Stop Severe Climate Disruption?" Belfer Center Newsletter, available at http://www.belfercenter.org/files/newsletterssummer007.pdf (last accessed October 2007).

3. James Hansen, Testimony before House Select Committee on Energy Independence and Global Warming, June 23, 2008.

4. Pacala and Socolow, "Stabilization Wedges: Solving the Climate Problem for the Next 50 Years with Current Technologies," *Science* 35 (August 13, 2004).

White House Communications and Press Operations

1. Carol Gelderman, *All the Presidents' Words: The Bully Pulpit and the Creation of the Virtual Presidency* (New York: Walker and Company, 1997), p. 172.

A New Office of Social Entrepreneurship

1. The Internal Revenue Code defines over 27 categories of organizations exempt from federal income taxes, including private country clubs, labor unions, business associations, fraternal organizations, universities, and many others. About 1.5 million of these organizations make up the "independent sector." The "independent sector" encompasses the charitable, social welfare, and faith-based portions of the non-profit sector. Throughout this section, when we refer to "non-profits" we are referring to these "independent sector" groups. See Leslie Crutchfield and Heather Grant, *Forces for Good: The Six Practices of High-Impact Nonprofits* (San Francisco: John Wiley and Sons, 2008).

2. Lester Salamon and S. Wojciech Sokolowski, "Employment in America's Charities: A Profile" (Baltimore: The Johns Hopkins Center for Civil Society Studies, December 2006), p. 3; Bureau of Labor Statistics, "Employment, Hours, and Earnings from the Current Employment Statistics Survey (National): Financial Activities" (U.S. Department of Labor), available at http://data.bls.gov/PDQ/servlet/SurveyOutputServlet?&series_id=CEU5500000001.

3. Roger L. Martin and Sally Osberg, "Social Entrepreneurship: The Case for Definition," *Stanford Social Innovation Review* 5 (2) (2007): 28–39.

4. William Foster & Gail Fine, "How Nonprofits Get Really Big," *Stanford Social Innovation Review* 5 (2) (2007): 46–55.

Economic Policy

Overview: A Pro-Growth, Progressive Economic Agenda

1. Bureau of Labor Statistics (2008).

2. This discussion on the new productivity decade is adopted from a previous description in Gene Sperling, "Rising Tide Economics," *Democracy: A Journal of Ideas* (Fall 2007).

3. U.S. Census Bureau (2008).

4. Goldman Sachs, "The Macro Effects of Rising Income Inequality," *U.S. Economics Analyst,* June 30, 2006.

5. Benjamin Franklin, "Information to Those Who Would Remove to America," September 1782, in *The Writings of Benjamin Franklin*, ed. Albert Henry Smyth. 10 vols. (New York: Macmillan Co., 1905–7).

6. For further discussion on the specific progressive values discussed here, see Gene Sperling, *The Pro-Growth Progressive* (New York: Simon & Schuster, 2005), pp. 33–40.

7. Andy Grove (speech to Global Tech Summit, October 9, 2003), available at http://www.globaltechsummit.net/press/GTS_AndyGrove.pdf.

8. See Gene Sperling, "How to Get Fewer Scientists," *The Washington Post*, July 24, 2007.

9. See Shirley Ann Jackson, "Pathways to Progress: Enhancing Engineering Education" (speech to WEPAN, 2008 Annual Conference, St. Louis, June 9, 2008), available at http://www.rpi.edu/president/speeches/ps060908-wepan.html.

10. Steven Greenhouse, *The Big Squeeze: Tough Times for the American Worker* (Knopf, 2008), pp. 247–249.

11. Ross Eisenbray, "On the Department of Labor's Final Overtime Regulations," Testimony before the Senate Health, Education, Labor and Pensions Committee, May 4, 2004.

12. Scott Lilly, "Beyond Justice" (Washington, DC: Center for American Progress, December 2007).

13. Spencer Hsu, "Report Faults Mine Safety," *The Washington Post,* November 17, 2007.

14. Anne-Marie Lasowski, Testimony on Fair Labor Standards Act (Government Accountability Office, July 15 2008).

15. Thea Lee, Testimony before the Committee on International Relations Subcommittee on Africa, Global Human Rights, and International Operations, "Human Rights in China: Improving or Deteriorating Conditions?" April 19, 2006.

16. For more see David Kusnet, Lawrence Mishel, and Ruy Teixeira, *Talking Past Each Other* (Economic Policy Institute, 2006), available at http://www.epi.org/books/talking/TalkingPastEachOther(full).pdf.

17. Richard Fry, "Latino Youth Finishing College: The Role of Selective Pathways" (Pew Hispanic Center, June 2004).

18. Arthur J. Rolnick and Rob Grunewald, "Early Intervention on a Large Scale," *Quality Counts*, January 4, 2007, available at http://www.minneapolisfed.org/Research/studies/earlychild/early_intervention.cfm; Robert Dugger, "American Kids, Workforce Quality and Fiscal Sustainability: A Multi-Year Plan for the Invest in Kids Working Group—Year 2," Invest in Kids Working Group Working Paper No. 4 (Committee on Economic Development, January 2005); Jeffrey Roth and David Figlio, "The Behavioral Consequences of Pre-kindergarten Participation for Disadvantaged Youth," in "The Economics of Disadvantaged Youth" (National Bureau of Economic Research, February 2008).

19. Laura L. Rendon, "Access in a Democracy: Narrowing the Opportunity Gap," in *Reconceptualizing Access in Postsecondary Education and Its Ramifications for Data Systems* (Report of the Policy Panel on Access, Washington, DC, September 9, 1999).

Overview: A Progressive Agenda for Competitiveness and Trade

1. One recent paper using four different methodologies concludes that growing U.S. openness to trade and investment flows since 1950 produced economic benefits of about $1 trillion per year by 2003 and explains over 10 percent of the average income gains enjoyed by American families during this period. See Scott Bradford, Paul Grieco, and Gary Hufbauer, "The Payoff to America from Global Integration," in Fred C. Bergsten, ed., *The United States and the World Economy* (Washington, DC: Institute for International Economics, 2005). For other considerably smaller estimates of the gains from globalization see Dani Rodrik, "The Globalization Numbers Game," Dani Rodrik's Weblog, May 7, 2007, available at http://rodrik.typepad.com/dani_rodriks_weblog/2007/05/the_globalizati.html; and Josh Bivens, "The Marketing of Economic History: Inflating the Gains of Trade Liberalization" (Washington, DC: Economic Policy Institute, 2007).

2. See Bradford, Grieco, and Hufbauer, "The Payoff to America from Global Integration." This study finds that imports cause about $54 billion a year in lifetime dislocation costs for workers who suffer job losses and lower wages.

3. Alan S. Blinder, "Offshoring: The Next Industrial Revolution?" *Foreign Affairs* 85 (2) (2006):113–118; Lori Kletzer, "Trade and Immigration: Implications for the U.S. Labor Market," Working Paper (University of California, Santa Cruz, 2007).

4. International Monetary Fund, "World Economic Outlook: Spillovers and Cycles in the Global Economy" (2007).

5. Robert Z. Lawrence, *Blue-collar Blues: Is Trade to Blame for Rising U.S. Inequality?* (Washington, DC: Peterson Institute for International Economics, 2008).

6. Claudia Goldin and Lawrence Katz, "Long-Run Changes in the U.S. Wage Structure: Narrowing, Widening, and Polarizing," Working Paper (Harvard University, 2007). Also forthcoming in Brookings Papers on Economic Activity (2008).

7. David Autor, Lawrence Katz, and Melissa Kearney, "The Polarization of the U.S. Labor Market," NBER Working Paper (Harvard University, 2006).

8. Goldin and Katz, "Long-Run Changes in the U.S. Wage Structure."

9. Andrew Tilton and others, "Immigration and the North American Economy," Global Economics Paper no. 168 (Goldman Sachs, 2008).

10. Laura Tyson, "Innovation and National Competitiveness," in Liber Amicorum for Klaus Schwab (Cologny/Geneva: World Economic Forum, 2008).

11. Peter Orszag, "Current and Future Investment in Infrastructure," Testimony before the Committee on the Budget and the Committee on Transportation and Infrastructure, May 8, 2008, available at http://www.cbo.gov/ftpdocs/91xx/doc9136/05-07-Infrastructure _Testimony.pdf.

12. Tom Kalil and John Irons, "A National Innovation Agenda: Progressive Policies for Economic Growth and Opportunity through Science and Technology" (Washington, DC: Center for American Progress, 2007).

13. The inadequacies of U.S. physical infrastructure manifest themselves every day. Congestion and traffic delays waste 1.8 billion gallons of fuel and cost an estimated $50.3 billion each year. According to the Department of Transportation, freight bottlenecks cost the U.S. economy $200 billion or about 1.6 percent of GDP each year. Bernard Schwartz, "Why Prosperity Requires Public Investment," In The Promise of Public Investment (New York: Schwartz Center for Economic Policy Analysis, 2008)

14. American Society of Civil Engineers, "Report Card for America's Infrastructure" (2005).

15. Orszag, "Current and Future Investment in Infrastructure."

16. Ibid.

17. Heidi Crebo-Rediker and Douglas Rediker, "Financing America's Infrastructure Needs," Working Paper (Washington, DC: New American Foundation, 2008).

18. "Transatlantic Balance Sheet: Environment Matters," The Globalist, Executive Edition, May 25, 2008.

19. Pers-Anders Enkvist, Tomas Naucler, and Jens Riese, "What Countries Can Do About Cutting Carbon Emissions," The McKinsey Quarterly (2) (2008): 34–45.

20. See, for example, Peter Ogden, John Podesta, and John Deutch, "A New Strategy to Spur Energy Innovation" (Washington, DC: Center for American Progress, 2008).

21. Richard Samans and Jonathan Jacoby, "Virtuous Circle: Strengthening Broad-Based Progress in Living Standards" (Washington, DC: Center for American Progress, 2007).

22. Wayne M. Morrison, "China-U.S. Trade Issues" (Washington, DC: Congressional Research Services, 2007).

23. "China—Soft Exchange Rate," available at http://www.federalreserve.gov/releases/ h10/Hist/dat00_ch.txt (last accessed August 2008).

Overview: Science, Technology, and Innovation Challenges

1. United States Commission on National Security/21st Century, "Road Map for National Security: Imperative for Change" (2001).

2. Clifford Winston, "Government Failure versus Market Failure" (Washington, DC: AEI-Brookings Joint Center for Regulatory Studies, 2006).

3. Henry Chesbrough, *Open Innovation* (Boston: Harvard Business School Press, 2003).

4. Eric Von Hippel, *Democratizing Innovation* (Cambridge, MA: MIT Press, 2005).

5. Federation of American Societies for Experimental Biology, "Federal Funding for Biomedical and Related Life Sciences Research: FY2008" (2007).

6. National Academy of Sciences, "Rising Above the Gathering Storm" (2007).

7. Paul M. Romer, "Should the Government Subsidize Supply or Demand in the Market for Scientists and Engineers?" Working Paper 7723 (National Bureau of Economic Research, 2000).

8. Richard B. Freeman, "Investing in the Best and Brightest: Increased Fellowship Support for American Scientists and Engineers," Discussion Paper 2006–09 (Hamilton Project, 2006).

9. Organisation for Economic Co-operation and Development, "OECD Broadband Statistics to December 2006" (2007).

10. Communication Workers of America, "Speed Matters: A Report on Internet Speeds in All 50 States" (2007).

11. See, for example, *The Broadband Deployment and Acceleration Act of 2007*, H.R. 1818, 110 Cong. 1 sess., introduced by Representative Doris Matsui (D-CA).

12. See, for example, Pierre de Vries, "Populating the Vacant Channels: The Case For Allocating Unused Spectrum In The Digital TV Bands To Unlicensed Use For Broadband And Wireless Innovation." Working Paper 14 (New America Foundation Wireless Future Program, 2006).

Overview: Economic Opportunity for All or a New Gilded Age?

1. Julia B. Isaacs, Isabel V. Sawhill, and Ron Haskins, "Getting Ahead or Losing Ground: Economic Mobility in America" (Washington, DC: Economic Mobility Project, 2008).

2. Center for American Progress, "From Poverty to Prosperity: A National Strategy to Cut Poverty in Half" (2007).

3. Isabel V. Sawhill and John E. Morton, "Economic Mobility: Is the American Dream Alive and Well?" (Washington, DC: Economic Mobility Project, 2007), p. 3.

4. Heather Boushey and Christian E. Weller, "What the Numbers Tell Us," in James Lardner and David Smith, eds., *Inequality Matters: The Growing Economic Divide in America and Its Poisonous Consequences* (New York: New Press, 2005), p. 36.

5. Isaacs, Sawhill, and Haskins, "Getting Ahead or Losing Ground," p. 62.

6. Ibid. p. 19.

7. Jared Bernstein, "You Can Take It With You," in Brian D. Smedley and Alan Jenkins, eds., *All Things Being Equal: Instigating Opportunity in an Unequal Time* (New York: New Press, 2007), pp. 28–29.

8. Isaacs, Sawhill, and Haskins, "Getting Ahead or Losing Ground," p. 75.

9. Ibid. p. 76.

10. Amaad Rivera and others, "State of the Dream 2008: Foreclosed" (Boston: United For A Fair Economy, 2008).

11. Ibid. p. 81.

12. Richard D. Kahlenberg, "The Century Foundation's Security & Opportunity

Agenda: Helping Children Move from Bad Schools to Good Ones" (New York: Century Foundation, 2006).

13. Center for American Progress, "From Poverty to Prosperity."

Overview: Meeting the Challenge of the Housing and Credit Crises

1. Edward M. Gramlich, "Booms and Busts: The Case of Subprime Mortgages," paper presented at the Federal Reserve Bank of Kansas City symposium, "Housing, Housing Finance, and Monetary Policy," in Jackson Hole, Wyoming, Aug. 31, 2007, available online at http://www.kc.frb.org/PUBLICAT/ECONREV/PDF/4q07Gramlich.pdf.

2. *The Mortgage Reform and Anti-Predatory Lending Act of 2007*, HR 3915, 110th Cong., 1st sess.

3. Michael S. Barr, "Credit Where It Counts," New York University Law Review 80 (2) (2005): 513–652.

4. Michael S. Barr, Sendhil Mullainathan, and Eldar Shafir, "Behaviorally Informed Home Mortgage Regulation," Working Paper (Joint Center on Housing Studies, November 2007).

5. Gramlich, "Booms and Busts."

Department of the Treasury:
Credibility and Flexibility for Economic Groth

1. See, for instance, John Podesta, Sarah Rosen Wartell, and David Madland, "Progressive Growth: Transforming America's Economy through Clean Energy, Innovation, and Opportunity" (Washington, DC: Center for American Progress, November 28, 2007); and John Podesta, Todd Stern, and Kit Batten, "Capturing the Energy Opportunity: Creating a Low-Carbon Economy" (Washington, DC: Center for American Progress, November 28, 2007).

2. "Press Gaggle by Ari Fleischer" (May 12, 2003), available at http://www.whitehouse.gov/news/releases/2003/05/20030512-1.html.

3. Andrew Pollack, "Dollar Hits Low Against Yen with More Declines Feared," *The New York Times*, October 21, 1994.

4. *The New York Times*, "Dollar Recovers as Bentsen Reverses Stand on Support," October 22, 1994.

5. *BBC News*, "Bush to announce new economic team," December 8, 2002.

6. *The Economist*, "The peso crisis, ten years on," December 29, 2004; Paul Blustein, *The Money Kept Rolling In (and Out)* (New York: PublicAffairs, 2005), pp. xix–xxi.

7. Seth Mydans, "Indonesia Asks I.M.F. and World Bank Aid," *The New York Times*, October 9, 1997; Beth Jinks and Laurent Malespine, "Reviving Thai 'ghosts,'" *International Herald Tribune*, June 20, 2006.

8. Yahoo! Finance, S&P 500 Historical Data: August–September 1997, available at http://finance.yahoo.com.

9. U.S. Department of the Treasury, Bureau of the Public Debt, "Debt to the Penny and Who Holds It" (April 15, 2008), available at http://www.treasurydirect.gov/NP/BPDLogin?application=np.

10. Steven R. Weisman, "U.S. ran a record trade deficit in 2006," *International Herald Tribune*, February 13, 2007.

11. Matt Fiedler, "Where Do Our Federal Tax Dollars Go?" (Washington, DC: Center for Budget and Policy Priorities, April 14, 2008).

12. Center for Medicaid & Medicare Services, "2008 Annual Report of the Board of Trustees of the Federal Hospital Insurance and Federal Supplementary Medical Insurance Trust Funds" (March 25, 2008).

13. Tom Kalil and John Irons, "A National Innovation Agenda: Progressive Policies for Economic Growth and Opportunity through Science and Technology" (Washington, DC: Center for American Progress, November 28, 2007).

14. Bureau of Labor Statistics, "Current Employment Statistics" (U.S. Department of Labor, 2008); Bureau of Economic Analysis, "GDP by Industry Data" (U.S. Department of Commerce, 2006).

15. U.S. Trade Representative, "U.S. Proposals for Liberalizing Trade in Services" (July 2002), available at http://www.ustr.gov/assets/Document_Library/Press_Releases/2002/July/asset_upload_file224_2009.pdf.

16. Bernard Hoekman and Aaditya Mattoo, "Services Trade and Growth," Policy Research Working Paper 4461 (Washington, DC: World Bank, January 2008).

17. Wendy Dobson and Pierre Jacquet, *Financial Services Liberalization in the WTO* (Washington, DC: Peterson Institute, 1998).

18. Daniel Pruzin and Gary G. Yerkey, "United States Proposes Broad Opening of Services Sector in WTO Trade Negotiations," *International Trade Reporter*, July 14, 2002.

19. Richard Samans and Jonathan Jacoby, "Virtuous Circle: Strengthening Broad-Based Global Progress in Living Standards" (Washington, DC: Center for American Progress, December 2007).

20. U.S. Department of the Treasury, "U.S. Fact Sheet: The Third Cabinet-Level Meeting of the U.S.-China Strategic Economic Dialogue" (December 13, 2007).

21. Mohammed El-Erian, "IMF Reform: Attaining a Critical Mass," in Edwin Truman, ed., *A Strategy for IMF Reform* (Washington, DC: Peterson Institute, April 2006), pp. 501–512.

22. Pedro Malan, et al., "Report of the External Review Committee on Bank-Fund Collaboration" (Washington, DC: International Monetary Fund, February 2007).

23. Daniel Tarullo, Testimony before U.S. Senate Committee on Banking, Housing, and Urban Affairs, "Reforming Key International Financial Institutions for the 21st Century," August 2, 2007, available at http://banking.senate.gov/public/_files/tarullo1.pdf.

24. Allan Meltzer, "IMF and World Bank Reform 2004," Testimony before Senate Committee on Banking, Housing, and Urban Affairs, "Congressional Oversight of the IMF and World Bank," May 19, 2004, available at http://banking.senate.gov/public/_files/meltzer.pdf.

25. Samans and Jacoby, "Virtuous Circle."

26. U.S. Civil Society Coalition, "Responsible Reform of the World Bank" (April 2002), available at http://www.essentialaction.org/imf/worldbank_report/IDA_FINAL_REPORT.pdf.

Office of Management and Budget: Ensuring Fiscal Responsibility and Government Accountability

1. Republicans used the CRA in the first weeks of the Bush administration to nullify an ergonomics rule issued at the end of 2000.

2. President Reagan's Order was E.O. 12291 (continued through the first Bush administration) and President Clinton's was E.O. 12866. President G.W. Bush's E.O. 13422, issued midway through Bush's second term, amended but largely left in place the Clinton Order.

3. Independent regulatory commissions, like the Securities and Exchange Commission and the Federal Communications Commission, have not been subject to centralized regulatory review except in very limited areas. This should continue to be the approach.

4. The Clinton E.O., unlike the one issued by President Reagan, was signed after extensive consultations with key players, which may have been instrumental in achieving buy-in from stakeholders with dramatically different views.

5. Bush had earlier amended the Clinton E.O. by removing the vice president from the regulatory review process, substituting the chief of staff and/or the director of OMB. If the president wants the VP-elect to be engaged in regulatory matters, the administration should rescind E.O.s 13422 and 13258.

6. Examples include: Information Quality Act Guidelines (2002); Circular A-4: "Regulatory Analysis" (Sept. 17, 2003); Final Information Quality Bulletin for Peer Review (Jan. 14, 2005); Agency Good Guidance Practices (Jan. 27, 2007); and OMB Memorandum: "Updated Principles for Risk Analysis" (Sept. 19, 2007).

7. The first budget of President George H.W. Bush was sent to Congress on February 9, 1989 (20 days after inauguration), President Clinton's first budget was sent on February 17, 1993 (+29 days), and President G.W. Bush's first budget was sent on February 28, 2001 (+39 days).

8. Presidents may issue E.O.s unilaterally and without any procedural requirements; E.O.s are a means of establishing substantive standards or processes by which *agencies* carry out their work, but cannot directly affect individuals, businesses, or state and local governments.

9. See, for example, Protecting the Property Rights of the American People (E.O. 13406, concerning "takings" of property); Protecting American Taxpayers from Payment of Contingency Fees (E.O. 13433, on tort reform); Actions Concerning Regulations That Significantly Affect Energy Supply, Distribution, or Use (E.O. 13211, on energy policy); and Notification of Employee Rights Concerning Payment of Union Dues or Fees (E.O. 13201, on unions).

10. See http://www.ombwatch.org/article/articleview/4090/1/90?Topic1D=1, "White House Attempts to Entrench PART at Federal Agencies," November 20, 2007.

11. This section describes OMB's role in building the budget. Depending on how the administration chooses to organize the White House, various White House policy counsels also play a role in developing priorities and major policy initiatives.

Office of the United States Trade Representative: Responding to the Changing Global Challenge

1. *Trade Act of 1974, U.S. Code 19, § 2171.* As summarized in the leading study of American trade politics, "the Trade Expansion Act of 1962 created the position of the president's special representative for trade negotiations. (STR) After two Nixon administration efforts to weaken or abolish it, the Trade Act of 1974 made the STR a statutory unit in the Executive Office of the President. Five years later, Congress forced the Carter Administration to carry out a trade reorganization that increased the office's size and power and renamed it

USTR." I.M. Destler, *American Trade Politics*, 4th ed., (Washington, DC: Institute for International Economics, 2005), p. 113.

2. *Trade Act of 1974, U.S. Code* 19, § 2155.

3. Pew Research Center for the People and the Press, "Doubts About China, Concerns About Jobs: Post-Seattle Support for WTO," survey conducted by the Princeton Survey Research Associates (February 9–14, 2000), available at http://people-press.org/reports/pdf/44.pdf (last accessed August 2008).

4. Los Angeles Times/Bloomberg Poll, "National Investor Survey" (May 1–8, 2008), available at http://www.calendarlive.com/media/acrobat/2008-05/38819516.pdf (last accessed August 2008).

5. See, for example, Steven Castle and Mark Lander, "After Seven Years, Talk Collapse on World Trade," *The New York Times*, July 30, 2008, p. 1.

6. *Trade Act of 1974, U.S. Code* 19, § 2241.

7. *Trade Act of 1974, U.S. Code* 19, § 2242(a)(2).

8. Ambassador Charlene Barshefsky, Testimony before the Senate Finance Committee, July 29, 2008, p. 10.

9. This point has been made by many trade experts. See, for example, Daniel K. Tarullo, "The Case for Reviving the Doha Round" (Washington, DC: Center for American Progress, January 2007).

10. This recommendation was made by Charlene Barshefsky in her July 29, 2008, testimony to the Senate Finance Committee.

11. The astonishing increase of bilateral FTAs being negotiated around the world has been observed by many commentators. See, for example, Claude Barfield, "U.S. Trade Policy: The Emergence of Regional and Bilateral Alternatives to Multilateralism," *Intereconomics—Review of European Economic Policy* 42 (5) (September/October 2007): 239–249; Bruce Stokes, "Bilateralism Trumps Multilateralism," *National Journal*, December 16, 2006, pp. 59–60; Greg Mastel, "The Rise of the Free Trade Agreement," *Challenge* 47 (4) (July–August 2004): 41–61.

12. Immediately after the breakdown of the Doha Round, Brazil, a major trading nation that has, for the most part, avoided negotiating FTAs, said that it would have to shift course and begin doing so. BNA International Trade Daily, "Collapse of Doha Talks Signals Set Back for Brazil's WTO-Oriented Trade Strategy," July 31, 2008.

13. Nor would such an FTA necessarily be limited to Asian nations. But this is the region in which the United States faces the most serious challenges, and we must move vigorously to regain our position.

14. An initiative toward Asia will not be taken seriously in the region until the new administration addresses the Korea-U.S. FTA, negotiated by the Bush administration.

15. Daniel K Tarullo, "A Sensible Approach to Labor Standards to Ensure Free Trade" (Washington, DC: Center for American Progress, 2007).

16. Samuel Laird and Andre Sapir, "Tariff Preferences," in *The Uruguay Round: A Handbook on Multilateral Trade Negotiations*, Michael J. Finger and Andrezj Olechowski, eds. (Washington, DC: World Bank, 1987), cited in Comments submitted to the Office of the U.S. Trade Representative by the Women's Edge Coalition, Oxfam America, the German Marshall Fund of the United States, and Viji Rangaswami, Carnegie Endowment of International Peace, September 5, 2006, "Generalized System of Preferences (GSP): Initiation of Reviews and Request for Public Comments," 71 Fed. Reg. 45079 (Aug. 8, 2006).

17. Judith M. Dean, "Do Preferential Trade Agreements Promote Growth: An Evaluation of the Caribbean Basin Economic Recovery Act," USITC Office of Economics Work-

ing Paper, No. 2002-07-A (Washington, DC: USITC, July 2002), also cited in the Comments submitted to USTR, referenced in Note 16.

18. Ibid., p. 13.

19. This rationale also extends to the U.S.-Panama FTA, which, although less important than the other two agreements, has national security implications because of the Panama Canal. Congressional Democratic objections to the Panama FTA are not as deeply felt as the objections to the Colombia and Korea agreements; the opposition could dissipate this year if a Panamanian legislator, indicted for murder by the United States, decides to resign.

20. Although the trade representative is a cabinet official, USTR is situated within the Executive Office of the President. For that reason, the general counsel is not a Senate-confirmed official. Congress should consider changing that, in light of the importance of the role that the general counsel traditionally plays.

21. See, for example, Robert D. Atkinson, president, Information Technology and Innovation Foundation, "Combating Unfair Trade Practices in the Innovation Economy," Testimony before the U.S. Senate Committee on Finance, May 22, 2008.

22. This is the approach taken in a major piece of legislation introduced by House Judiciary Committee Chairman John Conyers.

23. See, for example, William Cline, "The Case for a New Plaza Agreement," Policy Briefs in International Economics (Institute of International Economics, December 2005); C. Fred Bergsten, "The Dollar and the Remnimbi," Testimony before U.S. Senate Committee on Banking, Housing and Urban Affairs, May 23, 2007; Morris Goldstein, "A (Lack of) Progress Report on China's Exchange Rate Policies," Working Paper Series (Peterson Institute for International Economics, June 2007).

24. This point is made by virtually all the leading experts.

25. Ambassador Schwab and the Bush administration made a good start in this direction by joining with the European Union and Canada to win a WTO case against China on auto parts. USTR has also vigorously prosecuted two cases involving China's avoidance of WTO obligations to the detriment of the U.S. copyright industries. These cases—one on piracy, and one on market access—have generated gratifying support from other countries.

26. Senate Finance Committee Chairman Max Baccus called for launching a negotiation of free trade in services between the United States, the European Union, and Japan. Speech to the Coalition of Services Industries, September 17, 2008.

27. The National Free Trade Council (NFTC) recently released a proposal on negotiation authority incorporating these ideas.

Department of Commerce:
Proving Ground for Sustainable Economic Growth

1. Former colleagues at the Department of Commerce who contributed invaluable substantive suggestions and insights to this chapter include Ev Ehrlich, Sally Ericcson, Bill Reinsch, Rob Stein, Loretta Schmitzer, and Sally Yozell. Ross Johnson provided editorial assistance.

2. Ken Jacobson, "Advanced Technology Program Board Perplexed by NIST's Decision to Shut the Program Down," *Manufacturing News* 13 (10) (2006): 2.

3. Robert Atkinson and Howard Wial, "Boosting Productivity, Innovation, and Growth Through a National Innovation Foundation" (Washington, DC: The Information Technology and Innovation Foundation and The Brookings Institution, 2008), available at http://

www.brookings.edu/~/media/Files/rc/reports/2008/04_federal_role_atkinson_wial/NIF%20Report.pdf.

4. Ibid.

5. Patricia Mulroy, "Diving in the Deep End: Help Water Agencies Address Climate Change" (Washington, DC: Brookings Opportunity '08, 2008).

6. "The Coastal Community Development Project," available at http://coastalmanagement.noaa.gov/partnership.html (last accessed June 2008); U.S. Commission on Ocean Policy, "An Ocean Blueprint for the 21st Century" (2004), available at http://oceancommission.gov/documents/full_color_rpt/000_ocean_full_report.pdf.

7. The Intergovernmental Panel on Climate Change, "Climate Change 2007: Impacts, Adaptation and Vulnerability" (2007), available at http://www.ipcc.ch/ipccreports/ar4-wg2.htm.

8. National Wildlife Federation, "Sea-Level Rise and Coastal Habitats of the Chesapeake Bay: A Summary" (2008), available at http://www.nwf.org/nwfwebadmin/binaryVault/NWF_Chesapeake-SLR-Report-Summary.pdf.

9. Government Accountability Office, "Federal Research: Policies Guiding the Dissemination of Scientific Research from Selected Agencies Should Be Clarified and Better Communicated" (GAO, 2007), available at http://www.gao.gov/new.items/d07653.pdf.

10. Andrew Reamer, "The Department of Commerce Budget Request for Fiscal Year 2008: Observations for Consideration," Testimony before the House Committee on Appropriations, Subcommittee on Commerce, Justice, Science and Related Agencies, March 6, 2007, available at http://www.brookings.edu/testimony/2007/0306useconomics_reamer.aspx?rssid=reamera.

11. Government Accountability Office, "Export Promotion: Trade Promotion Coordinating Committee's Role Remains Limited" (GAO, 2006), available at http://www.gao.gov/new.items/d06660t.pdf.

12. Government Accountability Office, "2010 Census: Bureau Needs to Specify How It Will Assess Coverage Follow-Up Techniques and When It Will Produce Coverage Measurement Results" (GAO, 2008), available at http://www.gao.gov/new.items/d08414.pdf.

13. The International Intellectual Property Alliance, "Copyright Industries in the U.S. Economy: The 2006 Report" (2006), available at http://www.iipa.com/pdf/2006Siwek Summary.pdf.

14. Pew Oceans Commission, "America's Living Oceans: Charting a Course for Sea Change" (2003), available at http://www.pewtrusts.org/uploadedFiles/wwwpewtrustsorg/Reports/Protecting_ocean_life/env_pew_oceans_final_report.pdf; and U.S. Commission on Ocean Policy, "An Ocean Blueprint for the 21st Century."

15. Farm, Nutrition, and Bioenergy Act of 2007, Public Law 110-234, 110 Congress. 2 sess. (May 22, 2008).

16. World Wildlife Foundation, "Sustainability at the Speed of Light" (2002), available at http://assets.panda.org/downloads/wwf_ic_1.pdf.

17. James Parks, "The Future of Manufacturing and America's Middle Class" (Washington, DC: AFL-CIO, 2007).

18. Atkinson and Wial, "Boosting Productivity, Innovation and Growth Through a National Innovation Foundation."

19. Academic research suggests, for example, that the gay and lesbian population was undercounted by 16 percent in 2000. M.V. Lee Badgett and Marc A. Rogers, "Left Out of the Count: Missing Same-Sex Couples in Census 2000" (Washington, DC, Institute for Gay and

Lesbian Strategic Studies, 2003), available at http://www.iglss.org/media/files/c2k_leftout.pdf.

Department of Labor:
Promoting Opportunity While Protecting Worker Rights

1. See Sarah Anderson, John Cavanagh, Chuck Collins, Sam Pizzigati, and Mike Lapham, "Executive Excess 2007: The Staggering Social Cost of U.S. Business Leadership," 14th annual CEO Compensation Survey, Institute for Policy Studies and United for a Fair Economy, August 29, 2007.

2. Nonfarm payroll employment increased from 109,725,000 in January 1993 to 132,469,000 in January 2001 and 137,318,000 in September 2008. Bureau of Labor Statistics data.

3. In FY2001 there were 17,667 full-time employees at DOL and in FY2008 16,142 full-time employees. There is an increase to 16,848 FTEs in the president's FY2009 request, but that would still be below FY2001 levels. See "DOL Fiscal Year 2009 Budget in Brief," available at http://www.dol.gov/_sec/budget2009/app.htm (last accessed July 2008).

4. Ibid. FY2001 discretionary spending at DOL was $11.753 billion, while it was $11.650 billion in FY2008 and is proposed to be $10.542 billion in FY2009.

5. See Harry J. Holzer, "Better Workers for Better Jobs: Improving Worker Advancement in the Low-Wage Labor Market" (The Hamilton Project, December 2007).

6. See Peg Seminario, Director Safety and Health, AFL-CIO, Testimony before the Senate Employment and Worker Safety Subcommittee of the Health, Education, Labor and Pensions Committee Hearing on "Is OSHA Working for Working People?" April 26, 2007. The number of establishments is estimated to have grown from 3.9 million in 1975 to 8.9 million in 2008.

7. See U.S. Department of Labor, "Summary of the Major Laws of the Department of Labor," available at http://www.dol.gov/opa/aboutdol/lawsprog.htm (last accessed July 2008).

8. The Inspector General of DOL issued "High Growth Job Training Initiative: Decisions for Non-Competitive Awards Not Adequately Justified," Report No. 02-08-201-03-390, November 2, 2007, which called into question the process for awarding 134 of 156 grants under this program. Ninety percent of the questioned awards had been noncompetitively issued. See also Scott Lilly, "Sole Sourcing: Handling Out Tax Dollars at the Labor Department" (Washington, DC: Center for American Progress, 2007), available at http://www.americanprogress.org/issues/2007/11/sole_sourcing.html.

9. John E. Baugher and J. Timmons Roberts, "Workplace Hazards, Unions & Coping Styles," *Labor Studies Journal* 29 (2) (2004): 83–106.

10. *Employee Free Choice Act of 2007*, H. Rept. 110-23, 110 Congress, 1st session, p. 7.

11. Executive Order 13208 was issued by President George W. Bush to amend this order to remove this preference.

12. See Brainard, Litan, and Warren, "A Fairer Deal for American Workers in a New Era of Off-Shoring" (Brookings Trade Forum, 2005).

13. Maurice Emsellem, National Employment Law Project, Testimony before the U.S. House of Representatives, Ways & Means Committee, Subcommittee on "Income Security & Family Support," March 15, 2007.

14. See Wayne Vroman, "Strengthening Unemployment Insurance," Briefing Paper #202 (Economic Policy Institute, October 23, 2007).

15. Ibid, p. 3.

16. U.S. General Accounting Office, "Unemployment Insurance: Role as Safety Net for Low-Wage Workers Is Limited" (December 2000), pp. 13–16.

17. Ibid, p. 3.

18. The federal UI surtax was supposed to be a temporary tax on employers to restore solvency to the UI system but has been in place since 1977. It has been extended four times by both Democrat and Republican majorities in Congress. Reed Act distributions are federal payments of unemployment insurance dollars to the states from the revenues the federal government holds in reserve.

19. Raymond J. Uhalde, Deputy Assistant Secretary, Employment and Training Administration, Statement before the Subcommittee on Human Resources, Committee on Ways and Means, United States House of Representatives, September 7, 2000.

20. For a discussion of S.1871 and H.R. 2233 Unemployment Insurance Modernization Act see Chad Stone, Robert Greenstein, Martha Coven, "Addressing Longstanding Gaps in Unemployment Insurance Coverage" (Center on Budget and Policy Priorities, August 7, 2007), available at http://www.cbpp.org/7-20-07ui.htm.

21. See U.S. Department of Labor, "FY2009 Department of Labor Budget in Brief," available at http://www.dol.gov/_sec/budget2009/app.htm.

22. See U.S. Government Accountability Office, "Trade Adjustment Assistance: Most Workers in Five Layoffs Received Services, but Better Outreach Needed on New Benefits," GAO-06-43 (January 2006) and "Trade Adjustment Assistance: Changes Need to Improve States Ability to Provide Benefits and Services to Trade-Affected Workers," GAO-07-995T (June 2007).

23. Department of Labor, "FY2009 Congressional Budget Justification, Occupational Safety and Health Administration," available at http://www.dol.gov/dol/budget/2009/PDF/CBJ-2009-V2-08.pdf, p. 33.

24. FY2001 proposed budget for OLMS was $30.6 million and 296 FTEs while the FY2009 proposed budget is $58.2 million and 369 FTEs.

25. See Brennan Center for Justice, "Protecting New York's Workers: How the State Department of Labor Can Improve Wage and Hour Enforcement" (December 2006).

26. Seminario, "Is OSHA Working for Working People?"

27. Ibid.

28. Ken Ward, "Mine Safety Efforts Still Stumbling," Sunday Gazette (Charlotte, WV), Feb. 19, 2008.

29. BLS Displaced Worker Survey Data 2003–05 shows that there were 8.2 million displaced workers over this period.

30. Holzer, "Better Workers for Better Jobs: Improving Worker Advancement in the Low-Wage Labor Market."

31. The secretary should also work with Congress to move the Office of Job Corps from the Office of the Secretary back to the Employment and Training Administration. This will aid in the development of a more integrated and comprehensive youth training strategy that seeks to build links across all of the youth programs at DOL.

32. Cathy Ruckelshaus and Rebecca Smith, "Holding the Wage Floor: Enforcement of Wage and Hour Standards for Low-Wage Workers in an Era of Government Inaction and Employer Unaccountability," Immigrant & Nonstandard Worker Project Policy Update (National Employment Law Project, October 2006).

33. Ross Eisenbrey, "Long Hours, Less Pay," EPI Briefing Paper #152 (Economic Policy Institute, July 14, 2004).

34. See Natwar Gandhi, "Tax Administration: Issues in Classifying Workers as Employees or Independent Contractors," Testimony before the Before the Subcommittee on Oversight Committee on Ways and Means, June 1996, GAO document T-GGD-96-130.

35. Seminario, "Is OSHA Working for Working People?" p. 7.

Securities and Exchange Commission:
Restoring the Capital Markets Regulator and Responding to Crisis

1. David Roche, "Insight: The fire threatens credit insurance," *Financial Times*, January 14, 2008, available at http://search.ft.com/ftArticle?queryText=credit+default+swaps+and+notional&y=0&aje=true&x=0&id=080114000361&ct=0 (last accessed March 9, 2008).

2. SEC Chairman Harvey L. Pitt, "Remarks Before the AICPA Governing Council," October 22, 2001, available at http://www.sec.gov/news/speech/spch516.htm.

3. Penelope Patsuris, "The Corporate Scandal Sheet," Forbes.com, August 26, 2002, available at http://www.forbes.com/2002/07/25/accountingtracker_print.html.

4. *Public Company Accounting Reform and Investor Protection Act of 2002*, Public Law 107-204, 107th Congress, 116 Stat. 745 (July 30, 2002).

5. Stephen Labaton, "3 Inquiries Begun into S.E.C.'s Choice of Audit Overseer," *The New York Times*, November 1, 2002; Stephen Labaton, "Government Report Details a Chaotic S.E.C. Under Pitt," *The New York Times*, December 20, 2002.

6. Stephen Labaton, "Markets & Investing; Defying Election-Year Tradition, S.E.C. Draws Up a Busy Agenda," *The New York Times*, January 2, 2004; Stephen Labaton, "S.E.C. Backs Rules on Fund Ethics and Disclosure," *The New York Times*, May 27, 2004; Stephen Labaton, "S.E.C. to Order That Funds Have Outsiders as Chairmen," *The New York Times*, June 22, 2004; Stephen Labaton, "S.E.C. at Odds on Plan to Let Big Investors Pick Directors," *The New York Times*, July 1, 2004; Stephen Labaton, "Member of S.E.C. Criticizes Inaction," *The New York Times*, October 9, 2004.

7. Jenny Anderson, "Strife Aplenty at S.E.C. Chief's Farewell Session," *The New York Times*, June 30, 2005.

8. Stephen Labaton, "Donaldson Announces Resignation as S.E.C. Chairman," *The New York Times*, June 1, 2005; Stephen Labaton, "S.E.C.'s Chairman Is Stepping Down from Split Panel," *The New York Times*, June 2, 2005.

9. Jesse Westbrook and Otis Bilodeau, "SEC Chief, Seeking Consensus, Draws Fire From Both Sides," *Bloomberg.com*, June 18, 2007, available at http://www.bloomberg.com/apps/news?pid=newsarchive&sid=ax1WWAMfrL6A (last accessed Feb. 29, 2008).

10. Department of the Treasury, *Blueprint for a Modernized Financial Regulatory Structure* (March 2008), available at http://www.treasury.gov/press/releases/reports/Blueprint.pdf.

11. Absolute Return, "Top Hedge Fund Assets Surpass $1.6 Trillion According to *Absolute Return* Survey," press release, March 4, 2008, available at http://www.hedgefundintelligence.com/images/590/55595/Billion%20Dollar%20Club%20-%20March%202008%20-%20press%20release.pdf; "Private equity firepower hits $2 trillion," *Financial News Online*, January 24, 2008, available at http://www.efinancialnews.com/investmentbanking/index/content/2349631961. "Private equity funds raised more than $500bn last year from investors, according to research provider Private Equity Intelligence." See David H. McCormick, under secretary for international affairs, Testimony before the Senate Committee on Banking, Housing, and Urban Affairs, "Sovereign Wealth Fund Acquisitions and Other

Foreign Government Investments in the U.S.: Assessing the Economic and National Security Implications Before the Senate Comm. on Banking, Housing, and Urban Affairs," November 14, 2007, available at http://www.ustreas.gov/press/releases/hp681.htm. "Today, what is new is the rapid increase in both the number and size of sovereign wealth funds. Twenty new funds have been created since 2000, more than half of these since 2005, which brings the total number to nearly 40 funds that now manage total assets in a range of $1.9–2.9 trillion. Private sector analysts have projected that sovereign wealth fund assets could grow to $10–15 trillion by 2015."

12. Editorial, "If the Price Is Right," *The New York Times*, October 18, 2006; Alison Vekshin, "Frank Says Hedge Funds Pose Potential Risks to System," Bloomberg.com, July 11, 2007, available at http://www.bloomberg.com/apps/news?pid=newsarchive&sid=aMYgw9EHnsXA (last accessed Feb. 29, 2008).

13. SEC Chairman Christopher Cox, "The Rise of Sovereign Business" (speech for the Gauer Distinguished Lecture in Law and Policy at the American Enterprise Institute Legal Center for the Public Interest, December 5, 2007), available at http://www.sec.gov/news/speech/2007/spch120507cc.htm.

14. *Stoneridge Investment Partners, LLC v. Scientific-Atlanta, Inc. et al.*, 128 S.Ct. 761 (2008); *Regents of the University of California et al. v. Credit Suisse First Boston (USA) Inc. et al.*, 482 F.3d 372 (5th Cir. 2007) cert. denied, 2008 U.S. LEXIS 1120 (2008).

15. *Stoneridge Investment Partners, LLC v. Scientific-Atlanta, Inc., et al.*, 128 S.Ct. 761 (2008), Motion for Leave to File Brief out of Time and Brief Amici Curiae of Former SEC Commissioners in Support of Petitioner (2007).

16. *Securities Exchange Act of 1934*, 48 Stat. 881 (June 6, 1934), codified at 15 U.S. Code § 78a et. seq.

17. Securities and Exchange Commission, "Summary Report of Issues Identified in the Commission Staff's Examinations of Select Credit Rating Agencies" (July 2008); Proposed Rules for Nationally Recognized Statistical Rating Organizations, Securities Exchange Act Release No. 57967 (June 16, 2008) [73 FR 36212 (June 25, 2008)] ("NRSRO June 16, 2008 Proposing Release"); References to Ratings of Nationally Recognized Statistical Rating Organizations, Investment Company Act Release No. 28327 (July 1, 2008) ("NRSRO Proposal").

18. California Public Employees' Retirement System, et al., Petition for Interpretive Guidance on Climate Risk Disclosure, before the Security and Exchange Commission, September 18, 2007, available at http://www.edf.org/page.cfm?tagID=13094 (last accessed March 4, 2008).

19. *AFSCME Employees Pension Plan v. American International Group, Inc.*, 462 F.3d121 (2d Cir. 2006).

20. Proposed Rule, "Disclosure Regarding Nominating Committee Functions and Communications between Security Holders and Boards of Directors," 17 CFR Part 240, October 14, 2003, available at http://www.sec.gov/rules/proposed/34-48301.htm.

21. *Shareholder Vote on Executive Compensation Act*, S. 1181, 110th Cong. (2007).

22. Floyd Norris, "S.E.C. Changes Reporting Rule on Bosses' Pay," *The New York Times*, December 27, 2006.

23. The Aspen Institute, "Long-Term Value Creation: Guiding Principles for Corporations and Investors" (2008).

24. Securities and Exchange Commission, "Statement of the Securities and Exchange Commission Concerning Financial Penalties," press release, January 4, 2006, available at http://www.sec.gov/news/press/2006-4.htm.

25. SEC Commissioner Paul S. Atkins, "Remarks before the U.S. Chamber Institute for Legal Reform" (February16, 2006), available at http://www.sec.gov/news/speech/spch021606psa.htm.

26. David Scheer and Jesse Westbrook, "SEC Penalties Fall Amid 'New Ethos' on Company Fines," *Bloomberg.com*, November 19, 2007, available at http://www.bloomberg.com/apps/news?pid=newsarchive&sid=aJKCRZoXEz71 (last accessed February 29, 2008).

27. David Evans and David Scheer, "SEC Aims to End Backdating Cases in 'Short Order' Thomsen Says," Bloomberg News, January 25, 2008, available at http://www.bloomberg.com/apps/news?pid=newsarchive&sid=avxEFbA2CFfs (last accessed March 7, 2008); see also the controversy involving the SEC's settlement of the single largest case, *California Public Employees Retirement System v. UnitedHealth Group, Inc.*; Chen May Yee, "Judge Tests His Authority in McGuire Settlement," *StarTribune.com/Minneapolis-St. Paul, Minnesota*, December 28, 2007, available at http://www.startribune.com/templates/Print_This_Story?sid=12871806 (last accessed March 3, 2008); Associated Press, "UNH Deal with Ex-CEO Under Scrutiny," Associated Press Business News, December 27, 2007, available at http://news.moneycentral.msn.com/printarticle.aspx?feed=AP&date=20071227&id=7882784 (last accessed March 3, 2008).

28. SEC Commissioner Paul S. Atkins, "Remarks Before the International Corporate Governance Network 11th Annual Conference," July 6, 2006; SEC Chief Accountant Conrad Hewitt, Letter to Financial Executives International and American Institute of Certified Public Accountants, September 19, 2006, available at http://www.sec.gov/info/accountants/staffletters/fei_aicpa091906.htm.

29. Securities and Exchange Commission, Final Rule, Investment Company Governance, 17 C.F.R. Part 270, *Federal Register 69*, No. 147: 46378 (August 2, 2004), available at http://www.sec.gov/rules/final/ic-26520.pdf.

30. *U.S. Chamber of Commerce v. Securities and Exchange Commission*, 412 F.3d 133 (DC Cir. 2005).

31. Emergency Order Pursuant to Section 12(k)(2) of the Securities Exchange Act of 1934 Taking Temporary Action to Respond to Market Developments, Exchange Act Release No. 58166 (July 15, 2008); see also Amendment to Emergency Order Pursuant to Section 12(k)(2) of the Securities Exchange Act of 1934 Taking Temporary Action to Respond to Market Developments, Exchange Act Release No. 58190 (July 18, 2008); Order Extending Emergency Order Pursuant to Section 12(k)(2) of the Securities Exchange Act of 1934 Taking Temporary Action to Respond to Market Developments, Exchange Act Release No. 58248 (July 29, 2008).

32. See homepage for Financial Industry Regulatory Authority, available at http://www.finra.org.

33. *Financial Planning Association v. Securities and Exchange Commission*, 2007 U.S. App. LEXIS 15169 (DC Cir. June 25, 2007)

34. Angela Hung and others, "Investor and Industry Perspectives on Investment Advisers and Broker-Dealers" (Rand Corporation, 2008), available at http://www.rand.org/pubs/technical_reports/TR556/.

35. SEC Advisory Committee on Improvements to Financial Reporting, "Progress Report of the SEC Advisory Committee on Improvements to Financial Reporting," progress report submitted to the United States Securities and Exchange Commission, Release No. 33-8896, File No. 265-24, February 14, 2008, available at http://www.sec.gov/rules/other/2008/33-8896.pdf.

36. Notice of Roundtable Discussion; Request for Commitment Securities Act Release No. 8947 (July 29, 2008). This footnote follows relaxation of the application of GAAP to foreign private issuers; Securities and Exchange Commission, Proposed Rule: Acceptance from Foreign Private Issuers of Financial Statements Prepared in Accordance with International Financial Reporting Standards Without Reconciliation to U.S. GAAP, 17 CFR Parts 210, 230, 239 and 249, *Federal Register* 72: 37962 (July 11, 2007) available at http://www.sec.gov/rules/proposed/2007/33-881fr.pdf.

37. Heather Timmons and Katrin Bennhold, "Calls Grow for Foreigners to Have a Say on U.S. Market Rules," *The New York Times*, August 29, 2007; Michael M. Phillips and Yuka Hayashi, "More Credit Shocks Could Revive Crisis: Global Bankers Warn of Lending Reductions Amid U.S. Slowdown," *The Wall Street Journal*, February 11, 2008.

38. Compare with Statement by Assistant to the President for Press Relations Fitzwater on the Formation of the Working Group on Financial Markets, March 18, 1988, available at http://www.reagan.utexas.edu/archives/speeches/1988/031888e.htm (last accessed March 3, 2008).

39. Prof. Michael Greenberger, Univeristy of Maryland School of Law, Testimony before the House Committee on Agriculture, "Hearing to Review Legislation Amending the Commodity Exchange Act," 2008.

40. *Gramm-Leach-Bliley Financial Services Modernization Act*, Public Law 106-102, 106th Congress, 113 Stat. 1338 (November 12, 1999).

Domestic Policy

Overview: America's Changing Demographics

1. Peter Brimelow and Ed Rubinstein wrote in 1997, in a very controversial article, that "[d]emography is destiny in American politics." See "Electing a New People," *National Review*, June 16, 1997. While not agreeing so much with Brimelow's views, whether in his book *Alien Nation* or in numerous articles since then, we must give credit to him for this phrase. His writings have focused almost entirely on how immigration and the growing Hispanic and immigrant population would hasten the demise of the Republican Party and, in his eyes, reshape this country into something different, and apparently unappealing.

2. Centers for Disease Control and Prevention and the Merck Company Foundation, "The State of Aging and Health in America, 2007" (Whitehouse Station, NJ: The Merck Company Foundation; 2007), p. III.

3. Ibid., p. 3.

4. Jeffery Passel, "Age Pyramids for Hispanics, Non-Hispanic White population: 1960, 2000, and Projected 2030," in Marta Tienda and Faith Mitchell, eds., *Multiple Origins, Uncertain Destinies: Hispanics and the American Future*, Panel on Hispanics in the United States, Committee on Population, Division of Behavioral and Social Sciences and Education National Research Council (Washington, DC: The National Academies Press, 2006), Figure 4-3, p. 63.

5. California Long Term County Data Book 2002, available at http://www.caads.org/ltcdata/ltc_data.html (last accessed July 2008).

6. "The State of Aging and Health in America, 2007," available at http://www.cdc.gov/aging/saha.htm, p.25.

7. Tienda and Mitchell, *Multiple Origins, Uncertain Destinies*, p. 23.

8. Pew Hispanic Center, "U.S. Population Projections: 2005–2050," February 11, 2008, available at http://www.pewhispanic.org/reports/report.php?ReportID=85.

9. Tienda and Mitchell, *Multiple Origins, Uncertain Destinies*, p. 3.

10. Manuel Pastor, "The New Economy, the New Demography and the New Inequality in California," presentation as part of panel, "An Economic and Labor Policy that Lifts All Boats: How Can We Make Sure the Labor Market Works for Latinos?" The 40th Annual Conference of the National Conference of La Raza, San Diego, California, July 13, 2008.

11. Tienda and Mitchell, *Multiple Origins, Uncertain Destinies*, pp. 45–46.

12. Samuel Huntington, *Who We Are? The Challenge to America's National Identity* (New York: Simon & Schuster, 2004).

13. Pew Hispanic Center, "Assimilation and Language" (2004), available at http://pew hispanic.org/factsheets/factsheet.php?FactsheetID=11.

14. In 2000, foreign-born Hispanics averaged 9.8 years of education, as compared to non-Hispanic whites at 13.6, non-Hispanic blacks at 12.6, and native-born Hispanics at 12.3. Data derived from U.S. Bureau of Census (2000).

15. Tienda and Mitchell, *Multiple Origins, Uncertain Destinies*, p. 60.

16. U.S. Census Bureau, "The Foreign-Born Population in the United States: 2003" (2004), available at http://www.census.gov/prod/2004pubs/p20-551.pdf.

17. Organisation for Economic Co-operation and Development, "Education at a Glance 2008: OECD Indicators" (Paris, 2008), available at http://www.oecd.org/edu/eag2008.

18. U.S. Census Bureau, "Minority Population Tops 100 million," May 17, 2007, available at http://www.census.gov/PressRelease/www/releases/archives/population/010048.html.

19. Some of the reasons include lack of legal channels for employment-based immigration, family backlogs, non-existent enforcement against employers who hire undocumented workers, demand for low-wage, low-skilled workers, and employer bias against domestic workers, especially African-Americans and little or no enforcement of labor standards.

20. See, e.g., National Asian American Pacific Legal Consortium, "2002 Audit of Violence Against Asian Pacific Americans" (2002), available at http://www.advancingequality.org/files/2002_Audit.pdf.

21. Center for American Progress, "Deporting the Undocumented: A Cost Assessment" (Washington, DC: Center for American Progress, 2005), available at: http://www.american progress.org/issues/2005/07/b913099.html.

22. U.S. Census Bureau, "America's Families and Living Arrangements: 2003" (November, 2004), available at http://www.census.gov/prod/2004pubs/p20-553.pdf.

Overview: Building a Vibrant Low-Carbon Economy

1. Stern Review "Report on the Economics of Climate Change" (Cambridge University Press: Cambridge, MA, 2008).

2. Norman Myers, "Environmental Refugees: An Emergent Climate Issue," Organization for Security and Co-operation in Europe, 13th Economic Forum, May 23–27, 2005, available at http://www.osce.org/documents/eea/2005/05/14488_en.pdf.

3. B. C. Bates and others, eds., "Climate Change and Water," Technical Paper of the Intergovernmental Panel on Climate Change (IPCC Secretariat, Geneva, 2008), p. 210.

4. Ibid.

5. Energy Information Administration, "Official Energy Statistics from the U.S. Government," August 7, 2008.

6. John Podesta, Todd Stern, and Kit Batten, "Capturing the Energy Opportunity: Creating a Low-Carbon Economy" (Washington, DC: Center for American Progress, 2007), available at http://www.americanprogress.org/issues/2007/11/energy_chapter.html.

7. Ibid.

8. Joel Makower, Ron Pernick, and Clint Wilder, "Clean Energy Trends 2008" (Clean Edge, 2008); F. Bresssand and others; "Curbing Global Energy Demand Growth: The Energy Productivity Opportunity" (McKinsey Global Institute, 2007).

9. Christopher Hall, personal communication with COWS (Center for Wisconsin Strategies), June 7, 2007.

10. Roger Bezdek, "Renewable Energy and Energy Efficiency: Economic Drivers for the 21st Century" (American Solar Energy Society, 2007). As noted above, Bezdek casts a very broad net, including direct and indirect jobs in both public and private sectors, with the largest concentrations in manufacturing, followed by recycling and construction. Whether one agrees with this counting method or not, Bezdek's discussion of selection criteria highlights many of the trickier aspects of analyzing green jobs data.

11. The original REPP roadmap is George Sterzinger and Matt Svrcek, "Wind Turbine Development: Location of Manufacturing Activity" (Renewable Energy Policy Project, September 2004). This national analysis was followed by a series of detailed state reports, including Wisconsin, Ohio, Pennsylvania, and Massachusetts, in which Sterzinger and his colleagues expand the wind model to include job estimates for component manufacturing in other renewable energy technologies.

12. Sarah White and Jason Walsh, "Greener Pathways: Jobs and Workforce Development in the Clean Energy Economy" (Center on Wisconsin Strategy, The Workforce Alliance, and Apollo Alliance, 2008).

13. David Sandalow, "Ending Oil Dependence" (The Brookings Institution, 2007).

14. An exhaustive description of cap and trade is beyond the scope of this chapter, but can be found in CAP's seminal report, "Capturing the Energy Opportunity," available at http://www.americanprogress.org/issues/2007/11/pdf/energy_chapter.pdf.

15. Terry Dinan, "Trade-Offs in Allocating Allowances for CO_2 Emissions" (Congressional Budget Office, 2007), available at http://www.cbo.gov/ftpdocs/80xx/doc8027/04-25-Cap_Trade.pdf.

16. Danny Fortson, "Power firms to pocket 6bn from carbon 'handouts' in new emissions regime," UK Independent, January 2, 2008, available at http://www.independent.co.uk/news/business/news/power-firms-to-pocket-6bn-from-carbon-handouts-in-new-emissions-regime-767623.html.

17. "World Energy Intensity: Total Primary Energy Consumption per Dollar of Gross Domestic Product Using Purchasing Power Parities: 1980–2005," International Energy Annual 2005 (Energy Information Administration, 2005).

18. John Urbanchuk, "Contribution of the Ethanol Industry to the Economy of the United States" (LECG Corporation, 2008), available at http://www.ethanolrfa.org/objects/documents/1537/2007_ethanol_economic_contribution.pdf.

19. Jaap de Hoop Scheffer, "NATO: The Next Decade," Speaking at the Security and Defense Agenda, Brussels, Belgium, June 3, 2008, available at http://www.nato.int/docu/speech/2008/s080603a.html.

20. "Contributions to Global Warming: Historic Carbon Dioxide Emissions from Fossil

Fuel Combustion, 1900–1999" Washington, DC: World Resources Institute, 2001), available at http://earthtrends.wri.org/text/climate-atmosphere/map-488.html.

Overview: Health Care Coverage, Costs, Chronic Illness, and Demographics

1. C. Schoen, S. Collins, J. Kriss, and M. Doty, "How Many Are Underinsured? Trends Among U.S. Adults, 2003 and 2007," *Health Affairs* 27 (4) (2008): w298–w309, available at 10/1377/hlthaff.27.4.w298. Underinsured is defined as out-of-pocket medical spending that exceeds 10 percent of income; deductibles that exceed 5 percent of income; and total out-of-pocket spending exceeding 5 percent of income for low-income individuals.

2. Centers for Medicare and Medicaid Services, "National Health Expenditure Accounts, 2006 Highlights" (Department of Health and Human Services, 2006), available at http://www.cms.hhs.gov/NationalHealthExpendData/downloads/highlights.pdf.

3. Organisation for Economic Co-operation and Development, "*OECD Health Data 2008*: How Does the United States Compare," available at http://www.oecd.org/dataoecd/46/2/38980580.pdf.

4. Gerard Anderson, "Chronic Conditions," *Expert Voices*, NICHM Foundation (January 2002).

5. Institute of Medicine, *Retooling for an Aging America: Building the Health Care Workforce* (April 2008); H. Mead and others, "Racial and Ethnic Disparities in U.S. Health Care: A Chartbook" (The Commonwealth Fund, March 2008).

6. Stan Dorn, "Uninsured and Dying Because of It: Updating the Institute of Medicine Analysis on the Impact of Uninsurance on Mortality" (The Urban Institute, January 2008).

7. Families USA, "Paying a Premium: The Added Cost of Care for the Uninsured" (2005), available at http://www.familiesusa.org/assets/pdfs/Paying_a_Premium731e.pdf.

8. Schoen and others, "How Many Are Underinsured?"

9. D. Himmelstein, E. Warren, D. Thorne, and S. Woolhandler, "Illness and Injury as Contributors to Bankrupty," *Health Affairs* Web Exclusive, February 2, 2005, available at DOI10.1377/hlthhaff.w5.63.

10. Centers for Medicare and Medicaid Services, "National Health Expenditure Data," available at http://www.cms.hhs.gov/NationalHealthExpendData/03_NationalHealth AccountsProjected.asp#TopOfPage.

11. McKinsey Global Institute, "Accounting for the Cost of Healthcare in the United States" (January 2007).

12. Jeanne Lambrew, "McCain's Health Plan Puts at Least 56 Million People with Chronic Disease at Risk of Losing Health Coverage," Center for American Progress Action Fund, April 29, 2008, available at http://www.americanprogressaction.org/issues/2008/chronic_disease.html.

13. Henry J. Kaiser Family Foundation, "Women and Health Care: A National Profile—Key Findings from the Kaiser Women's Health Survey," available at http://www.kff.org/womenshealth/7336.cfm.

14. Group Health Cooperative MacColl Institute, "Does the Chronic Care Model Work?" available at http://www.improvingchroniccare.org/index.php?p=Multimedia&s=160, current as of January 2007.

15. Ibid.

16. H. Mead and others, "Racial and Ethnic Disparities in U.S. Health Care: A Chartbook."

17. Trust for America's Health, "Prevention for a Healthier America: Investments in Disease Prevention Yield Significant Savings, Healthier Communities" (July 2008), available at http://healthyamericans.org/reports/prevention08/Prevention08.pdf.

18. For more information on the Chronic Care Model, see http://www.improving chroniccare.org.

19. U. Reinhardt, "Does the Aging of the Population Really Drive Demand for Health Care?" *Health Affairs* 22 (6) (2003): 27–39.

20. American Geriatrics Society Core Writing Group of the Task Force on the Future of Geriatric Medicine, "Caring for Older Americans: The Future of Geriatric Medicine," *Journal of the American Geriatrics Society* 53 (2005): S245–S256.

21. A.R. Seghal, "Impact of Quality Improvement Efforts on Race and Sex Disparities in Hemodialysis," *Journal of the American Medical Association,* February 23, 2003, 289 (8): 996–1000; H. Mead and others, "Racial and Ethnic Disparities in U.S. Health Care."

22. S. Gehlert and others, "Targeting Health Disparities: A Model Linking Upstream Determinants to Downstream Interventions," *Health Affairs* 27 (2) (2008): 339–349.

Overview: Teaching All Our Children Well

1. The National Center for Education Statistics, "National Assessment of Educational Progress," average 2007 scaled scores, available at http://www.nces.ed.gov/nationsreport card/.

2. National Center for Education Statistics, "Digest of Education Statistics: 2007" (U.S. Department of Education), available at http://www.nces.ed.gov/programs/digest/d07 (last accessed August 2008).

3. Education Week, "Diplomas Count 2008: School to College" (2008), available at http://www.edweek.org/ew/toc/2008/06/05/index.html (last accessed August 2008).

4. The Education Trust, "College Results Online Database," available at http://www.collegeresults.org (last accessed July 2008).

5. Dan Goldhaber, "Teacher Pay Reforms: The Political Implications of Recent Research" (Washington, DC: Center for American Progress, 2006).

6. National Center for Education Statistics, "National Public Education Financial Survey, Fiscal Year 2006" (Washington, DC: U.S. Department of Education 2007). The federal contribution varies dramatically by district, however. In the 100 largest districts in the United States, it ranges from 2.2 percent in Douglas County School District in Colorado to 18.6 percent in Brownsville Independent School District in Texas.

7. Steven Barnett and Leonard Masse, "Funding Issues for Early Childhood Care and Education Programs," in Debby Cryer and Richard Clifford, eds., *Early childhood education and care in the USA* (Baltimore: Paul H. Brookes Publishing, 2002).

8. William C. Sonnenberg, "Federal Support for Education: Fiscal Year 1980 to Fiscal Year 2003" (Washington, DC: Department of Education, National Center for Education Statistics, 2004).

9. Steven Barnett and Donald J. Yarosz, "Who Goes to Preschool and Why Does It Matter?" (New Brunswick, NJ: National Institute for Early Education Research, 2007); Karen Schulman, "Overlooked Benefits of Prekindergarten" (New Brunswick, NJ: National Institute for Early Education Research, 2005).

10. William T. Dickens, Isabel Sawhill, and Jeffrey Tebbs, "The Effects of Investing in Early Education on Economic Growth" (Washington, DC: Brookings Institution, 2006).

11. Goodwin Liu, "How the Federal Government Makes Rich States Richer" (Washington, DC: Education Trust, 2006).

12. Bob Wehling and Carol Schneider, *Building a 21st Century U.S. Education System* (Washington, DC: National Commission on Teaching and America's Future, 2007).

13. See House Committee on Education and Labor, "Teacher Excellence for All Children Act of 2007 Summary" (U.S. House of Representatives), available at http://edlabor. house.gov/publications/TEACHActsummary0507.pdf (last accessed August 2008).

14. Government Accountability Office, "Improved Accessibility to Education's Information Could Help States Further Implement Teacher Qualification Requirements," GAO-06-25 (November 2005), p. 33.

15. Government Accountability Office, "No Child Left Behind Act: Education Should Clarify Guidance and Address Potential Compliance Issues for Schools in Corrective Action and Restructuring Status," GAO-07-1035 (September 2007).

16. Robert Balfanz and Nettie Legters, "Locating the Dropout Crisis—Which High Schools Produce the Nation's Dropouts? Where Are They Located? Who Attends Them?" (Baltimore, MD: Johns Hopkins University, September 2004).

17. The American Diploma Project, "Ready or Not: Creating a High School Diploma That Counts" (2004).

18. Don McLaughlin and others, "Comparison between NAEP and State Mathematics Assessment Results: 2003" (Washington, DC: U.S. Department of Education Institute of Education Sciences, 2008); Don McLaughlin and others, "Comparison between NAEP and State Reading Assessment Results: 2003" (Washington, DC: U.S. Department of Education Institute of Education Sciences, 2008).

19. Robert E. Slavin, "Evidence-Based Reform: Advancing the Education of Students at Risk" (Washington, DC: Renewing Our Schools, Securing Our Future National Task Force on Public Education, Center for American Progress and Institute for America's Future, 2005).

20. Jay P. Greene and Marcus W. Winter, "Public High School Graduation and College-Readiness Rates: 1991–2002" (New York: Manhattan Institute, 2005).

21. U. S. Department of Education, National Center for Education Statistics, http://nces.ed.gov/surveys/peqis/inc/displaytables_inc.asp.

Overview: Immigration Reform Can Be Orderly and Fair

1. Emily Bazar, "Strict Immigration law rattles Oklahoma businesses," *USA Today*, Jan 10, 2008, p. A1.

2. Federal Bureau of Investigation, *Uniform Crime Report: Hate Crime Statistics, 2006* (U.S. Department of Justice, 2007), Table 1.

3. Pew Hispanic Center, "2007 National Survey of Latinos: As Illegal Immigration Issue Heats Up, Hispanics Feel a Chill" (December 13, 2007).

4. Janet Murguia and Cecilia Muñoz, "From Immigrant to Citizen," *The American Prospect*, Special Report, November 2005.

5. Amy Goldstein and Dana Priest, "Some Detainees Are Drugged for Deportation: Immigrants Sedated Without Medical Reason," *The Washington Post*, May 14, 2008.

6. Rajeev Goyle and David Jaeger, "Deporting the Undocumented: A Cost Assessment," Center for American Progress, July 2005. http://www.americanprogress.org/kf/deporting_the_undocumented.pdf.

7. Randy Capps, Rosa Maria Castaneda, Ajay Chaudry, Robert Santos, "Paying the Price: The Impact of Immigration Raids on America's Children," Washington, DC: Urban Institute and National Council of La Raza, 2007.

8. Julia Preston, "Immigration Dilemma: A Mother Torn from a Baby," *The New York Times*, November 17, 2007.

9. Douglas Massey, "Backfire at the Border: Why Enforcement Without Legislation Cannot Stop Illegal Immigration," Center for Trade Policy Studies, June 2005. http://www.freetrade.org/pubs/pas/tpa-029.pdf.

10. Jeffrey Passel, "The Size and Characteristics of the Unauthorized Population in the U.S.," Pew Hispanic Center, March 2006. http://pewhispanic.org/files/reports/61.pdf.

11. Randy Capps, Michael Fix, Jason Ost, Jane Reardon-Anderson, and Jeffrey S. Passel, "The Health and Well Being of Young Children of Immigrants" (Washington, DC: Urban Institute, 2004).

12. See Michael Fix, ed. *Securing the Future: U.S. Immigrant Integration Policy, A Reader* (Washington, DC: Migration Policy Institute, 2007).

13. Border Network for Human Rights, "The Status of Human and Civil Rights at the Border 2007" (2007).

14. Karen Lee Ziner, "Probe into detainee's death widens," *The Providence Journal*, August 11, 2007.

15. "Citizenship Blues," *The New York Times*, February 17, 2008.

Overview: Government Transparency in the Age of the Internet

1. Deborah Fallows, "China's Online Population Explosion: What It May Mean for the Internet Globally . . . and for U.S. Users" (Washington, DC: Pew Internet and American Life Project, July 12, 2007), available at http://www.pewinternet.org/pdfs/China_Internet_July_2007.pdf.

2. "Electronic Freedom of Information," available at http://www.usobe.gov/index.aspx (last accessed June 2008).

3. "How to Obtain Employee Benefit Documents from DOL," available at http://www.dol.gov/ebsa/publications/how_to_obtain_docs.html (last accessed June 2008).

4. OMB Watch and Center for Democracy and Technology, "Hiding in Plain Sight: Why Important Government Information Cannot Be Found through Commercial Search Engines" (December 2007), available at http://www.cio.com/article/31729/The_E_Government_Act_The_Cost_the_Hurdles_the_Future/ (last accessed June 2008).

5. OMB Watch and Center for Democracy & Technology, "Hiding in Plain Sight."

6. TRAC, "About Us," available at http://trac.syr.edu/aboutTRACgeneral.html (last accessed June 2008). See also "FOIA Activities," available at (last accessed June 2008).

7. Coalition of Journalists for Open Government, "Still Waiting After All These Years: An in-depth analysis of FOIA performance from 1998 to 2006" (August 8, 2007), available at http://www.cjog.net/background.html (last accessed June 2008).

8. National Freedom of Information Coalition, "The FOI Advocate," September 7, 2007, available at http://nfoic.org/advocate/advocate_090707.html (last accessed June 2008).

9. OpenTheGovernment.org, "Secrecy Report Card 2007," available at http://www.openthegovernment.org/otg/SRC2007.pdf (last accessed June 2008).

10. Jim Morris, Alejandra Fernandez Morera, Marina Walker Buevara, and Brendan Mc-

Garry, "Shadow Government" (Washington, Center for Responsive Politics, 2008), available at http://www.publicintegrity.org/shadow/ (last accessed June 2008).

11. "Earmarks," available at http://earmarks.omb.gov/ (last accessed June 2008).

12. OMB Watch, "Previous Proposals for Federal Government Transparency: A Preliminary Report" (October 2007).

13. Ibid.

14. David Ardia, "Bush Signs FOIA Reform Bill" (Citizen Media Law Project, January 1, 2008), available at http://www.citmedialaw.org/blog/2008/bush-signs-foia-reform-bill-new-definition-news-media-will-benefit-bloggers-and-non-tradit.

15. Citizen Media Law Project, "Bush Refuses to Fund New FOIA Ombudsman, Takes the Heart Out of Open Government Reform Law" (Feb. 7, 2008), available at http://www.citmedialaw.org/subject-area/foia.

16. Elizabeth Williamson, "Is Ombudsman Already in Jeopardy?" *The Washington Post*, February 6, 2008, available at http://www.washingtonpost.com/wp-dyn/content/article/2008/02/05/AR2008020502840.html.

17. House Committee on Oversight and Government Reform, Minority Staff, "Secrecy in the Bush Administration" (Government Printing Office, Sept. 14, 2004), available at http://oversight.house.gov/features/secrecy_report/index.asp.

18. Occupation Safety and Health Administration, U.S. Department of Labor, "OSHA eTools and Electronic Products for Compliance Assistance," available at http://labor commission.utah.gov/UOSH/Outreach/ConstructionCD/www.osha.gov/dts/osta/shasoft/index.html.

19. Michael Fix and Katherine Lotspeich, "E-Government and Regulation: The Department of Labor's Web-based Compliance Assistant Resources" (Washington, DC: The Urban Institute, August 2003), available at http://www.urban.org/UploadedPDF/410845_e-government.pdf.

20. Alan Sipress, "Open Call from the Patent Office," *The Washington Post*, March 5, 2007, available at http://www.washingtonpost.com/wp-dyn/content/article/2007/03/04/AR2007030401263_pf.html.

21. Steven Aftergood, "The Next President Should Open Up the Bush Administration's Record," *Nieman Watchdog*, February 7, 2008, available at http://www.niemanwatchdog.org/index.cfm?fuseaction=ask_this.view&askthisid=00321.

22. Thomas Jefferson, "Letter to Dr. Price, January 8, 1789," in Adrienne Koch and William Peden, eds., *The Life and Selected Writings of Thomas Jefferson* (New York: The Modern Library, 1998).

Overview: Renewing Our Democracy

1. Caltech/MIT Voting Technology Project, "Voting—What Is, What Could Be" (July 2001), available at http://www.votingtechnologyproject.org/2001report.htm.

2. Help America Vote Act of 2002, Public Law 107-252, 107th Congress (2002).

3. Charles Stewart III, "Residual Vote in the 2004 Election," Working Paper, Version number 2.3 (Caltech/MIT Voting Technology Project, February 2005), available at http://www.vote.caltech.edu/media/documents/vtp_wp21v2.3.pdf.

4. See Lawrence Norden and others, "Better Ballots" (Brennan Center for Justice, July 2008).

5. R. Michael Alvarez, Co-Director of Caltech/MIT Voting Technology Project, "Voter

Registration: Past, Present and Future," Written Testimony Prepared for the Commission on Federal Election Reform, June 17, 2005, available at http://american.edu/ia/cfer/0630test/alvarez.pdf.

6. *Crawford v. Marion County Election Board,* 553 U.S. ___ (2008).

7. See Alexander Keyssar, *The Right to Vote: The Contested History of Democracy in the United States* (New York: Basic Books, 2000), p. 122.

8. Steven Hill, *10 Steps to Repair American Democracy* (Sausalito: PoliPoint Press, 2005), p. 37.

9. See Demos, "Election Day Registration," available at http://www.demos.org/page18.cfm.

10. R. Michael Alvarez and Stephen Ansolabehere, "California Votes: The Promise of Election Day Registration" (Demos, 2002), p. 12, available at http://www.vote.caltech.edu/media/documents/california_votes.pdf; see also, Mary Sullivan, "The Triggering Effects of Election Day Registration on Partisan Mobilization Activities in U.S. Elections," paper prepared for presentation at the Annual Meeting of the American Political Science Association, Washington, DC, August 31–September 3, 2005, available at http://www.allacademic.com/meta/p_mla_apa_research_citation/0/4/1/5/2/p41525_index.html.

11. See Lorraine Minnite, "Election Day Registration: A Study of Voter Fraud Allegations and Findings on Voter Roll Security" (Demos, 2004), available at http://www.demos.org/pubs/edr_fraud_web.pdf.

12. See, e.g., Lawrence Norden et. al, "The Machinery of Democracy: Protecting Elections in an Electronic World" (Brennan Center for Justice, 2006), available at http://brennan.3cdn.net/52dbde32526fdc06db_4sm6b3kip.pdf.

13. Jeff Manza and Christopher Uggen, *Locked Out: Felon Disenfranchisement and American Democracy* (New York: Oxford University Press, 2006), pp. 248–250.

14. Erika R. Wood, "Restoring the Right to Vote" (Brennan Center for Justice, 2008), available at http://brennan.3cdn.net/8782cc82daf02b9431_29m6ibzbu.pdf.

15. Deborah Hastings, "Voting Commission Plagued By Problems, Limited Funds," Associated Press, June 26, 2008, available at http://www.boston.com/news/nation/articles/2008/06/16/voting_commission_plagued_by_problems_limited_funds/?rss_id=Boston.com+--+National+news (last accessed on June 19, 2008).

16. See Brooks Jackson, *Broken Promise: Why the Federal Election Commission Failed* (New York: Century Foundation, 1990).

17. See *Vieth v. Jubelirer,* 541 U.S. 267, 274 (2004) (Scalia, A.).

18. *Lulac v. Perry,* "Brief of Samuel Issacharoff, Burt Neuborne, and Richard H. Pildes, As Amicus Curiae in Support of Appellants," p. 2, available at http://moritzlaw.osu.edu/electionlaw/litigation/documents/Brief_Amici_Curiae_Issacharoff_Neuborne_Pildes.pdf.

19. See Justin Levitt with Bethany Foster, "A Citizen's Guide to Redistricting" (Brennan Center for Justice, July 2008), available at http://www.brennancenter.org/page/-/Democracy/2008redistrictingGuide.pdf.

20. Fair Vote, "Who Picks the President?" (2005), available at http://www.fairvote.org/media/research/who_picks_president.pdf.

Department of Justice:
Restoring Integrity and the Rule of Law

1. See, e.g., Memorandum from Jay S. Bybee, Assistant Att'y Gen., to Alberto R. Gonzales, Counsel to the President (Aug. 1, 2002). The Bush administration ultimately disavowed

this memo in the face of public outrage when it leaked to the public and OLC eventually issued a replacement memorandum. Memorandum from Daniel Levin, Acting Assistant Att'y Gen., to James B. Comey, Deputy Att'y Gen. (Dec. 30, 2004). See also Memorandum from U.S. Dep't of Justice (Jan. 19, 2006), reprinted in David Cole & Martin S. Lederman, "The National Security Agency's Domestic Spying Program: Framing the Debate," 81 *Indiana Law Journal* 1355, 1374 (2006).

2. Charlie Savage, *Takeover: The Return of the Imperial Presidency and the Subversion of American Democracy* 73 (2007)

3. Jack Goldsmith, *The Terror Presidency* 89 (2007).

4. *Id.* at 10.

5. *Boumediene v. Bush*, 553 U.S.—(2008); 128 S.Ct. 2229 (2008); *Hamdan v. Rumsfeld*, 548 U.S. 557 (2006); *Rasul v. Bush*, 542 U.S. 466 (2004); *Hamdi v. Rumsfeld*, 542 U.S. 507 (2004).

6. Office of the Inspector General & Office of Professional Responsibility, U.S. Department of Justice, "An Investigation of Allegations of Politicized Hiring in the Department of Justice Honors Program and Summer Law Intern Program" (June 24, 2008).

7. Office of the Inspector General & Office of Professional Responsibility, U.S. Department of Justice, "An Investigation of Allegations of Politicized Hiring by Monica Goodling and Other Staff in the Office of the Attorney General" (July 28, 2008).

8. Commission of Inquiry into the Actions of Canadian Officials in Relations to Maher Arar, *Report of the Events Relating to Maher Arar* (2006).

9. See, e.g., "Symposium: Ideas for a New Administration," *Harvard Law & Policy Review* 2(2)(2008), including Senator Edward M. Kennedy, "Restoring the Civil Rights Division"; Janet Reno & Geoffrey M. Klineberg, "What Would Jackson Do? Some Old Advice for the New Attorney General"; James K. Robinson, "Restoring Public Confidence in the Fairness of the Department of Justice's Criminal Justice Function"; Lois J. Schiffer & Richard J. Lazarus, "The Environment and Natural Resources Division of the United States Department of Justice: Planning for the Transition to the Next Administration"; P. J. Crowley, "Homeland Security and the Upcoming Transition: What the Next Administration Should Do to Make Us Safe at Home"; Timothy E. Wirth, "A Way Forward on Climate Change."

10. Robinson, *supra* note 9, at 267.

11. Dawn E. Johnsen, "Faithfully Executing the Laws: Internal Legal Constraints on Executive Power," *UCLA Law Review* 54 (6) (2007): 1559–1611 (reprinting and elaborating upon the OLC Guidelines).

12. Am. Bar Ass'n, Task Force on Presidential Signing Statements and the Separation of Powers Doctrine (Aug. 24, 2006); Neil Kinkopf, *Signing Statements and Statutory Interpretation in the Bush Administration*, 16 *William & Mary Bill of Rights Journal* 307 (2008); Trevor W. Morrison, "Constitutional Avoidance in the Executive Branch," 106 *Columbia Law Review* 1189 (2006); posting of David Barron et al., to Georgetown Law Faculty Blog, http://gulcfac.typepad.com/georgetown_university_law/2006/07/thanks_to_the_p.html (July 31, 2006); posting of Laurence Tribe, to Balkinization, http://balkin.blogspot.com/2006/08/larry-tribe-on-aba-signing-statements.html (Aug. 6, 2006).

13. See Dawn E. Johnsen, "What's a President to Do? Interpreting the Constitution in the Wake of Bush Administration Abuses," 102 *Boston* University Law Review (2008).

14. See "Presidential Authority to Decline to Execute Unconstitutional Statutes," 18 Op. Off. Legal Counsel 199 (1994); "The Legal Significance of Presidential Signing Statements," 17 Op. Off. Legal Counsel 131 (1993); "The Attorney General's Duty to Defend and Enforce Constitutionally Objectionable Legislation," 4A Op. Off. Legal Counsel 55 (1980).

15. *Adarand Constructors v. Pena*, 515 U.S. 200 (1995).

16. See Schiffer & Lazarus, supra note 8,

17. *Gideon v. Wainwright*, 372 U.S. 335 (1963).

18. American Bar Association, *"Gideon's* Broken Promise: America's Continuing Quest for Equal Justice" (Chicago, 2004).

19. *Washington v. Davis*, 426 U.S. 229 (1976); *McClesky v. Kemp*, 481 U.S. 279 (1987).

Department of Health and Human Services:
Delivering Efficient and Effective Health Care for All Americans

1. Kaiser Family Foundation and Health Research and Educational Trust, "Employer Health Benefits 2007 Annual Survey" (Menlo Park, CA: Kaiser Family Foundation, 2007).

2. U.S. Census Bureau, *Table H1A-1, Historical Health Insurance Coverage Status and Type of Coverage by Sex, Race, and Hispanic Origin: 1999 to 2007*, available at http://www.census.gov/hhes/www/hlthins/historic/hihistt1.html.

3. Jeffrey A. Rhoades and Steven B. Cohen, Agency for Health Care Research and Quality, *The Long-Term Uninsured in America, 2002–2005*, Statistical Brief No. 183 (U.S. Department of Health and Human Services, August 2007).

4. Jack Hadley, "Insurance Coverage, Medical Care Use, and Short-Term Health Changes Following an Unintended Injury or the Onset of a Chronic Condition," *Journal of the American Medical Association* 297 (10): 1073–1084, March 14, 2007; Stan Dorn, "Uninsured and Dying Because of It: Updating the Institute of Medicine Analysis on the Impact of Uninsurance on Mortality" (Washington, DC: The Urban Institute, January 2008).

5. Cathy Schoen et al., "Taking the Pulse of Health Care Systems: Experiences of Patients with Health Problems in Six Nations," *Health Affairs* Web Exclusive, W5-509-525, November 3, 2005.

6. Ellen Nolte and C. Martin McKee, "Measuring the Health of Nations: Updating an Earlier Analysis," *Health Affairs* 27 (1) (2008): 58–71.

7. HealthGrades, "HealthGrades Patient Safety in American Hospitals Study" (April 2008).

8. Friends of NCHS, Fact Sheet for the FY 2009 Budget, available at: http://www.chsr.org/nchsfactsheet.pdf.

9. S. Jay Olshansky, Douglas J. Passaro, Ronald C. Hershow, Jennifer Layden, Bruce A. Carnes, Jacob Brody, Leonard Hayflick, Robert N. Butler, David B. Allison, and David S. Ludwig, "A potential decline in life expectancy in the United States in the 21st century," *New England Journal of Medicine* 352 (11) (2005): 1138–1145.

10. Office of Management and Budget, *Budget of the United States Government, Fiscal Year 2009* (Executive Office of the President, 2008).

11. U.S. Department of Health and Human Services, available at: http://www.hhs.gov/about/whatwedo.html/.

12. Office of the Actuary, Centers for Medicare and Medicaid Services, *Projected National Health Expenditures* (Department of Health and Human Services), available at: http://www.cms.hhs.gov/NationalHealthExpendData/Downloads/proj2007.pdf.

13. For the text of the directive, see: http://www.cms.hhs.gov/smdl/downloads/SHO081707.pdf.

14. Donna Cohen Ross, Aleya Horn, and Caryn Marks, "A 50-State Update on Eligibility Rules, Enrollment and Renewal Procedures, and Cost Sharing Practices in Medicaid and

SCHIP in 2008" (Washington, DC: Kaiser Commission on Medicaid and the Uninsured, January 2008).

15. Donna Cohen Ross, "New Citizenship Documentation Requirement Is Taking a Toll: States Report Enrollment Is Down and Administrative Costs Are Up" (Washington, DC: Center on Budget and Policy Priorities, March 13, 2007).

16. Congressional Budget Office, "Medicare, Medicaid, and SCHIP Administrative Actions Reflected in CBO's Baseline" (February 29, 2008), available at: http://www.cbo.gov/budget/factsheets/2008b/medicaremedicaid.pdf.

17. Kaiser Commission on Medicaid and the Uninsured, "Children's Health Insurance Program Reauthorization Act of 2007 (CHIPRA): The Revised CHIPRA (H.R.3963) Compared to the Original Bill (H.R. 976)" (November 2007).

18. Jeanne M. Lambrew, "Conservative Health Reform: Why It Could Deepen Our Health System Crisis" (Washington, DC: Center for American Progress Action Fund, 2008).

19. Tricia Neuman, "Medicare Advantage: Key Issues and Implications for Beneficiaries," Testimony before U.S. House of Representatives Committee on the Budget, June 28, 2007.

20. Peter C. Hebertson, "Selling to Seniors: The Need for Accountability and Oversight of Marketing by Medicare Private Plans," Testimony before U.S. Senate Committee on Finance, February 7, 2008.

21. Robert Pear, "Methods Used by Insurers are Questioned," *The New York Times,* May 7, 2007.

22. For a review of existing guidance, see Kerry Weems, Acting Administrator, Centers for Medicare and Medicaid Services, Testimony before U.S. Senate Committee on Finance, "Selling to Seniors: The Need for Accountability and Oversight of Marketing by Medicare Private Plans," February 13, 2008.

23. Ellen O'Brian and Jack Hoadley, "Medicare Advantage: Options for Standardizing Benefits and Information to Improve Consumer Choice" New York: The Commonwealth Fund, April 2008).

24. Committee on Government Reform, Minority Staff, "Politics and Science in the Bush Administration" (Washington, DC: U.S. House of Representatives, August 2003).

25. Shankar Vedantam, "Racial Disparities Played Down at Request of Top Officials, Report on Health Care Differs from Draft," *The Washington Post,* January 14, 2004, p. A17.

26. Richard Carmona, MD, Former Surgeon General, Testimony before U.S. House of Representatives Committee on Oversight and Government Reform, "The Surgeon General's Vital Mission: Challenges for the Future," July 10, 2007, available at: http://oversight.house.gov/documents/20071127162330.pdf.

27. These ideas and others have been proposed in *The Surgeon General Independence Act,* H.R. 3447, 110 Cong. 1 sess.

28. AcademyHealth, "Historical Analysis & Publication Rights in Government Contracts for Health Services Research" (July 2007).

29. For the range of options and considerations, see AcademyHealth, "Placement, Coordination, and Funding of Health Services Research within the Federal Government" (September 2005); Gail Wilensky, "Developing a Center for Comparative Effectiveness Information," *Health Affairs* 25 (6) (November/December 2006): w572–w585.

30. Centers for Disease Control and Prevention, "Indicators for Chronic Disease Surveillance," *Morbidity and Mortality Weekly Report* 53 (RR11) (Sept. 10, 2004): 1–6.

31. Shin-Yi Wu and Anthony Green, "Projection of Chronic Illness Prevalence and Cost

Inflation," prepared for Partnership for Solutions (Baltimore, MD: Johns Hopkins University, 2000).

32. Centers for Disease Control and Prevention, "National, State, and Urban Area Vaccination Coverage among Children Aged 19–35 Months: United States, 2006," *Morbidity and Mortality Weekly Report* 56 (34) (August 31, 2007): 880–85.

33. Elizabeth A. McGlynn, S.M. Asch, J. Adams, et al, "The quality of health care delivered to adults in the United States," *New England Journal of Medicine* 348 (26) (June 26, 2003): 2635–2645, available at: http://content.nejm.org/cgi/content/abstract/348/26/2635.

34. Eric A. Finkelstein, Phaedra S. Corso, and Ted R. Miller, *The Incidence and Economic Burden of Injuries in the* United States (New York: Oxford University Press, April 2006).

35. Richard Hillestad, James Bigelow, Anthony Bower, Federico Girosi, Robin Meili, Richard Scoville, and Roger Taylor, "Can Electronic Medical Record Systems Transform Health Care? Potential Health Benefits, Savings and Costs," *Health Affairs* 24 (2005): 1103–17.

36. Dana P. Goldman, David M. Cutler, Baoping Shang, Geoffrey A. Joyce, "The Value of Elderly Disease Prevention," *Forum for Health Economics & Policy*, Forum: Biomedical Research and the Economy: Article 1, available at: http://www.bepress.com/fhep/biomedical _research/1/.

37. For a discussion of the broader economic benefits of investments in health care, see David M. Cutler, *Your Money or Your Life* (Oxford: Oxford University Press, 2004).

38. Denise Fraga, Garrett Groves, Laurie Seremetis, and Jeanne Lambrew, "Consumer-Driven Health Plans May Preempt, Not Promote, Prevention" (Washington, DC: Center for American Progress, April 10, 2008), available at: http://www.americanprogress.org/ issues/2008/04/prevention.html.

39. The ideas of a cross-agency council or undersecretary for public health and prevention have been developed by the Trust for America's Health in a forthcoming set of transition recommendations.

40. For more on the idea of a Wellness Trust, see Jeanne M. Lambrew and John D. Podesta, "Promoting Prevention and Preempting Costs: A New Wellness Trust for the United States" (Washington, DC: Center for American Progress, 2006); Jeanne M. Lambrew, "A Wellness Trust to Prioritize Disease Prevention" (Washington, DC: The Hamilton Project, Brookings Institution, 2007).

41. Gerry Fairbrother, Melinda J. Dutton, Deborah Bachrach, Kerry-Ann Newell, Patricia Boozang, and Rachel Cooper, "Cost of Enrolling Children in Medicaid and SCHIP," *Health Affairs* 23 (1) (2004): 237–43.

42. See, for example, Thomas M. Selden, Julie L. Hudson, and Jessica S. Banthin, "Tracking Changes in Eligibility and Coverage Among Children, 1996–2002," *Health Affairs*, 23 (5) (2004): 39–50; Karl Kronenbusch and Brian Elbel, "Simplifying Children's Medicaid and SCHIP," *Health Affairs* 23 (3) (2004): 233–46.

43. See 42 CFR 433.112(c) and 42 CFR 433.111(b)(3) that exclude "eligibility determination systems" from enhanced federal matching payments.

44. For a description of the options and barriers to automatic enrollment in Medicaid and SCHIP, see Stan Dorn and Genevieve M. Kenney, "Automatically Enrolling Eligible Children and Families into Medicaid and SCHIP: Opportunities, Obstacles, and Options for Federal Policy Makers" (New York: The Commonwealth Fund, June 2006).

45. Dahlia K. Remler and Sherry A. Glied, "What Other Programs Can Teach Us: Increasing Participation in Health Insurance Programs," *American Journal of Public Health* 93 (1) (2003): 67–74.

46. John Iglehardt, "Pursing Health IT: The Delicate Dance of Government and the Market," *Health Affairs* 24 (5) (2005): 1100–101.

47. Kenneth W. Kizer, Testimony before U.S. House of Representatives Committee on Ways and Means, Subcommittee on Health, March 6, 2006.

48. Karen Davenport, "Navigating American Health Care: How Information Technology Can Foster Health Care Improvement" (Washington, DC: Center for American Progress, May 2007).

49. New York and Iowa, for example, included implementing electronic medical records as part of their Medicaid 1115 waivers.

50. Arthur L. Kellerman, "Crisis in the Emergency Department," *New England Journal of Medicine* 355 (13) (2006): 1300–1303.

51. Crystal Franco, "Billions for Biodefense: Federal Agency Biodefense Funding, FY2008–FY2009," *Biosecurity and Bioterrorism: Biodefense Strategy, Practice and Science* 6 (2) (2008): 131–46.

52. David J. Dausey, Nicole Lurie, and Alexis Diamond, "Public Health Responses to Urgent Case Reports," *Health Affairs, Web Exclusive*, W5-412-419, August 30, 2005; Nicole Lurie, "The Public Health Infrastructure: Rebuild or Redesign?" *Health Affairs*, 21 (6) (November/December, 2006): 28–30.

53. Jeanne M. Lambrew and Donna E. Shalala, "Federal Health Policy Response to Katrina: What It Was and What It Could Have Been," *Journal of the American Medical Association* 296 (11) (2006): 1394–1397.

54. For ideas on improvements, see the AMA/APHA Linkages Leadership Summit, "Improving Health System Preparedness for Terrorism and Mass Casualty Events" (Chicago: The American Medical Association, 2007).

55. Trust for America's Health, "Ready or Not? Protecting the Public's Health from Disease, Disasters, and Bioterrorism" (Washington, DC: Trust for America's Health, 2007).

56. National Center for Health Statistics, *Health, United States, 2007* (Centers for Disease Control and Prevention, 2007).

57. Agency for Healthcare Research and Quality, *2007 National Healthcare Disparities Report* (Department of Health and Human Services, 2008).

58. Institute of Medicine, "Unequal Treatment: Confronting Racial and Ethnic Disparities in Health Care" (Washington, DC: National Academy of Sciences, 2002).

59. David Satcher, in Tavis Smiley, ed. *Covenant with Black America* (New York: Third World Press, 2006).

60. McKinsey Global Institute, "Accounting for the Cost of Health Care in the United States" (January 2007).

61. Kaiser Family Foundation, "Dual Eligibles: Medicaid's Role for Medicare's Low-Income Beneficiaries" (Washington, DC: Kaiser Commission on Medicaid and the Uninsured, July 2005).

62. One idea for change is to link Medicare's limited benefit to private insurance to develop a seamless system; see Jeanne M. Lambrew, "Affordable Long-Term Care," *Democracy: A Journal of Ideas* 8 (Spring 2008).

63. Jochen Hartwig, "What Drives Health Care Expenditures? Baumol's Model of 'Unbalanced Growth' Revisited," Working Paper 06-133 (Zurich: KOS Swiss Economic Institute, March 2006).

64. Conor Dougherty, "Factories Fading, Health Care Steps In," *The Wall Street Journal*, April 15, 2008, p. A1.

65. Thomas Bodenheimer, "Primary Care: Will It Survive?" *New England Journal of Medicine* 355 (9) (2006): 861–64.

66. Natasha Singer, "For Top Medical Students, an Attractive Field," *The New York Times*, March 19, 2008.

67. See, for example, *Medical Education Trust Fund Act of 2001*, S. 743, 107 Cong. 1 sess.

68. Jeanne M. Lambrew and John D. Podesta, "Promoting Prevention and Preempting Costs."

69. Kevin Sack, "In Massachusetts, Universal Coverage Strains Care," *The New York Times*, April 5, 2008.

Food and Drug Administration:
Protecting Public Health Through Science

1. Food and Drug Administration Science Board, Subcommittee on Science and Technology, *FDA Science and Mission at Risk* (November 2007).

2. The report was conducted by the FDA Science Board, an advisory committee to the FDA Commissioner, consisting of outside experts from industry, academia, and other government agencies.

3. FDA Science Board, *FDA Science and Mission at Risk*.

4. Gail H. Cassell, Testimony before the Subcommittee on Oversight and Investigations of the Committee on Energy and Commerce House of Representatives, "Science and Mission at Risk: FDA's Self Assessment," January 29, 2008, available at http://energycommerce. house.gov/cmte_mtgs/110-oi-hrg.012908.FDASelfAssessment.shtml.

5. FDA Science Board, *FDA Science and Mission at Risk*.

6. Ibid.

7. Ibid.

8. This amount includes user fees and would account for even less, about 1.5 cents a day, if it did not include user fees paid by industry.

9. Government Accountability Office, *Preliminary Findings Suggest Recent FDA Initiatives Have Potential, but Do Not Fully Address Weaknesses in Its Foreign Drug Inspection Program*, GAO-08-701T (Washington, DC: April, 2008).

10. Andrew C. von Eshenbach, "State of the FDA" (speech before Food and Drug Law Institute Annual Conference, Bethesda, MD, April 12, 2007), available at http://www.fda. gov/oc/speeches/2007/fdli041207.html.

11. Ibid.

12. GAO, *Food and Drug Administration, Effect of User Fees on Drug Approval Times, Withdrawals, and Other Agency Activities*, GAO-02-958 (Washington, DC: September 2002).

13. Cassell, Testimony on "Science and Mission at Risk: FDA's Self Assessment."

14. Cathy Dombrowski, "FDA's 'Dysfunctional' Hiring System May Be Good for Safety Databases," *The Pink Sheet*, March 3, 2008.

15. GAO, *Federal Oversight of Food Safety: FDA's Food Protection Plan Proposes Positive First Steps, but Capacity to Carry Them Out Is Critical*, GAO-08-435T (Washington, DC: Jan. 29, 2008).

16. Ibid.

17. FDA Science Board, *FDA Science and Mission at Risk*.

18. GAO, *Federal Oversight of Food Safety*.

19. Ibid.

20. Institute of Medicine, *The Future of Drug Safety: Promoting and Protecting the Health of the Public* (September 2006).

21. Interagency Working Group on Import Safety, *Action Plan for Import Safety: A Roadmap for Continual Improvement* (November 2007).

22. GAO, *Preliminary Findings Suggest Recent FDA Initiatives Have Potential*.

23. GAO, *Drug Safety: Preliminary Findings Suggest Weaknesses in FDA's Program for Inspecting Foreign Drug Manufacturers*, GAO-08-224T (Washington, DC: Nov. 1, 2007).

24. GAO, *Federal Oversight of Food Safety*.

25. GAO, *Preliminary Findings Suggest Recent FDA Initiatives Have Potential*.

26. National Academy of Sciences, *Animal Biotechnology: Science-Based Concerns* (August 2002).

27. FDA, "Calories Count, Report of the Working Group on Obesity" (March 12, 2004), available at http://www.cfsan.fda.gov/~dms/owg-toc.html.

Department of Housing and Urban Development: Meeting 21st-Century Metropolitan Challenges

1. Lawrence Thompson, "A History of HUD" (2006), available at http://www.hudnlha.com/housing_news/hud_history.pdf. U.S. Office of Personnel Management, Federal Human Resources Data, March 2008.

2. U.S. Department of Housing and Urban Development, "Public and Indian Housing, Resident Characteristics Report," September 30, 2008.

3. Martin D. Abravanel, "Do We Know More Now? Trends in Public Knowledge, Support and Use of Fair Housing Law" (U.S. Department of Housing and Urban Development, 2006).

4. According to data from the federal Home Mortgage Disclosure Act, Hispanics were twice as likely as white people to get high-cost loans. Blacks were 2.3 times as likely as whites to receive high-cost loans. See http://www.nytimes.com/2007/11/04/weekinreview/04bajaj.html?_r=1&scp=1&sq=race%20foreclosure&st=cse&oref=slogin.

5. Mortgage Bankers' Association, Q1 data, 2008.

6. Peter S. Goodman, "For Hispanics in U.S., a dream is going sour," *Herald Tribune*, May 12, 2008.

7. RealtyTrac, "Detroit, Stockton, Las Vegas post highest 2007 metro foreclosure rates," February 13, 2008.

8. Andrew Jakabovics, "HOPE NOW Needs Help: Housing Crisis Requires Federal Action," Center for American Progress, March 4, 2008, available at http://www.americanprogress.org/issues/2008/03/hope_now.html. Updated data from "HOPE Now, Mortgage Loss Mitigation Statistics," August 2008.

9. FHASecure, Press Release (FHASecure, August 29, 2998).

10. David Abromowitz, "Addressing Foreclosures: A Great American Dream Neighborhood Stabilization Plan" (Washington, DC: Center For American Progress, 2008), available at http://www.americanprogress.org/issues/2008/01/gardns.html.

11. Government Accountability Office, "Federal Housing Administration: Decline in the Agency's Market Share Was Associated with Product and Process Developments of Other Mortgage Market Participants" (2007), available at http://www.gao.gov/new.items/d07645.pdf.

12. Alan Mallach, "Tackling the Mortgage Crisis: 10 Action Steps for State Government" (Brookings Institution, 2008).

13. Ibid.

14. For further discussion of land banking, see forthcoming Brookings paper by Frank Alexander.

15. Annie Clark and Kalima Rose, "Bringing Louisiana Renters Home," PolicyLink, 2007; Amy Liu, "Building a Better New Orleans"(Brookings Institution, 2006).

16. Amy Liu and Allison Plyer, "The New Orleans Index, Anniversary Edition: Three Years after Katrina" (Brookings Institution and the Greater New Orleans Community Data Center, August 2008).

17. Council of Large Public Housing Authorities, Statement on proposed 2009 budget (CLPHA, February 4, 2008).

18. NAHRO 2008 Legislative and Regulatory Agenda, available at http://www.nahro. org/legislative/2008/leg_agenda_08.pdf.

19. Alan Berube, "MetroNation: How U.S. Metropolitan Areas Fuel American Prosperity" (Brookings Institution, 2007).

20. Brookings analysis of Census Zip Code Business Patterns, 2004.

21. Brookings analysis of U.S. Census data; salaries calculated in 2005 dollars.

22. Bruce Katz and Margery Austin Turner, "Rethinking U.S. Rental Housing Policy" (Brookings Institution, 2008); U.S. Census, American Community Survey, 2006.

23. Joint Center for Housing Studies of Harvard University, "America's Rental Housing: the key to a balanced national policy" (2008).

24. Bruce Katz and Margery Austin Turner, "Rethinking U.S. Rental Housing Policy" (Brookings Institution, 2007).

25. Barbara Lipman, "A Heavy Load: The Combined Housing and Transportation Burdens of Working Families" (Center for Housing Policy, 2006).

26. Marilyn Brown, Frank Southworth, and Andrea Sarzynski, "Shrinking the Carbon Footprint of Metropolitan America" (Brookings Institution, 2008); Energy Information Administration data.

27. Michael Stegman, Roberto Quercia, and Walter Davis, "The Earned Income Tax Credit as an Instrument of Housing Policy" (Brookings Institution, 2003).

28. LIHTC figures based on analysis of HUD National LIHTC Database, 2005 update. Brookings analysis of HUD State of the Cities Data.

Department of Education: Restoring Our Nation's Commitment to an Equitable Education for All Americans

1. Department of Education Organization Act (DEOA) 20 USCS §3401, §3402 (1)-(4). Three additional purposes are articulated in the Act: to improve the coordination of federal education programs; to improve the management and efficiency of federal education activities, especially with respect to the process, procedures, and administrative structures for the dispersal of federal funds, as well as the reduction of unnecessary and duplicative burdens and constraints, including unnecessary paperwork, on the recipients of federal funds; and to increase the accountability of federal education programs to the president, the Congress, and the public.

2. The No Child Left Behind Act [hereinafter NCLB], 20 U.S.C. 6301 *et seq.* is the 2002 reauthorized Elementary and Secondary Education Act first enacted in 1965 under Presi-

dent Lyndon B. Johnson. Title I of the Act provides state and local education agencies with federal funds based on the number of poor children in the state and local school districts.

3. See, e.g., Student Right-to-Know and Campus Security Act, Pub. L. 101-542 (1990).

4. The reauthorization bill for ESEA (NCLB) is pending in Congress. The HEA was reauthorized as the Higher Education Opportunity Act, P.L. 110-315 (August 14, 2008).

5. Congress has often extended reauthorization beyond the required five years. The No Child Left Behind Act was passed in 2002 and should have been reauthorized in 2007. The Higher Education Act was scheduled for reauthorization in 2003.

6. For example, the name and stand alone status of the current Office of Vocational and Adult Education appears outmoded—by name certainly—and might be organized to concentrate on high school reform and innovative linkages to postsecondary education and workforce development and career opportunities.

7. Democratic Staff, Committee on Education and Labor, U.S. House of Representatives, February 4, 2008, available at http://edlabor.house.gov/publications/2009Bush BudgetEdSummary.pdf (last accessed on February 28, 2008).

8. Ibid.

9. Ibid.

10. 20 U.S.C. §6212 (Waiver authority of Secretary of Education).

11. See "Lifetime Effects: The High/Scope Perry Preschool Study Through Age 40" (2005) available at http://highscope.org/Content.asp?ContentID=219 (last accessed on June 2, 2008). This longitudinal study examined the lives of 123 African Americans at age 40 and determined that those who had been enrolled in preschool programs had higher earnings, were more likely to hold a job, had committed fewer crimes, and were more likely to have graduated from high school than adults who did not have preschool.

12. Title II HEA, §201.

13. Ibid. §201(d).

14. Pub. L. 110-227 (May 7, 2008).

15. Students attending less competitive four-year institutions, community colleges, and for-profit universities are finding it more difficult to secure federally backed loans as a result of the credit crisis. Some of the nation's largest banks have dropped these institutions and their students from their list of eligible borrowers, potentially forcing these students to forgo attending college; to take out loans with less attractive terms, increasing the possibly they will default on the loans; or to work at second or third jobs, becoming less successful as students. *The New York Times*, June 2, 2008, A1.

16. More than 40 percent of all undergraduate students attend community colleges. Ibid. These students are disproportionately poor students and students of color commuting from home to work to school. They need access to high-quality, affordable, and geographically accessible community college programs that are both flexible in course offerings and scheduling.

17. See, e.g., Neil A. Lewis, "Bush Names Affirmative Action Critic to Civil Rights Post," *The New York Times*, March 30, 2002, available at http://query.nytimes.com/gst/fullpage. html?res=950CEEDB163AF933A05750C0A9649C8B63.

18. Some of the proactive enforcement efforts that OCR might pursue include combining its analysis of its own surveys of local education agencies with the data that each state must provide under §1418 of the Individuals with Disabilities Education Act (20 U.S.C. 1400 *et seq.*) on the number of children with disabilities by race, ethnicity, and disability who are, *inter alia*, receiving early intervention or who are placed in separate classrooms, schools, and facilities. OCR should also work with the program staff administering NCLB and

reviewing disaggregated AYP data on the proficiency levels of racial, ethnic, ELL, and disabled subgroups of students to identify patterns of disparity and to target areas of interest from both a civil rights and school/student achievement perspective to investigate or consider opportunities for joint or crosscutting compliance, enforcement, and technical assistance efforts across the department.

19. U.S. Department of Education, "Annual Report to Congress of the Office for Civil Rights, Fiscal Year 2006" (Washington, DC, 2007), p. 2.

20. *Parents Involved in Community Schools v. Seattle School District No. 1, et al.*, No. 05-908 (U.S. June 28, 2007); *Meredith v. Jefferson Cty. Bd. of Educ.*, No. 05-915 (U.S., June 28, 2007).

21. 20 U.S.C. §7914 (2004); see also 20 U.S.C. §7861 (c) (7) (2004).

22. U.S. Department of Education, "Supplemental Educational Services. *Non-Regulatory Guidance*" at C-3 (Washington, DC, 2005).

23. Legislation introduced on January 24, 2008, by Sen. Edward M. Kennedy (D-MA) and Rep. John Lewis (D-GA) and cosponsored by Sens. Clinton (D-NY) and Obama (D-IL), among others, would permit individuals to seek relief when recipients of federal funds engage in practices that have a discriminatory effect on the basis of race, national origin, color, disability, age, or gender. Currently, the regulations implementing the civil rights laws enforced by the Department of Education give it the authority to find violations even where there is no discriminatory intent but where practices have the effect of discriminating against students and others who are protected under those laws. See, e.g., 34 C.F.R. §100.3(b) (2). However, this legislation is necessary because currently individuals have no private right of action to sue to eliminate practices that have a discriminatory impact on protected individuals.

24. Goodwin Liu, "Interstate Inequality in Education Opportunity," 81 *N.Y.U. L. Rev.* 2044 (2006), available at http://www.law.nyu.edu/JOURNALS/LAWREVIEW/ISSUES/vol81/no6/NYU603.pdf.

25. Ibid.

26. See Southern Education Foundation, "A New Majority: Low Income Students in the South's Public Schools" (2007).

27. Liu, "Interstate Inequality in Education Opportunity," 2044.

28. Ibid., 2117.

29. Ibid.

30. Ibid., 2117–2126.

31. Ibid.

32. Ibid., 2105–2113.

33. Ibid., 2108.

34. See, e.g., Linda McSpadden McNeil and others "Avoidable Losses: High Stakes Accountability and the Dropout Crisis," *Education Policy Archives* 16 (3) (2008 available at http://epaa.asu.edu/epaa/v16n3/.

U.S. Department of Transportation:
Green Reforms for Environmental and Consumer Safety

1. Energy Information Administration, "Petroleum Basic Statistics" (Department of Energy, 2006 except where noted), available at http://www.eia.doe.gov/basics/quickoil.html (last accessed June 18, 2008).

2. National Highway Traffic Safety Administration, "Traffic Safety Facts 2002," DOT HS 809 612 (Department of Transportation, 2002), available at http://www-nrd.nhtsa.dot.gov/

Pubs/2002ovrfacts.pdf (last accessed June 19, 2008); National Highway Traffic Safety Administration, "Economic Impact of U.S. Motor Vehicle Crashes Reaches $230.6 Billion, New NHTSA Study Shows," U.S. Department of Transportation, 2002.

3. Federal Motor Carrier Safety Administration, *Large Truck Crash Facts 2006*. (Department of Transportation, 2008).

4. *To amend the Safe, Accountable, Flexible, Efficient Transportation Equity Act: A Legacy for Users to make technical corrections, and for other purposes*, H.R. 6233, 109 Cong. 2 sess.

5. *Safe, Accountable, Flexible, Efficient Transportation Equity Act: A Legacy for Users*, Public Law 109-59, 109 Cong. 1 sess. (Aug. 10, 2005).

6. National Surface Transportation Policy and Revenue Study Commission, *Transportation for Tomorrow: Report of the National Surface Transportation Policy and Revenue Study*, vol. II, chp. 4 (2007).

7. Matthew Wald, "Travelers Shift to Rail as Cost of Fuel Rises," *The New York Times*, June 21, 2008.

8. National Highway Traffic Safety Administration, "Traffic Safety Facts," DOT HS 810 809 (Department of Transportation, 2006), available at http://www-nrd.nhtsa.dot.gov/Pubs/810809.pdf (last accessed June 19, 2008).

9. National Surface Transportation Policy and Revenue Study Commission, *Transportation for Tomorrow: Report of the National Surface Transportation Policy and Revenue Study*, vol. II, chp. 5 (2007).

10. Williams Buechner, "History of the Gasoline Tax" (American Road and Transportation Builders Association, 2008), available at http://www.artba.org/economics_research/reports/gas_tax_history.htm (last accessed June 18, 2008).

11. National Surface Transportation Policy and Revenue Study Commission, *Transportation for Tomorrow: Report of the National Surface Transportation Policy and Revenue Study*, vol. I, p. 1 (2007).

12. National Highway Traffic Safety Administration, "Traffic Safety Facts 2002." DOT HS 809 612 (Department of Transportation, 2002), available at http://www-nrd.nhtsa.dot.gov/Pubs/2002ovrfacts.pdf (last accessed June 19, 2008).

13. Federal Motor Carrier Safety Administration, "Large Truck Crash Facts 2006" (Department of Transportation, 2008).

14. Ibid.

15. National Highway Traffic Safety Administration, "Traffic Safety Facts 2006," DOT HS 810 805 (Department of Transportation, 2008), available at http://www-nrd.nhtsa.dot.gov/Pubs/810805.PDF (last accessed June 27, 2008).

16. National Highway Traffic Safety Administration, "Economic Impact of U.S. Motor Vehicle Crashes Reaches $230.6 billion, New NHTSA Study Shows" (Department of Transportation, 2002).

17. National Highway Traffic Safety Administration, "Traffic Safety Facts 2002," DOT HS 809 612 (Department of Transportation, 2002), available at http://www-nrd.nhtsa.dot.gov/Pubs/2002ovrfacts.pdf (last accessed June 19, 2008).

18. National Highway Traffic Safety Administration, "Counts of Frontal Air Bag Related Fatalities and Seriously Injured Persons" (Department of Transportation, 2008), available at http://www.nhtsa.dot.gov/portal/nhtsa_static_file_downloader.jsp?file=/staticfiles/DOT/NHTSA/NCSA/Content/SCIQtrly/Current/Biannual_Report.pdf (last accessed June 30, 2008).

19. National Safety Council, "Injury Facts 2008 Edition" (2008) available at https://www.usw12775.org/uploads/InjuryFacts08Ed.pdf (last accessed June 30), p. 94.

20. *Public Citizen et al. v. Federal Motor Carrier Safety Administration*, 374 F.3d 1209 (DC Cir. 2004).

21. Joan Claybrook, Testimony before the House Committee on Energy and Commerce Subcommittee on Commerce, Trade and Consumer Protection, "Reauthorization of the National Highway Traffic Safety Administration," Mar. 18, 2004.

22. *Safe, Accountable, Flexible, Efficient Transportation Equity Act: A Legacy for Users* Public Law 109-59, 109 Cong. 1 sess. (Aug. 10, 2005), available at http://www.nhtsa.dot.gov/nhtsa/Cfc_title49/MotorVehicleSafetyProvisions.pdf.

23. Kids and Cars, "U.S. Fatalities by Type (2002–2007)" (Leawood, Kansas, 2008), available at http://www.kidsandcars.org/bottom_statistics.html (last access July 3, 2008).

24. *Cameron Gulbransen Kids Transportation Safety Act of 2007*, P.L. 110-189, 110 Cong. 1 sess. (Government Printing Office, 2007).

25. Federal Highway Administration, "Western Uniformity Scenario Analysis" (Department of Transportation, 2004).

26. National Transportation Safety Board, "Factors That Affect Fatigue in Heavy Truck Accidents," NTSB SS-95/01 (Department of Transportation, 1995).

27. 72 FR 71247, 71270 (July 3, 2008).

28. Consumer Affairs, "Motorcycle, Pedestrian Deaths Rising," August 31, 2006, available at http://www.consumeraffairs.com/news04/2006/08/motorcycle_deaths.html (last accessed June 18, 2008).

29. U.S. Fatality Analysis Reporting System, "National Statistics" (Department of Transportation, 2008), available at http://www-fars.nhtsa.dot.gov/Main/index.aspx (last accessed July 3, 2008).

30. Advocates for Highway and Auto Safety, "2008 Roadmap to State Highway Safety Laws" (District of Columbia, 2008).

31. Advocates for Highway and Auto Safety, "Graduated Drivers Licensing" (District of Columbia, 2008).

32. Advocates for Highway and Auto Safety, "2008 Roadmap to State Highway Safety Laws" (District of Columbia, 2008).

33. National Highway Traffic Safety Administration, "Open Container Laws" (Department of Transportation, 2008).

34. *Motor Carrier Safety Improvement Act.* § 210, *amending* 49 U.S.C. § 31144.

35. Bureau of Transportation Statistics, "National Transportation Statistics" (Department of Transportation, 2008).

36. "Grounded: Reauthorization of the Federal Aviation Administration Is Stuck on the Legislative Tarmac," *The Washington Post,* May 28, 2008, p. A12.

37. National Safety Transportation Board, "Most Wanted Transportation Safety Improvements: Aviation Issue Areas" (Department of Transportation, 2008), available at http://www.ntsb.gov/recs/mostwanted/aviation_issues.htm (last accessed May 20, 2008).

38. Federal Aviation Administration, "Next Generation Air Transportation System 2006 Progress Report" (2007), available at http://www.faa.gov/news/fact_sheets/news_story.cfm?newsId=8336 (last accessed June 2, 2008).

39. Matthew Wald, "A Long List of Big Issues for FAA," *The New York Times,* May 8, 2008, available at http://www.nytimes.com/2008/05/08/business/08faa.html?partner=rssnyt&emc=rss (last accessed June 8, 2008).

40. John Prater, Testimony before the House Committee on Transportation and Infrastructure Subcommittee on Aviation, on "Runway Safety," Feb. 13, 2008.

41. Energy Information Administration, "Demand" (Department of Energy, 2008), available at http://www.eia.doe.gov/pub/oil_gas/petroleum/analysis_publications/oil_market_basics/demand_text.htm (last accessed June 18, 2008).

42. 73 FR 24352, 24484 (May 2, 2008), p. 24479.

43. Energy Information Administration, "Weekly Retail Gasoline and Diesel Prices" (Department of Energy, 2008), available at http://tonto.eia.doe.gov/dnav/pet/pet_pri_gnd_dcus_nus_w.htm (last accessed June 18, 2008).

44. Energy Independence and Security Act of 2007, P.L. 110-140 § 108, 110 Cong. 1 sess.

45. Sholnn Freeman, "Flying Is Going to Get Even Less Fun: Rising Fuel Costs Test Airlines, and the Way We Travel," *The Washington Post*, June 14, 2008, p. D01.

46. Associated Press, "Like Motorists, Airlines Are Reducing Their Speed to Save Fuel Costs," *The New York Times*, May 2, 2008, available at http://www.nytimes.com/2008/05/02/business/02air.html?_r=1&oref=login (last accessed June 16, 2008).

Environmental Protection Agency: Restoring Scientific Integrity, Sound Regulation, Fair Enforcement, and Transparency

1. Union of Concerned Scientists, "Interference at the EPA: Science and Politics at the Environmental Protection Agency" (Cambridge, MA: April 2008).

2. House Committee on Oversight and Government Reform, "Committee Report: White House Engaged in Systematic Effort to Manipulate Climate Change Science" (United States House of Representatives: December 12, 2007).

3. Julie Gerberding, director of the Centers for Disease Control and Prevention, "Climate Change and Public Health," Testimony before the Senate Committee on Environment and Public Works, "Examining the Human Health Impacts of Global Warming," draft and final versions, October 23, 2007.

4. *Massachusetts v. U.S. E.P.A,* 549 U.S. 497; 127 S.Ct. 1438 (2007).

5. Felicity Barringer, "White House Refused to Open Pollutants Email," *The New York Times,* June 25, 2008.

6. United States Clean Air Act, U.S. Code 42, ch. 85 (2006) § 7571(a)(1)(A).

7. *New Jersey et al. v. EPA,* No. 05-1097 (DC Cir. Feb 8, 2008). EPA's petition for a rehearing was denied on May 20, 2008.

8. *North Carolina v. U.S. Environmental Protection Agency,* No. 05-1244 (U.S. Court of Appeals for the District of Columbia, July 11, 2008).

9. Environmental Protection Agency and Department of the Army, Corps of Engineers, "Advance Notice of Proposed Rulemaking on the Clean Water Act Regulatory Definition of 'Waters of the United States,'" *Federal Register* 68, no. 40 (January 25, 2003): 9613–9614; *Solid Waste Agency of Northern Cook County v. U.S. Army Corps of Engineers,* 531 U.S. 159 (2001); *Rapanos v. U.S. E.P.A.,* 547 U.S. 715 (2006).

10. EPA and ACE, "Clean Water Act Jurisdiction Following the U.S. Supreme Court's Decision in *Rapanos v. United States & Carabell v. United States*" (June 5, 2007), available at http://www.epa.gov/owow/wetlands/pdf/RapanosGuidance6507.pdf.

11. *Riverkeeper, Inc., et al. v. U.S. Environmental Protection Agency,* No. 04-6692-ag(L) (2nd Cir. January 25, 2007).

12. The Supreme Court granted cert. on April 14, 2008, on three consolidated cases regarding this matter. Oral arguments have not yet been scheduled.

13. John Solomon and Juliet Eilperin, "Bush's EPA is Pursuing Fewer Polluters," *The Washington Post*, September 30, 2007, p. A01.

14. Donald S. Welsh, EPA Regional Administrator, Letter to William Kovacs, U.S. Chamber of Commerce, June 22, 2007.

15. *New York et al. v. Johnson and U.S. Environmental Protection Agency*, No. 07 CV 10632 (Southern District Court of New York, filed November 28, 2007).

16. John B. Stevenson, "EPA Needs to Ensure That Best Practices and Procedures Are Followed When Making Further Changes to Its Library Network," Testimony before the House Committee on Science and Technology Subcommittee on Investigations and Oversight (General Accounting Office, 2008).

17. American Society of Civil Engineers, Testimony before the House Transportation and Infrastructure Committee Subcommittee on Water Resources and the Environment, January 19, 2007.

18. Environmental Working Group, "The Unintended Environmental Consequences of the Current Renewable Fuel Standard: A Guide to Future RFS Policy" (2007).

19. See Daniel C. Esty and Reece Rushing, "Governing by the Numbers," Center for American Progress, April 2007, available at http://www.americanprogress.org/issues/2007/04/pdf/data_driven_policy_report.pdf, and also Center for American Progress, *Progressive Priorities*, page 251, "Moving Government Into the Information Age" (2005), available at http://www.americanprogress.org/projects/progressivepriorities/govtforinfoage.html.

20. Katherine N. Probst and David M. Konisky, *Superfund's Future: What Will It Cost?* (Washington, DC: RFF Press, 2004).

21. Ibid.

22. Environmental Protection Agency, "Chemical Information Collection and Data Development (Testing)," available at http://www.epa.gov/oppt/chemtest/ (last accessed August, 2008).

23. Richard Denison, "Environmental Defense Fund's Comments on ChAMP: EPA's Recent Commitments and Possible New Initiatives for Existing Chemicals" (May 2008), available at http://www.edf.org/documents/7871_Comments_ChAMP_May08.pdf (last accessed August 2008).

Department of Agriculture:
Tackling Food and Energy Crises Amid Global Warming

1. Globally, aid donors neglected the agriculture sector for decades, with bilateral aid for agriculture slipping from 18 percent of foreign assistance in 1980 to about 4 percent today. Like other aid donors, the United States has neglected agriculture in developing countries. U.S. assistance for agricultural development is at an all-time low of about $283 million. Only $91 million of this is for Africa. This is down from $589 million, including $172 million for Africa in FY05. No non-emergency food aid funding or Millennium Challenge Corporation funding is included. From Emmy Simmons' unpublished paper, "USAID/EGAT/AG."

2. Under authority granted both agencies in the Bioterrorism Act of 2002.

3. Debate continues in Colorado and Idaho over proposed modifications to the 2001 Clinton roadless protection strategy. The governors of these states should be consulted to determine if their proposed revisions to the Clinton roadless rule should be adopted instead.

4. Richard Louv, *Last Child in the Woods* (Algonquin, 2004).

5. Government Accountability Office, "Climate Change: Agencies Should Develop Guidance for Addressing the Effects on Federal Land and Resources," GAO-07-863 (2007).

6. According to a study by the Australian National University, unlogged forests store three times more carbon dioxide than estimated by the U.N. Intergovernmental Panel on Climate Change and 60 percent more than cyclically logged plantation forests, arguing for strategies that preserve intact forests. A National Farmers Union program for capturing and storing carbon has generated $8 million in income for producers since 2006.

Federal Communications Commission:
Preparing the Way for Ubiquitous Broadband

1. John Horrigan, "Home Broadband 2008" (Pew Internet and American Life Project, June 2008).

2. Federal Communications Commission, *Policy Statement* (FCC 05-151, August 5, 2005).

3. Stephen Blumberg and Julian Luke, "Wireless Only and Wireless Mostly Households: A Growing Challenge for Telephone Surveys" (Center for Disease Control and Prevention, 2008).

4. American Library Association and Information Institute, "Libraries Connect Communities: Public Libraries Funding and Technology Access Study 2007–2007" (College of Information, Florida State University, 2007).

5. Comscore, "Number of Online Videos Viewed in the U.S. Jumps 13 Percent in March to 11.5 Billion" (press release May 2008).

6. Consumers Union, "Democratic Discourse in the Digital Information Age: Legal Principles and Economic Challenges," available at http://www.consumersunion.org/telecom/0102mediaexec.htm.

7. Government Accountability Office, "Media Ownership: Economic Factors Influence the Number of Media Outlets in Local Markets, While Ownership by Minorities and Women Appears Limited and Is Difficult to Assess," GAO-08-383, March 2008.

8. S. Derek Turner and Mark Cooper, "Out of the Picture 2007: Minority and Female TV Station Ownership in the United States" (Free Press, 2007).

9. CTIA, "Estimated Current U.S. Wireless Subscribers" (2008), available at www.ctia.org.

10. John Horrigan, "Mobile Access to Data and Information" (Pew Internet and American Life Project, March 2008).

11. Mark Stell, "Customers Complain After Cellphone Switchover," Minnesota Public Radio, October 30, 2007, available at http://minnesota.publicradio.org/display/web/2007/10/30/alltellprobs/.

12. GAO, "FCC Has Made Some Progress in the Management of Its Enforcement Program but Faces Limitations, and Additional Actions Are Needed," GAO-08-125 (February 2008).

Federal Trade Commission:
Consumer Protection for a 21st-Century Economy

1. Federal Trade Commission, "Generic Drug Entry Prior to Patent Expiration: An FTC Study" (2002), available at http://www.ftc.gov/os/2002/07/genericdrugstudy.pdf.

2. See Edward F. Cox, Robert C. Fellmeth, and John E. Schultz, "The Consumer and the Federal Trade Commission" (1969); and American Bar Association, "Report of the American Bar Association Commission to Study the Federal Trade Commission" (1969). Both reports harshly criticized almost every aspect of FTC's performance and raised serious questions about whether the agency should be abolished.

3. See Federal Trade Commission Staff Report, "Anticipating the 21st Century: Consumer Protection Policy in the New High-Tech, Global Marketplace" (1996), available at http://www.ftc.gov/opp/global/report/gc_v2.pdf. The report set the consumer protection agenda for the next five years of Chairman Robert Pitofsky's term and served as the foundation for the consumer protection program of the next chairman, Timothy Muris, as well.

4. Federal Trade Commission Staff Report, "Anticipating the 21st Century: Competition Policy in the New High-Tech, Global Marketplace" (1996), http://www.ftc.gov/app/global/report/gcv1.pdf.

5. Although the agency does produce a plan in accordance with the Government Performance and Accountability Results Act, that plan focuses on performance measures rather than identifying clear priorities for the agency's enforcement agenda.

6. The term "Chicago School" is typically used to refer to analytical precepts that focus on efficiency explanations and that were advanced by legal scholars such as Robert Bork, Richard Posner, and Frank Easterbrook. See William E. Kovacic and Carl Shapiro, "Antitrust Policy: A Century of Economic and Legal Thinking," *Journal of Economic Perspectives* 14 (1) (2000): 43–60.

7. U.S. Department of Justice and Federal Trade Commission, *Horizontal Merger Guidelines* §0.1 (1992, revised 1997).

8. For example, the FTC has testified in support of legislation that would ban payments by brand-name drug companies to generic drug companies as part of patent litigation settlements that result in delaying the market entry of the generic drugs. The FTC also should consider using its rulemaking authority to develop a rule relating to patent settlements in the pharmaceutical industry that could provide an evidentiary basis for legislation or serve as an alternative, should legislation not be forthcoming.

9. See, e.g., James M. Lacko and Janis K. Pappalardo, "The Effect of Mortgage Broker Compensation Disclosures on Consumers and Competition: A Controlled Experiment," Federal Trade Commission Bureau of Economics Staff Report (2004), available at http://www.ftc.gov/os/2004/01/030123mortgagesummary.pdf; Macro International, Inc., "Design and Testing of Effective Truth in Lending Disclosures," submitted to the Board of Governors of the Federal Reserve System (2007), available at http//www.federalreserve.gov/dcca/regulationz/20070523/Execsummary.pdf; Mary J. Culnan, "Consumers and Privacy Notices" (2001), Interagency Public Workshop: Get Noticed: Effective Financial Privacy Notices, available at http://www.ftc.gov/bcp/workshops/glb/presentations/culnan.pdf.

10. See, e.g., *Telemarketing Sales Rule*, 16 C.F.R § 310.4 (2007); *Credit Practices Rule*, 16 C.F.R § 444.2 (2008).

11. See Paul C. Light, *A Government Ill Executed: The Decline of the Federal Service and How to Reverse It* (Cambridge, MA: Harvard University Press, 2008).

12. This program implements 5 U.S.C. § 5379, which authorizes agencies to set up their own student loan repayment programs.

13. See Federal Trade Commission Press Release, "FTC Staff Proposes Online Behavioral Advertising Privacy Principles" (December 20, 2007), available at http://www.ftc.gov/opa/2007/12/principles.shtm.

14. See Center for Democracy & Technology Press Release, "Privacy and Consumer Groups Recommend 'Do Not Track List' and Other Policy Solutions to Offer Consumers More Control Over Online Behavioral Tracking" (October 31, 2007), available at http:// www.cdt.org/press/20071031press.php.

15. *U.S. SAFE WEB Act* of 2006, Pub. L. No. 109-455, 120 Stat. 3372 (codified as amended in scattered sections of 15 U.S.C.).

16. See Federal Trade Commission Press Release, "FTC Chairman and Commissioners Testify Before Senate Committee on Commerce, Science, and Transportation on proposed 'Federal Trade Commission Reauthorization Act of 2008'" (April 8, 2008), available at http://www.ftc.gov/opa/2008/04/reauth.shtm.

17. The Magnuson-Moss amendments to the FTC Act enable the Commission to adopt trade regulation rules concerning unfair and deceptive practices, and to institute civil actions and obtain civil penalties to address violations of such rules. 15 U.S.C. § 57a.

18. The Fair Credit Reporting Act imposes requirements on consumer reporting agencies as well as on entities that use consumer credit reports. The act also provides consumers with a right to learn about the information maintained about them, and a procedure for disputing the accuracy of information contained within their credit reports. 15 U.S.C. § 1681-1681u.

Corporation for National and Community Service:
Supporting Civic Action to Solve America's Problems

1. Howard Husock, "The AmeriCorps Budget Crisis of 2003: (A) Why the National Service Movement Faced Cutbacks and How It Responded," John F Kennedy School of Government Case Studies in Public Policy and Management (2004).

2. "National service" refers to substantial service, usually full-time, provided in exchange for a benefit, such as an educational scholarship. AmeriCorps is a national service program. "Community service" and "volunteer service" typically refer to service that does not include such benefits.

3. Unpublished poll by Peter D. Hart Research Associates (February 2008).

4. Corporation for National Service and Abt Associates, "Still Serving: Measuring the Eight-Year Impact of AmeriCorps on Alumni" (2008).

5. See transcript for "The American Role in Education Reform," Center for American Progress, available at http://www.americanprogress.org/events/2008/02/americorps.html (February 13, 2008).

6. Andrew Hahn, Thomas D. Leavitt, Erin McNamara Horvat, and James Earl Davis, "Life After YouthBuild: 900 Graduates Reflect on Their Lives, Dreams and Experiences" (Somerville, MA: YouthBuild USA, 2004).

7. Center for American Progress Task Force on Poverty, "From Poverty to Prosperity: A National Strategy to Cut Poverty in Half" (Washington, DC: Center for American Progress, 2007).

8. Shirley Sagawa, "Summer of Service: A New Rite of Passage?" (Washington, DC: Innovations in Civic Participation, 2004).

9. Susan Dentzer, "Service Credit Banking," in Stephen L. Isaacs and James R. Knickman, eds., *To Improve Health and Health Care, Volume V* (Robert Wood Johnson Foundation, 2002).

10. Aspen Institute Nonprofit Sector and Philanthropy Program, "Ten Nonprofit Policy

Proposals to Strengthen U.S. Communities" (2008); Michele Jolin, "Innovating the White House," *Stanford Social Innovation Review* (Spring 2008).

11. America Forward Coalition, "America Forward: Invent, Invest, Involve" (2007).

National Security Policy

Overview: Containing the Terrorist Threat

1. This is based on findings in the RAND/MIPT database. A report by Simon Fraser University in Canada argues that the increase in terrorism reported by the U.S. government and other sources, including RAND/MIPT, is skewed by the inclusion of civilian deaths in Iraq, where a civil war is underway. See Simon Fraser University, "Human Security Brief 2007" (May 21, 2008), available at http://www.humansecuritybrief.info. But the American Security Project finds an increase in terrorism even if Iraq is not included. See American Security Project, "Are We Winning? Measuring Progress in the Struggle against Violent Jihadism" (September 2007), available at http://www.americansecurityproject.org/issues/reports/are_we_winning.

2. United States Government Accountability Office Report to Congressional Requestors, "Combating Terrorism: The United States Lacks Comprehensive Plan to Destroy the Terrorist Threat and Close the Safe Haven in Pakistan's Federally Administered Tribal Areas" (April 2008) available at http://www.hcfa.house.gov/110/GAO041708.pdf; National Intelligence Estimate, "The Terrorist Threat to the U.S. Homeland" (July 2007) available at http://www.dni.gov/press_releases/20070717_release.pdf.

3. 9-11 Commission, "Final Report of the National Commission on Terrorist Attacks upon the United States" (July 22, 2004).

4. See, for example, Stephen M. Walt, "Beyond Bin Laden: Reshaping U.S. Foreign Policy," *International Security* 26 (2001): 57–58. See also, Kenneth N. Waltz, "The Continuity of International Politics," and Colin Gray, "World Politics as Usual after September 11: Realism Vindicated," in Ken Booth and Tim Dunne, eds., *Worlds in Collision* (London: Palgrave, 2002).

5. For example, see remarks by Defense Secretary Robert M. Gates in Thom Shanker, "Gates Says New Arms Must Play Role Now," *The New York Times*, May 14, 2008. See also Josh White, "Defense Secretary Urges Military to Mold Itself to Fight Iraq-Style Wars," *The Washington Post*, May 14, 2008, p. A04.

6. The term "jihad," which means to strive, has been appropriated by terrorists who consider violent jihad to be a sixth pillar of Islam. For an explanation, see Assaf Moghadam, *The Globalization of Martyrdom: Al Qaeda, Salafi Jihad, and the Diffusion of Suicide Attacks* (Baltimore: Johns Hopkins University Press, 2008).

7. For more on the impact of globalization, see Philip Bobbitt, *Terror and Consent: The Wars for the Twenty-first Century* (New York: Random House, 2008).

8. This is Bruce Hoffman's terminology. See "Does Our Counter-terrorism Strategy Match the Threat?" Testimony before the House International Relations Committee, Subcommittee on International Terrorism and Nonproliferation, September 29, 2005, available at http://www.rand.org/pubs/testimonies/CT250-1/.

9. Gregory Katz, "FBI Informant Crucial to Terror Plot Probe; Inmate Provided Help to Reduce His Prison Sentence," *The Houston Chronicle*, June 10, 2007; David Kocieniewski, "6

Men Arrested in a Terror Plot Against Ft. Dix," *The New York Times*, May 9, 2007; Rob Olmstead and Joseph Ryan, "FBI Thwarts Mall Attack Arrest Made in Rockford Area," *Chicago Daily Herald*, December 9, 2006; Associated Press, "Man Sentenced in SoCal Terrorism Probe," June 23, 2008.

10. For more on this see Jessica Stern, *Terror in the Name of God* (New York: HarperCollins, 2003). See also Archive.org, "Third Interview with Dr. Ayman Zawahiri 5/2007," available at http://www.archive.org/details/Third-Interview.

11. Ibid.; IntelCenter, "al-Qaeda Videos Vol. 74—Interview with Sheikh Ayman al-Zawahiri, April/May 2007 (English Subtitles)," available at http://www.intelcenter.com/audio-video/qaeda.html.

12. Joby Warrick, "U.S. Cites Big Gains Against Al-Qaeda; Group Is Facing Setbacks Globally, CIA Chief Says," *The Washington Post*, May 30, 2008, p. A01.

13. Intelligence Community Statement before the Senate Select Committee on Intelligence, "Annual Worldwide Threat Assessment," February 5, 2008, available at http://www.dni.gov/testimonies.htm, p. 8.

14. Ibid, pp. 7–8.

15. This is the mandate of the Hoover Institution Task Force on National Security and Law. See http://www.hoover.org/taskforces/taskforces/nationalsecurity.

16. General David Petraeus, Lt. General James Alos, and Lt. Colonel John A. Nagl, *The U.S. Army/Marine Corps Counterinsurgency Field Manual* (University of Chicago Press, 2007), p. 45.

17. See John Esposito and Dahlia Mogahed, "What Makes a Radical?" excerpt from *Who Speaks for Islam?* (New York: Gallup Press, 2007), available at http://www.gallup.com/poll/104941/What-Makes-Radical.aspx.

18. For an excellent discussion of terrorists' tendency to seek renown, see Louise Richardson, *What Terrorists Want* (New York: Random House, 2006).

19. David Galula, *Counterinsurgency Warfare: Theory and Practice* (1964, repr., Westport, CT: Praeger Security, 2006), p. 53.

20. Program on International Policy Attitudes at the University of Maryland, "Muslims Believe U.S. Seeks to Undermine Islam" (April 24, 2007). PEW found similar results in its 2004 polling in Jordan, Morocco, Pakistan, and Turkey.

21. Ibid.

22. John L. Esposito and Dalia Mogahed, "What Makes a Radical? An Excerpt from *Who Speaks for Islam?*" Muslim-West Facts Initiative (March 17, 2008), available at http://www.muslimwestfacts.com/mwf/105514/What-Makes-Radical.aspx.

23. Peter Bergen and Paul Cruickshank, "The Unraveling," *The New Republic*, June 11, 2008, available at http://www.tnr.com/politics/story.html?id=702bf6d5-a37a-4e3e-a491-fd72bf6a9da1; Lawrence Wright, "The Rebellion Within: An Al Qaeda Mastermind Questions Terrorism," *The New Yorker*, June 2, 2008, available at http://www.newyorker.com/reporting/2008/06/02/080602fa_fact_wright; see also Intelligence Community Statement before the Senate Select Committee on Intelligence, "Annual Worldwide Threat Assessment."

24. See summary in Bergen and Cruickshank, "The Unraveling."

25. This effort should build on studies that are already underway. See, for example, George Washington University Homeland Security Policy Institute/ University of Virginia Critical Incident Analysis Group Report on Internet-Facilitated Radicalization, "Networked Radicalization: A Counter-Strategy" (May 3, 2007), available at http://www.gwumc.edu/

hspi/pubs/hspi_pubs.htm. See also Radical Middle Way website, available at http://www.radicalmiddleway.co.uk/.

26. Some terrorism experts see our enemies as entirely rational, focused on changing our policies. See, for example, Anonymous, *Through Our Enemies' Eyes: Osama Bin Laden, Radical Islam, and the Future of America* (Potomac Books, 2003); Anonymous, *Imperial Hubris: Why the West Is Losing the War on Terror* (Brassey's, Inc., 2004); Marc Sageman, *Understanding Terror Networks* (University of Pennsylvania Press, 2004); Peter Bergen, *Holy War, Inc.* (Free Press, 2002).

27. Shibley Telhami, "Does the Palestinian Conflict Still Matter: Analyzing Arab Public Opinion," Analysis Paper (Washington, DC: Brookings, June 2008).

28. Ibid.

29. Terrorism is an "uncertainty" rather than a "risk," in the sense that it is not possible to calculate the probability of an attack.

30. William D. Nordhaus, "Bad, Worse, and Worst Cases and How to Think about Them" (presented at Terrorism, Climate Change, and Beyond: A Discussion of Cass Sunstein's *Worst Case Scenarios* conference, October 4, 2007); see also Cass Sunstein, *Worst Case Scenarios* (Cambridge, MA: Harvard University Press, 2007).

31. Richard Zeckhauser and Anthony Patt, "Action Bias and Environmental Decisions," *Journal of Risk and Uncertainty* 21 (1) (July 2000).

32. Ibid.

33. Cass Sunstein points out that we can be precautionary in regard to the identified problem, in this case terrorism. But we could also be precautionary in regard to side effects, so that the notion of a precautionary approach does not really make sense. See Cass Sunstein, *Laws of Fear: Beyond the Precautionary Principle* (Cambridge: Cambridge University Press, 2005). See Sunstein, *Worst Case Scenarios*.

34. Petraeus, Alos, and Nagl, *The U.S. Army/Marine Corps Counterinsurgency Field Manual*, pp. 151–152.

35. Secretary of Defense Robert M. Gates, remarks delivered to Air War College (Maxwell, AL, April 21, 2008), available at http://www.defenselink.mil/speeches/speech.aspx?speechid=1231.

Overview: The Costs and Benefits
of Redeploying from Iraq

1. Tom Shanker, "Gates Endorses Pause in Iraq Troop Withdrawals," *The New York Times*, February 12, 2008.

2. Speech of President George W. Bush at the National Defense University, September 9, 2008. Speech can be accessed at http://www.whitehouse.gov/news/releases/2008/09/20080909.html.

3. As of the time of publication. Iraq Coalition Casualty Count, available at http://www.icasualties.org.

4. Robert Burns, "Mullen: Afghanistan Isn't Top Priority," Associated Press, December 11, 2007.

5. Interview with Bob Woodward, *PBS Frontline*, September 8, 2004, available at http://www.pbs.org/wgbh/pages/frontline/shows/choice2004/interviews/woodward.html.

6. Michael Duffy with Mark Kukis, "The Surge at Year One," *Time*, January 31, 2008.

7. For more on this subject see: Lawrence Korb, Max Bergmann, Sean Duggan, and Peter Juul, "How to Redeploy: Implementing a Responsible Drawdown of U.S. Forces" (Washington, DC: Center for American Progress, August 2007).

8. Ibid.

Overview: Reducing Global Poverty
Is a Moral and Security Imperative

1. The United States Commission on Helping to Enhance the Livelihood of People around the Globe, "Beyond Assistance: The HELP Commission Report of Foreign Assistance Reform" (2007), p.10.

2. The World Bank, "Meeting the Challenge for Rural Energy and Development" (Washington) available at http://siteresources.worldbank.org/INTENERGY/Resources/Rural _Energy_Development_Paper_Improving_Energy_Supplies.pdf (last accessed June 2008).

3. HELP Commission, "Beyond Assistance," p. 12.

4. William Easterly, *The White Man's Burden: Why the West's Efforts to Aid the Rest Have Done So Much Ill and So Little Good* (New York: Penguin Books, 2006), p. 8.

5. Economic Commission for Latin America and the Caribbean, "Poverty and Income Distribution" (2003), available at http://www.eclac.org/publicaciones/xml/6/15086/ ChapterI2003%20ing.pdf (last accessed June 2008), pp. 72–724.

6. Oxfam International, "Adapting to Climate Change: What's Needed in Poor Countries and Who Should Pay," Briefing Paper Number 105 (2007) available at http://www. oxfam.org/en/files/bp104_climate_change_0705.pdf/download (last accessed June 2008).

7. Oxfam International, "Rigged Rules and Double Standards: Trade, Globalization, and the Fight Against Poverty" (2002), p. 9.

8. The World Bank, "Agriculture for Development: The 2008 World Development Report" (Washington, DC: The World Bank, 2008), p. v.

9. Johannes Kotschi, "Coping with Climate Change and the Role of Agrobiodiversity," Tropentag 2006, University of Bonn, October 11–13, 2006: Conference on International Agricultural Research for Development, available at http://www.tropentag.de/2006/ abstracts/full/625.pdf (last accessed June 2008), p. 2.

10. The CNA Corporation, "National Security and the Threat of Climate Change" (2007), available at http://securityandclimate.cna.org/report/National%20Security%20 and%20the%20Threat%20of%20Climate%20Change.pdf (last accessed May 2008).

11. International Action Network on Small Arms, Oxfam International, and Saferworld, "Africa's Missing Billions: International Arms Flows and the Cost of Conflict," Briefing Paper Number 109 (2007) available at http://www.oxfam.org/en/files/bp107_africas_missing _billions_0710.pdf (last accessed June 2008), p. 9.

12. Ibid.

13. Ian Smillie and Larry Minear, eds., *Humanitarian Action in a Calculating World* (Connecticut: Kumarian Press, 2004), p. 10.

14. Calculations made from "Global Policy Forum" (Peacekeeping Tables and Charts), available at http://www.globalpolicy.org/security/peacekpg/data/index.htm (last accessed June 2008).

15. Susan E. Rice and Stewart Patrick, "Index of State Weakness in the Developing World" (Washington, DC: The Brookings Institution, 2008), p. 17.

16. United States Congress, "Letter to the President," available at http://www.usglc. org/documents/FY09_150_House_Senate_sign_on_letters.pdf (last accessed June 2008).

17. Millenium Challenge Corporation website, http://www.mca.gov/press/index.php (last accessed June 2008).

18. WorldPublicOpinion.org, "U.S. Role in the World: General International Engagement," available at http://www.americansw7rld.org/digest/overview/us_role/general_principles.cfm (last accessed June 2008).

19. The PIPA/Knowledge Networks Poll, The American Public on International Issues, "Americans on Addressing World Poverty" (June 30, 2005), available at http://www.pipa. org/OnlineReports/ForeignAid/WorldPoverty_Jun05/WorldPoverty_Jun05_rpt.pdf (last accessed June 2008).

20. Stuart E. Eisenstat and Congressman John Edward Porter, co-chairs, "Commission on Weak States and U.S. National Security" (Washington, DC: Center for Global Development, 2004), available at http://www.cgdev.org/section/initiatives/_archive/weakstates (last accessed June 2008), p. 6.

21. HELP Commission, "Beyond Assistance," p. 1.

22. Steven Radelet, "Foreign Assistance Reforms: Successes, Failures, and Next Steps," Testimony before the Senate Foreign Relations Subcommittee on International Development, Foreign Assistance, Economic Affairs, and International Environmental Protection, June 12, 2007, available at http://www.senate.gov/~foreign/testimony/2007/Radelet Testimony070612.pdf (last accessed May 2008).

23. Robert M. Gates, "Landon Lecture (Kansas State University)" (November 26, 2007), available at http://www.defenselink.mil/speeches/speech.aspx?speechid=1199 (last accessed May 2008).

24. Congressional Research Service, "Kenya: The December 2007 Elections and the Challenges Ahead" (Washington, DC: U.S. Library of Congress, 2008), available at http:// www.fas.org/sgp/crs/row/RL34378.pdf (last accessed May 2008), p. 16.

25. Stewart Patrick and Kaysie Brown, "The Pentagon and Global Development: Making Sense of the DoD's Expanding Role," Working Paper Number 131 (Washington, DC: The Center for Global Development, November 2007), available at http://www.cgdev.org/content/publications/detail/14815/ (last accessed May 2008).

26. Lawrence Korb, Testimony before the Senate Foreign Relations Committee, Subcommittee on International Development and Foreign Assistance, December 6, 2007.

27. Craig Cohen, "A Perilous Course: U.S. Strategy and Assistance to Pakistan" (Washington, DC: Center for Strategic and International Studies, 2007), available at http://www. csis.org/media/csis/pubs/071214_pakistan.pdf (last accessed May 2008).

28. Oxfam America, "Smart Development: Why U.S. foreign aid demands major reform" (2007), available at http://www.oxfamamerica.org/newsandpublications/publications/briefing_papers/smart-development/smart-development-may2008.pdf (last accessed June 2008), p. 6.

Overview: Prepare Our Homeland for the Worst, but Prepare Smartly

1. Homeland Security Council, "National Strategy for Homeland Security" (October 2007), p. 41, available at http://www.whitehouse.gov/infocus/homeland/nshs/NSHS.pdf.

2. Ibid., p. 3.

3. Insurance Information Institute, *Insurance Fact Book 2007* (New York: Insurance Information Institute, 2007), p. 113.

4. Stephen E. Flynn, "The Brittle Superpower," in Philip E. Auerswald and others, eds., *Seeds of Disaster, Roots of Response, How Private Action Can Reduce Public Vulnerability* (Cambridge University Press, 2006), p. 26.

5. "National Security Strategy of the United States of America" (September 17, 2002), p. viii, available at http://www.whitehouse.gov/nsc/print/nssall.html.

6. In a concession to its political base, the Bush administration formed the Department of Homeland Security at the existing level of resources. While some supplemental funding was available immediately after 9/11, the amount available for DHS decreased substantially once the United States invaded Iraq.

7. P. J. Crowley and Bruce Butterworth, "Keeping Bombs Off Planes" (Washington, DC: Center for American Progress, May 2007), p. 7, available at http://www.americanprogress.org/issues/2007/05/air cargo.html.

8. Federal Emergency Management Agency, briefing on May 1, 2008, Washington, DC.

9. Department of Homeland Security, "Budget-in-Brief, Fiscal Year 2007" (2007), p. 69.

10. Michael Sheehan, Deputy Commissioner of Counter Terrorism, interview with New York City Police Department, January 30, 2004.

11. Homeland Security Council, "National Strategy for Homeland Security," p. 19.

12. New York Police Commissioner Raymond Kelly, discussion with Ford Foundation, New York City, December 3, 2007.

13. Richard A. Clarke, *Against All Enemies: Inside America's War on Terror* (Free Press, 2004), p. 259.

14. Irwin Redlener, *Americans at Risk: Why We Are Not Prepared for Megadisasters and What We Can Do* (Knopf, 2006), p. 231.

15. "National Security Strategy of the United States of America," p. 1.

16. David Cohen, Deputy Commissioner for Intelligence, discussion with New York Police Department, Ford Foundation, New York City, December 3, 2007.

17. Stephen Flynn, *America the Vulnerable: How Our Government Is Failing to Protect Us from Terrorism* (HarperCollins, 2004), p. 98.

18. Irwin Redlener, *Americans at Risk: Why We Are Not Prepared for Megadisasters and What We Can Do* (Knopf, 2006), p. 23.

Overview: National Security, Human Rights, and the Rule of Law

1. See, e.g, *Boumediene v. Bush*, 553 U.S. —, — (2008), 128 S.Ct. 2229 (2008); *Hamdan v. Rumsfeld*, 548 U.S. 557 (2006); *Rasul v. Bush* 542 U.S. 466 (2004); *Hamdi v. Rumsfeld* 542 U.S. 507 (2004).

2. See, e.g., David Bowker and David Kaye, "Guantanamo by the Numbers," *The New York Times*, November 10, 2007.

3. See, e.g., Frederick A.O. Schwarz, Jr. and Aziz Z. Huq, *Unchecked and Unbalanced: Presidential Power in a Time of Terror* (New Press, 2007); Charlie Savage, *Takeover: The Return of the Imperial Presidency and the Subversion of American Democracy* (Little, Brown and Company, 2007); Jack Goldsmith, *The Terror Presidency: Law and Judgment Inside the Bush Administration* (W. W. Norton, 2007); Barton Gellman, *Angler: The Cheney Vice Presidency* (The Penguin Press HC, 2008); Eric Lichtblau, *Bush's Law: The Remaking of American Justice* (Pantheon,

2008); Jane Mayer, *The Dark Side: The Inside Story of How The War on Terror Turned into a War on American Ideals* (Doubleday, 2008); James Risen, *State of War: The Secret History of the CIA and the Bush Administration* (Free Press, 2006).

4. Any ongoing military commissions cases should be terminated, and the suspects re-categorized into one of these four categories, which derive from detailed recommendations in Ken Gude, "How to Close Guantánamo" (Washington, DC: Center for American Progress, June 2008), available at http://www.americanprogress.org/issues/2008/06/pdf/guantanamo.pdf; Human Rights First, "How to Close Guantanamo: Blueprint for the Next Administration" (New York and Washington, DC: August 2008), available at http://www.humanrightsfirst.org/pdf/080818-USLS-gitmo-blueprint.pdf; and Sarah E. Mendelson, "Closing Guantánamo: From Bumper Sticker to Blueprint" (Center for Strategic & International Studies, July 13, 2008), available at http://www.csis.org/media/csis/pubs/080715_draft_csis_wg_gtmo.pdf.

5. *Authorization for Use of Military Force Resolution*, September 18, 2001, Public Law 107-40, S. J. RES. 23, 107th Cong., 115Stat.224 (2001).

6. For elaboration, see the chapter by Samuel Berger and Thomas Donilon in this book. Thanks to Mark Green & Michele Jolin, to whom I owe this suggestion.

7. *Boumediene v. Bush*, 553 U.S. —, — (2008), 128 S.Ct. 2229 (2008) (slip op. at 36) (ruling that the Guantánamo detainees have a constitutional right to habeas corpus).

8. For a description of what such national security legislation could look like, see generally Harold Hongju Koh, *The National Security Constitution: Sharing Power After the Iran-Contra Affair* (Yale University Press, 1990).

9. *Hamdan* v. *Rumsfeld*, 548 U.S. 557 (2006).

10. See, e.g., Benjamin Wittes and Mark Gitenstein, "A Legal Framework for Detaining Terrorists: Enact a Law to End the Clash over Rights" (Washington, DC: The Brookings Institution, 2007), p. 12, available at: http://www.brookings.edu/papers/2007/~/media/Files/Projects/Opportunity08/PB_Terrorism_Wittes.pdf; Andrew McCarthy and Alykhan Velshi, "We Need a National Security Court," in *Outsourcing American Law 43* (forthcoming); Jack Goldsmith and Neal Katyal, "The Terrorists' Court," *The New York Times*, July 11, 2007 (urging that detention determinations be made by life-tenured Article III judges, selected by the Chief Justice of the U.S. Supreme Court, similar to the selection of judges who serve on the Foreign Intelligence Surveillance Court).

11. See Richard B. Zabel and James J. Benjamin, Jr., "In Pursuit of Justice: Prosecuting Terrorism Cases in the Federal Courts" (New York and Washington, DC: Human Rights First, 2008), available at http://www.humanrightsfirst.info/pdf/080521-USLS-pursuit-justice.pdf (including quantitative analysis and based upon interviews with judges, prosecutors, and defense lawyers with firsthand experiences in terrorism cases).

12. *Hamdan* v. *Rumsfeld*, (underscoring value of proceeding in regularly constituted courts); *Boumediene v. Bush*.

13. See John R. Bolton, under secretary of state for arms control and international security, to Kofi Annan, U.N. secretary general, May 6, 2002, available at http://www.state.gov/r/pa/prs/ps/2002/9968.htm. Although the United States initially refused to accede to the Rome Statute of the International Criminal Court, President Bill Clinton ultimately signed the treaty on December 31, 2000, just before leaving office. See Clinton's Words: "The Right Action," *The New York Times*, January 1, 2001, p. A6.

14. See Genocide Prevention Task Force, available at http://www.ushmm.org/conscience/taskforce/ (last accessed September 2008).

Overview: Public Diplomacy
Can Help Restore Lost U.S. Credibility

1. *Changing Minds, Winning Peace: A New Strategic Direction for U.S. Public Diplomacy in the Arab & Muslim World,* Report of the Advisory Group on Public Diplomacy for the Arab and Muslim World, Edward P. Djerejian, Chairman, Submitted to the Committee on Appropriations U.S. House of Representatives, October 1, 2003.

2. Comprehensive global studies by the Pew Research Center show that the United States' image has declined in most parts of the world. According to Pew, since 2003, "Favorable ratings of America are lower in 26 of 33 countries for which trends are available. The U.S. image remains abysmal in most Muslim countries in the Middle East and Asia, and continues to decline among the publics of many of America's oldest allies. Favorable views of the U.S. are in single digits in Turkey (9 percent) and have declined to 15 percent in Pakistan. Currently, just 30 percent of Germans have a positive view of the U.S.—down from 42 percent as recently as two years ago—and favorable ratings inch ever lower in Great Britain and Canada." Also from Pew: "Of even greater concern: Critiques of the U.S. are not confined to its policies, however. In much of the world there is broad and deepening dislike of American values and a global backlash against the spread of American ideas and customs." Pew Research Center, "Global Unease with Major World Powers" (2007).

3. United States Advisory Commission on Public Diplomacy, *Getting the People Part Right: A Report on the Human Resources Dimension of U.S. Public Diplomacy* (Department of State, 2008).

4. "From the U.S. Advisory Commission on Public Diplomacy: no one in PD conducts PD overseas," available at http://mountainrunner.us/2008/06/from_the_us_advisory_commission.html (last accessed June 2008).

Department of State:
Rebuilding and Repositioning America's Diplomatic Strength

1. See generally, The White House Transition Project Archives, http://WhiteHouse TransitionProject.org. And also see Martha J. Kumar, George C. Edwards, III, James Pfiffner, and Terry Sullivan, *Meeting the Freight Train Head On: Planning for the Transition to Power* (The White House 2001 Project, August 18, 2000), p. 2.

Department of Homeland Security:
Rebuilding to Create What Should Have Been from the Beginning

1. Speech by Rep. Henry Waxman, Chairman of the United States House of Representatives Committee on Oversight and Government Reform, May 14, 2007, available at http://oversight.house.gov/story.asp?ID=1318.

2. Government Accountability Office, Department of Homeland Security, "Improved Assessment and Oversight Needed to Manage Risk of Contracting for Selected Services," September 2007, GAO-07-990.

3. Spencer S. Hsu, "Homeland Security's Use of Contractors is Questioned," *The Washington Post*, October 17, 2007, A3.

4. *Implementing Recommendations of the 9/11 Commission Act of 2007*, 110th Congress.

5. Remarks by Secretary of the United States Department of Homeland Security Michael Chertoff on the Electronic System for Travel Authorization, June 3, 2008, available at http://www.dhs.gov/xnews/speeches/sp_1212584527732.shtm.

Federal Emergency Management Agency:
Rebuilding a Once Proud Agency

1. Michael D. Selves, President, International Association of Emergency Managers, Testimony before the Subcommittee on Economic Development, Public Buildings, and Emergency Management, Committee on Transportation and Infrastructure, U.S. House of Representatives, April 26, 2007, page 4 of prepared text.

2. From "FEMA History," available at www.fema.gov/about/history.shtm (last accessed April 2008).

3. "The Stafford Act" refers to the *Robert T. Stafford Disaster Relief and Emergency Assistance Act*, as amended. This legislation defines FEMA's role and authorities in disaster preparedness, mitigation, response, and recovery vis-à-vis the states and local governments.

4. See "Emergency Management Performance Grants," Federal Emergency Management Agency, available at www.fema.gov/emergency/empg/empg.shtm, February 27, 2007 (last accessed April 2008).

5. Only two of the 15 National Planning Scenarios are associated with natural disasters, which form the core of traditional capabilities to be supported with EMPG funding. See David Howe, Senior Director for Response and Planning, "Planning Scenarios: Executive Summaries" (Homeland Security Council, July 2004).

6. To its credit, when Congress approved the Hurricane Katrina Recovery Act of 2006, they authorized substantial additional funding for EMPG: $375 million in 2008 and $535 million in 2009. Unfortunately, the current administration did not recognize the full importance and need for this funding as compared to other budget priorities, recommending far less in their budget submissions. For example, in FY 2008, the Bush administration recommended only $200 million for EMPG, a more than 46 percent reduction from authorized levels (Congress later increased that appropriation to $300 million, which after management costs were subtracted, resulted in the $291.45 million shown in the chart above). The FY 2009 funding request is also for $200 million, a more than 62 percent reduction from authorized levels.

7. The cost-effectiveness was later confirmed through two congressionally mandated reports, one completed by the Multi-Hazard Mitigation Council and one by the University of Colorado.

8. Criteria for being designated a "high-performing" state related to these programs should be developed to ensure financial and programmatic accountability, and states should be periodically re-evaluated to ensure that they continue to meet these standards.

Department of Energy:
Implementing the New Energy Opportunity

1. See history of oil prices at Energy Information Administration, "Cushing, OK WTI Spot Price FOB," available at http://tonto.eia.doe.gov/dnav/pet/hist/rwtcd.htm.

2. See "Climate Change 2007: Synthesis Report: An Assessment of the Intergovernmental Panel on Climate Change" (2007), available at http://www.ipcc.ch/pdf/assessment-report/ar4/syr/ar4_syr.pdf.

3. Executive Order no. 13423, "Strengthening Federal Environmental, Energy, and Transportation Management," *Federal Register* 72, no.17 (January 26, 2007): 3919; Executive Order no. 13123, "Greening the Government Through Energy Efficient Management," *Federal Register* 64, no. 109 (June 8, 1999): 30851; Executive Order no. 12902, "Energy Efficiency and Water Conservation at Federal Facilities," *Federal Register* 59, no. 47 (March 10, 1994): 11463; Executive Order no. 12759, "Federal Energy Management," *Federal Register* 56, (April 19, 1991): 16257; Executive Order no. 12261, "Gasohol in Federal Motor Vehicles," *Federal Register* 46 (January 8, 1981): 2023; Executive Order no. 12217, "Federal Compliance With Fuel Use Act Prohibitions," *Federal Register* 45 (June 20, 1980): 41623.

4. Executive Order no. 13423, at Sec. 2(a).

5. Executive Order no. 13124, at Sec. 201.

6. Executive Order no. 13423, at Sec. 2(g).

7. *Energy Policy and Conservation Act of 1975*, §§ 6231, 6234, codified at *U.S. Code* 42 §§ 77.

8. Department of Energy, Energy Information Administration, "U.S. Weekly Crude Oil Ending Stocks SPR (Thousand Barrels)," available at http://tonto.eia.doe.gov/dnav/pet/hist/wcsstus1w.htm (last accessed March 3, 2008).

9. *Energy Policy Act of 2005*, § 301(e).

10. See *Strategic Petroleum Reserve Fill Suspension and Consumer Protection Act of 2008*, Public Law 110-232, at Sec. 2(a).

11. See, e.g., Tom Doggett, "Bush Won't Release Emergency Oil to Ease Prices," Reuters, January 2, 2008, available at http://www.reuters.com/article/domesticNews/idUSN028636420080102. ("'This president will not use the SPR to manipulate (oil prices),' White House spokeswoman Dana Perino said. 'Doing a temporary release of the SPR is not going to change prices very much.'")

12. Oil may not be released from the SPR unless the president finds that a "severe supply emergency" exists, defined as "a national energy supply shortage which the president determines (A) is, or is likely to be, of significant scope and duration, and of an emergency nature; (B) may cause major adverse impact on national safety or the national economy; and (C) results, or is likely to result, from (i) an interruption in the supply of imported petroleum products, (ii) an interruption in the supply of domestic petroleum products, or (iii) sabotage or an act of God." *U.S. Code* 42 § 6241(d). The secretary may initiate an exchange of oil in the SPR for other oil to be placed in the SPR as a management tool. For instance, the secretary may exchange oil of one quality for oil of a different quality in order to conform the profile of oil in the SPR to the profile of U.S. refineries.

13. In fact, when President Bill Clinton authorized a 30 million barrel exchange in 2000, it was characterized as a response to "overall heating oil inventories [that were] more than 20 percent lower than they were [the previous] year; 50 percent lower on the East Coast; more than 60 percent lower in New England." President Clinton also noted that the "underlying cause of low inventories is the high price of crude oil," but did not characterize the exchange as a response to high prices.

14. Department of Energy, Office of Fossil Energy, "Strategic Petroleum Reserve—Quick Facts and Frequently Asked Questions," available at http://www.fossil.energy.gov/programs/reserves/spr/spr-facts.html (last accessed March 3, 2008).

15. Department of Energy, Office of Fossil Energy, "Releasing Crude Oil from the

Strategic Petroleum Reserve," available at http://www.fossil.energy.gov/programs/reserves/spr/spr-drawdown.html#desertstorm (last accessed March 3, 2008).

16. U.S. Department of Labor, "Identifying and Addressing Workforce Challenges in America's Energy Industry," President's High Growth Job Training Initiative, U.S. Department of Labor Employment Training Administration (March 2007), p. 4.

17. National Petroleum Council, "Hard Truths: Facing the Hard Truth About Energy" (2007), p. 177.

18. U.S. Department of Labor, "Identifying and Addressing Workforce Challenges in America's Energy Industry," p.4.

19. Energy Information Administration, "Annual Energy Review 2007," Table 5.24.

20. *Energy Independence and Security Act of 2007*, § 202(a), codified at *U.S. Code* 42 § 7545(o)(2).

21. *U.S. Code* 26 §§ 6426(b)(2)(a), (b).

22. EIA forecasts ethanol production of 740,000 barrels of ethanol per day in 2010 and 930,000 barrels per day in 2015. See Energy Information Administration, "Annual Energy Outlook, 2008," Table A11. With the current ethanol credit set at 45 cents per gallon, see the *Food, Conservation, and Energy Act of 2008*, Public Law 110-246, Sec 15331. The subsidy would cost $6.12 billion in 2010 and $7.7 billion in 2015.

23. DOE's total energy technology research, development, and deployment budget in FY2008 was $2.9968 billion. The administration requested $3.2393 billion for FY2009. Laura Diaz Anadon, Kely Sims Gallagher, and Matthew Bunn, "DOE FY09 Budget Request for Energy Research, Development & Demonstration—Commentary" (Belfer Center for Science and International Affairs, Kennedy School of Government, 2008), p. 11.

24. Energy Information Administration, "International Energy Outlook 2008—Highlights," Figure 3, available at http://www.eia.doe.gov/oiaf/ieo/index.html (last accessed on July 31, 2008).

25. Former Secretary of Energy Bill Richardson has called the United States "a superpower with a Third World [power transmission] grid."Editorial, "'Third World' Power Grid," *Los Angeles Times*, August 15, 2003, p. B12.

26. National Commission on Energy Policy, "Siting Critical Energy Infrastructure, An Overview of Needs and Challenges, A White Paper Prepared by the Staff of the National Commission on Energy Policy" (2006), p. 16; Bernard C. Lesieutre and Joseph H. Eto "Electricity Transmission Congestion Costs: A Review of Recent Reports" (Ernesto Orlando Lawrence Berkeley National Laboratory, 2003), pp. vii., 2, 21–27; U.S. Department of Energy, "National Transmission Grid Study" (2002), pp. 16–19.

27. See David Cay Johnson, "Grid Limitations Increase Prices for Electricity," *The New York Times*, December 13, 2006; U.S. Department of Energy, "National Electric Transmission Congestion Study" (2006), p. 28. The department did not make an estimate for the Western grids.

28. Ibid., p. 47; Department of Energy, "Interim Report of the U.S. Department of Energy Power Outage Study Team: Findings From the Summer of 1999" (2000).

29. This estimate is in 2005 dollars. See Anaon, Gallagher, and Bunn, "DOE FY09 Budget Request for Energy Research, Development & Demonstration—Commentary," p. 2.

30. See National Academy of Engineering, "Concerning Federally Sponsored Inducement Prizes in Engineering and Science. Report of the Steering Committee for the Workshop to Assess the Potential for Promoting Technological Advance Through Government-Sponsored Prizes and Contests" (National Academy Press, 1999), p. 4, avail-

able at http://www.nap.edu/catalog/9724.html (last accessed March 3, 2008); see website of X Prize Foundation at http://space.xprize.org/ansari-x-prize (last accessed on July 30, 2008).

31. See Newt.org, "National Prizes Foster Innovative Solutions," available at http://newt.org/EditNewt/NewtNewsandOpinionDB/tabid/102/ArticleType/ArticleView/ArticleID/803/PageID/872/Default.aspx (last accessed March 3, 2008); see National Research Council of the National Academies of Science, "Innovation Inducement Prizes" (National Academy Press, 2007), available at http://www.nap.edu/catalog.php?record_id=11816 (last accessed March 3, 2008); National Academy of Engineering, "Concerning Federally Sponsored Inducement Prizes in Engineering and Science" (1999), available at http://www.nap.edu/catalog.php?record_id=9724 (last accessed March 3, 2008).

32. Eric Hirst, "Electric Utilities and Energy Efficiency," available at http://www.ornl.gov/info/ornlreview/rev28_2/text/uti.htm; Matthew L. Wald, "A $30 Million Carrot; Whirlpool and Frigidaire in Refrigerator Contest," *The New York Times*, December 8, 1992; Office of Technology Assessment, "Energy Efficiency Challenges and Opportunities for Electric Utilities," Box 4-c, pp. 75–76, available at http://books.google.com/books?id=_F99TkyNXbgC&pg=PT86&lpg=PT86&dq=%22golden+carrot%22+refrigerator&source=web&ots=K0X-dvVncl&sig=W5N78isBzlPawgVNizgo5Dc6DDY&hl=en&sa=X&oi=book_result&resnum=9&ct=result#PPT12,M1.

33. *U.S. Code* 42 § 6295.

34. Ibid.

35. Energy Conservation Program for Consumer Products: Energy Conservation Standards for Rsidential Furnaces and Boilers, *U.S. Code* 10 § 430 (2007).

36. *State of New York et al. v. Bodman/NRDC et al. v. Bodman*, Nos. 05 Civ. 7807/7808 (JES) (S.D.N.Y. November 6, 2006).

37. *Energy Independence and Security Act of 2007*, §§ 301–325 (codified as amended in scattered sections of *U.S. Code* 42).

38. Energy Information Administration, "Electric Power Annual 2006," Table 7.2.

Department of Veterans Affairs:
Seriously Caring for Our Wounded Warriors

1. *Veterans' Health Care Eligibility Reform Act of 1996*, Public Law 104-262, 104th Cong. (Oct. 9, 1996).

2. Department of Veterans Affairs, "Facts about the Department of Veterans Affairs" (December 2007), available at http://www1.va.gov/opa/fact/docs/vafacts.pdf.

3. Ibid.

4. Office of Management and Budget, "Budget FY 2009—Department of Veterans Affairs," available at http://www.whitehouse.gov/omb/budget/fy2009/veterans.html (last accessed August 2008).

5. Daniel Bertoni, Government Accountability Office, "Veteran's Disability Benefits: Claims Processing Challenges Persist, while VA Continues to Take Steps to Address Them," #GAO-08-473T, Testimony Before the Committee on Veterans' Affairs, Subcommittee on Disability Assistance and Memorial Affairs, "Examining the U.S. Department of Veterans Affairs' Claims Processing System," February 14, 2008, available at http://www.gao.gov/new.items/d08473t.pdf.

6. Terri Tanielion and Lisa Jaycox, ed., "Invisible Wounds of War: Psychological and Cognitive Injuries, Their Consequences, and Services to Assist Recovery," RC552.P67T34 2008 (Rand Center for Military Health Policy Research, 2008), available at http://www.rand.org/pubs/monographs/2008/RAND_MG720.pdf.

7. Veterans' Disability Benefits Commission, "Honoring the Call to Duty: Veterans' Disability Benefits in the 21st Century" (October 2007), available at http://www.vetscommission.org/pdf/eReport_prepub_9-27.pdf.

The Intelligence Community:
Making the Newly Created Bureaucracy Work

1. The views expressed in this paper do not reflext the views of the members of staff of the House Intelligence Committee. This paper is derived completely from open course material and contains no classified information.

2. The 16 agencies are: the Central Intelligence Agency; the National Security Agency; the National Geospatial-Intelligence Agency; the National Reconnaissance Office; the Defense Intelligence Agency; the National Security Branch of the Federal Bureau of Investigation; the Office of Intelligence and Counterintelligence of the Department of Energy; the Bureau of Intelligence and Research of the Department of State; the Office of Intelligence and Analysis of the Department of Homeland Security; the Office of Intelligence and Analysis of the Department of Treasury; the Office of National Security Intelligence of the Drug Enforcement Administration; Air Force Intelligence; Army Intelligence; Naval Intelligence; Coast Guard Intelligence; and Marine Corps Intelligence.

3. In 1997, the intelligence budget was $26.6 billion (a number declassified by then-CIA Director George Tenet). For FY 2008, the National Intelligence Program was $47.5 billion (declassified pursuant to a statute by Director of National Intelligence Mike McConnell). This number does not include the Military Intelligence Program and assorted other pots of intelligence money.

4. "Special Report: Worldwide Defense Spending," *Defense News*, September 22, 2008, p. 11.

5. Defense News, "Study: Intel Contract Employees Costly," September 1, 2008, p. 24.

6. *Intelligence Authorization Act for Fiscal Year 2009*, H.R. 5959, 110th Congress, Sec. 425.

7. Office of the Director of National Intelligence, "Statement by the Office of the Director of National Intelligence on the North Korea Nuclear Test," press release, October 16, 2006, available at http://www.fas.org/nuke/guide/dprk/odni101606.pdf.

8. The deputy director of national intelligence for analysis serves as chairman of the National Intelligence Council, which provides the DNI and senior policymakers with the intelligence community's most authoritative written judgments concerning national security issues. The NIC is comprised of 13 national intelligence officers, who serve as chief analysts on a particular topic. These officers are responsible for writing National Intelligence Estimates, which provide consensus judgments on the most important intelligence questions. The DDNI for analysis also oversees the preparation of the President's Daily Briefing and other articles for senior policymakers.

9. National Intelligence Estimate, "Iraq's Continuing Programs for Weapons of Mass Destruction" (October 2002), available at http://www.fas.org/irp/cia/product/iraq-wmd.html.

10. This list is derived from Henry B. Hogue, "Presidential Appointee Positions Requiring Senate Confirmation and Committees Handling Nominations," Congressional Research Service Report (March 18, 2008), available at http://assets.opencrs.com/rpts/RL30959_20031027.pdf.

11. William Jackson, "Chertoff Outlines Goals of National Cybersecurity Initiative," Government Computer News, April 8, 2008, available at http://www.gcn.com/online/vol1_no1/46080-1.html.

Acknowledgments

Change for America would not exist without the dedication and support of many Americans who prove that the highest patriotism is the persistent pursuit of a better America.

The Center for American Progress Action Fund and the New Democracy Project are especially grateful to this volume's authors, who lent considerable time and talent to their work, as did the following authors whose work appears in the expanded online version of *Change for America*: Jared Bernstein; Rebekah Diller; Ross Eisenbrey; Michele A. Flournoy; George T. Frampton, Jr.; Pamela Gilbert; Mark Greenberg; Fred P. Hochberg; Alice E. Hunt; Simon Lazarus; Mark Shields; Winnie Stachelberg; Max Stier; Lauren Strayer; and Christine Varney. The editors similarly thank the numerous policy experts whose advice challenged our authors to create new ideas and better policies.

This volume also belongs to the following generous individuals and institutions who saw the value of *Change for America* before even one word was written: Roger Altman; Robert H. Arnow; Dr. Gail Furman; Wade Greene; Francis Greenburger; Anne Hess and Craig Kaplan; Michael Goodwin, president of OPEIU; William E. Little, Jr.; Robert McKay; Douglas H. Phelps and the Fund for Public Interest Research; Bernard L. Schwartz; David E. Shaw; the Campaign Reform Project; the Open Society Institute; and several anonymous donors. Our sincere gratitude goes to Doug Wilson and the board of the Howard Gilman Foundation, whose generosity contributed untold energy to this project.

The editors offer their deepest gratitude to the managing director of the *Change for America* project, Sam Davis. Sam managed with great skill and patience an enormous number of moving pieces that led to *Change for America*.

The editors offer special thanks to the entire Center for American Progress Action Fund editorial team: Annie Schutte, Andrew Pratt, Robin Pam, and Dan

Wagener. Your detailed and thoughtful work on tight deadline is a real testament to your skill.

In particular, we thank Ed Paisley, who leads and inspires his team with talent, focus and good-humor. Ed's extensive work has made this book better in every way.

Moreover, several individuals deserve thanks for their unique contributions to *Change for America*'s success: Debby Goldberg; Erica Payne; Jessica Raatz; Peter Schwartz; and the staff of the White Oak Plantation and Conference Center in Jacksonville, Florida.

The editors offer thanks for the generous institutional and intellectual support provided by the staffs of the Center for American Progress Action Fund and the New Democracy Project. In particular, we thank: Tamara Chao; Ian Hoffmann; David Malinsky; Anne Strahle; and Marshall Verdi.

Finally, the editors give enormous thanks to Melody Barnes, who launched this effort and managed it through the most critical decisions about structure and content before she left to join the Obama for America campaign. Her wisdom, insights and singularly strong judgment shaped this project in all of the best ways.

Mark Green
Michele Jolin
November 2008

Appreciation

Jeremy Bash would like to thank Mike Delaney, Brian Morrison, Larry Hanauer, Caryn Wagner, Mieke Eoyang, and Marcel Lettre for their assistance with writing "The Intelligence Community." (The views expressed in this chapter do not reflect the views of the members or staff of the House Intelligence Committee. This chapter is derived completely from open source material and contains no classified information.)

Gail R. Wilensky would like to thank Hal Blair, Bill Brew, Karen Guice, Sue Hosek, and Marie Michnich for their assistance with writing "Department of Veterans Affairs."

Cynthia G. Brown would like to thank Robin Chait and Amy Subert for their assistance with writing "Overview: Teaching All Our Children Well."

Carol M. Browner would like to thank Jonathan Cannon, Brandon Berkeley, and Elizabeth Raulston for their assistance with writing "Environmental Protection Agency."

P. J. Crowley and *Steve Richetti* would like to thank Stephen Flynn, Rand Beers, Michael Signer, and Mark Wentworth for their assistance with writing, "Overview: Prepare Our Homeland for the Worst, But Prepare Smartly."

Rudy deLeon would like to thank Winny Chen, Bryan Thomas, and Bruce van Voorst for their assistance with writing "Department of Defense."

Peter Edelman and *Angela Glover Blackwell* would like to thank Amy Block, Milly Hawk Daniel, Julia Isaacs, Jared Bernstein, and Mark Greenberg for their assistance with writing "Economic Opportunity for All or a New Gilded Age?"

Tom Freedman would like to thank Lisa Brown, Michele Jolin, Elena Kagan, Ann O'Leary, Ed Paisley, John Podesta, Bruce Reed, Michael Waldman, Sam Gill, Jessica Goad, Matt Lindsey, and David Beier for their assistance with writing "Domestic Policy Council."

Bracken Hendricks and *Van Jones* would like to thank Benjamin Goldstein, Jason Walsh, Nicole Henderson, Kit Batten, Bob Sussman, Gayle Smith, Todd Stern, and Sam Davis for their assistance with writing "Building a Vibrant Low-Carbon Economy."

Dawn Johnsen would like to thank Preeta Bansal, David Barron, Lisa Brown, Walter Dellinger, Jamie Gorelick, Eric Holder, Neil Kinkopf, Marty Lederman, Bill Lann Lee, Margaret Love, Wendy Patten, James Robinson, Laurie Robinson, Lois Schiffer, and Mark Agrast for their assistance with writing "Department of Justice."

Mitchell Kapor would like to thank Thomas Kalil and Julius Genachowski for their assistance with writing "Chief Technology Officer."

Bruce Katz would like to thank Shoshana Lew and Margery Austin Turner for their assistance with writing "Department of Housing and Urban Development."

Sally Katzen and *Jack Lew* would like to thank Jill Blickstein, Michael Fitzpatrick, Alice Rivlin, Robert Reischauer, Jason Furman, Robert Greenstein, Gary Bass, and John Koskinen for their assistance with writing "Office of Management and Budget."

Lawrence J. Korb would like to thank Peter Juul, Max Bergmann, and Sean Duggan for their assistance with writing "The Costs and Benefits of Redeploying from Iraq."

Jeanne Lambrew would like to thank Art Kellerman for his assistance with writing "Department of Health and Human Services."

Ellen S. Miller would like to thank Bill Allison, Micah Sifry, and Mike Smith for their assistance with writing "Government Transparency in the Age of the Internet."

Edward Montgomery would like to thank Harry Holzer, Ray Uhalde, Michael Kerr, Richard Freeman, and Ric McGahey for their assistance with writing "Department of Labor."

Cecilia Muñoz would like to thank Charles Kamasaki and Cassandra Butts for their assistance in writing "Immigration Can Be Orderly and Fair."

Shirley Sagawa would like to thank Ann Maura Connolly, Deborah Jospin, Alan Khazei, and Kelly Ward for their assistance with writing "Corporation for National and Community Service."

Jonathan Sallet would like to thank Ev Ehrlich, Sally Ericcson, Bill Reinsch, Rob Stein, Loretta Schmitzer, Sally Yozell, and Ross Johnson for their assistance with writing "Department of Commerce."

Ira Shapiro would like to thank William A. Reinsch, Michael B. Levy, Clyde Prestowitz, Viji Rangaswami, and Kent Hughes for their assistance with writing "United States Trade Representative."

Gene Sperling would like to thank Josh Picker, Sara Aronchick, and Victoria Palomo for their assistance with writing "Overview: A Pro-Growth, Progressive Economic Agenda."

Joshua Steiner would like to thank Roger Altman, Bill Dauster, Peter Fisher, Gene Ludwig and Lee Sachs, and Amias Moore Gerety for their assistance with writing "Department of Treasury."

Jessica Stern would like to thank Bruce Hoffman for his assistance with writing "Overview: Containing the Terrorist Threat."

Laura D. Tyson would like to thank Naoko Nakamae, Will Straw, Michele Jolin, Sarah Wartell, Thomas O'Donnell, and Charlene Barshefsky for their assistance with writing "Overview: New Rules for Globalization and Trade."

Doug Wilson would like to thank Rosemary Crockett, Rudy DeLeon, Mara Rudman, Judith Siegel, Robert Coonrod, and Tara Sonenshine for their assistance with writing "Public Diplomacy Can Restore Lost U.S. Credibility."

Judith Winston would like to thank Cynthia G. Brown, Joan Baratz-Snowden, Michael Cohen, Fritz Edelstein, Scott Fleming, David J. Goldberg, William L. Taylor, Steve Y. Winnick, and Cynthia E. Winston for their assistance with writing "Department of Education."

James Lee Witt would like to thank Jane Bullock, George Haddow, Hans Kallam, David Miller, Michael Herman, and Michael D. Selves for their assistance with writing "Federal Emergency Management Agency."

About the Contributors

Editors

Mark Green is the author or editor of 22 books on public policy, including the bestselling *Who Runs Congress?* (1972) and *The Book on Bush* (2004). He was the elected Public Advocate for New York City (1994–2001) and is currently president of Air America Media and the New Democracy Project.

Michele Jolin is a senior fellow at the Center for American Progress Action Fund. She was a vice president at Ashoka and was chief of staff for President Bill Clinton's Council of Economic Advisers.

Ed Paisley is vice president for editorial at the Center for American Progress Action Fund. He joined the Center after 20 years in journalism covering business and finance on five continents for *The Deal*, the *Far Eastern Economic Review*, and *Institutional Investor* magazine, where he won an Overseas Press Club award for his coverage of the handover of Hong Kong from Britain to China in 1997.

Lauren J. Strayer is executive director of the New Democracy Project, co-author of *Defend Yourself!* (2006), and a former producer at Air America Radio.

Contributors

Michael Barr, a senior fellow at the Center for American Progress Action Fund and a law professor at the University of Michigan, is also a non-resident senior fellow at the Brookings Institution and recently co-edited *Building Inclusive Financial Systems*.

Jeremy Bash is the chief counsel of the House Permanent Select Committee on Intelligence. In this position, he advises the Committee Chairman and the other 11 Members of the Committee's Majority on policy and oversight matters related to the operations of the nation's 16 intelligence agencies. He is a former counsel at the law firm of O'Melveny and Meyers. In 2000, he served as national security issues director for the Gore-Lieberman campaign.

Sandy Berger was national security advisor to President Bill Clinton from 1997 to 2001 and now is co-chairman and co-founder of Stonebridge International, LLC.

Jodie Bernstein, former director of the Bureau of Consumer Protection at the Federal Trade Commission and general counsel and assistant administrator at the Environmental Protection Agency, is of counsel to Bryan Cave, LLP.

Angela Glover Blackwell served as senior vice president of the Rockefeller Foundation, and is founder and CEO of PolicyLink.

Lisa Brown, former counsel to Vice President Al Gore, is currently the executive director of the American Constitution Society for Law and Policy.

Cynthia G. Brown, director of education policy at the Center for American Progress Action Fund, was the first assistant secretary for civil rights at the Department of Education, and has spent over 35 years working in a variety of professional positions addressing high-quality, equitable public education.

Carol Browner, former administrator of the Environmental Protection Agency, is a founding principal at The Albright Group, LLC.

Shaun Casey is associate professor of Christian Ethics at Wesley Theological Seminary in Washington, D.C., where he directs the National Capital Semester for Seminarians.

Joe Cirincione, former director for nonproliferation at the Carnegie Endowment for International Peace, was a senior fellow and director for nuclear policy at the Center for American Progress Action Fund. He is now president of the Ploughshares Fund.

Henry Cisneros is the former secretary of the U.S. Department of Housing and Urban Development and a four-term mayor of San Antonio. He is now chairman of CityView, which provides an attractive project financing alternative for experienced homebuilders and developers who demonstrate a commitment to quality and want a long-term, multiple-project relationship.

Joan Claybrook, former administrator of the National Highway Traffic Safety Administration, is president of Public Citizen and founder of Public Citizen's Congress Watch.

Virginia Cox spent nearly a decade at the Food and Drug Administration and the Department of Health and Human Services, and is now senior vice president at the Consumer Healthcare Products Association.

Gregory Craig was assistant to the president and special counsel during the Clinton administration. He also served as senior assistant to Senator Edward Kennedy (D-MA) for Foreign Policy and National Security Affairs. The former director of policy planning at the Department of State and a former White House special counsel, he is currently a partner at Williams and Connolly.

P. J. Crowley formerly served as special assistant to President Bill Clinton for national security affairs and principal deputy assistant secretary for public affairs at the Department of Defense. He is a senior fellow and director of homeland security at the Center for American Progress Action Fund.

Karen Davenport, director of health policy at the Center for American Progress Action Fund, was a senior program officer at the Robert Wood Johnson Foundation, and a legislative assistant to Senator Bob Kerrey (D-NE).

Rudy deLeon, former deputy secretary at the Department of Defense, is the senior vice president for national security and international policy at the Center for American Progress Action Fund.

Tom Donilon was assistant secretary of state for public affairs under President Bill Clinton, and has held a wide range of White House and presidential campaign advisory positions. Since 1986, he has served as a senior advisor to the chairman of the Senate Judiciary Committee on Supreme Court nominations.

Maria Echaveste was former assistant and deputy chief of staff to President Bill Clinton, and is a lecturer in residence at UC Berkeley's School of Law, Boalt Hall. She is a senior fellow at the Center for American Progress Action Fund.

Peter Edelman, former assistant secretary for planning and evaluation at the Department of Health and Human Services, has been a professor at Georgetown Law since 1982.

Christopher Edley, Jr. served in two White House administrations and was a professor at Harvard Law for 23 years. He is dean of UC Berkeley's School of Law, Boalt Hall.

Clark Kent Ervin, former inspector general of the Departments of Homeland Security and State, is director of the Homeland Security Program at the Aspen Institute. He is the author of *Open Target: Where America Is Vulnerable to Attack*.

Tom Freedman served as senior advisor to the president in the Clinton administration. He is president of Freedman Consulting, LLC, a strategic consulting firm, a visiting scholar at Resources for the Future, and a senior fellow at the Progressive Policy Institute.

David J. Hayes is the global chair of the Environment, Land & Resources Department at Latham & Watkins. Mr. Hayes served as the deputy secretary of the interior during the Clinton administration. As deputy secretary, he was second in command at Interior under Secretary Bruce Babbitt.

Bracken Hendricks, a senior fellow at the Center for American Progress Action Fund working on climate change and energy independence, was a special assistant to Vice President Al Gore and served with the Department of Commerce's National Oceanic and Atmospheric Administration.

Elgie (Elwood) Holstein served in the Clinton administration as special assistant to the president for economic policy.

Larry Irving, former assistant secretary of commerce for communications and information for President Bill Clinton, is president of the Irving Information Group, an information technology consulting firm.

Dawn Johnsen, former acting assistant attorney general for the Office of Legal Counsel, was legal director of NARAL and is a professor at the Indiana University School of Law, Bloomington.

Van Jones, a senior fellow at the Center for American Progress Action Fund working on climate change and energy independence, is the founder and president of Green For All; a founding board member of the Apollo Alliance and 1Sky; and author of the bestseller *The Green Collar Economy* (Harper One, 2008).

Elena Kagan is the Charles Hamilton Houston Professor of Law and dean of Harvard Law School. From 1995 to 1999, Kagan served in the White House, first as associate counsel to the president (1995–96) and then as deputy assistant to the president for domestic policy and deputy director of the Domestic Policy Council (1997–99).

Tom Kalil, former deputy director of the White House National Economic Council, is special assistant to the chancellor for science and technology at UC Berkeley. Tom is also a senior fellow at the Center for American Progress Action Fund.

Mitchell Kapor has been at the forefront of information technology for 30 years as an entrepreneur, software designer, activist, and investor. He was involved in founding the Lotus Development Corporation, the Mozilla Foundation, and Linden Research, the creator of Second Life.

Bruce Katz, former chief of staff at the Department of Housing and Urban Development, is vice president and director of the Metropolitan Policy Program at the Brookings Institution.

Sally Katzen, former administrator of the Office of Information and Regulatory Affairs, deputy director of the National Economic Council, and deputy director for management at the Office of Management and Budget, is a lecturer and public interest/public service fellow at the University of Michigan Law School.

Harold Hongju Koh is dean of Yale Law School, where he is the Gerard C. and Bernice Latrobe Smith Professor of International Law. From 1998 to 2001, he served as assistant secretary of state for democracy, human rights and labor.

Lawrence J. Korb, former assistant secretary of the Department of Defense (1981–1985) and a retired captain in the Naval Reserve, is author, co-author, editor, and contributor to 20 books, a senior fellow at the Center for American Progress Action Fund, and a senior advisor to the Center for Defense Information.

Jeanne Lambrew is a senior fellow at the Center for American Progress Action Fund and an associate professor of public affairs at the Lyndon B. Johnson School of Public Affairs at the University of Texas. From 1997 to 2000, she worked on health policy at the White House as the program associate director for health at the Office of Management and Budget and as the senior health analyst at the National Economic Council.

Neal Lane is the Malcolm Gillis University Professor at Rice University and is a senior fellow of the James A. Baker III Institute for Public Policy. He has served in various government positions, most recently as assistant to the president for science and technology and director of the White House Office of Science and Technology Policy for President Clinton.

John Leshy was associate solicitor of Interior in the Carter administration, and solicitor (general counsel) of Interior throughout the Clinton administration. He is currently the Sunderland Distinguished Professor of Law at Hastings College of the Law, University of California, San Francisco.

Jack Lew was director of the Office of Management and Budget from 1998 to 2001 and executive director of the House Democratic Steering and Policy Committee from 1985 to 1987.

Jim Lyons served in the Clinton administration as undersecretary for natural resources and environment in the Department of Agriculture, and is vice president for policy and communications at Oxfam America.

Ann Malester, former deputy director of the Federal Trade Commission's Bureau of Competition, is a partner at Weil, Gotshal & Manges.

Ellen S. Miller, a noted campaign finance and ethics expert, is co-founder and executive director of the Sunlight Foundation, a Washington-based, non-profit catalyst that is using new technology to open up Congress.

Ronald Minsk was former director of the National Economic Council and special assistant to President Bill Clinton.

Edward Montgomery, former deputy secretary and chief economist at the Department of Labor, is dean of the College of Behavioral and Social Sciences at the University of Maryland.

Cecilia Muñoz, a noted immigration expert, is senior vice president for the Office of Research, Advocacy, and Legislation at the National Council of La Raza.

John Podesta, president and CEO of the Center for American Progress Action Fund, was chief of staff to President Bill Clinton from October 1998 to January 2001 and is a professor at Georgetown Law.

Steve Richetti was a deputy chief of staff to President Clinton and is now principal of Richetti, Inc.

Shirley Sagawa, an appointee in the administrations of President George H.W. Bush and President Bill Clinton, is a visiting fellow at the Center for American Progress Action Fund with the goal of creating a comprehensive national service policy.

Richard Samans is a senior fellow at the Center for American Progress Action Fund and managing director of the World Economic Forum. Before joining the forum, Rick served as special assistant to the president for international economic policy in the United States, and was senior director of the National Security Council's International Economic Affairs directorate in the White House.

Jonathan Sallet, partner with The Glover Park Group, served under President Clinton as assistant to the secretary and director of the Office of Policy & Strategic Planning of the Department of Commerce, focusing on economic and technology policy.

Ira Shapiro, former general counsel and trade ambassador in the Office of the United States Trade Representative, is an international trade lawyer at Greenberg Traurig, LLP.

Gayle Smith, former journalist, special assistant to the president, and senior director for African Affairs at the National Security Council, is a senior fellow at the Center for American Progress Action Fund.

Gene Sperling is a senior fellow at the Center for American Progress Action Fund, U.S. chair for the Global Campaign for Education, and co-chair for the Education Partnership for Children of Conflict. Previously, Sperling served as national economic advisor to President Clinton from 1997 to 2001 and deputy national economic advisor from 1993 to 1996.

Joshua L. Steiner, former chief of staff at the Department of Treasury and managing director at Lazard, is a managing principal of Quadrangle Group, LLC.

Jessica Stern, former director for Russian, Ukrainian, and Eurasian Affairs at the National Security Council, is the author of two books on terrorism and a lecturer in public policy and faculty affiliate at Harvard.

Todd Stern, former White House staff secretary and assistant to President Bill Clinton, was also counselor to the Secretary of the Treasury. He is currently a partner at Wilmer Hale and a senior fellow at the Center for American Progress Action Fund.

Laura D. Tyson, former chair of the National Economic Council and former chair of the President's Council of Economic Advisers, is a professor at the Haas School of Business, UC Berkeley and a senior fellow at the Center for American Progress Action Fund.

Michael Waldman, former assistant to the president and director of speechwriting for President Bill Clinton, is the author of several books, including *My Fellow Americans* and *A Return to Common Sense*. He is executive director of the Brennan Center for Justice at the NYU School of Law.

Sarah Rosen Wartell was deputy director of the National Economic Council and worked at the Federal Housing Administration. She is the executive vice president for management at the Center for American Progress Action Fund and oversees its economic program.

Gail Wilensky, former director of Medicare/Medicaid, deputy assistant to the president on health and welfare issues, and Dole-Shalala Commissioner, is an economist and senior fellow at Project HOPE.

Doug Wilson, former congressional director and senior advisor at the United States Information Agency and principal deputy assistant secretary for public affairs at the Department of Defense, is co-founder of the Leaders Project and a member of the board of directors of the Howard Gilman Foundation.

Judith Winston was general counsel and undersecretary of the Department of Education during the Clinton administration and formerly a law professor at American University. She is founder and principal at Winston, Withers Associates.

James Lee Witt, former director of the Federal Emergency Management Agency, is CEO of James Lee Witt Associates, a part of GlobalOptions Group, the nation's premiere crisis management and preparedness services consulting firm.

Center for American Progress Action Fund

The Center for American Progress Action Fund is a progressive think-tank dedicated to improving the lives of Americans through ideas and action. It is creating a long-term, progressive vision for America—a vision that policy makers, thought-leaders and activists can use to shape the national debate and pass laws that make a difference.

www.americanprogressaction.org

The New Democracy Project is a public policy institute established in 1981 to promote democratic participation, economic fairness and social justice. Due to relationships with leading progressive scholars and advocates, government officials, labor leaders, and the media, NDP can counter the conservative consensus with new progressive ideas.

www.newdemocracyproject.org